FREDERICK J. McDONALD

Stanford University

Wadsworth

EDUCATIONAL PSYCHOLOGY

SECOND EDITION

Publishing Company, Inc., Belmont, California

FREDERICK J. MCDONALD
EDUCATIONAL PSYCHOLOGY, SECOND EDITION

© 1959, 1965 by Wadsworth Publishing Company, Inc., Belmont, California. All rights reserved. No part of this book may be reproduced in any form, by mimeograph or any other means, without permission in writing from the publisher.

L. C. Cat. Card No.: 65–17551

Printed in the United States of America

THIRD PRINTING, JANUARY 1966

For Jan

PREFACE

This book is written for those readers who believe that teaching is more than technique, that learning to teach requires learning more than the "tricks of the trade." The central, dominating theme is that teaching requires thinking—thinking by hypothesizing about the effects of the teacher's strategies to produce learning; thinking about the factors likely to bring about significant changes in students.

This book is about educational psychology, an applied science. It will be most useful to those readers who want to apply the concepts and generalizations of psychology to teaching. It is written to stimulate thinking about the psychological problems of teaching—to induce the reader to begin thinking *psychologically* about teaching problems.

My belief is that a first course in educational psychology, a basic book about educational psychology, should help the reader to acquire the intellectual habits of psychologists and the technical skills developed by psychologists for teaching. It should give him the spirit of inquiry; a grasp of the importance of empirical methods; an appreciation of the need for theorizing and hypothesizing and for testing one's theories and hypotheses.

Studying educational psychology ought to be a stimulating, challenging enterprise; it ought to open windows and let in fresh air on teaching; it ought to command the best of your abilities. I hope this book provides such an experience for you; I have tried to respect your intelligence, imagination, and creative abilities.

My revision of this book reflects developments in psychology and in my own experiences. First, educational psychology is clearly moving in the direction of an applied science—becoming more systematic, more committed to the use of theoretical models, making more use of a wide range of psychological ideas and data. Hence, the emphasis in this edition on the concept of instructional strategies, on the use of the feedback model. Second, my own thinking about educational psychology has been stimulated by my active involvement in an experimental program of teacher training. This opportunity made me think through the kinds of conceptual models I have presented in this edition, and it enabled me to see teaching from the viewpoint of the teacher who has to learn how to teach. What I have written represents my conviction, after this experience, that a teacher's success—his productivity, his creativity—depends on the understanding he achieves about the psychology of educating.

The first chapter introduces the student to the spirit in which the book was written; it is the first invitation to critical inquiry. The second and third chapters present conceptual models for thinking about teaching and learning. The remainder of the book goes into the specifics of educational psychology and represents my selection of the content most relevant, given the approach I take in these early chapters.

Your attention is called to one aid added in this edition, the glossary. Terms whose understanding may require a ready reference, or terms frequently used in the text, have been printed in **bold-face type.** These terms are defined in the glossary.

Each chapter has a summary, which provides an overview of the principal concepts and generalizations discussed in the chapter. Questions at the end of each chapter are designed to stimulate thinking about the issues and problems discussed; some projects to encourage application, usually of a modest nature, are also suggested. By each of these means, I have tried to provide a self-contained instructional system, one component in the system built into the course in educational psychology.

I wish to express my appreciation of the helpful comments made by many users of the first edition, both teachers and students. Dr. Merle C. Wittrock of the University of California at Los Angeles deserves my special thanks for his stimulating and encouraging critique of the revision, and for the pleasure and privilege of sharing ideas with him.

Dr. Arthur P. Coladarci, Miss Rebecca Hayden, and Mrs. Mary Warner deserve remembrance for their contributions to the first edition. Tre Ford valiantly typed the revision at all hours and deserves my special thanks for acceding to unreasonable demands on her time and energy. Dorothy Ohliger bore her editorial responsibilities with remarkable fortitude. Her editorial assistance was invaluable to me.

The dedication of the book to my wife is a small remembrance for her continued patience with my working habits and her unflagging encouragement.

FREDERICK J. MCDONALD
STANFORD, CALIFORNIA

CONTENTS

BASIC CONCEPTS AND PRINCIPLES

CHAPTER ONE

TEACHING BEHAVIOR AND THE LOGIC OF SCIENTIFIC INQUIRY

Of all the kinds of people in the world, few have been exposed to our scrutiny as frequently and as continuously as have teachers. We have watched them scanning the kindergartner's art, leading a class in song, marshaling easily distracted observers on a field trip, bending over a test tube in a laboratory, delivering a lecture, reading a poem. Is the teacher at these times only a manager, a friendly commentator, a dispenser of supplies, a ready reference? How does he make a poem interesting, a theorem intelligible? How did you learn to write a sentence, to count by tens, to give a speech? Twelve or more years ago you had a modest speaking vocabulary, a few simple physical skills, and the rudiments of civilized behavior. How did those interveners the teachers help to transform you from that small child to an adult competent to engage in the democratic process, aware of depth psychology and relativity, reasonably knowledgeable in art or literature or music or science or economics or history?

Your abilities and interests, your enthusiasms, your effort were necessary. But these too were learned. You were not born appreciating Bach or Picasso, or wanting to paint or to play tennis. Something had to be done to bring about these changes; they did not just happen. The significant, though not exclusive, role played by teachers in your development is obvious. But how did they bring about these changes in you? And, equally important, can you learn to do the same things for other students?

This book is about learning and teaching. The questions raised in the preceding paragraphs admit of no simple, one-word, one-sentence answers. To make a theorem intelligible, a poem exciting; to help students acquire the behavior necessary for participating intelligently in the democratic process; to stimulate their curiosity—all of this requires an understanding of the learning process, which in turn requires an understanding of psychology.

RELATION OF PSYCHOLOGY TO EDUCATION

The purpose of a course in psychology is to help you think psychologically. To think psychologically means to use the concepts and principles of psychology to understand human behavior. It also means to adopt the methods and tools of behavioral science. The function of any science is to describe and explain the events of the phenomenal world (the world as perceived) that are in its area of concern and study. Each science has marked off for itself, as it were, sets of observable events that are the object of study in that science. Physics, for example, describes and explains the relationships between matter and energy.

THE SCIENCE OF PSYCHOLOGY

Psychology, as a science, *describes and explains the observable behavior of organisms.* The psychologist asks, for example: What conditions in the life of a child bring about "aggressive" actions or behavior? What experiences enable a child to learn to read or to write? Why do people choose the occupations they enter? Why are some people better than others at problem solving?

The method that psychologists use to explain behavior is essentially that used by any scientist. They observe a given kind of behavior and attempt to relate this behavior to other observable factors. This is substantially what we do in everyday life when we attempt to explain the behavior of other people. For example, teachers and students alike feel that performance on tests in various courses depends upon factors other than knowledge of the subject being tested. We often hear an explanation such as "Johnny did poorly on this test because he wasn't feeling well." But we must raise a question here as we do about all explanations: Is the explanation a valid one? We can answer this only by systematic observation of the behavior of many people. Only when we know whether or not feeling states tend to influence test performance can we assign the explanation of Johnny's test performance to this factor. Also, in analyzing the relationship between test performance and the way Johnny feels, we must be sure we have not overlooked other factors that may account for his test performance. Perhaps he simply did not understand the test directions.

The teacher in this example has to answer two questions: (1) What factors are likely to affect test performance? (2) Which of these factors actually are influencing *this* test performance? The second question depends upon the first, and the teacher usually makes decisions related to the second. The teacher and the psychologist, then, continually seek to answer the question: What factors are related to this observed behavior?

THE PRESENT STATE OF EDUCATIONAL THEORY

What role does educational psychology—the proper subject of this text—play in the development of an educational science and in the practice of education? The practice of any art begins to improve with the development of new ways of viewing the activities that comprise it. New concepts and new theories enable us to give meaning to the activity in which we are engaged, to increase our understanding of this activity, and to predict and control the course of the activity. Ideally, the underlying science of the activity should provide the basis for this understanding and control; however, since we have no general and comprehensive educational theory or science, educational theory has drawn largely on those theories and sciences that seem to be most relevant to the educational process. Among these are the behavioral sciences and, in particular, psychology.

Psychologists have always taken a great interest in the educational process, and educational psychologists (notably, E. L. Thorndike,[1] with

---

[1] See "Thorndike's Connectionism," in E. R. Hilgard, *Theories of Learning*, 2nd ed. (New York: Appleton-Century-Crofts, 1956), Chapter 2. Thorndike is cited because his contributions laid the foundations of educational psychology, and because he led in applying psychology to educational practice.

his conception of learning as a set of stimulus-response bonds or connections) have had considerable influence on educational practice. The mental-test movement is another example of the contribution of psychologists to educational practice.

These are some of the comparatively specific contributions. It should be equally obvious that the general subject matter of psychological investigation is of relevance to educational practice. The psychologist investigates the learning process, the development of personality, the interrelations between children and their environments, and a host of other problems— all of which are related to educational problems. Psychology is the science of behavior change, and the function of the educational process is to promote desirable behavior changes.

The teacher studying psychology, however, should not expect to find simple answers to his questions. The psychologist will probably ignore the question about what to do specifically when Johnny throws spitballs. For as much as psychologists do know about learning, only an uncautiously brave, and perhaps foolhardy, psychologist would describe specific teaching procedures that would be universally applicable.

If psychology does not provide simple recipes for teaching, of what value is the study of psychology for the educator? Psychology contributes to the development of the teacher in two ways: (1) *by providing the teacher with a set of concepts and principles* that will enable him to view human behavior more critically and to increase his understanding of this behavior; (2) *by providing the teacher with skills* that are directly related to the educational process, such as ways of interpreting intelligence test and achievement test scores.

This chapter assumes that the improvement of educational practice requires critical study of the psychological theories and hypotheses underlying teaching practice, and systematic evaluation of the operations that apply these ideas. This analysis and evaluation is carried out by many people, and much of it must be done under controlled rather than classroom conditions. However, the teacher, as a professional, must maintain a stance of critical inquiry toward his own practices.

PROFESSIONAL KNOWLEDGE AND CRITICAL INQUIRY

A practitioner who claims professional status rests his claim on his expertise. He can cure or alleviate illnesses, or build bridges, or design automobiles or space vehicles. It is not, however, simply his skill in carrying out these activities but what he knows about the activity that determines his expertise. His knowledge gives him greater insight into problems and provides him with more varied ways of solving them. He is more adaptable, more flexible, more inventive—in part because he knows more than the nonprofessional.

This idea should not be oversimplified. Obviously, there are noncreative, inflexible professionals with varying degrees of ability and skill. Similarly, there are individuals of considerable expertise who lack such symbols of professionalism as a degree or membership in a professional society. However, the characteristic mark of the professional, as distinct from the craftsman or technician, is his grasp of the knowledge that supports his practice. This knowledge is theoretical as well as practical; that is, the professional knows not only what to do but why it ought to be done.[2]

Obviously, understanding of learning processes prepares a teacher to modify his teaching behavior to meet the specific problems he faces. He will be more observant of pupil behavior because his theoretical knowledge prepares him to look for subtle cues he might otherwise ignore. He is prepared to interpret what he observes, to consider more possibilities. His greater theoretical knowledge will prepare him to be a more adaptive problem solver. The press toward understanding, the search for data to support the practice, the construction of theories and hypotheses to improve practice mark the professional mentality. The professional sees the intimate relation between theory and practice.

THEORY AND PRACTICE

You have undoubtedly heard the statement "It's good in theory but poor in practice." The wide appeal of this statement should not obscure the fact that it does not describe the relation of theory to practice. A theory that does not explain or predict or help us to control something is a poor theory. It is good only in the sense that it seemed like a good explanation until it was tested. Such a theory ought to be rejected or modified.

On the other hand, sometimes the theory is good but the practice is poor; many of the principles of aerodynamics were known before a plane

---

[2] These ideas are based on distinctions made by Alfred North Whitehead in *Adventures of Ideas* (New York: The Macmillan Company, 1933), pp. 72–73; paperback (New York: Mentor Books, 1955), pp. 64–65.

was flown. And there are theories that have not yet been applied; knowledge about the chemical structure of the gene has not as yet led to methods for modifying genetic structure. Finally, many practical human activities were conducted quite effectively before theories were constructed to explain them. But all of these relations between theory and practice are examples of man's attempts to make sense out of his experiences, and to make experiences out of his ideas.

THEORY AND PRACTICE IN TEACHING

In a practical art such as teaching, a theory is a way of explaining how learning may be produced. Because theories may be more or less valid, more or less general, predictions from a theory may be more or less accurate. In a complex set of functions such as teaching, there may be subtheories and even competing theories to account for the actions taken in the profession. There may be seemingly contradictory explanations or suggestions.

Despite these qualifications, it is important to understand that each practitioner is theorizing. He makes assumptions and predictions. He has preferred ways of looking at the phenomena that characterize the profession. Gage states this idea as follows:

Yet, of course, all men . . . are theorists. They differ not in whether they use theory, but in the degree to which they are aware of the theory they use. The choice before the man in the street and the research worker alike is not whether to theorize but whether to articulate his theory, to make it explicit, to get it out in the open where he can examine it. Implicit theories—of personality, of learning, and indeed of teaching—are used by all of us in our everyday affairs. Often such theories take the form of folk sayings, proverbs, slogans, the unquestioned wisdom of the race. The scientist on the other hand explicates his theory.[3]

CONCEPTS AND METHODS OF SCIENTIFIC INVESTIGATION

Scientific method is no more than a set of logical rules for validating assertions about observable events. As a thinking tool, it can be applied to

---

[3] N. L. Gage, "Paradigms for Research on Teaching," in N. L. Gage, ed., *Handbook of Research on Teaching* (Chicago: Rand-McNally and Company, 1963), pp. 94–95.

any set of observables to yield greater understanding of them. We may reject the overweening claims of some scientists. We may dislike some of the applications of scientific knowledge. We can hardly reject a logical tool.

In this section we will examine some of the principal concepts and methods of scientific investigation. This study can provide greater appreciation of scientific method as a tool for critical inquiry in education. It can help a teacher use psychological research in evaluating and devising educational practices. It can give him a way of thinking that will facilitate critical inquiry. Hopefully, it will stimulate him to seek additional opportunities for training in psychological and educational inquiry.

THE STARTING POINT

Scientific investigation begins in curiosity—a question, a problem. Why do some men seem to learn more rapidly and more easily than other men? How do feelings and emotions influence thinking? Can emotions inhibit learning? Do some people have greater capacity to learn mathematics than others? Why is some information easily remembered, other items quickly forgotten? How does a group of people work together to solve a problem? Can we predict who is more likely to profit from a learning experience? Why do some teachers seem to produce greater learning in their students, more commitment to learning to learn?

How a question comes to be asked the first time may be obscure. Interestingly, this problem is itself the object of considerable current investigation.[4] Several processes seem to account for the initiating of a question or a problem, though the mechanism in each case is not clear. One of these is the ruminations of the investigator or theorist. Einstein was bothered by the traditional concept of time and began asking such questions as "What if one were to run after a beam of light?" A seemingly foolish question perhaps, but one that prompted him to ask seriously, "What is the velocity of light?" The results of his asking that question are well known.

Another source of stimulation is the press of observations, some of great practical importance. Why does blood flow from a wound? Are diseases transmitted from man to man or animal to man? Can we predict who will

[4] A growing body of literature on creativity attests to current interest in this problem. Some representative approaches may be found in H. E. Gruber, G. Terrell, and M. Wertheimer, eds., *Contemporary Approaches to Creative Thinking* (New York: Atherton Press, 1963).

profit from traditional schooling and identify who will need special educational provisions?

Some questions arise when someone wonders whether something that has always been assumed is in fact so. For example, Van Wagenen and Travers [5] observed, as many teachers have, that a teacher asks questions of a relatively small number of students in any class hour. Can we assume that other students are learning from the responses made by the student answering? These investigators arranged an experiment in which some students responded to questions and others did not. The responding student was told whether his answer was correct. Nonrespondents listened to these interchanges. On the last day of the experimental week, students were tested on items that had been taught. The group that had interacted directly with the experimenter received a **mean score** of 54 per cent correct. The group that had only listened to the interactions received a mean score of 44.3 per cent, and showed a marked decrement in performance over the week.

This example should reassure those readers who thought that question asking is a special ability reserved for the Einsteins, the Pasteurs, and other great innovators, theoreticians, and experimentalists. You have spent hundreds of hours in classes where this teaching procedure has been used. From there it is one short step to the question. The first step in critical inquiry can be made by anyone who is willing to ask a question. Question asking probably depends on our willingness to play with ideas and to suspend judgment.

Problem solving may also generate new problems. In the Van Wagenen and Travers experiment, why did the students who only listened learn less? The investigators hypothesized that the task had become dull for them and that the method did not control task orientation. Does encouraging participation by question asking generate interest? If so, why? May not the questions or the content be dull? This experiment did not answer these questions. But its results may stimulate other questions, which may lead to further experimentation.

THE CONCEPT OF VARIABLES

Some questions ask simply "what," "where," and "how many." What is the average class size in the local school district? How many teachers are

[5] R. K. Van Wagenen and R. M. W. Travers, "Learning under Conditions of Direct and Vicarious Reinforcement," *Journal of Educational Psychology*, 54 (1963), 356–362.

there in the state of California? What is the chemical composition of sugar? What is the range of verbal aptitude scores in my class? Where did Columbus first touch land?

There are many reasons for asking such questions. Frequently, a teacher needs to answer them before he can solve a problem or make a decision. For example, he needs to know the range of ability in his class in order to formulate instructional plans. If there is a wide range of ability, he may decide to break the class into smaller groups.

Another kind of question is about relationships. "What is the relation between ability grouping and achievement?" "What is the relation between map coloring and a child's ability to locate countries?" These questions name two or more quantities: ability grouping and achievement, map coloring and locating countries. Ordinarily, we seek answers to this kind of question because we want to know whether quantities like these change with respect to each other. Why have a child color a map? If map coloring does not help him locate countries, or enjoy geography, or relax him, or relieve boredom, or arouse his curiosity, why have him do it?

Sometimes, answers to questions of the first kind suggest questions of the second kind. An analysis made by the research department of the Los Angeles City Schools illustrates how facts can lead to ideas for relations.[6] Table 1–1 reports the extent of emotional problems of students assigned to remedial reading classes. On the basis of the data examined, the author of the report concluded that a substantial number of pupils in the sample had "emotional problems sufficiently obvious to be reported." Do emo-

TABLE 1–1. *Frequency of emotional difficulties in students assigned to remedial reading classes* (N = 142).

Category	Emotional Difficulties (per cent) *
General Health	39.5
School	55.7
Home	34.3

* Of the 142 students studied, 46 per cent showed emotional difficulties in more than one category.

[6] *An Analysis of Data Regarding Pupils Assigned to Remedial Reading Classes 1951–57* (Los Angeles: Los Angeles City School Districts Division of Elementary Education, Guidance and Counseling Section, January 1958).

tional difficulties cause the reading difficulties, or do they result from the reading difficulties? These data cannot tell us. But they do suggest some relationship between reading and emotional difficulties. Controlled experiments can then be devised to determine more about the relationship.

Each time a relation is sought, we begin by choosing factors that we think might be related. Our first step is a categorization, a classification. These categories have names or labels, like "emotional difficulties" or "reading difficulties." They may prove to be too broad or too narrow; and we will abandon them if we learn little or nothing by using them. Such categories or factors are called **variables.** A variable is a category for classifying phenomena. However, some categories may be more meaningful and measurable than others. The category "emotional problems" is very general; it might include, for instance, such more specific variables as "withdrawal," "anxiety," "aggression," and "hostility." The category "reading difficulties" might include "inadequate sight vocabulary," "poor work habits," and "limited speaking vocabulary." Each category groups events that are observable in various amounts or degrees, and that differ from one another in amount or degree.

In any study, a major task of the researcher is to define clearly the variables being studied, and to refine the method of measuring them.

Hypotheses as Relations among Variables

A **hypothesis** states a relation of dependency among variables. It predicts that a change in one variable will be accompanied by or will produce changes in another variable.

Here are some examples of hypotheses: *The characteristics of the college a student attends will be related to the scores he obtains on the Graduate Record Examination.*[7] The first variable is "college characteristics"; the second, "examination scores." *Attitude toward school will be related positively to the amount of biology retained.*[8] Attitude toward school is one variable, since not all students have the same attitude; amount of biology retained is another variable. The hypothesis predicts that positive attitudes will be associated with greater retention.

Hypotheses are frequently stated in the form "If *A*, then *B*": "If positive attitude toward school, then greater retention of subject matter." When a

---

[7] R. C. Nichols, "Effects of Various College Characteristics on Student Aptitude Test Scores," *Journal of Educational Psychology*, 55 (1964), 45–54.

[8] C. M. Garverick, "Retention of School Learning as Influenced by Selected Affective Tone Variables," *Journal of Educational Psychology*, 55 (1964), 31–34.

hypothesis is stated in this form, the dependency relation is made clear: Retention of subject matter depends on a positive attitude toward school.

This latter hypothesis should stimulate several questions. Intuitively, you may think that retention of subject matter depends on other variables as well as a positive attitude—on ability, interest, study habits, teaching method. But this hypothesis does not preclude these other possible relations. It simply states that there is a relation between attitude and retention of biology. If you are tempted to say, "That's obvious," you may not be pleased to know that the study cited found no such relation.

A hypothesis may state a relation between more than two variables. For example, "If the attitude toward school is positive, and if the student is interested in biology, then he will retain more biology information."

"But," you may ask, "why couldn't it be the other way around? Maybe the person who is easily learning a subject *develops* a positive attitude." At this point, two possibilities are available. And these alternative statements lead us into different theories about the organization among these variables. If we think of attitudes as relatively stable, influencing other behavior, then we would expect attitude toward school to influence retention. If, however, we think that the attitudes are developed and easily influenced by concurrent experience, then we would expect school experience to influence attitudes.

This example makes clear that a hypothesis is not an isolated idea, but part of a context of concepts and assumptions. The research scientist will ordinarily designate his context and any supporting theory, and will also marshal any available data to support the plausibility of the hypothesis as he has stated it. This careful thinking is economic, though it may occasionally blind an investigator to new ideas or approaches.

Measurement of Variables

We come now to one of the distinguishing marks of the scientific method—the observation of phenomena. The preceding phases can be conducted in the comfort of one's armchair, or discussions in the teachers' lounge may produce an occasional hypothesis worth testing. But the hypothesis has to be put to the test; otherwise, it is speculation— interesting but of unknown validity. *A hypothesis is tested by interrelating observations of the variables described in it.* These observations are *measurements* of the variables. The *measurements* are the products of a systematic method of measurement.

What do we mean when we say a variable is measured? Essentially, we mean that we have some way of describing its variations. The first step is to define the variable in terms of observables, behavior that can be seen and counted. Bandura, for example, wanted to find out whether children who observe aggressive acts are later likely to commit such acts.[9] He defined an aggressive act as one likely to hurt, either physically or verbally. Bandura first showed his subjects a film, in which the film model punched, struck with a mallet, and threw a doll into the air. Simultaneously, the model emitted such hostile remarks as "Hit him in the nose." After his subjects had seen the film, Bandura placed them in a play room containing materials that could be used for aggressing; and he counted the number of times the materials were used aggressively. His definition of imitative aggression indicates how this variable was specified:

This category includes acts of striking the Bobo doll with the mallet, sitting on the doll and punching it in the nose, kicking the doll, tossing it in the air, and the verbally aggressive responses "Sock him," "Hit him," "Kick him," "Throw him in the air," and "Pow" (p. 6).

These acts can be seen; they can be counted. In this sense they have been measured.

Necessary characteristics of the measurement procedure. The description of the behavior to be measured introduces the problem of **validity.** Whatever procedure is used, it must actually measure what it purports to measure. Assume that your class has been studying poetry, and you want to know whether they like poetry more than they did when they began its study. You must first ask yourself what you mean by "liking poetry," what you will accept as the criterion of liking poetry. For instance, do they *say* they like poetry? Do they read poetry without being required to? Do they even perhaps try writing poetry?

Here again we run into some problems. Suppose a person says he likes poetry but rarely, if ever, reads any? Would you conclude that he likes poetry? Or, if you choose the reading of poetry as your criterion, you must devise some way to assess how much poetry reading your students are doing. Or you may scale these different behaviors, with stated liking being the lowest degree and writing poetry the highest. Again, you must construct some way of observing these behaviors.

We frequently express our ideas in generalities such as "liking poetry."

---

[9] A. Bandura, D. Ross, and S. Ross, "Imitation of Film-Mediated Aggressive Models," *Journal of Abnormal and Social Psychology,* 66 (1963), 3–11.

To measure "liking," we must select one or more of the above possible meanings as our definition in this instance. For example, you may decide that liking poetry means how much poetry the person actually reads. This behavior, reading poetry, is the **criterion behavior.**

The general principle to be applied in devising the measurement procedure is that either the criterion behavior or some behavior known to be highly related to it must be observed. The experiment by Bandura illustrates the first method; an experiment by Edling illustrates the second.[10] Edling showed a group of high school students two films designed to motivate students to attend college, and tried to find out whether the films produced their intended effect. He could have simply found out how many *did* eventually go to college. However, since he wanted to see the immediate effects of the films, he devised a paper-and-pencil attitude scale. (There was also a good experimental reason for this immediate testing; later matriculation might be attributed to other factors than the film message.) However, he first had to demonstrate that responses on the attitude scale were related to college attendance. Therefore, he collected attitude responses and data on college attendance on another but similar group of high school students. He found that 66 per cent of students who received scores above the mean enrolled in college, but only 11 per cent of students below this point enrolled. He could conclude, then, that the attitude scale did measure, though not perfectly, behavior related to college attendance. The relation was substantial enough to justify the use of the attitude scale in the experiment.

The measurement procedure must also be **reliable**—that is, accurate. What would you do with a scale that gave your weight one day as 140 pounds; the next day as 150; and the next as 160 (assuming no evidence for rapid gain or loss)? Although all measurement scales are only relatively accurate, the degree of accuracy has to be known. When the error of measurement is large, the scale readings may be useless. In all cases the conclusions drawn from the measurements have to be related to the accuracy of the measuring instrument.

The third principal characteristic of a measurement procedure is that it must be **standardized**—that is, the conditions of measurement must be held constant. The logic of this principle is simple. If the conditions of measurement change, differences in behavior may be ascribed to the

---

[10] J. V. Edling, *A Study of the Effectiveness of Audio-Visual Teaching Materials When Prepared According to the Principles of Motivational Research,* Final Report, Project No. 221, National Defense Education Act (Washington, D. C.; Office of Education, U. S. Department of Health, Education, and Welfare, 1963).

method of measurement. This principle is not violated when an investigator uses two different tests—provided he can demonstrate that the two tests are measuring the same behavior. To eliminate **practice effects** (the learning that takes place simply because the subject has taken the test), for example, an investigator may change tests from before to after measurements, but he will provide evidence to show that the tests are measuring the same behavior.

Each of these principles is a logical requirement if we want to draw conclusions from our observations. Testing the validity of an observation ensures that we observe what we want to observe. Reliability ensures confidence in our description. Standardization of the procedure ensures that the same kinds of data are gathered in each instance of observation.

Application of principles of measurement. We may apply these principles in two ways. First, in our reading of psychological and educational research, we may inquire about methods of measurement. Does an author carefully describe his methods of measurement? Does he define the variables to be measured? Does he report the technique for evoking the desired behavior? What statements does he make about the validity of measurement procedures? Does he provide information on reliability? What were the conditions of measurement?

We may also apply these principles to our observations of behavior. A teacher may say, for example, "Jimmy doesn't get along well with other children" or "Susy is very creative in her art work." One is not very fussy if he asks what the teacher means by "not getting along well." Does Jimmy hit other children, or refuse to talk to them, or sulk when refused a request? In what way is Susy more "creative" than other students? Has the teacher had comparable opportunities for evaluating the creativity of other children? Has the teacher seen only one instance of Susy's creativity; if so, would you have confidence in the description?

THE EXPERIMENTAL METHOD AND HYPOTHESIS TESTING

Measurement of behavior is a necessary step in scientific method, but it is only a means to an end. The purpose of scientific method is to determine the relations among variables. The most powerful tool for assessing these relations is the experimental method.

The essence of the experimental method is to produce change in one variable (or more) and study the effect of this variation on changes in a second variable. Two technical terms will be useful here. The **indepen-**

dent variable is the one deliberately varied. The **dependent variable** is the variable predicted to be affected by manipulations of the independent variable. When hypotheses are stated in standard form, the independent variable is readily identified; it is the variable in the "if" clause. In the hypothesis "If someone makes overt responses while learning, the learning will be greater," the independent variable is method of responding, and the dependent variable is the amount of learning.

An experiment by Krumboltz and Weisman to test this hypothesis illustrates both the experimental method and examples of the measurement principles discussed above.[11] First, the measurement problems. What is meant by "greater learning"? These investigators constructed a test designed to measure a student's familiarity with concepts and principles described in a teaching program. Since they wanted to measure what the students learned immediately after the teaching and two weeks later, they constructed two forms of the test. Learning was measured by the scores obtained on the test. Since each test item could be answered correctly by a knowledge of the content in the instructional program, students who received higher scores had learned more. The reliability of the test was determined and found to be high.

How was variation in the independent variable, method of responding, produced? An instructional program was used, in which each item of content was presented in a "frame," along with a question about that item. There were four groups of subjects. Three of these groups were **experimental groups**: The *overt* group wrote out the answer to each question. The *covert* group was instructed to compose an answer but not to write it out. The *reading* group read each item and its answer, which was provided for the student. A fourth group, called the **control group**, worked through a program on a different topic.

The overt group did not obtain significantly higher scores on the immediate criterion test than the covert or reading groups. Students in this group did perform better than those in the control group—which is hardly surprising, since the latter studied different content. However, the overt group did significantly better on the test taken two weeks later. The original hypothesis seems to require modification. We may now say that active responding during the acquisition phase of learning probably yields greater long-term retention.

[11] J. D. Krumboltz and R. G. Weisman, "The Effect of Overt and Covert Responding to Programed Instruction on Immediate and Delayed Retention," *Journal of Educational Psychology,* 53 (1962), 89–92.

Experimental Control

An experimenter must arrange his variables in such a way that the influence of the independent variable is unambiguous and incontestable. *An experiment is a logical design to test what is called the* **statistical hypothesis:** *that the independent variable has only an unsystematic and chance influence on the dependent variable.* Experimental arrangements are devised to control the potential influence of other variables. When non-chance effects are found, the statistical hypothesis of no influence may be rejected.

Bandura's experiment (see p. 14) illustrates these ideas. The children in his experiment included both boys and girls. Since our society tolerates more physical aggression from boys than girls, more imitative aggression might be found in groups composed only or primarily of boys. If it were, we would attribute differences between the groups to their composition rather than to the influence of the model. Therefore, Bandura assigned both boys and girls to the various treatments.

To eliminate or to reduce the probability of systematic differences among groups, experimenters usually assign individuals *randomly* to groups—by assigning numbers to the experimental subjects and then assigning them to groups by using a table of random numbers, in which numbers corresponding to subject numbers occur in random order.

Experimenters further test for possible chance results by using *control groups. A control group resembles treatment groups in as many relevant ways as possible, except that its members are not exposed to the independent variable.* Krumboltz and Weisman's experiment (see p. 17) is illustrative. First, students in this group were placed there randomly from the pool of available subjects. Second, they too studied a program but of different content, responding in writing to the program questions. If the control group had scored as high as any of the experimental groups, we could not conclude that the independent variable was producing an effect. When experimental groups exceed the control group significantly, we can logically attribute the differences to the influence of the independent variable.

However, what if the members of the control group had read a book, or had been in another room? Differences among the groups could be attributed to these factors. Experimental control is achieved by making sure that a variable likely to influence the results has an equal opportunity of affecting all subjects. In the Krumboltz and Weisman experiment, for example, all subjects had been told that they were using new instructional materials. If using new materials influences learning, the influence is equally likely to occur in all groups.

These experiments illustrate the kind of logical game a scientist plays. They also illustrate that experimenting requires careful thinking and imagination. Most important, they demonstrate why experimenting is necessary. The world of observables is complex. Experimenting simplifies it and controls it just long enough to help us understand how variables are related.

Evaluation of Experimental Conclusions

Repetition of experiments. Any experiment is a sample of all the experiments that could be conducted to test the hypothesis. By chance alone, a small percentage of all experiments that could be conducted would support the hypothesis. How can we be certain that this experiment is not the one producing the seemingly significant but chance results? We can never be completely certain. We can only reduce the probability of uncertainty. Therefore, one requirement of the scientific method is that experiments be repeated; the term used is **replicated.** If the same or similar results are obtained again and again, confirming or invalidating a hypothesis, confidence in the conclusion rises.

Practically, the repetition of experiments is expensive and intrigues the scientist hardly at all unless he feels something is awry. The principle is still relevant; experiments should be replicated. However, two other tests are used to ameliorate the stringency of this requirement.

Consistency of results. The *test of consistency* is applied to experimental results. Do the results fit with previous experimentation; are they consistent with predictions from well-established theory? Krumboltz and Weisman, for example, in concluding their report, recognize that their results contradict a hypothesis that has experimental support. Rather than rejecting the hypothesis, they relate their data to suggestions of other investigators and attempt to explain how the results might be consistent with the general hypothesis. They say, "The advantages of overt responding may not become clearly apparent until some time after the study period." [12] This supposition suggests why other investigators have failed to find overt responding highly effective; these other investigators failed

[12] Krumboltz and Weisman (see note 11), p. 92.

to measure long-term retention. Again, we see that a hypothesis must be viewed in the context of the ideas of which it is a part.

Plausible rival hypotheses. Another test to evaluate experimental conclusions is to seek for competing hypotheses that might explain the results equally well. For example, in the Krumboltz and Weisman experiment, the subjects in the covert and reading groups may have been brighter and learned more easily, thus overcoming the handicaps of the instructional method. This explanation is a **plausible rival hypothesis.** However, the investigators attenuated the *plausibility* of this rival explanation by random assignment of subjects. Or perhaps subjects improve simply as an effect of instruction, regardless of its characteristics. To eliminate the plausibility of this hypothesis, the experimenters used a control group, which received a comparable instructional procedure but different content exposure; this group did significantly poorer than the other groups. Another rival hypothesis: The kind of content may influence the ease of learning it. To control this potential influence, common content is used in all experimental treatments.

Plausible rival hypotheses are eliminated by careful experimental design. Therefore, in judging the meaning of the results of an experiment, we must evaluate the amount of experimental control in its design. The greater the control, the greater our confidence in the results. The fewer the number of competing hypotheses that might explain the results, the greater our confidence in our conclusions.

The emphasis on *plausibility* indicates that we should identify a genuine source of potential explanation not accounted for by the design of the experiment. There are several common sources of such alternative explanations, and we consider them now.[13]

Experiments conducted over relatively long periods of time with human subjects may be influenced by what happens to the subjects in the intervening periods. Suppose, for example, that I were conducting an experiment designed to test the effects of several ways of presenting information on the relation of smoking to lung cancer. During the course of the experiment, an investigator reports that the data gathered on these effects antedated the widespread use of filters. He further points out that filters have reduced the amount of cancer-producing agents reaching the

---

[13] The ideas treated in this section are developed in greater detail in D. T. Campbell and J. C. Stanley, "Experimental and Quasi-Experimental Designs for Research on Teaching," in N. L. Gage, ed., *Handbook of Research on Teaching* (see note 3), Chapter 5, pp. 171–246.

smoker. What effect might this extra-experimental influence have on my results?

A similar extra-experimental effect may be produced by maturation of the subjects in the experiment. To study the effects of a physical-fitness program, we should design our experiment so that the results could not be attributed to maturation of the subjects. One way to do this is to assign subjects randomly to the treatments, so that maturation is a constant effect in all groups. Another way would be to use subjects unlikely to mature on the behavior being studied, if this is possible.

In long-term studies subjects are usually lost through death or because they refuse to participate further in the study, or move away and cannot be located. The characteristics of the remaining subjects might account for the experimental results. Many school experiments conducted over time run this risk. Assume that you want to know the effects of four years of college on a class. You are interested in finding whether college has changed students' attitudes toward scholarship, intellectuality, and willingness to tolerate uncertainty and doubt. You measure their attitudes in these respects at entrance and at the end of each year in college. The results are reasonably attributed to the college's influence only if the group is intact at the end of the four years. Perhaps the remaining students are those most receptive to the college's influence.

Since many problems of this kind are significant both theoretically and practically, and since it is impossible to eliminate dropouts, an experimenter will try to salvage his data. He will compare dropouts and retainees to see whether they differ in any way relevant to the variables being measured. In this way he tests the credibility of the rival explanation—that the characteristics of the subjects account for the results.

A comparable problem arises when an experiment uses volunteers, particularly when the study is likely to deter some people from participating. Characteristics associated with volunteering, rather than the experimental treatment, may explain the results.

One source of rival explanation, the effect of being in the experiment, is known as the **Hawthorne effect.** The Hawthorne effect is the behavior change that accrues simply because a subject receives the special treatment that any experiment provides. Some people are so impressed with the possibility of this effect that they explain away all educational experimentation as being the result of it. This point of view ignores the principle that a rival explanation must be *plausible.* The Hawthorne effect is a plausible rival explanation when the experiment compares a treatment and a no-treatment group. For example, an investigator may want to compare a new method of teaching reading with the customary method. Students in the experimental group might easily become aware that they were being taught reading in a different way. In such cases a Hawthorne effect is a plausible rival explanation of any results obtained. However, a shrewd investigator will invent ways of disguising the conduct of an experiment, in order to eliminate this effect. Or, as in the Krumboltz and Weisman experiment, he will treat a control group as much like the experimental groups as he can, making it difficult for the subjects to know which are experimental treatments.

THE CORRELATIONAL METHOD AND HYPOTHESIS TESTING

The experiment as a logical tool has been discussed at length because of its importance in scientific method. The correlational method is another tool for making inferences, particularly important to the educational practitioner because of its widespread use in psychological and educational research.

A **correlation** is an *association between two or more variables.* For example, if a teacher tabulates the aptitude scores and the grade-point averages at the end of the first semester for each student in his class, he will probably find a relation between these two sets of data. In Figure 1–1 is a plot of data of this kind. This plot is called a **scattergram** and is made as follows. Take the scores of a student. Read across to his aptitude score and up to his grade-point average score. Plot each set of scores similarly, and a diagram like Figure 1–1 results. We·are now in a better position to make a judgment about the data because we have used all of them: high aptitude scores do tend to go with high grade-point averages, and similarly at the low ends of the scales.

This example is an instance of a *positive correlation*. A positive correlation is one in which individuals high on one measure tend also to be high on a second measure, and correspondingly for individuals at the low end of the scale. A *negative correlation* is one in which individuals high on one measure tend to be low on the second, and those low on the first tend to be high on the second.

An example of the correlational method is Fleming and Weintraub's study of the relation between creativity and rigidity.[14] Other investigators, using samples of older children and adults, had found creative

---

[14] E. A. Fleming and S. Weintraub, "Attitudinal Rigidity as a Measure of Creativity in Gifted Children," *Journal of Educational Psychology,* 53 (1962), 81–85.

behavior correlated with measures of personality characteristics, such as greater emotional and ideational freedom. Fleming and Weintraub wanted to know whether these relations would be found in younger children of high ability.

What is meant by verbal creativity is best described by how it is measured. An experimenter gives a problem to a child and asks him to solve it. The problem is stated in words, and the child's solution is given in words—hence the label "verbal." The creativity of the solution is judged by its unusualness. Fleming and Weintraub measured verbal creativity by

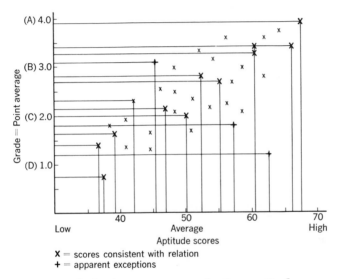

X = scores consistent with relation
+ = apparent exceptions

FIGURE 1–1. *A scattergram, plotting aptitude scores and grade-point average.*

posing such questions as "What would you do to try to become educated, if all schools were abolished?"

Rigidity was defined as intolerance of ambiguity; the behavior of casting ideas, opinions, and feelings in "black and white." A paper-and-pencil test measuring this attitude was used to obtain rigidity scores. When the sets of scores were correlated, they were found to be negatively related. High verbal creativity is associated with low rigidity, and low verbal creativity is associated with high rigidity in this sample of children (see Figure 1–2). Tests were also used to measure nonverbal creativity. One of the tasks required each child to draw a picture using a colored shape. Scoring methods were devised for rating these productions. The

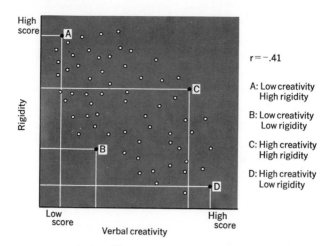

FIGURE 1–2. *Illustrative scattergram of relationship between verbal creativity and rigidity (adapted from Fleming and Weintraub).*

correlation between nonverbal creativity and rigidity was small, and should be treated as if there were no relation.

Applications of Correlational Method

Two applications of the correlational method are very common. Recall that we said a test must be shown to measure what it purports to measure; that is, the test must be valid. An achievement test, for example, may be designed to measure knowledge of English usage. Do scores on this test correlate positively with other measures of this knowledge—for instance, the grades students receive in English courses? A correlation of English-usage scores and English grades will show whether an association exists between the test performance and the criterion measure. A relatively high correlation indicates that the two measures are probably measuring the same behavior.

Another application of correlational method is in estimations of the reliability of measuring instruments. If a test were administered twice to a group of students, we would expect their scores to be correlated (assuming that the students were not studying in the intervening period and that nothing unusual had occurred to affect their performances). We would question the accuracy of the instrument if students high on one occasion were low on another. There are other methods of computing the reliability, but each involves a correlation between two performances.[15]

The Correlation Coefficient

Formulas have been developed for translating the amount of a relationship into a number. Although the details of these formulas will not be explained here, the concept will be described. A perfect relationship means that the highest score on one variable is accompanied by the highest score on the second, and similarly for each score down to the lowest. A lack of relation is easily symbolized by zero. The numerical value of the correlation must reflect these variations from zero to perfect correlation. The purpose of the statistical formula is to produce a number that indicates the amount of relation. One of the most widely used correlational methods, the **Pearson Product-Moment correlation coefficient,** produces numbers in the range from $+1$ to -1. Intermediate relations are represented by such numbers as .54, .32, .49, $-.30$, $-.72$. The absolute value of the number, the number without the sign, indicates the *degree* of relationship. The larger this absolute value, the greater the association between the two variables.

The sign indicates the *direction* of the correlation. A **positive correlation** is one in which scores are arranged similarly on two measures; highs on one tend also to be highs on the other, and similarly for low scores. A **negative correlation** is one where scores on the two measures are oppositely arranged, high on one and low on the other.

Assume, for example, that a correlation of .90 is obtained between two sets of scores on two different tests. We note first that the coefficient is positive, which means that high scores on one test are associated with high scores on the other, and similarly for low scores. Second, we note that the absolute value of the coefficient is near 1.00, which means that the association between the two sets of scores is high. The closer the numerical value is to zero, the less association there is between two sets of scores.

There are different numerical ways of expressing the degree of association between two variables. The above examples use the Pearson Product-

[15] Elaboration of these concepts and technical details may be found in A. Anastasi, *Psychological Testing,* 2nd ed. (New York: The Macmillan Company, 1961), and L. J. Cronbach, *Essentials of Psychological Testing,* 2nd ed. (New York: Harper & Row, 1960).

Moment coefficient, the one you are likely to encounter in reading test manuals and research articles. It is readily identified by the symbol *r*.

TESTS OF STATISTICAL SIGNIFICANCE

The sheer numerical value of a correlation does not indicate that an association exists. Suppose that you are studying the relation between aptitude scores and performance in a geometry class. You collect aptitude and achievement scores on a **sample** of students. It is a sample because these students are some of all the students studying geometry. Let us arbitrarily say that there are 150 students in this sample. Assume that you could obtain the same data on 100 such samples. That is, in Sample 1 you

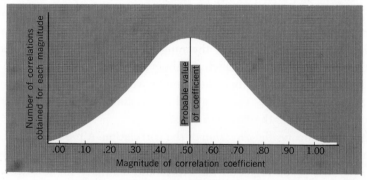

FIGURE 1–3. *Distribution of correlation coefficients between aptitude scores and scores on geometry achievement test.*

have 150 aptitude scores and geometry achievement test scores; similarly, for Sample 2 and Sample 3; and so on for 100 such samples.

Compute the correlation between the two sets of scores separately for each sample. The results might look something like this: Sample 1, r = .90; Sample 2, r = .75; Sample 3, r = .45; . . . Sample 95, r = .20; Sample 96, r = .85. You have not obtained identically the same coefficient for each sample. But you would expect some consistency in the results. These hundred correlation coefficients would probably be distributed something like Figure 1–3. From such an arrangement, you can make an *inference* about the *probable* value of the amount of correlation; that is, the value you would obtain if you had data for every student studying geometry.

In practice, an investigator rarely has one hundred samples of this kind. However, he must determine whether the coefficient he has obtained could have arisen as the result of chance factors or whether it is an approximation of the probable relation between the variables. To answer this question, he applies a *test of statistical significance*. This test is a mathematical manipulation that permits an inference about the probability that the figure he obtained is due to chance factors.

Fleming and Weintraub indicate which of the ten correlation coefficients they report are statistically significant; that is, which ones are unlikely to have arisen by chance alone (see Table 1–2). Let us study this table of correlation coefficients to apply what we have learned. We note that with one exception all of the correlations are negative. Four of the six correlations are between .30 and .45, one is larger than the rest, another

TABLE 1–2. *Correlations of creativity batteries (from Fleming and Weintraub).*

Variables	Rigidity [a]	Nonverbal Creativity	Chronological Age	IQ
Verbal Creativity	−.41 *	.53 *	.08	.04
Verbal Originality	−.37 *			
Verbal Fluency	−.40 *			
Verbal Flexibility	−.32 *			
Nonverbal Creativity	−.15		.02	.06
CA	−.50 *			

[a] Partial *r* (age held constant) between rigidity and verbal creativity = −.43.
* Significant at the .01 level.

smaller. Five of the correlations have an asterisk attached, referring to the note "significant at the .01 level." This statement tells us the probability that a correlation as large as the one obtained would arise by chance alone.

Significance levels are reported in this way. Another way is as follows: $p < .01$, which is read "probability less than one one-hundredth." Some statement of this kind should accompany every research report, although some results will not be significant and not all will reach the .01 level. Note that an asterisk is not attached to the correlation between nonverbal creativity and rigidity.

The statistical method of testing for significance pits two hypotheses against each other. One hypothesis is the *research hypothesis*. Recall that Fleming and Weintraub expected to find a negative relation between creativity and rigidity, since other investigators had found one and there were theoretical reasons for expecting one. Their research hypothesis: There will be a negative correlation between the variables creativity and rigidity.

The other hypothesis, against which the experimental hypothesis is pitted, is the *statistical hypothesis*—that the correlation between variables is zero. The statistical test of significance leads to a probability figure, such as noted above, which tells us the probability that the obtained correlation is likely to be a chance departure from zero.

We are in the position of choosing between the hypotheses on the basis of a probability. When the probability is small, usually .05 or less, we reject the statistical hypothesis of zero correlation. This statistical hypothesis is called the **null hypothesis.** In rejecting the statistical hypothesis, we are logically accepting the research hypothesis. By accepting or rejecting the statistical hypothesis, we are evaluating the research hypothesis. When we reject the statistical hypothesis, we tentatively accept the research hypothesis, and contrariwise.

This concept of statistical significance also applies to the data produced in experimental studies. Such studies usually present results in the form of mean differences between groups; for example, the mean scores on an achievement test for two experimental groups may differ. Sometimes the data are reported in percentage differences: "50 per cent of group *A* reached criterion level (a predetermined score) on a performance test, but only 20 per cent of group *B*." The reasoning used above must be applied to these kinds of data. The statistical significance of these differences is calculated. In so doing, the investigator is answering the question "What is the probability that a difference of this magnitude would arise by chance alone?" If the differences are statistically significant, we infer that the differences may be attributed to the experimental variations, if appropriate experimental controls have been used.

Many technical details have been omitted in this discussion. We have not described how to compute the various tests of significance. Nor have we given the principles for selecting the appropriate test. These matters are properly discussed in depth in statistics courses and books. However, *the behavior to be acquired as a consequence of this discussion is relatively easy to specify:* (1) *in any study that you read, look for statements about statistical significance;* (2) *relate these statements to the conclusions drawn.* This last action is prompted by asking yourself the following questions: What is the research hypothesis? What is the statistical hypothesis? What is the probability that a difference or correlation of this magnitude would arise by chance? Is this probability small enough (usually .05 and below) to justify the risk of rejecting the statistical hypothesis? If the statistical hypothesis is or is not rejected, what do I say about the research hypothesis?

We have pointed out many reasons for accepting hypotheses tentatively. The above description of the experimental and correlational methods and of the concept of statistical significance should make clear what is meant by tentativeness. It is not obstinacy, nor is it a compulsive perfectionism. First, data of some kind must be available. Second, those data must be evaluated. The preceding discussion of experimental and correlational method prepares you to estimate the validity of the inferences to be drawn. The analysis of statistical significance makes abundantly clear that acceptance and rejection is a matter of probabilities. Third, the conclusions of the study must be related to many other factors: Have other investigators obtained similar results? How generalizable are the results? What contradictions or inconsistencies are suggested by the data? These assessment operations are ways of judging the validity of the hypothesis.

Tentativeness means assessing the probable validity of a hypothesis and acting consistently with this estimate. It also means being prepared to revise the judgment when evidence suggests such a need. It means continually examining the validity of the hypothesis as it is tested in new situations and under new conditions.

This spirit of continually examining and testing ideas is recommended to teachers in the belief that this attitude is necessary for the improvement of educational practice. Understanding the logic of scientific method is no more than acquiring methods for verifying ideas. This approach can make the act of teaching an exciting intellectual enterprise. Its expected consequence is greater reliability in fostering learning in children.

EXPERIMENTATION IN THE CLASSROOM

The most common objection to experimenting is that an experiment is not "lifelike." Teaching is a complex process. There are many variables influencing both teaching behavior and the learning process. An experiment studies only a few of these many variables. So the argument runs.

The point is valid but irrelevant. An experiment does not replicate life in all its complexity; it simulates aspects of it. The purpose of the experimental method is to control the influence of some variables to study the relations among others. As we have seen, the credibility of a conclusion depends on the amount of control the experimenter can exert.

The experiment is a tool to produce reliable knowledge. The experimental method is more likely to be efficient in this respect than induction from our experience. Our experience is complex because it does not occur in an orderly fashion, and because we cannot parcel out the influence of all the factors in it. How would you, for example, determine whether overt responding is a necessary condition for efficient learning from your ordinary classroom experience? Or that the effect is more likely to be on long-term than short-term retention?

Obviously we learn from our experience; at least, we draw conclusions from what we observe. Simply having more experience, however, does not guarantee greater understanding. A teacher ought to think critically about the day-by-day events, experimenting vicariously by interrelating his experiences. "Today when I asked questions, students seemed eager to answer. Yesterday, hardly a hand was raised. Why? Was it the question? Was it the way I asked it? Has something happened to the students in the meantime?" So the teacher questions and hypothesizes. This conceptual rearranging of events is necessary to make any sense out of one's experience.

The next step is to arrange direct control of these events. Systematic questioning of some students may be related to their performance on other questions, or on a test, for example. These manipulations do not produce sufficient experimental control to draw highly valid conclusions. But a teacher may repeat a procedure with different students, with new subject matter, to test a hypothesis and plausible rivals.

The author and his associates had a group of teachers record one of their class sessions. These teachers tabulated the frequency of responses of each student in the class. They were instructed to reward the participation of low participators and eliminate reward for high participators in the succeeding class sessions. The study was short term, so that harmful effects were not anticipated. The teachers recorded a second session after this treatment, tabulating again participatory responses. They found, as was predicted, that low participators were now participating more frequently, and high participators less frequently.

This was a quasi-experiment—systematic manipulation of a variable was used, but experimental control was minimal. Other variables may be influencing the results. Perhaps the rewarded participators felt more confident on the subjects being discussed. Repeat the procedure with new content. Perhaps the effect varies with the ability of the students. Vary the procedure by ability level, rewarding and not rewarding both high and low ability students. In these ways a teacher may apply the logic of experimentation in testing hypotheses about teaching plans and procedures.

These approximations of formal experimentation can be carried out by teachers in their classrooms. A little imagination, curiosity, and confidence may be all that is required. Consider this problem. A teacher was convinced that model building increased his students' interest in ancient history and improved their knowledge of the subject. How could he find out whether his convictions had any validity? Why not experiment?

The first step is defining the behavior changes we expect to occur. How will we judge greater interest? More questions asked in class? More reading? Expressions of interest? Pick one or more criteria of this kind and decide how the behavior will be measured. Similarly, define the way in which greater understanding will be shown. Next, construct some model-building assignments. One activity might be to construct a model of the Forum, another of the Coliseum. Describe what is to be done and what is to be learned. Then devise an alternative way of learning the same things, such as drawing schemas of the same buildings and their surroundings. Or, as a third method, develop a set of reading materials on the same items.

Make these activities as nearly alike as possible in all respects except the model-building and drawing activities. For example, all three methods should cover the same time; you should devote equal attention to each group. Since teachers have considerable freedom in arranging assignments, randomly assign your class members to each of these activities. Record your observations of these students during the learning period. At the end of the activities, test for the various groups' understanding and information. Assuming a significantly superior performance for one or more groups, what are the plausible rival explanations?

THE PROBLEM OF APPLYING RESEARCH

We will asume that you have grasped the idea that a scientific study does not replicate life, that its purpose is to find relations among a limited number of variables. The problem in a practical situation is that many variables may be influencing effects. To apply research results to a practical problem, it is necessary to judge the correspondence between the simulated situation of an experiment and the complexity of the "real" situation.

Research studies may be classified by their approximation to the situation where we will apply what we have learned. Let us consider two experiments on the same general problem. Teachers argue about the value of making a learning task more or less difficult. Some say that students will learn more if they are challenged; others claim that they will become discouraged. We present two experiments that contrast markedly in their correspondence to classroom conditions.

Sax and Reade, interested in this problem, constructed a "hard" and an "easy" examination, which they administered to a university class as a six-week examination.[16] The two exams were distributed randomly to the class. Precautions were taken so that students would not learn they had received different exams. Both groups took the same final examination, which fell between the hard and easy exams in difficulty. The mean scores on the final exam differed significantly, the group which took the harder exam scoring higher. The authors report a probability figure of .001 ($p = .001$). What does this figure mean?

They analyzed the results by comparing the performances of the brighter and less bright students under the two conditions. They found that brighter students who took the hard exam did better than those who had the easy exam. Similar results were not obtained for the less bright students. Since teachers usually give easier exams to grade students, Sax and Reade recommend the following decision rule. "Use fairly difficult examinations throughout the semester and . . . fairly easy examinations for grading purposes at the end of the semester" (p. 25). Are you wondering about the effect of such a rule on the less able students? Remember that these investigators did not find any relation between difficulty of exams and achievement for the less able student.

What do you think about applying this decision rule to other teaching situations? Do you think that the age and educational level of the students might be related to the effects? If you do, what differences would you expect? Might some teacher characteristics interact with the examination procedure to affect the results? You cannot claim these other variables will change the results. You may predict it.

Contrast this experiment with one reported by Lawrence and Festinger, who were also interested in the relation of effort to learning. Lawrence and Festinger randomly assigned rats to two experimental treatments.[17]

---

[16] G. Sax and M. Reade, "Achievement as a Function of Test Difficulty Level," *American Educational Research Journal*, 1 (1964), 22–25.

[17] D. Lawrence and L. Festinger, *Deterrents and Reinforcement* (Stanford, Calif.: Stanford University Press, 1963), pp. 141–143.

In one treatment the rats had to run up an incline of 25 degrees to reach the food box; in the other, up an incline of 50 degrees. The rats in the second condition had to work harder during the learning trials. The criterion of learning was the number of trials required to extinguish the learned behavior. If a learned behavior is difficult to extinguish, we assume that the original learning was greater. Lawrence and Festinger found that extinction occurred more quickly with rats who had to expend less effort to learn.

Before you say that rats are not students, remember that these experiments have been presented to study the correspondence between the experiment and "real life." Infra-human organisms are useful experimental subjects because the experimenter can achieve greater experimental control by using them. These animals do not have a learning history for the kinds of tasks on which the experimenter trains them. The students in the Sax and Reade experiment are experienced learners. Although the effects of their learning history are controlled by random assignment to groups, we have no way of knowing if and how learning history interacts with the experimental variables.

The experimental animal lives in a highly controlled environment. We give little thought to parental and peer group influences on his learning. But Sax and Reade had to disguise their treatments so that students would not influence each other. We are surer that learning history and other influences are not affecting the results in the Lawrence and Festinger experiment because there is greater control over them. But we cannot tell from either experiment what influence such variables may have.

Other experiments must be performed to assess the effects of the many variables present in the actual classroom learning situation. As this knowledge becomes available, it may be applied in the design of instructional systems. These systems manipulate variables that are likely to produce desired behavior changes. An analogy may be helpful to understand this idea.

Engineers, by experimenting, study the effects of stress variables on the stability of structures. They have also accumulated considerable experience in constructing stable structures. Each of these applications is also tested. The design or first phase of this sequence applies what is known about stress variables to the creation of a particular structural system. The second phase is called the developmental phase, during which models are tested and field trials are run. The development phase tests the design to determine its practicality.

Experimentation is a strategy for discovery; development, a strategy for invention. Unfortunately, in education we do not progress systematically from experimentation to development.[18] However, the day is not too far distant when we will carry out these sequences to construct instructional systems. But even then a portion of the development task will remain with the teacher, who will need to adapt tested instructional systems to the realities of his classroom.

THE RESEARCH-DEVELOPMENT CONTINUUM

We initiated this discussion with a problem. How do we apply what we have learned by experimenting to develop instructional systems? The greater the correspondence between the experimental situation and the one it simulates, the closer we are to the design and development phase.

Hilgard [19] describes six steps along the research-development continuum (see Figure 1–4). On the pure research end of the continuum are

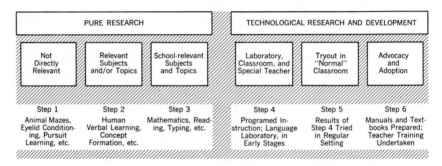

FIGURE 1–4. *Steps in research on learning—pure research to technological development (from Hilgard).*

the studies like the experiments we have been discussing in this chapter. Step-1 experiments are usually designed to test theoretical notions. The tasks are not directly relevant to the learning tasks in a classroom, but they are important because of the general knowledge they produce. The Lawrence and Festinger experiment (p. 32) illustrates this step.

Step-2 experiments usually use human subjects and deal with content

[18] For an interesting discussion of the problems of research and development in psychology and education, see A. Melton, "The Science of Learning and the Technology of Educational Methods," *Harvard Educational Review*, 29 (1959), 96–106.
[19] E. Hilgard, "A Perspective on the Relationship between Learning Theory and Educational Practices," in E. Hilgard, ed., *Theories of Learning and Instruction*, Sixty-third Yearbook of the National Society for the Study of Education (Chicago: University of Chicago Press, 1964), pp. 402–415.

nearer to that taught in schools (e.g., nonsense-syllable memorizing and retention). The Van Wagenen and Travers experiment (see p. 10) is illustrative. These experiments test theoretical principles applicable to education, not educational practices as such.

Step 3 is illustrated by the Krumboltz and Weisman (p. 17) and the Sax and Reade (p. 32) experiments. Here, the subjects are school-age children and the content is actual subject matter taught in schools. Again, however, experimental results are not applied to teaching practices.

Step 4 represents the first step in the development sequence. At this step a model of an instructional system is built and tested under controlled conditions. We could take the program Krumboltz and Weisman developed, build similar programs on other topics, and try them out in special laboratory classrooms. After these preliminary tests we would be ready for Step 5—more extensive tests in "normal" classrooms.

Step 6 represents the extensive application of a tested instructional system. Here, approaches found successful in Steps 4 and 5 are "packaged" for wider use. In this phase, materials are developed, teachers retrained to use the system, and problems of public acceptance resolved.

If our research knowledge were developed along these lines, the problem of application of research knowledge would be largely solved. Greater understanding of the value of these sequences by teachers will hasten the day when they will be carried out extensively.

THE TEACHER AND THE DEVELOPMENT SEQUENCE

It is obvious that the teacher's activities are like those in the development sequence. The teacher's task is in large part clinical, requiring the application of general procedures and systems to particular individuals.

Teaching and learning are dynamic activities. What happens next is modified by what happened before. In this ongoing activity, the teacher also uses decision rules. Both in the over-all strategies he invents and in their implementation the teacher is testing the hypotheses from which the decision rules are derived. He needs the habit of critical inquiry both to think intelligently about research data and theories and their application and to evaluate his teaching strategies and their implementation.

The point of view advocated throughout this book, and especially in this chapter, is clearly presented in the following quotation from John Dewey:

Facts which are . . . interrelated form a system, a science. The practitioner who knows a system . . . is evidently in possession of a powerful instrument for observing and interpreting what goes on before him. This intellectual tool affects his attitudes and modes of response in what he does. Because the range of understanding is deepened and widened, he can take into account remote consequences which were originally hidden from view and hence were ignored in his action. Greater continuity is introduced; he does not isolate situations and view them in separation as he was compelled to do when ignorant of connecting principles. At the same time, his practical dealings become more flexible. Seeing more relations he sees more possibilities, more opportunities. He is emancipated from the need of following tradition and special precedents. The ability to judge being enriched, he has a wider range of alternatives to select from in dealing with individual situations.[20]

As Dewey suggests, the improvement of educational practice requires teachers who can think critically about the processes of education. Such an approach promises much for the teacher himself. Educational activity conceptualized in this way can be a challenging enterprise. No longer will we view the teacher as a simple craftsman who has learned the "tools of his trade." Rather, we will see him as immersed in a potentially creative and imaginative task in which he can find intellectual stimulation by the continual analysis of the educational process.

SUMMARY

This chapter describes the principles of critical inquiry and their application in psychological and educational research. These principles are shown to be relevant to the activities of the effective classroom teacher. *Teaching activity requires critical inquiry. Teaching acts are generated from hypotheses about learning.* These hypotheses may be improved by a study of psychology. They may also be evaluated by applying the logic of critical inquiry in an analysis of their effects.

1. Psychology is the science whose object of study is human behavior. Psychological research establishes generalizations about human behavior, which enable us to predict and control that behavior.

2. This science contributes to educational theory and practice: (a) the teacher learns *concepts* and *generalizations* that he may use in developing

---

[20] John Dewey, *Sources of a Science of Education* (New York: Liveright Publishing Corp., 1929), pp. 20–21.

and evaluating teaching activities. (b) The teacher learns the *skills* developed by this science—skills directly related to the educational process. (c) The teacher learns to apply the *logic of the scientific method* to teaching practice.

3. The basic principles of the scientific method are easily grasped and of wide applicability. Critical inquiry begins with a question, with curiosity prompted by observation or generated from theories or hypotheses Questions may be formulated as *hypotheses.*

4. Hypotheses state a relation among *variables.* Variables are categories for classifying observable events that differ from one another in amount or degree.

5. Scientific method is the logic used in testing hypotheses. The first step in hypothesis testing is measurement of the variables described in the hypothesis. Measurement involves *carefully controlled observation.* The measurement procedure must be *valid* (that is, measure the behavior it purports to measure), *reliable* (measure that behavior accurately), and *standardized* (the conditions of measurement held constant).

6. The most precise way to test the relations among variables is to conduct an experiment. In an experiment, one variable, called the *independent variable,* is manipulated by the experimenter; and the effect of this manipulation on a second variable, called the *dependent variable,* is studied. The experiment is constructed in such a way that the influence of other variables is *controlled.*

7. The purpose of control is to eliminate or reduce the plausibility of other factors that might account for the changes in the dependent variable. Experimenters try to achieve experimental control by selecting subjects *randomly* and by using a *control group,* whose members are like those in the experimental conditions except that they do not receive the experimental treatment.

8. To evaluate experimental conclusions, researchers (a) repeat (*replicate*) the experiment if possible; (b) show that their results are *consistent* with previous experimentation; (c) explicitly rule out *plausible rival hypotheses.*

9. Some well-known sources of rival hypotheses must be controlled in experiments. The influence of events occurring outside the experimental treatment must be shown irrelevant to the results. Results must not be attributable to maturation of the experimental subjects, or must not have been produced because certain types of subjects remained in the experiment while others dropped out. Results must not be influenced by the behavior change that occurs because subjects receive the special treat-

ment provided by the experiment; this effect of being in an experiment, called the *Hawthorne effect,* may be controlled by making the treatment of experimental and control subjects as much alike as possible except for the experimental manipulation.

10. The *correlational method* is another way of testing the relation among variables. A correlational method is a mathematical way of measuring the fact of and amount of association among two or more variables. A *positive correlation* means that measurements on two variables are related in the same way; for example, an individual high on one measurement will be similarly, though not necessarily identically, high on the second measurement. A *negative correlation* means that measurements on two variables are related in opposite ways.

11. Correlational methods are used also in computing the reliability and validity of measuring instruments, an application the teacher will frequently encounter. The *Pearson Product-Moment correlation coefficient* (r) is one commonly used coefficient, whose values range from $+1$ to -1.

12. The statistical method compares two hypotheses—the *research hypothesis* (that there *is* a relationship between the variables being studied) and the *statistical* or *null hypothesis* (that there is no relationship and that contrary experimental results are merely the result of chance factors).

13. To test for the possibility that a difference in effects between experimental and control treatments, or an obtained correlation between two variables, may be the result of chance factors, *a test of statistical significance* is applied. If the results are found statistically significant, the research hypothesis may be tentatively accepted.

14. The application of the results of careful studies is not always a simple matter. The experiment only simulates aspects of the practical situation in which we are interested. If an experiment simulates the conditions of ordinary teaching, its results may be applicable to actual practice. However, a *research and development sequence* ought to be carried out. In the first phases of this sequence thorough experimental research under laboratory conditions is usually required, followed by more experimentation under conditions like those in the classroom. When reliable information has been gathered about relations among variables, this knowledge is used to invent a technology. This technology is a practical application of the ideas in an instructional strategy or design for producing learning. This application is then tested out in practice. The study of the application in practice is called developmental research.

15. Many designs for producing learning must be invented and tested

by the teacher. Using psychological knowledge, imagination, and the products of the critical evaluation of his experience, the teacher creates teaching-learning designs. The habit of critical inquiry and a knowledge of its logic is required to evaluate these inventions.

STUDY AND DISCUSSION QUESTIONS

1. Some educators have argued that, since educational theory is not highly developed at the present time, the safest procedure to use in improving educational practice is to develop educational practice by a process of trial and error. How would you respond to this argument?

2. Some people argue that the teacher is too busy and the classroom situation too complicated to permit systematic critical inquiry into the validity of educational procedures. How would you respond to this argument?

3. Some people claim that a concern for predicting and controlling the events of a classroom situation is a mechanistic approach to education. In what respects may this argument be valid? What assumptions are implicit in it? In what respects is an attempt to predict and control the events of the educative act a defensible description of the process of organizing learning experiences?

4. How would you respond to the statement that a teacher's experience is the best basis for deciding what are appropriate educational procedures? In what sense is this statement defensible? What assumptions are implicit in it? How would you qualify it?

5. What hypotheses would you offer to account for the fact that some educators appear to fear or mistrust a theorizing approach to educational practice?

6. Is an "art of teaching" incompatible with a "science of education"? In what ways might the art and science be related?

7. Some educators argue that psychological experiments do not duplicate classroom conditions. Present a defensible argument to demonstrate that such experimentation might be helpful in organizing learning experiences.

8. How do you account for the fact that many apparently "successful" teachers know very little psychology? How do you explain the fact that some teachers who have studied psychology are not "successful" in the classroom?

9. Literary men often show great insight in describing human behavior. Why is a science of psychology necessary as long as we have these other observations of human behavior? Might not the same argument be made for the observations of an experienced teacher?

10. Suggest some explanations for the following observed events:

    a. John reads any book on the Middle East that he can find.

    b. Rick quit the basketball team after it lost its last game.

    c. Jim collects butterflies and stamps.

    d. Joe is usually late for class.

11. Review your explanations for the above events and analyze the origins or sources of your explanations. Which of these explanations were based on your observations; which were derivations from some general psychological principles you hold?

12. Critically evaluate your explanations by attempting to determine what observations influenced them. How many observations did you make before formulating the principles you used? Were these observations systematically made, or did they "just happen"? What factors may have influenced your judgments of what you observed?

13. Below is a list of statements (not necessarily correct) about behavior change and such factors as teaching procedures, home influences, and personality characteristics. For each statement, (1) identify and describe the variables in the statement; (2) rearrange the statement in hypothetical form ("If . . . , then . . ."); (3) identify the independent and the dependent variable in each statement; (4) suggest ways in which the variables might be measured.

    a. Pupils learn better with frequent tests.

    b. Bright students are frequently bored in class.

    c. Girls are better than boys at English.

    d. Children should be taught number concepts by having them manipulate objects in various combinations.

    e. Spelling is learned more efficiently if taught as needed.

    f. Geography is more interesting if realistic models of terrain and other physical objects are used.

    g. Students of plane geometry should do considerable construction work with ruler and compass so that they will learn geometric principles.

    h. Geometry can be learned better when students build objects requiring an application of geometric principles.

    i. The way a child feels about another child depends on the kind of home in which he is being raised.

    j. Cooperation among children is improved when children work on projects together.

    k. Students are more likely to be interested in school work when it is related to their problems.

    l. The best-liked teachers are friendly and helpful.

14. What is your judgment of the correctness of these statements? How did you arrive at your judgments; are they based on casual or systematic observations? What assumptions about people and how they learn are you making?

15. What variables, other than the independent variable in each hypothesis, might produce the changes in the dependent variable? List several rival hypotheses.

16. Select one of the hypotheses that interests you and devise an experimental study to test its validity. Specify the variables being controlled. Indicate the methods of measuring the variables. Describe how the independent variable will be manipulated in an experimental study.

17. State a hypothesis or develop a question about teaching and learning. Design a study to answer the question or to test the hypothesis.

18. Select a study that interests you from a recent issue of the *Journal of Educational Psychology* or the *American Educational Research Journal*.

   a. What are the author's hypotheses? Identify the variables.

   b. How does he support the reasonableness of testing them?

   c. Is the study an experiment or is the correlational method used?

   d. What measurement procedures are used? What does the author report about the reliability and validity of the measurements?

   e. What results were obtained; how is the statistical significance of the results reported?

   f. Are the author's conclusions justifiable?

   g. How do the results fit with previous work?

   h. What suggestions are made for additional research?

   i. How does the research apply to teaching and learning?

   j. Locate the study on the research-development continuum. What steps are needed to use the results in educational practice?

RECOMMENDED READINGS

The teacher interested in the results of research he might apply will find the first two readings highly usable sources. The other readings will extend and supplement ideas presented in this chapter.

Encyclopedia of Educational Research, 3rd ed.; C. Harris, ed. New York: The Macmillan Co., 1960.

Handbook of Research on Teaching, N. L. Gage, ed. Chicago: Rand McNally, 1963.

J. Dewey, *The Sources of a Science of Education.* New York: Liveright Publishing Corp., 1929.

A. Kaplan, *The Conduct of Inquiry: Methodology for Behavioral Science*. San Francisco: Chandler Publishing Co., 1964.

The following articles in the Sixty-third Yearbook of the National Society for the Study of Education, Part I, *Theories of Learning and Instruction*, E. Hilgard, ed. Chicago: University of Chicago Press, 1964:

> F. J. McDonald, "The Influence of Learning Theories on Education (1900–1950)," pp. 1–26.

> R. Glaser, "Implications of Training Research for Education," pp. 153–181.

> A. A. Lumsdaine, "Educational Technology, Programed Learning, and Instructional Science," pp. 371–401.

> E. R. Hilgard, "A Perspective on the Relationship between Learning Theory and Educational Practices," pp. 402–415.

The following periodicals regularly carry articles of interest to teachers: *Journal of Educational Psychology, American Journal of Educational Research, Journal of Educational Research, Journal of Experimental Education.*

CHAPTER TWO

A PSYCHOLOGICAL MODEL OF TEACHING BEHAVIOR

This chapter introduces you to a point of view about teaching: as a process of making and testing decisions that produce learning in students. These decisions are based on special knowledge, the kind of knowledge that a study of educational psychology provides. One cannot learn to make them in the course of everyday living, since they depend on an understanding of how people learn.

To begin, we need to study the activity of the teacher as a psychological phenomenon. Therefore, the following sections describe a model of teaching activity as a decision-making process.

THE TEACHER AS DECISION MAKER

We learn in many ways. Some of our learning occurs by chance: a child happens on a bird snatching tatters for its nest. Much of our learning is planned and controlled: someone contrives or invents a situation from which we can learn. Teaching is this kind of contrivance or invention.

If learning is planned for, or controlled, does this mean that the teacher dominates the learner in an authoritarian manner? No such implication is intended. Rather, by "planning" or "controlling," he arranges stimuli to evoke certain kinds of behavior, to preclude others. Consider the child learning to read. He could, at great cost in time and effort, decipher the alphabet or words by himself. The teacher simplifies his task by giving him reading instruction. Reading behavior is demonstrated for him, or the responses he has available are linked to visual symbols.

The arrangements for learning may be looked at as deliberate plans for producing learning. The effectiveness of a plan may be judged from the learning it produces. This concept of *plans for learning,* or *teaching strategies,* is the principal and critical component in the conception of teaching behavior to be described here.

A teacher executes a plan for learning. Teaching behavior is the set of actions which engage the learner in a situation from which he can acquire new or modified ways of behaving. This definition is admittedly broad. It points up the essential character of teaching activity as a deliberate construction to produce learning, although it does not specify what that learning should be.[1] It excludes plans for evoking habits or for utilizing customary responses. If I say "hello" to a colleague, I expect a similar response. My colleague does not have to learn how to respond; this learning has long since occurred. Similarly, we do not think of a concert pianist as learning the concerto he is performing; his performance demonstrates what he *has* learned.

PLANS AS A PSYCHOLOGICAL CONCEPT

A plan is a guide for action. Plans are directive and controlling. They are more or less specific. They take many forms: blueprints, lecture notes, auto-club routings, dress patterns, cookbook recipes, movie scenarios, outlines, and computer programs. The plans, however, are only partially represented by these symbols. A plan is generated in the thinking of the planner; it is his conception of how to do something, the kinds of actions to be taken and their order. A plan includes a conception of a goal and the means for reaching it.

---

[1] For a general discussion of the theoretical ideas underlying these ideas, see C. K. Packer and T. Packer, "Cybernetics, Information Theory, and the Educative Process," *Teachers College Record,* 61 (1959), 134–142.

Plans are made by making choices, by making decisions. *A plan is a set of decisions.* The decisions guide action in the sense that a person chooses or selects what actions he will take. A teacher, for example, decides that he will discuss a historical novel in his English class. This choice or decision determines, and in that sense guides, what he will do.

Ordinarily, a decision of this kind is related to a number of other decisions. The decision to select a novel is prior to the decisions about how to discuss it, what assignments to make, what ideas to stress, and how to stimulate interest in the reading. Although a person may not actually plan each decision step by step, and may not clearly foresee all the choices he will make, his plans are an arrangement, an ordering of choices. Obviously, the more carefully thought out a plan, the more apparent is the ordering of the decisions.

We are now prepared for a formal definition of this concept, *plans.*

"A plan is any hierarchical process in the organism that can control the order in which a sequence of operations is to be performed."[2]

The principal characteristic of this process is that it is a *control* process. A plan *directs* and *determines* the actions a person takes to achieve something he has set out to do. The steps in the process occur in a predetermined sequential order. Some of the actions in a plan are necessary before other actions may be taken, or they make later steps easier. It is in the sense of one action's leading to another or preparing for another that a plan may be thought of as a control process. For example, I am about to leave my home for class. I cannot get into my car without leaving my house. I usually gather my materials before leaving the house, and I have yet to start the car before entering it. To get from here to class, I first pack my materials, move out the door, then into the car, through the operations of starting and driving it, and finally to leaving the car and entering the classroom.

Consideration of this simple example will help us derive some other characteristics of a plan and some assumptions implied in our definition. Some of the operations of a plan are interchangeable. I may start my car, and then return to the house for my briefcase. I can start the engine of the car from under the hood. In each instance the set of operations leads to my goal. Ordinarily, I will evoke a set of criteria for selecting the order. If I am a car buff, I may choose to demonstrate my skill by starting the car in

[2] G. A. Miller, E. Galanter, and K. H. Pribram, *Plans and the Structure of Behavior* (New York: Holt, Rinehart and Winston, 1960), p. 16.

the more difficult way. On a cold morning, I may start the car first to warm it up while I am making my other preparations for leaving.

One decides *the components of a plan and their sequence and timing by relating them to a goal or a set of goals.* A teacher, for example, wants to encourage an interest in careful observation of natural phenomena, such as the movement of cloud formations and the state of the weather. His goal is to produce this interest in his students. He will devise some plan for producing it. He will decide, for instance, what observations he wants his students to make, what questions he will ask, whether or not he will encourage them to record information. When he has made this selection of things to do, he will have formulated a plan, which describes a sequence of actions to be taken by him and his students. What he does, when he does it, and how he does it are determined by his goal—to produce in his students an interest in careful observation.

The enactment of a plan may lead to a revision of the plan. As the actions of the plan unfold, new information is received which leads the planner to see new possibilities, makes him aware of unanticipated difficulties, or changes the characteristics of the problems to be solved to attain his goal. Errors in the conception or the tactical execution of the plan become apparent. This **feedback** from the effects of executing the plan acts as a *control mechanism* to reshape the plan or to replace it with a new plan.[3]

A plan is described as a *hierarchical* process because the attainment of a goal typically requires an ordered sequence of action. Some of these steps, as we have seen, may be interchangeable. They may be modified to some extent in action. There may be several different plans for attaining a goal. But the successful achievement of a goal depends on some sequencing of actions, in which some actions must occur before others.

TEACHING PLANS AND LEARNING

A teaching plan is essentially a small theory about how to produce learning. From the feedback the teacher receives as he executes the plan and as he evaluates its effects, he may learn its strengths and weaknesses. He may use this information to modify the plan, and this modification in turn may be tested. He will then adopt those plans that lead to desired goals, the changes in student behavior. He has learned a new behavior pattern to be used in teaching.

[3] The conception used here is a cybernetic model of human action and learning. This kind of a model is described in G. T. Guilbaud, *What Is Cybernetics?* (New York: Criterion Books, 1959).

This learning process does not proceed as smoothly as the above description may suggest. The teacher may be insensitive to feedback available to him. He may not know how to modify the plan. He may execute plans that cancel each other out (he may, for example, encourage students to speak in a foreign language but at the same time punish every mistake—thus effectively discouraging their attempts). Or the theory of the plan may be weak, because the teacher does not himself have adequate knowledge of the learning process or does not use what he does know. For instance, a speech teacher who wants to develop persuasive skills in his students may carefully describe the arts of persuasion; his lecture is a model of exposition, and his students know what he means. But how many of them will become persuasive speakers if they do not write and give speeches, if they have no opportunity to test their skills? This teacher has overlooked some important requirements for learning: a learner usually needs to attempt desired responses and to receive information (feedback) on their appropriateness. We cannot blame a teacher every time a student fails to learn. We can, however, expect teachers to use whatever knowledge may be presently available in developing plans for producing learning.

The model of the teacher as a plan-making and plan-executing organism has been introduced in this chapter to point out that learning on the teacher's part is an essential characteristic of teaching. This conception also emphasizes the problematical and hypothetical characteristics of teaching actions. It provides a way of approaching the study of educational psychology by describing the relation between formal knowledge and its use. Another way of looking at plans is needed before these ideas can be developed.

THE DECISION COMPONENTS IN TEACHING PLANS

Consider this example. You want to teach your students what a ballad is. First, *you have to decide exactly what you want them to know about ballads.* Presumably, you will want them to know the ideas and emotions that typically are treated in the ballad form; you will also want them to know the rhythm and rhyme structure of the ballad. You may also want them to understand the social functions of the ballad.

Second, *you must decide what student behavior will be observed, to see whether your teaching strategy has achieved the desired effects.* How will you know that the students understand the social functions of the ballad? Or that they can recognize its rhythm pattern?

Third, *you will have to plan a strategy for producing the desired learning.* Will you begin by defining a ballad, or will you give the students a set of ballads and prompt their discovery of the characteristics? Will you introduce other forms of poetry or prose? How many examples do you think you will need either to illustrate the definition or to prompt its discovery?

All of these questions invite you to make a decision. In each of the categories of questions, there are choices to be made among the alternatives available. The plan you eventually develop will reflect these choices. Some of your choices must be postponed, and some may be only anticipated as possibilities. Suppose that you decide to ask the students to give examples of ballads, and nobody gives one. Perhaps you asked the question too soon, before the students grasped the idea; they may be reluctant to give an example, or they may not know any. These possibilities may be anticipated. But you will have to decide *in class* whether or not the students are reluctant, and you will have to decide what to do. As you develop the plan and as you execute it, decision making is continually required.

As the above discussion suggests, some of the decisions in teaching plans are made before the plan is executed in action. Others may be only anticipated and are made as the plan is executed. However, these decisions will usually fall into one of three categories: (1) What is the student to learn? (2) How can the teacher determine whether the student is learning? (3) How can the desired learning be brought about?

Professional training prepares for decision making by describing the kinds of decisions the professional process characteristically requires. It also provides the theoretical base for decision making and some supervised experience in the process. Throughout this book you will be invited to make decisions, to formulate the hypotheses and theories that support your choices; and you will learn ways of testing for the effects of your decisions. You are encouraged to invent new plans and variations on old ones. In these ways, you are being led into the decision-making process, which is the core of professional teaching.

THE DECISION-MAKING MODEL

The act of decision making is the act of choosing among alternatives.[4] What factors are involved in the choice?

[4] The conception of the decision-making process used here is described in I. D. J. Bross, *Design for Decision* (New York: The Macmillan Company, 1953).

ALTERNATIVES AND CONSEQUENCES

The decision-making process is more easily analyzed as it appears in *problematic situations*—that is, when the way to attain a desired goal is unknown or only partially known, or when several ways are available. These ways—or paths to the goal, as they are sometimes called—are the alternatives. *An alternative is a probable way of attaining a goal.*

Each alternative ordinarily will have predictable consequences. *Consequences are the effects we expect if the alternative is carried into action.* Recall the example of teaching about the ballad. You had the choice of asking the class for their examples, or asking them for examples of other poetic forms, or of not asking for any examples. One of the consequences of asking for an example is that you may not get one, or you may get only a few, or you may get poor or erroneous ones, or you may get several excellent examples.

Associated with each consequence is an *estimate* of the likelihood of its occurrence. This estimate is a calculation of the probabilities that a particular consequence will happen when you enact the alternative. Obviously, before you can make this estimate, you need certain information—information about how people in general, and your students in particular, are likely to respond to your question. Highly personal questions, for instance, are likely to yield few answers; similarly, questions asked in a threatening manner are likely to discourage answers.

PROBABILITY ESTIMATES

Numbers representing degrees of **probability** may be used to symbolize the estimate. A highly probable event is given a value near 1. For example, a highly probable event would be said to have a probability value of .90 or .95 or .80. These estimates are read as follows: There are nine chances out of ten, or nine and a half chances, or eight chances, that X will occur. An unlikely event has probability values near 0. A probability value of .20 means that there are two chances in ten that X will occur.

In our decision making, then, we act in the light of probability estimates, although we may not always formalize the estimate in a percentage. If the consequences are of great importance, we try to get as precise a figure as our methods permit. Ships at sea and farmers pay considerable sums to obtain precise weather information. Families planning picnics can usually tolerate more imprecision and larger margins of error.

Objective Probability

The objective-probability estimate is a numerical description of the probabilities based on evidence.[5] We obtain this estimate by determining how often an event has occurred under known conditions. For example, to calculate the probability that a student will participate in a class discussion, I would have to observe him during those times when the teacher opens up a topic for discussion. I count how often he offers an opinion, disagrees or agrees with another student, or asks a question. If I observed him for one month, I would obtain a record of his participation. From it I may derive an estimate of the student's future participation.

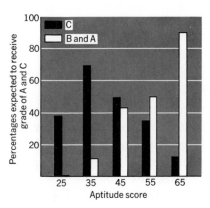

FIGURE 2-1. *Relation between aptitude-test scores and grade-point average.*

Another way to estimate objective probabilities is to predict one event on the basis of another event with which it is correlated. Weather prediction is a familiar example of this method. There is a known correlation between the rise or fall of a barometer and the probability of rain. By observing one phenomenon, we can predict the second. Figure 2–1 is based on the measured **correlation** between an aptitude measure and college success as measured by grade-point average. The arrangement of the bars shows the percentage at each score level expected to maintain a satisfactory average. Will each student in the high success range necessarily do well, and will each student in the low range necessarily do poorly? Obviously not; but these figures represent the probabilities of success at each level. If the data are reliable, and if unexpected factors do not intervene, judgments based on the data are more likely to be as predicted than not.

Another way to estimate objective probabilities is by using a principle or theory or **model**. Principles and theories describe the relations among **variables**. When these relations can be stated precisely, as in the mathematical formulation for the speed of a falling body, fairly precise predic-

[5] An application of this and related concepts is illustrated in R. S. Tedley and L. B. Lustad, "Reasoning Foundations of Medical Diagnosis," *Science*, 130 (1959), 9–21.

tions may be made. When the relation is known but cannot be stated in such precise terms, it is still possible to make a prediction but with less precision.

Developing generalizations that state a relation among variables is a first step on the road to more precise predictions. Designing and carrying out an experiment to test the generalization is a second step. Consider the following reasoning, which leads to a generalization. Begin by thinking of students as goal directed. See their behavior as functional, as a way of attaining these goals. Next, think about a dependent student—that is, one who leans on the teacher for direction, who is not likely to undertake learning without the prompting and encouraging of a teacher, who needs support and direction. What would such a student be likely to learn in your class?

Amidon and Flanders [6] predicted that such a student would be more concerned with following the suggestions and directions of the teacher than he would be with learning what was being taught. They reasoned that a dependent person is likely to have learned to comply as a way of satisfying his dependency needs. If this were so, then he would be particularly sensitive to directions from the teacher and less interested in what was being taught. The experiment they designed tested how susceptible to teacher influence such students were.

Amidon and Flanders randomly assigned 140 dependent-prone students to four kinds of teaching sessions, during which they were taught a few geometrical concepts. Two variables were manipulated: the clarity of the goals and the directness of the teacher influence. In the *clear* condition, the uses of what was to be learned were pointed out; in the *unclear* condition, the students were warned that they could not be sure how this information would be used. In the *direct*-influence treatment, the teacher gave a lecture, asked questions, and worked problems. In the *indirect*-influence treatment the teacher conducted a discussion on the material, explaining and illustrating problems. The four groups were (1) clear goals, direct influence; (2) unclear goals, direct influence; (3) clear goals, indirect influence; (4) unclear goals, indirect influence. Which of these groups learned more geometry? Would a help-seeking person be more influenced on a learning task by the clarity of the goals of the task or by the way the teacher handled the learning experience, giving more or less direct help?

[6] E. Amidon and N. A. Flanders, "The Effects of Direct and Indirect Teacher Influence on Dependent-Prone Students Learning Geometry," *Journal of Educational Psychology*, 52 (1961), 286–291.

Amidon and Flanders found that the dependent-prone students were not affected by the clarity of the goals. However, they learned more geometry when the teacher used indirect influence. These investigators reasoned as follows in explaining their results:

As the teacher becomes more directive, this type of student finds increased satisfaction in more compliance, often with less understanding of the problem solving steps carried out. Only when he is free to express his doubts, to ask questions and gain reassurance, does his understanding keep pace with his compliance to the authority figure. Lacking this opportunity, compliance alone may become a satisfactory goal and content understanding may be subordinated to the process of adjusting to teacher directives (p. 290).

A generalization may be made that indirect-influence procedures are more likely to facilitate achievement in dependent-prone students. The exact probability figure as well as the limitations of the generalization need to be discovered.

Each of the three methods described in the preceding paragraphs— numerical description of observed data, prediction based on correlated data, prediction based on tested principle or theory—is a means of estimating probabilities by using data. They yield more or less precise estimates depending on the **reliability** of the methods of measurement, the adequacy of the **sampling** procedures used, and the degree of control exercised over influences on the events being studied. Their use yields information in which we have some degree of confidence.

Each of us, however, makes many decisions based on estimates which have not been carefully evaluated. "By guess and by gosh" and "guesstimates" describe in clichés the kind of information we frequently have. Yet we act as if we have some conception of what the probabilities might be. Since we cannot always wait for precise information, it is worth considering how this behavior relates to the decisions a teacher has to make.

Subjective Probabilities

Teaching behavior requires hundreds of decisions. For many of these decisions, precise data will not be available on the probabilities of consequences. The reasons are twofold: first, many predictions or hypotheses have not been studied; second, many decisions are about events that occur only once or infrequently, and their relative uniqueness precludes their study. In these cases the teacher must apply whatever knowledge he has available to test the validity of his decisions.

Inevitably, teachers, like many other practitioners, come to rely heavily on their experience, and develop their own sets of beliefs about expectancies. These *personal beliefs about probabilities* are *subjective* because their validity has never been tested. They may be the products of unique or uncommon experiences, or they may be developed from ordinary experiences that a teacher has learned to handle in his own way. In either case the beliefs are untested in any systematic way.

Some of these beliefs are overgeneralizations from limited experience. Other beliefs are the products of faulty logic, which leads to similar errors in estimation. Others are the product of a teacher's own reaction to what has happened to him—a reaction that might not have been shared by another teacher.

We cannot, of course, test everything we believe, count every consequence; but when the consequences are important, most of us try to assess the objective probabilities, to base our judgments on data rather than on unanalyzed hunches or feelings. The consequences of teaching decisions are important. These decisions deserve to be made in the most intelligent way that we can.

This implied exhortation is not intended to make you feel guilty if you cannot be as objective as is being urged. The problem is not yours alone. Extensive research needs to be done by many people on teaching problems. But you can profit from what we already know; you can catch the spirit of curiosity; you can support and even participate in data-gathering activities. You can acquire the habit of critical inquiry about teaching behavior. In this book you are invited to move from the unanalyzed hunch, the self-serving rationalization, the intuition that is little more than the projection of your needs, to the continuing effort to verify your predictions and to ground them in theory and in research evidence.

VALUES OF A DECISION

To this point we have been describing decision making as if it were determined primarily by our knowledge of what is likely to happen when we act. If this were true, decision making could be improved if we knew more about the probabilities of consequences. Return to our example of the teacher's question asking. If you knew (that is, if you were highly certain) that you would get poor examples when you called for examples, would you ask the question? Probably not. Obviously, the value or desirability of the consequence has also influenced your decision. Associated with the consequences of actions are judgments of the desirability of these consequences.

The sources of these judgments are complex. Some derive from our philosophy of life or of education. Some reflect the social standards accepted in our society, our culture, or our profession. Some are derivations from experience, the products of studying a chain of actions and their accumulated effects. Some are carefully thought out; others are unanalyzed preferences. Some are matters of style.

Attempts to quantify these judgments have not been highly successful, since it is difficult to obtain a scale that preserves an invariant relation among our values. You are familiar with this concept of **invariance** in scales. An invariant property of an object or an event is a characteristic that does not change under some conditions. The colors of objects, for example, do not change if they are exposed to constant atmospheric conditions, and if the internal chemical properties remain constant. Color is an invariant property of objects. Weight is also. (But remember, the conditions under which the property is invariant must be specified.)

A linear scale, using inches or centimeters as the metric, preserves an invariant relation among objects measured with this scale. An individual 6 feet tall is always taller than one 5 feet 10 inches, if we use a rigid instrument for measuring and start from a common point of measurement, and if the individuals' heights remain constant during the period of measurement. But try to find a scale that will similarly order your valuing of jazz, pizza, baseball, classical music, Shakespeare's plays, colonial furniture, Paris fashions, calculus, Salinger's fiction, satire, and summer days.

Typically, some of these objects and events, such as your music preferences or food preferences or your interest in school subjects, can be ordered in subsets. Tests have been developed which order these subsets so that the person who prefers music to mathematics can be distinguished from the person who prefers physics to psychology.[7] Moreover, although the problem of measuring values with greater precision remains to be solved, people *act as if* their behavior were controlled by their values, and rough approximations of these values may be inferred from their

[7] Vocational interest tests are examples. For a discussion of their construction, use, and limitations, see L. J. Cronbach, *Essentials of Psychological Testing*, 2nd ed. (New York: Harper and Row, 1960), Chapter 14.

behavior. These assumptions about behavior are sufficient to warrant the assumption that these values are likely to influence decision making.

DECISION RULES

In the act of making a decision, one usually must select among the combinations of probabilities and values. First, he conceptualizes a set of alternative ways of acting and considers the possible consequences of each. For example, I want to go fishing and I want to catch fish as well as enjoy the scenery, the exercise, and the solitude. The alternatives are the many places I may go fishing. One stream has produced limits for the past two weeks but is 200 miles away, is difficult to get to, and has poor camping facilities. A second stream has had moderate yields, is 15 miles away, but also has poor camping facilities. A third stream has had mediocre yields, is also 15 miles away, and has good campgrounds. How do I select a stream?

Obviously, my decision depends on the combination of probabilities and values. The probabilities of what I am likely to find have been given: good or poor fishing, near or far-away locations, and good or poor camp facilities. If the value of catching fish is high and the importance of traveling distance and good campgrounds comparatively low, I will probably select the first stream. By choosing it, I am highly likely to achieve what I highly value. If the distance is significant, I am more likely to choose the second stream, because my chances of catching fish are reasonably good and I achieve two things that I value.

In some such way, we combine probabilities and value estimates. We then need a "rule" for selecting among these combinations so that we are likely to obtain favorable outcomes—the attainment of our goal or the resolution of our problem. *A decision rule is a principle to be used in selecting among the alternatives when the probability and value estimates are known.*

You hear many of these "rules" in the statements people make about the reasons for their actions. "If you don't give homework, they won't study." This statement is a generalization about students but also tells you something about how that teacher is going to act. He will give homework whenever he wants to be sure that his students work at learning. He probably will give homework regularly. Notice that the decision rule is hidden; the teacher does not explicitly formulate it. But we expect him to act consistently with his beliefs.

Sometimes the decision rule is stated explicitly. "I always start a history lesson with a set of questions that I want them to be able to answer." "I'd rather have them get the sense of the story, so I encourage them to read on even if they don't know each word." "When I have a problem with a child, I talk to the parents." These statements tell us how the persons who made them will probably act. Although they do not state all the alternatives—with their associated consequences, probabilities, and values—these options usually are apparent, so that the choice to be made is clear. The statements may be poor guides for effective action. Their authors may not always act consistently with them. But each of them is a generalization that probably guides the person's actions to some degree.

Development of Decision Rules

Decision rules, like the probabilities and values of consequences, are learned. This learning is mediated by feedback. A decision rule is used in action, and the effects of its use are available as information to the decision maker. The effectiveness of feedback depends on its frequency, the conditions under which it is obtained, and the decision maker's interpretations of the feedback.

Many decision rules are the products of accumulated experience. Proverbs are familiar examples: "A stitch in time saves nine"—that is, it is better to take action now than run the risk of greater difficulties later. Consideration of this homely example will illustrate the characteristics of decision rules.

First, the rule is obviously not to be applied invariantly (though it does not always say so). For instance, if the problem conditions are ambiguous, like a shadowy figure approaching on a poorly lighted street, it is better to resolve the ambiguity to some extent than to act, here either by flight or by attack. The expert decision maker is recognized by his superior knowledge of the limitations of the decision rule. It is important to know the conditions under which a decision rule is likely to be effective. Failure to know and to appreciate the significance of these limitations leads to misinterpretations and errors. A teaching plan predicated on an overgeneralization of a decision rule will lead to the failure of the plan or to less success than was desired.

Second, the use of the rule will not always bring about desired outcomes. Sometimes, action—even when appropriate—does not ward off later difficulties. Ideally, a good rule should always lead to desired results—that is, predict outcomes nearly perfectly. But these rules are like other generalizations; they have varying degrees of **validity.**

Third, the known validity of the decision rule depends on the testing the rule has received. Our proverb, as mentioned, is probably the product of considerable, if informal, testing. The decision rule, like other generalizations, is a statement that can and should be tested by empirical methods. If we do not perform such tests, our judgment about the validity of the rule is at best an educated guess. Controlled observation has been a powerful tool for assessing the validity of common-sense notions. Decision rules derived from theories, attractive as they may be, need also to be tested.

Formal decision rules are derived from controlled observations. These observations are **samples** of all the observations that could be made. They permit an estimate of what would be observed if the totality of observations could be made. It is practically impossible, for example, to observe all teacher-student interactions. We observe a sample of them, and generalize to similar situations; our statements are descriptions of what will probably occur in these other cases. If, for example, observations of teacher-student interaction are made in the primary grades, generalizations from them apply to situations where *the same conditions* obtain. "The same conditions" does not mean "all the identical conditions"; if it did, thousands of rules and descriptions would be needed. It means all those conditions known or believed to be related to what the rule predicts.

Decision Rules and Personal Style

Decision rules account for the *pattern of choices* a person himself makes in solving a problem or carrying out a plan of action. One of the more interesting lines of research is the relation between these patterns and other personality characteristics. Psychologists study decision-making behavior by placing a person in a situation (for instance, in a betting game) where choices are available to him and by studying the pattern of his choices.[8] They have found that individuals do form decision strategies and that these strategies differ with different individuals.[9] Figure 2–2 illustrates differences among three individuals in risk-taking

[8] W. Edwards, "The Theory of Decision-Making," *Psychological Bulletin,* 51 (1954), 380–417.

[9] N. Kogan and M. Wallach, *Risk Taking: A Study in Cognition and Personality* (New York: Holt, Rinehart and Winston, 1964).

behavior.[10] Mosteller and Nogee studied what individuals would risk in a betting game. The line marked "fair offer" in Fig. 2–2 represents what a bet ought to be worth in terms of the probabilities of winning. The solid lines represent what the persons in the experiment actually bet: some bet more (lines plotted above "fair offer"), some less (lines below "fair offer"). Some subjects risked more, some less; their respective subjective value and probability estimates are reflected in their wagers.

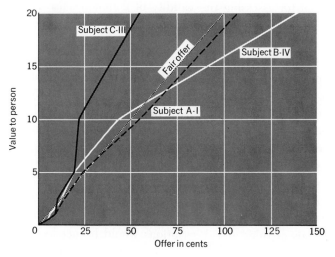

FIGURE 2–2. *Differences in risk-taking behavior (adapted from Mosteller and Nogee).*

If decision behavior is an integral aspect of personality—not an attachment of some kind, or a factor operating occasionally—then we should be able to predict an individual's behavior if we know the decision rules he typically uses. Although the study has yet to be performed, we could describe differences among teachers by noting differences in the decision rules they seem to prefer. The "child-centered" teacher, for instance, characteristically makes decisions by considering the effects of teaching strategies on the child's image of himself and his attitude toward learning. Other teachers decide on strategies by considering other outcomes. Personal style in teaching may then be thought of as the kinds of decision rules a teacher typically uses.

[10] F. Mosteller and P. Nogee, "An Experimental Measure of Utility," *Journal of Political Economy*, 59 (1951), 371–404.

DYNAMICS OF THE DECISION-MAKING PROCESS

The elements described in the preceding sections are the major components of a decision-making model. However, listing the components does not describe the process. The question to be answered is: How does a plan, which is a set of decisions, control behavior? Three behavior sequences are used to describe the dynamics of the decision-making process.[11]

Input Sequence

The input sequence is that phase in which the person assimilates and interprets information, and organizes it into a set of instructions for action. This phase may be relatively simple (a teacher noting a pupil's raised hand) or complex (a teacher analyzing the results of a test).

The program for action is developed in this sequence; the plan or some part of it is formulated. This operation may occur as rapidly as stimuli are transmitted through the nervous system, or there may be a large time gap between reception of information and action.

Operation Sequence

The operation sequence, the phase of decision making that is directly observable in behavior, carries the plan into action. The sequence of actions may be simple responses, such as a movement or a word (the teacher pointing to the student who has raised his hand), or a complex set of interrelated actions (the teacher leading the fifth-grade class on a field trip).

Test Sequence

In this sequence, the person tests the effects of the plan. He receives feedback, information about the effects of the decisions made. This feedback is used as new input to revise plans where necessary. This phase, like the input phase, may proceed with the speed of nerve impulses (some of

---

[11] The model presented here is one kind of feedback model. Models of this kind vary in the number of elements they include. For a general model, see A. Newell, J. C. Shaw, and H. A. Simon, "Elements of a Theory of Human Problem Solving," *Psychological Review*, 65 (1958), 151–166.

the actions occurring so quickly that they have been called "reflexes") or may be extended in time (an elaborate system of experimentation in the development of a drug, or a car, or an achievement test).

CHARACTERISTICS OF THE DECISION-MAKING PROCESS

Figure 2–3, a **cybernetic** model of human behavior, represents the decision-making process. The word "cybernetic" derives from a Greek word meaning "steersman." In this model, then, feedback provides the kind of control that a steersman gives to a ship. The navigator, to pursue this analogy briefly, has a plan, charted as a course. The ship is set on this

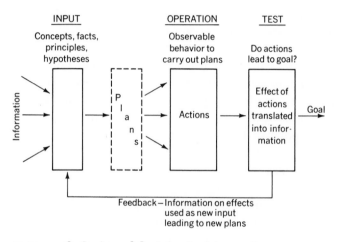

FIGURE 2–3. *A model of the decision-making process.*

compass course, and the navigator controls its movement in relation to the plan by using the steersman's feedback information about the ship's position. Human behavior is an analogous process. A person controls the enactment of a plan by utilizing feedback information from the effects of his actions. The decisions that form the plan serve as a set of instructions; and these instructions order the behavior sequence in relation to a goal to be achieved.

This conception, of course, is only a model—a simplification and an abstraction, to be used for descriptive and explanatory purposes. This model assumes that teaching behavior is goal directed—the goal, broadly stated, being some change in student behavior. The input information is the material the teacher uses to construct the plan or strategy. The operations sequence is the plan in action, manifested in the observable behavior of the teacher. Feedback is information received by the planner on the effects of the plan.

This model conceives of the teacher as active, as a constructor of events, as responsive to information he is continually receiving from the effects of his actions. He is not a passive recipient of stimuli. Neither is he a digital computer capable only of enacting a fixed program. He can modify his own programs, and he can control the feedback process—that is, he can select both the amount and kind of feedback he will use.

USES OF THE DECISION-MAKING MODEL

Why has this model been introduced? Each teacher has some theory of human behavior, some conception of how humans learn, and some notion of the functions and purposes of a teacher. Naturally, the way a teacher views the world of teaching will shape his teaching strategies. The author once knew a teacher who viewed every class as a setting for an uprising and every student as a potential plotter. He interpreted any deviation from rigid attention as a sign of insurrection. Almost all his teaching strategies were designed to control attention; the feedback of importance to him was any sign of inattention. A happier example is represented by the teacher who uses test information on student ability to modify the difficulty level of a learning session.

A model is offered as a way of presenting a theory of teaching. This model may or may not fit with your conceptions of what teaching is. It is introduced here because we want to look at teaching and learning as decision-making behavior and because we want to use psychological knowledge as a way of improving these decisions. The advantages of using this model are worth noting.

A model of any phenomenon focuses our attention on selected aspects of that phenomenon. This model of teaching behavior directs attention to the modifiability of teaching behavior, and to the effects of teaching behavior on student behavior.

Modifiability is to be studied by considering what information a teacher uses in constructing and changing his teaching strategies: that is, how does the teacher conceptualize teaching and student behavior; what principles does he use to interpret and to describe these behaviors; what are his value judgments and his probability estimates of the consequences of his decisions?

We also want to study teaching strategies objectively. If plans are deliberate constructions, then we should be able to describe the factors that need to be considered in developing teaching strategies. If a teacher has a theory of learning, we should be able to evaluate that theory and to see its relation to decision making.

This book invites you to engage in a critical analysis of teaching strategies. A course in educational psychology introduces you to the study of human learning. The ideas and information you will acquire may be used to construct teaching strategies. This knowledge will not be given in the form of nostrums, simple rules of the game, or psychological patent medicine. In the following section an important aspect of the model presented will be discussed.

DECISIONS AND HYPOTHESES

Decisions are hypothetical; that is, assuming a certain set of conditions, they predict certain effects. They state a relation between the set of conditions and an effect. You decide to start your automobile; that is, you predict that if you turn the key to connect the ignition circuit, an electric current will be set up that will fire an explosive mixture in the cylinders, which in turn will move a mechanical system that will rotate the wheels. This sequence of events occurs if a set of conditions prevails: no breaks in the electric circuit, gasoline in engine, the mechanical parts properly connectèd. Change any of these conditions and the automobile either will not start or will not move when started.

This example may seem trivial until we recall how much knowledge was necessary to construct a system of such high reliability. The system has been so contrived that the decision to start an automobile depends on personal considerations, not on technical ones. I decide only whether I want to use the system. Only rarely do I have to think about the system itself.

Teaching plans are similar systems in principle. They too are constructions designed to achieve specific effects. But admittedly they rarely have the high reliability of the ignition system of an automobile. Why not? In the first place, our knowledge of human learning is neither so extensive nor so precise as our knowledge of the electrochemical and mechanical systems of an automobile. Second, our knowledge of teaching plans as instructional systems is comparably deficient. However, if perfectly reliable knowledge were needed to act, mankind would be immobilized. Considerable knowledge is available, and our problem is to learn to use it to produce more knowledge.

The response of many individuals is to fall back on "tried-and-true" methods, usually something a teacher has found "works for me." Although this reaction may provide a feeling of security, it hardly does justice to the complexity of the problems a teacher faces. This approach strips teaching of its challenge and depreciates the curiosity that it may both excite and satisfy.

The model of teaching behavior used here implies that decisions and sets of decisions formulated as plans be treated as hypotheses.

DECISIONS AS HYPOTHESES ABOUT LEARNING

Each of the decisions that a teacher makes in formulating and enacting a teaching plan is a hypothesis about learning. Although the teacher may not formulate his plans in hypothetical language, what he does may be stated in propositions something like this: "If I introduce these words into the vocabulary lesson, then the pupils will have more words available to read Scott's *The Lady of the Lake.*" A general teaching strategy is also a hypothesis. Language teachers, for example, believe that students should, as soon as possible, speak in the language being learned. They are hypothesizing that extensive practice in hearing and speaking the language will enable students to use the language without having to translate consciously as they speak. These hypotheses, simple or complex, are predictions about the behavior that will result from certain kinds of learning experiences. In principle, such hypotheses have varying degrees of probable validity.

Coladarci points up the essential characteristics of this kind of thinking:

Intelligent hypotheses are not chosen randomly nor are they found full-blown. An intelligent hypothesizer thinks along the lines of the following model: "*On the basis of what I know now* about individual differences and the reading process, I hypothesize that this kind of grouping-for-reading will lead to the kind of pupil-progress in reading that I would like to bring about."[12]

An example will make clear how a teacher's choices can shape what a child will learn. A fourth-grade teacher was introducing a unit on "Pioneer Life." He asked the students what they wanted to study about

[12] A. P. Coladarci, "The Relevancy of Educational Psychology," *Educational Leadership,* 18 (1956), 489–492. See also A. P. Coladarci, "The Teacher as a Hypothesis-Maker," *California Journal for Instructional Improvement,* 2 (1959), 3–6.

"Pioneer Life" and what kinds of questions they should raise concerning the subject. As the discussion proceeded, the children suggested the usual categories for studying a history unit—namely, the pioneer's food, shelter, and clothing. One child mentioned that he had seen a Western movie in which a man accused of horse stealing was immediately hanged. This comment on the movie evoked considerable interest in the group, and one of the children asked why the man was hanged right away. The teacher dismissed this question as irrelevant to a discussion of pioneer life. The decision not to utilize this question in effect set the stage for the kinds of things that the pupils would talk about. Had the teacher chosen to capitalize upon this question, topics concerning pioneer conceptions of justice and due process of law, the function of law-enforcing bodies, and the validity of citizens' arrests could have been developed. These topics did not emerge in the ensuing discussion, nor were they included as relevant points in the outline of topics to be studied under the heading of "Pioneer Life." The teacher's decision at this point, then, determined the character of what the children could learn.

Would this teacher have profited by thinking about his decisions, by examining the hypotheses he held about the effects of his teaching? For example, did this teacher predict that his students would understand pioneer conceptions of justice? It seems unlikely that they would when questions about these ideas are quickly dismissed. Had he tested to see what the students were learning about these conceptions, the result might have prompted him to modify his teaching strategy. He would also have learned that the hypotheses which supported his original decisions were probably invalid.

The first step in learning to view teaching behavior as hypotheses being tested in action is to see the effects of teachers' decisions on learning. Prescott has described this relation as follows:

These accumulating decisions create the conditions under which the pupils live and learn at school. For example, they determine the freedom or restriction of movement, of speech, of access to materials, of spontaneous inquiries or comments, of choice of experiences. They profoundly influence the kinds of relationships the children are able to establish and maintain with adults in the school and with each other in the classroom, on the playground, and everywhere about the school. These decisions often determine the actual learning experiences to which the children are exposed, the content upon which attention is focused, and the food for mental, social, and spiritual growth that is offered each child. They determine the aspects of life and the world with which the pupils are brought into contact, and they evoke or fail to evoke the various steps of the reasoning process, and encourage or discourage curiosity and imagination. They promote certain codes of conduct and imply the validity of certain attitudes and values for living in our times and in our society. These judgments permit some adjustment processes and mechanisms to operate and discourage others. They emphasize certain meanings as valid and condemn others as untrue and unacceptable.[13]

The second step is to see the hypothetical character of these decisions, to examine one's conceptions of the learning process as they influence the formulation of these hypotheses. The third step is to learn to test these hypotheses, to utilize the feedback process to reshape teaching plans.

In the following chapter the student as a learner and the instructional process will be discussed. The concepts used here will be developed into a model of the learning organism and a model of instructional strategies. In the remainder of the book, we will discuss the basic generalizations of psychology and suggest the kinds of hypotheses about teaching and learning that might follow from an understanding of them. You will be encouraged to hypothesize, to criticize, and to evaluate these ideas within the framework of the models presented in this and the following chapter.

SUMMARY

The purposes of this chapter are twofold: (1) to describe a model of teaching behavior; (2) to use this model to analyze teaching behavior as decision making, and teaching decisions as hypotheses about ways to produce learning. This model is used to suggest the ways in which a teacher applies what he has learned about psychology to educational practice. It is also the kind of model most consistent with the conception of the teacher as a hypothesis maker.

1. The central idea of the chapter is that learning is planned for and controlled by the *teaching strategies* the teacher initiates. These strategies are *plans for learning*—that is, plans to bring about new or modified ways of behaving.

2. A teaching plan is a process within the teacher, a set of decisions made by the teacher which guide and control his actions. The plan is designed to achieve goals, which are the behavior changes in students.

[13] D. A. Prescott, *The Child in the Educative Process* (New York: McGraw-Hill Book Company, 1957), pp. 6–7.

This plan is a process composed of sequences of action which are initiated and carried out in an orderly, hierarchical way. The most important characteristic of the plan, as a psychological construct, is that it controls action. Plans are not merely concepts or designs—they determine behavior.

3. It is not necessary to assume that all plans are deliberately conceived or, once conceived, are inflexible. Plans grow and develop and are modified through experience, *feedback*. They are changeable even as the planner enacts them.

4. *Plans are structures of decisions.* Three general kinds of decisions are required in teaching plans: (a) What kinds of behavior change is your teaching plan going to bring about? (b) How will you know that the plan has been effective? (c) What will you do to bring about the desired learning? The consequences of decisions must also be anticipated and evaluated.

5. Our *decision-making model* has the following components: (a) The decision maker selects among *alternatives;* considers the *consequences* of selecting a particular alternative; and *estimates* the probability that a particular consequence will occur.

6. When a probability estimate is based on adequate information—and usually expressed numerically—the estimate is *objective*. When it is based on personal experience alone—particularly when that experience has not been evaluated—the probability is *subjective*. Predictions may be made objectively by using correlational methods or by developing generalizations from experimenting.

7. Associated with each of the consequences of an alternative is a *judgment about its value*. The sources of these value judgments are one's philosophy of life, cultural and professional standards, and a pragmatic evaluation of one's experience. These values are not easily quantified.

8. A *decision rule* is a principle for making a judgment among alternatives. Decision rules are generalizations and have varying degrees of validity. This validity is not absolute, only relative; that is, the rule will be effective only under certain conditions. Even under these conditions, it will not always bring about the desired results. It is most likely to be effective if it has been substantially tested.

9. Decision-making behavior is learned and becomes an aspect of *personal style*. Certain types of teachers, for example, characteristically make certain types of decisions.

10. The decision-making process has three major components: (a) an *input sequence,* in which information is assimilated and formulated into a

plan; (b) an *operation sequence,* in which the plan is carried into action; (c) a *test sequence,* in which *feedback* is received, evaluated, and used as part of the new input for the next cycle of action.

11. The decision-making model is useful in enabling us to evaluate teaching strategies objectively. It also provides us with a way of talking about teaching strategies as designs and of introducing the concepts and principles that may be used in constructing and in improving these designs.

12. Decisions and teaching plans are *hypotheses* about what may produce learning. These plans, because our knowledge of how people learn is still developing, are not perfectly reliable. Because they are not, plans must be thought of as probably valid, and the act of teaching should be seen as a test of their validity. The psychology of learning provides the broad generalizations for hypotheses about teaching. The teacher, in formulating teaching plans, makes a second and third order of hypotheses. These hypotheses are specific to the teacher's class and the conditions under which his students are learning.

This chapter has presented a point of view, a way of thinking about teaching. This conception is used to organize the ideas presented in the remaining chapters. The teacher will need to learn to see how his decisions are important determinants of what his students will learn, to learn to think of these decisions as hypotheses to be tested, and to learn to test these hypotheses by utilizing the feedback he receives and can receive. The educational psychology he will learn offers him concepts, generalizations, and data that can be used in generating hypotheses and teaching plans. He will also learn some of the skills necessary to test these hypotheses.

STUDY AND DISCUSSION QUESTIONS

1. A sixth-grade teacher of social studies organizes a learning experience on the transportation system of the local community. As part of this learning experience, he takes the children on trips on the buses which are part of this transportation system. He finds that the pupils ask many more questions about the operation of the transportation system and seem to have a clearer understanding of its purposes and functions. The teacher hypothesizes that this procedure is effective in producing greater understanding of the complexities of the transportation system. What characteristics of the class and the teaching plan need to be considered if the teacher wants to generalize his teaching strategy to other students? Be specific about the ways in which you think changes in these variables would affect the results.

2. Assume that this same teacher is organizing a learning experience related to the operation of city government. He hypothesizes that a visit to the city council will increase the pupils' understanding of the functions of city government. He feels reasonably certain that the predicted behavior changes will occur because of his experience with the field trip in the study of the transportation system of the city. What variables in these situations may limit the extent to which the teacher may generalize results from the first experience to the second? What assumptions is the teacher making about relationships among these variables when he generalizes from his previous experiences? What factors in the second experience that may not have been present in the first experience might limit the effectiveness of this procedure?

3. Suggest ways in which the following hypotheses need to be clarified before they can be tested and before conclusions can be drawn about their generality.

   a. The use of films in social studies classes improves the students' grasp of concepts.

   b. The use of films in social studies classes improves the students' ability to understand cultural differences.

   c. Field trips make the isolated and abstract facts of the text come to life.

   d. Effective problem-solving behavior results when students work on problems that have meaning for them.

4. A general hypothesis, for which there is some experimental support, is that verbal approval (including praise) will improve a student's learning. What characteristics of students may be related to the effects of giving approval of this kind? Select one and state a hypothesis relating it and verbal approval to learning.

5. Think of a person whom you know well. How would this person react to verbal approval? Would his reaction change if the learning task or the person giving approval changed? Give a set of decision rules to be used with this person.

6. Assume that you had a film on the role of transportation in the development of the American economy and that the content of the film was also covered in the text you were using. How could you determine whether the use of the film alone, the text alone, or the use of both is more likely to be an effective procedure for improving students' understanding of this topic? Describe how you could arrange learning experiences to derive data from which you could draw conclusions in this respect. What kinds of pupil change would you predict would be affected by the film that may not be effected by reading the test? What kinds of changes is reading the text more likely to produce than seeing the film? What kinds of pupil behavior would you observe or test in order to gather data to validate your hypotheses?

7. Consider the following hypothesis: An authoritarian teacher is less likely to effect significant pupil changes than a democratic one. Identify and de-

fine in precise terms the variables and relationships suggested in the above hypothesis. Attempt to develop more specific hypotheses when you have clarified the meaning of the concepts and relationships included in this hypothesis.

8. Some teachers use daily quizzes in their classes. What hypotheses about behavior changes are implicit in this practice?

9. A fifth-grade teacher encourages his pupils to make scrapbooks of pictures of different parts of the United States. What hypotheses might this teacher be making about behavior change?

10. A history teacher asks a local judge to discuss civil rights with his class. Formulate several hypotheses relating this practice to behavior change.

11. Devise a teaching plan to have somebody learn to tie a simple knot (or some other comparably simple behavior). List the behavior changes which will be produced. Describe the steps in the teaching strategy. What will be the test of the effectiveness of the plan? What hypotheses about learning does your plan assume? Try your plan out on someone and report its effects.

12. Devise teaching plans for the learning of a simple concept like that of an animal or kind of person or piece of equipment. Again describe what is to be learned and how you will bring about this learning. Perform analyses similar to those described in Question eleven.

13. Go over each of these teaching plans and list the decisions you made. What alternatives were available? What were the consequences you anticipated? How did you estimate their probabilities? How did you judge their desirabilities? List your decision rules. These questions and directions prompt you to make your decision-making processes as explicit as possible.

14. What hypotheses are implied in the choices you made in these teaching plans? What do you know about their validity?

15. Describe the information you need about students to formulate your teaching plans. How is this information to be used in making decisions? What information will you need as the teaching plan is enacted?

RECOMMENDED READINGS

W. Ross Ashby, *An Introduction to Cybernetics.* New York: John Wiley and Sons, 1958.

I. Bross, *Design for Decision.* New York: The Macmillan Co., 1953.

G. T. Guilbaud, *What Is Cybernetics?* New York: Grove Press, Inc., 1960.

G. Miller, E. Galanter, and K. Pribram, *Plans and the Structure of Behavior.* New York: Henry Holt and Co., 1960.

Sixty-third Yearbook of the National Society for the Study of Education, Part I, *Theories of Learning and Instruction*, E. Hilgard, ed. Chicago: University of Chicago Press, 1964:

N. L. Gage, "Theories of Teaching," pp. 268–285

K. H. Pribram, "Neurological Notes on the Art of Educating," pp. 78–110

CHAPTER THREE

INSTRUCTIONAL STRATEGIES AND LEARNING

This chapter presents two major ideas: (1) a **model** of the **learning organism** and (2) a model of **instructional strategies.** These models are descriptions. They may be used as analytic tools for thinking about problems of instruction and learning. They also may be used as organizing rubrics, as schema for classifying the information and ideas you will gather as you read the remainder of the book.

We need a model of the learning organism for the same reason that we needed a model of teaching behavior. It provides a common frame of reference for analyzing learning problems. If you and I are going to communicate, we need some shared concepts. Even if we did not agree completely on the details of the model, we still would need some simplifying device to reduce the sheer mass of detail. Of course, the main reason for presenting a model is that it is a reasonable facsimile of what the learning organism is like.

We can present a model of an instructional strategy because we now know enough to be able to say what general characteristics any such strategy ought to have. The details have to be varied with the instructional problem and with the student, but there is enough regularity to describe.

A MODEL OF THE LEARNING ORGANISM

"Learning organism" may sound sterile and abstract. Obviously, we are talking about people; but we use the more abstract label to direct attention to the characteristic of people in which we are primarily interested here—their capacity to learn. In this section, as we said, we will present a model of people as learners. That is, we will consider how we need to think about a person in order to interact with him as a potential learner.

People, of course, are more than just learners. The most obvious characteristic of people is their complexity. A human being is an enormous collection of cells and processes, capable of making a very large number of responses. It is impossible to embrace all this complexity. Therefore, our conceptions of other persons are *functional simplifications*. We simplify by ignoring a mass of detail. As you talk to a friend, you do not, I assume, think about the flow of blood through his veins or the electrochemical discharges in his nervous system. If you are an internist, however, the person's physiological properties and processes are what you attend to. This example suggests the meaning of functionality in simplification. Your purposes in interacting with a person determine what aspects of his person capture your attention. Good examples are provided by artists. An artist wishes to portray what he feels to be the significant aspects of some observable, be it a stream, a cloud, an ashcan, or a human being. Andrew Wyeth put the idea this way, when he described one of his pictures, dominated by a single color:

I saw that house once in just that light and wanted to paint it. I remembered the miller who lived there and how he used to come to the door, when I went there as a child, all covered with flour dust, all one color except his eyes, which were reddened by the dust. My reason for painting it was just that tone, that light.[1]

[1] E. P. Richardson, "Andrew Wyeth," *Atlantic Monthly*, 213 (1964), 64.

You may think that the artist has great freedom to see the world as he chooses. In one sense, he does. But he sees it as light, color, and form. The musical composer sees the world as sound. Each of us, for his own purposes, sees the world and people in a simplified way.

KINDS OF MODELS

There are, then, many ways of reconstructing experience. Let us consider some kinds of models so that you may understand the properties and uses of the particular model of the learner that we will use.[2]

One kind of model is the *replica*, a scaled construction that reproduces the important features of the original. Replicas are tangible; you can see them, touch them, hear them. A globe map is a replica model; a mockup of a Gemini capsule is also. The kind of model we will use is *not* a replica model.

Another kind of model, the kind we will use to describe the learning organism, is the *symbolic model*. Symbolic models are intangible except as lines and words on paper or sounds from a speaker describing the model. They use abstract concepts and symbols to portray parts and their interrelations. A diagram of an automobile engine, an electrical diagram of a circuit, a Mercator projection map, the bar charts you can find in any newsmagazine, the diagrammatic representations of battle movements, house plans, dressmaking patterns—all are symbolic models. A symbolic model abstracts aspects of the original. Some abstractions (for example, an equation for a chemical reaction) are highly symbolic. Others (for instance, a road map) are less abstract.

We use symbolic models in thinking about people. Some of these symbols are poetic and metaphorical: "A pretty girl is like a melody." Others are more descriptive: a health officer thinks of people as potential objects of invasion by infectious agents.

DANGERS IN USING MODELS

There are a number of problems in using models, pervasive as they are in our thinking. A symbolic model is an analogy. Like all analogies, there

[2] For a general discussion on the use of models, see A. Chapanis, "Men, Machines, and Models," *American Psychologist*, 16 (1963), 113–131; for some applications to education, see N. L. Gage, "Paradigms," in N. L. Gage, ed., *Handbook of Research on Teaching* (Chicago: Rand-McNally, 1963), Chapter 3.

is only a partial correspondence between the model and its original. The following quotation makes this point well:

> In certain superficial ways the behavior of an electronic digital computer is something like that of the brain. Once we admit so much, the next step is easy. We forget that this is only an analogy and we lapse quickly into calling the computer a "brain." The next step is equally easy. Now we find ourselves saying, and, I am afraid, believing, that the computer *is* a brain. This is just so much rubbish! A computer is no more a brain than the Palomar telescope is an eye, or a bulldozer a muscle.[3]

The author of this quotation says that every time someone uses the word *model,* he substitutes the word *analogy.* The effect, he claims, is like a cold shower in clearing the cobwebs from the discussion, a mixed but pointed metaphor.

Models are also approximations. A model works only something like the original. A model of the learner enables us to predict how he will behave under certain conditions. But we must also observe how he actually does behave.

Since models are human inventions, they may be more or less correct. They are means to the end of predicting and controlling. They postulate processes and variables. The description may be simply inaccurate, and the model need to be revised.

None of these difficulties with models is an argument against using them. They are simply warnings about man's fallible logic.

The symbolic model of the learner, presented in the following sections, describes only the major behavioral systems of a person. This simplification calls attention to those features that are most significant in learning. As such, they must be considered when one is organizing instructional strategies.

ASSUMPTIONS ABOUT THE LEARNING ORGANISM

Our first assumption is that the learner is an information-processing organism. By information, we mean no more than the stimuli that impinge on the learner, which he uses in some way. Second, we assume that the learner is goal-directed, that he behaves to achieve certain desirable

[3] A. Chapanis (see note 2), p. 126.

states. Third, we assume that he uses information to achieve these goals. The utilization of information to achieve the goals is mediated by **feedback** processes. *A feedback process is a link between an information source and an information user.* A teacher correcting a question or student's work is a feedback mechanism because he is giving information which the learner uses to achieve his goals more effectively.

What is **learning** in this conception? *It is the process by which the learner acquires those responses necessary to attain a goal.* What does the model suggest about the necessary characteristics of a learning experience? First, a learning experience must be goal-directed from the viewpoint of the learner. He must have goals that he is trying to attain. A learning experience is simply a device for putting the learner in a situation where he can attain these goals.

A second implication is that the learning experience must be information providing in the sense that it systematically gives the learner the feedback necessary for goal attainment.

Let us use an example to make clear how this model shapes instructional decisions. Suppose we want to teach a child to recognize letters of the alphabet. Devising an instructional strategy is fruitless if the child has no reason to learn the alphabet. He cannot participate in the learning experience without some conception of the purposes to be achieved and without wanting to achieve those purposes. Since he has a limited number of responses available for letter recognition, we must devise a system of using the responses available. A common procedure is to display a letter, pronounce it, and invite the child to repeat the sound. If he could not make the sound, we would have to begin a step back and teach him. As he makes the sound, he needs feedback to tell him whether he is making correct recognitions. This is usually provided by the teacher, who also trains him to provide his own feedback by listening to the sounds as he enunciates them.

Notice that the strategy is built to use the assumed characteristics of the learner. If we did not assume that he could or would utilize feedback, there would be no reason to provide the correction procedure. We also assume that he processes the visual symbols in some way. We expect him to be able to recognize variations in line arrangements in the letters. Where the discriminations may be subtle, as between *a* and *o*, a teacher will initiate a strategy to teach this discrimination. This strategy may show the desired response or prompt the desired discrimination. It must also provide feedback on the correctness of the child's attempts to make the desired discrimination.

ASSUMPTIONS ABOUT
LEARNING PROCESSES

When we say that the learner is a goal-seeking organism, we must be able to point to some observable behavior with distinctive characteristics as a referent for this label. For *processes are response systems,* always identifiable in the last analysis by observable behavior. You may think of them as generally similar to physiological processes, many of which are not directly observable and which can be understood only by a study of their effects. Do not carry the analogy too far. You are not going to lay open the person and find a motivational system. But it is likely that neurophysiological correlates and determinants of these processes would be found.[4] At present we are about where physiology and anatomy were several centuries ago; physiologists and physicians knew that blood flowed and that something had to be going on inside the skin, but their descriptions of the mechanisms seem ludicrous in the light of later knowledge.

The details of these intervening response systems will be described in succeeding chapters. Here we list them, give a brief description, and in the next section point up their implications for designing instructional strategies. We assume that the following response systems [5] are available in some form in the learner:

1. *A motivational system:* the capacity of the learner to select and seek goals. A major directive or orienting system, the motivational system accounts for variations in energy expended and the complex choices of approaching and engaging in learning experiences or of avoiding them.

[4] For a summary of recent progress and its implications for understanding learning processes, see K. H. Pribram, "Neurological Notes on the Art of Educating," in E. R. Hilgard, ed., *Theories of Learning and Instruction,* Sixty-third Yearbook of the National Society for the Study of Education, Part I (Chicago: University of Chicago Press, 1964), Chapter IV, pp. 78–110.

[5] Some scholars are literally revulsed by the postulation of intervening processes such as these systems. The current and most forthright spokesman for this view is B. F. Skinner: see *The Behavior of Organisms* (New York: Appleton-Century-Crofts, 1938); *Science and Human Behavior* (New York: The Macmillan Company, 1953); and "Reinforcement Today," *American Psychologist,* 13 (1958), 94–99. Others consider only the processes and give meager attention to their behavioral referents. Here, we consider *both* the processes and the behaviors which define them.

For three statements on this problem—the first, a historical critique; the second and third, summaries of research utilizing the concept of mediating responses—see A. E. Goss, "Early Behaviorism and Verbal Mediating Responses," *American Psychologist,* 16 (1961), 285–298; C. E. Osgood, "On Understanding and Creating Sentences," *American Psychologist,* 18 (1963), 735–751; I. E. Farber, "The Things People Say to Themselves," *American Psychologist,* 18 (1963), 185–197.

2. *A cognitive system:* the set of responses by which the learner organizes and orders the stimuli around him. It also is the system by which he symbolically recalls or reinstates these stimuli and his conceptualizations of them. Finally, it is the system by which he interrelates his conceptualizations and solves problems.

3. *An attitudinal system:* the evaluative system of the person, by which he judges the "goodness" or "badness," for him, of the stimulus information he receives.

4. *A self system:* a complex integration of concepts of oneself as a learner and an associated evaluation. We assume that the person "sees" himself in some way as a successful or not very successful learner, as having or not having certain learning capacities. This self-image determines his "openness" to learning; whether he will, for example, even participate in a learning experience.

In Figure 3–1 is a symbolic model of this learner. He is only a set of lines and boxes, and we regret that he has been stripped of some of his more attractive features. Note that we have symbolized the interactions among these systems.

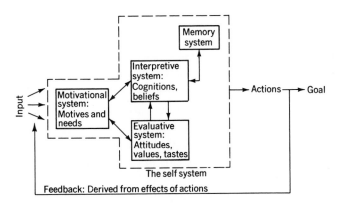

FIGURE 3–1. *Symbolic model of the learner.*

1. The self system and motivational system are portrayed as two major controlling systems. These systems determine what learning opportunities will be learning experiences. They determine the **approach-avoidance responses** the learner will make when he meets a new learning experience. In a classroom you will observe some students whose negative self-evaluations are impeding their learning. For them the learning ex-

perience is not effective, because their self-image acts as a stimulus to avoid participation. They can withdraw only in minor ways, but these withdrawals are usually frequent enough to interfere with learning.

2. The cognitive-attitudinal system is a sorting system that interprets the information the learner is receiving. As we will see, it is frequently impossible to separate the influence of these two systems. They interact. Our cognitions influence our evaluations, and our evaluations influence our cognitions. In later chapters we will explore these interrelations.

3. We have placed a memory system as a component of the cognitive system. This is the storage system, an information bank the person uses in each new learning experience.

All of these mechanisms or systems are what the learner brings to the learning experience. Decisions about instructional strategies are dependent on information about them. A teacher trying to influence attitudes about civil rights had better know something about how his students think and feel about minority groups.

What the learner does in the learning situation is dependent on the stimulus and feedback controls. What he learns about his environment depends on what is available in it, the information he receives from it. This relation is portrayed in Figure 3–1 as the feedback loop, which shows the constant interrelation between the environment and the learner.

The learner processes information from his environment and from his internal systems. This information processing acts as a stimulus to evoke behavior directed to attaining a goal. He receives feedback, which is a control mechanism for signaling him that his responding is bringing him toward or taking him away from his goal.

Some general principles may be stated by implication from this model. Remember that these response systems are learned: a child is not born with a complex cognitive system or a set of values; his self-evaluations are acquired gradually. The arrangement of a curriculum, therefore, demands two kinds of decisions, which are always necessary. First, at each new step or phase in the organization of learning opportunities, the teacher must gauge the effects of previous learning. Second, he must estimate the usefulness of what is to be learned—that is, the extent to which it will promote future learning.

In order to assess the effects of a student's prior learning, the teacher needs diagnostic skills and evaluative strategies. Too often, he may decide that a student has learned something just because he has been exposed to it. When a teacher finds that exposure and learning are not coincident, he frequently responds with, "You should have learned that." Although this reaction is understandable as a frustration response, it solves neither the teacher's nor the student's problem.

A second implication, to be discussed in detail later in this chapter, is that a teacher must carefully consider the demands that a learning situation will put on the student. Frequently a learning task must be broken into its components, and the student engaged in learning each of these components. For example, studying a period of history in a history class involves many learning tasks: the learner must acquire **concepts** and **generalizations;** he must remember specific bits of information; he must relate what he is learning to other problems. The teacher may also be expecting to influence attitudes through this study. To achieve the goals of the learning experience, he must engage and mobilize the learner's total system.

Although many teachers are aware of these complexities, they err by making invalid assumptions about the relations among these systems. For example, it is not generally true that providing information either produces conceptualizing behavior or influences attitudes. Yet many instructional strategies meant to change attitudes are little more than ways of distributing information.

In this book we study each of these response systems, as a perusal of the table of contents will show. In each chapter we describe the characteristics of the response system and the **variables** that influence their acquisition. We also discuss the interrelations among the systems, when they are known. The chapters then conclude with suggestions about evaluative decisions and instructional strategies. The learning objectives are:

1. To describe the observable behavior that is the referent for the response system. This behavior we label the *criterion behavior.*

2. To list the variables now known to influence the acquisition of the responses.

3. To estimate their relative influence and interactions.

4. To identify the critical instructional decisions that are consequent on this understanding.

5. To describe the general patterns of instructional strategies designed to produce these response acquisitions.

6. To identify the instructional and evaluative decisions required.

Before we take up these matters in detail, we consider a model of instructional strategies. This model is derivative from that of the learner. Because a learner has certain characteristics, those described in the model, an **instructional strategy** must meet certain requirements if learning is to be produced.

A MODEL OF INSTRUCTIONAL STRATEGIES

The construction of an instructional strategy is work, most of which is thinking. To plan a learning experience that is effective is no small accomplishment. To carry it out, to test it, and to modify it requires technical skill. Most of this book will be devoted to the kinds of decisions that must be made in planning instructional strategies. Before we begin this study, let us look for a moment at the kinds of planning decisions a teacher needs to make.

An educative act is the learning experience from the viewpoint of the teacher. It has the following components: (1) a formulation of the goals of the learning experience; (2) a plan for the instructional strategy; (3) a plan for evaluating the effects of the strategy.

FORMULATION OF GOALS

We now discuss the starting point of any instructional strategy, a conception of the desired changes in the student. Some teachers believe that each child sets his own objectives. In one sense this is a valid proposition. We implied this possibility when we described the learner as a goal-setting and goal-seeking organism. But the teacher sets the goals of a learning experience. His problem is to establish some consonance between the goals of the individual learners and his purposes in designing the learning experience. The teacher must also be responsive to the student's re-evaluation of his purposes, his willingness to go ahead and to inquire on his own. These developments are usually consonant with most teachers' purposes.

Perhaps the easiest way to avoid this problem is to see the classroom as something other than a battlefield with the teacher's purposes on one side and the learner's on the other. The purposes are simply conceptions of what kinds of changes are desired. They usually involve value choices. But many of these choices are general and matters of common agreement. In particular learning episodes, the teacher can formulate the behavior changes desired without threatening the values of students. Specifying the behavior changes desired in reading or arithmetic or history classes usually can be done without personal threat and without undermining the democratic way of life.

Educational Objectives

An **educational objective** is a statement about desired behavior change. Such a statement can be formulated at many different levels of abstraction. We can state that we want pupils to "have an appetite for learning," that we want a first-grade child to "learn to share materials with his fellow students," or that we want a fifth-grade child to "learn an appropriate concept of *peninsula*." The first of these objectives is highly abstract and generalized. To acquire an "appetite for learning" requires many complex changes in the individual. The second objective is relatively less abstract; the third, fairly specific.

A clear conception of the desired behavior change is necessary if learning experiences are to be organized to produce these behavior changes and if evaluation procedures are to be established for assessing the extent of the behavior change. While we may agree that all students should have an "appetite for learning," such a statement does not tell us the behavior that characterizes an individual who *has* an "appetite for learning." We must know how such a person will act, think, and feel. We must be able to answer the question "How can we recognize or identify a person who has an appetite for learning?"

Many educational objectives are stated at such a high level of abstraction that they have no utility for the organization of learning experiences or evaluation procedures. What behavior is implied in the phrase "an appetite for learning"? What concepts, generalizations, attitudes, and values have been acquired by a person who has "an appetite for learning"? What behavior distinguishes this person from one who does not have "an appetite for learning"? These questions can also be raised about objectives such as "the school should foster the development of intelligent participation in the processes of democratic government" or "the school should foster the development of cooperative behavior." Until we have defined these objectives in specific behavioral terms, we cannot organize a learning experience to foster these changes. Furthermore, we cannot determine whether these desired changes have occurred, since we have at best only a vague conception of the behavior to be observed or measured.

TABLE 3-1. *A statement of objectives for American schools (from Educational Policies Commission, National Education Association).*

THE OBJECTIVES OF SELF-REALIZATION

The Inquiring Mind. The educated person has an appetite for learning.

Speech. The educated person can speak the mother tongue clearly.

Reading. The educated person reads the mother tongue efficiently.

Writing. The educated person writes the mother tongue effectively.

Number. The educated person solves his problems of counting and calculating.

Sight and Hearing. The educated person is skilled in listening and observing.

Health Knowledge. The educated person understands the basic facts concerning health and disease.

Health Habits. The educated person protects his own health and that of his dependents.

Public Health. The educated person works to improve the health of the community.

Recreation. The educated person is participant and spectator in many sports and other pastimes.

Intellectual Interests. The educated person has mental resources for the use of leisure.

Esthetic Interests. The educated person appreciates beauty.

Character. The educated person gives responsible direction to his own life.

THE OBJECTIVES OF HUMAN RELATIONSHIP

Respect for Humanity. The educated person puts human relationships first.

Friendships. The educated person enjoys a rich, sincere, and varied social life.

Cooperation. The educated person can work and play with others.

Courtesy The educated person observes the amenities of social behavior.

Appreciation of the Home. The educated person appreciates the family as a social institution.

Conservation of the Home. The educated person conserves family ideals.

Homemaking. The educated person is skilled in homemaking.

Democracy in the Home. The educated person maintains democratic family relationships.

THE OBJECTIVES OF ECONOMIC EFFICIENCY

Work. The educated producer knows the satisfaction of good workmanship.

Occupational Information. The educated producer understands the requirements and opportunities for various jobs.

Occupational Choice. The educated producer has *selected* his occupation.

Occupational Efficiency. The educated producer succeeds in his chosen vocation.

Occupational Adjustment. The educated producer maintains and improves his efficiency.

Occupational Appreciation. The educated producer appreciates the social value of his work.

Personal Economics. The educated consumer plans the economics of his own life.

Consumer Judgment. The educated consumer develops standards for guiding his expenditures.

Efficiency in Buying. The educated consumer is an informed and skillful buyer.

Consumer Protection. The educated consumer takes appropriate measures to safeguard his interests.

THE OBJECTIVES OF CIVIC RESPONSIBILITY

Social Justice. The educated citizen is sensitive to the disparities of human circumstance.

Social Activity. The educated citizen acts to correct unsatisfactory conditions.

Social Understanding. The educated citizen seeks to understand social structures and social processes.

Critical Judgment. The educated citizen has defenses against propaganda.

Tolerance. The educated citizen respects honest differences of opinion.

Conservation. The educated citizen has a regard for the nation's resources.

Social Applications of Science. The educated citizen measures scientific advance by its contribution to the general welfare.

World Citizenship. The educated citizen is a cooperating member of the world community.

Law Observance. The educated citizen respects the law

Economic Literacy. The educated citizen is economically literate.

Political Citizenship. The educated citizen accepts his civic duties.

Devotion to Democracy. The educated citizen acts upon an unswerving loyalty to democratic ideals.

Statements of abstractly defined objectives are useful for describing the role of the school in society. Table 3–1 lists objectives for the American school taken from a statement by the Educational Policies Commission of the National Education Association. The over-all objective, the Commission states, "is the fullest possible development of the individual within the framework of our present industrialized democratic society. The attainment of this end is to be observed in individual behavior or conduct." [6]

The Commission identifies four aspects of educational objectives and outlines more specific statements in each of these categories (see Table 3–1).[7] These statements define the responsibilities of the American school in the socialization of the child. These statements, however, must be refined by specifying the behaviors implied in the objectives as they are stated. Before we can hypothesize what curricula and what particular learning experiences will foster the attainment of these objectives, we must have a more complete statement, one that specifies the desired behavior changes more clearly.

Immediate and Ultimate Objectives

If we study closely the list of objectives outlined by the Educational Policies Commission, we will notice that these objectives represent end points to be reached. They are descriptions of what a person ought to be like when he has gone through a series of educational experiences. The objective of the learning experience organized today may be the acquisition of information about the American Revolution, the development of the concept of a neutron, or facility in playing a musical score. In such cases the objective is immediate, and it is presumably attainable within a limited period of time.

But immediate objectives should be related to ultimate objectives. The child is acquiring a certain set of facts or a skill because such changes in

[6] *The Purposes of Education in American Democracy* (Washington, D. C.: Educational Policies Commission, National Education Association, 1938), p. 41.

[7] Although this list is dated, it is representative of the kinds of objectives that have been stated as the purposes of American education for three decades. Changes in lists of this kind reflect changes in emphasis, frequently stimulated by social changes. This list is from *The Purposes of Education in American Democracy* (Washington, D. C.: Educational Policies Commission, National Education Association, 1938). A recent statement relates these purposes to a central purpose, the development of man's capacity to think rationally. See *The Central Purpose of American Education* (Washington, D. C.: Educational Policies Commission, National Education Association, 1961).

behavior are consistent with his becoming a person who has an appetite for learning, or who understands his society, or who appreciates beauty. In developing a statement of objectives, we may proceed from generalized statements of ultimate objectives, such as those represented in the report of the Educational Policies Commission, to more immediate objectives, which, when attained, are presumed to contribute to the attainment of the broader and more abstract objectives.

The teacher in a classroom is organizing learning experiences that do more than affect the child at this particular time in his life; they will have a permanent effect on him. The sequence of learning experiences is designed to provide for a systematic and orderly development of the child's personality. Table 3–2 shows teacher objectives for a kindergarten class and for a sixth-grade class studying India. Note the specificity of these objectives when compared to the statement of objectives by the Educational Policies Commission. The assumption in the kindergarten or sixth grade is that the attainment of these immediate objectives will contribute to the attainment of the ultimate objectives.

Ideally, the objectives of any particular learning experience ought to be derived from some conception of what the person is to be like when he has gone through a sequence of learning experiences. This ideal arrangement, however, is not always realized in practice.

Unfortunately, this ideal relationship among ultimate objectives, immediate objectives, and the content and methods of instruction has only rarely been approximated in actual practice. Some of the content of current instruction, if derived at all from sound and accepted ultimate objectives, has been derived from them by a process of faulty inference, and contributes much less to the realization of the objectives than other content which should be substituted for it. More unfortunately, a portion of the present content of school instruction is there only by reason of the organization of the curriculum by "subjects," and because of the practice of introducing new materials in intact subject units, or subject by subject, often without any careful selection for detailed content of those subjects. As a result of this practice many detailed elements which have no relationship whatever to any ultimate objectives have entered the curriculum simply because they "belong" in the same broad category of knowledge, or in the subject, with other content which could be readily justified, and because of which the subject as a whole was selected.[8]

---

[8] E. F. Lindquist, "Preliminary Considerations in Objective Test Construction," in E. F. Lindquist, ed., *Educational Measurement* (Washington, D. C.: American Council on Education, 1951), p. 121.

TABLE 3–2. *Teacher objectives for a kindergarten and a sixth-grade class.*

Kindergarten	Sixth-Grade Class
I. TEACHER'S OBJECTIVE: To help the child learn to conform to the daily routine of the group. *Expected Behavior Changes* 1. The child obeys school rules, which he has helped discuss and which he accepts. 2. He listens attentively, so that he carries out directions properly. 3. He willingly participates in art, music, and physical activities.	I. TEACHER'S OBJECTIVE: To help the child gain knowledge of the physical world of India. *Expected Behavior Changes* 1. The child has a general idea of the physical features of India. 2. He knows what cholera is and how it is controlled. 3. He can explain some of the effects of altitude, temperature, and rainfall upon the economic and social conditions.
II. TEACHER'S OBJECTIVE: To ease the child's adjustment to school situations. *Expected Behavior Changes* 1. The child seeks answers to questions by making inquiries of the teacher and classmates. 2. He solves problems by himself. 3. He takes part in group play and activities.	II. TEACHER'S OBJECTIVE: To help the child gain skill and competence in using knowledge about India's physical world. *Expected Behavior Changes* 1. The child can make accurate measurements of physical phenomena such as rainfall, temperature, and wind speed. 2. He can interpret charts, maps, diagrams, and tables. 3. He can perform simple experiments in physical science.
III. TEACHER'S OBJECTIVE: To teach the child to share with others. *Expected Behavior Changes* 1. The child offers to share his toys with other children. 2. He waits in line to use play equipment, lavatory, and drinking fountain. 3. He is willing to share the place of prominence (first in line, holding the teacher's hand).	III. TEACHER'S OBJECTIVE: To help the child develop new attitudes and interests. *Expected Behavior Changes* 1. The child shows enthusiasm for movies and television programs with a scientific theme. 2. He is interested in new experiments in medicine. 3. He is interested in learning how men modify their environments.

Guides for Formulating Objectives in Behavioral Terms

Formulating objectives in behavioral terms is not a simple task. In the first place, most people have a difficult time separating words about behavior from a careful description of the behavior itself. In addition, the conditions for evoking the behavior are not always present and may have to be created. If I want to know whether a student understands a concept or a generalization, or if I want to see how he organizes ideas, I have to invent a situation that will evoke this behavior.

The problem is not insuperable if one continually thinks in concrete, definite terms. A good rule, as previously suggested, is to avoid broad terms like "know," "appreciate," "understand." These may be good first approximations. They identify the domain of behavior in which you are interested, and point you to the psychological systems of the learner about which you will be concerned. But the remaining steps are to simplify and to make more concrete these general descriptions.

Mager [9] suggests three steps in formulating objectives. First, name the desired behavior, which is frequently called the **terminal behavior.** State what the learner must *do* or *perform* to show that he has attained the objective. Second, specify the conditions under which the behavior may be expected to occur; that is, specify the test situation for assessing the behavior change. Third, specify an acceptable level of performance.

Component task analysis. Another way to approach the problem of objectives is to look at the characteristics of the learning tasks. Most learning tasks are complex. Reading, for example, is an extended series of tasks from simple letter and word identifications to critical analysis of literary forms. At any one level the task may be analyzable into several components. If this can be done, the behavioral demands of each task may usually be specified.

This analysis has the further advantage of sensitizing the teacher to the instructional requirements of the task. It also prompts decisions about the interrelations of the various acquisitions, appropriate sequencing, and the necessity for extended instruction on the subtasks.

Behavioral taxonomies. The unpleasant fact of the matter is that we have not developed taxonomies of behavioral demands in learning tasks.[10]

[9] R. F. Mager, *Preparing Objectives for Programmed Instruction* (San Francisco: Fearon Publishers, 1961).

[10] This problem is discussed extensively in A. W. Melton, ed., *Categories of Human Learning* (New York: Academic Press, 1964).

However, some analyses of the behavioral referents of educational objectives have been made. The following is a breakdown of a sample of such objectives.[11] These classifications may be used as guides in sharpening up your statements of objectives.

Knowledge: recall of specifics and universals, methods and processes, pattern, structure, or setting.

Knowledge of Specifics: recall of specific and isolable bits of information.

Knowledge of terminology: referents for specific symbols.

Knowledge of specific facts: dates, events, persons, places, etc.

Knowledge of Ways and Means of Dealing with Specifics: knowledge of ways of organizing, studying, judging, and criticizing.

Knowledge of conventions: characteristic ways of treating and presenting phenomena.

Knowledge of trends and sequences: processes, directions, and movements of phenomena with respect to time.

Knowledge of classifications and categories: classes, sets, divisions, and arrangements fundamental to a field, purpose, argument, or problem.

Knowledge of criteria: standards by which facts, principles, opinions, and conduct are judged.

Knowledge of methodology: methods of inquiry, techniques, and procedures employed in a field.

Knowledge of the Universals and Abstractions in a Field.

Knowledge of principles and generalizations: particular abstractions which summarize observations of phenomena—useful in explaining, predicting, describing, or in determining appropriate action or direction to be taken.

Knowledge of theories and structures: the body of principles and generalizations which present a systematic view of a complex phenomenon, problem, or field.

Comprehension: understanding what is communicated; can use what is communicated without necessarily being able to relate to other ideas or see all implications

Translation.

Interpretation.

Extrapolation.

---

[11] From B. S. Bloom, ed., *Taxonomy of Educational Objectives: Handbook I: Cognitive Domain* (New York: Daniel McKay Company, 1956). The definitions in this list have been simplified from those provided in the original. Two kinds of objectives are illustrated here: (1) those specifying the kinds of knowledge to be acquired; and (2) those specifying intellectual responses to be learned. In the second category, only the definitions for the main divisions have been given. See also D. R. Krathwohl, B. S. Bloom, and B. B. Masia, *Taxonomy of Educational Objectives: Handbook II: Affective Domain* (New York: Daniel McKay Company, 1964).

Application: use of abstractions in particular and concrete situations.

Analysis: breakdown of a communication into constituent parts or hierarchy of ideas.
   Analysis of Elements.
   Analysis of Relationships.
   Analysis of Organizational Principles.

Synthesis: combining to form a whole; arranging into a pattern or structure not clearly there before.
   Production of a Unique Communication.
   Production of a Plan.
   Derivation of a Set of Abstract Relations.

Evaluation: judgments about the value of material and methods for given purposes.
   Judgments in Terms of Internal Evidence.
   Judgments in Terms of External Criteria.

As you read this book, note that the discussions of instructional strategies in each chapter include a description of the criterion behavior for that particular kind of strategy. These descriptions are general guides for describing the specific behavior changes the strategy is meant to produce.

PLANNING THE INSTRUCTIONAL STRATEGY

Let us take a simple-minded view of what goes on when someone learns. First of all, he is confronted with or immersed in a set of stimuli. Second, he has to do something in that situation. We say he makes responses, only some of which we can see. When he acquires new responses or modifies old ones, he learns. How is this modification brought about? Obviously, it has something to do with what he has when he comes to the situation, and it has a lot to do with the characteristics of the situation. The environment is controlled in some way to increase the probability of his making desired responses. That is, an environment limits in some ways the range of response alternatives; and in designing learning experiences we deliberately limit these alternatives in the interests of producing learning. The idea applies when the desired learning is the kind thought to be most dependent on the internal resources of the person. As we will see in the chapter on problem solving, to induce problem-solving behavior in students, one must create a problem-solving atmosphere. The teacher signals the students that problem solving is desired, not answer giving or dredging up stale old facts. If he does not, problem solving is not likely to occur.

But how does the learner find out how to respond in a learning experience? Obviously, he has to have a way of determining what are appropriate and relevant responses. He must also try the responses. If they are fairly simple, he may make them quickly and appropriately. If they are complex, or require multiple coordinations, he may require extensive practice. As he makes the responses, he needs feedback.

In teaching, we are not playing games with the learner. We want to maximize his learning. Our model of an instructional strategy is a conservative one—at times, far too conservative. At points in the book we describe learning situations where acquisitions have been achieved without all the components of the model. But as a general guide, an instructional strategy probably should have the components described below.

Components of an Instructional Strategy

Think of a learning experience as an instructional episode. To be effective, this episode needs three components or phases: (1) a **response-guidance** phase, (2) a **response-practice** phase, (3) a **feedback** phase. In the response-guidance phase, the learner determines the characteristics of the desired response. In the response-practice phase, he tries the response. In the feedback phase, he obtains information that keeps him goal-directed.

The form and sequence of these components vary considerably, depending on what is to be learned and our resources for providing effective environmental manipulations. Each component may also be an extended instructional episode in itself. The learner may be shifted from one phase to another and back again. The three phases may be difficult to distinguish in some learning experiences.

Response-guidance phase. Response guidance does not always mean that the learner is shown what to do. In some cases, this is the most effective method; for example, when the desired behavior can be modeled or demonstrated, a display technique is likely to be highly effective.[12] In other cases, the desired response is impossible or too difficult to demonstrate; and the only way the response can be learned is by trying alternatives.

[12] A. Bandura, "Social Learning through Imitation," in M. R. Jones, ed., *Nebraska Symposium on Motivation* (Lincoln: University of Nebraska Press, 1962), pp. 211–269.

Another form of response guidance is a set of instructions—operating manuals or rules for spelling. In some of these instances the learner may already know how to enact some of the responses, so that response guidance consists of describing how to sequence the responses. The plans and instructions for assembling a model or for operating a machine usually assume that the user is able to make many of the movements required—how to move and lift, how to watch for signals, and how to position head, hands, and body. Therefore, the instructions are mainly guides for integrating these previously learned responses.

The essential idea of this phase is to use stimuli to prompt, evoke, and model the desired response. The student learns the form of the response and the cues to which it is attached.

Response-practice phase. An example of the response-practice phase is students' writing, in which they try to make the responses according to the concepts and rules for effective writing. Trying a dance step, enacting a basketball play, answering questions requiring a factual answer, translating verbally or in writing from a foreign language are other examples.

The complexity of the response to be practiced is a problem requiring careful analysis. Take the example of writing. We probably would begin with writing sentences, then paragraphs, and finally essays. Actually, the student is not practicing identically the same responses in each case. Writing a paragraph requires organizing responses that relate one sentence to another and each to the major idea of the paragraph. Similarly, for the essay, which also requires considerable conceptualization, utilization of sources, management of time, and reproduction of the manuscript. Again, a careful analysis of the response demands of the task is required. However, ability to write a sentence does not automatically guarantee ability to write a good paragraph. Similarly, one may be able to translate a list of foreign words and still be unable to translate sentences. In both these examples, acquisition of the first response is necessary for acquiring the second one because it is included in the second, more complex response.

Feedback phase. As the learner makes responses, he needs feedback on the correctness of his response. Sometimes this is provided directly on making the response. The example that comes painfully to mind is hitting a golf ball. The course of the ball is feedback on the correctness of the swing. The player has to know enough about the swing to utilize the feedback. Feedback is interpretative information, and the learner has to be able to interpret correctly. In other cases the feedback has to be provided through mechanical means or by the teacher—for instance, correcting problems and saying "That's right" or "That's wrong." Even aversive (that is, disagreeable) stimuli can be informative feedback of this kind.[13]

The kind of reinforcement provided is that associated with goal attainment. We have been assuming that the learner is motivated in this learning sequence, that by participating in it he is seeking goals significant to him. Attaining these goals is need satisfying and reinforces both the goal choices and the responses instrumental in attaining the goals.

Suppose that you are required to take a special course to learn how to operate a computer. You will probably learn how to operate the computer if relevant feedback is provided during the learning sequence. Your only reward—if you are taking the course merely because it is required—is completing the course without failing or without drastically affecting your grade-point average. If the desired learning is to be reinforced, however, the achievement of the goal of the learning task should have reward value —not necessarily money, but perhaps the reward of being able to understand and to cope with one's environment, the satisfaction of making sense out of the world, or having available new ways of responding.

One of the goals of an instructional strategy is to teach the learner how to provide feedback for himself—for instance by locating his mistakes or by learning alternate methods of solving a problem. These devices are simply ways of encouraging the learner to provide feedback to himself; that is, as he checks his work or tries alternate methods, he is learning something about the correctness of his responses. He is finding out what responses lead to goal attainment. It is not always recognized that responses like these are learned. One has to learn the specific method of checking and also the generalized response of learning to check. After years of hearing teachers say, "Why don't you check your answers," one can only wonder why it has not occurred to them that instructional strategies must be designed to teach this response specifically.

Instructional Problems and Psychological Issues

We are assuming that your problem is the construction of instructional strategies. To this task you bring what you will learn about the influence of various variables on learning. You will build these variables into the

---

[13] For a comprehensive review and analysis of this problem, see R. Solomon, "Punishment," *American Psychologist*, 19 (1964), 239–253.

components of an instructional strategy. It will not be long before you find that things do not work as easily as you thought they would. Why?

The instructional strategy is an extension from the learning paradigms of the experimental studies. The strategy is not an exact replica of the experimental situation, in which the influence of the variable is clear. Now there are many variables operating, and it may be difficult to assess how each will influence learning.

Another problem: You may not have done a good job of designing a mechanism for bringing the variable into the situation. Skinner has pointed out that ordinary teaching methods are weak technologies for utilizing the controlling force of feedback.[14] The teacher ordinarily reinforces a limited number of responses of all those the child makes. He might do well to revise the method so that more reinforcements can be given more frequently.

There are a number of issues on which the psychological literature gives mixed results, or on which sufficient information is not available. For example, a practice phase in some form is usually required in an instructional strategy. But how much practice to provide varies with the complexity of the response being learned and with effectiveness of the response-guidance phase. Ordinarily, considerable practice is required to hook complex responses to multiple cues—language habits are familiar examples. But if the response-guidance phase is an artful demonstration, simplified to highlight the significant steps and cues, much practice may be eliminated.[15] The teacher, of course, has only to observe the behavior carefully to judge when the practice has produced a desirable level of performance. Another issue concerns the scheduling of feedback. A **feedback schedule** is simply the timing and the amount of information the learner receives. If every response I make is corrected, I am receiving immediate feedback; whereas, if every fifth response is corrected, I am receiving feedback a fixed percentage of times. The feedback also may vary in how much information I receive—simple indications of correctness or appropriateness, or detailed explanations of mistakes and suggestions for improvement.

Different schedules of feedback have different effects.[16] These varieties

---

[14] B. F. Skinner, "The Science of Learning and the Art of Teaching," *Harvard Educational Review*, 24 (1954), 86–97.

[15] S. M. Roshol, "Film-Mediated Learning with Varying Representations of the Task: Viewing Angle, Portrayal of Demonstration, Motion, and Student Participation," in A. A. Lumsdaine, ed., *Student Response in Programmed Instruction* (Washington, D. C.: National Academy of Sciences, National Research Council, 1961), pp. 155–175.

[16] C. B. Ferster and B. F. Skinner, *Schedules of Reinforcement* (New York: Appleton-Century-Crofts, 1957).

of schedules are being tried in human learning situations, but our knowledge of their precise effects in these cases is extremely limited. There is no question, however, that immediate feedback is an effective method of behavior control. The practical problem is to arrange the learning situation in such a way that immediate feedback can be given.

In the succeeding chapters it may be useful to organize the material presented into three categories: (1) variables influencing response evocation and guidance; (2) variables influencing practice; (3) variables associated with feedback. In the next section is an example of an application of psychological principles in an instructional system.

Programming as an Instructional System

Practically everyone has heard about programmed learning and teaching machines. We discuss the topic here as an illustration of a carefully conceived instructional strategy.

Figure 3–2 contains a sample of several program frames.[17] What do you observe as characteristic of this display? Notice that the material is broken up into "frames," separate units, quite different in presentation format from the material you are now reading. At each frame the student is required to make a response, which is immediately corrected in the next frame.

The stem of the frame, the introductory and explanatory material, is the response-prompting phase of the strategy; the response writing is the practice phase; and the feedback is the correct answer given immediately. Notice particularly that the frame prompts a response both by actually suggesting it in the introductory statement, and cueing it in the response panel.

This is a simple, straightforward application of well-known psychological principles: get the learner actively involved [18] and provide him with feedback on his performance.[19] The rationale for the breaking up of the

---

[17] S. M. Markle, *Good Frames and Bad: A Grammar of Frame Writing* (New York: John Wiley and Sons, 1964).

[18] This principle has been generally accepted, but its precise meaning is not clear and its empirical validity debatable. Active responding may be necessary so that desired responses can be reinforced by the teacher or some other means. For a discussion of the issues, see F. D. Sheffield, "Theoretical Considerations in Learning of Complex Sequential Tasks from Demonstration and Practice," in A. A. Lumsdaine, *Student Response in Programmed Instruction* (note 15), pp. 13–32.

[19] The value of providing "knowledge of results" is well established. See R. Ammons, "Effects of Knowledge of Performance: A Survey and a Tentative Theoretical Formulation," *Journal of General Psychology*, 54 (1956), 279–299. However, Skinner was applying the results of his research on operant conditioning to instruction. See B. F. Skinner, "Teaching Machines," *Science*, 128 (1958), 969–977.

When you have completed Skinner's article, turn to Panel 1–2 and inspect its contents. Note that this panel contains a glossary of terms important in linear programing. For those whose psychology is rusty, an extra list is provided containing a few key terms frequently used in discussions of linear programing. Although very few of you will want to read through the glossary, you may find it helpful at certain points in this program. You may refer to it at any time.

THE FIRST PRINCIPLE

1. In his article Skinner states "there is a constant exchange between program and student," and "the machine does not simply present something to be learned; it induces sustained activity."

In these and other statements, Skinner makes clear his position on one of the main necessities governing learning. In order for learning to occur, the student must _____.

---

respond, or do something, or be active, etc.

2. From what Skinner says about "lectures, textbooks, and their mechanized equivalents," (refer to Panel 1–1 if you wish) would you say that *listening*, *reading*, and *watching* a film or TV presentation are responses of the sort that Skinner intends to have the student make?

The question asks what you would say. If you find yourself tending to say "yes," reread the first paragraph of Skinner's article. Note the emphasis on making sure that the student understands before he is allowed to go on.

---

3. A basic principle derived from the learning theory on which linear programing is based is:

In order for learning to occur, a response must be made by the learner. It follows that if we give a student two bits of information, both of which we expect him to learn, he should respond to

    (a) either of them

    (b) both of them.

(b) both of them.

4. Suppose a student has been led to respond correctly to the question "What is the capital of France?" In psychological terms, we can say:

    In the presence of the stimulus "capital of France," the student responds "Paris."

Is this the same situation as that represented by the following?

    In the presence of "Paris is the capital of what country?" the student will respond "France". _____.

FIGURE 3–2.   *Illustration of program frames (from Markle).*

If your answer is "yes," go to item 4a.
If your answer is "no," go to item 4c.

[On new page]

4a. Your answer was "yes." When the sentence "Paris is the capital of France" is broken into a *stimulus* part and a *response* part, it can be made into several different combinations of stimulus and response:
  "What country is Paris the capital of?" is one question to which the correct response is "France."
  "What is the capital of France?" is another question to which the correct response is "Paris."
According to the principle of active responding, the student who has learned the answer to the first question has *not necessarily* learned the answer to the second question. The principle has been supported—often to the chagrin of program authors who assume that reading is an adequate response—by data drawn from all levels of student age and ability.
  Minor wording changes (what we call "synonymous" phrasing) may be made without changing the stimulus-response relationship. One item is different from another whenever the stimulus is changed and a different response is asked for.
  Are the following questions the same or are they different?

> Q1. "What do we call the meaningful unit that goes in front of a root?"
> A1. "A prefix."
> Q2. "When a meaningful unit precedes a root, it is a _____."
> A2. "prefix."

For any student for whom "precedes" = "goes in front of," the items are the same.

4b. In the presence of the stimulus "The particles that circle the nucleus are called . . . ," the student responds "electrons."
  Is this the same situation as when in the presence of "Electrons circle around the . . . ," the student responds "nucleus"?

4c. Answer to 4 and 4b: No.

Note. Although the question may seem obvious to you, the failure to discriminate that such situations are different has led to criticisms of linear programs as being too repetitive (i.e., asking the student to do the same thing over and over again), when in fact they might not be. Go on to item 5.

material is that the small steps provide successive approximations to the desired response. Each step evokes some part of the total response. The cues in the response panel are gradually eliminated ("faded"). The response is finally linked with the appropriate stimulus.

While the idea is simple, it is not particularly easy to write good programs. Programmers have, however, been pragmatic and carefully tested each program, revising it when frames were ambiguous and particularly when the error rate of a frame was high.

What has happened to programming since its early days, which is not very long ago, is an interesting study in experimenting with an instructional strategy. The first innovation was to provide branching programs. Crowder argued that the structure of the content of a program could be organized logically, so that if a student was making few errors he could be advanced. Inevitably, the Skinnerian or linear programming was pitted against Crowderian or branched programs. Silberman's experiment [20] to compare these two program types was more complicated than a simple comparison of the two program types. He found that branching took less training time, as might be expected, but the learners under the two treatments did not differ significantly on the criterion test. He also found that "small-step" programs produce more effective learning than "large-step" programs.

The method of responding inevitably was varied. In the Silberman experiment cited above, the learners in one condition chose the correct response in a multiple-choice display; in another condition, they constructed the response. The former condition required less time, but the criterion performance of subjects in the two groups did not differ significantly.

Keislar and McNeill varied the response mode in a different way.[21] One group of subjects responded "overtly" by pressing a button for their answer choice. If they were correct, a green light flashed. A nonovert-response group did not press a button; but a five-second pause followed each question, after which the green light appeared in front of the correct answer. The experimenters found negligible differences between the groups. One of the suggestions for a lack of a difference, also found by

[20] H. Silberman, R. Melaragno, J. Coulson, D. Estevan, "Fixed Sequence versus Branching Autoinstructional Methods," *Journal of Educational Psychology,* 52 (1961), 166–172.

[21] E. R. Keislar and J. D. McNeill, "A Comparison of Two Response Modes in an Autoinstructional Program with Children in the Primary Grades," *Journal of Educational Psychology,* 53 (1962), 127–131.

other investigators,[22] is interesting. They think that the response-guidance procedure was so effective that the reinforcement procedure added nothing. They point out that the response guidance was carefully programmed. The overt response was a weak one, and making it did not elicit additional implicit behavior.

In a comparable experiment, Goldbeck and Campbell used a reading group, which performed as effectively on the criterion as the program group.[23] In another experiment, they varied the difficulty level of the program items and found that the overt-responding group did less well on the criterion when exposed to a low-difficulty program, but did significantly better when exposed to intermediate-difficulty programs.

These experiments were designed to test the effectiveness of the components of programming strategies. Although Skinner had described the major features of this strategy, these other investigators were attempting to provide experimental support for Skinner's application of his ideas to human learning tasks. Some, like Crowder, also thought that variations in the procedure might profitably be tried.

There is no question that people learn effectively when instructional material is presented through programming. However, is the procedure so effective that it ought always to be considered a substitute for other methods? [24] The research cited in the preceding paragraphs has not provided a "yes" or "no" answer to that question.

One of the principal features of these techniques is that they elicit an overt response from the learner. But, as we have seen, some learners succeed even though an observer cannot detect any overt response other than watching or apparent listening. This result is not entirely surprising, since we expect people to learn when they are seemingly passive. The surprise is that they apparently learn as well as when overtly responding.

The source of the confusion about these ideas on activity and responding is our conception of what we mean by "active." Since we cannot judge what the learner is doing unless we can see him making a response, we

[22] F. J. McDonald and D. W. Allen, "An Investigation of Presentation, Response, and Correction Factors in Programmed Instruction," *Journal of Educational Research*, 55 (1962), 502–507. The June–July 1962 issue of the *Journal of Educational Research* is worth studying for data on the effectiveness of programming.

[23] R. A. Goldbeck and V. N. Campbell, "The Effects of Response Mode and Response Difficulty on Programed Learning," *Journal of Educational Psychology*, 53 (1962), 110–118.

[24] For a comparison of instructional methods, see A. Roe, M. Massey, G. Weltman, and D. Leeds, *Automated Teaching Methods Using Linear Programs* (Los Angeles: University of California, Department of Engineering, 1960), Report No. 60–105. See also June–July 1962 issue of *Journal of Educational Research*.

usually equate "active" and "overt." However, the response we see may not be the one that the learner has to make in order to learn. In the Keislar and McNeill experiment, button pushing did not contribute in any measurable way to learning; to learn, the child had to make the responses necessary to identify a concept and to select it on the machine's display panel. When these responses were made, the child learned; and pushing the button was incidental. Although Skinner has argued that composing an answer by writing it out is necessary, perhaps writing is helpful only when the form of the written response requires that the answer be thought out. In whatever way the learner does that thinking—whether he writes out the answer or selects it from a display—he learns.

Another of Skinner's ideas on programming is that the learner should receive immediate feedback at each step in the program. This recommendation is also probably more conservative than is required for all kinds of learning and learners. Immediate feedback is most likely to be beneficial when the response is being "shaped" by the method of successive approximations. However, when the response can be easily demonstrated, it is debatable whether this kind of feedback is invariantly the best for the acquisition phase of learning.

What conclusion should the teacher draw from this discussion? Prompting learners to respond overtly—by speaking, by writing, by making movements—is clearly useful in facilitating learning. Obviously, when the overt response is the one to be learned, it has to be made to be learned. In other cases, the overt response is simply a way of making sure that the student is responding implicitly. From Goldbeck and Campbell's experiment we learn that overt responding was more effective with more difficult frames. But, was this effectiveness achieved by the overt responding or by the feedback—which, of course, can be provided most directly when the learner responds overtly? The latter possibility seems likely.

The careful experimentation that followed the development of programming is a model of the approach that should be used in evaluating instructional strategies. The first step should be to test the components of the strategy, and to find out what makes it effective. This research leads to the improvement of the strategy. The problem is to determine the characteristics of an effective strategy, to find out which elements in it are essential and which ones are not. Response mode, response-guidance characteristics, and feedback characteristics need to be varied systematically. The strategy needs to be tried with different response classes and with different types of content. Finally, programs and other instructional strategies need to be tested on different types of students. The goal is unmistakable—to determine what strategies are effective with what pupils. The development of programmed instruction is a useful model of an effective instructional strategy, which, if carefully studied, can be made more effective.[25]

PLANS FOR EVALUATING THE STRATEGY

There are two reasons for evaluating a strategy: to assess its effectiveness and to assess the progress of each learner. The first of these purposes may be achieved in two ways, one of which is clearly the teacher's work.

The teacher must know whether the strategy is producing a desirable level of learning. At the end of an hour or week of reading instruction, how well do the children read? In a mathematics class, can the students work a certain class of problems or understand a mathematical concept?

Research is necessary to assess the effects of an instructional strategy and to identify those conditions under which these effects are optimum. The first chapter described the methods that are used for this evaluation and the role the teacher can play in the development of effective instructional strategies. Since many of the strategies that the teacher will use are his own invention, the spirit and the method of critical inquiry is required.

The other type of assessment measures behavior change in the individuals in the teacher's class. This kind of measurement is routine for all teachers. The principles of measurement necessary for this activity are discussed at various points in this book. In the first chapter the basic concepts were introduced; they are used in the succeeding chapters. The whole topic is treated in detail in the last three chapters. Here we will indicate the principal concepts to be used in constructing an evaluative strategy.

A teacher begins planning an evaluative strategy by defining the behavioral goals of the strategy as concretely as possible. This clarification must be made before appropriate methods of measurement can be selected or devised.

The second step is to weigh the importance of these objectives. Some objectives are very important because they represent what a student must

[25] This view is developed by A. Lumsdaine, "Educational Technology, Programed Learning and Instructional Science," in E. R. Hilgard, ed., *Theories of Learning and Instruction,* Sixty-third Yearbook, National Society for the Study of Education (Chicago: University of Chicago Press, 1964), Chapter XVI, pp. 371–401. In the same volume, see also S. L. Pressey, "Auto-instruction: Perspectives, Problems, Potentials," Chapter XV, pp. 354–370.

have acquired if the learning experience is to be considered a success. Other objectives are less important, or important only as a step in a sequence of behavioral acquisitions.

The third step is to devise appropriate tests, methods of measuring the students' level of attainment of the objectives. These tests must be both **valid** (measure the behavior they purport to measure) and **reliable** (measure that behavior accurately).

The distribution of methods of measurement should reflect the importance of the objectives they measure. If one of the most important objectives of an instructional strategy is the acquisition of skill in critical inquiry, the methods of measurement should heavily emphasize the testing of these behaviors—not the student's knowledge of obscure bibliographic references in a text.

Finally, the data from the measurement procedures must be quantified, collated, and usually summarized so that the teacher can communicate to the student a judgment of his achievement.

Evaluation strategies ought to be used to plan for student improvement, an obvious idea but one not always carried out. If the strategy is to be used effectively for this purpose, it has to be designed so that the teacher can diagnose the students' difficulties.

In this book the intimate relation between measuring behavior change and planning instructional strategies is stressed. In the succeeding chapters, where we discuss mainly hypotheses, experiments, and data about learning, we also point out the relevant measurement procedures and problems in assessing concept development, attitude change, the acquisition of problem-solving behaviors, etc. In the last three chapters the technical skills required to develop appropriate measurement procedures are described in greater detail.

SUMMARY

This chapter introduces two major constructions which are used throughout the book: (1) *a model of the learning organism;* (2) *a model of instructional strategies.* Each of these models is a general description of the characteristics and processes which a learner and an instructional strategy may be thought to have.

1. Any phenomenon is so complex that not all of it—but only certain features of it—can be studied at one time. A simplification, an abstraction, of this kind is what is meant by *a model.* By means of a model, we sim-

plify by focusing our attention and interest on significant characteristics of what we are studying.

2. There are two general kinds of models. One kind is the *replica model,* in which the model portrays as closely as possible selected features of what it represents. Such models look like what they represent. Another kind of model is the *symbolic model.* In this kind of model characteristics are represented by means of abstract symbols. These symbolic representations may be quite abstract, as in a mathematical equation for a process; some, such as road maps, are less abstract. Some are descriptive; others are poetic.

3. Models are analogies. As such, they represent only *a part* of some phenomenon. Since models are human inventions, they may be more or less correct, more or less accurate descriptions of something.

4. Our symbolic model of the learner assumes (a) that the learner is an information-processing organism; (b) that the learner is goal-directed; (c) that he utilizes information from his environment to achieve these goals.

5. These assumptions imply that learning experiences have certain characteristics: (a) The learning experience must be goal-directed from the viewpoint of the learner. A learning experience is a way of putting the learner in a situation where he can attain these goals. (b) The learning experience must be information-providing in the sense that it provides the learner with feedback necessary for attaining his goals.

6. We also make assumptions about learning processes—specifically, that these processes are response systems manifested in observed behavior. The following response systems are assumed to be available in some form in each learner: (a) a motivational system, the set of responses that accounts for the goal-oriented behavior that we observe; (b) a cognitive system, a set of responses by which the learner organizes and orders stimuli impinging on him, and by which he interrelates his conceptions of these stimuli; (c) an attitudinal system, a set of responses by which the learner evaluates the stimulus information he is continually receiving; (d) a self system, a set of responses by which the learner conceptualizes himself as a learner and evaluates himself in this respect.

7. These response systems interact. The self system and the motivational system are essentially controlling systems. They determine the degree of involvement of a learner in an educational experience. The cognitive and attitudinal systems form a sorting system, which interprets the information the learner receives from his environment. Associated with this system is a memory system, which stores information. The

learner processes information from his environment and his internal systems. This information processing acts as a stimulus to evoke behavior directed to attaining a goal. He receives feedback, which indicates to him the extent to which he is attaining his goal. To the degree that his goal is reached, the feedback acts as a reinforcing mechanism.

8. This conception of the learner has two general implications for thinking about instructional strategies and for making instructional decisions. First, the curriculum may be thought of as a device for modifying these systems. The objectives of instruction may be stated as changes in these systems and related observable behaviors. Practically, the teacher must identify the status of the development of these systems as a first step in designing an instructional strategy. Second, the kind of instructional strategy the teacher designs must take into account the demands placed on these systems by the strategy.

9. This book is designed to familiarize the student with general learning objectives: (a) the observable behavior associated with these response systems; (b) the variables known to influence the acquisition of these response systems; (c) the known interactions among the systems. This knowledge may be used to identify critical instructional decisions that are the consequence of understanding these relationships; to describe the general patterns of instructional strategies that will produce these response acquisitions; and to identify the instructional and evaluative decisions required to produce these changes.

10. Any particular educative act may be thought of as having three parts: (a) *formulation of the goals* of the learning experience; (b) *development of a plan* for the instructional strategy; (c) the formulation of a plan for *evaluating the effects* of the strategy.

11. The formulation of objectives requires that the teacher distinguish between immediate and ultimate purposes. In either case the objectives need to be stated in terms of behavior that may be observed. To state objectives in behavioral terms, the teacher first describes what a learner must do or perform to show that he has attained the objective. Second, he must specify the conditions under which the behavior may be expected to occur. Third, he must determine acceptable levels of performance. Another way to approach the description of purposes is to analyze the learning tasks that the learner must master in the situation that the teacher has devised. This analysis has been called *component task analysis.*

12. The model of instructional strategies presented includes three major components: (a) the *response-guidance* phase of the strategy, in

which the learner has displayed for him the desired behavior change; (b) a *response-practice phase*, in which the learner attempts the desired behavior change; (c) a *feedback phase*, during which the learner receives information on the correctness of his response, and during which he has the opportunity to attain significant goals by his response acquisition. In planning a specific strategy, the teacher manipulates specific variables in each of these three major categories.

13. Programmed instruction is an example of a carefully conceived instructional strategy. In this instructional strategy, the response-guidance phase consists of presentations of small amounts of instructional stimuli; the practice phase is provided by the learner's responding to questions at each step in the program; the feedback phase consists of giving the learner immediate information on the correctness of his response. This strategy has been and is continuing to be investigated extensively. The results at the present time are mixed. Not all of the components of this strategy have been proved to be necessary for learning. Further, it seems clear that if one component is changed, another component may not need to be carried out in the manner originally prescribed for programming. The research done on programmed instruction illustrates the necessity for experimenting with any particular kind of instructional strategy.

14. One evaluates a strategy (a) to assess its effectiveness and (b) to assess the learner's progress. Research, tests, and measurements are required if one is to evaluate adequately. The following chapters relate measurement of behavior change to the planning of instructional strategies.

STUDY AND DISCUSSION QUESTIONS

1. Invent a replica model of one of the objects or processes listed below. Select a medium for constructing the replication. Describe the relationship between the original and the replica. Identify the amount of correspondence in size, material, arrangement, color, and other important features. In what way is your model a simplification of the original? What can we learn about the original from your model?

   a. A model of the traffic movement in your classroom.

   b. A model of the major instructional centers of your school.

   c. A model describing the relationship between students' residences and the major instructional areas.

    d. A model of the relationship between students' residences and the major recreational areas.

2. Invent a symbolic model for the objects or processes described below. Indicate the features of the original which are omitted in the model. Describe the relationship between the components of the model and the parts of the original. Explain the meaning of the symbolism in the model. Also explain what can be learned about the original from the model, and what cannot be learned.

    a. A model of the pattern of questioning and answering between teacher and students in one of your classes.

    b. A model of the typical presentation procedures used by you, if you are teaching, or by one of your teachers.

    c. A model of the steps in executing a simple skill or procedure, such as hitting a golfball, writing a paragraph, baking a cake.

    d. A model of the basic plan of some simple game with which you are familiar.

    e. A model of the basic strategic moves in this game.

    f. A symbolic model of one of the replica models described in the first question.

3. Select some simple response that you would like somebody to acquire—a simple skill, a concept or generalization, or the solution to a simple type of problem. Using the model of the learning organism presented in this chapter:

    a. Describe the goals a learner might achieve by learning what you want him to learn.

    b. Describe the information that will be presented to him as part of the learning process.

    c. Indicate how the learner will receive feedback on goal attainment if he acquires the desired response.

4. In constructing your learning experiences, what assumptions have you made about:

    a. The motives the learner probably will bring or ought to bring to the learning experience.

    b. The cognitions about the learning experience that will need to be acquired or should be available at the time of learning.

    c. The attitudes necessary for learning, or which are acquired as part of the process of learning.

    d. The way in which the self system of the learner is influenced by and influences the learning experience.

5. State as concretely as possible the behavioral objectives of the learning experience that you have chosen to construct. Indicate which of these objec-

tives are immediate, and describe their relationship to the ultimate objectives of the learning experience. Also describe the component tasks of the learning experience.

6. Invent an instructional strategy for teaching the desired response. Break down your description of this strategy into the three components described in this chapter. For each component give the steps to be taken by the instructor, or instructing device, the amount of practice and involvement required of the learner, and the feedback procedures to be used.

7. Try this instructional strategy on somebody who is willing to learn what you want to teach him. Before you test the strategy, describe the behavior observations you will make to evaluate the effectiveness of the strategy. After you test the strategy, evaluate its effectiveness. On what evidence do you base your conclusions about its effectiveness? What assumptions about the characteristics of the components of the strategy seem less valid on the basis of the information you now have?

8. Perform a component task analysis for one of the following:

   a. Learning to solve a quadratic equation.

   b. Learning to write an acceptable paragraph.

   c. Learning to read a simple sentence.

   d. Learning to identify the letters of the alphabet.

   e. Learning to chair a meeting.

   f. Learning to conduct a discussion on a topic of current and controversial interest.

9. Select a unit in some subject that you are teaching or may teach. Define the specific behavior changes that the learning experiences of this unit will promote. Describe in detail the criteria that you will use for determining the amount of behavior change to be regarded as satisfactory.

10. Below are listed three general educational objectives. Describe each of these objectives in specific behavioral terms. Relate the attainment of these objectives to particular learning experiences at different levels in a school system. In what ways do the experiences in elementary school and high school contribute to the attainment of these objectives? What levels of behavior change may be expected at various points in the child's education?

   a. The educated person should write the mother tongue effectively.

   b. The educated person can work and play with others.

   c. The educated citizen seeks to understand social structures and social processes.

11. Given the objective: *The educated citizen respects the law,* what behavior changes would you expect to observe if a child learns to respect the law? Be specific about the behavior expected and the context in which you expect to see this behavior. What is the school's contribution to this behavior change?

12. Write a short program on some subject of interest to you (see footnote 17 for a source on writing programs). Try programming the description of the difference between a symbolic and a replica model as a preliminary exercise.

RECOMMENDED READINGS

R. Gagné, ed., *Psychological Principles in System Development* (New York: Holt, Rinehart and Winston, 1962).

R. Glaser, ed., *Training Research and Education* (Pittsburgh: University of Pittsburgh Press, 1962).

A. A. Lumsdaine and R. Glaser, eds., *Teaching Machines and Programmed Learning* (Washington, D. C.: National Education Association, 1960).

"Learning Theory and AV Utilization," *Audio-Visual Communication Review,* 9 (1961). This issue is devoted to articles describing the relevance of learning theory to instructional systems employing audio-visual devices. The ideas have broad applicability.

S. M. Markle, *Good Frames and Bad: A Grammar of Frame Writing* (New York: John Wiley and Sons, 1964.)

S. L. Pressey, "Autoinstruction: Perspectives, Problems, Potentials," in Sixty-third Yearbook of the National Society for the Study of Education, *Theories of Learning and Instruction,* E. Hilgard, ed. (Chicago: University of Chicago Press, 1964), pp. 354–370. See also J. B. Carroll, "The Analysis of Reading Instruction: Perspectives from Psychology and Linguistics," pp. 336–353.

PART TWO

THE PROBLEMS
OF LEARNING

CHAPTER FOUR

MOTIVATION AND LEARNING

Teachers are very much aware of the importance of motivation in facilitating learning, and they use a variety of techniques—devices such as grades, honor rolls, gold stars, achievement medals, praise, and blame—to induce pupil motivation. In this chapter we will describe **motivation**, the relationships between motivation and learning, and the process by which teachers can assess the motivational processes of their students. We will not give specific techniques guaranteed to produce motivation for learning in any and all students. However, a study of motivation should make the teacher sensitive to the complexity of this problem and aware of motivational principles that can guide his educational practices, although there are as yet no infallible specific guides to action. As Hilgard and Russell have observed, there is "no panacea for all the ills of indifference, dislike, and rebellion encountered in children placed in unsuitable school environments. If there is any conclusion from recent research of which a teacher may be sure, it is that there is no known formula or infallible set of procedures to motivate all pupils at all times. . . . The evidence seems rather clear, too, that motivation is not something applied apart from the learning situation but is an intrinsic part of it." [1]

WHAT IS MOTIVATION?

As a basis for developing an understanding of the concept of motivation, consider the following example:

John and Bill are members of the junior class at Lincoln High School, and both are enrolled in the physics course. Both have been "A" students and are among the students obtaining the best grades on each of the tests given by Mr. Richards, the physics instructor. Mr. Richards has announced a test for next week on the topic "Electricity." Both boys study intensively for this test, and both receive high grades.

John is quite concerned about his grade, a 91, and sees Mr. Richards about his paper. He wants to discuss his paper with Mr. Richards because he feels that he should be given a few more points. He would like to get a 92 or a 93 because this grade will affect his over-all average, which is important to him because he wants to be considered for an officership in the ROTC unit at the school. Mr. Richards points out that John's answers do not justify changing his mark. The discussion becomes somewhat heated, and John is obviously upset when he realizes that his grade will not be changed. After his discussion with Mr. Richards, he complains to several of his fellow students that he doesn't think he is being treated fairly and that Mr. Richards is too demanding in what he expects.

Bill, who is interested in becoming an engineer, also goes to Mr. Richards about his paper. He is concerned because he has missed questions, but the basis of his concern is the inadequacy of his own knowledge. He spends some time discussing with Mr. Richards the questions that he missed. When he finishes his discussion with Mr. Richards, he feels satisfied that he now knows the subject matter of the test better than he did before. His comments to his classmates are remarkably different from those of John. Bill sees Mr. Richards as a helpful teacher, one who is interested in seeing that his students learn. Bill states that he likes having teachers who expect you to perform at your best because he feels that this is the best preparation for the kind of career that he is planning.

[1] E. R. Hilgard and D. H. Russell, "Motivation in School Learning," in *Learning and Instruction*, Forty-ninth Yearbook of the National Society for the Study of Education, Part I (Chicago: University of Chicago Press, 1950), p. 37.

In the above example, note that the behavior of the two boys is in many respects substantially the same. Each has studied intensively for the test; each has performed at about the same level on the test; each has gone to the teacher to discuss his paper with him. But the reasons for their behavior are radically different. John is interested in obtaining good grades, because they are means for his securing an officer rank in the ROTC unit. Bill, on the other hand, is interested in becoming an engineer, and knowledge of physics is important to him as a means to attaining this goal.

A second example will elaborate these ideas. In the first example, the behavior of the two boys was quite similar; in this example it is quite different.

The teacher proposes that the class visit a California mission as part of their study of early California history. Judy is excited about this possibility and works hard to organize a group of her classmates to gather information on the missions. She reads several books, asks many questions, puts together a notebook that can be used on the trip.

Susy couldn't care less. She reads books about the missions only after considerable urging by the teacher, and then slowly and not very carefully. She asks no questions, does not participate in any discussions, and on the day of the trip drags along at the end of the group.

You probably would explain the differences between the two girls by saying that Judy is interested and Susy is not. We know in a vague way what you mean by "interested"; you mean concerned, alive, active. But why is Judy interested and Susy not?

Another example might be two girls who are interested in being popular with their fellow students. One seeks to win this popularity by being "social," the other by managing class activities.

In these three examples, note that sometimes the persons' goals are similar, but the observed behavior is different; sometimes the behavior is similar, but the goals are different. In each case, however, the behavior was the way in which the person sought to obtain what he wanted.

MOTIVATION AS AN EXPLANATORY CONSTRUCT

The behavioral differences illustrated in the simple examples above represent a class of behaviors that we will call **arousal phenomena**. We want to explain why the human organism is aroused in some situations and not in others. To do this, we use an explanatory **construct**, motivation.

An important characteristic of motivated behavior is its directedness. The person is not like a vibrating string, or a running engine. He makes selections; he emits some responses but not others. If we look closely at Susy's behavior, we suspect that she is also expending energy to avoid actively participating in the trip.

The construct motivation is used to explain why some situations or events or persons arouse this directed behavior. This concept, however, explains only this selective character of behavior. It does not entirely explain how the person acquired the responses he makes. Judy's ability to gather information is not accounted for by saying she is interested in the project, nor is her reading ability or her skills at participating in a discussion. *Motivation is a necessary but not a sufficient condition for learning.* If a person is not motivated, he will not expend the psychological energy necessary to acquire responses; he will avoid the learning situations which will produce the desired changes. But other conditions, such as response guidance and reinforcement, must be provided before learning is ensured.

MODEL OF THE MOTIVATIONAL PROCESS

Motivation, an energy change within the person, is characterized by affective arousal and anticipatory goal reactions. This definition contains three elements:

1. *Motivation begins in an energy change in the person.* Although we know the organic base for some energy changes (the hunger motive typically originates out of physiological changes in the digestive system of the person), for many motives (for instance, those of John and Bill) the exact organic nature of this energy change is unknown.

2. *Motivation is characterized by affective arousal.* A number of terms have been used to describe this "feeling" state. Subjectively it may be characterized as "emotion." When a child tells us that he was "mad" when he struck a companion, he is describing the feeling state accompanying this motivated behavior. This affective arousal need not be intense, and the person may not even be conscious of a change in his affective state. The student working quietly at his desk gives very few, if any, manifestations of affective arousal, except the intentness with which he appears to be working. But we infer that this very intentness is a manifestation of the psychological change that has occurred within him.

3. *Motivation is characterized by anticipatory goal reactions.* The motivated person makes responses which lead him to a goal, the function of

which is to reduce the tension created by the energy change in him. Motivation, in other words, leads to goal-seeking responses. Judy, whose goal presumably is to learn as much as she can about missions and to use the trip to satisfy her curiosity, seeks information because it will lead to the attainment of her goal. John and Bill study hard for the physics test, and find out why they made mistakes, because these responses contribute to their respective goals.

This description of motivation is a model of the process from arousal to goal attainment. Its elements are (1) an arousal of the person, (2) goal-seeking behavior, (3) goal attainment, (4) reduction of the arousal state.

We have deliberately simplified the relationship between the motivated state of the person and his goal-seeking behavior. We have assumed, first of all, that the person is capable of making the responses necessary to lead to the goal which will reduce his psychological tension—but, in many instances, the person may select unattainable goals. Second, we have been assuming that the goal when attained is satisfying to the individual—but the person's estimate that a certain goal will satisfy his needs may be incorrect.

MOTIVES AND NEEDS

We observe numerous instances of specific goal-seeking behavior. A child seems to be reading intently. Johnny gathers up his mitt and bat and runs out to the ball game. A college student enrolls in an English literature course. You take off for a day at the beach.

However, not everyone wants to go to the beach or listen to Bach. You are offered a ticket to the opera; you politely decline, and a friend offers to take the ticket. If we observe many instances of your declining opportunities to listen to musical performances, we say that you have no interest in that type of activity. We describe you as a person who "doesn't like music."

Consider a contrasting case: a person who likes to compete. Start a game, and he chaffs until he can participate. He wants to win and seems to enjoy the effort required to do so. We say that he has a competitive instinct, or a desire to win.

In both of these cases we are making a prediction that certain kinds of potential goals are likely to motivate the person. Musical performances do not stimulate you to make "going-to-musical-performance" responses. We predict that they will not arouse goal-seeking behavior. Our competitor offers a safe bet; he is highly likely to be aroused by competitive situations. Our competitor is presumably satisfying some need by engaging in competitive activities. We may not be sure what it is. By analyzing the situations that arouse his competitive behavior and by studying his other behaviors, we make inferences about the specific goals he is seeking. Friendly games seem to bore him; sloppy play by partners angers him; he is energized mainly by situations in which he has an opportunity to win. From these observations we conclude that what he seems to want is to win. Remember that we see only *instances* of these motivated behaviors. But, from a number of similar instances, we *infer* that the individual has a tendency to be motivated in certain ways.

Note what our inferential problems are. We have to have an adequate sample of his behavior from which to induce a hypothesis. We have to find ways of testing this hypothesis. This we do by offering him competitive opportunities or by observing him to see whether he seeks them out or accepts them when they are offered in the ordinary course of events.

A **motive** is an instance of motivated behavior, an instance of goal-seeking behavior. A child's motive in striking a playmate is the goal he is seeking by that action. He may be striking his companion to demonstrate that he is bigger and stronger. He may be relieving his hostile feelings. Bill's motive in talking with Mr. Richards is to correct his mistakes. Bobby's typical motive is to get the teacher's attention.

Motives arise out of needs. When a person is motivated specifically, he is attempting to satisfy some need. **Needs** describe the relatively permanent tendencies in persons to be motivated in specific ways, and we infer them from the commonalities among the goals that the person appears to be seeking. Needs are aroused or activated either by internal changes within the individual or by stimulus events in the environment. Once the internal change has taken place, the energy basis for goal-seeking behavior is available. (See page 151 for definitions of the difference between *normative needs* and *psychological needs*. This chapter is concerned with the latter type.)

What evidence do we have that internal changes take place, since they are not observable? The evidence for the existence of changes in an individual's psychological need system is based upon knowledge of what happens when goal-seeking behavior is interrupted or frustrated. We could be reasonably certain that a change of sufficient strength was operating if a person persisted in attempts to attain a goal.

An interesting experiment demonstrated this point. Ovsiankina [2] set up a laboratory situation in which she had students work on a variety of tasks, such as solving puzzles and modeling animals in clay. The tasks were presumably interesting, but of no personal importance to the students. When a student became interested in one task, the experimenter interrupted and asked the student to move on to a new task. The student was allowed to complete the second task and then was free for a short period after he had completed this task. Two results were apparent. First, the students resisted the initial interruption and took on the second task only with persuasion. Second, without prompting from the experimenter, the students frequently returned to finish the interrupted task; 79 per cent of the interrupted tasks were resumed spontaneously by the students. [3] In explaining these data, we may infer a tension which is reduced only by completion of the task.

Zeigarnik [4] produced a similar effect under entirely different experimental conditions. She gave her experimental subjects a series of twenty simple but varied tasks, each requiring a few minutes of work. Half of these were interrupted, and half were not. At the end of the work period the subjects were asked to recall as many as possible of the twenty tasks. Subjects recalled 68 per cent of the uncompleted tasks, and only 43 per cent of the completed tasks.

In these experiments the subject's tendency to return to an incomplete task cannot be explained by immediate environmental influences. The experimenter neither required nor urged the subjects to finish all tasks. We infer that the persistency in completing tasks is related to the strength of some need to finish the task. Experimental evidence suggests that the character of the need involved may be quite complex. [5] We could postulate several specific needs as the probable bases for motivation. The experimentation demonstrates that under the influence of an internal process, called *motivation*, the individual's behavior persists until a goal

---

[2] N. Ovsiankina, "The Resumption of Interrupted Tasks," *Psychologische Forschung*, 11 (1928), 302–379.

[3] A similar result was obtained with nursery school children. See E. Katz, *Some Factors Affecting Resumption of Interrupted Activities by Pre-school Children* (Minneapolis, University of Minnesota Press, 1938), Institute of Child Welfare Series, No. 16.

[4] B. Zeigarnik, "Uben das Behalten von erledigten and unerledigten Handlungen," *Psychologische Forschung*, 9 (1927), 1–85.

[5] For a review of these studies, see W. C. H. Prentice, "The Interruption of Tasks," *Psychological Review*, 51 (1944), 329–340; for a critical analysis of experimentation, see G. W. Boguslavsky, "Interruption and Learning," *Psychological Review*, 58 (1951), 248–255.

has been reached. The goal in these experiments was the completion of the tasks. On attainment of the goal the behavior leading to the attainment of the goal subsides.

We see many instances of the effects of **need arousal** in everyday life. The student who wants to be a physician enters willingly on a long career of preparation, during which he foregoes many immediate satisfactions and pleasures to attain his long-term goal. The teacher who has trouble getting Johnny to do his school work is sometimes surprised at the long hours of arduous practice that Johnny will put in on the baseball field. For the motivated learner difficulties and problems are met willingly, and seemingly unpleasant tasks no longer have the flavor of being chores.

THE NEED SYSTEM

Presumably the child begins life with a limited system of needs; as he develops into a mature person, his need system becomes more complex. The young child under the close supervision of his parents may have acquired comparatively strong dependency needs, which he manifests by such behaviors as seeking help from his parents, continually questioning them, staying close to them, holding his parent's hand when he crosses the street, and wanting to know where his mother is. As he develops and becomes increasingly able to handle his own affairs without the assistance of adults, his dependency need tends to diminish, a change which we infer from the fact that his help-seeking behaviors become fewer and fewer.[6] We now may notice behaviors which we could classify as evidences of a need for independence. At a later age the child prefers to make decisions on his own. The extent to which changes in needs take place and the particular forms that these changes assume is a function of many factors, such as the way the child's needs at any stage of his life are met, changes in available goal objects for satisfying his needs, and demands made upon him by his environment.[7]

Are there needs common to all individuals? Or does each individual have his own unique pattern of needs? Is the need system of a person

[6] This relationship between independence and dependence needs has been simplified in this discussion. Experimental work suggests the complexity of this relationship; see E. K. Bellar, "Dependency and Independency in Young Children," *Journal of Genetic Psychology*, 87 (1955), 25–36.

[7] For a comprehensive study of relationships of this kind, see R. R. Sears, E. E. Maccoby, and H. Levin, *Patterns of Child Rearing* (Evanston, Ill.: Row, Peterson and Company, 1957).

highly stable and unchangeable? Questions like these have great practical importance for educators. If we knew the common needs of children, we could organize their environment so that their needs would be satisfied. We could also utilize these needs to bring about desirable kinds of learning. A basic principle of a current curriculum theory is that the curriculum must meet the needs of the child. Such a principle presupposes the needs of children can be described, and probably also assumes some commonalities among the needs of individual children. The questions that we are raising here, therefore, have both theoretical and practical importance.

CLASSIFICATION OF NEEDS

Because human behavior is so variable that need satisfaction takes many different forms, attempts to classify the common needs of human beings have been largely ineffective. There are probably as many lists of needs as there are psychologists who have attempted to formulate these lists. As yet there is comparatively little experimental evidence to support these speculations. One student strives for excellence in academic activities, another for excellence in athletic activities. Are these students motivated by different needs, or is it that each is motivated in essentially the same way but has learned that different goals satisfy his common needs? This is essentially the problem the psychologist faces when he attempts to classify and to organize the goal-seeking behaviors of human beings.

We will not attempt a new classification, nor will we adopt some standard list of needs. It is probably more profitable for the prospective teacher to be familiar with the processes of inference involved in identifying the needs of an individual than it is for him to memorize some relatively arbitrary list of needs. Below are several lists developed by psychologists. You will notice in these lists some agreement and considerable differences among the needs catalogued. The lists differ both in number of needs included and in kinds and definitions of needs. Each compiler, however, is classifying needs according to concepts and principles that he thinks are important. Murray [8] defines the needs in detail and attempts to distinguish them from each other. Cronbach [9] develops a list of needs which are generally defined but appear to have relevance for

[8] From H. A. Murray, *Explorations in Personality* (New York, Oxford University Press, 1938).
[9] From L. J. Cronbach, *Educational Psychology*, 2nd ed. (New York: Harcourt, Brace and World, 1963).

interpreting behavior. Maslow [10] suggests an organizational principle for a system of needs. He has developed an integrated system of needs arranged in hierarchical order based on the relative importance of the satisfaction of the needs. According to Maslow, higher-order needs do not develop until lower-order needs are minimally satisfied. Since no clear agreement has been reached on a common classification, it hardly is worth the teacher's time to memorize lists. He may use them as examples; however, it is more important that he understand how such lists are developed. He will use the same kinds of inferential and classification processes in making judgments about students.

Murray's List

Abasement. To surrender. To comply and accept punishment. To apologize, confess, atone.   Self-depreciation. Masochism.

Achievement. To overcome obstacles. To exercise power. To strive to do something difficult as well and as quickly as possible.

Acquisition. To gain possessions and property. To grasp, snatch, or steal things. To bargain or gamble. To work for money or goods.

Affiliation. To form friendships and associations. To greet, join, and live with others. To cooperate and converse sociably with others. To love. To join groups.

Aggression. To assault or injure. To belittle, harm, blame, accuse, or maliciously ridicule a person. To punish severely. Sadism.

Autonomy. To resist influence or coercion. To defy an authority or seek freedom in a new place. To strive for independence.

Blamavoidance. To avoid blame, ostracism, or punishment by inhibiting asocial or unconventional impulses. To be well behaved and obey the law.

Counteraction. Proudly to refuse admission of defeat by restriving and retaliating. To select the hardest tasks. To defend one's honor in action.

Cognizance. To explore. To ask questions. To satisfy curiosity. To look, listen, inspect. To read and seek knowledge.

Construction. To organize and build.

Deference. To admire and willingly follow a superior. To cooperate with a leader. To serve gladly.

Defendance. To defend oneself against blame or belittlement. To justify one's actions. To offer extenuations, explanations, and excuses. To resist "probing."

Dominance. To influence or control others. To persuade, prohibit, dictate. To lead and direct. To restrain. To organize the behavior of a group.

Exhibition. To attract attention to one's person. To excite, amuse, stir, shock, thrill others. Self-dramatization.

Exposition. To point and demonstrate. To relate facts. To give information, explain, interpret, lecture.

Harmavoidance. To avoid pain, physical injury, illness, and death. To escape from a dangerous situation. To take precautionary measures.

Infavoidance. To avoid failure, shame, humiliation, ridicule. To refrain from attempting to do something that is beyond one's powers. To conceal a disfigurement.

Nurturance. To nourish, aid, or protect the helpless. To express sympathy. To "mother" a child.

[10] From A. H. Maslow, "A Theory of Human Motivation," *Psychological Review*, 50 (1943), 370–396; also A. H. Maslow, "Some Theoretical Consequences of Basic Need Gratifications," *Journal of Personality*, 16 (1948), 402–416.

Order. To arrange, organize, put away objects. To be tidy and clean. To be scrupulously precise.

Play. To relax, amuse oneself, seek diversion and entertainment. To "have fun," to play games. To laugh, joke, and be merry. To avoid serious tension.

Rejection. To snub, ignore, or exclude. To remain aloof and indifferent. To be discriminating.

Retention. To retain possession of things. To refuse to give or lend. To hoard. To be frugal, economical, and miserly.

Sentience. To seek and enjoy sensuous impressions.

Sex. To form and further an erotic relationship. To have sexual intercourse.

Succorance. To seek aid, protection, or sympathy. To cry for help. To plead for mercy. To adhere to an affectionate, nurturant parent. To be dependent.

Superiority. This need is considered to be a composite of achievement and recognition.

Understanding. To analyze experience, to abstract, to discriminate among concepts, to define relations, to synthesize ideas.

Cronbach's List

Affection
Approval by Authority
Approval by Peers
Independence
Competence and Self-respect

Maslow's List

Physiological needs
Safety needs
Love and belonging needs
Esteem needs (needs for achievement and recognition)
Self-actualization needs
Desires to know and understand

PRINCIPLES OF CLASSIFICATION

The following are some of the principles relevant to the determination of common needs:

1. *There is a set of basic needs;* that is, physiological conditions for these needs are common to all men, and the environment is sufficiently stable to provide conditions for satisfying these needs. An example is the need for food. Changes in an individual's physiological condition lead to changes in the state of his hunger **drive.** Other examples are needs for air, elimination, activity, and rest. These drive states and their associated needs are intimately related to human survival, and, as we suggested earlier, the physiological basis for these needs is known.

2. *Some needs are characteristically acquired within cultural contexts.* A need for success, or a need for achievement, characterizes many members of American society. Other societies reward achievement and excellence so infrequently that the need for achievement does not characterize the members of those societies. Among the Alorese, for example, "strength does not rate very high; neither does skill; nor are these qualities greatly admired. They have no skilled artisans who take pride in achievement and special talent, which, even if it did exist, would get no special

esteem." [11] Stability in the patterns of reward and in the goals that an environment provides influences the consistency with which needs are acquired by members of a given cultural or subcultural group. The variability in environments suggests that the need systems of children will vary considerably, even though we may be able to identify some commonalities in needs among children.

3. *The need system of individuals is dependent in part on their state of development.* The very young child has limited needs—needs for physical nurturance and support and emotional warmth. Later, he develops needs related to approval of his behavior from adults; still later this need comes to include the goal of peer approval. Needs for achievement begin to develop—that is, to be learned—when and if opportunities for striving are made worthwhile. The need system of the child is adequate to the demands of his age. We expect the motivational systems of adults to be more complex than those of children because adults have been exposed to more opportunities to acquire new motives and because their experience has stimulated them, though not always successfully, to develop new motives.

These three principles imply a hierarchy of needs. [12] First, there are some needs common to men irrespective of their cultural environments. Second, some needs will be common to members of the same society, but will vary from one society to another. Third, needs will develop as the individual's experience expands. Commonality in needs among individuals results from common experiences, and variability from differences in experience. [13]

IDENTIFICATION OF NEEDS

In attempting to describe the need system of a child, we may be looking for the motivational basis of his behavior in a particular instance; for example, we may be attempting to determine why a child is crying at this moment, or is annoying another pupil, or picks a science book from the

[11] A. Kardiner, *Psychological Frontiers of Society* (New York: Columbia University Press, 1945), p. 235.

[12] For one writer's conception of this hierarchy, see A. H. Maslow, "A Theory of Human Motivation" (see note 10); and "'Higher' and 'Lower' Needs," *Journal of Psychology*, 25 (1948), 433–436.

[13] For an analysis of one aspect of this problem, see R. R. Sears, J. W. M. Whiting, V. Nowlis, and P. S. Sears, "Some Child-Rearing Antecedents of Aggression and Dependency in Young Children," *Genetic Psychology Monographs*, 47, No. 2 (1953), 135–234.

library shelf. Or we may be interested in determining the need system that underlies most of the child's behavior; for example, we may want to find out whether a child is motivated by a need to achieve, a need for affection, or a need for status. Whether we are attempting to determine a motive or a need, the process of inference is essentially the same.

An Investigation of the Relations between Needs and Behavior

The problem of the relationship between behavior and motivation requires extensive scientific investigation. A scientific investigation of this relationship formalizes and refines inferential processes of a kind that we have suggested the teacher will be using. One study,[14] which attacked this problem directly, illustrates this refinement of observation. It also exemplifies that relationships between specific behaviors and needs are not obvious and straightforward.

The purpose of the study was to discover the relations between inferences about needs and the behavior that had been observed. First, the investigator put together a list of needs assumed to be characteristic of most adolescents. She also classified the behavioral ratings that had been made on a group of children. These needs and the behavior classifications are listed below. Second, judges rated each child in the group (1) on each

Needs

Need for autonomy. Striving for independence and freedom; desire to be free from social ties, to shake off influence, coercion, and restraint; relatively little care for conventions and group ideology; tendency to act as one pleases.

Need for social ties, social acceptance. Desire to be generally well-liked; to conform to custom, to join groups, to live sociably, to be accepted by a group in any form, to make contacts.

Need for achievement. Desire to attain a high standard of objective accomplishments; to increase self-regard by successful exercise of talent, to select hard tasks; high aspiration level.

Need for recognition. Desire to excite praise and commendation, to demand respect, social approval and prestige, honors and fame.

Need for abasement. Tendency to self-depreciation, self-blame or belittlement; to submit passively to external forces, to accept injury, blame, criticism, punishment; tendency to become resigned to fate, to admit inferiority and defeat, to confess, to seek punishment and misfortune; masochistic tendency.

Need for aggression. Desire to deprive others by belittling, attacking, ridiculing, depreciating.

Need for succorance. Desire for support from outside; from people, institutions, or supernatural agencies.

Need for control (dominance). Desire to control one's human environment, by suggestion, by persuasion or command.

[14] E. Frenkel-Brunswik, "Motivation and Behavior," *Genetic Psychology Monographs*, 26 (1942), 121–265.

Need for escape. Tendency to escape all unpleasant situations; to avoid blame, hardship, etc.; to project own failures on others or on circumstances; to gain immediate pleasure with inability to postpone pleasure; use of fantasy, etc.

Examples of Behavior Categories

Grooming activity. Obviously spends a great deal of time in grooming self. Frequently arranges or combs hair, brushes off clothes, puts on make-up.

Energy output. Overtly active practically all the time, including gross movements and aggressive contacts with physical environment; eager, animated, bodily movements.

Interest in opposite sex. Continually initiates contacts with and takes every opportunity to attract attention of members of opposite sex, for activities in which sexes are mixed.

Social participations. Takes every opportunity for social contact allowed by the nature of the situation. Continually directs attention toward others, talks to them and participates in activities with them.

Seeking of adult company. Seeks out adults in preference to children in a group. Hangs around adults making frequent bids for attention. Identifies self with adults. Very cordial to adults.

Resistance to authority. Deliberately breaks rules. Refuses to comply with requests of person in charge. Subtly resists authority; evasive, sly, two-faced, smooth, in contrast to: Eager to comply with adults' wishes; anticipates what adults must want; asks adult assistance in enforcing regulations; extremely suggestible with adults.

Social self-confidence. Very assured behavior with both adults and children. Takes failure in matter-of-fact way. Invites new situations requiring poise and confidence.

Attention seeking. Constantly seeks to put self in a conspicuous position; bluffing, showing off. Exerts strenuous efforts to gain recognition of associates.

Sensitivity and dependence on approval. Excessively concerned about the sort of impression he makes on his associates. Very sensitive and easily "hurt." Reacts strongly to praise or blame. Constantly leaning on others for approval of his actions, or help in his decisions.

Leadership. Highly successful in influencing the group either directly or by indirect suggestion. Competent in organizing and handling group activities. Comments or suggestions welcomed by the group and readily accepted.

need, classifying it from strong to weak, and (2) on each behavior category, classifying from frequent to infrequent exhibition of the behavior. For example, Susy might be rated as having a very strong need for social ties; she might also be rated as showing considerable grooming activity—which meant that she had been frequently observed arranging her hair or putting on make-up.

The judges had known and studied the children for a long period of time. Their independent ratings of each child were found to agree to a sufficiently high degree (**reliability** of measurement). The data from which they worked had been gathered over many years, so that the individual's stable tendencies could be identified.

What was the relationship between any particular inferred need and the behavior description? Let us use the need for recognition for illustrative purposes. No relationship between the strength of the need for recognition and attractive appearance was found; that is, children with a high need for recognition were neither more nor less attractive than those children who had a low need for recognition. However, there was a comparatively high relationship between the need for recognition and grooming activity; that is, children who had a high need for recognition were also rated as spending more time in grooming activities. There was also a significant relationship between the need for recognition and energy output. Other significant relationships of need for recognition were with interests in the opposite sex and reference to the opposite sex, seeking of adult company, social self-confidence, attention seeking, self-assertion, dependence on approval, and leadership. In general, behaviors which we might characterize as "overt social activity" are related to the need for recognition. However, not all adolescents with a strong need for recognition engaged in the same social behavior to the same degree.

Some relationships illustrate the complexity of the problem of relating a particular need to specific kinds of behavior. For example, there was a relationship between need for recognition and exuberance when boys were studied, but no such relationship was found in the sample of girls. Also, the need for recognition was related to irritability, selfishness, and irresponsibility among girls, but no such relationship was found in the sample of boys. On a common-sense basis we would not predict that a person who is selfish satisfies a need for recognition through his selfish behavior. But the data in this study suggest the possibility of such a relationship, at least for girls who have a high need for recognition. On a common-sense basis we might also have predicted that either a boy or girl with a strong need for recognition would be exuberant, but the data do not support this prediction.

These data illustrate that **need satisfaction** may take a variety of forms. Both the need for recognition and the need for aggression were related to behavior items in the category "Overt Social Activity." A child with a strong need for recognition may be satisfying it in the same way as a child who has a strong need for aggression, or each of these needs may be satisfied in distinctive ways.

The data from this investigation also illustrate the complexity of the relationship of motivation to observed behavior. In everyday life we frequently make inferences about the motives of students and other people, but long experience with children does not guarantee that our inferences will be reliable. The teacher who expects to have accurate knowledge about the need systems of children should, in the first place, have extensive behavior data about these children. The somewhat casual observations of the classroom are a poor substitute for systematic and extended observation. Furthermore, the teacher must continually check his inferences by making predictions about behavior to be expected, assuming the presence of a specific need disposition in the personality of a child. These inferences must be revised continually and checked as the teacher acquires more information about the child.

Methods of Inferring Needs

Inferences about motivation and need systems are made from the persistency and direction of a person's behavior. Such inferences may be made in two ways: (1) by observing goals for which the individual appears to be continually striving; (2) by observing the effects that occur when what appear to be goal objects are denied the individual.

Inferring needs from goals. If we are applying the first principle, we infer the character of the need from the kind of goal object sought. We assume the existence of the need from the fact that goal objects of a given kind are persistently striven for. For example, we infer that a child is motivated by a need for prestige if he seems interested in positions and activities that carry prestige. In the second instance, we infer the presence of a need from the fact that the person may continue to seek a goal object even when it has been removed. For example, if a student loses an election to a club presidency, but tries for this officership again, we infer that he is motivated by a need for the goal that the officership represents to him.

Assume that a student in one of our classes is a persistent worker, who completes all assignments on time and who does his work carefully. Assume also that on several occasions he has inquired about the exact nature of an assignment, has attempted to determine whether he has done the work correctly, and has shown interest in the grades he has received on his assignments and tests. We can use this observed behavior as evidence of motivation, and assume that by these activities the student is attempting to satisfy some needs. We infer that he is motivated to do well in academic work. But this statement tells us comparatively little about what goals he is seeking and what needs he is attempting to satisfy by striving to succeed in his school work. If the student tells us that he wants to be on the honor roll or to win a scholarship or a prize for academic achievement, we have additional evidence to support our inference that the student is striving for success in his school work.

However, only if we observe the student striving for other goals will we be able to make inferences about an underlying need that motivates much of his behavior. For example, does he go out for varsity sports because he wants to win a letter, or enter the debating contest to win prizes? If we observe that he attempts to be best in whatever he does, we have additional evidence for an inference about an underlying need. But shall we say that this student is striving for academic success? Does he want to achieve success irrespective of the nature of the activity? Or is it the prestige that goes with the obtaining of a prize that he is seeking? We can arrive at a reliable inference about needs only by careful observation of the student in many situations. It is all too easy to misjudge the character of the motivation because of inadequate observation of the child.

We may also make faulty inferences about needs by generalizing from particular instances of goal-seeking behavior to general patterns of goal-seeking behavior. We may infer that the student who is striving for academic success has a need to achieve, and then assume that he can satisfy this need by achieving in many different ways. However, the student may satisfy his need for achievement simply through striving for academic success, and may be indifferent to other kinds of achievement.

We may also be misled by inferring a commonality among goal objects, whereas the person we are observing does not see this commonality at all. The student who strives for both academic success and a varsity letter in football may be satisfying different needs in each case. Academic success may satisfy his need for achievement, and winning a varsity letter may satisfy his need for prestige and status. Therefore, when we make inferences about needs from the goals that individuals appear to be seeking, our inferences about needs should be checked against new observations.

The teacher, once he has assumed that a child is motivated by a given need, should make predictions about what kinds of behavior would be expected if a child were motivated by such a need. He can then test these predictions by observing the behavior of the child. If he infers that a student is motivated by a need for achievement, he may predict that this student will attempt to do his best in situations that offer an opportunity to excel. If the student does make persistent attempts to excel in a variety of situations, the hypothesis about his need system is probably true.

Inferring needs from behavior in frustrating experiences. A more reliable test of the existence of a need is what the individual does when a presumed need is frustrated in some way. If we remove some goal object that we have inferred a person is striving for, and the individual gives up striving for the goal, we can infer that the need motivating the goal-seeking behavior is not a strong one. While laboratory situations can be devised in which needs are frustrated in a limited way, the practical requirements of everyday life and the value standards that we generally accept do not permit us to frustrate the needs of other individuals extensively. However, in the ordinary course of circumstances the needs of individuals will be frustrated; and, from the behavior that we observe at these times, we may make inferences about the presence of needs in the motivational system of an individual. A child who is striving for academic success may not achieve this success or may not achieve it to the degree that he has desired. At such a time we can observe the effects of this frustrating condition upon him. If he becomes highly disturbed or makes renewed efforts to achieve success, or if he criticizes the teacher for failure to give him a good grade, we may infer that his need for success is a strong motivating force in his personality.

Mildly frustrating conditions can be established in experimental situations to study the effects of frustration on motivation. Hartup [15] studied the effects of withdrawing social approval for a task children were performing. Two groups of children were given approval by adults while they were working. One group of children continuously received the approval of an adult while they worked; a second group of children worked for a short period during which they received approval, and then for a period during which they did not receive the approval of an adult. Both groups of children were then asked to learn two simple tasks. Children in the second group, the group deprived of adult approval preceding the learning period, took fewer trials to learn the task and made fewer errors in the process. The results supported the hypothesis that withdrawal of approval stimulates learning. The children in the second group had experienced mild frustration of their need for approval; as a consequence, the strength of this need became greater and motivated the learning behavior. The children in the first group did not have to work so hard because their needs for approval were being met.

When a frustrating situation leads to problem-solving behavior and where there is evidence of increasing striving, we can infer the existence of a need disposition, which the person is attempting to satisfy by goal-seeking behavior. In more technical terms, *the facilitation of performance is a function of the strength of the motivation.* We infer the strength of the motivation from the degree and extent to which behavior changes. As we

---

[15] W. W. Hartup, "Nurturance and Nurturance-Withdrawal in Relation to the Dependency Behavior of Pre-school Children," *Child Development*, 29 (1958), 190–201.

noted earlier, social conditions will frequently produce frustrating situations, and the teacher, on occasion, inadvertently may deprive children of goals that they are seeking. The teacher who is sensitive to the relationship between frustrating circumstances and the strength of motivation should be able to infer the particular needs of a child from the effect of the frustrating situations on the behavior of the child.

HOW MOTIVES AND NEEDS ARE LEARNED

Although the theory of how motives and needs are acquired has not been worked out and tested to all psychologists' satisfaction, some general notions are accepted as tentative descriptions of this learning.

When we identify a motive, we are really describing either the kinds of **reinforcers** a person seeks (which we have called goals) or the kinds of behavior that have been typically reinforced. Most descriptions of needs and motives are mixtures of these two ways of labeling. For example, a need for achievement is usually defined in terms of a broad class of reinforcers—the attainment of the symbols of excellence.

One way in which motives are acquired is through **reinforcement** of specific responses. A child is rewarded with smiles, loving attention, cuddling, and warm words by his mother every time he does something she has asked. The desired behavior becomes a permanent part of his behavior repertoire; that is, the set of responses he is most likely to enact. To the observer he appears to be motivated to pick up his toys; or, if we observe his mother reinforcing him for these actions, we infer that he is motivated to seek his mother's approval.

Motives are also learned when one reinforcer is paired with another event which we want to become a reinforcer for the person. For example, we use approval to encourage a child to learn, but we also make the learning opportunity pleasant and stimulating in other ways so that the child finds the activity of learning a rewarding one. We also make what he learns useful for achieving other reinforcers. He learns to make change so that he can handle money. Being able to handle money means that he can buy what he wants at the store with a minimum of supervision. He learns to value counting and change-making activities because they lead to a wide variety of events that are reinforcing.

These reinforcers are usually called goals in this chapter. We assume that an individual seeks out situations in which he will attain the goals he has come to value; that is, the goals that are reinforcing for him. Statements about his motives and needs are ways of describing the kinds of events he finds reinforcing and the kind of behavior he is most likely to enact because it has been reinforced in the past.

NEED SATISFACTION AND REINFORCEMENT OF BEHAVIOR

Behavior that has led to satisfaction of needs tends to be repeated when the needs are aroused. By writing a feature article for the school newspaper, Jane has won her classmates' approval. When she is motivated again to seek approval, she will probably try this or similar means a second time. The behavior that led to the goal is *reinforced and strengthened; that is, when the person is again motivated in the same way, the behavior is likely to occur.*

From the teacher's point of view, many instances of classroom behavior are inexplicable and difficult to eradicate, simply because they have been strongly reinforced through need satisfaction. The child who is continually talking in class, answering out of turn, and generally disruptive of classroom procedures may be attempting to satisfy a strong need for attention. Since his behavior is obviously attention getting, angry outbursts and reprimands on the part of the teacher produce the very effect that the behavior is designed to stimulate.

Even in situations presumably rewarding to a child, deviant kinds of behavior may be learned. In the following example, Bobby has learned that deviant behavior brings him the attention that he wants. The more attention he receives, the more likely he is to be disruptive.

Every year, in this area, children go from door to door in the neighborhood selling seeds to raise money for incidental expenses of the school. The children buy the seeds in school from ten to twenty cents a pack and sell them. The fact that no package is less than a dime is generally well known to the children. Nevertheless, Bobby tries to buy a package for a nickel. He says to the teacher, "Any for five cents?" And the teacher says, "No, dear, they're all at least a dime. You just need one more nickel, don't you?" And Bobby says, "I'll get it tomorrow."

Bobby was the only child in the class to make this mistake. In correcting him, the teacher gently called him "dear" and gave him another chance in close contact with her by having him bring the extra nickel the next day. No other child got a second try at teacher. Thus, Bobby's erratic behavior was inadvertently reinforced by the teacher.[16]

[16] J. Henry, "Working Paper on Creativity," *Harvard Educational Review*, 27 (1957), 152.

The conditions for learning motives are complicated and varied. We describe the major influences on this learning in this section. In the first part we discuss the general social influences which prompt certain kinds of goal-seeking behaviors and which reward learning to seek these goals. In the second part we describe the factors that influence a person in setting goals for himself.

SOCIAL INFLUENCES ON THE ACQUISITION OF NEEDS

Such needs as the need for approval, the need for status, the need for achievement, the need for affection are not inborn.[17] Needs of this kind are acquired or learned as the individual interacts with other persons in his environment.[18] The environment in which a child is raised is a complex system; it provides a child with opportunities for specific kinds of learning and rewards this learning. The process of inducing behavior change by rewarding certain kinds of behaviors and punishing or not rewarding other kinds is the *process of socialization*.

Socialization practices vary in different societies and subsocieties. The American child is socialized in somewhat different ways, depending upon the social class in which he is being raised. Sociologists and psychologists discriminate layers or strata of American society by the level of occupation that characterizes the members of these strata, the amount of income, the level of education, and other objective criteria of this kind.[19] The objectively differentiated classes have been shown to differ in child-rearing practices.[20] The differential patterns in child rearing tend to reinforce the learning of differential needs and goal expectations.

[17] Psychologists differ on what needs are learned and the manner in which they are learned. For a discussion of this problem, see J. Deese, *The Psychology of Learning* (New York: McGraw-Hill Book Company, 1958), pp. 108–114.

[18] For experimental evidence that needs can be acquired, see N. E. Miller, "Studies of Fear as an Acquirable Drive: I. Fear as Motivation and Fear-Reduction as Reinforcement in the Learning of New Responses," *Journal of Experimental Psychology*, 38 (1949), 89–101. For a discussion of learned motives, see N. E. Miller, "Learnable Drives and Rewards," in S. S. Stevens, ed., *Handbook of Experimental Psychology* (New York: John Wiley and Sons, 1951).

[19] W. L. Warner et al., *Social Class in America* (Chicago: Science Research, 1949).

[20] A. Davis and R. J. Havighurst, "Social Class and Color Differences in Child Rearing," *American Sociological Review*, 11 (1946), 698–710. Also, E. Maccoby et al., "Methods of Child Rearing in Two Social Classes," in A. P. Coladarci, *Educational Psychology: A Book of Readings* (New York: The Dryden Press, 1955), pp. 97–121.

Social Class and Need Acquisition

The social class of a person is that group of individuals with whom a person is most likely to associate on a more or less intimate basis and who share common ideals, values, attitudes, and ways of behaving. This social milieu creates a learning environment for the growing child. The environment provides him with available goals for which he may work and rewards him for striving for these goals.

Within each of these participation levels, with their cultural environments, a child learns characteristic behavior and values concerning family members, sexual and aggressive acts, work, education, and a career. A child of middle status, that is, acquires different social goals, different needs, different codes of right and wrong, and he experiences different psychological rewards and punishments from those learned by a child of either upper or lower status.[21]

The home is an important influence on the pattern of needs acquired by a child. Home influences are related to the social status of the family and to specific child-rearing practices within any home. Children from homes of a given social status are likely to have a common pattern of needs and a relatively common set of goal expectations. But within any social class we will find differences among children, depending upon the kinds of child-rearing practices emphasized in the home.

Home Influence and Goal Orientation

A study by Kahl [22] demonstrates the relationship between the social status of a family, as measured by the father's occupation, and the educational and occupational aspirations of the boys in the family. In Table 4–1 the boys have been classified on the basis of their fathers' occupations and their own levels of intelligence. As the data in the table indicate, the largest percentage of boys who expect to go to college are those who have the highest intelligence and whose father's occupation is of the highest level. However, among all of the boys who fall into

[21] A. Davis, "Socialization and Adolescent Personality," in Forty-third Yearbook of the National Society for the Study of Education, Part I (Chicago: University of Chicago Press, 1944), p. 203.

[22] J. A. Kahl, "Educational and Occupational Aspirations of 'Common Man' Boys," *Harvard Educational Review*, 23 (1953), 186–203.

the highest intelligence category, the percentage of those who expect to go to college decreases as we move down the scale of occupations.

In this same study, Kahl interviewed 24 boys intensively. All of these boys had sufficient intelligence to go to college, but half of them planned to go to college and half did not. All of them came from working-class homes, and had done satisfactorily in school. Kahl was interested in determining the extent to which parents encouraged these boys to go to college. The data in Figure 4–1 suggest a strong relationship between the amount of parental pressure toward college and the son's aspiration to go to college. As is evident from these data, practically all of the boys who were not aspiring to go to college were also living in homes in which there

TABLE 4–1. *Percentage of boys who expect to go to college, by IQ and father's occupation (3,348 cases) (from Kahl).*

| | IQ quintile | | | | | |
| | (Low) | | | | (High) | All |
Father's occupation	1	2	3	4	5	quintiles
Major White Collar	56%	72%	79%	82%	89%	80%
Middle White Collar	28	36	47	53	76	52
Minor White Collar	12	20	22	29	55	26
Skilled Labor & Service	4	15	19	22	40	19
Other Labor & Service	9	6	10	14	29	12
All Occupations	11	17	24	30	52	27

was no parental pressure to go to college. The majority of boys who expected to go to college were living in homes in which there was parental pressure to go to college.

On the basis of extensive interviewing with the parents, real differences in attitudes and expectations could be found among these homes. The homes in which there was little pressure to improve one's lot by going to college were described as follows:

. . . concerned with balancing the budget each week, with living for the moment in a smooth manner. They looked neither to the past nor to the future. The father wanted a job which offered congenial workmates, an easy boss, a regular pay check. . . . The children were told to stay in high school because the diploma was pretty important in getting jobs nowadays, but they were allowed to pick their own curriculum according to taste. The value "doing what you like to do" was applied to school work, to part-time jobs, and to career aspirations. Rarely was the possibility of a college education seriously considered: "we can't afford such things," or "we aren't very bright in school." Indeed, their perception of college and the kinds of jobs college-trained people held were exceedingly vague. . . . In some, they felt that common people like themselves were lucky to have a regular job, that the sons would be like the fathers, that such was life and why think about it (pp. 192–193).

On the other hand, the homes in which there was considerable pressure for advanced education were described as remarkably different in their attitudes:

. . . the parents who believed in "getting ahead" were more sensitive to social hierarchies and thought more about the subject than those who

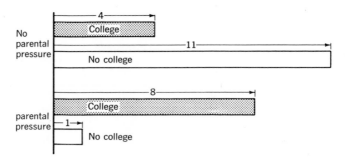

FIGURE 4–1. *Relation between parental pressure and son's aspiration for college (24 boys) (after Kahl).*

were satisfied with their lot. They used the middle class as a reference group that was close enough to have meaning, though far enough away to be different. They kept thinking: "There, but for a few small difficulties, go I." The difficulty they usually referred to was lack of education. These people spoke with monotonous regularity about their handicap of poor education. Sometimes they blamed themselves for not taking advantage of their opportunities when young; they said that they did not realize when they still had time how important it was to get advanced training. . . . They saw an occupational world stratified according to the basic principle of education, and education was something you got when you were young (p. 193).

The differences in these homes illustrate the differences in the kinds of environment that lead to differential goal expectations and needs in children. The various social strata in American society may be differen-

tiated on the basis of differences in attitudes and values, in goal expectations, and in rewards provided for appropriate goal striving.[23] The middle-
class family, for example, places greater emphasis upon *attainment* and
striving for success. The middle-class family typically emphasizes independence training, which is begun earlier than in lower-status families.
Success and striving for success are highly rewarded in such families, with
the consequent development of strong needs for achievement in children
of middle-class families. However, while middle-class families have many
characteristics in common, the environment created within each of these
families is not identical. Not every child of a middle-class family will be
motivated to achieve to the same degree. However, middle-class children
as a group are more likely to be motivated by achievement needs than are
children coming from lower-status families.

These distinctions have important implications for the teacher who
must attempt to assess the motivations of his students. Generally, children
from different status levels in society will be characterized by different
motivational systems, will have different goal expectancies, and will be
motivated by different kinds of rewards. Since the American school
typically has children from practically all levels of society, the teacher is
faced with the complex problem of motivating children who have different need systems. One of the major problems of the American school is
motivating children from lower-status homes. The child who has not
learned to value education or the goals to which it leads is not likely to be
motivated to participate actively in school work. Whatever the teacher
does to motivate lower-status children will probably involve a substantial
reorganization of their need systems and goal expectancies. Recall the
general principle cited earlier in this chapter—that the relationship between goals and need satisfaction is learned. New needs and goal expectations will have to be acquired by a child who does not expect to find
satisfaction in the goals achieved through formal education.[24]

While differences of the kind described here characterize the various
strata of American society, the teacher studying the individual child cannot be certain that every middle-class child is highly motivated to achieve

---

[23] For interesting descriptions of such differences, consult the following: A. B. Hollingshead, *Elmtown's Youth* (New York: John Wiley and Sons, 1949); W. L. Warner
et al., *Who Shall Be Educated?* (New York: Harper and Brothers, 1944); W. L. Warner and P. S. Lunt, *The Social Life of a Modern Community* (New Haven: Yale
University Press, 1941).

[24] The suggestion has been made that school experiences be reorganized to meet the
needs of lower-class children. In this suggestion the term "needs" is being used differently from what it is here.

and every lower-class child is not motivated to achieve. As we have suggested, the learning of these needs depends upon the characteristics of each family. As the study of working-class boys (see Figure 4–1) suggests, even within the strata of a society which would be classified as lower status, certain families place considerable emphasis on achievement and have goal expectations similar to those of middle-status families. The problem for the teacher always resolves itself into a determination of the need systems of a particular child. The teacher must ask such questions as "What is it that this child wants? What is it that this child is willing to work for?"

Child-Rearing Practices and Need Acquisition

Winterbottom [25] has studied the relationship between the demands made by parents on their children and the achievement needs of the children. In this study mothers were interviewed to obtain information on the demands that they made of their children and the age at which they made these demands. Then the children were tested to determine the strength of their needs for achievement. As Figure 4–2 illustrates, children with high achievement needs, up to about age nine, come from homes in which the mothers make greater demands. For example, the mothers of children with high *n* achievement (need for achievement) expected their children to know their way around the city, to try new things for themselves, to do well in competition, and to make their own friends. McClelland states:

The mother of a son with high *n* Achievement is interested in her son's developing away from her, in urging him to master things on his own, whereas the mother of a son with low *n* Achievement is willing to let such things slide and let him remain somewhat more dependent on her. . . . *Achievement motivation in boys is associated with stress on independence training by their mothers.*[26]

The same study investigated the relationship between the kind of reward provided for achievement and the strength of the child's achieve-

[25] M. R. Winterbottom, "The Relation of Childhood Training in Independence to Achievement Motivation," cited in D. McClelland et al., *The Achievement Motive* (New York: Appleton-Century-Crofts, 1953), pp. 297–306.
[26] D. C. McClelland et al., *The Achievement Motive* (New York: Appleton-Century-Crofts, 1953), pp. 303–304.

ment need. The mothers were asked in what manner they rewarded a child when he did something that they wanted him to do. The data indicate that "mothers who used physical rewards for fulfillment of achievement demands have sons whose average n Achievement score is twice that of mothers who used more attenuated means of affective arousal" (p. 306). The data in this study illustrate that the strength of needs varies with the goals which children are encouraged to strive for and the rewards which are given for striving for these goals.

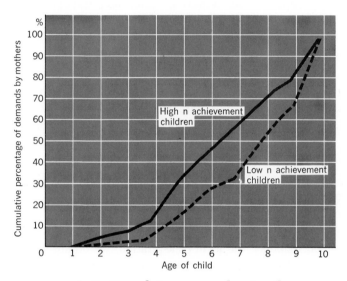

FIGURE 4-2. *Cumulative curves showing the proportion of total demands made up to each age level as reported by mothers of children scoring high and low on* n *achievement (from Winterbottom).*

What a child comes to believe important for him, what he wants to work for, where he sees himself going in life, depend on the kinds of influences we have been discussing. Some of these influences are in the form of directives about what is important; others are the parents' habitual way of treating the child. But, in all cases, parents and others are prompting the child to seek goals they deem desirable and are rewarding him for doing so.

The child comes to school with some conception of himself, with some idea of the activities he finds satisfying. However, school opens up a new world for him; hopefully, he will develop new goals. The experience he has in school, we suspect, strongly influences the development of his motives and needs. The child's reaction to later school experience is influenced by earlier experience.

EFFECTS OF SCHOOL EXPERIENCE ON GOAL SETTING

A person's expectation of how he will perform a task is called his **level of aspiration.** Suppose that we have been teaching fractions in arithmetic to a group of children. They have worked a number of problems and have had the basic processes explained to them. We present the children with ten problems and ask each child how many he expects to get correct. One child will expect to get all of the problems correct because, during the learning experiences, he has been repeatedly successful with problems of this kind. Another child will state that he expects to get only a few problems correct because he has been experiencing difficulty with this kind of problem. Each child has an estimate of his own abilities based on his experience with an activity or task. On the basis of this estimate of his own ability, he predicts how he thinks he will do. Some children will set expectations for themselves considerably beyond a level that they could reasonably be expected to achieve. Other children will set their *level of aspiration* below what can be achieved. However, by studying the factors which influence the level of aspiration, we obtain an estimate of the factors which are likely to influence a child's goal expectations.[27]

SUCCESS AND FAILURE AND LEVEL OF ASPIRATION

A relationship between success and failure and the level of aspiration has been demonstrated in a number of experimental studies.[28] In some of these studies the child had little or no experience with the kind of task that he was asked to perform in the experiment, and success and failure experiences were fabricated by the experimenter. In other studies the effects of long-term success and failure on the level of aspiration in tasks

[27] P. S. Sears, "Levels of Aspiration in Relation to Some Variables of Personality: Clinical Studies," *Journal of Social Psychology,* 14 (1941), 311–336. See also H. M. Schroder and D. E. Hunt, "Failure-Avoidance in Situational Interpretation and Problem Solving," *Psychological Monographs,* No. 342 (1957).

[28] A review of these studies and a critical analysis can be found in K. Lewin et al., "Level of Aspiration," in J. McV. Hunt, ed., *Personality and the Behavior Disorders* (New York: Ronald Press Company, 1944), pp. 333–378.

with which the child was familiar have been studied. The general conclusion from both kinds of studies is substantially the same—that success tends to raise the level of aspiration, and failure tends to depress it. However, the relationships between previous experience and immediate success or failure are complex, and a study by Sears has demonstrated the effects of these variables on the level of aspiration.[29]

In her study, Sears chose three groups of children who were in the fourth, fifth, and sixth grades. The first group, called the "success" group, contained children who had experienced success in school, as evidenced by their grades, and who felt that they had been successful. A "failure" group was composed of children who, by the same criteria (school grades and how they felt about their school experience), had experienced failure. A mixed group, called the "differential" group, was made up of children who had had successful experiences in reading and unsuccessful experiences in arithmetic. The three groups were comparable in age, intelligence, and the number of boys and girls in each group.

Each group of children was given tasks under what were called "neutral" conditions. These were reading and arithmetic tasks of the type that children usually do in elementary school and on which they are frequently tested. The children were administered a series of these tasks and, after each one, were asked to estimate their time on the succeeding task. In this "neutral" condition we have a measure of each child's level of aspiration as he moves from one reading task to another, and from one arithmetic task to another.

If we compare the levels of aspiration in these groups of children, we have some estimate of the relationship between previous success or failure in reading and arithmetic and the level of aspiration that the child sets for himself in a situation which is nonthreatening. Figure 4–3 illustrates the differences between the three groups. Each child is located by the difference between his estimate and the actual amount of time he took on the tasks. A child who thought he would take longer than he actually did on the task just finished is located on the negative side—his goal is below what he has shown he can do. A child who estimates he will do better than he has just done is on the positive side. A large positive discrepancy means that the child thinks he is going to complete the task in much less

[29] P. S. Sears, "Levels of Aspiration in Academically Successful and Unsuccessful Children," *Journal of Abnormal and Social Psychology*, 35 (1940), 498–536. For a critique of the relevance of level-of-aspiration studies to educational practice, see D. Sivertsen, "Goal Setting, Level of Aspiration, and Social Norms," *Acta Psychologia*, 13 (1957), 54–60.

time than he has. The children who had previous experiences of failure were more variable in setting levels of aspiration for themselves on these tasks. The children who had experienced some success appeared to be more realistic in setting their level of aspiration.

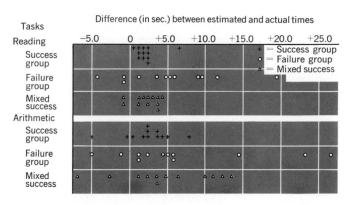

FIGURE 4–3. *Effects of previous success on levels of aspiration. Each symbol represents one child (from Sears).*

After this initial experience the children in each group were called back to perform on tasks similar to the ones they had performed under "neutral" conditions. However, half the children in each group were told that they had been highly successful in their performance under the "neutral" conditions, and half the group were told that they had done very poorly on the tasks in the initial testing. Figure 4–4 gives the data for the groups after the experience of success and failure.

The effects of immediate success and failure are similar to the effects of long-term success and failure. Under success conditions the level of aspiration tends to correspond realistically to the performance level of the child. Under failure conditions there are large discrepancies between performance and level of aspiration. In general, the children under failure conditions are more variable in their estimates of their expected performance than are the children under success conditions.

The data presented suggest the general relationships between success and failure and the individual's level of aspiration. Sears further explored the meaning of setting an expected goal for one's self by comparing three groups of children: (1) a group that set the level of aspiration slightly above actual performance, (2) a group whose level of aspiration was set considerably above actual performance, (3) a group that consistently set the level of aspiration below performance level. For example, children's performance and level of aspiration would follow a pattern similar to this:

	High Positive Discrepancy	Low Positive Discrepancy	Negative Discrepancy
Performance Level, Last Task	8 sec.	8 sec.	8 sec.
Level of Aspiration, Next Task	2 sec.	6 sec.	9 sec.

It seemed apparent that the behavior of setting a goal had different meanings for each of these three groups:

1. *The Low-Positive-Discrepancy Group.* This is a group that consistently sets the level of aspiration above performance level on the last task. *For these children the discrepancy measure was usually smaller after success and larger after failure.* The level of aspiration seems to be affected by immediate performance. "They take account in a practical way of their previous good and bad performances as reported . . . They react rather strongly to success and failure. . . . The levels of aspiration of this group might be described as closely tied to a (for them) satisfactory reality, but easily modified in response to a change in the reported performance" (pp. 522–523).

2. *The High-Positive-Discrepancy Group.* This group showed a large discrepancy between level of aspiration scores and performance scores. *For these children high-positive-discrepancy scores decrease under success and increase under failure conditions.* "Frequently the children of this group set initially a level of aspiration which is far removed from their performance scores and they maintain this level almost rigidly . . . If the performance should approach the level of aspiration, the latter is immediately raised so that a large discrepancy continues to be present. These subjects seem to be inwardly compelled to do so, as if they never felt that they were doing well enough. . . . If the goal is achieved, however, there is no such satisfaction and relaxation of tension . . . Under the failure conditions sluggish, apathetic behavior sometimes appears . . . " (pp. 523–524).

3. *The Negative-Discrepancy Group.* This is the group of children who persistently set their level of aspiration below their performance scores. *Under both success and failure the discrepancy between the level of*

aspiration and performance was increased. "In responsiveness and flexibility the members of this group resemble the low positive discrepancy children . . . in the low positive group the subjects are responsible and flexible in terms of a stated goal which is ahead of their performance; in the negative discrepancy group the responsiveness and flexibility are directed toward avoiding the failure of a performance *worse* than that prescribed by the level of aspiration. . . . Their aim is to be always on the safe side—an aim which seems to them most probable of achievement when the level of aspiration is placed just equal to or lower than the performance immediately previous" (pp. 524–525).

This analysis shows the reinforcing effect of attaining a goal. Some children avoid a punishing consequence by setting their expectations

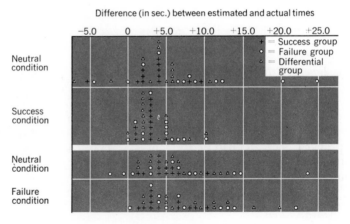

FIGURE 4–4. *Effects of recent success and failure on level of aspiration (from Sears).*

below what they probably can do. Some children "hope" for a reward by setting their goal high. The fluctuation in level of aspiration is a behavioral manifestation of how success or failure has influenced the child.

INFLUENCE OF THE GROUP ON GOAL-SETTING BEHAVIOR

Experimental evidence has demonstrated the influence both of a child's previous experience and of his immediate experience upon his goal-setting behavior. Is a child likely to be influenced by the group with which he is working, or does he set his standards solely in terms of what he knows about himself and his abilities? Does the bright child adjust his standards of performance to the class average, and would he raise his standards of performance if he were placed in a group with high standards? Will the child who has not been performing successfully set higher standards for himself if he is placed in a group whose average performance is above his own? Obviously, these are important practical questions related to the psychology of motivation. Experimental data do suggest that the child's level of aspiration is influenced by the standard of performance within his own group.

Effect of Knowing Performance Rank in a Group

Anderson and Brandt [30] conducted an experiment to answer some of the questions raised above. These investigators set up two groups, an experimental and a control group, and attempted to motivate the children in the two groups in different ways. Both groups were given a simple cancelation task to perform. On successive days the children in the experimental group were given their relative standing in class, whereas the children in the control group were not. Each child in the experimental group knew where he stood with respect to the group, and was asked to set a standard for himself on the task. The experimental group was significantly superior to the control group in achievement on the task. We infer that the motivation produced by knowledge of where one stands in the group is related to this difference in achievement. This conclusion is consistent with data from other studies, which indicate that knowledge of how one is doing tends to enhance performance and motivation for improvement.[31]

This study also produced important data on the goal-setting behavior of the children in the experimental group. Each time these children were told their relative position in the group, they were asked to set a new standard for themselves. Children who were in the lowest ranks of actual achievement consistently set goals considerably above their past achievements, whereas those in the upper ranks consistently set goals consider-

[30] H. H. Anderson and H. F. Brandt, "Study of Motivation Involving Self-Announced Goals of Fifth Grade Children and the Concept of the Level of Aspiration," *Journal of Social Psychology*, 10 (1939), 209–232.

[31] Experimental data on this point are reviewed in R. S. Woodworth and H. Schlosberg, *Experimental Psychology* (New York: Henry Holt and Company, 1954), pp. 686–688. See also L. Plowman and J. B. Stroud, "The Effect of Informing Pupils of the Correctness of Their Responses to Objective Test Questions," *Journal of Educational Research*, 36 (1942), 16–20. For a more recent study, see E. B. Page, "Teacher Comments and Student Performance: A Seventy-four Classroom Experiment in School Motivation," *Journal of Educational Psychology*, 49 (1958), 173–181.

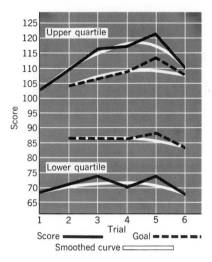

FIGURE 4–5. *Mean achieve-ment scores and mean goals by trials for upper and lower quartiles of achievement (from Anderson and Brandt).*

ably below their preceding achievement (see Figure 4–5). There appears to be some type of group standard toward which the children are tending. This group standard represents a wished-for or hoped-for level of achievement for the child who is not doing well. Apparently, the child who is achieving well above this standard can maintain his feeling of success even by lowering his own goals in the direction of the level of the group average.[32]

Effect of Knowing Other Groups' Performances

Does a group tend to establish its standard by reference to the standards of other groups? For instance, will a group of freshman algebra students establish a standard of performance relative to the performance of other freshmen students taking algebra courses, or will each group be influenced principally by its own previous experience? This question was investigated by Chapman and Volkmann.[33] Four groups of college students were given a test of literary ability. The first group was given instructions about the test; the second group was given, in addition to the instructions, the mean score obtained on this test by a group of literary experts; the third group was given the mean score of a group of college students on the test; and the fourth group was given the mean score of a group of laborers on the test. The students in each group were then asked to estimate their expected performance. When the mean estimates of how the students expected to do were computed, the investigators found the second group—that is, the students who knew the aver-

[32] For comparable results with a group of college students, see E. R. Hilgard, E. M. Sait, and G. A. Magaret, "Level of Aspiration as Affected by Relative Standing in an Experimental Social Group," *Journal of Experimental Psychology*, 27 (1940), 411–421; and M. Hertzman and L. Festinger, "Shifts in Explicit Goals in a Level of Aspiration Experiment," *Journal of Experimental Psychology*, 27 (1940), 439–452.

[33] D. W. Chapman and J. Volkmann, "A Social Determinant of the Level of Aspiration," *Journal of Abnormal and Social Psychology*, 34 (1939), 225–238.

age score of literary experts—set their level of aspiration much lower than any of the other groups. The group that was told the performance of the laborers set their level of aspiration higher than that of any of the groups. Since none of the students in these groups knew how he would actually perform on the test, he was presumably estimating his performance by comparing himself with what he knew about how other groups had performed. In a second part of the experiment, another group of students was given similar instructions, but not until after they had taken a first form of the test. Under these conditions the students estimated their expected performance more in terms of their own previous performance than in terms of the known performance of the other groups.

Effects of Grouping Practices on Level of Aspiration

The level of aspiration of a child is influenced by his knowledge of how his group and other groups perform, and by his own experience with a task. Teachers are frequently urged to encourage a child to set his standards in relation to his own abilities. However, a child's conception of his own ability is determined in part by his evaluation of the performances of others. A child who is relatively unsuccessful in reading or arithmetic has learned to judge his performance by what he has seen of the performances of his fellow students. As long as the child is able to determine where he stands with respect to other children, his feelings of success and failure and his consequent goal-setting behavior will be influenced by his knowledge of his place in the group.

Frequently teachers will divide a class into several groups of differing ability levels and encourage each of these groups to work at its own pace. Whether this is an effective technique for producing feelings of success is not known. Its effectiveness would probably depend upon the children's information about the relative standings of the three groups. Common-sense observation suggests that children would easily learn the status differences between the three groups. A child can recognize that the teacher spends considerable time with one of the groups while permitting another group to work independently. Even the most cursory inspection of the materials being used will tell a child that there are differences in the complexities of these materials. It is not difficult for a child to determine that he is in the "low group," even though the group may never be labeled as such. Consequently, the possibility of developing a personal standard of excellence or achievement in ignorance of the standards set by a group does not seem likely.

Furthermore, since each group sets its own standards, a child is more likely to regulate himself by the standard of his own group. If the group is a low group, this standard will inevitably be a lower standard. The teacher is left with a dilemma. Should he place poor students in groups in which the level of performance is considerably above theirs, or should he construct groups in which the level of the performance is not radically different from that of most of the members of the group? If he chooses the first plan, he may induce continued feelings of failure on the part of the poorer students. If he chooses the second, the group standard may be so easy to meet that a student will not be motivated to achieve higher standards. The experienced teacher will probably use both arrangements. By placing a student in groups of children with the same level of ability, the teacher can encourage him to work up to his capacities and maximize the probability of his having successful experiences. By his membership in many groups of varying ability levels, the child will be able to form a realistic conception of his own ability. But he will have had sufficient success experiences to minimize the relative failure he may experience when working with students of higher ability.

MOTIVATION AND INSTRUCTIONAL STRATEGIES

Every instructional strategy must include some kind of motivational strategy—some plan for engaging the learner's interest and attention, so that he will expend the effort necessary to learn. For instance, the teacher may decide to present his material in an unusual or striking or different manner; or he may provide material that he knows will interest the learner. An example of the first strategy is provided by the teacher who heats a bimetallic bar while holding it in such a way that it bends upward —a phenomenon most students have not observed and which seemingly contradicts their ordinary experience. The second strategy is demonstrated by the teacher who assigns a novel about an adolescent's problems as a way of stimulating interest in literature.

The first strategy is an **arousal strategy.** It is designed to activate the learner, to focus his attention, to stimulate his curiosity. The psychological principle exemplified in this strategy is that changes in stimulation are arousing and sensations associated with arousal are motivating.

The second strategy is a common one. It exemplifies a conditioning conception of how interests are learned. The event, lesson, reading, discussion that we want the learner to be interested in is associated with things he is known to be interested in. Knowledge of plot line in analyzing a story may be dull for many adolescents; but when the plot concerns events in an adolescent's life, the task becomes more meaningful. Literary analysis thus becomes associated with discussing topics of interest; because the latter is rewarding, the former becomes so.

A variation on this strategy makes one event a means of obtaining a desired goal. Assume that students like to read a set of books available in the classroom. The teacher says that they may use the class library when they have finished writing a brief essay. More reading time will be given to those students who do a careful job of writing and who try to make their essays interesting and original. In this example, the teacher is reinforcing writing responses—using the opportunity to read as the reinforcer. Some spread of interest from reading activity to writing activity is expected.

A better reward would be one that is intimately associated with the activity of writing. The child would learn what rewards can be produced by writing well. In the paragraph above, the connection between the writing and the reinforcer was "artificial" in the sense that the teacher could have used any reinforcer attractive to the children. The writing of letters to the school board or to the principal to call attention to a student problem may be rewarded by action removing the problem. An essay published in the school paper may similarly reinforce writing activity.

The object in this variation on the strategy is to link the activity to the rewards that it ought ordinarily to bring. The general principle is obviously sound. However, these kinds of connections are often difficult to arrange, or some of them are relatively unpredictable. The school board becomes angry, or the problem is ignored—the consequences may turn out to be punishing. For other activities the important and meaningful rewards associated with the activity are delayed. For the boy who wants to become a medical doctor, biology and chemistry are potentially interesting subjects; the reward value that he may find greatest, however, is postponed. It may be approximated if he is encouraged to read and to experiment on applications of these subjects to health problems.

On some occasions, the motivational strategy is lost sight of, and both teacher and students become involved in the activity selected as a means of rewarding acquired interests. Model building or mural painting, introduced as a way of motivating students, becomes the goal itself, and its instrumental value may be lost. The activity is motivating, but its educational value must be reconsidered in the light of the time and attention being devoted to it.

Each of the above strategies involves finding a way of initially stimulating the student and of reinforcing his interest. Practically, the teacher is sometimes limited in what he may do in either of these respects, though imaginative teachers are highly and surprisingly inventive. Not infrequently, the teacher falls back on the kinds of **incentives** that are typically available. The psychology of their use deserves consideration here.

INCENTIVES AND MOTIVATION

An *incentive* is a reward or source of **need satisfaction** that a person *may* obtain. The possibility of attaining this reward or goal induces motivated behavior. An incentive is something proffered to a learner to engage him in the actions of learning. The teacher makes a judgment about the reward value of something he offers to students. In our earlier example, he offered the opportunity to read interesting books as an incentive to stimulate writing activity. The teacher knew that the students liked this reading. By making it available, he introduced an incentive; the students who were allowed to read considered themselves rewarded.

Obviously, the teacher must know what is likely to be rewarding or need satisfying for his students. The teacher will need to study individuals to assess their specific interests and needs. He may also generalize with caution from what he knows about students of a certain age level or social background.

School environments typically provide many kinds of rewards for successful performance, such as grades, prizes, teacher approval, and the approval of classmates. These rewards are also called *incentives* because we assume that they will motivate students to work harder and to perform better.

Grades as Incentives

Grades are an example of a standard incentive introduced into practically all learning environments in schools. As motivational devices, grades are useful incentives only insofar as children's needs will be satisfied by attaining high grades. As every experienced teacher is aware, for many children grades do not serve as an incentive; they are motivated by needs that are not satisfied by attaining high grades. Other children will work for grades in order to satisfy a variety of needs, as our example of John and Bill illustrated. A child who receives praise and approval from his parents for receiving high grades has different expectations about the value of grades than does a child whose parents ignore or minimize the value of high grades.[34]

Since grades give a student information on his performance, we would then expect them to influence a student's level of aspiration. Treat[35] studied the relations of grading practices to students' performances and levels of aspiration. In one class, grades were distributed on a normal curve—that is, the percentage of each letter grade was fixed. In another class, the grading system varied with performance, so that higher grades were given if performance improved. Treat found improved performance and more realistic level of aspiration in the class in which the ascending grade scale was used. The students in this group were like the children in Sears' "low-positive-discrepancy" group. In the class in which a fixed grade system was used, performance did not improve systematically, and the level of aspiration was less realistic. Achieving good grades is a success experience; so motivation and performance improved when grades were administered to create a success experience.

The Teacher's Behavior as a Source of Incentives

The way a teacher acts toward his students may be a source of rewards for them. The teacher shows in many ways his estimate of the student and of his work. Some of these ways are quite direct, verbal comments; others, such as avoidance or lack of interest, are more subtle. A teacher may abruptly terminate a conversation of interest to the student. He may look out the window or shuffle through his papers. Or a teacher may provide powerful incentives to induce the student to participate in a learning experience, to keep him working, and to stimulate him to work more effectively. An experiment by Page provides some experimental support for this hypothesis.[36]

This experiment was performed in 74 high school classrooms with more

[34] T. R. Ford, "Social Factors Affecting Academic Performance," *School Review*, 65 (1957), 415–422. Also J. J. Kurtz and E. J. Swenson, "Factors Related to Over-Achievement and Under-Achievement in School," *School Review*, 59 (1951), 472–480.

[35] W. C. Treat, "Motivational Effects of an Ascending Grade Scale," unpublished doctoral dissertation (Stanford, Calif.: Stanford University, 1950).

[36] E. B. Page, "Teacher Comments and Student Performance: A Seventy-four Classroom Experiment in School Motivation," *Journal of Educational Psychology*, 49 (1958), 173–181.

than two thousand students. Each teacher administered an objective test, one that would ordinarily occur as part of the regular instruction. The teachers scored the tests in the usual way. They then randomly assigned the papers to one of three treatments. In the "no-comment" treatment, the papers were returned with grades but without comment. In the "free-comment" treatment, the teacher made whatever comments he thought the papers required. "Specified-comment" subjects received their papers with a comment that had been designated in advance for each letter grade. For example, A papers were accompanied by the comment "Excellent! Keep it up." F papers were labeled "Let's raise this grade!" The scores on the next objective test were used to estimate whether the comments had an effect on performance.

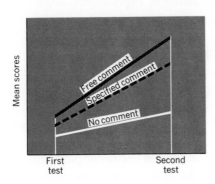

FIGURE 4–6. *Effects of teachers' comments on student learning (from Page).*

Page found that students receiving comments did significantly better on the second test than those who did not receive comments. The free-comment group obtained higher scores than the specified comment, but the difference was not significant. See Figure 4–6 for a display of these results, which amply illustrate the incentive value of the teacher's behavior.

Classroom Use of Incentives

Teachers and the school environment provide incentives which may or may not be related to the goals that a child is seeking. *The goal is what the child is seeking; the incentive is what the teacher provides.* Furthermore, the teacher is limited in the number of incentives that he can provide, and he cannot assume that any incentive will invariably motivate all children.[37] Most children are motivated to some extent by a need for approval, but not all children are motivated by a need for either adult approval or the approval of teachers specifically. A child who has received comparatively little approval from his parents will not neces-

[37] See, for example, G. G. Thompson and C. W. Hunnicutt, "The Effect of Praise or Blame on the Work Achievement of 'Introverts' and 'Extroverts,'" *Journal of Educational Psychology,* 35 (1944), 257–266.

sarily be strongly motivated to seek the approval of teachers. Even a child who has consistently received approval from adults cannot be motivated indefinitely by more and more approval. For such a child, a temporary withdrawal of approval may act as more of an incentive than additional approval.

The teacher must learn to use incentives in a variety of ways and to expect different results with different pupils as he uses these incentives. Here again the teacher hypothesizes about what incentives are likely to motivate a particular student and continually revises his estimates of the value of incentives on the basis of the performance of students when these incentives are provided. Hilgard and Russell have pointed out:

The proper motivation of learning is one of the basic essentials of any set of educational experiences. Learning seems to be more complete and more efficient when it is energized and directed by strong motivational factors. Accordingly, a large part of the teacher's task is to understand the motives of children and to use them in stimulating desirable learnings.

Motivation must be considered, not as a temporary device to stimulate interest, but as a complex of the needs of the child in the social situation in which he lives. As such, motivational factors are continually shifting as the child develops and as new elements enter the home-school-community pattern. The teacher, accordingly, is alert to the dynamic qualities of motivation and to shifts in patterns affecting behavior and learning.

Because of the large number of factors comprising a motivational pattern, the teacher can never expect a single teaching device or a larger group of procedures to stimulate different children or adolescents in the same way. In general, that teacher is most successful who can provide a variety of purposes and satisfactions in the learning process. Directing interests and activities towards social approval, or esthetic satisfaction, stimulating mental curiosity relating to both immediate and more remote goals, capitalizing on a variety of interests—all these and other procedures are needed in a well-motivated school program.[38]

EDUCATIONAL OBJECTIVES AND THE LEARNER'S GOALS

Educational objectives are statements of desired behavior changes. From the viewpoint of the teacher, educational objectives represent goals for which students should strive. What is the relationship of these goals to the needs of students? If the student attains the goals represented by

[38] E. R. Hilgard and D. H. Russell, "Motivation in School Learning," in *Learning and Instruction*, Forty-ninth Yearbook of the National Society for the Study of Education, Part I (Chicago: University of Chicago Press, 1950), pp. 66–67.

educational objectives, will his needs be satisfied? Or must he acquire new needs in order to attain these goals?

Most statements of educational objectives—for example, "The educated person can work and play with others" or "The educated person appreciates the family as a social institution"—represent long-range accomplishments for the individual.[39] However, a child or even an adolescent cannot look into the future and visualize with any great clarity the kind of a person that he is likely to be. He is immersed in present activities and immediate goals. The teacher must interrelate these specific goals with the long-term goal if it is to be achieved. The specific goal in the second-grade classroom may be that of getting along with one's classmates. The attainment of this goal will be part of a process which will eventually lead to the long-range goal of appreciating the value of other people, respecting their rights, and recognizing the importance of institutions such as the family.

The second-grade child may study the relationship of his family to the community, and may be concerned with such specific things as how the family contributes to the community and how the community in turn supports and maintains the family. In these activities he presumably is motivated by specific goals which can be attained within a relatively short period of time. But each of these goals may be part of a general structure of goals which lead to the abstract goal represented in the statement of educational objectives. The first problem, therefore, in organizing learning experiences in terms of goals is to organize these experiences on the basis of fairly specific and attainable goals, which are related to the more general goals represented in the usual statement of educational objectives.

The question still remains whether or not the goals of education, as they are reflected in statements of educational objectives, are in fact the goals that will satisfy children's needs. Modern educators have attempted to solve this problem by constructing curricula which relate the needs of children to educational objectives.[40] When educators speak of building a curriculum related to the "needs of children," are they using the term "needs" as it has been used in this chapter? Most curriculum conceptions built upon the needs of children begin with an analysis of present society and then proceed to a statement of what children need in order to adjust to this society. However, *what children need to adjust to this society is not*

---

[39] See *The Purposes of Education in American Democracy* (Washington, D. C.: Educational Policies Commission, National Education Association, 1938).

[40] For a discussion of the relationship of the needs of children to the organization of the curriculum, see V. T. Fair, C. Zachry, and R. Kotinsky, *Reorganizing Secondary Education* (New York: Appleton-Century-Crofts, 1939).

necessarily what children desire or want. Wright makes this point in the following statement:

Children need optimum health; they need vocational preparation. Here we are talking about what, in the opinion of adults, children ought to have, but seldom if ever strive to get. Children need recreation; they need rewarding social contacts. Now we are talking about what, in their own living, children very often strive to get, whether adults like it or not.[41]

In the above discussion, we have made a distinction between two ways in which the concept of need is used. For the sake of convenience, the two categories of needs embraced in this distinction may be called **normative needs** and **psychological needs.** *Normative needs* represent adult expectations of what a child *should* need—whether he knows it or not. A *psychological need*, on the other hand, is a state of tension within the child; it is the basis for the child's striving for particular kinds of goals. Psychological needs provide motive power, whereas normative needs do not. Psychological needs become linked to goals and the child strives for these goals because he expects them to satisfy his needs. Normative needs are conceptions of what a person ought to be like. We say a person needs to be able to read, to compute, to write clearly. He needs these behaviors if he is to function adequately in our society. If he wants to be a nuclear physicist, he needs to learn higher mathematics. Statements of this kind describe what a person *ought* to acquire to achieve certain purposes. General statements of what the school hopes to accomplish are frequently formulated as descriptions of what the person ought to be like. They are normative in the sense that they represent a standard against which accomplishment may be measured.

Psychological needs, on the other hand, influence children to seek specific goals, which may or may not be related to the goals reflected in statements of educational objectives.[42] A child entering school may not want to learn to read. Some children never develop any powerful motives for learning mathematics or science; nor do they all acquire a taste for literature and art.

The teacher must utilize the actual motives and goals of children in

[41] H. F. Wright, "How the Psychology of Motivation Is Related to Curriculum Development," *Journal of Educational Psychology,* 39 (1948), 149–156.

[42] For a comprehensive discussion of the concept of need and its relations to educational theory, see R. D. Archambault, "The Concept of Need and Its Relation to Certain Aspects of Educational Theory," *Harvard Educational Review,* 27 (1957), 38–62. Also, B. P. Komisar, " 'Need' and the Needs-Curriculum," in B. O. Smith and R. H. Ennis, eds., *Language and Concepts in Education* (Chicago: Rand McNally, 1961), pp. 24–42.

such a way that they will strive for goals which will result in behavior stated as desirable.

Curriculum organization has profited from the conception of basing the curriculum on the needs of children. Much subject matter which is no longer useful in any sense has been eliminated from the curriculum, and a broader and more realistic conception of education has resulted. Modern educators have built a curriculum derived from conceptions of what the majority of children will need in order to be useful members of society, with provisions for the needs of particular groups of children. This reorganization of the curriculum has not simplified or resolved the problem that has always confronted teachers—the problem of motivating students to work for specific goals. The teacher faces children with varying needs and learned goal expectations. The teacher's task is to broaden children's conceptions of their goals, foster the acquisition of new needs, and through this process enhance the total development of the child.

This shaping of the child's motivational system is an important teaching task. The child needs to learn new goals and to new acquire new motives. This learning is achieved by applying a principle with which you are now familiar. Place the child in a situation that will provide maximum need satisfaction for acquiring new behaviors; that is, in this case, new interests, new motives, and new goals.

PROVIDING SUCCESS EXPERIENCES

The data from the Sears study clearly indicate the relationship between previous experience and the level of performance or goals that an individual is willing to set for himself. Out of his past experience the individual develops a conception of what he is likely to be able to do and adjusts his standards accordingly. The child who has experienced failure to some degree in his previous experience with a task may not expect to do well when confronted with the task again. But apparently some children with failure experiences set unrealistic goals, as if they wished to perform at this unrealistic level even though they may not expect to do so. Even providing success experiences for children who have had failure experiences in the past does not guarantee that they will become more realistic in their conceptions of their goals. It is frequently recommended that every child should have some experience of success in some activity. While this is probably sound advice, the teacher should not assume that a few success experiences can immediately offset the effects of previous experiences with failure. A child who has learned that he does not do well in reading is not likely to change his conception of himself nor of his goals by a few experiences of success with reading tasks. To offset the effects of a relatively long history of failure, a correspondingly long sequence of success experiences must be provided.

Recall that the programming technology recommended by Skinner utilizes a progression of small steps to shape behavior. The argument is that reducing the difficulty of the task at each step simplifies the learning demands. The learner is practically sure of making a desired response, for which he is reinforced. The inhibitory effects of failure are minimized. This is essentially the idea being recommended here and generalized to the whole pattern of school tasks. By controlling the arrangement of learning experiences, the teacher has control over the success-failure variable.

The nature of the task and the general expectations about what constitutes success and failure in this task influence the levels of performance that an individual will set for himself. A child who has learned to read materials at the second-grade level is not likely to feel that he is a failure because he cannot read materials at the fifth- or sixth-grade level. The child has learned that there is a range of acceptable performance, and has corresponding feelings of success or failure within this particular range. The child in the second grade who is reading well below the level of second graders is not likely to feel successful because he can read better than children in the kindergarten. A child's expectation or goal for his own performance in a task is influenced by the generally accepted levels of performance for children with his experience and of his age level. Therefore, it is probably impossible to induce motivation by raising the standard of success above a level which most children would consider realistic for themselves. However, as long as the standard is within the acceptable range for children at a given age level or grade level, successive elevations of the success standard may motivate students to set higher standards for themselves, provided they have had success in meeting the previously established standards.

SUMMARY

This chapter describes the concept of motivation and the relationship of motivation to learning. The major purpose of the chapter is to introduce the teacher to the process by which motives are inferred, and to describe the ways in which the motivations of students may be utilized to engage them in learning.

1. Motivation has been defined as an energy change occurring within a person; it is characterized by a state of affective arousal and by behavior changes called anticipatory goal reactions. Motivational states with these characteristics are inferred from observable behaviors. The concept of motivation is used to explain the goal-seeking behavior that we observe.

2. The motivational process, then, involves (a) arousal, (b) goal-seeking behavior, (c) goal attainment, (d) reduction of the arousal state.

3. We call *motives* those instances of directed behavior which we observe. This behavior is recognized by the direction of the person's energies to achieve some result, which is usually referred to as the goal of his actions.

4. From observations of many instances of motivated behavior, we make inferences about stable and relatively permanent dispositions, called *needs*. In making judgments about motivation, we first make inferences about motives; we then make inferences from the motives to generalizations about needs.

5. The concept of a *need system* describes the kinds of motivational dispositions that characterize a person. Such systems may be quite simple or very complex. Attempts to classify various kinds of needs into systems have been attempted. No single classification is completely satisfactory.

Any system of classifying needs should probably describe needs in each of the following categories: (a) needs related to the biological survival and development of the person; (b) needs acquired because the individual's environment consistently rewards certain kinds of goal-seeking behavior.

6. Needs are identified by one or both of two general methods. In all cases a need or motive is inferred from some observable behavior, which is characterized by direction and persistency. One method for inferring needs is to identify the goals that a person persistently seeks. Another method is to observe the effects of frustration on a person's behavior: the more frustrated a person becomes when blocked in goal attainment, the more likely it is that the goal is significant to him.

7. Most of the motives and needs that characterize the personality system are learned. The general principle that accounts for this learning is that motives and needs which have been reinforced by goal attainment are acquired as permanent response tendencies. An analysis of this learning points us to look at social influences on learning. Reliable evidence sug-

gests that variations in such factors as one's social-class background, the kinds of goals and goal-seeking behavior that are rewarded in the home, and certain kinds of child-rearing practices produce specific kinds of motivational dispositions.

8. The school attempts to produce motivations in students that stimulate them to seek the goals implicit in the objectives of the school. Substantial evidence suggests that success and failure in learning experiences in school affect students' goals and their *level of aspiration,* their expectations about their performance of various tasks.

9. Since many school learning experiences are conducted with children in groups, and since the children are generally aware of the abilities and motivations of their peers, the influence of the group's level of performance and aspiration is also a significant factor. Group levels of performance tend to be adaptations between the potential performances of the best and poorest performers. Similarly, groups also tend to set their expectations for themselves by a comparison with the achievements of comparable groups.

10. One of the teacher's major tasks is to invent motivational strategies which engage the learner in the activities from which he will learn. One of the ways to bring about motive arousal in a learner is to provide *incentives* for learning. Incentives induce goal-seeking behavior.

11. Another strategy for inducing learning is to make the goals of the learning experience consonant with the kinds of goals the learner is seeking. A distinction between our conception of what a learner needs (normative needs) and what he wants (psychological needs) is important to make when using this kind of motivational strategy.

STUDY AND DISCUSSION QUESTIONS

1. Refer to the example of John and Bill presented in the first part of this chapter. What are the *motives* of each of these boys in the situation described? What *needs* would you infer from these motives? What predictions would you make about other motives that you would expect these boys to have if your inference is accurate?

2. A student participates quite actively in class discussions. What motives might underlie this behavior? What needs would you infer from these motives?

3. Suggest several motives for each of the following instances of behavior:

   a. A student pushes another student as they stand in line.

   b. A student insists on rewriting his papers when they are corrected.

    c. A student joins the debate team and the student newspaper.

    d. A child collects stamps and rocks.

    e. A student does not attend school dances.

    f. A student signs up for the French course.

4. Using the motives you suggested in the above examples, describe the needs that may underlie these motives. Predict the kinds of behavior you would expect to observe if the students were motivated by these needs.

5. What needs might be satisfied by a boy who is interested in working on automobiles? How might these activities be learned as a source of need satisfaction?

6. Some students are intensely interested in interscholastic athletic activities even though they are not members of the varsity teams. What needs might be satisfied by attending games and "rooting" for the team? Suggest some ways in which these sources of need satisfaction may have been learned.

7. How do you account for the fact that some students do not find intellectual activities a source of need satisfaction? How might such activities be learned as sources of need satisfaction?

8. In the Ovsiankina experiment cited earlier, the students were interested in tasks of no apparent relevance to their usual activities. How do you account for this fact? In what ways might this situation be similar to some of the learning experiences provided for children in school? Can you expect interest to develop in a comparable manner in these learning experiences? If not, why not?

9. Define each of the following kinds of needs in terms of the behavior from which you would infer the need. Describe the behaviors specifically, and the situations in which you would expect the behaviors to occur.

    a. A need for approval.

    b. A need for affection.

    c. A need for independence.

10. What differences in goals and needs would you predict might characterize the following children? Describe the kinds of behavior you would look for to check your predictions.

    a. A boy whose father is an engineer.

    b. A boy whose father is a steelworker.

    c. A girl whose father is an engineer.

    d. A girl whose father is a steelworker.

11. Dependency needs characterize many young children. In what ways might a dependency need be manifested in the behavior of an older child and an

adult? If you observe behavior from which you infer a need for independence, can you conclude that the person has no dependency needs or that a dependency need was not a motivating force in his behavior at some earlier period in life? In what ways may these two kinds of needs be related?

12. How do you explain Frenkel-Brunswick's finding that girls with strong needs for recognition were characteristically more irritable and selfish? May we assume that girls with this kind of need are more likely to be irritable and selfish?

13. Under what conditions would you use withdrawal of social approval as a means of increasing motivation in a learning experience? What kinds of children might not be motivated by such a procedure? If this procedure did not achieve the desired effect, what explanation would you offer?

14. What kind of behavior in learning experiences would you predict would characterize a child whose mother urged him to be independent? Assume that you observed him to be particularly dependent in school; how would you account for his behavior?

15. Two children are doing poorly in arithmetic. One, however, is achieving below his ability. The other is achieving consistently with his ability. What hypotheses would you offer about the relationship of their "failure" experiences to the kinds of goals they set for themselves? Would they be equally "unrealistic" in their estimates of future success? Would you attempt to provide "success" experiences for the child who is achieving below his ability? What hypotheses are implicit in the procedures you would use with this child?

16. Some people argue that "failure" experiences are necessary, since children will have to meet such experiences "in life." Evaluate this argument in the light of the experimental evidence presented in this chapter.

17. A child is achieving below his ability. Would you place him in a group of students of comparable ability or lesser ability? Formulate the hypotheses implicit in the procedure you recommend.

18. Some people argue that "gifted" students should be grouped together. They maintain that these students will work harder, since they will be in a group for which the expectations will be higher. Does the evidence presented in this chapter support this argument? Would you expect this procedure to achieve its purpose for all gifted students? What other factors might influence motivation in this kind of a situation?

19. Some students claim that they are interested in learning, but not in grades. What needs might characterize such a student? In what ways might he be motivated differently from a student who "works for grades."

20. Below are several *normative* needs. How might a child with a strong need for independence be motivated to strive for the goals involved in these needs?

a. Children need to compute accurately.

b. Children need to know how to read.

c. Children need a knowledge of their country's history.

21. Some people argue that the needs of children are better provided for in the activity program of the school than in the classroom. Would such an argument be valid if the "needs" referred to are normative needs? Psychological needs?

22. Select a simple game with which you are familiar and that you will teach to a fellow student or to an elementary or high school child. Describe the way in which you would introduce the learning of this game to the child or the student. How would you interest him in learning to play? What motives of his are you appealing to?

23. Select a concept or generalization from your major field. Again, construct a motivational strategy to induce the student to learn the concept or generalization. What incentives will you use to induce learning? Are they intrinsic to the nature of the learning activity itself or do they appeal to motives which are not directly related to the learning?

24. You are teaching a class, and you notice that the class seems bored. Is a motivational strategy called for? If so, what would you do? Invent your own situation and apply your ideas to it.

RECOMMENDED READINGS

R. D. Archambault. "The Concept of Need and Its Relation to Certain Aspects of Educational Theory," *Harvard Educational Review*, 27 (1957), 38–62.

J. W. Atkinson. *An Introduction to Motivation*. New York: D. Van Nostrand Co., 1964.

R. Dreikurs. *Psychology in the Classroom*. New York: Harper & Brothers, 1957.

E. R. Hilgard and D. H. Russell, "Motivation in School Learning," in the Forty-ninth Yearbook of the National Society for the Study of Education, Part I, *Learning and Instruction*. Chicago: University of Chicago Press, 1950, pp. 36–68.

K. B. Madsen. *Theories of Motivation*. Cleveland: Howard Allen, Inc., 1961. This book summarizes and compares all modern theories of motivation; it is an excellent reference for the student who wishes to delve deeply into this topic.

D. C. McClelland. *Studies in Motivation*. New York: Appleton-Century-Crofts, Inc., 1955.

N. E. Miller. "Learnable Drives and Rewards," in S. S. Stevens, ed., *Handbook of Experimental Psychology*. New York: John Wiley and Sons, 1951, pp. 435–472.

P. S. Sears and E. Hilgard. "The Teacher's Role in the Motivation of the

Learner," in the Sixty-third Yearbook of the National Society for the Study of Education, Part I, *Theories of Learning and Instruction,* E. Hilgard, ed. Chicago: University of Chicago Press, 1964, pp. 182–209. In the same volume, see also F. T. Tyler, "Issues Related to Readiness to Learn," pp. 210–239.

CHAPTER FIVE

LEARNING AND THE COGNITIVE PROCESSES: CONCEPT FORMATION

Ask that mythical person, the average man, what the schools ought to do for students and he is likely to answer, "Make them think." The prestigious Educational Policies Commission, which periodically has pointed to the significant goals of American education, has most recently urged that the development of thinking processes be recognized as the major task of the American school.[1]

Before this laudable purpose can be realized, we need to be clear on what we mean by "thinking." To some, thinking is being well informed; to others, it means solving problems or inventing or creating. It is used synonymously with reasoning and remembering, interrelating ideas, and evaluating evidence. How many times have you heard a teacher

[1] *The Central Purpose of American Education* (Washington, D. C.: Educational Policies Commission, National Education Association, 1961). See also *Deciding What to Teach* (Washington, D. C.: Project on the Instructional Program of the Public Schools, 1963).

say, "Think carefully" or "Why don't you think!" We are admonished to "think again," "think before you speak," "think twice." Many different kinds of behavior seem implied in these statements. "Think carefully" may mean "Check the data before you draw a conclusion" or "Try to remember" or "There is something elusive or tricky here; so be careful in drawing conclusions." A behavior analysis is required to identify the many kinds of responses implied in the usages of the term *thinking*.

Equally important: How is the teacher to evoke these different behaviors? What kinds of instructional strategies will encourage students to reason, remember, classify, hypothesize, experiment?

Thinking, as used commonly, includes evaluation and personal preference, and thus is not necessarily rational in the logical sense. A man who "thinks" about the United Nations may or may not like the organization; he may make value judgments about it. This distinction has practical importance. As we will see, developing understanding or increasing a student's knowledge about things, events, or people does not invariably produce a change in how he feels about them. His feelings and values may interfere with his ability to grasp ideas or even to remember facts.

In this and the following chapter we will study the cognitive processes and, in later chapters, the attitudinal and evaluative processes. *The cognitive processes are those processes by which man organizes and interrelates the data of experience.* Recall the model of the learning organism described in Chapter 3. The learner is conceptualized as an information-processing organism; he sorts and interprets sensory inputs. The cognitive processes are the responses he makes to sort and interpret this input.

Various kinds of behavior are associated with these processes: (1) *classifying behavior*—concept formation; (2) *interpreting behavior*—the making of generalizations (interrelations among concepts) and application of critical thinking; (3) *associative thinking*—storing of information as a means of interpreting experiences.

These cognitive processes are integral to man's personality. They are dynamic processes influencing the behavior we observe. In this chapter we will consider concept formation; in the following chapter, the learning of generalizations and associative thinking.

WHAT IS A CONCEPT?

✤ A third-grade class is studying a unit on "Ships, Harbors, and Cargoes." In this unit the children are to learn what a "harbor" is. The teacher describes a harbor as a "sheltered body of water having piers." Some teachers might be satisfied if the children are able merely to repeat this description of a harbor. However, if the teacher wants the child to acquire the *concept* of "harbor," a much more complicated process of learning is involved.

PROCESSES INVOLVED IN CONCEPT FORMATION

The formation of a concept is distinguished from the rote memorization of the verbal definition of a concept in the following ways:

1. *Discrimination is required.* The child must be able to distinguish a harbor from other geographical formations—particularly other bodies of water, such as rivers, lakes, seas, oceans.

2. *Generalization is required.* The child must be able to utilize the description of a harbor to identify many examples of harbors. The concept of a harbor is a categorization or a grouping which applies to many different kinds of harbors, each of which is characterized by a sheltered body of water and piers.

A concept, then, is a classification of stimuli that have common characteristics. The concept is not the stimulus itself, nor even the stimulus experience itself, but a *classification* of certain stimuli, events, or characteristics. In using the concept "harbor," a child may be thinking of harbors he has seen, or he may be thinking of the only harbor with which he has had any experience. But the concept is formed when this classification can be extended beyond this single experience or event. Thus, two processes are involved in learning a concept: first, the child *makes discriminations* by which he distinguishes one concept from another; second, he *generalizes* the concept to other examples of it.

In making these discriminations and generalizations, *a person must abstract or infer from the sensory data of his experiences.* If we take a child to see a harbor, he perceives literally thousands of events and phenomena. If the child is to learn the concept of a harbor, however, he must ignore many of these events and focus his attention on others. For example, the size of the harbor is irrelevant to the concept, as is the color of the water. The number of piers, the construction of the piers, the kinds of men employed on the piers, the details of loading and unloading cargo—all must be ignored. The child must focus instead on *selected, specific features*—the sheltered body of water and the piers—and must recognize these as the *defining characteristics* of a harbor. Thus, the process of abstraction or inference in concept formation is essentially one of focusing on the defining characteristics of the concept.

Failures to discriminate lead to misconceptions and consequently to incorrect interpretations. Such errors in discrimination can be made in two ways: (1) by omitting essential features or (2) by including features not essential to the concept. If a child notices a lighthouse located on the shore, and assumes that lighthouses are characteristic features of harbors, he can err in either of two ways. He can identify any formation that has a lighthouse as a harbor, or he can fail to identify as harbors those that do not include a lighthouse. Similarly, the small child who calls every man "daddy" has focused on certain features of his father that are characteristic of other men but do not distinguish his father from these other men. Failure in discrimination in this instance leads to overgeneralization.

Thus, a child may utilize a class or category name, such as "daddy" or "harbor," but still may not have acquired an appropriate concept for that category or class. The process of learning concepts consists of more than memorizing the definitions for class names. Moreover, many concepts learned in and out of school are difficult to define in any precise way; consequently, the processes of discrimination and generalization required to learn these concepts are not easily promoted. Consider, for instance, the teacher's attempt to teach the principles of democracy and the importance of "democratic" behavior in political, social, economic, and interpersonal affairs; "democratic" behavior is not easily defined. Furthermore, such concepts are revised as the child grows up; the meaning of the concept shifts with new associations as the child's field of experience broadens.

FUNCTIONS OF CONCEPTS

Concepts enable the individual to interpret his experiences. The observable behavior of the person will vary with the conceptual interpretations he makes of his environment. The child whose concept of a teacher is defined by such evaluations as harsh, demanding, overbearing, punitive, and unsympathetic will behave differently from the child who sees the teacher as helpful, kind, sympathetic, and rewarding.[2]

[2] H. H. Anderson and J. E. Brewer, "Studies of Teachers' Classroom Personalities, II: Effects of Teachers' Dominative and Integrative Contacts on Children's Classroom Behavior," *Applied Psychology Monographs*, No. 8 (1946). See also P. Sears and V. Sherman, *In Pursuit of Self-Esteem: Case Studies of Eight Elementary School Children* (Belmont, Calif.: Wadsworth Publishing Company, 1964).

Man invents categories necessary to interpret his environment and to deepen and broaden his understanding of the phenomena that he perceives. The principles discussed here have been summarized as follows:

We begin with what seems a paradox. The world of experience of any normal man is composed of a tremendous array of discriminably different objects, events, people, impressions. There are estimated to be more than 7,000,000 discriminable colors alone, and in the course of a week or two we come in contact with a fair proportion of them. No two people we see have an identical appearance, and even objects that we judged to be the same object over a period of time change appearance from moment to moment with alterations in light or in the position of the viewer. All of these differences we are capable of seeing, for human beings have an exquisite capacity for making distinctions.

But were we to utilize fully our capacity for registering the differences in things and to respond to each event encountered as unique, we would soon be overwhelmed by the complexity of our environment. Consider only the linguistic task of acquiring a vocabulary fully adequate to cope with a world of color differences! The resolution of this seeming paradox—the existence of discrimination capacities which, if fully used, would make us slaves to the particular—is achieved by man's capacity to categorize. *To categorize is to render discriminably different things equivalent, to group the objects and events and people around us into classes, and to respond to them in terms of their class membership rather than their uniqueness.* [Italics added.] Our refined discriminative activity is reserved only for those segments of the environment with which we are specially concerned. For the rest, we respond by rather crude forms of categorical placement.[3]

THE LEARNING OF CONCEPTS

The concepts, generalizations, and principles a child learns become a part of his personality, resulting in a personality quite different from that which would develop were he exposed to other concepts and generalizations. These differences in personality structure resulting from different kinds of concept formation vary among cultures and societies and even within the same culture. They also vary from individual to individual within the same society.[4] Every child, for example, learns a concept of

[3] J. S. Bruner, J. J. Goodnow, and G. A. Austin, *A Study of Thinking* (New York: John Wiley and Sons, 1956), p. 1.

[4] Cultural differences in concept formation appear in the generalized "images" people hold about each other's countries. The following studies will be of particular inter-

"my country." The child living in the eastern part of the United States, however, differs somewhat in his concept of "my country" from a child living in the Southwest. The American child, the French child, and the Russian child have different meanings for the concept "native country," because the relevant experiences differ in their own countries. These and other concepts shape the child's orientation to his environment. As these concepts become stabilized, they become difficult to change and become an integral aspect of personality.[5]

The process of concept formation is intimately tied to the total development of the child's personality. The child who is beginning school has already developed a system of concepts and characteristic ways of perceiving and organizing the stimuli from his environment. Learning experiences extend, diversify, and reorganize this conceptual system. As this conceptual system changes, the child's personality changes.

FORMAL AND INFORMAL CONCEPT FORMATION

In this chapter we will discuss principally the learning of *formal* concepts—concepts that the school systematically inculcates, such as electron, photosynthesis, equalitarianism, rationalism, the expanding frontier, states' rights, compound sentence. Each of these and many others are concepts used to interpret the subject matter of different areas of knowledge. These formal concepts differ from those the child acquires informally, in that their meanings have generally been clarified to some extent, and are shared and communicable, whereas the concepts the child acquires informally may be highly subjective and personal.

Children come to school with a system of concepts informally acquired; therefore, the teacher must determine the present stage of concept development of each child and its significance to the acquisition of new concepts. Most "reading-readiness" tests given to kindergartners and first

est to American college students, since they suggest the "images" of America held by college students from foreign lands: C. P. Loomis and E. A. Schuler, "Acculturation of Foreign Students in the United States," *Applied Anthropology*, 7 (1948), 17–34; R. B. Zajonc, "Aggressive Attitudes of the 'Stranger' as a Function of Conformity Pressures," *Human Relations*, 5 (1952), 205–216; W. H. Sewell, R. T. Morris, and O. M. Davidson, "Scandinavian Students' Images of the United States: A Study in Cross-Cultural Education," *The Annals of the American Academy of Political and Social Science*, 295 (1954), 126–135; K. Gezi, *The Acculturation of Middle Eastern Arab Students in Selected American Colleges and Universities* (Washington, D.C.: American Friends of the Middle East, Inc., 1959).

[5] See J. Watson and R. Lippitt, "Cross-Cultural Learning: A Study among a Group of German Leaders," *Institute of International Education News Bulletin*, 30 (1955), 2–5.

graders are essentially tests of concept formation. From these tests the teacher may estimate whether the child has an adequate grasp of concepts for which he will be learning the word symbols. The child entering the primary grade has acquired concepts of many kinds; he has concepts for most of the objects in his environment, such as the persons in his family, his home, the family car, and the utensils he uses. He has also developed relational concepts, such as "inside of," "outside of," "from," "to," "up," "down." He may have only the vaguest grasp of some other kinds of concepts, such as "smaller than" or "larger than." [6]

At any level of education there will be varying degrees of concept formation within any group of children.[7] Even the concepts introduced in school in a systematic manner will be influenced by the kinds of experiences that a child may have out of school. History books frequently emphasize the concept of America as a land of opportunity. A child growing up in the slums and one coming from a better section of the city will not have the same experiences for forming this concept. To the child from the slums, the concept of "opportunity" may very well be no more than a word. He may have no experiential base for the concept symbolized by the word.

INFLUENCE OF PREVIOUS LEARNING ON CONCEPT FORMATION

The child's interpretations of new concepts will be influenced strongly by the concepts he has already developed, both formally and informally.[8] The concept of fractions, for example, is introduced after the concept of a whole number; the child is taught addition of fractions after he has learned the concept of addition of whole numbers. Logical arrangements of this kind are perhaps most satisfactory where the out-of-school experience of the child is not likely to be related to the concepts he is being taught in school, and where the concepts are not likely to have personal

---

[6] For a review of literature on children's number concepts, see W. E. Martin, "Quantitative Expression in Young Children," *Genetic Psychology Monographs,* 44 (1951), 147–219.

[7] For one discussion of this problem, see W. A. Brownell, "Readiness and the Arithmetic Curriculum," *Elementary School Journal,* 38 (1938), 344–354. For a critical discussion of the concept of "readiness," see F. Tyler, "Issues Related to Readiness to Learn," in E. R. Hilgard, ed., *Theories of Learning and Instruction,* Sixty-third Yearbook of the National Society for the Study of Education, Part I (Chicago: University of Chicago Press, 1964), Chapter IX, pp. 210–239.

[8] M. E. Oakes, "Children's Explanations of Natural Phenomena," *Teachers College Contributions to Education,* No. 926 (New York: Columbia University Press, 1947).

and social meanings. When concepts relate to experiences that a child may be having out of school, these concepts may be clothed in emotional and imaginative meanings.

This point may be illustrated by the following experiences of a group of sixth graders. The students were working on a unit on India. The teacher invited a university student from India to speak to the children and to describe his country for them. During the talk the speaker illustrated his points with slides, showing pictures of various scenes in India. In this situation the children were exposed to a wide variety of events relating to "India" in a fairly unsystematic fashion. After the talk, the teacher asked the children to write down their impressions of India. Each child responded in terms of the concepts that he had already developed. Here are some of the impressions of "India" reported by the children after the visitor's remarks:

Wayne: I'm thinking of the sweeping beauty of a temple, its semi-precious stones gleaming in the morning mist, remains of a ruined Buddha in the age-old temple, the creeping vines growing up through the crack in the ancient rock, its huge bulk a monument to the ancient ones who built it.

Ruth: A village home with oxen screeching and stamping up and down the walks.

Sandy: The Taj Mahal with its beauty and luster. The Black Pagoda, cold, black and sinister. The Red Forts, worn with battle but still beautiful. The palaces and the temples all symbolize the want for beauty of the Indian people.

Layne: The people on the boardwalk seemed so natural, the way they were just sitting there, thinking and talking, with children playing. Everything they did was just so natural.

Scott: Drinking water where the cows take a bath seems like eating mud.

Bryan: It was interesting how the man put a cobra and a mongoose together and let them fight. It seemed sort of stupid because he sat with his legs crossed and let the two fight right in front of him. If the cobra struck at the mongoose and missed, he would be bit. Also, the cobra might turn on him.

This rich variety of impressions is all the more striking when we recall that each of these children heard the same words and saw the same pictures. The children had essentially the same stimulus experience, but each child interpreted and selected from the stimuli in terms of his own conceptual system and his attitudes and feelings. One child responds to the beauty of the temples; another, to the awesome sight of a cobra and a mongoose fighting. Another child sees the personal habits of the people as repulsive; still another sees the people as natural and as human as the people he knows.

These children will probably develop concepts about India which have common characteristics. They will remember the Taj Mahal as a large, white, beautiful building. They will know the details of dress and the personal habits of the people of India. In these respects their concepts will be fundamentally alike, but each concept will still have a different meaning for each child. The total system of concepts of each child will be unique because common concepts will have different associations—that is, meanings, feelings, and emotions associated with them.

These variations in the conceptual systems among children influence the learning of any given concept. Too frequently, we assume that the mere presentation of a learning experience guarantees that each child will learn concepts in identically the same fashion. The child who sees the habits of the people as repulsive and the child who sees the people as "natural and human" will make different interpretations about the significance of life in India. The school influences concept formation by controlling the experiences to which children are exposed. While the teacher has little control, if any, over the out-of-school experiences, the teacher may influence the development of concepts by the kinds of experiences he provides for the child in the process of learning a concept.

CONCEPT FORMATION AND APPROPRIATE EXPERIENCE

Concepts cannot be learned without some relevant experience with the phenomena to be conceptualized. The third graders studying the concept of "a harbor" can be provided with a variety of experiences to help them identify a harbor. They may study harbor formations on maps and distinguish these configurations from other configurations illustrated on maps; they may visit a harbor and observe the harbor formation directly; they may watch a film on harbors of the world, which illustrates the essential characteristics of a harbor.

Experience enables the child to make the necessary discriminations. The range of these experiences will vary from those that are direct and immediate to experiences that are more or less remote from the direct sensory experience of the phenomenon being conceptualized. The child studying harbor formations on maps is having a direct sensory experience of maps, but not of harbor formations.

The kinds of concepts children develop will be limited by the kinds of experiences that are available to them.[9] Some experiences cannot be provided for children because they have not reached the stage of development which permits them to participate in the appropriate activity.[10] The primary-grade child does not study international affairs because he does not have sufficient experience with any form of social organization beyond that of his own family. We familiarize him with the concepts of local government, and gradually proceed to concepts of national and international organization when he has experiences from which he can formulate these concepts, or when he can be easily introduced to the relevant experiences.

Social and family conditions provide the child with a set of experiences from which concepts are developed.[11] One of the difficulties in developing geographical concepts, and such concepts as time and distance, may be the relative immobility of the child and his family. A child who has not traveled beyond his own neighborhood, who has never flown in an airplane, who has not traversed large sections of this country, forms his concepts of distance, transportation time, and location from abstract and indirect experiences. It may not be necessary for a child to traverse time zones to develop an understanding of the concept of time zones; many people have a basic understanding of time zones without ever leaving their local community. But many concepts may be difficult for a child to understand because his home, community, and school cannot provide him with the requisite experiences for developing them adequately.

The author had occasion to visit a small school in a farming community. In one of the classrooms visited, the teacher was discussing "white-collar workers." The teacher was trying to convey some idea of what was meant by the "white-collar worker," the conditions of his work and life, and his general social position. In the course of discussion, the author happened

[9] J. M. Deutsche, *The Development of Children's Concepts of Causal Relations,* University of Minnesota Institute of Child Welfare Monographs (Minneapolis: University of Minnesota, 1937); G. M. Peterson, "An Empirical Study of the Ability to Generalize," *Journal of Genetic Psychology,* 6 (1936), 90–114.

[10] Age differences have been consistently found in concept formation: see L. A. Welch, "A Preliminary Investigation of Some Aspects of Hierarchical Development of Concepts," *Journal of Genetic Psychology,* 22 (1940), 359–378; M. G. Colby and J. B. Robertson, "Genetic Studies in Abstraction," *Journal of Comparative Psychology,* 33 (1942), 385–401.

[11] H. Ordan, *Social Concepts and the Child Mind* (New York: King's Crown Press, 1945).

to look out a window and noticed a group of men in front of a feed store across the street. The men in this community were obviously not white-collar workers and probably wore white collars, literally speaking, only on Sundays. In this community the child would probably have difficulty in grasping the concept of a "white-collar worker." He has had no direct exposure to "white-collar workers," to the kinds of communities they live in, or to the kinds of jobs that they perform. In situations like this, the teacher decides, first, what kinds of experiences are likely to generate the concept and, second, whether these experiences can be provided with sufficient ease to justify the consideration of the concept at this time. In some cases, the learning of a concept may be so important that the teacher is willing to use less appropriate experiences, which will help the children to gain at least some understanding of the concept.

STEREOTYPED CONCEPTS

In one sense concepts are "pictures in our heads"; they are impressions, visualizations, representations of phenomena that actually have been observed or about which we know something even though we have not actually observed the person, the place, or the event which we have conceptualized.

Rigid but inaccurate concepts, impervious to experience, are called **stereotypes.** A stereotype is a "fixed impression, which . . . results from our defining first and observing second." [12] Stereotyping occurs when there is "a tendency to attribute generalized and simplified characteristics to a group of people in the form of a verbal label." [13] An individual cannot observe every phenomenon about which he has some concept. Frequently, he must rely on sources of information which may be unreliable or inadequate. A child may have a concept of Negroes, Jews, Russians, Germans, or Turks without ever having seen individuals who belong to these racial, ethnic, and national groups. What associations occur to you when you hear the words "hillbilly," "foreigner," "hick," "square"? Many of these stereotypes arouse strong emotional feelings. Stereotypes are developed because the individual does not think critically, does not observe, does not analyze.

[12] D. Katz and K. W. Braly, "Racial Stereotypes of One Hundred College Students," *Journal of Abnormal and Social Psychology,* 28 (1933), 287.

[13] W. E. Vinacke, "Explorations in the Dynamic Processes of Stereotyping," *Journal of Social Psychology,* 43 (1956), 105.

There seems to be a real difference between analytical, differentiated, and directed thinking or reasoning on the one hand, and the autistic, emotional, uncritical, memory and recognition thinking of stereotyping on the other. In stereotyping it almost seems as though the individual either judges not at all, or does so only via well-worn, dependable, swiftly traversable channels which require a bare minimum of defining, distinguishing, inducing, weighing of evidence, or any of the so-called higher mental processes.[14]

An important aspect of stereotyping is the character of the concepts embedded in the stereotype. Table 5–1 indicates descriptions of national groups according to traits attributed to these groups by college students. Certainly, not all the individuals in each of these national groups has each of the characteristics listed by the students in the study. Not all Negroes are superstitious and lazy, nor are all Chinese superstitious and sly, nor are all Englishmen sportsmanlike and intelligent. Most of the traits attributed to these national and racial groups reflect a vague, undifferentiated, socially shared picture of each of these groups. The concepts involved in these pictures are obviously inadequate and overgeneralized.

Stereotypes represent inadequate conceptualizations, and one of the responsibilities of the educational system is to develop adequate concepts of people, places, and events. The process of changing an individual's prejudices toward a particular group is not simply an intellectual process. Many children's concepts of people and events have developed in a haphazard manner. Other people's ideas and concepts have been accepted uncritically, and the child has had limited opportunity to be exposed to the necessary observation and information to develop adequate concepts.[15] The school serves an important social function by providing children with the experiences necessary to revise their concepts about other racial and national groups, and about individuals, places, and events with which they have had limited, if any, experience.

The conceptual system of the child is one of his interpretative processes, as we have noted continually throughout this chapter. The school's responsibility is to develop this conceptual system, to enlarge it, refine it. By encouraging careful discriminations and generalizations, and by pro-

---

[14] J. Fishman, "An Examination of the Process and Function of Social Stereotyping," *Journal of Social Psychology*, 43 (1956), 34–35.

[15] E. L. Horowitz, "The Development of Attitude toward the Negro," *Archives of Psychology*, No. 194 (1936). M. Radke and J. Sutherland, "Children's Concepts and Attitudes about Minority and Majority American Groups," *Journal of Educational Psychology*, 50 (1949), 449–468.

TABLE 5-1. *The twelve traits most frequently assigned to each of various racial and national groups by 100 Princeton students (from Katz and Braly).*

Traits checked, rank order	No.	Per cent	Traits checked, rank order	No.	Per cent
GERMANS			**NEGROES**		
Industrious	65	65	Superstitious	84	84
Stolid	44	44	Lazy	75	75
Intelligent	32	32	Happy-go-lucky	38	38
Scientifically-minded . . .	78	78	Ignorant	38	38
Methodical	31	31	Musical	26	26
Extremely nationalistic . .	24	24	Ostentatious	26	26
Progressive	16	16	Very religious	24	24
Efficient	16	16	Stupid	22	22
Jovial	15	15	Physically dirty	17	17
Musical	13	13	Naive	14	14
Persistent	11	11	Slovenly	13	13
Practical	11	11	Unreliable	12	12
ITALIANS			**IRISH**		
Artistic	53	53	Pugnacious	45	45
Impulsive	44	44	Quick-tempered	39	39
Passionate	37	37	Witty	38	38
Quick-tempered	35	35	Honest	32	32
Musical	32	32	Very religious	29	29
Imaginative	30	30	Industrious	21	21
Very religious	21	21	Extremely nationalistic . .	21	21
Talkative	21	21	Superstitious	18	18
Revengeful	17	17	Quarrelsome	14	14
Physically dirty	13	13	Imaginative	13	13
Lazy	12	12	Aggressive	13	13
Unreliable	11	11	Stubborn	13	13
ENGLISH			**CHINESE**		
Sportsmanlike	53	53	Superstitious	34	35
Intelligent	46	46	Sly	29	30
Conventional	34	34	Conservative	29	30
Tradition-loving	31	31	Tradition-loving	26	27
Conservative	30	30	Loyal to family ties . . .	22	23
Reserved	29	29	Industrious	18	19
Sophisticated	27	27	Meditative	18	19
Courteous	21	21	Reserved	17	17
Honest	20	20	Very religious	15	15
Industrious	18	18	Ignorant	15	15
Extremely nationalistic . .	18	18	Deceitful	14	14
Humorless	17	17	Quiet	13	13
JEWS			**JAPANESE**		
Shrewd	79	79	Intelligent	45	48
Mercenary	49	49	Industrious	43	46
Industrious	48	48	Progressive	24	25
Grasping	34	34	Shrewd	22	23
Intelligent	29	29	Sly	20	21
Ambitious	21	21	Quiet	19	20
Sly	20	20	Imitative	17	18
Loyal to family ties . . .	15	15	Alert	16	17
Persistent	13	13	Suave	16	17
Talkative	13	13	Neat	16	17
Aggressive	12	12	Treacherous	13	14
Very religious	12	12	Aggressive	13	14
AMERICANS			**TURKS**		
Industrious	48	48	Cruel	47	54
Intelligent	47	47	Very religious	26	30
Materialistic	33	33	Treacherous	21	24
Ambitious	33	33	Sensual	20	23
Progressive	27	27	Ignorant	15	17
Pleasure-loving	26	26	Physically dirty	15	17
Alert	23	23	Deceitful	13	15
Efficient	21	21	Sly	12	14
Aggressive	20	20	Quarrelsome	12	14
Straightforward	19	19	Revengeful	12	14
Practical	19	19	Conservative	12	14
Sportsmanlike	19	19	Superstitious	11	13

viding the experience necessary for the development of a concept, the school, through its teachers, encourages the development of a conceptual scheme which will enable the child to interpret his environment adequately and make the necessary behavioral adjustments to it.

VARIABLES INFLUENCING THE LEARNING OF CONCEPTS

In the preceding sections concepts were described as categories for classifying experience. The person is thought of as a sorter and classifier when he is acquiring concepts. To sort he must first discriminate some features of his experience from others, a process we call abstracting. Second, he must treat things which are quite different in many ways as alike in some features. Usually, one categorizes objects, people, and events by attending to relatively few of their many characteristics. A car buff and the ordinary automobile owner attend to different characteristics of cars. The engineers who build them attend to still other features. However, the underlying psychological processes are the same in all these cases. The owner, the racing enthusiast, the collector of vintage autos, and the automotive engineer each attends to some features of automobiles and ignores others.

The psychological problem is to determine what variables influence a person to attend to certain critical features and ignore the rest. One reasonable hunch is that the instances or examples of the concept will somehow determine what I come to think the concept is.

USE OF EXAMPLES

The process by which the concept *harbor* is acquired, as distinct from memorizing the definition of harbor, consists in presenting the student with both examples and non-examples of harbors. With each presentation the student identifies or discriminates the features which characterize a harbor and, on the basis of this discrimination, classifies a geographical formation as either a harbor or a non-harbor. The examples of the concept are referred to as "positive instances," and the non-examples are referred to as "negative instances," or "positive" and "negative" examples. Negative examples of harbors would be other geographical formations. Some of these formations—for example, mountains or a peninsular formation— quite obviously have none of the characteristics of harbors. Other bodies of water would also be non-examples of harbors, but would have some of the characteristics of a harbor; for example, a lake is a body of water, but it may or may not be sheltered, and may or may not have piers. If a concept is ambiguously defined, or if it shares many characteristics in common with other concepts, discriminating this concept from others, even for the person who has learned the concept, may be a difficult task.

Essentially, the presentation of an example or a non-example of a concept is information giving. Some of the information is relevant to what is to be learned, and some is not. The learner is confronted with a complex sorting task. The problem for the teacher is to present him with sufficient information to facilitate the learning of the concept. The psychological question here is how much relevant information is necessary to learn a concept and how much irrelevant information impedes the learning.

What is the relationship of the examples used to illustrate a concept to the learning of the concept? Would it be possible for a student to learn what a harbor is if we presented him only with examples of non-harbors? Or should we present him only with examples of harbors? Or should we give him both examples and non-examples of harbors? In what order should these examples and non-examples, if we use both, be presented? Should we present all the examples simultaneously, or should we present them one at a time, waiting until the student has acquired all the necessary information for a particular example? Will the third grader understand the concept of a harbor better if we take him out and show him a harbor, or will he understand the concept better if we present him with a series of simplified pictorial representations of harbors? These kinds of questions are psychological questions which can be and have been investigated, and experimental literature provides us with some answers to them.

Non-Examples

Can a student learn a concept from exposure to negative examples only? Practically, this question may seem unimportant, since most teachers would probably build their instructional strategies around positive instances. Experimental study of the question, however, has provided insight into the process of concept formation.

The experimental literature seems to support the conclusion that learners can acquire a concept through negative instances, but the process is slow and not very reliable.[16] Even then, the learning seems to occur only when the subjects have some idea of the number and kinds of dimensions that are relevant. Let us use a simple-minded example to make this point clear. Suppose that you are learning the concept of a horse for the first time. We have pictures of a very large number of objects, and I hand them to you one at a time. You guess which is a horse and which is not, and I tell you when you are correct. If our stack of pictures includes a wide range of objects, your sorting job is extremely difficult. The first picture is an automobile; the second, a house; the third, an apple; and so on. You guess "horse" when I give you the picture of a house. After correction, you have eliminated one class of objects. Is it surprising that the learning is slow? And if I stop after thirty-five pictures, none of which is of a horse, you probably will not learn the concept. Progress appears only when you have some idea of what is relevant, such as animals and quadrupeds.

One explanation proposed for the difficulty in learning from negative instances is that this method places heavy demands on the memory of the learner.[17] He has to remember all the things that are not included in the concept, which usually far exceed the number included. This explanation will be used to account for other difficulties in concept learning. Remember it; we will use it to formulate a general decision rule for constructing instructional strategies.

The above discussion may well leave you with some reservations about using negative instances. However, some problem solutions *are* achieved by the use of negative instances. "Trouble-shooting" frequently requires an elimination or exclusion strategy, in which possibilities are systematically eliminated to find the difficulty. Mathematical proofs are sometimes built by proving what cannot be true to find what must be true. However, in a concept-learning experiment, Braley tried to get his experimental subjects to adopt an exclusion strategy.[18] He arranged the experimental task so that some subjects could learn the concept only in this way. Only two of thirty subjects were able to learn the concept. He concluded that

[16] See K. L. Smoke, "An Objective Study of Concept Formation," *Psychological Monographs*, No. 191 (1932); "Negative Instances in Concept Learning," *Journal of Experimental Psychology*, 16 (1933), 583–588; and "Experimental Approach to Concept Learning," *Psychological Review*, 42 (1935), 274–279. See also C. I. Hovland and W. Weiss, "Transmission of Information concerning Concepts through Positive and Negative Instances," *Journal of Experimental Psychology*, 45 (1953), 175–182.

[17] H. E. Cahill and C. I. Hovland, "The Role of Memory in the Acquisition of Concepts," *Journal of Experimental Psychology*, 59 (1960), 137–144.

[18] L. S. Braley, "Strategy Selection and Negative Instances in Concept Learning," *Journal of Educational Psychology*, 54 (1963), 154–159.

learners either cannot or will not use negative information efficiently for acquiring concepts.

He speculated that exclusion strategies are "higher-level" problem-solving strategies, which place considerable load on memory processes. A reasonable hypothesis from his data is that exclusion strategies, when required for problem solving, must be formally taught. A teacher cannot expect students to adopt them without instruction.

Combining Examples and Non-Examples

One general principle of sequence arrangements can be given. If students learn a concept through examples, they are typically better at recognizing examples than non-examples. If they practice on non-examples, they are better at recognizing non-examples than examples.[19] In learning with positive instances or examples, the learner is making discriminations of the appropriate characteristics of the concept. However, non-examples provide him with information also, since they expose him to phenomena which have none or only some of the characteristics of the concept. Two kinds of discrimination are required to learn a concept: (1) discrimination of the appropriate characteristics; (2) discrimination of the inappropriate characteristics. More experience with either kind of discrimination produces greater facility in making that kind of discrimination.

We cannot say that to teach a concept we must present only positive instances, or only negative instances, or a mixture of positive and negative instances. Students differ in their ability to profit from these kinds of series; however, more students prefer a mixture of positive and negative instances.[20] If negative instances are presented early in the learning sequence, they apparently confuse some students. The student does not have a sufficiently adequate grasp of the essential characteristics of the concept to be helped by the addition of a negative instance. Negative instances have a corrective value, however, and can serve as a checking device once the student has a reasonably adequate grasp of the basic dimensions of the concept. The introduction of negative examples tends to increase accuracy in discrimination.

The fact that some students prefer positive instances and others prefer mixtures of positive and negative instances suggests that the manner in

[19] A. H. Buss, "A Study of Concept Formation as a Function of Reinforcement and Stimulus Generalization," *Journal of Experimental Psychology*, 40 (1950), 494–503.
[20] Data are largely suggestive; consult studies cited in notes 16 and 19.

which students learn concepts tends to be individualized. There are probably some students who can learn better from the presentation of positive instances of a concept; others, from a mixture; still others, from a large proportion of negative instances in a series. The teacher arranges the presentations of the examples for a group, and usually does not know which student is likely to profit from a particular kind of sequence. Under these conditions a larger proportion of positive instances probably should be used in initial phases of learning a concept. As the learning progresses, negative instances may be introduced to ensure accuracy by facilitating the student's checking the correctness of his concept.

Number of Examples

How many examples should a teacher use in inducing concept learning? Superficially, it may appear that the more examples provided, within limits imposed by fatigue and boredom, the better the learning. This hypothesis, however, does not fit with our model of the learner. The model we use here assumes that learning depends on the information available to the learner and the amount of feedback he receives as he utilizes this information. Repeated examples would be effective only if they provided additional information and opportunities for corrective feedback.

The problem of how many examples to use seems to be one of carefully specifying what is to be learned. We will use the concept of *local kin group* to illustrate this specification problem. A local kin group may be defined as the largest group in the society whose members are related and live together. Such groups include families, clans, and larger groups called "demes," in which fifty or sixty related individuals reside together under one roof. The concept is illustrated by these many instances. Ordinarily, the teacher hopes that the student will be able to identify the full range of cases as examples of local kin groups. To get the idea across, he may arbitrarily provide many instances of the nuclear family (mother, father, children) and joint families. But he expects the students to make the correct identifications of clans and demes as local kin groups.

If the teacher wants errorless recognition of nuclear and joint families as local kin, his best strategy probably is to give many instances of each of these until the concept is grasped. If he expects transfer to clans and demes, and other organizations, he probably ought to reduce the number of instances in the interest of greater variety.

Two kinds of learning appear to be involved: (1) learning within the problem—for instance, grasping the concept of local kin by intensive study of nuclear and joint families; (2) transferring across problems—for instance, generalizing what has been learned to new cases like clans and demes. Mastery of the first task facilitates but does not guarantee mastery of the second. Increasing the variety of instances facilitates the second process.

Two strategies seem possible: (1) intensive training on the initial examples, followed by some training on additional cases; or (2) training across all the cases. Which of these is the more effective strategy is not known, and it seems unlikely that either would be for all kinds of concepts.

One other hypothesis on the number of examples is relevant. Consider a concept like *adjective*, which is usually defined as any word that "qualifies" a noun. Because of the inclusiveness of the word "qualifies," the learner must ask himself whether a particular word gives a quality, or specifies, or distinguishes—operations indicated in hundreds of different ways. To acquire such a concept, because of the abstruseness and number of discriminations involved, he would probably require relatively large numbers of examples.

Complexity of Examples

Focusing on essential characteristics. If we take students to a harbor with little or no introduction to the concept of a harbor, and then expect them to learn what a harbor is, we are presenting them with a complex problem in discrimination. They will have an extremely difficult task in sorting out the many stimuli and determining the essential characteristics of the concept. A teacher can simplify the problem by accentuating the *essential characteristics* of the concept; experimental evidence suggests that this may facilitate concept learning.[21] He may, for example, begin a discussion of harbors with a brief descriptive statement used as a definition. Then, using diagrams and pictures, he can give examples and non-examples of harbors. Finally, on a visit to the harbor, he can point out the essential characteristics. At each step the teacher is focusing the child's attention on the essential characteristics of a harbor. The teacher can also use the children's questions to keep the essential characteristics in

[21] C. L. Hull, "Quantitative Aspects of the Evolution of Concepts," *Psychological Monographs*, No. 123 (1920). Z. Y. Kuo, "A Behavioristic Experiment on Inductive Inference," *Journal of Experimental Psychology*, 6 (1923), 247–293.

focus. If a child asks, "Do harbors have lighthouses?" the teacher can point out that this is not an essential characteristic of a harbor.

An experiment [22] illustrates the utility of accentuating essential characteristics. Two groups of biology students were to learn how to identify the parts of flowers. One group was given "real" flowers and was taught the parts with the real flowers as examples. The second group was presented with a large and simplified diagram of the parts of a flower, from which the parts were to be learned. The students using the diagram learned the parts of a flower more accurately and easily. They also were able to generalize their knowledge to real flowers better than the first group.

Some educators will argue that simplifying the examples of concepts deprives the student of contact with the richness and variety of the phenomena being studied. The issue here is not whether the child is deprived of richness and meaning, but at what point in the learning sequence the child should be exposed to all the shadings and meanings that may be associated with a concept. The experimental evidence suggests that in the *initial* phases of concept learning, simplicity and clarity in the examples used will facilitate the learning of the concept. Once the differentiating characteristics of the concept have been grasped adequately, variety in meaning and association may be introduced. The child who has some concept of what a harbor is has already enriched his knowledge, and is able to cope with the complexities of a "real" harbor. He can develop a wealth of associations and interpretations, and can interpret his environment much more easily and efficiently if he has had a systematic understanding of the characteristics essential to the concepts.

The issue is not between learning from textbooks and learning from "real-life experiences." We do not know as yet what experiences are most likely to facilitate learning of many concepts. The teacher will undoubtedly use a variety of experiences, but the whole experience must be simplified so that the essential characteristics of a concept can be determined easily by the child.

Realistic versus simulated experiences. Initial learning of concepts in "real-life" situations may complicate learning because of the threatening nature of some real-life situations. Marks and Ramond [23] performed an experiment in which concepts were evoked in two different situations,

---

[22] G. W. Boguslavsky, "Psychological Research in Soviet Education," *Science,* 125 (1957), 915–918.

[23] M. R. Marks and C. Ramond, "A New Technique for Observing Concept Evocation," *Journal of Experimental Psychology,* 42 (1951), 424–429.

described as "real life" and "textbook." The subjects in the experiment were to form a complex size-position concept from a series of stimuli presented on cards. In the "real-life" situation, the subject performed the task with the cards by himself. In the "textbook" situation, the experimental subject was asked to help a person described to him as performing the task in a real-life situation. The concept-formation task was essentially the same for both groups, except that the subjects in the "real-life" situation actually performed the task themselves by manipulating the cards. The "textbook" group produced significantly more correct solutions at a significantly higher rate than did the "real-life" group. Marks and Ramond suggest that the "real-life" situation may inhibit the subjects. The "real-life" situation may be so complex that it is threatening to the subject; consequently, it may inhibit him in making analyses so that he does not adequately form the concept. Thus, when we expose students to "real-life" situations, we should give some preparatory introduction to the nature of the concept, so that the inhibiting effects of some real-life situations might be reduced.

Lifelike experiences have certain advantages that should not be overlooked. A visit to a harbor may be more motivating, and stimulate greater interest in the concepts to be learned, than would merely pictorial or graphic representations of harbors. The teacher can weigh the advantages to be gained, in motivation and interest, against those to be gained by simplicity and clarity of presentation of a concept. Here, again, the teacher operates as a hypothesis maker. Rather than utilize one kind or set of experiences, he can manipulate the experiences of the students so that the advantages of the various kinds of experiences may be maximized in the total learning. One set of experiences may produce motivation and interest, while another set of experiences may facilitate accuracy and ease in learning. A judicious combination and integration of experiences will produce the greatest amount of learning.

From simple to complex concepts. School practice typically builds from simpler to more complex concepts. The definition of a harbor given to the third-grade class presupposed that the third graders had already learned the meaning of such concepts as "sheltered," "body of water," and "piers." If the third graders did not understand these concepts, could they have learned the concept of harbor as easily or as quickly as a group that had adequate meanings for these other concepts? Common sense suggests that they could not.

Experimental evidence partially corroborates this common-sense notion. Kendler and Vineberg [24] used three groups of college students to study the acquisition of a complex concept, which was based on two simpler concepts. The first group learned the two simple concepts; the second group learned one of the simple concepts; and the third group learned neither. Then all three groups were tested on their ability to learn the complex concept. The group that had learned the two elements of the compound concept learned the compound concept fastest; the group that had learned one element was next in speed; and the group that had learned neither of the simple concepts was the slowest. This experiment demonstrates that the compound concept can be learned even though the elementary concepts have not been previously learned, but that the learning process is less efficient. The greater time spent in learning a compound concept—without previous experience with the concepts composing the compound concept—does not result in greater accuracy of learning.

PRACTICE AND CONCEPT ACQUISITION

Quite frequently, in learning situations, concepts are not introduced one at a time, but many concepts are introduced more or less simultaneously. The sixth-grade class that heard the talk on India was exposed to a large number of concepts. We would expect that the newer concepts would not be easily assimilated without additional learning experiences.

In learning concepts, would the learning be better promoted by working intensively on the acquisition of the concepts, or by spreading the learning out over a period of time? Oseas and Underwood [25] tested the effects of **massed** (that is, concentrated) **practice** versus **distributed practice** on learning concepts. Distributed practice produced faster learning than did massed practice, although retention of the concept was high under both sets of conditions. In later discussions on the effects of practice, the student will note that this conclusion is appropriate for practice in other kinds of learning.

The experimental data suggest that concept formation will be facilitated by repeated study of a concept over periods of time. Concepts will be learned accurately and easily if they are repeatedly used as new

[24] H. Kendler and R. Vineberg, "The Acquisition of Compound Concepts as a Function of Previous Training," *Journal of Experimental Psychology*, 48 (1954), 252–258.

[25] L. Oseas and B. J. Underwood, "Studies of Distributive Practice: V. Learning and Retention of Concepts," *Journal of Experimental Psychology*, 43 (1952), 143–148. See also B. J. Underwood, "Ten Years of Massed Practice on Distributed Practice," *Psychological Review*, 68 (1961), 229–247.

learning is taken up. Too frequently the concepts taught are treated as discrete units which may never be used again. Repeated use of concepts enhances learning.

One way to ensure repeated use of concepts is to organize the curricu-

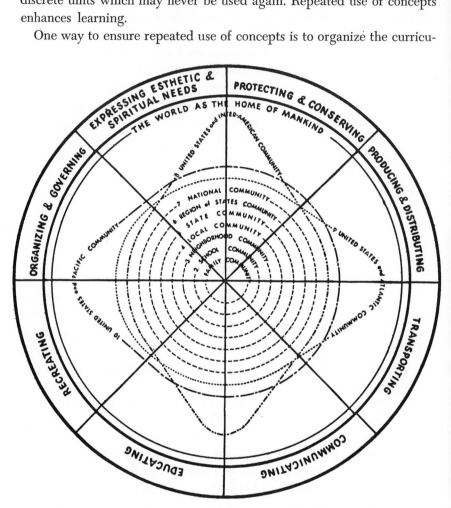

FIGURE 5–1. A social studies curriculum design (from Hanna).

lum around basic concepts. A proposal for organizing the social studies curriculum [26] divides human social activities into eight categories (see Figure 5–1). Each of these categories is a complex concept for interpreting social activity. These categories are used throughout the social studies

[26] P. R. Hanna, "Society–Child–Curriculum," in C. W. Hunnicutt, ed., *Education 2000 AD* (Syracuse, New York: Syracuse University Press, 1956).

program as particular societies are studied. For example: the first-grade child studies the family; the second-grade child, the school; the third-grade child, the community. They also analyze the activities of these various communities in terms of the basic concepts. As these concepts are used again and again, concept learning is strengthened. Also, new meanings and associations are developed for the concepts.

Such a curriculum arrangement incorporates a number of principles discussed above. The child learns the concept from his present experiences; the experiences are progressively more complex, but built on previous learning; the concepts are not mere memorized abstractions, but rather are ways of interpreting the environment.

REINFORCEMENT AND CONCEPT ACQUISITION

Reinforcement has a significant effect upon the learning of concepts. In an experimental situation, a reinforcement is an operation, arranged by the experimenter, that "rewards" a correct response. The experimenter, for instance, might reward a response by saying "That's right."

Carpenter [27] studied the effects of reinforcement on the learning of concepts. He formed four groups of students and had them learn a set of concepts, using simple materials. The reinforcement used in this experiment was the experimenter's statements, "That's right" or "That's wrong." In the first group, the experimenter reinforced a correct response—that is, a correct identification of an example of the concept—every fourth time. In the second group, every other correct choice was reinforced; in the third group, every correct choice was reinforced; in the fourth group, correct and incorrect choices were reinforced. (See Table 5–2.)

What is the effect of reinforcement on the learning of concepts? Does

TABLE 5–2. *Percentage of trials reinforced for each of four groups (from Carpenter).*

Group	No. Ss	Per cent of correct trials reinforced	Per cent of incorrect trials reinforced
1	23	25	
2	23	50	
3	23	100	
4	23	100	100

[27] F. Carpenter, "Conceptualization as a Function of Differential Reinforcement," *Science Education,* 38 (1954), 284–294.

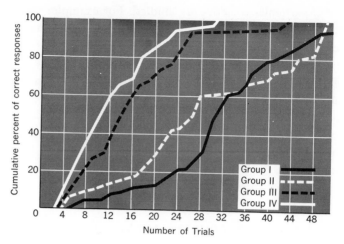

FIGURE 5–2. *Cumulative per cent of subjects reaching criterion by groups as a function of the number of trials (from Carpenter).*

the fourth group learn more quickly and easily than the first group? The results of this experiment indicated that the fourth, the group most frequently reinforced, learned the concept in the fewest number of trials and in the shortest amount of time. These results are shown graphically in Figures 5–2 and 5–3.

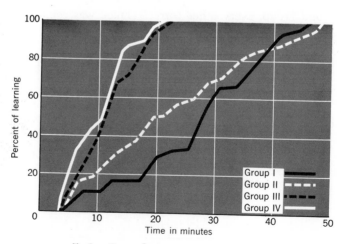

FIGURE 5–3. *Cumulative per cent of subjects who reached criterion as a function of time in minutes (from Carpenter).*

The foregoing experiment indicates the importance of reinforcement for the learning of concepts. The student should not conclude that for the learning of every concept complete positive and negative reinforcement must be given for every correct and incorrect use of the concept. We do not know what schedules of reinforcement will produce the most efficient learning for any and every kind of concept. However, the experimental data do suggest that frequent reinforcement is an important factor in the learning of concepts. Carpenter concluded:

This study suggests, together with what is already known, that the teacher may find profit in: (1) Being certain that the desired response is performed before assuming that learning has occurred. (Far too often teachers seem to operate on the assumption of osmosis and that this absorption of knowledge will guarantee sufficient transfer to the level of application.) (2) Noting the various responses that compose a skill, act, or complex behavior, and making sure that ample reinforcement is contiguous with them instead of rewarding only end results. This suggests that *we focus attention upon the behavioral processes instead of only products* (p. 293—Italics added).

Another characteristic of the reinforcement, or feedback, process is the speed with which it is given. For instance, in some classrooms students answer questions on paper and receive the corrections some time later. Sax [28] found that delaying the feedback increased significantly the number of trials required to learn the concept. The significant difference was between the group that had no delay but only 50 per cent feedback and the group that had 100 per cent feedback and a forty-minute delay. The latter group required twice as many trials to learn the concept. Delay of informative feedback, then, does not improve concept acquisition and probably impedes it.

VERBALIZATION AND CONCEPT ACQUISITION

Carpenter's experiment also provides evidence on another important aspect of conceptual learning. We frequently assume that a child has not acquired a concept unless he can verbalize it. However, 72 of Carpenter's subjects were able to operate with the materials in a manner indicating that they had learned the concepts, although only 18 per cent of these were able to verbalize the defining characteristics of the concepts. Other experimenters have observed the same phenomenon.[29]

[28] G. Sax, "Concept Acquisition as a Function of Differing Schedules and Delays of Reinforcement," *Journal of Educational Psychology,* 51 (1960), 32–36.
[29] C. L. Hull (see note 21) and K. L. Smoke (note 16).

The assumption that the child does not understand unless he can verbalize is consistent with the emphasis placed upon defining and memorizing in the schools. An important psychological and educational problem is to explain why subjects who apparently have mastered the concept cannot define it. Carpenter suggests an explanation:

> . . . that the non-verbal learning required establishment of different responses than the verbal learning and that it is not necessary to expect 100% transfer from one to the other. Also, there was no systematic reinforcement of verbalization during learning. But it is quite possible that Ss verbalized implicitly such that reinforcement was "sometimes" associated with the correct responses. Since S was told to seek for the identifying characteristics of each class, it may have been that much implicit verbalization accompanied the overt movements.[30]

An experiment by Johnson and O'Reilly confirms Carpenter's hypothesis that two different response modes are involved in classifying and verbalizing.[31] These investigators thought that poor verbalization is sometimes found in concept-acquisition experiments because the subjects are not required to verbalize their definitions during the experiment. They arranged an experiment to find out whether defining during learning yields better and more definitions. One group classified pictures of birds, discriminating between two kinds of birds. A second group classified verbal descriptions of the two kinds of birds. A third group classified pictures, but after each fifth card was asked to define the differences. The results were interesting. The group classifying verbal descriptions took few trials to criterion; that is, after a fewer number of trials they were able to make errorless classifications of the verbal descriptions. The picture-only group took the largest number of trials. If "good definitions" are compared, both the verbal group and the pictorial-defining group produced significantly more good definitions. The interesting comparison is that between the pictorial and the pictorial-defining groups, since it illustrates the necessity of training on the defining task. The pictorial-defining group gave almost twice as many good definitions. The investigators suggest that the verbal group found the verbal material easier to classify.

That some of the difficulty in defining may be attributed to the characteristics of the concept being defined is suggested by an experiment by

---

[30] F. Carpenter (see note 27), p. 292.

[31] D. Johnson and C. O'Reilly, "Concept Attainment in Children: Classifying and Defining," *Journal of Educational Psychology*, 55 (1964), 71–74.

Wilder and Green.[32] These investigators thought the difficulty in verbalizing a concept may result from shifting symbols. That is, sometimes (as in a mathematics class) subjects have to manipulate numbers, and then tell what they did in words. Does this shift from one kind of symbol or manipulation to verbal definition account for poor performance at the verbal task?

To test their hypothesis, Wilder and Green first had children watch two plants grow, one under light, the other in shade. After two weeks of watching the plants, the children were asked to describe and explain the differences. Half of them were to draw and half to write. When they finished this task, the experimenter introduced two other plants similarly treated but which the children had not watched. The instructions were the same, but half of those who drew now wrote, and half of those who wrote now drew. Four groups were formed in this way: one which wrote both times, another that drew both times, one which first wrote then drew, and a fourth which first drew then wrote.

When the investigators looked at each task separately, they found that for the first task those who drew differences to *describe* them did better than those who wrote about them. But those who wrote to *explain* the differences did better explaining than those who tried to draw an explanation. This second effect was also found on the second task. Wilder and Green argue that their data support the hypothesis that shifting from one medium to another, words to pictures and pictures to words, made describing and explaining in words more difficult.

Some of these difficulties seemed to arise because words or pictures were not available for ideas. How do you draw "because," for example, or express an abstraction like causality in pictures? The description of the specific differences is a comparably difficult task, placing great demands on one's vocabulary. Try describing the differences between two leaves in words.

These experiments are suggestive of the probable sources of difficulties in concept-learning tasks. The task of defining the concept, after exposure to instances of the concept, requires special training. Some of this training may be simple vocabulary acquisition, learning the words to describe the relevant characteristics or relations among characteristics. It probably also involves learning what constitutes an appropriate definition.

In the less artificial atmosphere of the classroom, the teacher who

[32] N. Wilder and D. Green, "Expressions of Concepts through Writing and Drawing and Effects of Shifting Medium," *Journal of Educational Psychology*, 54 (1963), 202–207.

expects the child both to acquire the concept and to be able to define the characteristics of the concept must teach for both kinds of responses. Reinforcement also will be beneficial in the learning of the verbalization. Thought should also be given to the special demands of the defining task. The phenomenon to be defined may be difficult to describe in words. The teacher decides on the importance of the defining task and what levels of performance may be regarded as adequate.

INSTRUCTIONAL STRATEGIES
AND CONCEPT LEARNING

If concept formation is to be facilitated, students will need a variety of examples of the concept. Accentuation of the important defining characteristics of the concept, simplification of the stimulus, preparation by training on basic concepts, and reinforcement of correct responses made in learning concepts tend to enhance the learning of concepts. The process, as well as the end result of learning concepts, is important. Reinforcement should not be postponed until the concept can be correctly defined, or even correctly used, but should be applied throughout the learning process to facilitate learning. Errors in concept formation are opportunities for learning, rather than mistakes to be dismissed or merely punished. An error in the process of acquiring a concept is an opportunity for revising the student's understanding of the characteristics of the concept.

In the process of concept formation, the child is performing as a hypothesis maker. The child formulates hypotheses about what he thinks the concept is. He then tests these by applying the concept correctly or incorrectly to examples and non-examples of it. Concept formation is an active process on the part of the learner. Concepts are much more efficiently acquired when the child is active (that is, formulating hypotheses about the nature of the concept and testing them) than if he acts merely as a passive recipient of stimuli.[33]

The first step in constructing instructional strategies to facilitate concept formation is selecting the experiences from which the concept is to be learned. How would you help a child grasp the concept of "county"? What phenomena are to be grouped in this category? Typically, teachers will define concepts of this kind. The definition simply points out the characteristics to be attended to in sorting stimuli. We want the child to dis-

[33] G. M. Della Piana, "Searching Orientation and Concept Learning," *Journal of Educational Psychology*, 48 (1957), 245–253.

criminate between cities and counties, between counties and states. To achieve these discriminations we need to know what stimuli are likely to prompt the desired sorting responses.

There is little experimental evidence to help the teacher make selections of this kind. Solving these problems requires hypothesis making and testing. The teacher must try different arrangements of experiences and evaluate their effects on the child's grasp of the concept. Instructional devices like books, field trips, movies, definitional statements are ways of presenting experiences hypothesized to be relevant to the learning task. Their use should be approached in the same hypothetical and critical spirit.

Although we do not know the particular experiences necessary for learning the multitude of concepts embraced in the school curriculum, we have made progress in identifying the variables influencing concept acquisition. The teacher may assess his selections by the degree to which they are likely to enhance the influence of these variables.

THE CRITERION BEHAVIOR

How do we know that a child has, in fact, acquired a particular concept? The criterion behavior, the behavior by which we judge that a concept has been learned, is the classifying responses the learner makes when required to sort stimuli. The simplest form of this behavior is the identifying response, in which the learner correctly labels instances of the concept. Another response by which we judge concept acquisition is identifying the non-exemplars of the concept. Figure 5–4 contains some examples of test items measuring concept acquisition.

LEARNING GOALS

The teacher decides on an acceptable classifying and identifying performance as the goal for the instructional strategy. This decision requires some thought about the range of instances and non-instances the learner will be expected to classify correctly. Here are some concepts selected at random from a history text: "capital," "trustee," "rebate," "philanthropy." How many instances of each of these concepts will the student be expected to identify? The range may be small or quite large, depending on the purposes that learning the concept will serve. In the chapter in which these concepts are introduced, the authors are describing different kinds of business organizations and methods of holding and distributing money.

The teacher, like the author, may find that a few instances are sufficient to explain the concept so that generalizations may be understood. Some concepts are so important that extensive identification of instances is desired.

The empirical character of this problem cannot be overlooked. The teacher judges the "cognitive worth" of a concept; how useful and logically necessary is it in developing understanding? The question of how many instances to provide is, however, decided by experimenting.

Each of the following items tests grasp of a mathematical concept:

1. Which of the following drawings suggests the fraction ¼?

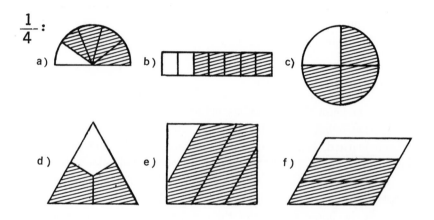

2. If the associative law [a(bc) = (ab)c] and distributive law [a(b + c) = ab + ac] are applied to △(□ + ○), which of the following statements are true?

(a) △(□ + ○) = □△ + ○
(b) △(□ + ○) = △ + □○
(c) △(□ + ○) = □△ + △○
(d) △(□ + ○) = □△ + ○△
(e) △(□ + ○) = (□ + ○)△

3. Applying the same idea, 42 may be written as

(a) 2(5 + 6)
(b) 5(2 + 6)
(c) 6(2 + 5)

FIGURE 5–4. *Test items measuring concept acquisition.*

PATTERNS OF CONTROLLING STIMULI

Recall that a basic idea stressed throughout this chapter is that the arrangement of instances of the concept is an important determinant of what is learned about the concept. Can we state what arrangements are likely to be most effective? Research on this problem is not very far advanced; so the ideas that follow are extrapolations. Treat them as hypotheses to be tested and patterns to be modified.

You already know some variables that should be considered in devising stimuli arrangements: number of instances, pattern of exemplars and non-exemplars, reinforcement ratio for identifying responses made by the learner, distinctiveness of relevant cues, and practice arrangements. An arrangement of stimuli in a concept-formation task requires varying all of these variables in some way. Some teachers argue that a good, hard example is worth many simple ones. Others argue that a few simple examples and three or four hard ones ought to do the job. Each of these decision rules, unrealistically prescriptive though they may be, describes patterns that some teachers predict will be effective. This section broadens your conception of relevant decision rules like these.

In concept-formation studies the experimenter plays a game somewhat different from the teacher's strategies. The experimenter makes the concept-acquisition task "hard" in some respects. He does not tell the learner what to look for except by the ways he presents stimuli. The learner may in some experiments select the instances from a pool to test a hypothesis which the experimenter confirms if he is correct. When this methodology is used, the selection strategies of the learners may be studied.

Suppose that we conduct a modified experiment here. The objects in Figure 5–5 illustrate a particular concept; that is, each object *may* illustrate the characteristics of the concept. Scan the figure to see whether you can identify the concept. As you do, keep a record of the steps you took. After you think you have identified the concept, answer the following questions. Are there any non-exemplars of the concept? If so, when did you identify them and how did you use them? What was your first hypothesis? When did you first think of it? How did you check it out? Did you study all of the figures first, and then check the hypothesis against each figure? Or did you make a guess from one figure and then test it successively against each of the others? The concept is "spherical surface," of which there are six positive instances and three negative instances.

Bruner reports a series of studies in which the methodology was similar to that employed in the above task.[34] He found that his experimental subjects could be classified into two kinds: *scanners* and *focusers*. A *scanning* strategy is identified by these behaviors: (1) the learner formulates a hypothesis and looks for instances of it; (2) he formulates new hypotheses as the original is disconfirmed. A *focusing* strategy is identified by these behaviors: (1) the subject picks a positive instance of the

Concept-formation diagram

FIGURE 5-5. *Objects illustrating a concept.*

concept and systematically varies its characteristics; (2) he changes hypotheses in relation to the positive instance, the focus.

Our experiment put you at a disadvantage since you had no way of knowing which examples were positive instances. In an experiment the subject is told when a figure illustrates the concept. Allowing for this disadvantage, were you a scanner or a focuser? A focuser probably would select one of the simpler figures such as the globe, and guess "round." His

[34] J. S. Bruner, J. J. Goodnow, and G. A. Austin, *A Study of Thinking* (New York: John Wiley & Sons, 1956).

next step is to check each of the figures against this guess. If his "round" hypothesis were not confirmed, he would stay with the focus instance but hypothesize from another of its characteristics, such as "spherical" or "large." A scanner might guess "objects to hold food," and then look for instances of this concept. Since only two other figures illustrate this concept, he would abandon it and try a new hypothesis. The difference is that the focuser works out from one example until he gets the concept, whereas the scanner keeps varying and checking his hypotheses until he hits the right one.

Is either of these selection strategies more efficient than the other? Bruner found in one of his experiments that scanners needed thirteen selections on the average to acquire the concept; focusers only five. Scanners made more redundant choices; that is, selections that gave them information they already had. Bruner summarizes these differences:

. . . modified focusing strategy is more efficient than modified scanning for attaining concepts when the instances are perceptually unavailable. Its superiority over scanning rests in its relative freedom from exacting memory and inference demands. *The superiority becomes the more marked when the amount of cognitive strain inherent in the task is increased* (p. 96—Italics added).

The general principle derived from these studies and to be used in constructing instructional strategies is that any pattern which reduces cognitive strain is likely to be effective and efficient. **Cognitive strain** means that the concept-acquisition task requires complex sorting behaviors, complicated hypothesis testing, and considerable remembering of information to sort and test.

Bruner had two parts to one of his experiments. In the first part, subjects looked for the concept with the instances in front of them. They worked two problems this way. The board with the instances was then removed (becoming *perceptually unavailable*), and they worked a third problem. The thirteen choices required by scanners was for this problem—an increase of three over the number required for the first two problems. The five choices needed by focusers was the same number as that required for the first two problems. For both kinds of problems, focusers were more efficient, and scanners became less efficient when they had to scan "in-the-head."

Cognitive strain may be described operationally by manipulation of variables that increase the discriminativeness of relevant cues and by stimuli arrangements that reduce the amount of information a learner has to retain as he progresses through the learning sequence. Practically, the teacher has to experiment with particular patterns applying these ideas. To make decisions, the teacher asks himself, "How do I increase the distinctiveness of the concept's characteristics, and how do I reduce the amount of information the learner has to carry to identify these characteristics?" A general decision rule for constructing instructional strategies may be formulated: Increase the availability and distinctiveness of the concept's characteristics, and reduce the amount of information to be remembered during the learning sequence.

DEDUCTIVE AND INDUCTIVE STRATEGIES

Concept-formation studies require a learner to induce the characteristics of the concept from the instances available. Informative feedback is given in a very limited way: this instance does or does not represent the concept. Teachers typically use a **deductive strategy.** They define or give a representative example of the concept as a focus, then supplement it with additional examples. The inductive strategy is less common as an instructional strategy because it is time-consuming. What are the effects of the two strategies comparatively?

This problem is discussed at greater length in the following chapter, since we want to consider it in relation to the development of cognitive systems. Summarily, inductive strategies are likely to produce greater transfer effects. The learner can apply his understanding to a greater variety of instances of the concept. Assuming that this is a consistent effect of **inductive strategies** (which we cannot say it is with a high degree of certainty at this time), the decision alternatives seem clear. One alternative is a reasonably adequate grasp of the concept with some loss in transfer power. The other is greater transfer power with whatever losses in additional concept formation may accrue from the time required for the strategy. The choice, then, depends on at least two factors: (1) the "logical worth" of the concept being learned and (2) its "psychological worth" in facilitating additional concept learning. The second alternative is obviously a matter for empirical test.

SUMMARY

This chapter describes the process of concept formation and the variables that influence the learning of concepts. Concept formation is one aspect of cognition—the process by which man organizes and interrelates data of his experience. Cognitive processes include *classifying behavior, interpreting behavior,* and *associative thinking.*

1. A concept is a classification of stimuli that have common characteristics. The acquisition of a concept requires *discrimination* of the characteristics of the concept and *generalization* of these characteristics to many particular instances of them. These processes of discrimination and generalization require that a person abstract and infer from sensory data of his experience.

2. Irrespective of the precision or vagueness of the concept, and whether the concept is learned *formally* as in school or *informally* as in the course of everyday experience, concepts serve as the means by which a person consistently interprets his environment.

3. Concepts apparently are learned relatively early in life. Learned concepts influence the acquisition of new concepts. The learned concepts serve as devices for sorting information, and this sorting process determines the way in which the person will organize new information into new concepts. In all cases, concept formation requires some kind of experience, either direct and immediate or abstract and symbolic, with the phenomena that are categorized in a concept.

4. Concepts formed on the basis of limited or inadequate experience with a phenomenon are called *stereotypes.* A stereotype is a fixed impression which results from defining first and observing second; that is, a person does not check his observations with his conceptions or his conceptions against his observations. Stereotypes of people are of personal and social significance because of their behavioral consequences in personal interactions. Many stereotypes of other people include characteristics which are not highly valued.

5. People learn concepts by sorting information from *examples* and *non-examples* of the concept. A *positive example* or instance of a concept contains the defining characteristics of the concept; a *negative example* does not. The learner acquires information from both positive and negative examples. From the former he learns what the characteristics are; from the latter, what they are not.

6. In organizing examples and non-examples for learning, teachers customarily provide many instances that illustrate the concept. Research indicates that the concept may be learned through negative instances, but the process is very slow and relatively unreliable. Learning from negative instances places too great a demand on the memory capacities of the learner. However, sometimes (as in trouble-shooting) the learning of

negative instances is a required strategy; here, the learner must be taught how to use negative instances in an exclusion strategy.

7. Rules for constructing instructional strategies which are combinations of positive and negative examples are not available. Evidence supports the hypothesis that individuals vary in their preferences for such combinations.

8. The number of examples to be used depends upon the type of concept involved. Providing many similar instances of a concept probably increases grasp of its defining characteristics. Providing a variety of instances of the concept probably promotes using the concept more broadly.

9. The learning of a concept may be facilitated if the examples of it are simplified. One of the problems in learning concepts from "real-life" experiences is that these experiences present very complex stimuli for the learner to sort. Also, these experiences may be threatening. A reasonable hypothesis is that initial learning may be facilitated by simplified and less lifelike examples. Breadth and depth of comprehension may be facilitated in the later stages of learning by more complex and lifelike stimuli. Similarly, when a concept may be broken down into more simple concepts, learning is facilitated if the learner proceeds from the simple to the complex; however, he can sometimes learn the more complex concepts without necessarily proceeding through the simpler ones.

10. Concepts that are frequently used are more likely to be retained. Reinforcement during the acquisition of concepts strengthens the learning of the concept. Generally, the more immediate the reinforcement for correct concept identifications, the more quickly the concept is learned.

11. Teachers are concerned that a child be able to describe a concept as well as make correct concept identifications in nonverbal ways. A concept may have been acquired even though the learner cannot verbalize all of its characteristics in a definition. One reason for the low correlation that is sometimes observed between correctness of identification and ability to describe the concept may be the result of genuine difficulty in finding words to define the concept. The behavior of defining in words the characteristics of a concept must be specifically taught for.

12. Instructional strategies designed to promote concept formation develop the concept by providing the learner with examples and non-examples, prompting, identifying responses by him, and reinforcing correct identifications. The criterion behavior by which concept acquisition is judged is the ability to make correct identifications of the concept. The precise number and range of the relevant identifications must be defined

by the teacher as part of the task of defining the behavioral objective of the concept-learning tasks.

13. There is some experimental evidence to support the general hypothesis that a concept-formation strategy which reduces *cognitive strain* is likely to be more efficient. The teacher can utilize this principle by presenting examples which clearly delineate the principal features of the concept and prompting the students to focus their attention on these examples.

14. Two general strategies—one an *inductive strategy*, in which the learner infers the characteristics from examples; the other a *deductive strategy*, in which the defining characteristics are described and the learner applies the definition—may be used. Generally, inductive strategies produce a greater ability to transfer what has been learned to new instances of the concept, and the concept may be retained longer. However, an inductive strategy is generally slow because of the amount of sorting activity demanded of the learner. The teacher chooses the amount of time to be spent in the learning of the concept in proportion to the importance of learning the concept thoroughly and the extent to which the concept will be used in later learning.

STUDY AND DISCUSSION QUESTIONS

1. List the major concepts in some course or subject you are likely to teach. Describe the defining characteristics of these concepts. What examples of these concepts would you use?

2. Analyze this list and the accompanying descriptions to determine to what extent the learning of any one concept is likely to facilitate the learning of other concepts. Explain in what way the learning of one of these concepts is likely to facilitate the learning of another concept. What hypotheses about concept formation are implicit in your stated relations?

3. Teachers frequently encourage learning of the concepts associated with cooperative behavior. How would you define "cooperation"? What kinds of experiences are likely to facilitate learning the discriminations and generalizations required to learn this concept? How would you determine that a child had acquired the concept of cooperation? If a child is cooperative, may you assume that he has learned the concept? Would you make a distinction between "being cooperative" and understanding the concept of cooperation?

4. Suggest some kinds of experiences from which children might infer the characteristics of the following concepts. What features of the stimulus events that you describe will have to be ignored? Do not recommend such unde-

fined kinds of experiences as "take a field trip." Be specific about the character of the experience.

a. Equal rights.

b. Sportsmanship.

c. "Hard work."

5. Describe some kinds of experiences that might have influenced a child's idea of these concepts. In what way might these previous associations interfere with or facilitate the learning of these concepts?

6. List some negative examples of the above concepts. What information is a child likely to acquire by learning that these are negative examples of the concepts?

7. Suggest some negative examples of the following concepts. Describe some ways in which they may be used to facilitate learning of these concepts:

a. Odd number.

b. Circular.

c. Flat.

d. Into.

8. Experimental evidence suggests that some students find concept learning easier with positive examples than with negative examples. What factors in their previous experience might account for this preference?

9. Assume that a child is developing a concept of "fair play." He is exposed, in the course of events, to quite a few negative instances of the concept, but fewer positive instances. How might these experiences influence the learning of other concepts in addition to that of "fair play"?

10. What kinds of experiences may have influenced a child to see members of some national or racial group as "sly," "superstitious," and "dirty"?

11. Under what conditions is information which contradicts a person's stereotyped thinking likely to influence a change in his thinking?

12. Is there a stereotype of the teacher? What factors might influence acquisition of such a stereotype by students?

13. Select a concept sufficiently simple that it may be taught in a relatively short period of time. Describe the defining characteristics of this concept. Devise a set of examples and non-examples for this concept. Construct a strategy for presenting these examples to several learners. Test the strategy, using, as a measure of learning, the number of trials (separate presentations of examples or non-examples) required to learn the concept.

14. Repeat the same experiment varying the reinforcement ratio. With several learners, give immediate reinforcement for every correct identification. For

several other learners, give reinforcement for every third correct identification. Now compare the number of trials for both sets to achieve the concept.

15. Using the subject matter with which you are familiar, select a key concept and define in behavioral terms the criterion by which you will recognize that a learner has achieved this concept. You should be specifying the kinds of identifications that the learner is expected to be able to make. Under what conditions are these identifications to be made? Have you simply asked the learner to repeat a definition of the concept?

16. Using a topic in a subject matter with which you are familiar, map out the principal concepts a student would need to learn in order to understand the major ideas of this topic. Then arrange these concepts in order of their relationship to each other, so that concepts which appear first in the order are necessary to learning of concepts which appear later in the order. What characteristics are transferred from the simple concepts to the more complex ones?

RECOMMENDED READINGS

W. A. Brownell and G. Hendrickson. "How Children Learn Information, Concepts, and Generalizations," in Forty-ninth Yearbook of the National Society for the Study of Education, Part I, *Learning and Instruction*. Chicago: University of Chicago Press, 1950, pp. 92–128.

J. Bruner. "The Act of Discovery," *Harvard Educational Review*, 31 (1961), 22–32.

J. Bruner, J. Goodnow, and G. Austin. *A Study of Thinking*. New York: Science Editions, Inc., 1962.

Roger Brown. *Words and Things*. Glencoe, Illinois: The Free Press, 1958.

E. B. Hunt. *Concept Learning: An Information Processing Problem*. New York: John Wiley and Sons, 1962.

R. C. Johnson. "Linguistic Structure as Related to Concept Formation and to Concept Content," *Psychological Bulletin*, 59 (1962), 468–476.

R. Leeper. "Cognitive Processes," in S. S. Stevens, ed., *Handbook of Experimental Psychology*. New York: John Wiley and Sons, 1951, Chapter 19.

D. H. Russell. *Children's Thinking*. Boston: Ginn & Co., 1956, Chapters 5 and 8.

C. M. Solley and G. Murphy. *Development of the Perceptual World*. New York: Basic Books, Inc., 1960.

W. E. Vinacke. "The Complexities of Thinking," *Psychological Bulletin*, 59 (1962), 450–456. In same issue, see I. Maltzman, "Motives and the Direction of Thinking," pp. 457–467.

CHAPTER SIX

LEARNING AND THE COGNITIVE PROCESSES: GENERALIZATIONS AND ASSOCIATIVE THINKING

In Chapter Five we discussed concept formation as one kind of cognitive process. We assume that concept formation is an essential ingredient in the development of cognitive processes. However, concepts are not discrete units stored in a child's head in some kind of mental filing system. Concepts are used to facilitate the kinds of cognitive processes that we will describe in this chapter: reasoning, the acquisition and use of generalizations or principles, and associative thinking.

These processes, like concept formation, enable a person to interpret his environment. A child who has learned that the evaporation of a liquid increases directly with the temperature of the liquid has acquired a principle he can use to understand such diverse phenomena as the drop in level of boiling water and the drying of creek beds in summertime. Such simple associations as "a red light means stop" prepare him to cross streets on his own. Here we will again be concerned with the variables in learning environments which influence the development of these cognitive processes.

THE ACQUISITION OF GENERALIZATIONS

Children are continually acquiring generalizations by making inferences from their experiences. A child who is warned repeatedly "not to speak out in class" may formulate the principle that "speaking out in class will be punished." He may, however, formulate another principle: "Expressing one's thoughts or feelings is undesirable." Irrespective of the appropriateness of either of these generalizations, the child has carried out essentially the same process in arriving at each of them. He has observed a number of events, he has conceptualized or categorized them, and he has related these sets of events to each other. The first principle states a relationship between a concept called "speaking out" and another concept called "being punished." The second principle is of the same general character.

DEFINITION OF A GENERALIZATION

A **generalization** is *a statement of relationship between two or more concepts.* The statement that "particles with charges of opposite sign attract each other" states a relationship between charged particles of opposite sign. Another example is the well-known generalization "The force of attraction between two bodies is directly proportional to the product of their masses and inversely proportional to the square of the distance between them." Three concepts—force, mass, and distance—are utilized in this generalization, and the relationship between them is a functional one stated in terms of proportionality.

A generalization is meant to be applied to more than a single event. The concepts included in the generalization refer to categories, and the statement of relationship between these categories is meant to be a relationship that applies to all particular instances of the concepts. For example, the generalization that the volume of a gas varies directly with the temperature of the gas applies to all particular instances of volume changes and temperature changes and to any gaseous substance. The child who has inferred that "good boys get good marks" will apply this generalization to different examples of "good boys" and many kinds of "good marks."

LEVELS OF UNDERSTANDING GENERALIZATIONS

A generalization can be learned simply by memorizing it. A student can memorize that "democracy flourishes when a free press is maintained." Many generalizations are learned in this way. The psychological process involved in acquiring principles at this level is essentially that of remembering. However, we wish to emphasize *the distinction between remembering a statement of a principle and understanding the principle.* The student's ability to repeat a generalization is not an adequate measure of his understanding of the generalization.

When understood, a principle can be applied in many instances. For example, the child *understands* the generalization "Volume and temperature of a gas vary directly" when he can use it to explain the increase in pressure in a tire on an automobile that has been driven for several hours. Similarly, a student understands principles about the relationships between wages and prices when he can explain the phenomenon of inflation by using these principles. The generalization "Democracy flourishes when a free press is maintained" is meaningless unless the student can use this principle to explain the relationship between the rise of a dictatorship and suppression of a free press. The important psychological question for the teacher is—"How can learning experiences be organized to facilitate the acquisition of generalizations at this level of understanding?"

ACQUIRING GENERALIZATIONS BY DEDUCTION AND INDUCTION

When a child learns a generalization, he organizes his experience into patterns which enable him "to make sense" of this experience. Generalizations can be developed in two ways: (1) by **deductions** from other generalizations; (2) by **inductions** from observations. The kind of reasoning used in geometry is a good example of the first process. Using such generalizations or assumptions as "Things equal to the same thing are equal to each other," we can develop other generalizations, such as "Equal central angles subtend equal arcs on the circumference of a circle." The cognitive process used in such derivations is that of logical reasoning: a person begins with a generalization and by logical reasoning arrives at other conclusions, which are themselves generalizations.

In the induction process a person begins with a set of observations and, on the basis of the observations, develops a generalization which appears either to explain or to predict the pattern of relationships that he has observed. Suppose that a teacher wants the children to learn the principles of the lever. He could begin by placing a board on a fulcrum; then he could place objects of different weight on each side of the fulcrum and balance the board by moving the objects to or away from the fulcrum until the board balances (see Figure 6–1). Such a demonstration could be carried out easily with pennies as weights, since the weight on each side of the fulcrum could be manipulated by adding or subtracting pennies. The teacher could have the children record the weight of pennies used on each side and the distance of the stack of pennies from the fulcrum. The

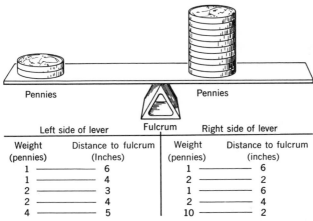

Left side of lever		Right side of lever	
Weight (pennies)	Distance to fulcrum (Inches)	Weight (pennies)	Distance to fulcrum (inches)
1	6	1	6
1	4	2	2
2	3	1	6
2	4	2	4
4	5	10	2

From the specific measurements can you generalize a quantitative relationship which is true for any condition?
Can you check the generalization with another example and observation? What degree of confidence do you have in making predictions from your generalization?

FIGURE 6–1

child now has a set of observations from which it is possible to infer a general principle about levers. The child might note that the lever balances when the heavier stack of pennies is moved closer to the fulcrum. The teacher now may develop the idea that the products of each weight times its distance from the fulcrum are equal. He could point out, for example, that "one times four equals two times two," using the data from the second observation.

As another example, assume that a teacher wishes to have students learn the generalization "Adjectives modify nouns." If the teacher presents a series of examples of words modifying nouns and then asks the children to *infer* the definition of an adjective, the children will use inductive processes to arrive at this definition. On the other hand, the teacher could define what is meant by an adjective, and then have children identify examples of adjectives. The second procedure encourages children to use deduction to develop an understanding of the principle. The method of stating definitions or generalizations and then requiring students to find examples or to check examples and non-examples of the generalizations is a fairly common teaching method. An important psychological question is, "Which of these two processes, induction or deduction, is likely to develop a clearer understanding of the generalization?"

RELATIVE EFFECTIVENESS OF INDUCTIVE AND DEDUCTIVE PROCESSES

The effects of using deductive or inductive processes in learning generalizations have not been adequately explored.

In an early study, Winch compared learning under conditions that encouraged inductive thinking and under conditions that encouraged deductive thinking.[1] The study did not demonstrate the general superiority of either method. Children taught by the deductive method did better when they were tested on the kinds of materials they had used in learning the generalization. However, the inductive method proved superior when children were tested on new but related materials. When children had learned a generalization by induction, they were able to use the generalization to interpret new material.

A related problem that has been explored is the relationship between "rote learning" and "meaningful learning." In a study of subtraction, Brownell and Moser compared learning by meaningful versus learning by mechanical procedures.[2] They compared the effectiveness of two methods of subtracting: the decomposition and the equal-additions methods. Both methods were taught in two different ways to 41 experimental classes. Some students were taught to use the methods mechanically. Other students were taught "meaningfully"; that is, subtraction was explained to them and they learned *why* the method led to correct results. On tests of accuracy given at the end of the learning experience, as well as six weeks later, groups that had learned by the "meaningful method" were superior in subtraction processes to groups that had learned by the mechanical method.

[1] W. H. Winch, *Inductive versus Deductive Methods of Teaching: An Experimental Research* (Baltimore: Warwick and York, 1913).

[2] W. A. Brownell and A. G. Moser, *Meaningful versus Mechanical Learning: A Study in Grade Three Subtraction* (Durham, N. C.: Duke University Press, 1949), Duke University Research Studies in Education, No. 8.

However, one interesting conclusion from this study illustrates that the differences in performance cannot be explained solely in terms of meaningful versus mechanical learning. In learning by either method, the students had used two-digit numbers. They were then required to subtract three-digit numbers. Those who had learned by the decomposition method were superior in applying their knowledge in this new task. In other words, although methods that emphasize understanding generally produce better results, some methods or approaches to content are more comprehensible than others. Processes which are taught meaningfully so that students are likely to understand them contribute to the development of superior performances. Research evidence generally supports the hypothesis that teaching "for meaning" is superior to teaching by rote methods; however, the teacher should distinguish between a process that he is able to explain and a process that the students are able to understand.[3]

Inductive and deductive strategies can be used in combination with a variety of other instructional procedures. They can be used for only some of the learning desired. A teacher may use an inductive strategy to start students on the learning of a principle. He may begin with a deductive strategy for some concepts and switch to an inductive one for others.

Recently, psychologists and educators have been urging that inductive methods be more widely used—mainly through "discovery-learning" techniques. The interest in this idea justifies a detailed analysis of the many conceptions included under this heading and an evaluation of the research to date and its implications for teaching.

DISCOVERY LEARNING

In the last ten years a remarkable and exciting series of curricular innovations has swept through the schools. Each of these programs has introduced new content into the curriculum. And, more important, each innovation has *reorganized* the conceptual structure of a discipline for presentation to elementary and high school students. **Set theory,** for example, used in teaching arithmetical and algebraic concepts is a conceptual tool for organizing mathematical concepts formerly taught as discrete and independent units. The argument is that conceptual organi-

---

[3] See C. L. Thiele, *The Contribution of Generalization to the Learning of the Addition Facts* (New York: Columbia University Press, 1939), Teachers College Contributions to Education, No. 763.

zations of breadth and power will produce greater understanding and appreciation of mathematical concepts and mathematical thinking. This argument is a general hypothesis about the relation between the structure of cognitive stimuli and ease, depth, and transferability of cognitive learning.

Simultaneous with the development of the new curricula has been a resurgence of interest in the processes by which cognitive behaviors are acquired. The cognitive processes of principal interest are those that require a learner to invent ideas, to sort complex stimuli, to make guesses, to test hunches, to ask questions. Correspondingly, ways of stimulating these processes in the classroom are being constructed. Heuristics, intuitive thinking, inquiry training, discovery learning are methodologies strongly recommended as necessary to achieve the goals of the innovations. These goals are described by Bruner:

Mastery of the fundamental ideas of a field involves not only the grasping of general principles, but also the development of an attitude toward learning and inquiry, toward guessing and hunches, toward the possibility of solving problems on one's own. . . . To instill such attitudes by teaching requires something more than the mere presentation of fundamental ideas. . . . it would seem that an important ingredient is a sense of excitement about discovery—discovery of regularities of previously unrecognized relations and similarities between ideas, with a resulting sense of self-confidence in one's abilities.[4]

To achieve these goals the learning experience must be structured to stimulate discovery, inquiry, invention, and to produce generalizing and organizing behaviors. **Discovery learning** is the label given to a set of methodologies designed to produce these behaviors. In this section we analyze critically this set of procedures.

The operations involved in discovery learning are essentially variations on what we have called inductive learning. The deductive and inductive processes can be distinguished in the following way. In the deductive process, the child is given the rule or generalization and must discover for himself many of the instances to which the rule or generalization applies. In the inductive process, the child discovers for himself the generalization as well as the instances to which the rule applies. To what extent do factors fostering discovery of a generalization influence the learning of this generalization and transfer of it to new instances?

[4] J. Bruner, *The Process of Education* (New York: Vintage Books, 1963), p. 20.

EXPERIMENTATION ON DISCOVERY LEARNING

Kersh experimented with the effects of independent discovery as compared to direction in discovery of a generalization.[5] He reasoned as follows: "If meaningful learning is the key concept, it should make no difference whether learning occurs with or without direction, so long as the learner becomes cognizant of the essential relationships. However, some learning procedures may be superior to others simply because they are more likely to cause the learner to become cognizant of the relationships" (p. 282).

Kersh set up three experimental groups to work on a series of problems involving arithmetical and geometrical relationships. The first group, called the "no-help" group, was required to discover the rules for working the problems without any assistance from the experimenter. The second group, called the "direct-reference" group, was given some direction, in the form of visual aids that would help to clarify the problems, and verbal instructions that directed their attention to the visual aids. The members of the third group, called the "rule-given" group, were told the rules directly and were given practice in applying the rules; they were not helped to understand the arithmetical or geometrical relationships involved in the problems. In this experiment, notice that the first two groups were to learn by inductive processes. The third group was to learn in a mechanical or rote way.

The results of the experiment suggest that the group called the "direct-reference" group, the group which received some direction in discovery, did understand the relationships involved somewhat better than did the other groups. The "no-help" group was, however, superior to the "rule-given" group. The experiment confirms that a procedure which facilitates meaningful learning is superior to rote learning. The results also suggested that transfer of learning to new situations was facilitated by independent discovery.

Kersh gathered data on students' motivation for the tasks at hand. After the experiment, the students were asked why they worked problems in certain ways, why they were unable to recall rules or generalizations when working on new problems, and how they felt about the learning situation. Kersh concluded that the students in the "no-help" group

[5] B. Y. Kersh, "The Adequacy of 'Meaning' as an Explanation for the Superiority of Learning by Independent Discovery," *Journal of Educational Psychology*, 49 (1958), 282–292.

appeared to be better motivated to continue working on the problems than were students in the other groups. While all students were motivated by external kinds of reward, such as the approval of the experimenter, the students in the "no-help" group developed an interest in the problems as such. One student in the "no-help" group reported that he was so intrigued with his success in discovering the rules that he told his friends of his experiences and tried out the problems on them. Other students in the "no-help" group went to the library in an effort to find formulas that would be useful in working the problems.

A second experiment by Kersh illustrates the complexity of the processes involved in discovery learning.[6] His results are important to a critical analysis of the methodologies now being used in and recommended for the new curricula. In this experiment three treatments were used: (1) a guided-discovery treatment, operationally similar to the direct-reference treatment in the first experiment; (2) a rote-learning treatment, comparable to the rule-given treatment; and (3) a directed-learning treatment, in which the subjects were taught the generalizations and given an explanation of them. A "no-help" group was not used in this experiment. To eliminate **practice effects** over the intervals, Kersh broke each of his treatment groups into subgroups of ten subjects each: one set took the tests three days after the experiment; the second set, three weeks later; the third, six weeks later. The behavior measured after the experimental treatments was recall of the generalizations, **transfer** of them to new problems, and self-reports of how frequently the generalizations had been used in the intervening period.

The results of the recall and transfer measures are reported in Table 6–1. Of the ten subjects who took the tests three days later, seven in the rote-learning group applied the rules correctly; six in the guided-discovery group did so also. A test of statistical significance indicates that the distribution of the subjects in these cells is non-chance. Recall what reasoning we go through with this information. We reject the hypothesis of no difference among the groups, and tentatively assume that the obtained differences may be attributed to the effects of the experimental treatments.

The surprising result in this experiment is that the rote-learning group was superior in applying and recalling the generalizations. However, the experiment was conducted to compare the guided-discovery and directed-learning groups; the rote-learning group was used as a control group. The

---

[6] B. Y. Kersh, "The Motivating Effect of Learning by Directed Discovery," *Journal of Educational Psychology*, 53 (1962), 65–71.

guided-discovery group was superior to the directed-learning group. The effects on continued use of the rules independently are in line with expectations but meager. Eleven out of thirty subjects in the guided-discovery treatment reported continued use, but only two in the directed-learning and six in the rote-learning groups.

In this experiment it appears as if the attempt to produce greater understanding was not highly effective. Kersh's explanation is intriguing, in part because he may be giving us a clue to the relative ineffectiveness of

TABLE 6–1. *Number of subjects (of 10 in each cell) who used and stated rules correctly on the retest (from Kersh).*

Treatment Groups	Used Rules*		Stated Rules*	
	Odd Nos. 1	Constant Diff. 2	Odd Nos. 3	Constant Diff. 4
Rote learning				
3 days	7	7	7	9
2 wks	7	6	2	6
6 wks	4	4	0	3
Guided discovery				
3 days	6	6	8	9
2 wks	3	5	3	4
6 wks	2	3	3	3
Directed learning				
3 days	4	3	3	4
2 wks	4	3	1	3
6 wks	0	3	1	1

* These rules, algorithms for adding series of numbers, are the rules that the subjects were taught, the principle of which some discovered.

teaching procedures thought to produce understanding. In the directed-learning treatment subjects were given the generalization and then had it explained to them. Kersh argues that this second activity, explaining, was an interpolated activity and interfered with retention. There were two learning tasks—rote grasp of the rule, and understanding of it. Placing the tasks in close contiguity produced inhibition of learning. There is no way of knowing whether this explanation is correct. It is plausible.

What may we conclude from these experiments? First, explanation does not necessarily produce understanding (an obvious but frequently ignored point). Second, understanding and discovery methods do not necessarily prolong retention. They may be expected to prove superior to rote methods when understanding has been achieved.

An important point is only suggested by these experiments. We cannot assume that a seemingly reasonable method of improving understanding does in fact improve it. In Kersh's second experiment the students' guided discovery was more effective than a carefully prepared and seemingly clear explanation. Obviously, in manipulating complex processes of the kind involved here careful task analysis is required.

The clearest effect appears in both experiments and should not be overlooked. Both a strong (no-help) and a weak (guided) discovery condition had better than average motivational effects. This increased interest presumably stimulates additional practice, which in turn facilitates learning.

Given our present state of knowledge about discovery learning, we may hypothesize that learning by independent discovery is likely to facilitate more comprehensive understanding; however, not all students in the "no-help" group were able to discover the generalization unaided within the time provided. Two factors may influence the probabilities of students discovering generalizations without help: (1) their general level of intelligence and (2) the amount of time provided for attempts at discovery. In general, learning through inductive processes appears to take longer than learning the applications of a given rule or generalization.

CURRICULAR STUDIES USING
DISCOVERY METHODS

The experimental studies discussed and cited above are short-term studies. The learning experience is limited. In studies conducted over a longer period of time, stronger effects might occur. Data on this point are meager.

Suchman has conducted an extensive **inquiry-training** study.[7] His experience is illuminating. First, a brief description of his method. Each training session begins with a demonstration on film. For example: a bimetallic bar is heated, it bends, it is plunged into water, it straightens

---

[7] J. R. Suchman, *The Elementary School Training Program in Scientific Inquiry* (Urbana, Ill.: University of Illinois Press, 1962).

out. The bar is turned over; the steps are repeated, except that this time the bar bends upward. The film concludes with the question "Why does the bar bend?" Another example is given in Figure 6–2.

In the discussion following the film, the teacher answers questions only with a "yes," "no," "maybe." He is a "responsive environment" for the learners as they test their hypotheses. The verbal feedback tells the children something about the validity of their hunches. The teacher also

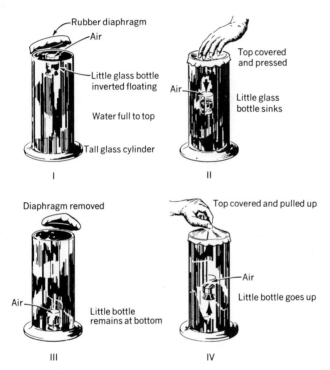

Why does the little bottle go down and then come up again?

FIGURE 6–2. *A problem scenario used to prompt inquiry.*

provides some guidance by helping a child out of difficulty when he has adopted a misleading strategy—but only by making clear the nature of the difficulty. After each session, the teacher conducts a critique to bring the children's attention to the inquiry strategies they have used.

Suchman's inquiry training was not a part of the regular classroom activity. The sessions were conducted only one or two times a week. Teachers conducting the inquiry sessions, although receiving some training, had only two practice sessions before beginning the training in their own classrooms. Each of these limitations probably weakened the power of the training.

Suchman compared two groups on tests designed to measure the students' understanding and use of the method of inquiry and their knowledge of specific scientific content. One group was made up of the children in the inquiry-training classes. The other group was composed of children in comparable classes in the same school but who had not had the inquiry training. Groups were located in twelve different schools.

One result was largely suggestive. Experimental groups in two schools obtained higher scores on a test measuring knowledge of content, the differences closely approaching significance. This is worth noting because the experimental groups had not had specific training on the content. However, it would be presumptuous to make too much of this slim reed of fact. The effect was not predicted. Why it occurs in some groups and not others is not clear. The suspicion is that it is an incidental effect. Other results were that the children with training were more fluent, asking 50 per cent more questions about the test problems. They also asked more analytical questions in contrast to diffuse questions.

The lack of differences between the two groups on what Suchman called product scores was the most disappointing result. Each of these scores measured what the child had learned as the "product" of the inquiry training. For example, in querying about any of the problems, the child could have learned the physical principles underlying the demonstrated phenomenon. A more complex kind of acquisition, similarly a product of inquiry, is recognizing the necessary conditions for the events occurring in the problem episode, and knowledge of the relevant parameters of the problem. See Figure 6–3 and the accompanying text for illustrations of both the problem and the test items. The children's responses were scored to produce three product scores on which the two groups, experimental and control, did not differ.

You may wonder why we bother to discuss nonsignificant differences. Because finding out what may be expected from this kind of training is important; because this kind of work may lead us somewhere even though these initial forays are disappointing; because this particular set of facts may be a badly needed antidote for readers infected with the "mystique" of discovery learning, as Ausubel calls it.[8]

---

[8] For a critique of discovery learning and related concepts, see D. Ausubel, *The Psychology of Meaningful Verbal Learning* (New York: Grune and Stratton, 1963), pp. 139–175. See also F. J. McDonald, "Meaningful Learning and Retention: Task and Method Variables," *Review of Educational Research*, 34 (1964), 530–544.

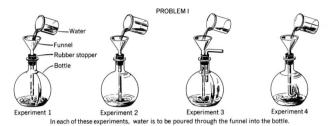

In each of these experiments, water is to be poured through the funnel into the bottle.

Part A. In which of the experiments will the bottle fill up with water most quickly?
1. Experiment 1.
2. Experiment 2.
3. Experiment 3.
4. Experiment 4.

Part B. Which of the following is necessary for the bottle to fill up with water?
1. The cork must fit tightly into the mouth of the bottle.
2. The liquid must be water or some other liquid that absorbs air.
3. There must be some way for the air in the bottle to escape.
4. The bottom of the funnel tube must always be higher than the water level in the bottle.

Part C. Which is the best rule to explain the correct answers to Parts A and B?
1. Water always flows down hill.
2. Water and air cannot occupy the same space at the same time.
3. Air absorbs water.
4. The flow of water is always from a high pressure to a low pressure.

FIGURE 6–3. *Problems and questions used to test effects of inquiry training (from Suchman).*

EVALUATION OF DISCOVERY LEARNING AS A TEACHING TECHNIQUE

The healthy and vigorous interest in discovery learning has been accompanied by strong claims for its effectiveness. As happens all too frequently in education, discovery learning has been offered, or at least taken, as a panacea for all the ills of indifferent, uninspired, rote teaching and poorly conceived organizations of subject matter. Let us look back over this exposition of both the experimental data from short-term studies and from Suchman's longer-term analysis.

The studies do indicate that the "discovery" learner is more interested in the instructional activity and the problem. He is more involved in the work, participates actively, and gets added practice because he is motivated to study the problem independently. We expect and predict that these factors will enhance learning. They appear to, but the amount of the effect is disappointing. One wants the discovery children to show a heady grasp of the principles, quick and easy facility in getting to the core of a new problem. Why are the effects so meager?

One reason may be that any one form of these methodologies prompts only some of the responses desired. One kind of training may be effective for producing more question asking than hypothesis testing, or more information seeking than hypothesis making. It does not follow that a procedure effective in producing one kind of response automatically produces other kinds.

Another difficulty is that we do not know what the response components are of the behavior we want to produce. Ultimately, a discovery method seeks skills and knowledge which will transfer to many other problems. What does one have to learn to be this generally effective when confronted with a new problem? We know so little about the response system we hope to produce that our training procedures may be irrelevant.

With the exception of the no-help condition in Kersh's study, inquiry training is essentially a highly controlled process of guided discovery. When the discovery is carefully programmed, it proves to be an effective method.[9] Probably the most reasonable conclusion at this stage of research is that inquiry training in the form developed by Suchman is effective in producing one of the necessary skills in cognitive behavior— that is, the learner learns to ask the kinds of questions that help him define the problem. He probably also in some ways learns to hypothesize. However, inquiry training does not, and probably will not in its present general format, produce organized and detailed knowledge of content. Transfer effects, which are expected to be the most attractive effect of such methods, have been weak but apparent. Ausubel suggests why discovery methods may produce transfer effects.

If learning by discovery promotes transfer in some unique way, it probably does so through the transferable experience of independently formulating and testing alternative hypotheses and through the transferable attitude of independent search. It still has to be demonstrated, however, that such experience and attitudes are transferable across disciplinary lines.[10]

[9] See R. M. Gagné and L. T. Brown, "Some Factors in the Programming of Conceptual Material," *Journal of Experimental Psychology*, 62 (1961), 313–321.
[10] Ausubel (see note 8), p. 161.

The functions of the teacher in this process are generally clear. First, he provides the stimulus conditions for searching and testing behavior; second, he acts as a feedback device, providing information on hypothesis testing. This last feature is characteristic both of the role of the experimenter and the inquiry trainer, but their function has been severely limited in studies. The effects of modifying and varying the kind and amount of feedback are unknown, and provide a fertile field for inquiry for the interested teacher and for the research specialist.

Suchman's comments about his experiment apply to other proposals for new discovery strategies:

One of the biggest dangers that accompanies each new teaching method that enjoys some measure of success is that it will be accepted rigidly and uncritically and used only in a limited sense. The Inquiry Training tested in this study can certainly be improved and adapted in many ways.[11]

COGNITIVE ORGANIZATION

The resurgence of interest in cognitive behavior has brought into sharp focus the problem of organizing subject matter and learning tasks. This problem may be described by applying the model of the learning organism presented in the third chapter. This model assumes that the learner has coding and sorting mechanisms, which determine how he uses the stimuli available to him. These coding and sorting behaviors are themselves acquired. An instructional system needs to provide for these responses by anticipating the ways in which the learner will react to stimuli. However, for relatively unfamiliar material, coding, sorting, and organizing responses are more directly under the control of the teacher. In these situations, the child learns the organization emphasized in the stimuli as they are presented to him—partly because the stimuli presented to him limit what he may do, and in part because the teacher rewards adopting the organizational principle presented.

A distinct issue is the question of the relative effectiveness of different kinds of organizing structures and principles. As interesting as this problem is, it is also quite complex. It does not bend easily to experimental thrusts. It is highly unlikely that one system of organization is equally effective for all learners. But our presentations leave the impression that

[11] Suchman (see note 7), p. 126.

we are insensitive to this idea. One book for many readers, one lesson for thirty different learners—such presentations are not likely to be maximally effective for these different persons. Although the requirements of mass instruction as it is presently organized limit how much these organizations may be varied, some organizations may be far more effective than others. This is the problem being attacked in the new curricula.

An interesting change in goal has also developed in recent years. The goal now is to present cognitive material so that the learner captures the spirit and way of thinking characteristic of an academic discipline:

Intellectual activity anywhere is the same, whether at the frontier of knowledge or in a third-grade classroom. What a scientist does at his desk or in his laboratory, what a literary critic does in reading a poem, are of the same order as what anybody else does when he is engaged in like activities—if he is to achieve understanding. The difference is in degree, not in kind. The school boy learning physics *is* a physicist, and it is easier for him to learn physics behaving like a physicist than doing something else.[12]

The problem is how to organize subject matter and teaching method to achieve this goal. The objective is clear. Shift from learning about a body of knowledge to learning its structure and method.

SEQUENCING COGNITIVE OPERATIONS

Learning must be staged in some way. Some things are prior, others subsequent. At any stage in this learning sequence, the student acquires information that he must retain for later stages, and operations that he will both use and transform into more complex behavior.

There have been two very general points of view about this problem. One is to organize in large units, working out from a major problem or theme to details. The other is to sequence from the smaller units progressively into the larger. This issue no longer seems as critical as it once did.[13] The problem has been attacked most recently as a straightforward problem in sequencing learning tasks, without the emotional and philosophical commitments that have confused earlier arguments.

---

[12] Bruner (see note 4), p. 14. Ausubel's comment on this statement is worth reading; see Ausubel (note 8), pp. 158–159; also pp. 145, 156.

[13] See B. J. Underwood, "Laboratory Studies of Verbal Learning," in E. Hilgard, ed., *Theories of Learning and Instruction*, Sixty-third Yearbook of the National Society for the Study of Education (Chicago: University of Chicago Press, 1964), pp. 143–144.

Gagné's research is representative of one approach.[14] The first step is a task analysis of the operations or behavior to be acquired working from the terminal behavior. Figure 6–4 illustrates such an analysis. At the top of the figure is the behavior that the student is to acquire, the **terminal behavior**. Immediately under this statement are listed the four behaviors presumed to be necessary to acquire the terminal behavior. Work back through the chain until you arrive at the initial behaviors listed in the two boxes at the bottom. These behaviors are assumed to be the necessary starting point.

This arrangement is itself a hypothesis about the sequence of behavior acquisitions a learner must go through to acquire the terminal behavior. Gagné has demonstrated that if one can perform operations lower in a sequence of this kind, he will be more likely to acquire the complex behavior represented in the terminal behavior.[15] The proposed theoretical explanation is that at each step the learner acquires learning sets, which transfer to the next step and facilitate his learning at that point.[16] This sequential arrangement is not simply a logical ordering of subject matter. It is *a psychological ordering of learning tasks*. The empirical task is to determine whether higher-order operations are dependent on the acquisition of lower-order operations. Gagné's work indicates that carefully programming the learner through the sequence of interdependent steps facilitates learning.

It should also be noted that the learning problems at each level are similar and present the same problems for decision making. For example, at any level, we have to decide on the number and kinds of examples, their characteristics, and feedback strategies. Each task level requires its own instructional strategy.

When Gagné compared groups with different arrangements of examples, he found that a group that had minimal variety learned significantly less than groups with examples of greater variety and even than a group with no examples. He argues that the learning task at each level is to acquire the behavior that facilitates generalization to the next level. A narrow range of examples inhibits or does not produce this generalizing behavior.

Another finding in this experiment is of interest because of its relevance

[14] R. M. Gagné and O. C. Bassler, "Study of Retention of Some Topics of Elementary Nonmetric Geometry," *Journal of Educational Psychology*, 54 (1963), 123–131.

[15] R. M. Gagné, J. R. Mayor, H. L. Garstens, and N. E. Paradise, "Factors in Acquiring Knowledge of a Mathematical Task," *Psychological Monographs*, No. 526 (1962).

[16] See R. M. Gagné, "The Acquisition of Knowledge," *Psychological Review*, 69 (1962), 355–365.

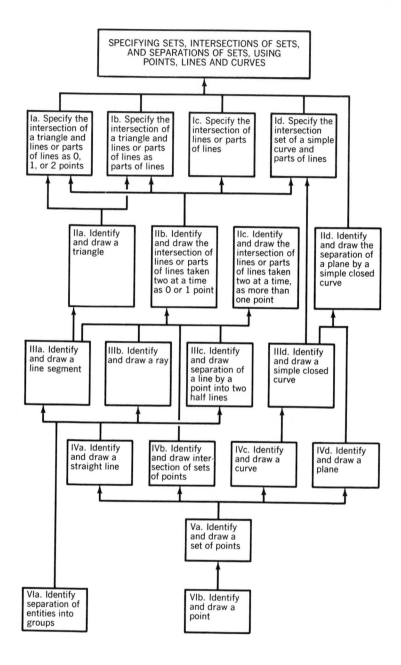

FIGURE 6–4. *Hierarchy of learning sets to be acquired as topics in the learning program employed during the original learning sessions (from Gagné and Bassler).*

to evaluation procedures used by many teachers. The experiment was designed to measure retention immediately after the learning experience and nine weeks later. The immediate retention was exceptionally high, 100 per cent in four of the five groups, and 71 per cent in the fifth group. As Gagné states, ". . . these scores do constitute good evidence that this kind of material, when learned by means of a carefully constructed instructional program, is *highly resistant to forgetting*." [17]

The interesting result referred to above was the pattern of forgetting of subordinate sets. Figure 6–5 illustrates what a student remembered at the two test periods.[18] Gagné devised a method to measure how many and

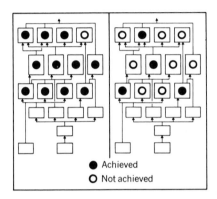

● Achieved
○ Not achieved

FIGURE 6–5. *Retention of subsets by one student (see Figure 6–4). Left diagram is retention pattern immediately after original learning. Right diagram is pattern nine weeks later (from Gagné and Bassler).*

which of the subsets were remembered. Significantly fewer of the subsets were retained at the end of the nine-week period. But, most strikingly, there appeared to be no order among the operations forgotten. "The forgetting of individual learning sets appears to be irregular, or random. Learning sets at one level do not appear to be forgotten with greater frequency than those at another level" (p. 128).

The relevance of this point to evaluation is that many teacher-made tests call for retention of subsets. For example, a teacher wants to test students' grasp of trends in American history. To grasp the larger trends, the students had to learn certain facts and subgeneralizations. As they acquired this information, the teacher related it to new information in

[17] Gagné and Bassler (see note 14), p. 127.
[18] Gagné and Bassler, p. 128.

order to shape the learning of the broad generalization. The teacher's test may include (and usually does) test items on these subsets of information.

How extensive the forgetting phenomenon described above is, or why it occurs, is not known. But the data are sufficiently suggestive to alert us that we may frequently test for behavior most likely not to be retained, even though the terminal or criterion behavior is retained. The teacher must ask himself, "Is or is not the retention of the subset necessary for some future learning? If the subset is forgotten, will it be reinstated?" A similar decision applies to the instructional strategy. If these subset operations need to be retained, review procedures to strengthen them are indicated.

INFLUENCE OF PRIOR LEARNING ON COGNITIVE STRUCTURE

We may conceptualize the learning problem in another way—as one in which the learner acquires **mediating responses** (see Figure 6–6). These responses are learned responses the person makes to associate stimuli and the overt responses we observe. For example, I am teaching second-grade children general concepts of community organization. One concept pertains to "community helpers"—the firemen, the police, sanitary engineers, and other public servants. The class is to learn the different functions of these groups. The instructional strategy will utilize what I have

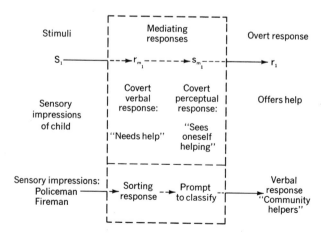

FIGURE 6–6. *Symbolic representation of mediating responses.*

learned about concept formation. But what assumptions am I making about learned responses the children may have available for this new learning? For instance, have they acquired the verbal responses "is like" or "is different from" to use in comparing and contrasting responses?

Using Familiar Materials

Teachers tacitly assume that learners have a complex repertoire of these mediating responses available—although, admittedly, elementary school teachers are aware of the child's probable limitations. Thus, they attempt to utilize what the child has already learned to mediate new learning; that is, they relate new things to something—words, ideas, objects, or personal experiences—*familiar* to the child. This generalization, though widely believed, is vague. A child may be familiar with the words and objects used to learn new ideas, but the ideas are unfamiliar. He may have had personal experiences that can be related to some new idea only by analogy. However, if we mean by *familiar* "abstract ideas expressed in concrete form," there is evidence to support the effectiveness of such an approach.

Brownell and Stretch [19] performed an experiment which demonstrates the relevance of the variable of "familiarity." Children were given the same problems in four different forms. In Form A, the problems were written in terms familiar to children. In Form B, relatively less familiar terms were used. In Form C, the terms used were not familiar to children, and Form D employed artificial terms. The children were tested on the problems written in each form. The percentages of problems worked correctly for each of the forms are given below:

Form A	Form B	Form C	Form D
64	58	57	51

Although these differences are not large, they are statistically significant and suggest the influence of the variable of familiarity in understanding and using generalizations.

In another experiment, Wilkins [20] presented students with syllogisms in familiar and unfamiliar terms, and asked them to say whether or not the

[19] W. A. Brownell and L. B. Stretch, *The Effect of Unfamiliar Settings on Problem Solving* (Durham, N. C.: Duke University Press, 1931), Duke University Research Studies in Education, No. 1.
[20] M. C. Wilkins, "The Effects of Changed Material on Ability to Do Formal Syllogistic Reasoning," *Archives of Psychology*, No. 102 (1928).

third statement followed from the first two. For example, the same syllogistic form would be presented in the following three ways:

1. No dogs are cats. No cats are men. Therefore, no men are dogs.	2. No blits are spuken. No spuken are lichts. Therefore, no lichts are blits.	3. No X's are Y's. No Y's are Z's. Therefore, no Z's are X's.

Wilkins found that students could understand syllogisms written in familiar terms somewhat better than syllogisms written in unfamiliar terms or symbols, as in columns 2 and 3.

The recommendation that the materials used should be familiar to students has been made so frequently that we may easily overlook the fact that familiarity is only one of the variables in learning a principle; furthermore, familiarity may inhibit as well as facilitate learning. Teachers may use events in students' lives to aid in the understanding of a historical period. Such a practice would be consistent with the hypothesis that familiar materials will facilitate the learning of a generalization, but if students assumed that Roman family life was not different from American family life, the procedure would produce an undesirable effect. We have also noted that some "familiar materials" may be anxiety-inducing. When familiar materials or problems are anxiety-inducing, learning is inhibited. Finally, our conception of what is familiar to a student is, in effect, a hypothesis about the effects of previous learning, and this hypothesis may not be valid. We may overlook materials that are familiar to students, or we may incorrectly assume that they are familiar materials available.

When students must learn generalizations for which they have not had relevant previous experiences, we may use a "pre-induction period," in which we familiarize the students with the materials from which they will formulate generalizations. Many teachers use what they call "exploratory periods," in which the child is allowed to play with or manipulate new materials to familiarize himself with them. For example, a fifth-grade teacher introduced a unit on "The Space Age" by placing models of rockets and pictures of the moon and stellar constellations around the room. The children began to ask questions about the materials, and the teacher used these questions to develop concepts and generalizations about space.

From this discussion we may formulate several hypotheses relevant to organizing learning experiences to aid the acquisition of a generalization. The learning of a generalization is likely to be fostered if the materials from which the generalization is to be learned are familiar to the student. Further, we may best promote such familiarity by exposing students to the materials and allowing them to explore and manipulate the materials. In such exploratory periods an individual may "learn how to learn"; he may be "practicing" observation of events and the testing of consequences.[21] He learns what is associated with what and what follows from what. However, familiarity with the materials from which a generalization is to be learned may inhibit learning if these materials are anxiety-inducing, or if students erroneously assume that what is to be learned is exactly like something previously learned.[22]

Advance Organizers

Ausubel approached the enormously complex problem of mediating responses by postulating an **advance organizer**.[23] These organizers take many different forms, but essentially they are sorting and classifying models. The label "advance" describes the necessary operation of providing these models as a learning task which precedes the learning task that is of paramount interest.

How do advance organizers affect learning and retention? Ausubel's advance organizers were concepts and generalizations into which the ideas to be learned could be assimilated. He presented information on the metallurgy of steel to two different groups. The experimental group read a passage describing the differences between metals and alloys, their advantages and limitations, and the reasons for making and using alloys;

[21] The data to support this hypothesis have been based largely on teachers' observations only. The experimental evidence available is based on infrahuman organisms. See, for example, H. F. Harlow, "The Formation of Learning Sets," *Psychological Review*, 56 (1949), 51–65; "Learning and Satiation of Response in Intrinsically Motivated Complex Puzzle Performance by Monkeys," *Journal of Comparative and Physiological Psychology*, 43 (1950), 289–294; "Analysis of Discrimination Learning by Monkeys," *Journal of Experimental Psychology*, 40 (1950), 26–39. Data from experiments in concept formation may be generalized as further support for this hypothesis. Davidon found that subjects allowed to manipulate materials in a concept-formation experiment did better in acquiring the concepts than those who were not permitted to manipulate the materials. See R. S. Davidon, "The Effects of Symbols, Shift, and Manipulation upon the Number of Concepts Attained," *Journal of Experimental Psychology*, 44 (1952), 70–79.

[22] Literature on the familiarity and personal relevance of a problem on efficiency in problem solving, in one area, is discussed in G. M. Wilson, "Arithmetic," in W. S. Monroe, ed., *Encyclopedia of Educational Research* (New York: The Macmillan Company, 1950).

[23] D. P. Ausubel, "The Use of Advance Organizers in the Learning and Retention of Meaningful Verbal Material," *Journal of Educational Psychology*, 51 (1960), 267–272.

this passage presented a set of concepts for organizing information about a particular alloy, such as steel. The other group studied a historical introduction to the material, presumably useful in creating student interest. The experimental group learned and retained significantly more information about metallurgy than did the other group.

Ausubel then attacked another problem: How can advance organizers affect the learning of units of cognitive material that are related by similarities and differences? [24] Suppose, for example, that we had presented a description of two different learning theories. To understand them, you would have to sort out the similarities and differences. Ordinarily, such units are studied one after the other. The problem is to keep from confusing the two theories. The reduction in confusion probably depends on two variables: (1) how well the first theory is learned, and (2) the degree to which its learning facilitates or inhibits learning the second theory. In one of Ausubel's experiments, subjects were given materials on Buddhism and Zen Buddhism. [25] The experimental group first studied materials that compared (1) Christianity and Buddhism and (2) Buddhism and Zen Buddhism. A control group studied introductory passages about Buddhism and Zen Buddhism; these passages were historical and biographical rather than comparative. On the first day of the experiment, prior to their reading the passages, all subjects were given a test of their prior knowledge of Christianity. Then, after they had studied the passages, they were given a test on Buddhism and another on Zen Buddhism. Again, the experimental group did better than the control group on tests of learning and retention (see Table 6–2).

An alternative hypothesis to account for these results is that those who did better may have had more religious knowledge or greater interest in religious topics. Ausubel argues that the advance organizer would be the more powerful variable, since it was more immediate to the task at hand. The effect of the advance organizer on learning and retention of Zen Buddhism material was not significant—a negative finding that Ausubel thinks was produced by the difficulties in discriminating between the two forms of Buddhism.

Although the absolute size of the differences between the groups in these studies seems modest, the effect has been consistently obtained; and

[24] D. P. Ausubel and D. Fitzgerald, "The Role of Discriminability in Meaningful Verbal Learning and Retention," *Journal of Educational Psychology*, 52 (1961), 266–274; and "Organizer, General Background and Antecedent Learning Variables in Sequential Verbal Learning," *Journal of Educational Psychology*, 52 (1962), 243–249.
[25] D. P. Ausubel and M. Youssef, "Role of Discriminability in Meaningful Parallel Learning," *Journal of Educational Psychology*, 54 (1963), 331–336.

the obtained differences fall within the significance level for rejecting the **null hypothesis.**

Much remains to be learned about advance organizers, but their potential value for organizing instructional strategies seems clear. Unfortunately, rules for constructing these arrangements are not available. Ausubel, Gagné, and other investigators proceed pragmatically, using a judicious mixture of common sense, logic, psychological knowledge, and careful testing of their materials. The teacher will have to proceed in the same way. The application of these ideas is a fruitful field for critical inquiry.

TABLE **6–2.** *The effect of cognitive organizers on retention (from Ausubel and Youssef).*

	Retention Scores on Buddhism Test	
	Experimental group (organizer)	*Control group*
Mean Total Score Buddhism Test[*]	19.4	17.6
Mean Total Score Zen Buddhism Test[*]	14.8	14.2

[*] Significance of differences: $p < .01$

ASSOCIATIVE THINKING

If you are asked what street you live on, you probably respond immediately and correctly. You probably learned this response originally by associating the name of the street with simple cues. One of these cues was the question "What street do you live on?" We teach children their own proper names, their house numbers and streets, and the names of many common objects through a process of associating these names and numbers with appropriate stimuli. We develop **associations** by attaching responses to certain stimuli, called **cues**—so that, when the cues or stimuli occur, the appropriate response to them is made easily and quickly. This cognitive process is somewhat simpler than deductive and inductive thinking, or acquiring concepts and generalizations. However, much thinking is of this character; and, like the other cognitive processes that we have studied, it enables an individual to make appropriate interpretations of his environment. Imagine the difficulties that would be involved if we had to reason out the name of every person whom we met or the name of every common object.

The educational significance of associative thinking is that desired behavior changes require the learning of associations. While we want children to understand the process of multiplication, we also wish them to learn the associations required in a multiplication table. When a child is given the stimulus "two times two equals," we want him to be able to respond "four" easily and quickly. Other examples of associations that we encourage children to learn are formulas of various kinds, foreign-language vocabulary, dates of historical events, and such conventions as "Capitalize the first word in a sentence."

THE MEANINGFULNESS OF ASSOCIATIONS

Some of the associations that we encourage children to learn can be given meaning when the principle underlying the association is explained or discovered. A child can understand why "two times two is four" when he understands the principles of combinations by multiplication. Many modern texts in arithmetic are designed to foster this understanding of arithmetic processes; for the sake of efficiency, we also encourage the child to remember the associations in the multiplication table. We will discuss at a later point in this chapter the relation between understanding and remembering.

Many of the associations to be learned in school are essentially mean-ingless. Statements such as "Sacramento is the capital of California" have to be learned even though we can give no rational meaning to the association between the term "Sacramento" and the place of the capital of California. Contrast the meaning that can be given to "two times two equals four." We may be able to explain how the capital of California came to be called Sacramento, but such an explanation gives no intrinsic meaning to the association. Another example of an essentially meaningless kind of association is the association between "red light" and "stop." The convention governing traffic signals is an arbitrary one; but, before a person can observe traffic rules, he must learn this association. It would be impossible to explain to a child why a red light means stop—other than to say that this is a matter of agreement.

In modern education considerable emphasis is placed on making learn-ing "meaningful." A distinction should be made at this point between giving meaning to learning a task and the meaning inherent in the character of the task. We may make the task of learning that Sacramento is the capital of California a meaningful task by relating the task to important concepts or generalizations that the child will have to learn in order to satisfy his needs. For example, children studying the history and government of their state need to understand geographical concepts and place orientations. They must be able to give the location of many governmental agencies, and to do this must learn the name of the state capital. Learning the name of the capital "makes sense" or has meaning in this larger context of learning. Note, however, that we have given meaning to the task of learning but have not added any intrinsic meaning to the association to be learned.

ASSOCIATION AND MEMORY

Associations, whether they are meaningful or not, depend heavily upon memory. An individual must retain an association if he is to use it. A child who cannot remember the multiplication tables is slow and inefficient in computational tasks. A discussion of associative thinking requires an understanding of factors that influence remembering and forgetting—so that learning experiences may be organized to facilitate the acquisition of these associations.

The experience of "remembering" is so obvious that we may overlook the fact that the process is not directly observable. We account for certain observations of human behavior by postulating a process called "memory." The behavior from which we infer the memory process may take any one of three forms. (1) If a person has studied a poem and can recite the poem at some time after he has studied it, the behavior that we observe is **recall behavior.** (2) The person may display **recognition behavior**—for instance, he may identify the correct date for the Declaration of Independence from a list of dates, even though he might not have been able to recall this date without having the list in front of him. (3) The person may show facility in **relearning** a task that he originally learned. If a child has memorized a list of vocabulary words, he will forget some of these words over a period of time; if he studies the list a second time, he probably will be able to learn the list much more quickly than he did the first time. We account for this phenomenon of rapid relearning by inferring that not all of the responses involved in the original learning had been forgotten and that those not forgotten were used in the relearning.

The behavior phenomenon that we observe in all these cases is that of **retention.** Memory is the process we use to account for the observed behavior called retention. What variables influence retention?

Reorganization and Retention

When a person meets a situation that is unfamiliar to him, he apparently strives to reorganize his impressions of the situation in terms of his previous experience. This attempt at reorganization enables a person to interpret a new experience and at the same time probably increases his retention of what is learned in the new experience. Deese [26] provides an interesting example of this tendency to organize the unfamiliar. Figure 6–7 gives a sample of the kind of picture that Deese presented to a group of subjects in an experiment. The subjects in this experiment were to remember a series of forms of this kind that were given to them. Deese found that his subjects typically applied some label to the forms; for example, the most frequent name assigned to the form in Figure 6–7 was "dog's head." These familiar labels presumably facilitated retention of the forms.

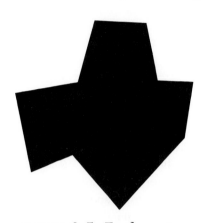

FIGURE 6–7. *Tendency to organize the unfamiliar. Subjects asked to identify this figure most commonly labeled it "dog's head" (from Deese).*

Bartlett [27] has also demonstrated the tendency to restructure as a way of organizing experience. He presented his experimental subjects with a series of pictures, and at a later time asked them to reproduce these pictures from memory. Figure 6–8 shows one such reproduction. Notice the sequence from a drawing fairly similar to the original to one which is radically different from the original but which preserves some of the features of the original. The memory of the original drawing apparently has been recoded in terms of a more familiar object. This reproduction of the Egyptian owl as a cat illustrates that this reorganization process has

[26] J. Deese, "Complexity of Contour in the Recognition of Visual Form," *WADC Technical Report,* No. 56–60 (1956).

[27] F. C. Bartlett, *Remembering: A Study in Experimental and Social Psychology* (Cambridge, England: Cambridge University Press, 1932).

disadvantages as well as advantages. The subject who recalled the original drawing as a cat, while he has retained some of the features of the original drawing, has apparently forgotten considerable detail.

An experiment by Carmichael [28] demonstrates that this process of reorganizing can be influenced. He presented a series of stimulus pictures to two groups of subjects. A stimulus word was given with each of the pictures; however, two different lists of stimulus words were used with two groups of subjects. After the subjects had seen the stimulus pictures and a set of associated words, they were asked to draw the pictures from

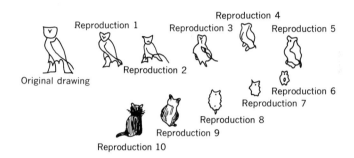

FIGURE 6–8. *A form reproduced from memory. The form is altered at each reproduction. The influence of labeling as a coding device is seen in the change from a conventional Egyptian symbol for an owl to a picture of a cat (from Bartlett).*

memory. Figure 6–9 shows the changes in the reproduced figure associated with the kind of stimulus word that was used with the picture. You will notice that the original figure has been changed in the direction of a figure more consistent with the stimulus word.

An important qualification needs to be made on the data from the experiments cited. We cannot tell to what extent the reproduction of a figure has been influenced by original inaccuracies of perception. The factor of inaccurate perception would account in part for distortions in the reproductions. However, the systematization of the successive reproductions, as in Bartlett's experiments, suggests the influence of a coding process.

[28] L. Carmichael, H. P. Hogan, and A. A. Walter, "An Experimental Study of the Effect of Language on the Reproduction of Visually Perceived Form," *Journal of Experimental Psychology*, 15 (1932), 73–86.

REPRODUCED FIGURES	WORD LIST I	STIMULUS FIGURES	WORD LIST II	REPRODUCED FIGURES
	Curtains in a window		Diamond in a rectangle	
	Bottle		Stirrup	
	Crescent moon		Letter "C"	
	Beehive		Hat	
	Eyeglasses		Dumbells	
	Seven		Four	
	Ship's wheel		Sun	
	Hour glass		Table	
	Kidney bean		Canoe	
	Pine tree		Trowel	
	Gun		Broom	
	Two		Eight	

FIGURE 6–9. *Influence of words upon reorganization. Groups presented with different word lists tended to reproduce drawings resembling the words they had associated with the stimulus figures.* (*From Carmichael et al.*)

All of the possibly influential factors in the recording process have not been explored adequately. The variable of familiarity appears to influence the recoding process and, consequently, the retention of what is learned.[29]

Three major processes appear to be involved in this system of reorganization: (1) a **leveling** process, in which irregularities or asymmetrical features are removed; (2) a **sharpening** process, in which striking or unusual features are accentuated; (3) an **assimilation** process, in which what is retained is changed in the direction of something more common

---

[29] See M. D. Arnoult, "Familiarity and Recognition of Nonsense Shapes," *Journal of Experimental Psychology,* 51 (1956), 269–276.

and familiar to the individual—the cat in the earlier illustration, for example.

We do not know which factors are more likely to initiate one of these processes than another. Experimental evidence suggests that the selection and recoding process appears to be strongly influenced by individual factors. Bartlett showed his experimental subjects a set of pictures and described the people in the pictures in conventional terms. For example, a pictured young man might be described as clean-cut, energetic, dynamic, and good-humored. The subjects' recall of the pictures appears to be strongly influenced by the attitude that the picture or description aroused. In Chapter Four, we cited Zeigarnik's experiment, in which individuals remembered more uncompleted tasks than completed tasks. Here we were provided with an example of the influence of motivational factors on what is remembered.

Understanding and Retention

The hypothesis that individuals try to "make sense" out of what they are experiencing suggests that an organizing principle introduced into the study of new material will facilitate learning and remembering this material. This hypothesis has been supported in a number of experimental studies. An example from Katona [30] will demonstrate the difference between the effects of what has been called "rote" learning and "meaningful" learning; that is, learning with and without organizing principles that give meaning to what is being learned. Katona used two groups of experimental subjects, each of which was to learn the following series of numbers:

$$5 \quad 8 \quad 1 \quad 2 \quad 1 \quad 5 \quad 1 \quad 9 \quad 2 \quad 2 \quad 2 \quad 6$$
$$2 \quad 9 \quad 3 \quad 3 \quad 3 \quad 6 \quad 4 \quad 0 \quad 4 \quad 3 \quad 4 \quad 7$$

The first group was told that a principle underlay the arrangement of the numbers. Most of the subjects soon discovered that the principle consisted of alternately adding 3 and then 4; for example, 5 plus 3 equals 8, 8 plus 4 equals 12, 12 plus 3 equals 15, and so on. The second group was to learn the numbers by rote. The experimenter suggested that the best method to use would be a rhythmical grouping of the numbers; for example, 2 9 3, 3 3 6, and so on. The subjects in this experiment were tested shortly after

---

[30] G. Katona, *Organizing and Memorizing* (New York: Columbia University Press, 1940).

the experiment and at a period three weeks later. The results of these tests are summarized in Table 6–3. The data in the table suggest there was little difference between the two groups in original learning. Three weeks later, however, a substantial proportion of the subjects who had learned with understanding had retained what they had learned.

TABLE 6–3. *Retention of number sequences learned with understanding (Class I) and learned by rote (Class II) (from Katona).*

| | Subjects who reproduced correctly | | Subjects who made 19 or more errors | |
	Class I	Class II	Class I	Class II
Half hour after learning	38%	33%	10%	7%
Three weeks later	23%	0%	15%	74%

There were 29 subjects in Class I and 30 in Class II for the original tests. Of these, 26 and 23 were available for the retests.

A study by Tyler [31] demonstrates that knowledge of principles and generalizations is more likely to be retained than is knowledge of less meaningful material, such as terminology. Tyler studied how much course content was retained after one year, using the terms learned in biology and zoology courses, knowledge of principles, and ability to interpret new experiments. The latter two processes depend heavily upon understanding, whereas the first process depends more typically on association. The results from this study are presented in Table 6–4. As the results indicate, much of the terminology is forgotten, but the principles and experiments are retained. The data suggest that the latter are known even better a year after the termination of the course. This retention of material which requires understanding may result from additional practice, if the students continued to use these principles or if they were restudied in other courses. While this possibility may account for some of the retention, it is not likely that it accounts for all of it.

These experiments demonstrate the utility of understanding and or-

[31] R. Tyler, "Some Findings from Studies in the Field of College Biology," *Science Education,* 18 (1934), 133–142.

TABLE 6–4. *Comparison of the results of the course examinations, the test one year later, and the standing of students at the beginning of the zoology course (from Tyler).*

Type of examination exercise	Mean scores at:			Per cent of gain lost one year later
	Beginning of course	Time of course examinations	One year later	
1. Naming animal structures pictured in diagrams	22.2	61.8	31.4	76.8
2. Identifying technical terms	19.7	83.1	66.5	26.2
3. Recalling information a. Structures performing functions in type forms	13.3	39.3	33.9	20.8
b. Other facts	21.4	62.6	54.1	20.6
4. Applying principles to new situations	35.2	64.9	65.1	Gain 0.7
5. Interpreting new experiments	30.3	57.3	64.0	Gain 24.8
Average for all exercises in the examination	23.7	74.4	63.3	21.9

ganization in facilitating retention. We hypothesize that if a teacher organizes material to be retained in terms of generalizations and principles, students are likely to retain this material longer. We must face the problem, however, that many things that are to be learned cannot be made meaningful. For example, we would want to know to what extent the students in Tyler's experiment needed to recall terminology in their future work. If this terminology were not important for future study, we would question the reason for having to learn it at all. But, in these and other courses, a knowledge of the special vocabulary is necessary if the student is to develop an understanding of the subject. Consequently, we must be concerned with factors likely to facilitate the retention of materials which are essentially meaningless or to which comparatively little meaning can be given.

Overlearning and Retention

Assume that a student is required to learn a list of twenty French vocabulary words. We will have him study these by going through the list. Each time he has gone through this list, we will ask him to recall as many French equivalents as he can. Each of these steps is a "trial." We can determine how many trials are required before the student can give us all of the equivalents correctly. Assume, for the purposes of discussion, that he has mastered all of the words after twenty such trials. We will refer to this level of retention—that is, his mastery of the list after twenty

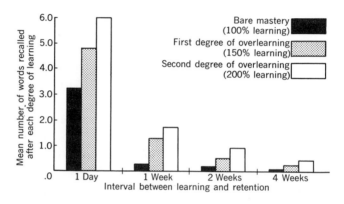

FIGURE **6-10.** *Effects of two degrees of overlearning on retention (from Krueger).*

trials—as "bare mastery." At this point we may say that the student has learned the equivalents. If he continues to practice on the list, beyond the point of "bare mastery," he is **overlearning** the words in the list.

What effect does overlearning have on retention? At the end of twenty trials the student has learned the list to the point where he can recall all of the words in the list. Will he be able to retain this knowledge better if he continues to study the list? Common sense suggests that this is likely, and experimental data support this common-sense hunch.

Figure 6–10, taken from a study by Krueger,[32] indicates the learning

---

[32] W. C. F. Krueger, "The Effect of Overlearning and Retention," *Journal of Experimental Psychology,* 12 (1929), 71–78. For additional data on this point, see H. F. Spitzer, "Studies in Retention," *Journal of Educational Psychology,* 30 (1939), 641–656.

curves for different degrees of overlearning. The 150 per cent overlearning means that the subjects in this experiment used half again as many trials in practice as they used on the original learning; and 200 per cent overlearning means that the subjects used twice again as many trials in practice as in the original learning. Based on our example, the level of "bare mastery" would be twenty trials; 150 per cent overlearning would be thirty trials, and 200 per cent overlearning would be forty trials. As the curve suggests, the amount retained is proportional to the amount of overlearning, even though all subjects gradually forget more and more of what they originally learned.

The teacher may organize learning experiences so that students overlearn what they have originally barely mastered. If learning experiences are organized in such a way that a student must continually re-use what he has already learned, he is overlearning. That is, he is continuing to practice on the material. In learning a foreign language, for instance, we may organize the writing and speaking exercises in such a way that a student continually re-uses words that he has already learned. Perhaps the students in Tyler's study quickly forgot terminology because they had little opportunity to overlearn words that they had "barely mastered."

Reviewing and Retention

Teachers frequently introduce review periods into learning sequences. A review is an opportunity for relearning and a way of implementing overlearning. How can such reviews be arranged to facilitate retention? To understand adequately some of the general principles relevant to this question, we must know what the general course of forgetting is. Figure 6–11 shows a curve of forgetting consistent with the data usually obtained in memory experiments.[33] As the figure illustrates, the greatest amount of forgetting occurs relatively soon after the initial learning has taken place. On the basis of the characteristics of this curve, we would hypothesize that overlearning or relearning in the form of review is most likely to be effective immediately after the original learning; however, some reviewing probably must also be done at other periods after the initial learning period. Experimental evidence suggests that more frequent reviews immediately after the initial learning, followed by rela-

---

[33] H. Ebbinghaus, *Memory*, trans. H. A. Ruger and C. E. Bussenius (New York: Bureau of Publications, Teachers College, Columbia University, 1913); cited in E. R. Hilgard, *Introduction to General Psychology* (New York: Harcourt, Brace and Co., 1953), p. 262.

tively widely spaced reviews over a period of time, is more likely to be effective in reducing forgetting.[34]

We cannot prescribe the exact number of days to allow between periods of review; still, we can state some general principles relevant to making decisions of this kind. The teacher will have to take into account four factors in deciding upon the appropriateness of the timing of review sessions: (1) the amount of overlearning at the time of initial learning; (2) the fact that the greatest amount of forgetting takes place immediately after learning; (3) the extent to which the original learned material is used in new learning; (4) the meaningfulness of the material originally learned. We have seen that three of these factors contribute

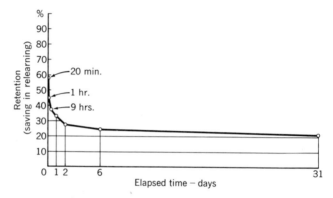

FIGURE 6–11. *Curve of retention for list of nonsense syllables (from Ebbinghaus).*

directly to the amount of material retained. When little time has been spent on overlearning, reviews probably will have to be more frequent. When material is not continually re-used, greater frequency of reviews will probably facilitate retention. The teacher may gather data on pupils' retention by systematically questioning students about material previously learned. From such data the teacher may make inferences about the extent of forgetting and plan appropriate reviews.

The word "review" may have two meanings. We have been using it here in the sense of "going over" previously learned material. It may also refer to a process of integrating previously learned material with new material; new relationships between the old and the new are developed. After students have learned a number of concepts or generalizations in a

[34] See L. Tsai, "The Relations of Retention to the Distribution of Relearning," *Journal of Experimental Psychology,* 10 (1927), 30–39.

course of instruction, the whole sequence of the material used to that point may be looked at in the light of these concepts and generalizations. This kind of review involves more than repeating previously learned responses. In any case, the process of review probably does not comprise a mere exact *repetition* of what has been learned. Since the student has been learning continuously between review periods, he will probably do some reorganizing and reintegrating of new material with old material. Since this continual reorganization and reinterpretation facilitates understanding, we would predict that it will also facilitate retention.

Recitation and Retention

Assume again that a student is memorizing a list of words. One of the ways in which he can memorize this list is by reading and rereading it to himself. He may also cover the list as he studies and attempt to recite the words to himself, or he may participate with another student in a mutual testing of knowledge of the list. Each of these possibilities suggests different levels of active participation in the process of remembering. Reading and rereading is a fairly passive process, while self-recitation or reciting to another person requires greater involvement of the individual in the task. Experimental evidence suggests that the latter processes facilitate retention. Figure 6–12 plots the per cent of material retained in relationship to the per cent of time devoted to self-recitation.[35] Since learning is facilitated when the learner participates more actively in the learning experience, the teacher may encourage students to use methods of self-recitation or mutual re-

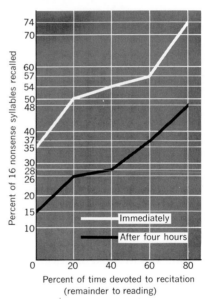

FIGURE 6–12. *The value of self-recitation in memorizing (from Gates).*

---

[35] A. I. Gates, "Recitation as a Factor in Memorizing," *Archives of Psychology*, No. 40 (1917). For additional evidence on the same point, see G. Forlano, *School Learning with Various Methods of Practice and Rewards* (New York: Columbia University Press, 1936), Teachers College Contributions to Education, No. 688; also, L. C. Seibert, *A Series of Experiments on the Learning of French Vocabulary* (Baltimore: Johns Hopkins, 1932), Johns Hopkins University Studies in Education, No. 18.

citation in studying; or he may organize such learning experiences himself. We would predict, for example, the periods of recitation used by teachers in vocabulary lessons will improve retention.

Interference Theory of Forgetting

Learning experiences are units or sequences of activity. As a learner moves from one learning experience to another, he encounters new activities, problems, and materials. Assume that a student has learned

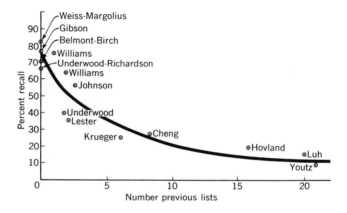

FIGURE 6–13. *Recall as a function of previous lists of similar material learned by the subjects. This curve was obtained by combining the data of a number of different investigators (from Underwood).*

twenty words of French vocabulary today. Tomorrow he learns twenty more, and the next day twenty more. Underwood [36] has studied the effects of these learning activities on successive attempts at learning vocabulary. Figure 6–13 shows the results from several studies based on this question. The curve shows the relationship between the amount recalled and the number of previous lists of similar material that subjects had to learn. It is clear that the greater the amount of similar material to be retained, the less the amount of material actually retained.

Data such as these have been used to support what is called the

[36] B. J. Underwood, "Interference and Forgetting," *Psychological Review,* 64 (1957), 49–60. L. Postman, "The Present Status of Interference Theory, in C. Cofer, ed., *Verbal Learning and Verbal Behavior* (New York: McGraw-Hill Book Co., 1961), pp. 152–178.

interference theory of forgetting. According to this theory, forgetting occurs because a person learns new responses between the time that he has originally learned a response and the time that he again is called upon to use it. Applying this conception to memory, we would say that between the time that a student learns a list of words and the time that he is called upon to use these words, he may have learned many more words. The more similar the intervening material, the more likely it is to interfere with the originally learned material when the student is required to recall it.

This hypothesis about factors influencing forgetting can be used as a basis for making decisions about organizing learning experiences. In general, the teacher should expect students to have difficulty retaining highly similar materials which are learned in close proximity to each other. However, any factor which strengthens retention of the original learning is likely to reduce the effects of interference. In other words, something that is well learned is likely to be retained, even though the person learns something else similar to the original learning, in either form or content.

Influence of Personal Factors on Forgetting

Personal factors play an important part in forgetting. Some experimental evidence suggests that pleasant associations are more likely to be recalled than unpleasant associations. Similarly, an individual's attitudes and values tend to influence what he will recall. This process has been called *selective forgetting*—that is, an individual, because of certain attitudes or feelings, is predisposed to forget some of the material he has presumably learned. A study by Levine and Murphy [37] demonstrates this phenomenon. In this experiment students' attitudes toward communism were determined. The students were then given both pro-communist and anti-communist selections to read, and their recall of the material in the selections was tested immediately after the reading. This process was repeated for three successive weeks, and recall tests were given for five weeks after this. The results of this investigation are given in Figures 6–14 and 6–15. As the figures indicate, anti-communists remembered more

[37] J. M. Levine and G. Murphy, "The Learning and Forgetting of Controversial Material," *Journal of Abnormal and Social Psychology*, 38 (1943), 507–517. See also H. Meltzer, "Individual Differences in Forgetting Pleasant and Unpleasant Experiences," *Journal of Educational Psychology*, 21 (1930), 399–409; and R. H. Thomson, "Experimental Study of Memory as Influenced by Feeling Tone," *Journal of Experimental Psychology*, 13 (1930), 462–467.

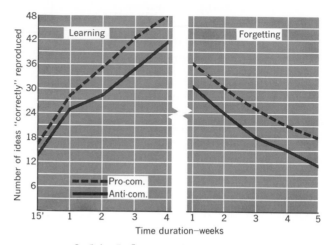

FIGURE 6–14. *Influence of personal factors on learning and forgetting. When pro-communists and anti-communists studied pro-communist selections, pro-communists learned more and forgot less rapidly (from Levine and Murphy).*

anti-communist material than did pro-communists, and pro-communists remembered more pro-communist material than did anti-communists. These differences were maintained over a relatively long period of time.

The term **selective forgetting** may suggest to some readers that the person *chooses* what he will forget. Perhaps we should call it instead **selective perception** and remembering. The Levine and Murphy study suggests that a person's initial perceptions of the material are influenced by his attitudes; that is, he is more likely to notice items of information or points of view consistent with his own. As a consequence, he may ignore items that contradict his own point of view. Selective perception, however, does not entirely explain the data: pro-communists, for example, did remember some anti-communist material and anti-communists did remember some pro-communist material—probably because they all read the material a number of times. However, the process of selective perception and selective remembering does determine the extent to which material consistent with one's own attitudes is retained.

The teacher is limited in the extent to which he can eliminate forgetting. However, through his arrangement of learning experiences, he can influence the extent to which the students are likely to retain what they have learned.

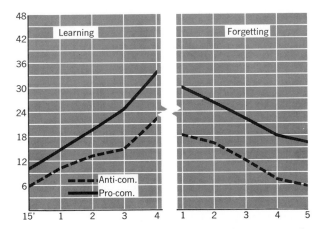

FIGURE 6-15. *Influence of personal factors on learning and forgetting. When pro-communists and anti-communists studied an anti-communist selection, anti-communists learned more and forgot less rapidly (from Levine and Murphy).*

INSTRUCTIONAL STRATEGIES FOR COGNITIVE DEVELOPMENT

Since the processes included in the category *cognitive learning* or *cognitive behavior* are extremely complex, we cannot outline a few instructional strategies that will promote and develop these many behaviors. We can, however, point up general patterns and the kinds of decisions that a teacher must make to plan and to conduct such strategies.

SELECTION OF OBJECTIVES

Instructional objectives in the domain of cognitive development are not always clear. "To develop understanding," admittedly too general, is difficult to specify—not always because one cannot say what he means but because he has so many choices. On page 87 is a sampling of specifications. These items, which classify cognitive behaviors, may be used to select and to clarify the objectives of an instructional.strategy.

An equally important decision is judging the interdependence of the behavioral goals. As we have seen in both Gagné's and Ausubel's analyses, programmatic arrangements of cognitive-learning tasks require that someone decide which tasks or concepts are related, and which ones must be learned first. This judgment is a hypothesis, a prediction; and the teacher will need to assess whether a particular hypothesis about interdependence is relatively valid.

THE CRITERION BEHAVIOR

How do we know when someone has acquired cognitive behavior? Essentially, such behavior is manifested by intellectual power; that is, in psychological terms, the ability to apply what has been learned—concepts, generalizations, process skills—to new material. Also, the learner acquires "learning-to-learn" behavior; he becomes increasingly autonomous, is more self-directive and, in a loose sense, self-instructive. He is, in short, able to **transfer** what he has learned—discovering new instances of the generalization, new problems for critical analysis.

In order to test whether an instructional strategy has, in fact, brought about cognitive development, the teacher should try to make the test problem similar to, but not identical with, the learning task. He should not ask students, for instance, to repeat instances of the generalization to which they were exposed in the acquisition phase, or verbal statements of laws, or descriptions and lists of process steps. One suspects that teachers use such measures to reassure themselves that students have learned *something*. Others may be convinced that storage of this kind indicates some ability to transfer what has been learned—a dubious point.

Measures of this kind may be defended when the teacher must assess whether necessary learning has been achieved. However, he must also distinguish between the minimal acquisition of cognitive behavior and that level of learning that facilitates transfer. If the teacher does not assess for transfer, he runs the risk of assuming that he has a powerful strategy when he has not.

INSTRUCTIONAL-STRATEGY PATTERNS

One way to analyze potentially effective instructional strategies is to begin by separating learning tasks and goals into **central tasks** and **peripheral tasks.** These two labels are chosen to call attention to the ordering of goals by the teacher. The central task and its associated goal is where the teacher hopes to bring the children. For example, a set of generalizations about city life is to be learned by fourth graders. These generalizations and related concepts are the advance organizers to be used in studying a wide range of kinds of cities, in identifying significant problems in city life, and in organizing factual information. They are to be used in making comparisons. This is the central task. The teacher expects the children to learn to make the desired comparisons, identifications, and classifications.

The teacher, however, will have to devote some time to tasks that are peripheral to this task but necessary to produce the learning required for the central task. The concepts and generalizations to be used have to be learned initially. Similarly, some factual information will need to be acquired. The teacher will need to prompt the children to use this information as new material is introduced.

These two kinds of tasks—central and peripheral—are not necessarily ordered in time. Some cognitive-learning experiences appear remarkably fluid, with rapid shifts from peripheral to central tasks and back again. Others seem to require systematic progression from peripheral to central. Suchman uses his type of inquiry training because he assumes that children must operate at a concrete level before they can begin to experiment mentally. The theory on which his procedures are based predicates this development as a necessary first step.[39] If, however, the children were capable of more complex cognitive behavior, the more difficult experimenting tasks might be the central task. Even then, it may be necessary to practice the lower skills at certain points to facilitate the more complex operations.

One strategy for proceeding from peripheral to central tasks has been developed by Taba.[40] She has been interested in helping children learn to treat generalizations as hypotheses, to learn to predict new events by understanding the antecedent-consequent relations in generalizations. For example, if a child understands the relation between climatic conditions and mode of life, he should be able to make a wide range of predictions when asked the question "What would happen if water came to the desert?" The central task is to bring the child to the level of understanding that will yield a wide range of relevant predictions. To reach this point, however, the child needs a store of concepts and generalizations about weather and its effect on living. To reach this

[39] B. Inhelder and J. Piaget, *The Growth of Logical Thinking from Childhood to Adolescence* (New York: Basic Books, 1958).

[40] H. Taba et al., *Thinking in Elementary School Children* (San Francisco: San Francisco State College, 1964), Cooperative Research Project 1574; H. Taba and F. Elzey, "Teaching Strategies and Thought Processes," *Psychological Record*, 65 (1964), 524–534.

level, Taba uses two peripheral tasks, which in this case are ordered in time. As the first task, she secures instances of relevant phenomena. For instance, a teacher might begin by listing all the things children can think of in the broad categories "mode of life" and "weather": "Tell me things people eat." "Tell me ways people work." "Tell me what clouds do." These questions stimulate information-producing behavior. In the second phase, children group the instances and begin to make interrelations among them. These groupings, prompted by the teacher, help the child see the relation between such things as the availability of water and the type of food eaten by the people, between seasonal variations in temperature and clothing worn, between temperature variations and kind of weather. When these interrelations are grasped, the children are presumably ready for the operations of prediction and higher-order generalization.

This latter task is the central goal of the strategy. The peripheral tasks are necessary, in theory, to bring the child to the point where he can engage in the higher-order operations. Taba has some data that suggest time ordering of the tasks is not necessary for all children. Some leap to high-order generalizations quickly and make predictions while generalizing. At other times it is necessary to work back from a generalization to specific details. In any case, by planning a sequence of tasks from peripheral to central, the teacher gives himself the opportunity to check where the children are. He may accelerate the strategy whenever this seems indicated.

One of the most interesting lines of recent research is on the sequencing of cognitive behaviors.[41] Some venerable beliefs are being seriously questioned. One of these, that cognitive learning must proceed from the concrete to the abstract, from the simple to the complex, has seen some bad days recently. First, Bruner asserted that even the most complex ideas can be taught in a meaningful way to the elementary school child. Then Suppes[42] introduced nonmetric geometry, then set theory, and finally mathematical logic into the primary grades. The various innovations in mathematics were underway by this time. How to help a child learn more complex material, not when it should be introduced, is now the question. And children do not seem to be traumatized by the more difficult cognitive content.

[41] See J. Bruner, "The Course of Cognitive Growth," *American Psychologist*, 19 (1964), 1–15. R. Brown, "How Shall a Thing Be Called," *Psychological Review*, 65 (1958), 14–21; also, R. Brown, *Words and Things* (Glencoe, Ill.: The Free Press, 1958).

[42] P. Suppes, "Modern Learning Theory and the Elementary School Curriculum," *American Educational Research Journal*, 1 (1964), 79–93.

These innovations must, of course, be evaluated; and it would be premature to accept Bruner's view at face value. But a climate of innovation and willingness to test accepted beliefs has developed, which hopefully will spread to the classroom teacher.

The accepted rules of proceeding from the simple to the complex, from the concrete to the abstract, ought to be regarded as reliable but probably fairly conservative decision rules. The curricular innovations and some experimental work [43] suggest that acquisition of supposedly complex cognitive behaviors depends at any time on the repertoire of behavior the child has available and the way in which the stimuli of a strategy are programmed. When the cognitive repertoire is limited, proceeding from the simple to the complex may be simply a way of enriching this repertoire.

A major function that an instructional strategy should serve is organizing the material to be learned. One method of organization is sequencing component tasks, Gagné's work on learning sets being representative of this approach. Another organizing device is the use of search and classifying models, Ausubel's concept of advance organizers being representative.

Another distinction in strategies is that between acquisition and retention strategies. The former produces initial learning, the latter strengthens it. In this and the preceding chapter we discussed the variables likely to be influential in each strategy.

A last distinction may be made between content and process strategies. The goal of the former is the acquisition of concepts, generalizations, models, theories, facts, problem solutions. The goal of the latter is the acquisition of certain kinds of skills, such as those taught children in inquiry training.

These distinctions are useful to keep in mind. First, awareness of them alerts the teacher to clarifying his purposes and points up the decisions to be made. The teacher must decide on the basis of his knowledge of the children being taught, and where he hopes to lead them, the strategy required at any one time. Second, they alert the teacher to use the variables known to be effective in producing the behavior changes envisioned as the goals of the strategy. We assume learning will be more effective if strategies are designed for specific purposes. As an incidental

[43] E. Keislar, "The Development of Understanding in Arithmetic by a Teaching Machine," *Journal of Educational Psychology*, 50 (1959), 247–253. Also, J. M. McNeil and E. Keislar, "Individual Differences and Effectiveness of Auto-instruction at the Primary Grade Level," *California Journal of Educational Research*, 12 (1961), 160–164.

benefit, these distinctions suggest an operational meaning for the time-worn concept of flexibility in teaching. Flexibility as here understood means selecting the strategy appropriate to the child's present cognitive accomplishments and relevant to the desired changes.

SUMMARY

This chapter describes the major variables influencing the learning of generalizations and associative thinking.

1. A generalization is a statement of relationship between two or more concepts. To learn a generalization the student needs to understand the various concepts involved and their relationship. A distinction should be made between simply memorizing a formal statement of a generalization and understanding it. Understanding is usually tested by the learner's ability to apply the generalization where it is relevant.

2. Generalizations may be learned in either of two ways, or some combination of them: (a) *inductively*, by inferring the generalization from observations of particular instances of the phenomena which it describes; (b) deductively, by deriving the generalization from higher-order statements which include it. Initial understanding of the generalization is achieved about equally well with either procedure; but generalizations learned inductively (although they are learned more slowly) appear to be remembered longer and to be used more extensively where they are relevant.

3. Inductive processes for promoting the learning of generalizations are being encouraged as new curricula are tried out in the schools. One form of such inductive learning has been called *discovery learning*, in which the learner is encouraged to formulate a principle from a set of experiences with minimal or no help. Limited experimentation suggests that some form of prompting or guidance is better than no help for producing learning of a principle. However, minimizing help seems to have some motivational effect; learners seek additional information to solve problems, or use the principle in non-experimental situations more frequently.

4. Inquiry training, a particular form of discovery learning, has been tested in school situations. The results indicate that the kind of inquiry behavior prompted and rewarded by the method is the kind of behavior likely to be learned. However, other forms of cognitive behavior—particularly those related to widespread transfer of what has been learned—do not seem to be facilitated as well.

5. A resurgence of interest in subject matter in the curriculum has stimulated research on cognitive organization—the organization of subject matter and learning tasks. One line of investigation has been the study of the *sequence* of cognitive operations required to learn a principle. This sequence may be studied by breaking the desired learning into a series of successive tasks thought to be necessary to reach the final stage. Such arrangements are called *learning sets,* which are hypothesized to have a general facilitating effect on learning. The experimental evidence at present is suggestive but not conclusive on the effects of acquiring such learning sets. One conclusion, however, is that learning sets acquired in this way are highly resistant to forgetting.

6. In general, experimental research indicates that prior learning influences cognitive structure, since the learner acquires *mediating responses* that enable him to understand new concepts.

7. Teachers attempt to use *familiar* material to mediate new learning. And this approach often does enhance the learning of a generalization. However, if the relationship between familiar and new is made too precise, it may be misleading. Also, realistic experiences may be threatening and, as a consequence, inhibit learning.

8. Another approach to developing cognitive structures is to use *advanced organizers* before exposing learners to the material from which they are to acquire generalizations. The advance organizer provides the learner with a sorting or organizing category system into which he can assimilate new information, and to which he can relate new information by comparison.

9. Cognitive processes are strongly influenced by *associative thinking.* An association is an established relationship between a response and a cue: when the cue occurs, the response follows easily and quickly. Some associations are meaningful in that they can be understood; that is, they "make sense." Other associations are relatively meaningless; they involve conventions or agreements, such as "Red light means stop," or "Capitalize the first word in a sentence."

10. The retention of these kinds of cognitive associations depends heavily on memory. Memory involves *recall, recognition,* and *relearning* ability—in short, *retention.* Meaningful material (material with organizing principles to give it meaning) is more likely to be remembered than nonmeaningful material. The retention of essentially meaningless material can probably be improved by relating it to meaningful contexts.

11. Retention is improved by *overlearning*—by continued practice on material after it has been "barely mastered." The teacher can provide an

efficient form of overlearning by arranging learning experiences so that students continually re-use what they have learned. Review periods are also useful in reestablishing original learning and are most likely to be useful if they are scheduled soon after the original learning period and are spaced over a period of time.

12. Retention tends to be reduced when new material being learned is highly similar to the original material. However, with more thorough original learning, the interference effect of new and similar material is reduced.

13. An important phenomena influencing retention is *selective perception*. What a person perceives in a situation is a function of the kinds of attitudes and similar predispositions that he brings to the situation. Similarly, what he remembers is also related to these same attitudes and values, probably because he learns better that toward which he is favorably disposed.

14. The criterion by which a powerful instructional strategy designed to foster cognitive development is judged is the learner's ability to transfer what he has learned from the strategy to a wide variety of situations. Another criterion is the learner's ability to acquire general learning responses, which will be useful to him in many new problem situations.

15. A major task in designing the strategy is to separate the *central* from the *peripheral* tasks. The distinction should be clear in a teacher's mind to avoid the unnecessary expenditure of effort on relatively unimportant learning tasks and to keep the importance of these tasks clearly in mind.

STUDY AND DISCUSSION QUESTIONS

1. List the most important generalizations to be learned in one of the following areas:

   a. Some course in your major field.

   b. Some course or subject that you are teaching or may teach.

   c. The content of the preceding chapter.

   Identify the concepts that are part of these generalizations and describe the relationships between these concepts.

2. In what sense is a concept a generalization?

3. Below are several generalizations. Describe how each of these generalizations might be learned by inductive and deductive processes. Be specific

about the kinds of experiences that would be used as examples of the generalizations, or as instances from which the generalization would be inferred.

a. A cooperative effort was necessary on the American frontier to preserve the American way of life.

b. Trial by jury is necessary to preserve individual freedom.

c. Radioactive fallout increases the concentration of strontium 90 in the bone structure of the body.

4. The above generalizations may require some modification or qualification. In what way would an individual learning these generalizations test their relative validity? Is a generalization tested when you find examples of it?

5. Some people argue that rote learning is necessary if the learning is to be retained. They cite as an example the necessity of memorizing the multiplication tables, or the parts of speech, or vocabulary in a foreign language. Evaluate this argument in the light of the discussion presented in this chapter on "meaningful" learning. What is the relationship between "meaningful" learning and retention?

6. Recall Kersh's experiments on the role of discovery in learning generalizations. Under what conditions would you expect a discovery group (that is, a "no-help" group) not to become interested in the problem situation, or to be less motivated toward problem solution than students who received help in problem solution?

7. How do you account for the consistent results obtained in experimental studies showing that students who acquire generalizations through understanding are better able to use these generalizations in new situations where they are appropriate?

8. What kinds of "familiar materials" could you use to stimulate students to learn the following generalizations?

a. Equals added to equals yield equals.

b. To every reaction there is an opposite and equal reaction.

c. In the United States the scope of governmental power depends upon the consent of the governed.

9. Many teachers use literary presentations which describe the realistic experiences of children and students like those who are reading the selections. These teachers argue that the children will learn readily from such readings because they will identify with the characters and thus understand the problems of the persons described in the selections. Evaluate this point of view by relating it to the discussion of the use of realistic and lifelike materials for understanding concepts and generalizations.

10. Select a unit or section of some subject you can teach. List all the generalizations to be learned in that section. Relate them to each other in a hierarchy of learning sets.

11. Construct at least two kinds of advanced organizers for use in learning the same material. Indicate the characteristics of the advanced organizers and why you think they will facilitate acquiring new information.

12. For this same topic, list all the associations to be learned and describe instructional strategies designed to induce them.

13. In what ways could learning experiences be organized so that long-term retention of the following materials would be improved?

a. A vocabulary list in a foreign language.

b. A list of spelling words.

c. A multiplication table.

d. The dates of important events in the American Revolution.

Explain in what ways you are using the principles discussed in this chapter in your suggested organizations of learning experiences.

14. Suggest ways in which review of materials in the previous question may be organized to improve retention. Again, explain the ways in which you are applying the psychological principles relevant to efficacy of review.

15. Students in high schools and colleges study many different subjects during the course of each day. Would you predict that this arrangement of courses would tend to reduce retention of what is being learned?

16. Devise an instructional strategy for the learning of generalizations and the learning of associations required in the sections of subject matter you selected in Questions 11 and 12. Indicate what variables you are manipulating in this strategy.

RECOMMENDED READINGS

D. P. Ausubel. *The Psychology of Meaningful Verbal Learning.* New York: Grune and Stratton, 1963.

F. Bartlett. *Remembering: A Study in Experimental and Social Psychology.* Cambridge, England: Cambridge University Press, 1932.

————. *Thinking: An Experimental and Social Study.* New York: Basic Books, Inc., 1958.

W. A. Brownell and G. Hendrickson. "How Children Learn Information, Concepts, and Generalizations," in Forty-ninth Yearbook of the National Society for the Study of Education, Part I, *Learning and Instruction.* Chicago: University of Chicago Press, 1950, pp. 92–128.

W. H. Burton, R. B. Kimball, and R. L. Wing, *Education for Effective Thinking.* New York: Appleton-Century-Crofts, 1960.

C. I. Hovland, "Human Learning and Retention," in S. S. Stevens, ed., *Handbook of Experimental Psychology.* New York: John Wiley and Sons, 1951.

R. Leeper. "Cognitive Processes," in S. S. Stevens, ed., *Handbook of Experimental Psychology*. New York: John Wiley and Sons, 1951, Chapter 19.

G. Polya. *Mathematics and Plausible Reasoning*. Princeton: Princeton University Press, 1954.

D. H. Russell. *Children's Thinking*. Boston: Ginn & Co., 1956, Chapter 10.

CHAPTER SEVEN

THE LEARNING OF PROBLEM-SOLVING AND CREATIVE BEHAVIOR

This chapter extends the description of the psychology of cognition to problem-solving and creative behavior. Although these kinds of human activities involve a person's attitudes, emotions, values, and skills, cognitive processes are central in them. Some forms of problem solving (for instance, scientific work) clearly depend on cognition. Others, such as literary and musical activity, seem more intuitive. But closer inspection of even these activities reveals that the intuitions of the artist are molded through his thinking.

Problem-solving behavior is the most complex behavior that a human being can acquire. To solve problems, any and all of his behavioral resources may be utilized. Furthermore, learning to cope with problems has pervasive effects on personality development. Engaging in and successfully solving problems teaches the person something about himself. He acquires a concept of himself as a successful problem solver, a concept that acts as a stimulus to prompt problem-seeking behavior. An education gives him the chance to confront social, personal, and intellectual problems—problems that excite, arouse, and involve him.

Our first task in this chapter is to clarify what we mean by problem-solving behavior. We will then consider how such behavior is acquired and, specifically, how the teacher may help students to acquire it. We will also examine a special case of problem-solving behavior, creative behavior.

PROBLEMS AND PROBLEM-SOLVING BEHAVIOR

As we indicated in Chapter 3, the learner is a hypothesis maker and tester. He formulates a plan, a set of hypotheses, to achieve a goal. Feedback informs him of the validity of his hypotheses for goal attainment. The kind of plan-making and plan-testing behavior he will acquire is determined by the situation in which he finds himself. For example, to understand the relation of human activity to environment, a person must learn to classify geographic and climatic phenomena. He needs plans for this kind of conceptualizing. He also needs plans for generalizing to interrelate these concepts.

To understand problem-solving behavior, therefore, we must consider the specific situation in which one is called upon to solve specific problems—in short, the *problem situation*.

PROBLEM SITUATIONS

Let us look at one such *problem situation*—the class studying a unit on India. Here, the children are exposed to many new and unusual experiences; they must assimilate new material, interpret it, and perhaps learn how to react to customs and ideas strange to them. In introducing this unit, the teacher must first help them to develop an understanding of the Indian culture. To achieve this goal—an exceedingly complex goal involving understandings, attitudes, and acquisition of information—the children must acquire complex sets of responses, new and unfamiliar ways of reacting and thinking and feeling.

A problem situation exists, then, when there is a goal to be attained, but the individual sees no well-defined, well-established means of attaining it; or when the goal is so vaguely defined or unclear to the person that he cannot determine what are relevant means for attaining it. If a child has already learned that he can understand other peoples by acquiring information about their customs and history, he knows that he will probably attain his goal of understanding the Indian culture if he studies Indian history and customs. Sometimes, however, a "goal" such as understanding the Indian culture may seem meaningless to a child because he does not know what is expected of him. He cannot determine whether the responses he is making are appropriate to attaining this goal.

Problem situations vary from person to person. You may recognize something as a problem; I may not. Reducing the tensions of the cold war is a problem for the persons who work toward such tension reduction as a goal. Getting to the moon is a problem for the individuals who want to get there. Finding a cure for cancer is a problem for many scientists. You may say that you know these are problems, but they probably are not *your* problems. Similarly, a problem situation cannot exist for a child unless there is a goal that he wishes to attain. If a child is not motivated to want to understand Indian culture and history, understanding the Indian people is not a problem for this child. However, even though he is not interested in understanding the Indian culture, he may have other goals and, consequently, other problems to solve—for instance, to maintain his standing in class or to keep out of trouble while working in a situation in which he is not interested.

Similarly, a problem does not exist for a child when he knows the means by which he can attain the goal. One of the major functions of the educational process is to teach children how to solve problems that they will meet frequently in the course of their development. Getting along with other people, for example, is a general problem. If we want to help a child to solve this problem under many and varied conditions, we introduce him to experiences in which he must solve this kind of problem. As he gains more and more experience—from frequent contacts with different groups of fellow students and adults—and if he profits from his experience by learning to react and adapt successfully in the different groups, he becomes more confident of his ability to get along with other people. He has available a wide variety of means that he knows are successful for attaining this general goal. When he is placed in a new interpersonal situation, he is prepared to analyze it and to decide on the likeliest means of attaining the goal.

TYPES OF PROBLEMS

From the viewpoint of the learner, a problem may be *presented* to him for solution, or it may be *discovered* by him.[1] Most educational experiences, including many of the present forms of discovery learning, present problems. When we say "Why did the bar bend?" we are presenting a problem. By "presenting a problem," we mean simply that the teacher creates a problem situation in which the learner may become engaged.

In some problem situations, the problem is *known;* in others, it is *unknown.* Many presented problems are known problems. A chemistry teacher gives a chemical solution to a class and asks the students to identify its elements. Both teacher and class know that the problem is to identify chemical elements. A social studies teacher conducting a discussion on the civil-rights problem has at least a general conception of what the problem is, although to the class the problem may be unknown.

There are two senses in which a problem is *unknown*—the first, suggested above, in which the learner does not know what the problem is, but somebody else does. Other unknown problems are those as yet undiscovered. That is, since man has continued to discover new problems, we assume that there are many problems still to be discovered. What is the educational relevance of this assumption? Does not our educational system hope to produce the creative scientist, philosopher, artist, mathematician, writer, social scientist, politician—one who will discover new problems, give us new ways of viewing life and experience? Is this not one of the goals of the problem-solving experiences we provide students?

A dimension of the problem's solution: in some situations, a method of solution is known; in others, it is unknown. Again, the method of solution may be known by the teacher but not by the learner; or it may be unknown by anyone.

Of what value are these distinctions? They suggest two major aspects of problem-solving behavior: (1) identifying the problem and (2) finding methods of solution. In the educational process, we must try to find problem situations that are most likely to produce both classes of behavior. But we must also ask whether general problem-solving behavior can in fact be taught. We have already implied that there is some uniqueness,

[1] J. Getzels, "Creative Thinking, Problem-Solving, and Instruction," in E. Hilgard, ed., *Theories of Learning and Instruction,* Sixty-third Yearbook of the National Society for the Study of Education (Chicago: University of Chicago Press, 1964), pp. 240–243.

some discreteness, in problem-solving behavior; but it is a uniqueness of combining many kinds of responses—combinations that may vary from problem to problem. Some seemingly contradictory facts are apparent. We teach logic as a problem-solving tool, yet find individuals who can use it only in limited ways. Is the method of teaching ineffective, or does problem-solving behavior involve many independent behavior patterns, each of which has to be learned?

A last word on this rough categorization of problems. A teacher can— and undoubtedly should—present known problems and known methods of solution; and students can learn these methods for these problems. But he should also create opportunities for the students to discover problems, to find methods of solution, to attack insoluble problems.

HOW PROBLEMS ARE SOLVED

Although the processes of problem solving have not yet been completely investigated, experimental evidence suggests the principal features of problem-solving processes.[2] Investigators have classified the steps or processes that they have observed when studying individuals in the act of trying to solve problems.[3] These experimenters create nonthreatening problem situations and analyze the results for possible common processes or similar behavior patterns.

Recently this methodology has been improved, since, with the aid of computers, investigators have been able to simulate problem-solving processes and steps.[4] Newell and his colleagues reproduced the operations used by human subjects in solving problems in a computer program,

[2] Comprehensive reviews and analyses of the experimental literature can be found in D. M. Johnson, *The Psychology of Thought and Judgment* (New York: Harper and Brothers, 1955); and W. E. Vinacke, *The Psychology of Thinking* (New York: McGraw-Hill Book Company, 1952).

[3] See, for example, H. E. Durkin, "Trial and Error, Gradual Analysis, and Sudden Reorganization: An Experimental Study of Problem-Solving," *Archives of Psychology,* No. 210 (1937); S. S. Sargent, "Thinking Processes at Various Levels of Difficulty: A Quantitative and Qualitative Study of Individual Differences," *Archives of Psychology,* No. 249 (1940). For a new approach, see H. Kendler and T. Kendler, "Vertical and Horizontal Processes in Problem Solving," *Psychological Review,* 69 (1962), 1–16.

[4] A. Newell and H. Simon, "Computer Simulation of Human Thinking," *Science,* 134 (1961), 2011–2016. See also C. Hovland, "Computer Simulation of Thinking," *American Psychologist,* 15 (1960), 687–693. The computer is a simulating device, not a thinking organism. However, it is a presently useful way of analyzing exceedingly complex processes. It has both promise and problems as a device for studying complex behavioral processes.

and then set the computer to solving the same problems the humans had worked. But they omitted some of the operations and rearranged the order of others. When the changes were made, problem-solving efficiency dropped off. Operations of this kind help pin down the details of processes that we can now describe in very general terms.

At least two common processes—*analysis of goal* and *analysis of situation*—appear in the various analyses of problem solving. Duncker's study is representative in this respect.[5]

He confronted experimental subjects with a variety of problems and asked them to "think aloud" as they attempted to solve the problems. For example, he gave the following problem to some of his subjects: "Given a human being with an inoperable stomach tumor and rays that can, at sufficient intensity, destroy organic tissue, how can one use the rays to free him of the tumor but avoid destroying the healthy tissue surrounding it?" Usually, the schematic sketch shown in Figure 7–1 was given to the

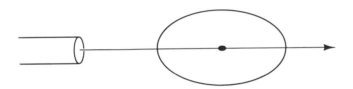

FIGURE 7–1. *Sketch given to subjects asked to solve a problem in which rays must destroy a tumor without destroying the tissue around the tumor (from Duncker).*

subject along with the problem. Below is the protocol of responses made by one subject. (The letter *E* prefixes comments made by the experimenter.)

PROTOCOL

1. Send rays through the esophagus.
2. Desensitize the healthy tissue by means of a chemical injection.
3. Expose the tumor by operating.
4. One ought to decrease the intensity of the rays on their way: For example—would this work?—turn the rays on at full strength only after the tumor has been reached. . . .
5. One should swallow something inorganic (which would not allow

[5] K. Duncker, "On Problem-Solving," *Psychological Monographs*, No. 270 (1945).

passage of the rays) to protect the healthy stomach walls. (*E:* It is not merely the stomach walls which are to be protected.)

6. Either the rays must enter the body or the tumor must come out. Perhaps one could alter the location of the tumor—but how? Through pressure? No.

7. Introduce a cannula. (*E:* What, in general, does one do when, with any agent, one wishes to produce in a specific place an effect which he wishes to avoid on the way to that place?)

8. (Reply:) One neutralizes the effect on the way. But that is what I have been attempting all the time.

9. Move the tumor toward the exterior. (Compare 6.) (*E* repeats the problem and emphasizes, ". . . which destroy at *sufficient intensity.*")

10. The intensity ought to be variable. (Compare 4.)

11. Adaptation of the healthy tissues by previous weak application of the rays. (*E:* How can it be brought about that the rays destroy only the region of the tumor?)

12. (Reply:) I see no more than two possibilities: Either to protect the body or to make the rays harmless. (*E:* How could one decrease the intensity of the rays en route? [Compare 4.])

13. (Reply:) Some divert . . . diffuse rays . . . disperse . . . stop! Send a broad and weak bundle of rays through a lens in such a way that the tumor lies at the focal point and thus receives intensive radiation. (Total duration about half an hour.) (pp. 2–8.)

How did the subject arrive at a solution to the problem? Did it just "pop" into his head? Did he flounder around until he hit upon a plausible solution without understanding why it was the correct solution until after he had hit upon it? On the basis of an analysis of this protocol and others like it, Duncker concluded that the two elements noted earlier must appear in a problem-solving process: *analysis of the goal* and *analysis of the situation.* These are processes, not necessarily phases or steps, that seem necessary to problem solution. They are probably intermingled in most problem solving. The person shifts from one kind of analysis to the other, using what he learns in each to help in the other kind of analysis.

ANALYSIS OF THE GOAL

In analyzing the goal, the person clarifies what is to be accomplished. In the foregoing problem, the subject had to keep clearly in view the character of the goal to be attained: to destroy the inoperable tumor by using the rays, but at the same time preserving the healthy tissue. The subject had to ask himself what could and could not be done. Before he had a relatively clear conception of the goal to be attained, the subject suggested solutions that were impractical or unrealistic (see items 4, 5, 6 in Protocol). When he proposed an operation for the tumor and an application of the rays without provision for protection, he apparently did not understand the goal.

ANALYSIS OF THE SITUATION

The problem-solving process also requires an analysis of the problem situation. In analyzing the problem situation, the person determines what he may and may not do to attain the goal, and what means are available for this purpose. The person attempting to solve a problem must first analyze the *conflicting elements in the problem:* rays could be used to destroy the tumor, but the rays could also destroy healthy tissue. The subject made several attempts to resolve this conflict; he suggested desensitizing the healthy tissues, turning the rays on at full strength only after the tumor had been reached, and neutralizing the effect of the rays on the way to the tumor. When he became aware that he must neutralize the rays in some way en route to the tumor, he came closer to resolving the conflict. If he had not been aware of this conflict at all, it would have been impossible for him to solve the problem.

Another way a person analyzes the problem situation is by determining the materials that are available for the solution of the problem. These materials may be either present in the situation or obtainable. In the above problem, the subject had first to formulate a principle: the rays had to be kept weak until they were in the locale of the tumor. After that, he had to use relevant information to answer the question of how the rays could be strengthened once they reached this locale. Knowing that lenses focus rays, the subject had only to suggest the use of a lens, and he had arrived at the basic elements in the solution of the problem. In some problem situations, the solution will require adaptation or utilization of materials already present in the situation. In other situations, the problem solver will have to call upon his general knowledge and experience in order to introduce into the situation available material that will facilitate the solution of the problem.

HYPOTHESIS MAKING

While these two phases, analysis of the goal and analysis of the situation, appear in the problem-solving process, they are not simple, discrete steps which guarantee the solution of a problem. Logical analyses of the problem-solving process usually suggest a series of four or five steps in the process,[6] but experiments in problem solving indicate that the problem solver does not necessarily go through these steps in a systematic order. One of the steps is hypothesis making. Before the problem solver can make reasonable hypotheses, he must have analyzed the goal and the situation. His first hypothesis may be highly inaccurate. When Duncker's subject suggested exposing the tumor, he had forgotten an important element in the problem situation. To abandon this hypothesis he needed only to remember this fact. But some of his hypotheses were untestable, such as the suggestion that "something" should be swallowed to protect the healthy stomach walls. Some hypotheses may be little more than wild guesses, while others may be developed by logical reasoning from assumptions. In the process of hypothesizing solutions, a person probably relies heavily on his previous experience. He will also be influenced by his prejudices, biases, and stereotypical thinking. The testing of hypotheses and their subsequent revision also may be somewhat haphazard and unsystematic. Logical analyses of problem solving are useful in calling our attention to the requirements of a logically satisfactory problem solution, but they do not describe how people actually solve problems or how they react in problem situations.

EFFECTS OF SUCCESS AND FAILURE
ON PROBLEM SOLVING

Lantz [7] studied the effects of success and failure in a problem-solving situation on children's intelligence-test performance. He placed his subjects within a barrier, and provided them with some tools; with these tools, they were to try to reach a ball placed outside the barrier (see Figures 7–2 and 7–3). In the first two problems the children were able to reach the ball; in the third problem the ball was placed well out of reach. To motivate the children, the experimenter permitted them to pick prizes they would obtain if they reached the ball in the third problem. Only half of the children could solve the third problem. Two groups were estab-

---

[6] See J. Dewey, How We Think (Boston: D. C. Heath and Co., 1933). This author warns that logical analyses of problem solving do not describe the way in which individuals attack problems. For a general discussion of this problem, see M. Henle, "On the Relation between Logic and Thinking," Psychological Review, 69 (1962), 366–378.

[7] B. Lantz, "Some Dynamic Aspects of Success and Failure," Psychological Monographs, No. 271 (1945).

FIGURE 7–2. *Ball-game situation for Problem I. Child stands behind barrier, with tools available behind barrier at his left. Examiner back of chair. Ball in rear corner of box on chair, which is slightly wider than box. Leash, to be placed on ball for Problem I, rests on right corner of back of chair. Folder with prizes on table within child's vision. Observer records at upper-right table. Examiner gives tests of Forms L and M, Stanford-Binet, at table at lower right. (From Lantz.)*

lished by this procedure—a success group and a failure group. Before and after the problem situation the children were given intelligence tests and were rated on a wide variety of behavior characteristics. Lantz found:

1. Success significantly increased average scores on the intelligence tests, but failure depressed scores. The answers to questions requiring thought processes, rather than rote memory, were significantly improved by success.
2. The children who were successful were rated significantly higher on such characteristics as self-confidence, social confidence, cooperation, alertness, friendliness, boldness, talkativeness, cheerfulness, quietness, persistence, and effort.
3. The success group spent less time working on the problems. The failure group took more time and showed more tension and desire to leave the problem situation.

FIGURE 7-3. *Ball-game situation for Problem III. Examiner, chair, and ball now 4 inches beyond child's farthest reach. Used tools in sight on table near observer. Prize selected also in full view on table near prize folder. (From Lantz.)*

4. Within the problem-solving situation, the failure group engaged in more fantasy behavior and less realistic problem-solving behavior.

As the data in this study indicate, a person who is failing in a problem situation is affected in many ways. His general mental efficiency is depressed, and he engages in a variety of behaviors that, we infer, are attempts to escape from the problem situation and that actually interfere with his successful solution of the problem. That long-term success or failure has pervasive effects on personality was demonstrated in the experiment by Sears (see pp. 136–140).

Repeated attempts at problem solving that are met with failure are discouraging and frustrating for the student. He can adjust to failure in a variety of ways. He can lower his expectation for himself so that he will not strive and persist in his problem-solving attempts. He may systematically avoid problems or attempt only those that he knows he can easily solve. The poor problem solver has less confidence in his ability to meet problems, is less willing to attack problems, lacks persistence and self-confidence, and resorts to fantasy and superstitious behavior as a way of attacking problems.

INDIVIDUAL REACTIONS TO FAILURE
IN PROBLEM SOLVING

Individuals react to problem situations in various ways. Some will search for solutions somewhat in the manner of Duncker's subject. Failing to find solutions, some may psychologically withdraw from the problem. Others may change it to one they *can* solve. Within the context of a particular problem, solutions that lead to the attainment of the goal are *adaptive;* those that fail to lead to the attainment of the goal are *maladaptive.* An effective solution may, nonetheless, be maladaptive in a more general sense because it is inconsistent with accepted value standards for appropriate solutions or interferes with the attainment of other desired goals. The class "bully" may resolve problems by force, but the method of solution is regarded as inappropriate and may interfere with the attainment of such desired goals as making friends. Some reactions in the problem situations we are discussing, such as aggressive attacks on objects and people, are maladaptive in both a specific and a general sense. Other reactions are maladaptive only in the sense that they do not lead to the attainment of a specific goal; they are not necessarily maladaptive in the more general sense because they may be adaptive ways of satisfying needs, even though particular goals cannot be obtained. Consider the premedical student who wishes to become a doctor but fails in chemistry; the attainment of his goal then becomes very unlikely. If there are no other means by which he can still continue in his premedical course, he will have to be satisfied with substituting some alternative goal that will satisfy his needs. If he wanted to become a doctor because of his desire to help people, for instance, he can probably satisfy his needs in another profession that involves working with people.

Repetition of Inappropriate Responses

Some individuals react to frustration in attaining a goal by continuing to make inappropriate responses. Compare the reactions of two students to difficulties in the following problem situation. The first graders were working on building activities, and Cris and Allen had both decided to build a small boat. The first step required sawing pieces of wood to a manageable size. Allen placed a piece of wood in a clamp and began sawing. But, because he had not adjusted the wood so that he could cut off the length he needed, the wood slipped. Allen looked around the class and then went back to his sawing. He continued sawing with great difficulty and finally managed to obtain a piece of wood that was much larger than what he wanted. The bell terminated his building activity. Cris began in exactly the same way, by placing a board in a clamp. As he sawed, he also ran into difficulties, because he too had not adjusted the wood to obtain the size that he wanted. Cris stopped work, opened the clamp, readjusted the piece of wood, tightened the clamp, and began the work over again. His sawing was easily completed, and when he was finished, he had a piece of wood of the size he desired. He was able to finish the boat within the alloted time.

Why did Allen persist in sawing in a way that prevented him from doing what he wanted to do? Because of inadequate information and faulty concepts, he may not have known what changes should be made in order to saw correctly.[8] Or he may have been afraid to try a new solution. Sometimes the problem solver *persists* in using a method of solution because he feels secure with this method of attacking a problem and found it successful in the past. He is afraid to try a new method or a new approach, even though the method that he has been using is inadequate for new problems. In other cases, the individual will revert to earlier modes of problem solution. Barker,[9] in an experiment with young children, found that when children are frustrated, their constructiveness of play decreases sharply; when prevented from reaching some attractive toys in another room, his subjects reacted as younger children would in an attempt to get to the toys.

An individual who is having difficulty solving a problem is probably motivated by several needs. Presumably he is motivated by the need that stimulated his goal-seeking behavior in the first place. When he is frustrated in his attempts to attain this goal, he probably is also motivated by a need to reduce the "painful" feelings associated with frustration. In this

---

[8] A number of studies have demonstrated that inadequate vocabulary development and reading difficulties are correlated with lack of success in problem solving. For reviews of studies in this area, see E. Eagle, "The Relationship of Certain Reading Abilities to Success in Mathematics," *The Mathematics Teacher*, 41 (1948), 175–179; K. L. Husbands and J. H. Shores, "Measurement of Reading for Problem Solving: A Critical Review of the Literature," *Journal of Educational Research*, 43 (1950), 453–465; H. C. Johnson, "Problem Solving in Arithmetic: A Review of the Literature," *Elementary School Journal*, 44 (1944), 396–403.

[9] R. G. Barker, T. Dembo, and K. Lewin, *Frustration and Regression: An Experiment with Young Children* (Ames: University of Iowa, 1941), University of Iowa Studies in Child Welfare, No. 1.

kind of situation, the individual may attempt to reduce his need—to avoid the painful effects of frustration—in such a way that his goal actually becomes the reduction of the tension associated with frustration. Persistence in making inappropriate responses, or reversion to earlier but currently maladaptive responses, may be effective in reducing this tension although ineffective in attaining the goal of the problem situation. The apparently inexplicable behavior of persisting in making inappropriate responses becomes intelligible if we find that the individual is satisfying some need by making these responses.

Aggressive Reactions

Another reaction to a frustrating situation is **aggression,** a hostile attack upon the problem situation or people in it.[10] Persons in the problem situation may be attacked verbally or physically; the person may throw down materials in anger, he may curse and swear or kick the nearest object. Whatever particular form the aggression takes, the individual is attempting to discharge his feelings of frustration and annoyance by directing them at other persons or things. The aggression is usually maladaptive since it does not solve the problem: once the aggressive attack is over, the person is still confronted with it.

An aggressive response may be attempted because in the past such a response has removed obstacles to goals. A child may have learned that when he becomes angry, he "gets his way." If such has been the case, an aggressive response may be an adaptive one in that it leads to goal attainment, though it may be socially undesirable or may prevent the child from attaining other goals such as friendship or approval. In other cases, an aggressive response may be a way of reducing the tension associated with frustration. Since the aggressive response may not be effective in removing the source of frustration, such a response would be only temporarily effective in reducing tension.

Dependency Reactions

Still another reaction to a problem situation is to seek help—not necessarily a maladaptive reaction. On the contrary, to solve problems effec-

[10] For a discussion of the relationships between frustration and aggression, see J. Dollard et al., *Frustration and Aggression* (New Haven: Yale University Press, 1939); and L. Berkowitz, "Aggressive Cues in Aggressive Behavior and Hostility Catharsis, *Psychological Review,* 71 (1964), 104–122.

tively, the learner must acquire ways of obtaining help—from models, bibliographical resources, measuring instruments, or even other persons as resources. Maladaptive help seeking utilizes other persons not to aid but actually to solve a problem. This behavior disengages the learner from the problem and deprives him of the opportunity to learn. He loses many of the rewards associated with achieving problem solution. Furthermore, if he is rewarded for having a problem solution—instead of for learning to solve problems—he may continue to avoid problem situations.

Goal Substitution

Still another reaction to frustration in attaining a goal is *substituting another goal for the desired one.*[11] Again, substituting one goal for another does not necessarily enable the person to solve his original problem. Frustration is reduced only if the substitute goal is capable of satisfying the needs and reducing the motivation that prompted the problem solver to seek the original goal. The more closely the substitute goal resembles the original goal, the more likely it is to produce need satisfaction. The student who wants to be an engineer but who does not have the necessary mathematical ability may find need satisfaction by becoming a highly skilled technician in a field where advanced mathematical training is not required.

Some individuals will attempt to attain the goal in *fantasy* by imagining that they are actually successful in attainment of the goal or by daydreaming about achieving the goal. The need satisfaction attained in this way is probably temporary and limited; however, some individuals will persist in fantasy solutions for relatively long periods of time. When an individual resorts to fantasy solutions for his problems, his mode of response is maladaptive even though it may be satisfying. As long as the individual remains in the problem situation, the fantasy solution can provide only a temporary escape from the demands of this situation. The adolescent who dreams of being an engineer or a doctor must eventually face his own limitations; his dreams must be within reach of his ability if he is to adjust to his environment.

The above modes of response to frustration in a problem situation are learned ways of responding to difficulties. The teacher who is analyzing

---

[11] For a review of experimental literature on substitute satisfaction, see S. Escalona, "Play and Substitute Satisfaction," in R. G. Barker, J. S. Kounin, and H. F. Wright, eds., *Child Behavior and Development* (New York: McGraw-Hill Book Co., 1943), pp. 363–378.

the behavior of his students in a problem situation has two problems: (1) to determine the probability that any of these responses will occur; (2) to infer what need systems could be satisfied through their behavior. For either of these tasks, we ordinarily need considerable information about a student's approach to problems. We begin by attempting to answer the question: What has been this student's *typical* response when frustrated in a problem situation? When the typical pattern of response has been identified, the next step is to discover what need is being satisfied by this way of behaving.

This explanation, a hypothesis, is used to find ways of reorienting the person to the goals of the problem situation. Is he satisfied by the rewards that being dependent provide? Or by being aggressive? If so, these goals must be made less attractive, if possible, or the goals of the problem situation increased in attractiveness. Although this principle is clear, its practical application is frequently difficult. The teacher may simply not have the means, or the effects of previous learning are so powerful that changes in the attractiveness of goals cannot be achieved. These difficulties should not, obviously, preclude trying to invent ways of bringing about such changes.

ALLEVIATING THE EFFECTS OF FAILURE IN PROBLEM SOLVING

Can these effects of failure in problem solving be alleviated? Is it possible to arrange the problem-solving situation to provide children with enough success so that they will not lose confidence and will persist in attempting to solve problems? Keister [12] conducted an experiment in which children attempted problems at which they had initially failed. Some of the children were put through a training program designed to improve their ability to solve problems by encouraging them to persist in their problem-solving attempts. Specifically, in the training program, the children were taught to persist even when the task was difficult, to depend less on help from adults, and to stop giving excuses for their failures. The training program began with a series of simple puzzles, similar to those on which the children had originally failed. Then the puzzles gradually became more difficult; as the children worked on these puzzles, the experimenter encouraged them to keep trying and rewarded

[12] M. E. Keister et al., "The Behavior of Young Children in Failure," in *Studies in Pre-School Education* (Ames: University of Iowa, 1937), University of Iowa Studies in Child Welfare, No. 14, pp. 29–82. Also summarized in R. G. Barker, J. S. Kounin, and H. F. Wright, eds., *Child Behavior and Development* (New York: McGraw-Hill Book Co., 1943), pp. 429–440.

successful responses. The experimenter at no time helped the children solve the problems, but she did ask questions designed to suggest new ways of attacking the problem or new ways of handling the materials. Figure 7–4 compares the amount of time the children spent in various responses before and after training. Note the rise in the amount of time spent attempting to solve the problem alone, and the reduction in time spent asking somebody else to solve the problem and rationalizing for failures. Interest in the problems also increased markedly.

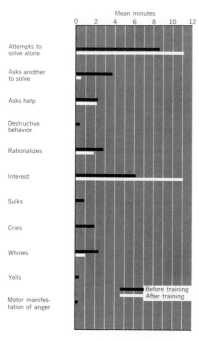

To determine the long-term effectiveness of the program, Keister gave another set of puzzles four and a half months after the original experimental period. In the original experiment one group of children had been retrained by the procedures outlined, and the other had not been trained. Figure 7–5 presents a comparison of the two groups after the interval of four and a half months. The trained group showed greater persistence, greater interest, and less rationalization than it had immediately after the training period, whereas the nontrained group performed about the same as it had during the original experiment.

FIGURE 7–4. *The responses of a trained group on puzzle-box test before and after training (from Keister).*

While this experiment was conducted with young children and the results must be generalized with caution, the experimental procedures suggest a number of hypotheses on how to organize learning experiences in order to promote problem-solving behavior. (1) The effects of failure are likely to be reduced if students work on problems within their capacities and for which they have appropriate information and skills. Here it is well to recall how the **variable** of familiarity is relevant to the learning of new material (see Chapter 6). (2) A period of preparation in which relevant information and skills are acquired will probably facilitate attempts to solve problems for which students are not adequately prepared. (3) The effects of failure are likely to be minimized if students are presented with problems graded according to difficulty. Success in solving the easier problems probably encourages interest and adaptive behavior. (4) Reward should be provided for correct responses made in attempting to solve problems, and the child should be given maximum encouragement as he attempts to solve them. The teacher can probably facilitate appropriate problem-solving behavior by pointing out difficulties, indicating errors, and suggesting new ways of looking at the problem situation.

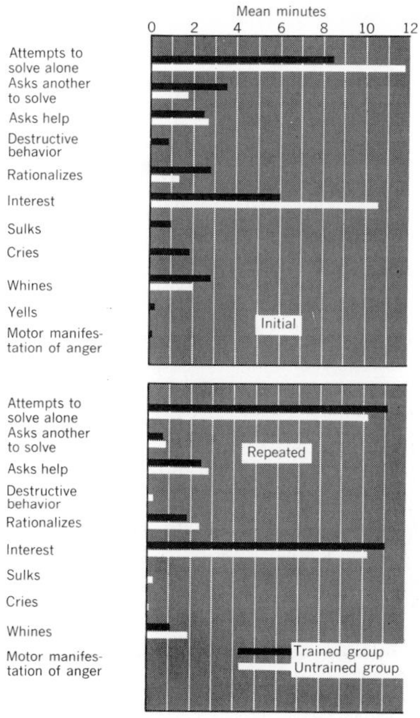

FIGURE 7-5. *The responses of trained and nontrained subjects on initial and repeated tests. Interval between tests averaged four and one half months (from Keister).*

INFLUENCE OF "SET" ON PROBLEM-SOLVING BEHAVIOR

The term **set** is used here to denote cognitive processes that predispose us to view and approach a problem situation in a given way.[13] An experimental problem used by Luchins[14] illustrates the influence of a "set" in solving problems. Luchins presented his subjects with three jars of different capacities and asked them to obtain a specified amount of water by using the measures of the jars available. Table 7-1 lists the problem

[13] Recall the discussion of Gagné's work on learning sets (see Chapter 6, p. 217). Set is here being used in the sense of orientation. Both this meaning and Gagné's imply that the learner is "prepared" to respond. For a discussion of learning set as a general phenomena, see R. Gagné, "The Acquisition of Knowledge," *Psychological Review*, 69 (1962), 355–365.

[14] A. S. Luchins, "Mechanization in Problem-Solving: The Effect of 'Einstellung,'" *Psychological Monographs*, No. 248 (1942). In another experiment (A. S. Luchins and E. H. Luchins, "New Experimental Attempts at Preventing Mechanization in Problem-Solving," *Journal of General Psychology*, 42 [1950], 279–297), Luchins found that students treated the problem as one to be reduced to a rule, even though he had made the problem more realistic by using smaller containers that the subjects could manipulate. See also R. P. Youtz, "The Relation between Number of Confirmations of One Hypothesis and the Speed of Accepting a New and Incompatible Hypothesis," *American Psychologist*, 3 (1948), 248–249.

numbers, the capacities of the jars in each problem, and the required amount of water to be measured using the given jars.

Luchins explained the first two problems to his subjects. In problem 1, 20 quarts can be obtained by filling the 29-quart jar and then pouring from it into the 3-quart jar three times ($29-3-3-3 = 20$). To solve the second problem the subject would need to fill the 127-quart jar, then pour off into the 21-quart jar, leaving 106 quarts; then, by filling the 3-quart jar twice, he could measure out the required number of quarts. Most of the following problems could be solved by this same procedure. To solve No.

TABLE 7-1. *The influence of set in solving problems (from Luchins).*

Problem	Given the following empty jars as measures			Obtain the required amount of water
1	29	3		20
2	21	127	3	100
3	14	163	25	99
4	18	43	10	5
5	9	42	6	21
6	20	59	4	31
7	23	49	3	20
8	15	39	3	18
9	28	76	3	25
10	18	48	4	22
11	14	36	8	6

7, however, the subject had only to pour from the 23-quart jar into the 3-quart jar to obtain the required 20 quarts. Problems 9 and 11 may also be solved by this simpler procedure.

Luchins administered this problem to a large number of students ranging from grade school through graduate school. Most of the students used the three-jar solution for all of the problems.

This experiment illustrates the influence of *set* in a problem-solving situation. Since the students were able to work all but one of the problems by using the first method, they continued to use this method. The set was disadvantageous to the extent that it made the problem situation more complicated and even prevented the solution to problem 9.

Luchins, working with the same set of problems, divided the students into two groups: one he allowed to work through the problems in the usual manner; to the other he gave the directions "Don't be blind" after the sixth problem. The majority of the students who heard the instruction "Don't be blind" shifted to the simpler solution.

The influence of **set induction** is further illustrated in an experiment by Wittrock.[15] Wittrock reasoned that introductory passages such as those used by Ausubel (see pp. 223–224) gave the learners a set toward the material as well as concepts for organizing it. "The sets produced by the written instructions . . . increase the probability that the subjects overtly or covertly rehearse certain pre-experimentally determined associations (Christianity) and that the occurrence of these responses facilitates the learning of related material (Buddhism)" (p. 85).

Wittrock did not give his subjects specific information on Christianity; however, he gave each of his four groups a different set of instructions before they studied the Buddhism passage. One group was instructed to note and remember the similarities between Christianity and Buddhism; the second group was to note the differences; the third group, the similarities and differences; and the fourth group was simply told to understand and remember the Buddhism content.

Two of the three experimental groups (second and third) scored significantly higher on the two Buddhism tests (which measured how much had been learned from the reading), both immediately after the experimental treatment and three weeks later. The first group scored higher than the fourth group, but the difference only approached statistical significance. When all three "set" groups were combined into one and compared to the fourth group, their mean score was significantly higher than that of the "understand and remember" group. The absolute size of the differences in these comparisons was not large, but the set-induction procedure utilized only a fifty-word passage.

The experimental treatments induced the learners to attend to selected aspects of the material and to organize it in the ways suggested. This kind of activity promotes greater knowledge of what is studied.[16] Wittrock, in

[15] M. Wittrock, "Effect of Certain Sets upon Complex Verbal Learning," *Journal of Educational Psychology*, 54 (1963), 85–88.

[16] A similar effect was obtained by Fischer. He gave identical passages to different groups; one group was told that the passage was about "Pittsburgh"; the second group, that it was about "smog"; the third group, that it was about "man and his environment." The two groups given specific sets performed better on a test of information in the reading than the third group. See L. Fischer, "The Influence of Teachers' Introductory Remarks on Student Perception of Written Materials," *California Journal of Educational Research*, 15 (1964), 221–225.

the above quotation, suggests one explanation for the effectiveness of sets in facilitating learning. Another hypothesis is that the set induction simplifies the learning task by pointing up what should be attended to and what may be ignored. The learner may then form some kind of schema into which the information is organized. Organized information is easier to assimilate and to retain, an effect apparent in better achievement on the knowledge tests.

Wittrock's experiment illustrates the ease with which a set is induced. Although set induction usually is a necessary and desirable feature of instructional strategies, it should not be too rigid or controlling; for effective problem solving requires diversity and flexibility in responding—behavior easily inhibited if the set-induction procedures discourage flexibility.

In their experiment on reading sets, Torrance and Harmon [17] illustrate the importance of *appropriate* set induction. They gave three groups of students three different instructions: (1) to apply creatively the content of assigned readings; (2) to evaluate the content critically; (3) to remember the content. Subsequent tests measured recall of the information, as well as creative and critical applications of the content to problems. For each type of test item, the group receiving a related set scored highest. Torrance and Harmon also found that the memory set was apparently easier to maintain over the three-week period of the experiment. They attribute this effect to the subjects' extended practice with this kind of set, the one most likely to be induced in many classes. The subjects' reactions are also interesting; memory sets evoked descriptions like "old," "boring"; creative sets, descriptions like "rash," "new," and "interesting."

SET AS A FUNCTION OF FAMILIARITY

In the experiments of Wittrock and Torrance, sets were induced to see what effect such instructions might have on learning. In the Luchins experiment, we saw that the learner seems to bring sets to problems. What produces these sets? An experiment by Maier [18] demonstrates that one variable operating to produce sets is the learner's familiarity with the

---

[17] E. P. Torrance and J. Harmon, "Effects of Memory, Evaluative, and Creative Reading Sets on Test Performance," *Journal of Educational Psychology*, 52 (1961), 207–214.

[18] N. R. F. Maier, "Reasoning in Humans: I. On Direction," *Journal of Comparative Psychology*, 10 (1930), 115–143.

stimuli in the problem situation. This familiarity predisposes him to see and to respond in customary ways.

In this experiment (see Figure 7–6), students were placed in a room containing pieces of wood, clamps, wires, chalk, and a heavy table which was not to be moved. They were asked to construct two pendulums suspended so that, in swinging, they would make marks with the chalk on the floor. To solve the problem the student would have to attach the chalk to the clamp, and the clamp to a wire; he would have to develop a support by attaching two pieces of wood together; then he would have to wedge the piece supporting the pendulums against the ceiling. The problem—in which familiar objects were to be used in unfamiliar ways —apparently was extremely difficult for the college students attempting it, and they were able to solve it only when the experimenter gave a general hint that the problem could be solved if there were some nails in the ceiling.

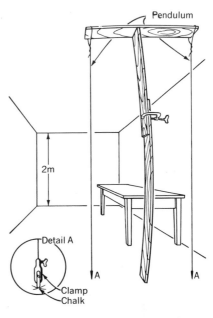

FIGURE 7–6. *Problem solving and "set." Here, subjects were required to use familiar objects in unfamiliar ways in order to solve a problem. Their familiarity with the objects made it difficult for them to solve the problem. (From Maier.)*

A comparable experiment [19] demonstrates even more clearly that a tendency to use materials in a specific way inhibits their use in new situations. In this experiment students were placed in a room which had two strings hanging from the ceiling. The problem was to tie the two strings together. The strings were placed sufficiently far apart so that they could not be held at the same time. To solve the problem, the subject would have to convert one of the strings into a swinging pendulum, so that he could stand at the second string and grasp the first as it swung toward him. Two objects were available: an electric switch and a relay. Even if he recognized that swinging one of the strings would solve the problem, the subject still had to devise a way of weighting the string so

[19] H. G. Birch and H. S. Rabinowitz, "The Negative Effect of Previous Experience on Productive Thinking," *Journal of Experimental Psychology*, 41 (1951), 121–125.

that it would act as a pendulum. Although many subjects needed a hint to recognize that the key to the problem lay in constructing a pendulum, they did recognize that one of the heavy objects could be used to construct the pendulum. The purpose of this experiment, however, was to determine whether previous experience with the objects would influence a choice of object when the subject constructed the pendulum. Before the problem-solving part of the experiment, the subjects worked with either the switch or the relay in a simple wiring problem. The investigators found that seventeen out of nineteen subjects did not use the object they worked with in the wiring problem when they constructed the pendulum. Apparently, these subjects saw an electrical switch or relay in terms of its proper use in wiring and could not make the shift to seeing these objects as potential pendulum bobs.

Although the experiments cited here are remote from many of the kinds of problems that are presented in classrooms, they illustrate an important principle of problem solving. Problem solving requires a fresh, direct attack on the problem at hand. Poor problem solvers rely too heavily on their old ways of looking at problem situations, even if they are no longer appropriate, and cannot view the elements in the problem in new ways.

To encourage a fresh approach to problems, the teacher should present students with problems that require new methods, new ideas, new concepts, new ways of using familiar materials, and should encourage students to be adaptive and creative in the problem-solving situation. One engineering professor, to encourage a creative approach to problems, requires his students to solve the engineering problems of an imaginary planet on which the conditions are radically different from those of the earth. Working with these problems, a student is forced to abandon the assumptions he has learned; he must work with new facts and find new ways of looking at what were familiar situations.

Earlier in this chapter, one of the forms of maladaptive problem-solving behavior was called "repetition of inappropriate responses" (see p. 263). One reason given for this repetition was that the learner had found old methods successful and thus had acquired a set for attacking a problem. Such persistence is most likely to occur when there are only a few methods of solution available and when the problem is especially difficult.[20] In a high-risk situation of this kind, it is not surprising that the problem solver falls back on tested methods.

[20] See E. A. Robinson, "An Experimental Investigation of Two Factors Which Produce Stereotyped Behavior in Problem Situations," *Psychological Bulletin*, 27 (1940), 394–410.

CONTROLLING THE INFLUENCE OF SET

If problems are arranged in such a way that the student achieves success by using one method, he persists in using this method. The teacher can reduce the influence of set in problem solving by arranging problems so that fresh attacks are required for each problem. If the student is continually required to vary his methods, his expectancy for the success of a given method is not unduly strengthened.

Admittedly, to produce problem-solving behavior, the teacher must induce a problem-solving set. However, if students assume that the customary rules of the game always hold, they will be set to respond in customary ways. One hears teachers complaining that students try so few approaches to problems, that they are unimaginative, that they want a formula or a rule, that they don't want to think. But have these teachers made clear that adaptability, flexibility, and inventiveness are desirable? Or have they stressed the importance of getting the "right answer," of producing an "acceptable" solution? If the teacher also rewards only the good solution, rather than the solving process as well, the student receives further information that his expectation was correct.

Although the effects of certain sets should be minimized, other sets will be deliberately invoked. The teacher needs to plan carefully the kinds of sets he wishes to induce, and to construct ways of doing so. By controlling set processes in this way, the teacher can facilitate learning.

INFLUENCE OF THE REALISM OF THE PROBLEM ON PROBLEM SOLVING

Students are supposed to apply the problem-solving behavior learned in school to later educational opportunities and to "life." Therefore, it is commonly held, problems presented at school ought to be "realistic" and "lifelike." Do students become better problem solvers if they work with "realistic" rather than "unrealistic" problem?

KINDS OF REALISTIC PROBLEMS

Before we attempt to answer this question, we should clarify the terms *realistic* and *unrealistic*. There are two possible meanings for the term *unrealistic*. Consider a problem such as the following:

A captain with fifty men comes to the edge of a river and finds only one boat, in which two children are playing. The boat is so small that it will hold only one man and not even a child in addition. How does the captain manage to get all his men ferried across?

This problem is little more than a puzzle. It is called "unrealistic" because it does not resemble the problems that people are likely to meet. Some problems are obviously artificial in this sense. Students may be interested in them and enjoy attempting to solve them, but the evidence needed for assessing their educational value is not available—possibly because we have not clarified what is to be learned by attempts to solve such problems, which frequently require the application of a generalization or a standard method of solution in order to solve them.[21] The so-called "work problems" or "thought problems" in mathematics are occasionally of this kind. They may be useful in developing ability to translate into symbols a problem stated in words, or in reinforcing the learning of a method for solution; however, they may have relatively little utility in preparing a student to solve "life" or "real" problems, such as those encountered in engineering and scientific work.

In addition, problems that resemble but do not duplicate "life" conditions are sometimes called "unrealistic" problems. Maier could have set up a miniature model of the materials in the room and asked students to attempt to solve the problem. The problem would have been unrealistic in that form, because it would not have duplicated the exact conditions of the situation in which the students were actually placed—in a room with full-size materials.

Many of the experiences and problem situations provided for students are necessarily artificial or are models of the real-life situation—with varying degrees of realism. The school is necessarily limited in the extent to which it can put students into real-life situations. If we are teaching students the problems involved in the operations of the United Nations, we might set up a mock UN Assembly. In the sessions we would try to duplicate conditions as they exist in the UN Assembly. The students can only approximate the feelings and attitudes of the members whose roles they are imitating; the mock assembly is not the real-life assembly. The students in the accounting or the typewriting class are solving problems

---

[21] Unrealistic problems of this kind, or logical games, may be used to teach principles of logic or methods of attack on problems as an introduction to "real" problems. For a preliminary investigation of such possibilities, see W. Shockley and F. J. Mc-Donald, *Teaching Scientific Thinking at the High School Level* (Washington, D. C.: U. S. Office of Education, 1964), Final Report, Project S-O90.

similar to the problems they may later solve in business, but the problem conditions are not exactly duplicated. Moving model cars in a driver-education class is not the same as actually driving a car down a crowded freeway, although such experiences may give preparation for solving real-life problems by teaching students appropriate methods of analyzing problems and techniques for resolving them. A student participant in a mock UN Assembly may learn the importance of understanding other people's views on a problem situation and develop skills in arbitrating differences of opinion. The driver-education class may prepare a student to anticipate the kinds of problems he may meet in driving and techniques for solving these problems.

LABORATORY VERSUS FIELD EXPERIENCES

In the preceding examples, it was impossible or unwise to place the student in the "real" problem situation. In other situations, however, is there any evidence to suggest that problem solving is improved when it is attempted in the actual situation? Here again, experimental evidence is limited, but available evidence suggests that the realistic situation is not necessarily or invariably superior in influencing the development of problem-solving behavior.

Lorge,[22] for example, presented ROTC students with a field problem. He divided the students into two groups: one group was to solve the problem in a laboratory situation; the other, in a field situation. In the laboratory situation the students had a model of the field problem. Lorge found that the same kinds of solutions were developed in both the laboratory and the field settings. More new elements or new ideas appeared during problem solving in the field setting, but these were not used in the final solutions. The field group did solve the problems more rapidly—perhaps because they were more interested or more involved in the problem, or because cues were more readily available to them.

This experiment does not settle the question of whether the degree of realism in a problem substantially improves problem-solving behavior in all respects. The more lifelike kind of problem may have greater transfer value to "real life." On the other hand, a realistic problem situation can be so complicated that effective problem-solving behavior is inhibited. A student who is confronted with a complex situation may not be able to

[22] I. Lorge et al., "Solutions by Teams and by Individuals to a Field Problem at Different Levels of Reality," *Journal of Educational Psychology,* 46 (1955), 17–24.

analyze it adequately. In the initial phases of solving a complex problem, refined and simplified problem settings will probably facilitate problem solving. To encourage problem-solving behavior, the teacher should plan learning experiences designed to provide genuine problems, which can be solved by the students within the limits of their experience. "Lifelike" situations may be more likely to be problem situations; however, the teacher must assess the student's readiness for handling particular problems and adjust the complexity of the problem-solving situation accordingly.

TRANSFER OF LEARNING IN PROBLEM SOLVING

Learning to solve problems usually has two purposes: (1) to acquire skills that may be used for many different problems; and (2) to learn to solve certain kinds of problems so that, when they are met again, a way of solving them is available. In either case, the teacher hopes to produce what psychologists call **transfer of training**—something "carried over" from one training problem to new problems. How may learning experiences—whether "realistic" or simulated—be organized so that the problem solving children do in school transfers to other problem situations, both in and out of school?

TRANSFER TO SIMILAR PROBLEMS

First of all, school problems should be in some respects similar to problem situations that may be encountered later; for the new problem is likely to evoke the problem-solving behavior that was effective in solving the original problem.[23] For example, if a chemist is asked to determine the chemicals in a compound, he can solve this problem by using the methods of qualitative analysis. He proceeds by a process of making and testing hypotheses, which eventually leads to the goal of isolating the constituents. The problem evokes behavior which has been effective in solving other problems of this kind.

Problem situations may be similar because the goals in the situations

[23] This hypothesis is consistent with experimental work on concept formation. See A. H. Buss, "A Study of Concept Formation as a Function of Reinforcement and Stimulus Generalization," *Journal of Experimental Psychology*, 40 (1950), 494–503. For a general discussion of transfer and stimulus generalization, see C. I. Hovland, "Human Learning and Retention," in S. S. Stevens, ed., *Handbook of Experimental Psychology* (New York: John Wiley & Sons, 1951), pp. 663–665.

are similar. Many interpersonal and social problems are good examples. You want to make friends among neighbors, classmates, professional colleagues. Communities—whether businesses, labor unions, professional organizations, or the bridge club—have similar goals of joining their members together in common purposes, in reducing friction, in stimulating interest in the group's activities. Similarly, units of subject content are frequently organized around common goals, such as learning to solve equations or to develop understanding of interrelated historical events or social forces. The learning achieved in solving a particular instance in one of these categories of problems is generalized to other cases as a way of attaining the same kind of goal.

Other problems will have similar features, usually component tasks that are alike, but the goals sought by problem solvers will differ. Writing is an example. Many different purposes are served by writing. Expository writing informs, instructs, challenges its readers. Narrative writing entertains, enlightens, and moves its readers. Few readers weep or laugh, except in desperation, after reading a scientific paper or the rules for comma placement. But writers need similar skills for each task: good sentence construction; tight, coherent paragraphs; and a system of organizing ideas to lead the reader to achieve the author's intent. Before you say too quickly that you have not found many novelists among scientists, or it has been some time since you read a scientific paper by a novelist, remember that we are not saying the writing problems are identical—only similar. The point to understand is that methods of approaching problems, component skills, even concepts and generalizations may be transferred across problems that are functionally dissimilar.

Problem-solving behavior learned in school, then, is more likely to be effective in the future if such behavior has a wide adaptability to the many kinds of problems students are likely to meet. Specifically, students may be taught appropriate methods for gathering information relevant to the problems they are solving.[24] Learning to use the library to gather appropriate information produces a set of behaviors that can be adapted to a wide variety of problem situations. Learning the operation of scientific instruments, such as the balance or the microscope, also has wide applicability to problems.

[24] See R. L. Thorndike, "How Children Learn the Principles and Techniques of Problem-Solving," in N. B. Henry, ed., Learning and Instruction, Forty-ninth Yearbook, National Society for the Study of Education, Part I (Chicago: University of Chicago Press, 1950), pp. 192–216.

TRANSFER OF GENERALIZATIONS

Many problems cannot be made similar to those with which the problem solver has had previous experience. Because the goals or the problem context is not directly transferable to a new problem. Nonetheless, a principle or generalization learned in one problem context may be adapted to the new problem situation. Considerable experimental work by Katona and others supports this conclusion.[25] In these experiments, subjects were given simplified problems that could be solved either by learning a relevant principle or by memorizing a method of solution. The memorization group was quicker in solving new problems that were identical or highly similar to the problems on which they practiced; but when the groups were presented with new problems that were not highly similar to the original problems, the "understanding" group was much more successful than the memorization group.

An experiment performed by Hendrickson and Schroeder[26] demonstrates how understanding a principle of solution facilitates solving other problems to which the principle of solution is applicable, even when the problems appear to be relatively similar. Hendrickson and Schroeder taught a group of eighth-grade students how to hit a submerged target with an air rifle. Although this experiment appears to require learning of a motor skill, a problem is involved. Since the target is submerged, the goal (hitting the target) cannot be attained by aiming as one would at a nonsubmerged target. Suppose that a student learns to hit the target at this depth, either by trial and error or by discovering that he must allow for the distortion of the image of the target. If the target is then raised slightly, he will be faced with a new problem relatively similar to the original problem. We assume that what has been learned in solving the original problem has transferred to the solution of the new problem if the student can solve this latter problem more quickly; that is, with fewer errors or with fewer unsuccessful attempts to hit the target.

In this experiment, the boys were divided into three groups. The boys in the first group were given a gun with no instructions except that they

[25] See G. Katona, *Organizing and Memorizing* (New York: Columbia University Press, 1940); also, E. R. Hilgard, R. E. Irvine, and J. E. Whipple, "Rote Memorization, Understanding, and Transfer: An Extension of Katona's Card Trick Experiments," *Journal of Experimental Psychology*, 46 (1953), 288–292.

[26] G. Hendrickson and W. H. Schroeder, "Transfer of Training and Learning to Hit a Submerged Target," *Journal of Educational Psychology*, 32 (1941), 205–213. This experiment is a modification of an early experiment: see C. H. Judd, "The Relation of Special Training to General Intelligence," *Educational Review*, 36 (1908), 28–42.

should practice until they could perform the task successfully. Those in the second group were given instructions on the principles of refraction of light; they were shown that the target was not where it appeared to be. The third group was given the same explanation, but was told that the deeper the lake, the farther the real rock would be from its image (see Figure 7-7). First, the students practiced hitting the target at a depth of 6 inches until they had mastered the task; then the target was moved to a depth of 2 inches. The number of trials required to perform the task successfully was the measure used to compare the groups. As the data in Table 7-2 indicate, the two groups that had received instruction were

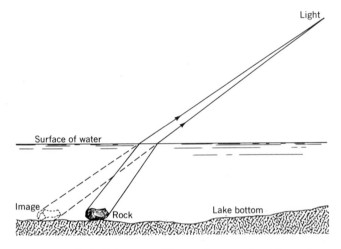

FIGURE 7-7. *Diagram illustrating explanation of re-fraction (from Hendrickson and Schroeder).*

both superior in performance; they required fewer trials to perform the task successfully. Furthermore, groups A and B were more successful than the control group in transferring what they had learned in the first task to the second task. Not all the boys in groups A and B were equally success-ful, because the problem also involved the development of skill in aiming. The data from this experiment support the hypothesis that understanding the principles involved in the solution of problems facilitates the solution of new problems to which the principles are applicable.

Two levels of understanding were provided for in this experiment, but the difference did not affect the results. Apparently the students who were told the principles of refraction without being given a specific application to the problem at hand were able to derive this application for themselves. Other experimental work supports the idea that transfer effects are greater when subjects derive the principle for themselves. Haslerud[27] gave subjects problems under two different experimental conditions. For some kinds of problems both the principles of solution and their application were explained to the subjects. For other kinds of problems no directions relevant to solutions were given. The subjects were given a test that included both kinds of problems. A week later a similar test was given. On the second test, Haslerud found that his subjects did significantly better on the kinds of problems for which they had to derive the principle in order to work the problem. Haslerud argues that a specific explanation blocks transfer because it prevents a subject from anticipating new applications of the principle.

TABLE 7–2. *Summary table showing improvement from first problem to second problem (from Hendrickson and Schroeder).*

Groups	Mean of trials required at 6"	at 2"	Gain in trials	Percentage of improvement
Control	9.10	6.03	3.07	34.1
Experimental group A	8.50	5.37	3.13	36.5
Experimental group B	7.73	4.63	3.10	40.3

This experimental evidence, then, supports the conclusion that transfer of learning is likely to occur when the original problem solving is accomplished through understanding of the principles involved in the solution. Such transfer also presupposes that a student understands that what he has learned in one problem context is applicable to other problems. The teacher may facilitate this transfer by pointing out that a principle of solution is relevant to other problems and having students apply a principle of solution to a wide variety of problems; and by preparing students to recognize problems similar to those on which they have worked and to anticipate the usefulness of solution principles in solving new problems.

PROBLEM SOLVING IN GROUPS

Group processes for solving problems are enjoying a popularity bordering on fanaticism. However, passionate convictions about their intrinsic

[27] G. M. Haslerud and S. Meyers, "The Transfer Value of Given and Individually Derived Principles," *Journal of Educational Psychology,* 49 (1958), 293–298.

value are met by a comparably passionate hostility to group activity, which is seen as a threat to individual freedom. Each of these extreme views is unwarranted. In a society where important decisions are jointly made in the political process, and where political conceptions of democratic action have diffused into other social systems in the society, children must learn how to relate to other people and how to work with them for common purposes. Some of the responsibility for this development has been shifted to the school because opportunities for this learning have decreased in what sociologists call the "nuclear family," mother, father, and children. Further, social behavior and responsibility are no longer centered around the family unit. Children need to learn to live and work effectively in a variety of social systems. On the other hand, they must not become merely dull-witted followers or one of the herd or dewy-eyed believers in the ineffable value of the group. The problem is to increase the area of individual choice by educating children to the influences any social system exerts on them and by helping them learn to shape the social influence a group exerts.

In this section, the small group, a combination of individuals selected to work together on a problem, is considered as a mechanism in an instructional strategy—as a way of producing desired behavior changes, either specific (learning a problem-solving skill) or general (learning to participate in group activity).

TRANSFER VALUE OF GROUP PROBLEM SOLVING

We may argue that group problem-solving activities are appropriate learning experiences if such activities have "transfer value." For example, we may hypothesize that participating in student-government activities prepares students for effective problem solving in civic affairs. Such hypotheses, however, need to be tested if we wish to maintain that students are being prepared to solve problems requiring group action.

Or we may claim that skills acquired in group problem solving are transferred to other problems requiring group action. We cannot assess directly the validity of so general a hypothesis until we specify both the particular behavior changes we desire to promote and the specific character of the group activities designed to promote them. Specific hypotheses—which are testable—may then be formulated.

For instance, we might hypothesize that when children participate cooperatively in planning the solution of a problem, they are more likely to "follow through" on carrying out the activities which will lead to its solution. In this hypothesis we have specified a group activity—cooperative planning—as the independent variable; and we have related it to a specific kind of behavior change—the development of "follow-through" behavior. Assume that the children are planning a field trip in conjunction with their study of local history. One of their problems is organizing transportation. They work out a transportation plan which involves assigning themselves places in the buses to be used. Each child knows in advance the bus on which he is to travel. If our hypothesis has considerable validity, the majority of the children should take their assigned places without direction from the teacher. If there is as much confusion in taking places as when the teacher assigns places, we question the validity of our hypothesis. In one study,[28] the investigators questioned the generality of this hypothesis when they noted that some children did not "follow through" after cooperative problem solutions had been planned. They studied the children who did not "follow through," and formulated the hypothesis that a child's feeling of being accepted by his group and his "follow through" are related. Further investigation suggested that children who feel more accepted by their group are more likely to follow through with group plans. In other words, other variables, as well as cooperative planning, influence "follow through."

One kind of transfer problem may be stated as follows: What is the effect of learning alone or in groups on subsequent learning? A transfer test of this kind assesses the power of the initial learning situation. Klausmeier, Wiersma, and Harris,[29] using a concept-formation problem, assigned subjects randomly to treatments in which they worked as individuals, in pairs, or in four-member teams. The experimental questions were: Which arrangement has the greatest effect on initial learning? Which, on an immediate transfer test? Which, on a delayed transfer test? In this experiment the subjects continued until they reached criterion—that is, until they had acquired the concepts. Differences among treatments were compared on the time required to reach criterion. The overall differences among the groups were statistically significant for immediate learning and transfer, but some of the differences between individual groups only approached significance. Working with another person (pairs or quads) favorably influenced the initial learning, mastering the concepts

[28] A. W. Foshay and K. D. Wann, *Children's Social Values* (New York: Bureau of Publications, Teachers College, Columbia University, 1954).

[29] H. Klausmeier, W. Wiersma, and C. Harris, "Efficiency of Initial Learning and Transfer by Individuals, Pairs, and Quads, *Journal of Educational Psychology*, 54 (1963), 160–164.

—although only one of these differences (quads over individuals) was statistically significant; pairs over individuals approached the selected significance level. But these results appeared to reverse themselves on the immediate-transfer test, where individuals were superior to pairs and quads (no significant differences appeared on the delayed-transfer test). The conclusion is that pairs and quads perform more efficiently at first, but the transfer advantage appears in the group that learned initially as individuals.

The authors offer this explanation for their results:

In the initial learning situation, the pairs and quads secured a large amount of information in a relatively short period of time, analyzed the information correctly, recalled the information, and deduced the correct concepts. Pairs and quads accomplished this better collectively than did individuals working alone; however, not all the members of the pairs and quads learned well. . . . Working alone initially, the individuals often guessed incorrectly what the concept was without having complete information, or did not analyze the information correctly, or did not recall it well. However, each individual was active and most of them improved performance across concepts during the initial learning and also learned how to go about the task. They continued improving in the transfer situation by applying the learning-to-learn procedures in the transfer situation (p. 164).

When we organize group activities, then, we should develop specific hypotheses about the relation of the activity to desired behavior changes. We are more likely to encourage these changes if we make the hypotheses explicit and if we revise them when we have evidence either that the desired changes are occurring or that they are not occurring with any greater frequency than they did as the result of some other organization of the learning experience. We need to specify clearly the desired behavior change and then formulate and test hypotheses about the relation of this behavior to effective group problem solving. Finally, we need to test our hypotheses about the relation between what is learned in one group problem-solving situation and what is effective in others. In the above example, we specified the desired behavior change as the development of "follow through." By its definition, this kind of behavior is related to effective group problem solving, since the problem is not solved "completely" or "in reality" if the proposed solution is not carried out. We also hypothesize that cooperative planning promotes this kind of behavior change; furthermore, we hypothesize that the development of this behavior in the group activities planned will carry over to other problem situations. This example illustrates the many kinds of hypotheses we need to formulate and test before we can assume that participation in group problem solving is preparing children to solve problems requiring co-operative action.

EFFECTIVENESS OF GROUP PROBLEM SOLVING

Is a group more efficient than an individual in solving problems? This question has never been adequately answered. We cannot say that groups invariably produce better solutions than do individuals for all kinds of problems. Efficiency in problem solving by groups depends on a variety of factors. A group will usually be superior to individuals when there is someone in the group who is capable of solving the problem and of communicating this information to the rest of the group. Suppose we randomly divide a class into two parts: one set of children will work as individuals; the other, in pairs. Ordinarily, the pairs will come up with more correct solutions to a set of arithmetic problems than will the group of children working as individuals. However, when the data are examined, we usually find that there is someone in each pair who is capable of solving the problems and who transmits his answers to the other member of the pair. In other words, a pair has twice as many chances of coming up with a correct solution as does an individual. New statistical procedures make allowance for this difference in the probability of achieving a correct solution.[30] But before we say more definitely that groups are more efficient in problem solving than individuals, we will need to explore the influence of such variables as the kinds of problems being solved and factors related to the group's operation.

Teachers, however, are not concerned merely with improving the number of correct answers obtained on a set of problems. They also want to develop the problem-solving abilities of children. What evidence is there to indicate that the child who works in a pair or a group is likely to do a better job than if he worked alone?

Bos,[31] in one experiment, worked with groups of children ranging from

[30] See I. Lorge and H. Solomon, "Two Models of Group Behavior in the Solution of Eureka-Type Problems," *Psychometrika*, 5 (1955), 139–148; I. Lorge et al., "A Survey of Studies Contrasting the Quality of Group Performance and Individual Performance," *Psychological Bulletin*, 55 (1958), 337–372; C. P. Duncan, "Recent Research on Human Problem Solving," *Psychological Bulletin*, 56 (1959), 397–429.

[31] M. C. Bos, "Experimental Study of Productive Collaboration," *Acta Psychologica*, 3 (1937), 315–426.

eleven to thirteen years of age. One group originally worked problems individually. After some weeks this group repeated the same tasks in pairs. A second group began as individuals and was retested individually. A third group began work in pairs and later worked as individuals. The task required the children to identify, from a set of paintings, those paintings that had been done by the same painter. In another experiment, Bos modified this task and worked with younger children. In both experiments, children working in pairs were more accurate than when they worked as individuals. Bos explains the results by suggesting that the children were more careful in their work when they had to communicate about it to other children. One of the principal effects of working in a group may be increased motivation to think more carefully and to work more efficiently. But these experiments do not duplicate the conditions of the classroom, in which the teacher also motivates the child to work carefully. We have no data that compare the effects of working in a group with working under the close supervision of a teacher.

We would predict, from what we know about group influences on individual behavior, that one of the major effects of working in a group would be improvement in accuracy and the encouragement of careful thinking. Where the group is highly motivated to work toward a common goal and where success depends upon the efforts of all the group members, thoughtlessness and carelessness are likely to be punished by the group. The more strongly a child is identified with a group, the more likely he is to be sensitive to these group pressures.

Communication in Groups

Another factor that probably facilitates problem solving in groups is the opportunity a group provides for *communication* among its members. A child attempting to solve a problem in a group can make a number of trial responses which, when made publicly in the group, can be criticized, analyzed, and evaluated. Since group members vary in their information and knowledge, a child can obtain information he does not have and can get clarification of concepts and generalizations that he does not adequately understand. Improved understanding should in turn facilitate problem solving.

Division of Labor in Groups

One of the major advantages of a group is that a *division of labor* for complex tasks is possible. This arrangement usually results in quicker solutions because the work can be organized so that parts of it can be easily and quickly accomplished by an individual in the group. Groups are not invariably quicker, for the rapidity of solution depends in part upon whether the task can be divided up in such a way that the individuals in the group can work on parts of it. Husband [32] had forty subjects work alone and eighty subjects work in pairs on three types of problems: a word puzzle, a jigsaw puzzle, and five arithmetic problems. Paired subjects were faster than individual subjects, except on arithmetic problems. Klugman [33] also found that pairs of children working on arithmetic-reasoning problems, while more accurate, needed significantly more time than did individuals. (Compare with Klausmeier's study, p. 284. Might these conclusions be related to the kinds of problem tasks used in each experiment?) Pairing off children, or placing them into groups, will facilitate accuracy and sometimes (depending on the task or problem) speed. However, the larger the group, the more complicated is the process of generating adequate group communication. The members of the group must become familiar with one another and assess the amount of information that each has before a common solution can be achieved. This communication process encourages individuals to think more carefully and to perform more accurately, but the communication process is so complicated that more time is required for achieving a complete solution.[34]

Leadership in Groups

Another factor contributing directly to the success of groups in problem solving is the quality of *leadership* provided in the group. Research evidence indicates that at least a minimum of leadership facilitates problem solution. Maier and Solem [35] used sixty-seven groups, each with five

[32] R. W. Husband, "Cooperative versus Solitary Problem Solution," *Journal of Social Psychology*, 11 (1940), 405–409.

[33] S. F. Klugman, "Cooperative versus Individual Efficiency in Problem-Solving," *Journal of Educational Psychology*, 35 (1944), 91–100.

[34] The following study provides evidence that under a time restriction larger groups reach consensus less frequently than do smaller groups: A. P. Hare, "Interaction and Consensus in Different Size Groups," *American Sociological Review*, 17 (1952), 261–267; see also E. J. Thomas and C. F. Fink, "Effects of Group Size," *Psychological Bulletin*, 60 (1963), 371–384. For the relation of group size to participants' and teachers' satisfactions with discussion groups, see W. J. McKeachie, "Research on Teaching at the College and University Level," in N. L. Gage, ed., *Handbook of Research on Teaching* (Chicago: Rand McNally, 1963), 1118–1172. See also R. F. Bales et al., "Channels of Communication in Small Groups," *American Sociological Review*, 16 (1951), 461–468.

[35] N. R. F. Maier and A. R. Solem, "Contribution of a Discussion Leader to the Quality of Group Thinking," *Human Relations*, 5 (1952), 277–288.

or six members, in a study of the effects of leadership on group problem-solving. Thirty-four of the groups were assigned a discussion leader, and the other thirty-three groups had a representative who acted as an observer. The tasks were mathematical problems, and in neither kind of group was the discussion leader or the observer permitted to express an opinion about the problem; the discussion leader, however, was to facilitate discussion in the group by ensuring that members had an opportunity to participate and by summarizing and clarifying. The group members were asked to record their answers to the problem before and after the discussion. Before the discussion, there was no significant difference in the number of correct solutions in the two kinds of groups. After the discussion, however, the leader-groups showed a significantly higher percentage of correct solutions.

When the data were analyzed, it was found that the major contribution of the discussion leader was that of protecting a correct minority opinion. In a leaderless group, the student with the correct answer can be overwhelmed by majority opinion. In a group that has at least a minimal kind of permissive leadership, the student is allowed to express his opinion on an answer and is partially protected from group pressures. As we suggested above, the efficiency of group problem solving depends upon the knowledge of its members and the amount of communication among them. In a leaderless group, the communication process is not maximized, because deviant members—those who disagree with the majority opinion—are not given an opportunity to express their views, or, if expressed, their opinions are rejected too quickly.

Throughout this discussion it has been suggested that the type of problem influences the effectiveness of group problem solving. In addition, sometimes a strong *executive structure*—an arrangement that produces a control function in a group—may be a necessary condition for any problem solving. Simon [36] provides an example that illustrates this idea. Ten persons are to cooperate to build a boat. Suppose that each has his own plan, but the ten people do not communicate their plans to each other. We would hardly be surprised if no boat resulted or if one did that sunk quickly out of sight. Simon says, "They would probably meet with better success if they adopted even a very mediocre design, and if they all followed this same design." The example is extreme and seems unlikely to happen in real life, but its point is unmistakable.

[36] H. Simon, *Administrative Behavior*, 2nd ed. (New York: The Macmillan Company, 1959), pp. 9–10.

Roby, Nicol, and Farrell [37] experimented with this problem and related the pattern of control to the type of problem being solved. One type of problem required that the actions of the group members be coordinated; the other, that the group be responsive to information received from the environment (**feedback**). One type of group used a leader who coordinated the information the group members had. In the other type, each

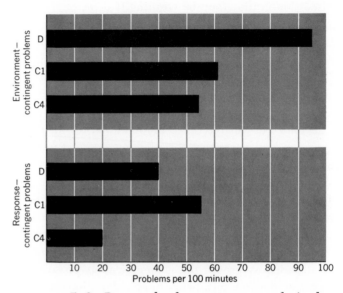

FIGURE 7–8. *Bar graphs show average speed of solving two types of problems under different conditions of executive structure. ("C1" refers to the scores made under the leadership of the "best" team member, "C4" indicates leadership by the "poorest" team member, and "D" indicates the condition in which all team members shared responsibility equally.) (From Roby et al.)*

group member was responsible for sharing his information and finding out what information the other members had.

Another variation was introduced. Two kinds of leaders were used: one with highest aptitude for the group task; the other, with the lowest aptitude. Figure 7–8 presents the results. Note that the "quality" of

[37] T. Roby, E. Nicol, and F. Farrell, "Group Problem-Solving under Two Types of Executive Structure," *Journal of Abnormal and Social Psychology*, 67 (1963), 550–556. See also M. Glanzer and R. Glazer, "Techniques for the Study of Group Structure and Behavior: II. Empirical Studies of the Effects of Structure in Small Groups," *Psychological Bulletin*, 58 (1961), 1–27.

leadership is an important variable; the low-aptitude leader has the least efficient groups. The interaction between problem type and leadership type was significant. Distributed responsibility is more effective when the group has to assimilate and organize "outside" information; centralized direction is more effective when the actions of the individuals in the groups is the major information to be processed.

Effects of Frustration in Group Problem Solving

We have discussed the effects of frustration on problem-solving behavior. One other advantage of the group situation for problem solving is that in a tightly knit group the effects of frustration are minimized. Wright [38] paired children in a frustrating situation and found that pairs of good friends showed more cooperative behavior and less conflict than did other pairs. More effective problem-solving behavior is likely to occur when frustration is reduced. Group problem solving may encourage the easily frustrated student to keep trying if he is strongly identified with the group.

INSTRUCTIONAL DECISIONS ON GROUP PROBLEM SOLVING

The first decision a teacher needs to make is whether to use some form of group activity to bring about a desired behavior change. This decision is contingent on whether the change can be learned only in a group setting. Some classes of behavior (e.g., listening to others' ideas, exchanging information with others, expressing one's own ideas in a group, and evaluating one's own and others' ideas) are evoked only in a group. Others (gathering information, assimilating and evaluating environmental feedback, identifying problems, hypothesizing, and testing hypotheses) can be learned individually but need to be adapted to group situations. Still others (performing an experiment, writing an essay, reading a book, working mathematics problems, operating a machine, and painting a picture) must be learned individually.

Other decisions require selection of the optimum learning conditions for any of these behavior changes. The use of groups to produce these changes requires that the group be organized for effective problem solving. In general, although we have seen that an effective group may

---

[38] M. E. Wright, "The Influence of Frustration upon Social Relations of Young Children," *Character and Personality*, 12 (1943), 111–122.

contain some ineffective learners, the conditions that make for group effectiveness are those that also make for effective individual learning.

In making these decisions, the teacher needs to interrelate two complex sets of factors: the type of problem and the structure of the group. *No one method of group organization is equally effective for all types of problems.* The following generalizations may serve as guides:

1. The group, like the individual, must be motivated to solve problems.

2. The group must be composed of individuals who have sufficient information and knowledge to be able to attack the problem, or who can acquire this information while working on the problem. This principle is equally valid for an individual working in a problem situation.

3. There must be free and open communication between all members of the group, if all are to participate in the problem solution.[39]

4. The pattern of leadership should maximize communication among members, and should supply a control function relevant to the group task.

5. Such factors as group size are significant to the degree that they inhibit or facilitate the variables affecting information gathering, processing, evaluating, and hypothesis formulating and testing. In general, the larger the group, the less likely it is that these conditions will be met and that all group members will participate actively in the group.

CREATIVE BEHAVIOR

Creativity has intrigued man for centuries. His response to the creative person has not, however, always been exemplary. Genius and madness have often been readily associated—a myth that persists in a disguised form in some theories of creativity.[40] Recent interest in the subject coincided with an increased awareness of the uses of talent in the Cold War. These highly selected illustrations exemplify the outstanding feature of creative behavior: It is in large measure a social phenomenon. Our common sense tells us that there is some apparent difference among people in

[39] See A. Bavelas, "Communication Patterns in Task-Oriented Groups," in D. Cartwright and A. Zander, eds., *Group Dynamics: Research and Theory* (Evanston, Ill.: Row, Peterson and Company, 1953), pp. 493–506. See also M. Glanzer and R. Glaser, "Techniques for the Study of Group Structure and Behavior: II. Empirical Studies of the Effects of Structure in Small Groups," *Psychological Bulletin*, 58 (1961), 1–27.

[40] For a critical discussion see R. May, "The Nature of Creativity" in H. Anderson, ed., *Creativity and Its Cultivation* (New York: Harper & Brothers, 1959), pp. 55–68.

originality and productivity, to which the label "creativity" is applied.[41] We ought to get about the business of analyzing the phenomenon to see whether it has distinctive attributes, whether it is rooted in the native endowments of the human organism, whether it is trainable. These are the problems and issues that recent research has attacked.[42]

DIFFERENCE BETWEEN ORIGINAL AND CREATIVE BEHAVIOR

As you read the previous analysis of problem-solving behavior, did the idea occur to you that problem-solving requires inventiveness and originality? Problem situations require the solver to hypothesize and test solutions until he finds one. The problem solver invents solutions; in some degree he is original. The more difficult and complex the problem for the solver, the less that is known or knowable about solving it, the more inventive, the more original, he must be.

What is the relationship between original behavior and creative behavior? Original behavior, it has been said, is behavior "which occurs relatively infrequently, is uncommon under given conditions, and is relevant to those conditions." [43] This definition is useful for two reasons: it is relatively easy to translate into behavioral specifications; and it places originality in the model of problem solving, obviating some of the difficulties in analyzing the creative process.

Creative behavior is behavior that results in products or achievements judged to be creative by relevant judges. Original behavior is a necessary condition for creative behavior. But not all original behavior results in creativity—either because an original idea is not translated into an achievement, or because such a translation is not judged to be creative. Creative is the label we apply to the products of another person's originality.

[41] For studies on this hypothesis, see A. Roe, *The Making of a Scientist* (New York: Dodd, Mead, 1953); and L. M. Terman, "Scientists and Nonscientists in a Group of 800 Gifted Men," *Psychological Monographs*, No. 44 (1954).

[42] See Anderson, *Creativity* (note 40); H. Gruber, G. Terrell, and M. Wertheimer, eds., *Contemporary Approaches to Creative Thinking* (New York: Atherton Press, 1963); D. MacKinnon, "The Nature and Nurture of Creative Talent," *American Psychologist*, 17 (1962), 484–495; and J. Getzels and P. Jackson, *Creativity and Intelligence* (New York: John Wiley and Sons, 1962).

[43] I. Maltzman, "On the Training of Originality," *Psychological Review*, 67 (1960), 229. See also E. Hilgard, "Creativity and Problem-Solving," in Anderson, *Creativity* (note 40), pp. 162–180.

VARIABLES INFLUENCING ACQUISITION OF ORIGINAL BEHAVIOR

One major theory of development of creative behavior, in this view not distinguished from original behavior, asserts that creativity is inherent in each person, and that the educator's task is to remove the obstacles to its growth. [44] This point of view assumes that creativity potential is available in all humans. This assumption probably means simply that a human being has the capacity for extended growth and modifiability, and that this growth potential will be used to its fullest if encouraged and not arbitrarily inhibited.

The first difficulty with this view is a theoretical one. How does the "encouragement of growth" produce creative behavior? Perhaps such encouragement stimulates the individual to try new ways of behaving, to abandon habits more easily when they seem ineffective. These developments seem necessary for being creative, but are they sufficient in themselves to produce creative behavior?

The second problem is a practical one. A teacher or a parent is told that he should not discourage growth. But how do we know when we are inhibiting an individual in such a way as to make him less creative. How do we stimulate his development in positive ways?

Both theoretically and practically, it seems to make more sense to think of creative behavior as learned rather than inherent—just as problem-solving behavior or conceptualizing behavior is learned. Then we may ask, "What are the specific variables that facilitate this learning?" When these are known, we may then incorporate them into instructional strategies and systems to foster creativity.

So far, the experimental work on original behavior has made no great or startling discovery. The first step has been to devise a model of what occurs when a person produces an original response. Investigators have assumed that original responses do not occur under ordinary conditions, but are likely to occur when certain associations are strengthened. In one experiment,[45] the test problem used was the string and pendulum problem

---

[44] One of the best spokesmen for this point of view is C. Rogers. See his chapter, "Toward a Theory of Creativity," in Anderson, *Creativity* (note 40), pp. 69–82. See also A. Maslow, "Creativity in Self-Actualizing People," in Anderson, pp. 83–95.

[45] A. Judson, C. Cofer, and S. Gelfand, "Reasoning as an Associative Process: II. 'Direction' in Problem-Solving as a Function of Prior Reinforcement of Relevant Responses," *Psychological Reports*, 2 (1956), 501–507. See also I. Maltzman et al., "The Facilitation of Problem-Solving by Prior Exposure to Uncommon Responses," *Journal of Experimental Psychology*, 56 (1958), 399–406.

in the Maier study discussed earlier in this chapter (pp. 288–289). Recall that its solution required an original response, using a heavy object such as a screwdriver for a pendulum bob. Before working the test problem, subjects in both the experimental and control groups were given a list of words, to which they **free-associated.** The list given to the experimental group contained words related to the problem solution. The examiners hypothesized that if associations to problem-related words were strengthened in this way, the problem situation should evoke some of these words from the free-association phase and cue off a solution. This prediction was confirmed—more solutions occurred in the experimental group.

In other studies Maltzman and his associates [46] found that when subjects were instructed to be original and were trained in making original responses, they were better able to solve problems requiring original responses. In one of these experiments they compared two different methods: (1) making many different responses to the same stimulus and (2) making different responses to different stimuli.[47] Though Maltzman found both methods effective, the first method produced greater transfer effects.

These studies are forays into a difficult terrain. But they demonstrate the potency of two variables—the training for originality and instructions to be original. An equally important fact is that **reinforcement** of original responses does produce transfer to a dissimilar situation.

Several more extensive studies have been conducted as classroom experiments, which apply the idea that originality must be specifically trained. The training methods have been derived from the influential ideas of Osborne,[48] the popularizer of the **brainstorming** technique.

Torrance [49] trained children in some of these principles and tested to see the effects of the training on original problem solving. The test problem was to produce ideas for improving a toy dog so it would be "more fun for boys and girls to play with." The training consisted in teaching children ways of getting new ideas; for example, put the object to new uses, adapt and modify it for other purposes, change it in color or motion or sound or odor or form or shape, enlarge it, make it smaller,

[46] I. Maltzman et al., "Experimental Studies in the Training of Originality," *Psychological Monographs,* No. 493 (1960).
[47] The methods are suggested in E. E. Slosson and J. E. Downey, *Plots and Personalities* (New York: Century, 1922).
[48] A. F. Osborne, *Applied Imagination* (New York: Scribner's, 1957).
[49] E. P. Torrance, *Explorations in Creative Thinking in the Early School Years: II. An Experiment in Training and Motivation* (Minneapolis: Bureau of Educational Research, University of Minnesota, 1959).

rearrange it, and change positions of parts. A control group was un-trained. All groups were instructed to produce ideas and were promised a reward for the best ideas. Two subgroups were specifically instructed (in accordance with one of the principles of brainstorming) to produce as many ideas as they could in an eight-minute period. The results of this experiment are graphed in Figure 7–9.

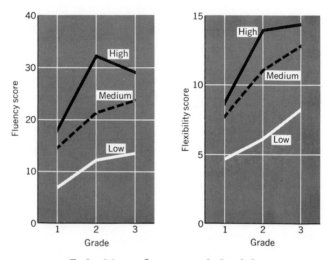

FIGURE 7–9. *Mean fluency and flexibility scores on toy-improvement problems of high-, medium-, and low-manipulation groups in Grades 1, 2, and 3 (from Torrance).*

Similarly, Taylor and others [50] found that sheer quantity of ideas does not necessarily produce better problem solving. However, Parnes and Meadow [51] found a significant improvement under "brainstorming" in-structions, and significant **correlation** (.64 to .81) between quantity and quality of ideas. This correlation is difficult to interpret because it is computed on subjects who had their first brainstorming experience in the experiment and subjects who had been in a creativity course. In two other

[50] D. W. Taylor, P. C. Berry, and C. H. Block, "Does Group Participation When Using Brainstorming Facilitate or Inhibit Creative Thinking?" *Administrative Science Quarterly,* 3 (1958), 23–47.

[51] S. Parnes and A. Meadow, "Effects of 'Brainstorming' Instructions on Creative Problem Solving by Trained and Untrained Subjects," *Journal of Educational Psychology,* 50 (1959), 171–176.

experiments [52] Parnes found significant improvement in the quality of ideas between the first and second halves of the subjects' idea-production period, suggesting some training effect. The subjects were untrained in the first experiment and trained in the second; the test period was brief (five minutes) in the first experiment and slightly longer (fifteen minutes) in the second experiment. Good ideas were produced in greater numbers in the latter parts of both experiments, supporting the hypothesis that idea production stimulates more idea production.

EVALUATION OF RESEARCH ON CREATIVITY

In all of these experiments, the creativity studied is fairly anemic when the content of the ideas or products is considered. However, the investigators are interested in variables that influence the process of creative thinking. Their use of relatively simple problems permits study of variables other than those associated with the complexity of the problem; or, as in Torrance's work, the problem is adapted to the interest and experience level of the subject.[53] So we must extrapolate these results, temporarily, to more complex problems and other kinds of problem-solving situations.

In addition, the studies have investigated what many would regard as only part of the process of creative and original behavior. The subjects in these experiments produce good ideas, but few experiments require them to test the ideas, to publish them, or put them into a product. Therefore, we should exercise caution in generalizing from what is known about one part of the creative process to other parts.

The experimental work supports the proposition, though not conclusively, that idea productivity improves with training and under the stimulus of free production (brainstorming). Groups become more productive, and individuals show transfer of originality to new problems after brainstorming instructions. These are notable effects; how powerful they are remains to be seen. Instructions in themselves, of course, may or may not have a productive effect. One of the assumptions made by some people interested in these problems is that the individual is being freed. This is a moot point. The argument involves a common fallacy that should be avoided: "If freed, then creative; creative, therefore, freed." Under origi-

---

[52] S. Parnes, "Effects of Extended Effort in Creative Problem Solving," *Journal of Educational Psychology*, 52 (1961), 117–122.

[53] For a study at the first-grade level, see C. Cartledge and E. Krauser, "Training First-Grade Children in Creative Thinking under Quantitative and Qualitative Motivation," *Journal of Educational Psychology*, 54 (1963), 295–299.

nality instructions individuals do produce more original responses, more inventive and creative ones. However, this does not prove that their creative powers were inhibited and have been released. And if teachers were to act on this assumption—that the individual automatically has original responses available and does not require specific training—they would undoubtedly be courting failure. In all of the experiments, some form of training was used.

With a few notable exceptions, creativity training is only a part of the curriculum or part of a class. As we saw with Suchman's inquiry training (pp. 210–215), no one knows what effects would occur if there were considerable press for creativity in all segments of a curriculum. There is probably a tolerance level of some kind, beyond which the press to creativity induces frustration and avoidance behavior.

Investigations of creative and less creative persons have provided some promising leads on characteristics likely to be related to high creativity.[54] Since these studies use the correlational method, we do not know to what extent these characteristics are necessary conditions for creativity. One of these factors is "openness to experience"—that is, the creative person seems more responsive to the diversity of his environment. In one experiment[55] individuals rated as high creatives used more cues in problem solving than did low creatives. At present we have at best general notions about how these characteristics may be acquired, and nothing specific enough to do more than provide a climate that encourages the development of creativity.

INSTRUCTIONAL STRATEGIES FOR THE DEVELOPMENT OF PROBLEM-SOLVING BEHAVIOR

The analysis presented in this chapter indicates that strategies for the development of problem-solving behavior, including creative behavior, are nonspecific. However, the object of the strategy clearly is to produce a broad class of transfer behaviors.

INSTRUCTIONAL GOALS

The instructional decisions require a distinction between specific problems to be attempted and specific methods of solution to be learned on the

---

[54] See MacKinnon (note 42).

[55] G. Mendelsohn and B. Griswold, "Differential Use of Incidental Stimuli in Problem Solving as a Function of Creativity," *Journal of Abnormal and Social Psychology,* 68 (1964), 431–436.

one hand, and general and diverse problems and general methods on the other. The pattern of the strategy varies with this choice. An evaluation decision is based on the same distinction. Testing procedures that assess a learner's knowledge of specific problems and methods give no information about general skills.

Since problem-solving behavior is a complex of skills and attitudes, a careful analysis of the learner's capacities and acquisitions is required. As in all instructional strategies the entering level of the learner determines what the strategy is designed to do. Studies have been performed to determine the interrelations among problem-solving capacities: such general characteristics as reading ability (required for problems in written form and for using written information), general intelligence, and ability to recognize the problem predict problem-solving success.[56] However, when we find that such factors as fluency make little contribution to the prediction we are left with a dilemma. The skill may not be related to performance, or with training of the skill problem-solving performance may be improved. A correlation study does not help us resolve this dilemma. Only by specific training and assessment of its effect on problem solving will we be able to determine what skills are necessary. Much of this kind of experimenting has to be performed by the teacher at present.

INSTRUCTIONAL-STRATEGY PATTERNS

Three factors are known to be related to the effectiveness of problem-solving strategies. First, the teacher must induce an appropriate *set*—a set to be original; to inquire; to solve the problem, not just get a correct answer. With such a set, the learner is more likely to transfer his methods and conceptions—to modify, abandon, or test them for their validity in the new situation.

Second, the teacher must select appropriate problems. Some problems have more potential than others for stimulating problem-solving behavior; they are more interesting, more demanding, more challenging. Unfortunately, we know too little about problem characteristics to be able to classify problems by their stimulus value for evoking certain kinds of problem-solving behaviors. We have to rely on the teacher's interest in problems, on his understanding of the problem area, and his willingness to be inventive.

Third, the teacher must provide appropriate feedback in the problem

[56] B. Harootunian and M. Tate, "The Relationship of Certain Selected Variables to Problem Solving Ability," *Journal of Educational Psychology,* 51 (1960), 326–333.

situation—feedback designed to reward problem-seeking and problem-solving behavior, as distinct from problem-accepting and answer-getting behavior. The rewards society provides for inquiry, highly adaptive problem solving, and creativity are not always great, and to the school-age child remote. Rewards associated with problem solving must be more immediate: the positive feedback from the teacher and the satisfactions derived from the resolution of doubt, ability to solve problems more effectively, and the satisfaction of curiosity.

Finally, the teacher must analyze the component tasks involved in problem solving.

Most important, he must distinguish between problem-discovering or problem-recognizing strategies and tasks, and problem-solving tasks. It is easy to assume that once a problem is identified, solution follows readily. This assumption may be misleading. Some problems (puzzles, certain mathematics problems) are so constructed that the process of identification leads easily to solution. In other problems (e.g., many important social problems) identification does not lead easily to solution. Recognizing the problem is a necessary condition for its solution; but it does not guarantee it.

Given the spirit of critical inquiry we recommend, as well as critical theoretical analysis, a teacher should feel free to experiment with various ideas for stimulating problem solving.[57] Many ideas recommended are of unknown validity, but they seem reasonable and are worth a try if we are willing to evaluate their effects critically.

SUMMARY

1. A problem exists (a) when there is a goal to be attained but the problem solver cannot identify means for attaining it or (b) when the goal is so unclear that the means for attaining it are unknown.

2. Problems may be classified as follows: (a) some problems are given to the solver, some are discovered by him; (b) some problems are known, others are as yet undiscovered; (c) sometimes, the solution to a problem is known, sometimes it has not yet been discovered by anyone.

3. Although the steps in problem solving are not precise and do not always occur in the same order, two processes seem to be required: (a)

[57] See, for example, Parts V and VI of S. Parnes and H. Harding, *A Source Book for Creative Thinking* (New York: Scribner's, 1962), and E. P. Torrance, "Developing Creative Thinking through School Experiences," in Parnes and Harding, pp. 31–47.

analysis of the goal of the problem; (b) *analysis of the problem situation.* The first process clarifies what is to be done; the second suggests how the problem may be solved.

4. These processes in problem solving may be looked at as processes of making and testing hypotheses. Learning to solve problems means learning to make hypotheses and learning how to test them.

5. Learning to solve problems is strongly influenced by an individual's success or failure in solving problems. Failure leads to avoidance of problems and other symptoms of frustration; success leads to better problem-solving behavior.

6. Some of the general reactions to failure in solving problems are (a) repeating inappropriate responses, (b) engaging in aggressive behavior, (c) depending on others to solve the problem, (d) substituting new goals.

7. The adverse effects of failure may be alleviated if, where such control is possible, the problems can be arranged so that the solver continually experiences some degree of success.

8. Problem solving may be made more difficult because the solver is predisposed to see the problem in ways that interfere with his thinking of new solutions. This behavior is called *set*. Such sets usually result from the solver's familiarity with the materials or context of the problem. He sees these features as he has always seen them, and cannot perceive them in ways that would facilitate solving the problem.

9. Teachers may utilize sets by deliberately calling the learner's attention to selected features of a problem or by directing him to produce certain kinds of problem-solving behavior. Frequently, solvers do not cope with problems successfully because they are not "set" to try many and different methods of solution, because they think that getting an answer rather than learning solving processes is what is expected.

10. The kinds of problems presented to learners determine what they learn about solving problems. Although some educators argue that all problems ought to be realistic, there is little evidence to support this contention. Sometimes, simplified, "unrealistic" problems may stimulate the learning of problem-solving behavior.

11. Problem solving is an important part of school experience because we want children to be able to solve problems later in life or outside the school itself. How can we be sure that the problem-solving training will *transfer* to other problems? This transfer is likely to occur when the training problems are similar to problems to be encountered later. Transfer also occurs when generalizations used in solving one problem can be

used in solving another, even though the problems may not appear to be similar.

12. Children are frequently placed in groups to solve certain problems. Groups are probably more effective than individuals (a) when the problem is complicated but can be subdivided, (b) when group members share their knowledge and skills in the service of solving the problem, (c) when the group has an organization for coordinating its efforts, (d) when its leaders stimulate cooperative endeavors, and (e) when the group is able to minimize the individuals' frustration in problem-solving situations.

13. The teacher frequently organizes groups as instructional mechanisms. When he does, he should be clear on what this procedure is to accomplish for the group members: are they to learn specific problem-solving techniques, or are they to learn how to get along and work with other people? In either case, the teacher needs to organize the group to make it productive; simply assigning people to groups does not guarantee this effectiveness.

14. Creative behavior is always original behavior—the capacity to solve problems in new and unusual ways.

15. Creative behavior is learned, although we are not yet sure exactly how it is learned. Experiments suggest that individuals specifically trained to be original in problem situations generally manifest more creative and original behavior than do untrained individuals. There is some evidence that stimulating idea production yields more ideas, some of which may be original.

16. In inventing instructional strategies to stimulate the learning of problem-solving and creative behaviors, the teacher should be clear and specific on the kinds of behavior that are included in these categories. The strategy must be designed, by the choice of problems and the ways in which the teacher encourages students to attack the problems, to evoke these kinds of behaviors. Emphasizing only the correctness of problem solutions may interfere with students' learning the processes of solving and creating.

STUDY AND DISCUSSION QUESTIONS

1. Describe how each of the following situations may require problem solving.
   a. Developing a concept of cooperation.
   b. Acquiring a favorable attitude toward athletics.
   c. Learning to play tennis.

2. Select a unit from some subject that you are teaching or plan to teach or from a section of this book. Describe the kinds of problems that students would be expected to solve after participating in the learning experiences associated with these units. Be specific about the goals represented in the problem situations, the problem context, and the alternative solutions required for problem solution.

3. In each of the situations listed below, describe the goal or goals of the problem situation, the important elements in the problem context, and the alternative solutions available to a problem solver.

   a. Becoming an engineer.

   b. Entering college for the first time.

   c. Writing an essay on the role of public education in American life.

4. A teacher plans a unit on America's participation in World War II. Suggest some problem situations that could be organized in connection with the study of this particular unit. Be specific about the goals and problem context in these problem situations.

5. Analyze the following problem situation from the viewpoint of a teacher who wants to help the student, specifying the goals and the elements in the problem context relevant to problem solution. Suggest some alternative solutions and attempt to predict the consequences of utilizing these solutions:

   Molly, a bright and attractive high school junior, is particularly uninterested in the study of American history. Her family is a typically upper-middle-class family; her father, a lawyer. Molly plans to go to college, and is primarily interested in mathematics. However, if she continues to perform at her present level, she may receive a failing grade in history. This low grade would jeopardize her college admission.

6. Suggest how Molly herself may view this problem situation and the ways in which she may attempt to solve the problem. Relate your solutions to this problem, as a teacher, to the kinds of solutions that the student may make of this problem.

7. Refer to the example of Cris and Allen and the discussion of persistence in problem solving. How could you determine whether Allen was persisting in inappropriate responses because he felt secure or because he did not have sufficient information to enable him to change his pattern of response?

8. Refer to the Lantz experiment discussed in this chapter. Assume that you are performing a similar experiment but that you arrange for an experimental group in which the children would fail at the first two problems. What hypotheses would you make about the effects of this failure experience on their intelligence-test performances and other behavior patterns? What relationships do you perceive between the results obtained in this study and the discussion of success and failure in the Sears study presented in Chapter 4?

9. Review both the Lantz and Sears experiments. Assume that Lantz asked the students to predict how they would do on a fourth problem. What effect would the success and failure experiences in this experiment probably have on students' levels of aspiration? Assume that you had a third experimental group that had failed on the first three problems; what predictions would you make about their level of aspiration with respect to a fourth problem?

10. Draw up a list of *specific* behaviors that you would expect to see when children are having difficulty solving a problem. Suggest what needs the problem solver may be attempting to satisfy through such behavior. What variations in these behavior patterns would you expect with children of different ages? Are there some behavior patterns that you might expect to observe in both a young child and an adult?

11. Discuss the Keister experiment as an illustration of transfer of learning. Draw up a list of behavior patterns that would have applicability in a wide variety of problem situations.

12. How do you account for the fact that simple directions from an experimenter, such as "Don't be blind," appear to "break" a set which is inhibiting efficiency in problem solving?

13. In what ways may a "set" in a problem situation be beneficial?

14. Some people argue that presenting students with realistic problems (that is, problems similar to those that students are likely to meet in their later lives) promotes better problem solving. In what ways may "lifelike" problems promote or inhibit student interest? In what ways may "lifelike" problems promote or inhibit transfer to other problem situations?

15. You are teaching a unit on the organization of local government. Describe some "laboratory" experiences that would facilitate the students' understanding of this organization. Also describe some "field" experiences that would contribute to the students' understanding of local government.

16. Assume that you take a class studying local government to a session of the city council. In what ways might this "field" experience interfere with the students' understanding of local organization? Assuming that this "field" trip occurs at the beginning of the learning experience, what benefits might it have in terms of enhancing greater understanding?

17. Assume that you are organizing a learning experience on the role of the railroad in American life. As a part of this experience, you take students to the local train depot, where they visit the trains and talk with the trainmen. What aspects of understanding the role of the railroad in American life will probably not be acquired from this kind of an experience? What "laboratory" or classroom experiences may facilitate understanding the role of the railroad? Be as specific as you can about the kinds of understanding that you would hope students would acquire from this learning experience, and suggest ways in which classroom and field experiences may contribute to the attainment of these objectives.

18. Some people argue that "group" activities in learning experiences actually interfere with the development of problem-solving behavior. Evaluate this argument, giving consideration to the behavior patterns that may and may not be learned in group problem-solving contexts.

19. A teacher is organizing a learning experience related to missiles and the space age. He divides the class into two groups. One group is to do library reading and make reports on the various kinds of missiles. The other group is to construct models of the various kinds of missiles. In what ways may these organizations be appropriately thought of as "group" activities? How might the learning experiences be organized so that the use of groups contributes to problem solutions? May the activities of both of these groups be organized in such a way that they are working on common problems?

20. Teachers occasionally organize discussion groups on current social problems. Some people argue that this kind of learning experience is inefficient, since many students who participate in these discussions are not well informed about the problems. Evaluate this criticism and suggest how this kind of learning experience might be organized so that the criticism would not be appropriate.

21. Some people argue that discussions of the kind noted in the question above are beneficial, even though students are not particularly well informed, because they learn how to listen to other people's opinions and how to interact with people in groups. For this purpose, these people argue, the content of the group discussion is not important. Again, evaluate this argument, giving due consideration to the objectives of this kind of learning experience and the organization of group activities designed to attain these objectives.

22. We noted that "follow-through" behavior may be associated with a child's feeling of acceptance in a group. On the basis of this hypothesized relation, would you argue that children should be allowed to organize their own groups when attempting problem solutions? Assume that children were free to make choices in situations of this kind; what factors do you think would influence their choice of group members?

23. Below is a list of three different activities. What aspects of these activities may be thought of as "individual" problems? What aspects of these activities may be regarded as "group" problems?

    a. Producing a class play.

    b. Learning the plays for the next varsity football game.

    c. Working a series of algebra problems in the algebra class.

24. In some subject you can teach, identify and describe the important problems that students should be able to solve when they have been exposed to this subject. Describe how solving these problems will help them attain the desired problem-solving behavior. Use the principles of transfer of training in this analysis.

25. What specific problem-solving skills are to be learned in this subject? How do these skills contribute to the learning of general problem-solving processes? Illustrate with concrete examples.

26. How would you recognize creative behavior in the subjects you can teach? What would you do to help students be more creative in these areas? Devise one illustrative instructional strategy to produce creative behavior.

RECOMMENDED READINGS

H. H. Anderson, ed. *Creativity and Its Cultivation.* New York: Harper & Brothers, 1959.

J. Bruner, "Some Theorems on Instruction Illustrated with Reference to Mathematics," in Sixty-third Yearbook of the National Society for the Study of Education, Part I, *Theories of Learning and Instruction,* E. Hilgard, ed. Chicago: University of Chicago Press, 1964, pp. 306–335.

B. E. Collins and H. Guetzkow. *A Social Psychology of Group Processes for Decision-Making.* New York: John Wiley and Sons, 1964.

J. W. Getzels, "Creative Thinking, Problem-Solving, and Instruction," in Sixty-third Yearbook of the National Society for the Study of Education, Part I, *Theories of Learning and Instruction,* E. Hilgard, ed. Chicago: University of Chicago Press, 1964, pp. 240–267.

H. H. Kelley and J. W. Thibaut. "Experimental Studies of Group Problem Solving and Process," in G. Lindzey, ed., *Handbook of Social Psychology,* Vol. II. Cambridge, Mass.: Addison-Wesley Publishing Co., 1954, Chapter 21.

G. Polya. *How to Solve It.* Princeton: Princeton University Press, 1945.

D. H. Russell. *Children's Thinking.* Boston: Ginn & Co., 1956, Chapters 9 and 13.

R. Strang. *Group Work in Education.* New York: Harper & Brothers, 1958.

R. L. Thorndike. "How Children Learn the Principles and Techniques of Problem Solving," in Forty-ninth Yearbook of the National Society for the Study of Education, Part I, *Learning and Instruction.* Chicago: University of Chicago Press, 1950, pp. 192–216.

E. P. Torrance. *Constructive Behavior: Stress, Personality, and Mental Health.* Belmont, Calif.: Wadsworth Publishing Co., 1965; see especially Chapters 11–23, pp. 187–393.

W. E. Vinacke. *The Psychology of Thinking.* New York: McGraw-Hill Book Co., 1952, Chapter 9.

M. Wertheimer. *Productive Thinking,* enlarged edition. New York: Harper & Brothers, 1959.

CHAPTER EIGHT

THE LEARNING OF ATTITUDES

In the preceding chapters we studied cognitive behaviors—orienting processes, ways in which man learns to look at his world and to solve its problems. In this and the following chapter we study another kind of orienting process—the kinds of preferences people acquire. These are the attitudinal and evaluative processes.

American schools have always attempted to influence attitudes. The little red schoolhouse was interested in teaching students the basic principles of American democracy, and in arousing positive feelings about American democracy and the American way of life. The modern school differs from its antecedents only in the range of attitudes that it attempts to develop. For example, we now want students to have appropriate attitudes toward sanitation and hygiene, toward safe driving, toward active participation in the affairs of government, toward ethnic, racial, and religious groups. The task is not a simple one.

Because man is a thinking and feeling organism, we cannot assume that merely exposing students to concepts and principles will guarantee the development of appropriate attitudes.

In a high school civics course, the teacher had spent a considerable amount of time emphasizing appropriate attitudes toward government and participation in the affairs of government. He particularly emphasized "respect for property" as one of the requirements of good citizenship. One of the students—who had been receiving *A* grades in this class—climbed the flagpole in the school yard during afterschool hours, hauled down the flag, and started a fire at the base of the flagpole. Whatever the reasons for his behavior, this student apparently had not learned the appropriate attitude toward property.

Although he had presumably developed abstract concepts related to law and order and the processes of government, he had not acquired appropriate *attitudes* about law and order and government.

We are not suggesting that it is the sole responsibility of the school to develop attitudes like these, or even that the school can be held accountable for the failure of the student to acquire them. The important point is that appropriate concepts and attitudes must be developed if desirable behavior is to be acquired. A school cannot develop responsible citizens merely by teaching verbal abstractions about government, law, and justice. If students are to be law-abiding and intelligent participants in the processes of democracy, they must acquire adequate concepts of government and positive attitudes toward the processes and symbols of government.

WHAT IS AN ATTITUDE?

What a person *thinks and feels* about Russians, Communists, Republicans, Democrats, the Constitution, his next-door neighbor, his closest friend, a book he has read, the color of a person's hair, colonialism, Picasso's art, the Yankees, or school integration depends on the **attitudes** that he has toward these subjects. Whether or not an individual's attitudes are based upon accurate or adequate concepts, whether or not his attitudes are appropriate to the subject toward which they are directed, does not concern us here. People do have attitudes, and these complex mediating processes influence almost all aspects of behavior.

An attitude is a predisposition to act in a positive or negative way toward persons, objects, ideas, and events. Like concepts, attitudes are *orientation processes;* as such, they provide *direction.* If I don't like

Negroes, or think that Jews are untrustworthy, I have a particular orientation toward Negroes and Jews. I have a way of thinking about Negroes and Jews which is different from any number of other ways that I could think about these people.

Attitudes are also *preferential processes* by which I evaluate, positively or negatively, persons or places or events or things. Preferences reflect the *selective* character of attitudes. I like, I dislike; I will or will not meet, talk to, or live in the same neighborhood or go to the same school with somebody. I *select* the food, the art, the plays, the books I *prefer*.

The fact that I think and feel in this specific manner means that I am *predisposed* to see Negroes and Jews in certain ways. I am not neutral or indifferent toward Negroes and Jews. I am *set, prepared, predisposed*, to think and feel in certain ways, and I tend to act in ways consistent with the way I think and feel. If I don't like Negroes, I probably will not want to live in the same neighborhood with them; I may not want to go to school with them; I will limit my contacts with them. On the other hand, if I have a different attitude toward Negroes, if I feel that they have the same rights as all other human beings, I will be predisposed to act consistently with this way of thinking and feeling. I will be for school integration and for integrated living areas; I will not hesitate to have Negroes among my friends or invite them into my home.

ATTITUDES AS ANTICIPATORY RESPONSES

An attitude is one kind of anticipatory response, but not all anticipatory responses are attitudes. A child of three or four can anticipate his mother's displeasure if he drags mud into the house, but it is unlikely that the child has an attitude about dragging mud into the house. If we are driving a car, we make numerous anticipatory responses, such as anticipating a change in lights or a sudden swerving of a driver in an adjoining lane; but such responses are not attitudes. The following characteristics differentiate attitudes from other kinds of anticipatory and other responses.

1. *Attitudes describe a general relation between a person and something else.* Anything that the person can distinguish as psychologically separate from himself can be an **attitude object**. We have attitudes toward groups of people, toward institutions, about particular people; we have attitudes toward physical objects, such as our home, our desk, our favorite book. An individual may also have attitudes toward himself. An adolescent may have an attitude toward his body; the fact that he talks

about his physical make-up as "his body" indicates that, to him, his body is an attitude object.

2. *Attitudes are directional orientations toward persons, places, or abstract ideas.* We are "for" or "against" something; we prefer one group to another group; we like and dislike. A person who has an attitude is not neutral toward the attitude object.[1]

3. *In describing people's attitudes, we can conceive of them as having varying degrees of strength or intensity.* If a person's attitude is relatively weak, if he does not feel strongly about Negroes, or Jews, or school, or baseball, we would predict that his observable behavior will not be greatly influenced by his attitude toward these subjects. On the other hand, if a person feels very strongly, either positively or negatively, about Negroes or Jews or baseball, we would predict that his observable behavior would be correspondingly more influenced by these attitudes.

4. *Attitudes are acquired.* A child is not born with a set of attitudes toward his environment. Attitudes require a **discrimination** and a **generalization** over many similar kinds of objects.[2] An individual may or may not have an attitude toward a particular Negro, a particular Jew, or a particular Boy Scout group. But if he has an attitude toward Negroes, Jews, or Boy Scouts, he has generalized his attitude to embrace any of the particular individuals who fall into these categories. A Negro, a Jew, or a Boy Scout will influence this individual to respond in a way in which he has responded to other Negroes, Jews, and Boy Scouts. Through the processes of discrimination and generalization, the individual develops a general pattern of response which we call an attitude.

One startling, unusual, or traumatic experience can influence an individual's attitude for the rest of his life.[3] Other attitudes are built up over a period of time; the individual has new experiences and interprets these

---

[1] In attitude studies, some individuals are identified as in a neutral position on an attitude continuum; that is, somewhere between the positive and the negative side of an attitude dimension. It would be equally correct to describe these people as having "no attitude," or to say that their attitude falls midway between the extremes of the attitude. The neutral point has meaning only with reference to the extreme positions on the attitude scale.

[2] A theoretical discussion of this relationship can be found in R. J. Rhine, "A Concept-Formation Approach to Attitude Acquisition," *Psychological Review,* 64 (1958), 362–370.

[3] Clinical studies on psychotherapy patients' reaction and adaptation to unpleasant stimuli supply some relevant evidence for this statement. See, for example, N. W. Shock and C. H. Coombs, "Changes in Skin Resistance and Affective Tone," *American Journal of Psychology,* 49 (1937), 611–620.

and integrates them into his ways of thinking and feeling. A child of two or three may have no strong attitudes toward school because he has had little experience with school or with teachers. When he starts kindergarten, he begins to react to the environment of the school: he forms clearer impressions; he develops stronger feelings about school; he develops some general orientations toward schooling. As he progresses through school, some of these reactions to school are strengthened and **reinforced**. His reaction to one teacher may be generalized to other teachers. Eventually, he reaches a point in his development where we can say with some assurance that he has a definite attitude toward school and teachers. The modern school emphasizes the importance of initial and continuing pleasant and rewarding school experiences for the child. The modern teacher is encouraged to be warm, pleasant, and friendly so that children may develop correspondingly positive attitudes toward him.

The process of acquiring an attitude, such as a positive attitude toward school, is complex. We cannot be sure that a pleasant kindergarten teacher or a pleasant kindergarten experience, or even a few years of a rewarding and agreeable school environment, will result invariably in the acquisition of a positive attitude toward school. A pleasant school environment may or may not offset the influence of a parent who continually rewards expressions of his own negative school attitude. Since attitudes are **sets** to respond to one's environment, the stimuli to which one is responding during attitude development are important determinants of the attitude that is learned.

5. *An attitude is a consistent way of interpreting and responding to one's environment.*

DIFFERENCE BETWEEN ATTITUDES AND MOTIVES

Attitudes and **motives**, like concepts, are not directly seen. Since both are inferred from behavior we observe, we should make a distinction between them.

An *attitude* prepares the individual to be motivated in specific ways, but it is not an existing motive. For example, a student who has a positive, constructive attitude toward school work will be predisposed to be motivated by assignments given by the teacher. A student with a negative attitude either will not study at all or will study poorly. Similarly, the student who likes school work is more likely to be motivated to achieve the awards given for a superior performance than is the student who feels negatively toward school work.[4]

A *motive* is more specific than an attitude. The student with a positive attitude toward school work will be motivated in many different but related ways, such as working for a high grade on a test, doing extra readings, studying his notes thoroughly. In each of these cases the student is working toward a particular goal; he works for these goals because he has a general attitude toward goals of this kind.

ATTITUDES AS INFERENCES FROM OBSERVED BEHAVIOR

We infer a person's attitudes by observing his behavior in situations where he has a choice of positive and negative ways of responding. We may, for instance, present him with a number of statements about objects, events, or ideas and ask him to indicate whether he likes or dislikes the various items (see Figure 8–1). From his pattern of likes and dislikes, we infer his attitude toward the objects to which the items refer. We also predict that he will respond similarly to other instances of the attitude object and to similar and related objects. If a boy typically behaves aggressively on the ballfield, kicking other players or cursing the umpire when he is annoyed, we may suspect that he will treat other players in other games and other people in other situations in much the same way. If he, in fact, does, we say he has an attitude.

On the other hand, a simple dislike for broccoli or last year's math teacher does not constitute an attitude as we are using the word here. Unless these dislikes are generalized to people—or foods—with similar characteristics, it seems simpler to treat the behavior as a single stimulus-response association, from which we can predict nothing about a typical way of responding.

VALIDITY AND RELIABILITY OF INFERENCES ABOUT ATTITUDES

How do we know whether our inferences about attitudes are **reliable** and **valid** (see pp. 14–15)?

---

[4] We are not concerned here with the complex personality reaction in which the individual may do that which he hates; our interest is with the more general case, in which attitudes predispose to motivations consistent with the attitudes.

COLLEGE QUESTIONNAIRE

Directions: There are not any right or wrong answers on this

questionnaire. You do not even have to put your name on it. ...

Answer quickly and frankly, don't think about special cases, and

Please Do Not Omit Any Item.

ALL YOU HAVE TO DO IS READ EACH OF THE STATEMENTS BELOW AND:

If you agree completely, encircle the - - - SA (strongly agree)

If you agree in general but want to

change it a little - - - - - - - - - - - - a (agree)

If you neither agree nor disagree,

encircle the - - - - - - - - - - - - - - - N (neutral)

If you disagree in general but not

with everything - - - - - - - - - - - - - d (disagree)

If you disagree completely, encircle the - SD (strongly

disagree)

(Sample Items)

1. A person who goes to college will live a happier and more profitable life than a person who does not go to college.

   S (a) N d SD

2. It is better for one to work hard now to get a college education
   than regretting it when it is too late.

5. Everyone should work a year or two before going to college.

10. All a person needs to get by on is an 8th grade education.

17. College is optional for women and essential for men.

29. College helps one to develop a better personality.

34. College just spoils you for working afterwards.

FIGURE 8-1. *An attitude scale (from Edling). The
use of this scale is described in Chapter 1 (see note 10).*

Reliability of Inferences

The person who constructed the attitude scale presented in Figure 8–1 was confronted with this question. First of all, to secure reliability, he tried to eliminate the ambiguity in the statements, so that each respondent would be confronted with a standard stimulus. He then had to make sure that individual responses did not change substantially when he administered the instrument on successive occasions.

The problem for the teacher in assessing the reliability of his inferences is logically the same. However, he usually cannot—as the scale constructor could—secure a standard condition. He observes how students treat each other in class, in the corridor, in the malt shop; and he must decide in what ways these conditions are comparable. In such situations he may make a risky generalization—that the situations are comparable in some respect for the student.

But the teacher faces a more serious problem in his attempts to assess attitudes. Under the ordinary conditions of schooling, he observes a limited **sample** of pupil behavior. Therefore, he cannot be sure that students respond similarly in *all* or even *most* comparable situations. He can improve the reliability of his observations, on which his inferences are based, only by sampling as many representative instances of a student's attitudes as he can.

Validity of Inferences

The problem of the validity of an inference about attitudes is also substantial. How can the teacher be sure that an observed behavior is really indicative of the attitude he infers? To take an extreme example: Ordinarily, physical attack may be interpreted as indicating intense dislike, but not always. Disturbed persons may not be striking the person they hit, but what that person represents; their dislike is not of the person struck, but of what he symbolizes. Or consider a less extreme example: A teacher may assume that some of his students have a negative attitude toward science or scientists. He has asked questions about science, and they have reacted negatively. Is his inference valid? Certainly, he would need more evidence before he drew conclusions about students' attitudes toward science. If he learns that these students do not enroll in science courses, never watch science programs on television, make disparaging remarks about science students, he can have somewhat more confidence that his inference is correct.[5]

HOW ATTITUDES ARE LEARNED

We have stressed the importance of the relationship between experience and attitude formation and development. The child acquires ways of responding to the set of stimuli or environmental events which form the pattern of his experience. The child who says, "Negroes are lazy" or "School isn't any fun," has learned a way of interpreting and responding to his environment.

Attitudes are responses, and acquiring an attitude is a behavior change. The general principles that explain behavior change apply to attitudes as well as to other kinds of behavior phenomena.

Behavior change begins in a motivated state of the organism. The **need system** of the person is aroused or energized, and the person makes responses to reduce the state of need. Attitudes, as responses, must be need satisfying, or must lead to responses which themselves are directly satisfying. The relationship of complex sets of responses, such as attitudes, to the need system of the organism is not obvious. Nonetheless, we can frequently trace the relationship of an acquired attitude to the satisfaction of a need.

REWARDS FOR LEARNING ATTITUDES

A child usually has a need for affection and love from his parents. To satisfy this need, the child learns to behave in ways which are pleasing to the parents. He may have learned that when he acts as his parents do, he receives strong approval and demonstrations of affection. He notices that his parents have certain ways of talking and acting when the subject of Negroes comes up, or he observes his parents in contact with Negroes. He hears his father making derogatory remarks about the living habits of Negroes and "detrimental effects that Negroes have on a neighborhood." He hears his mother's suspicions about the Negro employees at a local department store. If the child makes unkind remarks about a Negro playmate, he is not punished for them, but is rewarded by subtle demonstrations of approval or affection. This child may quickly learn that these

---

[5] One method to determine students' attitudes toward science used written essays on this subject. See M. Mead and R. Metraux, "Image of the Scientist among High School Students," *Science*, 126 (1957), 394–390.

particular responses and the implied ways of thinking and feeling, when expressed openly and verbally, bring reward and not punishment. Adult approval and rewards for behavior resulting from a given attitude serve as the mechanism by which the child learns that a given attitude is likely to satisfy his needs.

Since interpersonal relationships are the situations in which many of our social needs are satisfied, we would expect individuals to learn attitudes which maintain satisfying interpersonal relations. Many of the child's basic attitudes are learned in the context of the family, where the behaviors associated with these attitudes are consistently rewarded and intimately tied in with the child's needs for satisfaction. If a child wants to be loved and valued by his teachers, his classmates, parents, and neighborhood friends, he will probably acquire the attitudes which guarantee the maintenance of these friendly and satisfying relations.

CONFLICT IN ATTITUDES

A child may be in **conflict** over the appropriate attitudes to adopt, because he may be striving for two or more goals, both of which are desirable but which cannot be attained at the same time. For example, a child may want the approval of his parents and of his classmates. In some cases attaining the approval of both is incompatible. The child is in conflict because as he strives for the goal of parent approval, he also wishes to avoid the undesirable aspects of winning parent approval— namely, giving up the approval of his peers. As he strives for student approval, he wishes to avoid the undesirable aspects of winning student approval—namely, giving up parent approval. One aspect of this kind of conflict can be diagramed as in Figure 8–2.[6] As the child approaches one desirable goal, feelings of avoidance also arise. When the feelings of avoidance are strong enough, he withdraws from striving for the first desirable goal and returns to a point where his feelings of approach and avoidance balance each other. He then may strive for the second desirable goal, but the same process of approach and avoidance is repeated. He will approach this goal until his avoidance feelings are strong enough to pull him away from it.

We would expect to find the child in our example doing things to obtain parental approval but at the same time not committing himself whole-

---

[6] From J. Dollard and N. Miller, *Personality and Psychotherapy* (New York: McGraw-Hill Book Company, 1950), p. 356. By permission of the publisher.

heartedly to winning this approval. We would also expect to find him seeking to win student approval but, again, not committing himself wholeheartedly to winning this approval. He will appear to vacillate or to be in conflict over what he wants. He will remain in this state of conflict until one goal is more desired by him than the other or until neither becomes important.

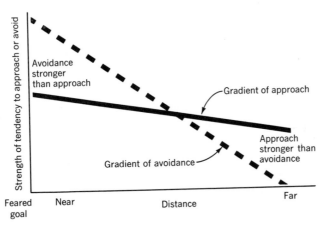

FIGURE 8–2. *Simple graphic representation of an approach-avoidance conflict. The tendency to approach is the stronger of the two tendencies when the subject is far from the goal, while the tendency to avoid is the stronger of the two when he is near to the goal. Therefore, when far from the goal, the subject should tend to approach part way and then stop. In short, he should tend to remain in the region where the two gradients intersect. (From Dollard and Miller.)*

Where there is a conflict between the attitudes for maintaining one kind of relationship and those appropriate for maintaining another, the child will choose the set of attitudes which promise the maintenance of the relationship which is more important to him, or he will work out sets of attitudes which are compatible with maintaining both kinds of relationships. He may appear to act as if he had one set of attitudes when relating to his teacher and another set when relating to his parents.

The diversity and conflicting nature of many special attitudes in our society frequently leave children in a state of indecision about what attitudes are most appropriate. This problem seems to be particularly acute as the child's world of social relations expands, and it becomes important for him to "get along with" a wide variety of people who hold divergent attitudes. As one teenager put the problem,

It's pretty hard to know what to think. Mostly kids in our school think that going steady is the thing to do. But my parents keep telling me that I shouldn't be tied down to one boy, that I'm too young to decide now about a boy. They want me to go to college, and keep saying that I shouldn't be thinking about marriage at my age. But if I don't go steady with a boy, I'll be left out of things around here. A girl who hasn't a steady is just a nobody. The other kids seem to think that there's something wrong with you if you can't tie a boy to you.[7]

This teenager is undecided and in conflict over discrepant attitudes toward dating. How she will resolve the conflict will depend upon what attitudes will ultimately lead to the greatest satisfaction of her needs. For the time being she vacillates between accepting the attitudes of her parents and those of her fellow students, a situation which is not entirely satisfactory to her and gives her only temporary relief from her uneasiness and self-doubt. Whatever attitude she develops, either momentarily or more permanently, will be a function of her needs and of the behavior that leads to the satisfaction of these needs.

This conflict is an example of the more general decision problem a person faces in attitude acquisition. The making of a decision among models, for example, is a choice among alternatives. Such choices require a person to select one alternative and to reject another. The choices are *dissonance producing;* that is, the person perceives them as incompatible. I can't say I am for civil rights and, at the same time, discriminate against minority-group members. I cannot say that I want to be a medical doctor and, at the same time, avoid a pre-med course. **Dissonance theory** predicts that a person in such situations will expend effort to reduce the dissonance.[8] The effort may be cognitive—devaluing one of the alternatives or readjusting the cognition in some way. I say that being a medical doctor isn't really very important, or that a particular act of discrimination is really a service to its object.

There is some evidence that a person in a dissonance-producing situa-

[7] H. H. Remmers and D. H. Radler, *The American Teenager* (Indianapolis–New York: Bobbs-Merrill Company, 1957), p. 164. Copyright 1957, used by special permission of the publisher.

[8] See L. Festinger, *Theory of Cognitive Dissonance* (Evanston, Ill.: Row, Peterson, 1957).

tion will expend effort to study the alternatives.[9] So we would expect people to think about the alternative attitudinal responses portrayed by models or advocated by them. There is also good support for the notion that having made a choice a person values it more highly than he did before he made it.[10]

In this section we have given a general principle by which the learning of attitudes may be explained. Responses that are rewarded become stable, general ways of responding called attitudes. But why does a person make the response at all? How does he know what kinds of responses to make? In the following section we discuss this question.

INFLUENCE OF MODELS ON THE ACQUISITION OF ATTITUDES

Recall your first few weeks in college, or your first few days in a new job. How did you find out what the appropriate ways of acting were in these new situations? You undoubtedly had acquired many behavior patterns that could be adapted to the requirements of the new social context. But there were many unknowns—simple things like the appropriate dress in certain places, or the range of permissible behaviors at certain events. Institutions like colleges frequently spell out the expectations, but even these formal prescriptions resolve only some of the ambiguities. In these and many similar situations, a person will identify another person who is successfully coping with the situation and will (either deliberately or unconsciously) imitate his behavior.

The idea of **imitation** (or **identification** with another—we use these terms interchangeably) has been in disrepute for some time among social scientists. However, recent studies [11] investigating this phenomenon have reawakened interest in what is an almost universal characteristic of behavior acquisition. Mainly, they have tried to discover the specific conditions under which one person will imitate another. In later sections we will discuss what is known about these conditions. A clear understanding of them is necessary to understand how attitudes are acquired.

---

[9] See E. Walster and L. Festinger, "Decisions among Imperfect Alternatives," in L. Festinger, *Conflict, Decision, and Dissonance* (Stanford, Calif.: Stanford University Press, 1964), pp. 131–145.

[10] L. Festinger, *Theory of Dissonance* (note 8).

[11] A. Bandura, "Social Learning through Imitation," in M. R. Jones, ed., *Nebraska Symposium on Motivation* (Lincoln: University of Nebraska Press, 1962), pp. 211–269. See also A. Bandura, *The Social Learning of Deviant Behavior* (New York: Holt, Rinehart & Winston, 1964); A. Bandura and R. Walters, *Social Learning and Personality Development* (Holt, Rinehart & Winston, 1963).

Attitudinal behavior may be acquired through problem solving. A person coping with a problem or adapting to a situation tries out a response and receives positive **feedback**. The behavior is learned because it is **reinforced**. Or this behavior may be an instance of response generalization. You may react to the characteristics of another person positively or negatively, but you acquired these ways of responding to such characteristics before you met this person. A negative reaction to bearded beatnik types might easily generalize to bearded citizens of high repute. The response has transferred to new cues.

However, much human behavior is probably learned by observance of other people's ways of responding. One person serves as a response guide, or **model**. A second person matches the behavior of the model.

Consistent with the model of the learning organism used throughout this text, we assume that matching (imitative) behavior has some reward value for the person who imitates another's behavior. Obviously, if the person is rewarded for imitating, we expect him to acquire the matching behavior. But what prompts him to match in the first place?

Variables Influencing Imitative Behavior

A recent experiment by Bandura makes clear the model characteristics that prompt imitative behavior.[12] In this experiment children were exposed to a model who controlled some highly attractive rewards (toys). Also present in the treatments were two other potential models; one of them received toys from the first model, and one of them did not. Since the children received toys some of the time from the controller, they could regard the second model as a rival. Whom would the children imitate—the model who controlled the rewards or the one who received them? The results were clear and significant: " . . . the model who possessed rewarding power was imitated to a greater degree than was the rival or the ignored model" (p. 531). Bandura interprets his results to support a social-power theory of influence. Persons who have social power are more likely to be imitated.

In a study of imitation of aggressive behavior, Bandura exposed children to an aggressive model and a nonaggressive model.[13] The aggressive model carted off all the toys in a playroom after displaying aggression. As

[12] A. Bandura, D. Ross, and S. Ross, "A Comparative Test of the Status Envy, Social Power, and Secondary Reinforcement Theories of Identificatory Learning," *Journal of Abnormal and Social Psychology*, 67 (1963), 527–534.

[13] A. Bandura, D. Ross, and S. Ross, "Transmission of Aggression through Imitation of Aggressive Models," *Journal of Abnormal and Social Psychology*, 63 (1961), 575–582.

expected, greater imitation of the aggressive model was found. When the children were asked whom they would like to be like, over 60 per cent of them said, "Rocky" (the aggressive model). When asked why, they responded, "Because he got all the toys."

Does the learner in these situations need to be rewarded for matching his behavior to that of the model? A study by Bandura and McDonald provides some information on this problem.[14] The behavior studied was an attitudinal behavior called moral judgment. The child was presented stories describing two children: one of them caused considerable damage while trying to be helpful; the other did little damage, but his intent was suspect. The child was asked to tell who "did the worse thing" and why. The children were tested on stories of this kind to see how they answered. Each child was then exposed to a model who responded to similar stories but in an opposite way. For example, if the child typically picked the well-intended but more destructive child, he was exposed to a model who picked the less destructive child whose good intentions were suspect.

Three experimental treatments were used. In one, the examiner reinforced the model by saying "Good" or "That's fine"; he also reinforced the child who imitated the model's choices. In the second condition, only the model was rewarded. In the third condition, no model was present but the child was rewarded if he shifted his mode of responding.

The results are graphed in Figure 8–3. As can be seen, reinforcing the child for imitating did not strengthen the treatment.[15] The important point is that the presence of the rewarded model was sufficient to instigate matching behavior.

However, this is not all the story. Mischel,[16] using a similar design, found that reinforcement is effective in maintaining the strength of the behavior change. During the acquisition phase, reinforcement again added nothing to the behavior change; but on a test a month later, reinforced subjects produced the imitated behavior at a higher level.

The conclusion from these studies is that the presence of a model possessing social power is sufficient to elicit matching behavior. If the learner is also reinforced during this acquisition phase, the behavior change will probably be maintained at greater strength.

Will the mere presence of a model with social power always produce

[14] A. Bandura and F. J. McDonald, "The Influence of Social Reinforcement and the Behavior of Models in Shaping Children's Moral Judgments," *Journal of Abnormal and Social Psychology*, 67 (1963), 274–281.

[15] The desired change seldom occurred; hence, the experimenter reinforced very few responses.

[16] W. Mischel and D. Schafer, "Effects of Devaluation of a Reinforcing and Non-reinforcing Model" (Stanford, Calif.: Unpublished manuscript, 1964).

imitative behavior in others? The model describes the necessary and sufficient conditions for attitude acquisitions. However, other variables do affect the likelihood that a person will be a model.

We are not surprised that small children imitate their parents and older brothers and sisters. Sheer availability seems the simplest explanation. But as the child moves into a larger social world, his model must have not only social power but *the kind of social power that the imitator wants*. If

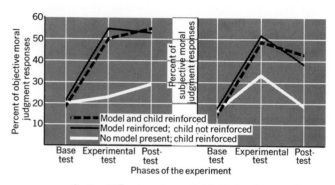

FIGURE 8–3. *Effects of models' behavior and reinforcing procedures on changes in children's moral judgments* (*adapted from Bandura and McDonald*).

the controller in the Bandura experiment had controlled stock certificates instead of toys, the children probably would not have imitated (identified with) him. Perhaps professors are not identification figures for all students, because the rewards they attain are not desired. In other cases, the rewards may be attractive but the behavior to be acquired to obtain them may elicit punishment in some form. Bandura found that girls less frequently imitated aggressive models.[17] Girls are not usually rewarded and are often punished for aggressive behaviors that are at least tolerated in boys.

A final word needs to be said on the characteristics of the imitative behavior itself. The popular assumption is that it is literal copying. Fads are an obvious example. Some matching behavior may be literal; some may not. The amount of literalness probably depends on the specificity of the behavior imitated, the social and physical constraints, and the range of situations to which the behavior is transferred. A gesture may be matched quite literally; a style of dress or a way of speaking may be only

[17] A. Bandura, D. Ross, and S. Ross, "Imitation of Film-Mediated Aggressive Models," *Journal of Abnormal and Social Psychology*, 66 (1963), 3–11.

generally copied and adapted to a variety of situations. Bandura found that the children in his experiments, where two models were present, put together combinations of each model's behavior.

From these conclusions, we may construct a model of a learning situation in which attitudes are likely to be acquired: *place a learner in the presence of a model who has high social power; reinforce the imitation; provide the conditions for rewarding the performance of the behavior when the model is no longer present.* As teachers, we observe children with attitudes. We assume that at some time in their experience they were in a learning situation like the one described above. If we wish to produce new attitude acquisitions, an analogous learning experience will have to be constructed.

Imitation and Identification

Does imitation occur only when the model is present? Since a person can be observed to be acting like another person who is not present, some theorists have treated this delayed imitation as a special process called *identification*. A distinction on this basis seems trivial. Another reason for making the distinction has been that some theorists think that imitative behavior occurs with relatively simple, easily observed behaviors, but that identification occurs with complex emotional and evaluative responses. The necessity of this distinction is weakened by a recent study, in which subjects responded with pain reactions when they were watching a model portraying pain—even though they themselves were not receiving a pain stimulus.[18] For convenience and to accommodate present usage, we will use the terms *identification* and *imitation* interchangeably. For example, the term *identification figure* is commonly used. We mean by it a model whose behavior is imitated, leading to the learning of new responses by the imitator which can be elicited independently under appropriate conditions. We also use the verb *identify* interchangeably with the verb *imitate*.

Educational Significance of Imitative Behavior

A child is exposed to many models. Since his family provides models for his earliest learning, and is a powerful source of rewards, we expect the child's attitudes to have been shaped principally by these influences.

[18] A. Bandura and T. Rosenthal, "Vicarious Classical Conditioning as a Function of Arousal Level," *Journal of Personality and Social Psychology* (in press).

However, such influences may work against the kinds of attitude changes the school is promoting. Consider the following example:

Tom was enrolled as a freshman in a pre-engineering program. He first came to the counseling bureau because he was academically deficient. Tom was having difficulty in applying himself to studying. Tom's interests were consistent with his plans, and he had sufficient ability to follow the pre-engineering program successfully. Why was he doing poorly in his academic work? Tom frequently referred to his father, who had not gone to college but was a highly successful insurance salesman; Tom enjoyed many of the benefits that resulted from his family's superior economic position. Tom thought highly of his father and admired his success. As he discussed his goals and his academic problems, he frequently said that he could be as successful as his father had been without pushing himself through a demanding academic program. Tom questioned whether it was worth his while to put off the rewards of success in business to go to college.

A short time later Tom's father came in to discuss Tom's academic problems. The father made it quite clear during the course of conversation that, while he thought college was important for Tom, he himself had been a success even though he had not had the opportunities for a college education. He subtly disparaged the values of a college education. If he spoke in this manner in Tom's presence, at least occasionally, it is highly probable that Tom's basic attitude toward the importance of college had been largely shaped by his father. If Tom wanted to be like his father, and he did, then he would think and act as his father did. This meant taking a deprecating attitude toward the values of college and feeling that the important thing was to get into business and push himself to success as his father had done before him.

This example, one of many that can be cited by almost every teacher, shows how the child's attitude toward school has been shaped by family members. When these attitudes are not consistent with those the school seeks to develop in the child, the school may have little influence on the child's attitudes.

The Bennington College study [19] provides interesting examples of how one school influenced some of its students but not others. Attitudes

---

[19] The complete details of the Bennington study appear in T. M. Newcomb, *Personality and Social Change* (New York: Dryden Press, 1943). Summaries and condensations appear in T. M. Newcomb and E. L. Hartley, eds., *Readings in Social Psychology* (New York: Henry Holt and Co., 1947), pp. 345–357; T. M. Newcomb, "Attitude Development as a Function of Reference Groups: The Bennington Study," in E. E. Maccoby, T. M. Newcomb, and E. L. Hartley, eds., *Readings in Social Psychology*, 3rd ed. (New York: Henry Holt and Co., 1958), pp. 265–275.

of the girls at Bennington College toward public affairs were studied over a four-year period. Many of the girls held conservative social and political attitudes. On the other hand, the faculty of the college strongly advocated a more liberal point of view and encouraged an active interest in public affairs. One of the major questions the study sought to answer was whether the Bennington atmosphere produced a substantial change in the attitudes of the girls who had spent several years there. Cited below are comments made by some of the most conservative girls; that is, girls whose attitudes had changed the least in their stay at Bennington. Included also are comments from girls who were the most liberal; that is, girls whose attitudes had changed the most during their stay at Bennington.

CONSERVATIVE GIRLS

F32: *Family against faculty has been my struggle here.* As soon as I felt really secure here I decided not to let the college atmosphere affect me too much. Every time I have tried to rebel against my family I found out how terribly wrong I am, and so I have naturally kept to my parents' attitudes.

D22: I would like to think like the college leaders, but I'm not bold enough and I don't know enough. So the college trend means little to me; I don't even realize how much more conservative I am than the others. *I guess my family influence has been strong enough to counterbalance the college influence.*

M12: It isn't that I have been resisting any pressure to become liberal. The influences here didn't matter enough to resist, I guess. *All that's really important that has happened to me occurred outside of college,* and so I never became very susceptible to college influences.

NONCONSERVATIVE GIRLS

H32: I accepted liberal attitudes here because *I had always secretly felt that my family was narrow and intolerant, because such attitudes had prestige value.* It was all part of my generally expanding personality—*I had really never been part of anything before.*

Q43: It didn't take me long to see that liberal attitudes had prestige value. But all the time I felt inwardly superior to persons who wanted public acclaim. Once I had arrived at a feeling of personal security, I could see that it wasn't important—it wasn't enough. *So many people have no security at all. I became liberal at first because of its prestige value.*

Qx: Every influence I felt tended to push me in the liberal direction: My underdog complex, *my need to be independent of my parents, and my anxiousness to be a leader here.*

Q63: *I came to college to get away from my family,* who never had any respect for my mind. Becoming a radical meant thinking for myself and, figuratively, thumbing my nose at my family. *It also meant intellectual identification with the faculty and students that I most wanted to be like.*

As the above comments illustrate, the girls most strongly identified with their families were also the girls whose attitudes changed the least; the girls who wished to break off their ties with their families or who wanted the reward of prestige approval were the girls who became most identified with the Bennington community and, consequently, changed their attitudes to the greatest extent. As the data from this study suggest, schools can influence attitudes, but the extent of the influence depends on how strongly a student is influenced by other people.

While in school, a student may resolve conflict between attitudes held by persons with whom he has strongly identified and the attitudes that the school is attempting to communicate. He may change temporarily while in school, and then change again when he returns to his home. He may work out a kind of temporary psychological isolation so that he is secure in school without radically changing his attitudes.

Kinds of Identification Figures

There are three principal kinds of potential identification figures present in the school environment: (1) historical personages, prominent individuals in contemporary society, idealized conceptions of men and women; (2) the teachers themselves; (3) fellow students.

Heroes of history are typical figures held up to students as models for appropriate attitudes and behavior. Many of these people, however, are comparatively remote from the life of the students. The differences in social conditions from one era to another, the unusual dramatic lives led by these people, suggest to the student that they are models for admiration but not for identification. The American schoolboy, born in a hospital and reared in a large city, who attends elementary school and high school without ever having to worry about obtaining a basic education, would probably have some difficulties seeing the Lincoln of the log cabin as a behavior model. However, from reading Lincoln's life, students are not expected to learn how to split rails—but something about work, perseverance, and responsibility. Are they capable of learning such attitudes from a model who is not physically present? Apparently, models portrayed through media do facilitate the acquisition of behavior. Bandura [20] found that children imitated aggressive models when they were portrayed on film. Bandura and Mischel [21] found that children imitated a model if they knew how the model had approached a problem—even if what the model had done was described only in a written statement read by the imitator.

The teachers in a school are also potential identification figures. Some students identify with their teachers, even to adopting the teachers' ways of speaking and mannerisms. However, teachers as a group do not present a wide range of identification models. The **stereotype** of the teacher in modern society has been that of a middle-aged female, frequently unmarried, relatively restricted in her social life by community conventions and mores. The elementary and high school teacher has not even been thought of as a member of an intellectual elite.

But when the American hears the words "school teacher"—to the extent that he fills it in in a general way and not merely with an image of Miss Jones of the fourth grade, to whom he took flowers or who caught him smuggling worms into class—the image will be something like this. He will think of a grade-school teacher who teaches perhaps the third or fourth grade; this teacher will be a woman of somewhat indeterminate age, perhaps in the middle thirties, neither young nor old, of the middle class, and committed to the ethics and manners of a middle-class world. In the emotional tone which accompanies the image there will be respect, a little fear, perhaps more than a little affection, an expectation that she will reward his efforts and struggles to learn and conform, and a spate of delighted memories of those occasions when he himself perpetrated feats of undetected mischief. She stands in his mind on the borderline of childhood, urging, beckoning, exhorting, patiently teaching, impatiently rebuking a child in whom the impulse is strong to escape the narrow bounds of the school room into the outdoors where birds are nesting, or the sun-lit pavements are waiting for marbles.[22]

Certainly not all American teachers fit this stereotype; yet this stereotype may dominate our thinking of what a teacher is like.[23]

---

[20] See note 17.
[21] A. Bandura and W. Mischel, "Modification of Self-imposed Delay of Reward through Exposure to Live and Symbolic Models," *Journal of Personality and Social Psychology* (in press).
[22] M. Mead, *The School in American Culture* (Cambridge: Harvard University Press, 1951), p. 5.
[23] An interesting description of this stereotype, as it appears in literature, can be found in A. Foff, "Scholars and Scapegoats," *The English Journal,* 47 (1958), 118–126.

Insofar as the teacher represents something more than the stereotyped image of the typical American school teacher, the possibility exists that students will identify with their teachers. An experimental study illustrates the relationship we have been discussing.[24] The experimenter measured the extent to which teachers' behavior was seen as warm and friendly by students. He also measured the amount of required work done by students and the amount of work that students initiated on their own. Significant positive relationships were found between the extent to which the students described the teacher as friendly and warm and the amount of self-initiated and required work that they did. While this study does not directly demonstrate the relationship between identification with teachers and change in pupil behavior, the experimenter suggested that the identification process could account for the relationship found. Teachers frequently advocate "working on one's own." However, the extent to which a student works on his own is a measure of the relationship between his attitudes and those of the teacher. The pupil works on his own because in identifying with the teacher he has taken on the teacher's values about the importance of self-initiated work.

The school is not entirely responsible for the image of the teacher that is so common in American society, but the school can do something about invalidating this image in choosing the teachers that are employed to staff our schools. Providing the kinds of teachers with whom students will identify is not simply a matter of having a faculty of young teachers or of married teachers, but of having a faculty of teachers who are sensitive to the world in which they and the children are living. The teacher must be the kind of person whose behavior has meaning and relevance for his students, as the principles discussed suggest.

INFLUENCE OF GROUPS ON ACQUISITION OF ATTITUDES

Individuals identify with groups as well as with other individuals. When a person identifies with a group, he sees himself as a member of

---

[24] M. L. Cogan, "Behaviors of Teachers and the Productive Behaviors of Their Pupils," *Journal of Experimental Education*, 27 (1958), 18–24; see also H. Levin, T. L. Hilton, and G. F. Liederman, "Studies of Teacher Behavior," *Journal of Experimental Education*, 26 (1957), 81–91. "Warmth" may promote identification, but recent experimental work suggests the importance of other variables in facilitating this relationship. For a discussion of this problem, see R. R. Sears, E. E. Maccoby, and H. Levin, *Patterns of Child Rearing* (Evanston, Ill.: Row, Peterson, 1957). A comparable discussion can be found in A. Bandura and R. H. Walters, *Adolescent Aggression* (New York: Ronald Press, 1959).

that group. He thinks of himself as having the attitudes of the members of this group; and he is influenced by the prevalent attitudes of the groups to which he belongs. The group is a behavior model for him.

However, not everyone who belongs to a group necessarily shares the attitudes and values of the group, or identifies with the group. We can distinguish between **membership groups** and **reference groups.** *A membership group is a group in which an individual is formally enrolled or a group of which he is regarded as a member. A reference group is a group which influences the attitudes of an individual because he identifies with the group, even though he may not be formally a member of this group.* At Bennington College, in the study referred to above, all of the girls were formally enrolled in the college organization. Bennington was the membership group for all of these girls. However, for some of these girls Bennington was not a reference group; the college group had comparatively little influence on their attitudes. The girl who said that the main influence on her life was her home, is a member of two groups—her family and the Bennington College group—but only the family is her reference group.

This distinction between membership-group and reference-group behavior explains a wide variety of behavior that can be observed in almost any school. Every student is a member of a school, of classes in the school, and frequently of other groups within the school. Teachers and administrators are often puzzled by the lack of influence of the school, or of particular groups within it, on the behavior of some pupils. These discrepancies are easily explained when we realize that formal group membership does not guarantee that the psychological processes of group identification will be initiated. In almost every class there are "outsiders," students whose interests seem to lie primarily outside of the school and who have no close ties with any of the groups within the school. In other cases, students' identification with groups preclude the influence that the school is capable of having on their attitudes. A student who joins the "Dirty Dozen," a group primarily interested in having fun, is not likely to be strongly influenced by the more academic groups, nor is he likely to be appropriately affected by the experiences which the school provides for the purpose of encouraging particular kinds of attitude development.

Need Satisfactions Provided by Groups

How does a group influence the attitudes of its members? People join groups for a variety of reasons related to the satisfaction of their basic needs. Some people join a group because the project the group is working on is one in which they are interested. These individuals will obtain their satisfactions from the achievements of the group. Others will join a group because they like people and the social interaction resulting from group membership.

Groups are also sources of prestige and status. The prestige of the group spreads to its members. In a complex organization like the school there are many groups, and a hierarchy of prestige can be found among them. Gordon [25] studied the social organization of a high school and found the following groups among the students:

1. *Athletic Crowd:* The athletic clique contained five varsity football members. . . . They were known as the "beer drinking crowd, who go over to the westside sometimes for sexual experimentation. . . . They have cars, dates, money, and usually liquor, and are highly clothing-oriented.

2. *Music and Club Activity Crowd:* The music clique concentrated on intramural and second-line prestige sports. They were more grade-oriented than the athletic group.

3. *Dating Crowd:* The dating clique concentrated slavishly on dress, intramural sports, and less prestige varsity sports. They were all "steady dates." They were not considered "big wheels" by cliques 1 and 2. They considered themselves "big wheels." Their major focus was on spending money in the proper manner, playing the social game, and religious adherence to dress.

4. *The "Brainy" Crowd:* The "brainy" clique's major focus was on scholastic achievement. Four members were elected to the National Honor Society. They combined participation in organizations of various kinds with extreme emphasis on scholarship. . . . Conformity on dress and dating was much more casual.

5. *The Hunting and Fishing Crowd:* The hunting and fishing clique "rated" with the "people who didn't rate." Out-of-school-oriented, they were members of the Outdoor Club, a low prestige organization. They were not as conforming to dress and dating as the other four cliques. There were several nonresident students among them.

The above ranking of these groups represents the order of prestige of the groups in the school. Each of these groups provides special kinds of rewards and satisfactions for their members. A student who belongs to the

[25] C. W. Gordon, *The Social System of the High School* (Glencoe, Ill.: The Free Press, 1957), p. 120.

athletic crowd can satisfy his needs for high social prestige and prominence in the school. A student who belongs to the hunting and fishing crowd can satisfy his needs for outdoor activities, but he could not satisfy a need for social prestige. Such cliques control a wide variety of social behavior within the school; even the dating behavior of these students may be group-controlled to some extent.

That the groups provide rewards for their members is apparent in the following sample of statements by clique members.

The clique you belong to has a definite bearing on your prestige. If you belong to a fast moving athletic clique, you are usually the same and this tends to build up your prestige outside of school and in dating more than would the other organizations of the school.

When you are in a good clique I think it helps your dating. For instance Mary Sands just recently started going around with us. It wasn't planned, but it just sort of happened. When she started going around with us she automatically got more dates (pp. 106–108).

These kinds of groups provide even more subtle rewards and satisfactions. One of the functions of the cliques in a school is to provide security for members, even when their school achievement is not entirely satisfactory. If one belongs to the "athletic crowd," poor achievement may not be important, and many compensations are provided for failure to achieve successfully in school. These groups also provide status for the individual; they open ways for acquiring things that must be competed for, such as dates and school offices. They provide the individual with a sense of adequacy and security, and they set the standards for behavior which, if maintained by group members, bring with them the rewards and satisfactions that the group can provide.

Table 8–1 summarizes data on the relationship between rewards accorded students and the degree to which they conformed to the prevailing attitudes at Bennington.[26] The PEP scores are on a scale of "political and economic progressivism." Low scores on this test indicate nonconservatism, which was the prevalent attitude at Bennington. High scores represented conservatism. The students were asked to nominate the five students "most worthy to represent the college" at an intercollegiate gathering. As the data in the Table indicate, students whose attitudes were most consistent with the dominant attitudes at Bennington were also

[26] T. M. Newcomb, *Personality and Social Change* (see note 19), p. 55.

accorded the most prestige by their fellow students. This relationship was consistent in all four college classes.

Group Pressures to Conformity and Attitude Change

The power of the group to influence the attitudes of its members results in part from the pressures that the group sets up to encourage conformity. When an individual joins a group, he is made aware of the standards and

TABLE 8–1. *Mean PEP scores, classified according to frequency of being chosen as representative (from Newcomb).*

Frequency of Choice	Freshmen		Sophomores		Juniors-Seniors		Entire College	
	N	Mean	N	Mean	N	Mean	N	Mean
40–89	—	—	3	60.3	5	50.4	8	54.1
12–39	—	—	5	65.6	15	57.6	20	59.7
5–11	—	—	5	65.3	18	62.2	23	62.7
2–4	10	64.6	18	68.6	19	61.6	47	65.3
1	12	63.4	17	68.6	15	62.1	44	65.0
0	61	72.8	39	71.3	14	69.0	114	71.7
Total	83	70.5	87	69.2	86	61.5	256	67.1

values of that group in both obvious and subtle ways.[27] Deviation from the accepted attitudes and values is punished by the group with rejection, exclusion, ignoring of the deviant member, and deprivation of the rewards that the group can provide.

By the time you are a senior, you should know when to wear heels, earrings, etc., and when to wear flats. People that would wear earrings to school or flats to the American theater naturally don't know anything. . . . Of course, you wouldn't wear saddles with hose or black suede flats with bobby socks. That would be unforgivable.

Vance keeps everyone else in line on dress. He is always making fun of someone else's clothes. He'll say, "Look at that guy's socks. Is he 'fruit!' You gradually get on to what to wear." [28]

The influence of the group on opinions of individuals has been demonstrated experimentally by Asch,[29] who used a simple experimental task,

[27] See L. Berkowitz, "Group Norms among Bomber Crews: Patterns of Perceived Crew Attitudes, 'Actual' Crew Attitudes, and Crew Liking Related to Aircrew Effectiveness in Far Eastern Combat," *Sociometry*, 19 (1956), 141–153.

[28] Gordon (see note 25), pp. 117–118, 120.

[29] S. E. Asch, "Effects of Group Pressure upon the Modification and Distortion of

that of matching a line of given length with one of three unequal lines. In this experiment the subject asked to do the matching did so in a group. The other members of the group had been instructed by the experimenter to make deliberate errors in the matching. The subject was confronted with a situation in which the opinions of the group members flatly contradicted his own observations. Some of the "errors" made by the other members of the group were obviously large. What was the effect of the majority opinion on the judgment of these subjects?

1. There was a marked movement toward the majority. One third of all the estimates in the critical group were errors identical with or in the direction of the distorted estimates of the majority. The significance of this finding becomes clear in the light of the virtual absence of errors in the control group, the members of which recorded their estimates in writing (see Table 8–2).

2. At the same time the effect of the majority was far from complete. The preponderance of estimates in the critical group (68%) was correct despite the pressure of the majority.

3. We found evidence of extreme individual differences. There were in the critical group subjects who remained independent without exception, and there were those who went nearly all the time with the majority. . . . One fourth of the critical subjects was completely independent; at the other extreme, one third of the group displaced the estimates toward the majority in one half or more of the trials (pp. 176–177).

These laboratory groups were artificial groups, since the subjects were assigned to the groups in a random manner. The group members associated with each other as a group only in the experimental situation. The evidence from this experiment is all the more striking when we recall that the task required the subjects to use the evidence provided by their own observations. There was little ambiguity, little room for opinion, in the essential nature of the task. We would expect that the influence of the majority would be even greater where there is room for differences of opinion. A group of high school students deciding on appropriate dress would be such a situation. The rules for proper dress are comparatively arbitrary. The group is free to set up its own standards, and the individuals in the group have no clear criteria for deciding what is appro-

Judgments," in E. E. Maccoby, T. M. Newcomb, and E. L. Hartley, eds., *Readings in Social Psychology* (New York: Henry Holt and Company, 1958), pp. 174–183. The same data are also reported in S. E. Asch, "Effects of Group Pressure upon the Modification and Distortion of Judgments," in H. Guetzkow, ed., *Group Leadership and Men* (Pittsburgh: Carnegie Press, 1951).

priate, other than the group standard. In such situations we would predict that the influence of the majority opinion would be all the more marked.

In the above experiment a large percentage of subjects was not strongly influenced, or was not influenced at all, by the opinions of the group. This result can be explained in the following ways: (1) Some individuals in the group felt it important to maintain an independence from majority opinion. (2) Some individuals were withdrawn from the group activity and reacted to the experimental task as an individual problem. (3) Some

TABLE 8–2. *Distribution of errors in experimental and control groups (from Asch).*

Number of critical errors	Critical group* (N = 50)	Control group (N = 37)
0	13	35
1	4	1
2	5	1
3	6	
4	3	
5	4	
6	1	
7	2	
8	5	
9	3	
10	3	
11	1	
12	0	
Total	50	37
Mean	3.84	0.08

* All errors in the critical group were in the direction of the majority estimates.

individuals were committed to performing the task as well as they could, irrespective of other people's judgments. These individuals probably had not formed identifications with their groups.

We would expect to find people in formally organized groups for whom these groups are merely membership groups, not reference groups. When this kind of a relationship exists between an individual and a group to which he belongs, the influence of the group on his opinion is relatively small. But when an individual is strongly identified with a group, and particularly in those areas of group concern for which there are no clear-cut criteria, the individual is likely to be influenced by the prevalent opinion in his group.

In another experimental situation, Schachter [30] set up groups which were to decide on the disposition of a problem in human relations. He introduced three members into each group: one member agreed with the majority opinion; another deviated slightly from the majority opinion; and a third member deviated considerably from the majority opinion. Schachter then studied the acceptance of these individuals in the group and the way members talked to them. He found that the largest number of communications were addressed to the most deviant member, particularly when group members were highly interested in the group activity. The group member who agreed with the majority had no more communications addressed to him than did any other member of the group. The slightly deviant member had some communications addressed to him until he shifted to a position of agreement with the group.

At the end of the experimental session the members were asked to nominate individuals to committees: one, an executive committee which had high prestige; the other, a correspondence committee which had low prestige. The deviates were nominated much more frequently for the correspondence committee than were any other members and were undernominated for the executive committee. This experimental study illustrates group pressures for conformity, even in groups which are artificially and temporarily formed.

A group communicates its standards, its prevalent attitudes and values, to its members—both openly, through direct statements, and subtly, through suggestions and hints. One can identify the rewarding of conforming behavior and the punishing of nonconforming behavior. The student who shows up at school in dress which does not conform to the pattern for his group is told, either directly or indirectly, that his dress is inappropriate. When the group is highly attractive to the student, when he expects to obtain rewards by being a member of the group, when it is important for him in any way to belong to the group, these pressures will tend to produce conformity to the group standard. If the student does not conform, if he is not interested in the group, if the group is merely a membership group and not a reference group for him, he will tend to be

[30] S. Schachter, "Deviation, Rejection, and Communication," *Journal of Abnormal and Social Psychology*, 46 (1951), 190–207. Also in D. Cartwright and A. Zander, *Group Dynamics: Research and Theory*, 2nd ed. (Evanston, Ill.: Row, Peterson, 1960), pp. 260–285.

isolated and cut off from the group. If he is free to leave, he may join another group that will provide rewards for him.[31]

INSTRUCTIONAL STRATEGIES FOR ATTITUDE ACQUISITION

In this chapter we have approached attitude acquisition as a social-learning and social-influence phenomenon. We have talked about how people influence each other, how one person learns from another. The instructional strategies derivable from these principles require manipulations of social systems and interpersonal relations.

THE CRITERION BEHAVIOR

First of all, the teacher must clarify the behavioral objectives of a strategy for inducing attitude acquisition. Otherwise, the students may adopt appropriate verbal behavior without the accompanying action behavior; they may say they like poetry, or mathematics, or that they believe in equal justice—and yet never read a book or associate with Negroes and Jews. The teacher should specify those actions that will characterize the attitude. These will always be the observable behavior that marks the attitude, and from which others would infer that the person held the attitude.

Sometimes, of course, verbal-behavior changes are appropriate goals of an instructional strategy. For example, we want students to talk certain ways about other people so that stereotypes are not communicated. The teacher would therefore define the ways of talking that represent the attitude.

As in preceding analyses, a **component task analysis** of the attitudinal domain is appropriate. From this analysis the teacher should be able to generate statements about the kinds of behavior change (both actions and words) required for the attitudinal acquisition.

PATTERNS OF STIMULUS ARRANGEMENTS

We said above that the model of attitude acquisition used here requires manipulation of the social conditions for learning. Three generalizations guide these constructions:

---

[31] See E. P. Hollander, "Conformity, Status, and Idiosyncrasy Credit," *Psychological Bulletin*, 65 (1958), 117–126.

1. The social situation must be designed to elicit the desired behavior. A sixth-grade teacher, interested himself in music, wanted to create a similar interest in his students. He could have talked about the joys of music listening, and he did. But he did much more than that. He played music for them and asked them to tell him what they thought of it; he loaned them his records to play; he worked up a trip for them to the opera, for which he carefully prepared them and which was a huge success. After this trip they had a long discussion of their impressions and reactions. Sometimes the desired situation for eliciting a behavior can only be simulated. Acting-out behavior in a **sociodrama** is a way of simulating attitude behavior.

2. Response guidance must be provided. This is what the model does. He portrays the desired behavior.

3. The strategy must provide rewards for the desired attitudinal response. A teacher may, for example, place a child in a work group that he thinks will both elicit and reward an attitudinal response. However, if this is to be a really rewarding environment, the teacher may have to plan the composition of the group carefully, and give it appropriate direction.

These principles are broad guides for decision rules. Although the teacher is limited by the institutional constraints under which he teaches, the constraints are not so compelling and restricting that the teacher cannot use his classroom as a social laboratory. He may also seek out-of-class opportunities for creating strategies consistent with the generalizations given above.

EVALUATIVE JUDGMENTS

As in any instructional strategy, the teacher first must assess the initial attitudes of his students. We do not have simple devices for making these assessments. The teacher may construct them, or he may use interviewing techniques, questioning in class, written reports, sociodramas, and direct observations. For example, asking the students to write up their reactions to a civil-rights demonstration may yield considerable information on how the students feel about minority-group members and their activities. The teacher should also be alert to other sources of information—a student's parents, other teachers, and friends. The problems of utilizing these resources are the same as those for any measuring instrument: How does one get reliable and valid data? With this problem in mind, attention is called here to these possible resources to encourage teachers to think of many different ways of assessing students' attitudes.

SUMMARY

1. An attitude is a predisposition to act in a positive or negative way toward persons, objects, ideas, and events.

2. As predispositions, attitudes are anticipatory responses. They describe a relation between a person and something else—an object, another person, or even one's own self conceived as an object. They are directional in the sense that they represent a positive or negative preference for the attitude object. They vary in intensity. They are learned ways of consistently interacting with and responding to the stimuli of one's environment.

3. Attitudes are general response patterns—ways of acting similarly toward classes of objects or people or events. Motives are specific—particular instances of goal-seeking behavior. Attitudes predispose a person to be motivated in ways consistent with the attitude.

4. Attitudes are inferred from observed behavior. Such inferences must be made from a representative sample of a person's behavior. The inference should also predict how a person is likely to behave in situations where we expect to see the attitude expressed.

5. Attitudes are learned primarily through rewards for attitudinal behavior—rewards in the form of need satisfaction or reinforcement given by another person.

6. Much attitudinal behavior may be learned by imitating others. Imitative behavior is likely to be induced from observing a model who achieves rewards for his way of behaving. This condition is sufficient to produce the learning of attitudinal responses. However, if the behavior is also reinforced, it is maintained in strength for a longer period of time.

7. Behavior learned by imitation is not necessarily a literal copying of the model's behavior. The learner frequently adapts the observed responses, or may create combinations of responses from observing more than one model.

8. The models to which children are exposed influence the attitudes they acquire. This learning is educationally significant, since it may be either consistent with or contrary to the kind of attitude learning the school is promoting.

9. The school's influence is considerably ameliorated when students identify strongly with persons whose attitudes contradict those the school is promoting.

10. The teacher sometimes does not serve as a model for desired attitude learning, because the students do not see him as achieving the kinds of rewards they desire. Also, a typical portrait of the teacher is not flattering and may discourage students from thinking about the teacher as a model.

11. The groups to which an individual belongs usually influence his attitudes. Holding certain attitudes may even be a necessary condition for belonging to some groups.

12. Groups exert pressures to conformity by the ways their members communicate with each other and by the way they reward attitudes shared by the group members.

13. In devising instructional strategies for attitude learning, the teacher must define both the actions and the words to be associated with the attitude.

14. Exposing the learner to models, real or abstract, directly or vicariously, and rewarding the attitude behavior when it occurs are the principles that should characterize all strategies designed to produce attitude change.

STUDY AND DISCUSSION QUESTIONS

1. From what student behaviors that you could observe, would you infer the following:
   a. He does not like teachers.
   b. He feels that students from lower socio-economic groups are inferior to him.
   c. He thinks the study of history is valuable.
   d. He feels that participation in athletic competition is childish.

2. You infer that a student has a positive attitude toward achievement in school; in what ways would you predict that he would be specifically motivated?

3. You infer that a student feels it is important to get along with other people; again, predict the ways in which this student is likely to be motivated.

4. What attitudes would you infer from the following instances of motivated behavior?
   a. A student works hard for a scholarship.
   b. A student tries hard to win a place on a varsity team.
   c. A student works actively on the student newspaper.

5. In responding to Question 4, have you suggested only one attitude that may be inferred from each of these instances of motivated behavior? Review your list of inferred attitudes and predict other instances of motivated behavior that you would expect to observe if the student held these attitudes.

6. Below is a list of activities. Suggest some conflicting attitudes that a student may hold relevant to them. Explain what factors may influence a conflict in attitudes relevant to these goal objects.

   a. Going to college.

   b. Using the family car.

   c. Steady dating.

   d. Being a top student.

7. Suggest the need satisfactions that may be attained by a student who identifies with the following people:

   a. Mother or father.

   b. A teacher.

   c. A popular classmate.

8. What models do you think parents would suggest a boy imitate if he is to learn his masculine sex role? What models probably would be suggested to girls if they are to learn their feminine sex role?

9. Some people argue that TV programs and movies that portray the lives of criminals have a bad influence on children. Evaluate this argument in the light of the discussion of imitative behavior presented in this chapter.

10. What factors in the Bennington environment may have increased the probability that girls attending Bennington would identify with the Bennington community? What differences between Bennington and other colleges and universities might account for the fact that students at other institutions may identify to a lesser degree with their respective college communities? What factors associated with attending a high school may inhibit strong identification with the high school community?

11. Some people argue that boys in the elementary schools have difficulty in assimilating the attitudes teachers try to develop in students because the teachers are frequently women. Evaluate this argument.

12. Are there some student attitudes that teachers are less likely to influence? If you think so, explain what factors would account for the fact that these attitudes are not likely to be changed.

13. Describe some student organizations with which you are familiar in terms of the dominant group attitudes of these organizations as you perceive them. What pressures to conformity are typically exerted by the members of these groups?

14. Groups may be more or less attractive to their members. What prediction would you make about the relationship between the attractiveness of a group to its members and the pressures to conformity in these groups? Check your predictions by reading Schachter's study of this relationship.

15. What kinds of need satisfactions may be obtained by a group member who adheres to the group standards for behavior?

16. You observe that a student does not seem to have any group associations in your school. What hypotheses would you offer to explain this observed behavior? How could you determine whether this student had been "rejected" by other students?

17. What attitudes do you wish students in your class, or who will take some subject you will teach, to acquire? What is the behavior that defines these attitudes? How will you know that students have acquired the attitudes?

18. Are the attitudes you described in Question 17 specific to what you are teaching, or are they general attitudes that might be learned in any class?

19. Describe the attitude learning you defined above as a problem in transfer of training.

20. Give one example of an instructional strategy designed to produce one of these attitude changes. List the stimuli to which students are exposed, how they will make the attitudinal responses, and the reinforcement procedures.

RECOMMENDED READINGS

S. E. Asch. *Social Psychology*. Englewood Cliffs, N. J.: Prentice-Hall, Inc., 1952, Chapters 16, 18, 19.

A. Bandura and R. Walters. *Social Learning and Personality Development*. New York: Holt, Rinehart and Winston, 1963.

J. S. Coleman. *The Adolescent Society*. New York: The Free Press of Glencoe, 1961. See Chapters II, III, VII, and X.

D. B. Harris. "How Children Learn Interests, Motives, and Attitudes," in Forty-ninth Yearbook of the National Society for the Study of Education, Part I, *Learning and Instruction*. Chicago: University of Chicago Press, 1950, Chapter 5.

J. Kagan. "The Concept of Identification," *Psychological Review*, 65 (1958), 296–305.

T. M. Newcomb. *Social Psychology*. New York: The Dryden Press, 1950, Chapters 4, 6, 7.

H. H. Remmers and D. H. Radler. *The American Teenager*. Indianapolis-New York: Bobbs-Merrill Co., 1957.

D. H. Russell. *Children's Thinking*. Boston: Ginn & Co., 1956, Chapter 6.

M. Sherif and H. Cantril. "The Psychology of 'Attitudes,'" *Psychological Review*, 52 (1945), Part I, 295–323.

B. F. Skinner. *Walden Two*. New York: The Macmillan Co., 1948 (paperback, 1962).

CHAPTER NINE

THE LEARNING OF ATTITUDES: COMMUNICATION PROCESSES

In the preceding chapter we used an interpersonal-influence **model** of attitude acquisition. The elements of this model appear in an attenuated form in another model of attitude influence, the communication model. The persuasive communication is the most commonly used method of influencing attitudinal responses. The behavioral goals are usually quite clear: buy a car, a perfume, a cigarette; support this candidate, this party. This suggestion of Madison Avenue, this hint of the pitchman, may repel you. But these are merely examples to remind you that persuasion is one of the most elemental of the human arts. It charges men for battle; it stirs political waters; it brings men to churches and synagogues and drives them to ridicule the same institutions. The Greeks had a name for it—rhetoric; we have many names for it—oratory, advertising, preaching, and teaching.

Our use of persuasion is a testimonial to our belief, justified or not, in the power of words to shape behavior. Teachers rely heavily on persuasive communications to produce behavior changes. In this chapter we study the variables that influence the effectiveness of persuasive communications.

EXPERIMENTAL STUDIES OF PERSUASIVE COMMUNICATION

The problem of attitude changes brought about by persuasive communication is complex and has been studied intensively for several decades.[1] We begin by discussing a characteristic experiment.[2]

One hundred and sixty-two high school students participated in this experiment. Initially, the students were tested to determine whether, and to what extent, they were prejudiced toward groups of people other than their own racial, ethnic, or religious group. The students were then divided into three groups. All three groups contained students with high, low, and intermediate degrees of prejudice. The first group was shown a film on prejudice, and the members participated in a discussion of the film after the showing. The second group only saw the film. The third group did not see the film, nor did the students discuss the subject of prejudice; they merely were tested for prejudice. The film, *The High Wall*, treats group prejudice as a "communicable disease" and traces its origins in the family and community. After the first group had completed its discussion of the film, all three groups of students took the same tests they had taken before the film, as well as an information test on the content of the film.

Does this kind of persuasive communication influence the attitudes of students? Does the predisposition of the student have any influence on whether or not his attitudes will be changed? Will the student who is highly prejudiced be less prejudiced after seeing this film? Does the experimental treatment—that is, whether a student saw the film with or without discussion—affect attitude change?

The results of this experiment were as follows:

1. Significant reductions in prejudice as measured by the test were

[1] For a survey of results obtained in studies of intergroup attitudes and a critical analysis of research in this area, see R. Williams, *The Resolution of Intergroup Tensions* (New York: Social Science Research Council, 1948). Another but less critical survey of a selected area of studies can be found in P. E. Jacob, *Changing Values in College* (New Haven: Edward W. Hazen Foundation, 1957).

[2] L. L. Mitnick and E. McGinnies, "Influencing Ethnocentrism in Small Discussion Groups through a Film Communication," *Journal of Abnormal and Social Psychology,* 56 (1958), 82–90.

produced in both experimental groups; that is, the groups that had seen the film. The reduction in prejudice was not related to the predisposition of the students, however, but to the kind of experimental treatment.

2. When the students were tested at a period one month later, students who had participated in discussion maintained the greatest change over that period of time. As Figure 9–1 indicates, the groups that had seen the film showed a significant shift in attitude immediately after the film, but

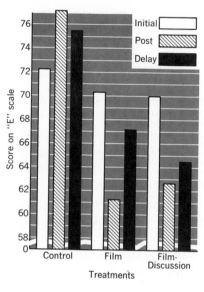

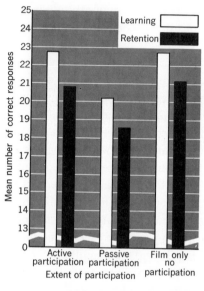

FIGURE 9–1. *Initial, post-treatment, and delay scores on the "E" scale (a measure of prejudice) for each treatment (adapted from Mitnick and McGinnies).*

FIGURE 9–2. *Mean learning and retention of information scores for each level of participation (adapted from Mitnick and McGinnies).*

gradually changed back to their original attitudes. Groups that discussed the film after they had seen it changed back least.

3. The amount of information learned from the film was related to the initial attitude of the students. Those individuals who were low in prejudice learned more factual information from the film than did those who were high in prejudice (see Figure 9–3).

This experiment illustrates the variety of factors that influence attitude change and that must be taken into account in any methodology the teacher may devise: (1) The predisposition of the student—the attitude that he brings to the learning situation—influences the amount of factual content he will learn from the film. He may not even get his facts straight, and he may not remember them if he is negatively predisposed to the subject presented. (2) Some general principles of learning also apply. The film conveys a mass of concepts, ideas, principles, and facts that are difficult for students to assimilate. The discussion period after the film probably clarifies ideas. We can only speculate on other values of the discussion, such as expressing feelings openly and discovering that other

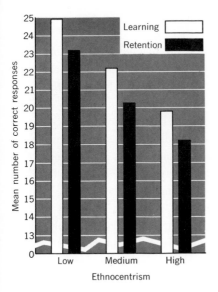

FIGURE 9-3. Mean scores on the learning and retention test for each predisposition group (adapted from Mitnick and Mc-Ginnies).

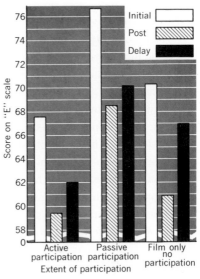

FIGURE 9-4. Initial, post-treatment, and delay scores on the "E" scale for each level of participation (adapted from Mit-nick and McGinnies).

people take the same position. (3) The extent to which a student partici-pates actively in the discussion is related to the amount of attitude change (see Figure 9-4). We do not know what personality variables determine the extent to which a student will participate in the discussion. These unknown variables may be the crucial factors producing attitude change.

Several important factors were not taken into account in this experi-ment. For example, suppose that discussion groups, instead of having subjects with varying degrees of prejudice in each group, were organized so that all persons with the same degree of prejudice were in the same group. We would have groups with high-prejudice members and other groups with low-prejudice members. Would the discussion now make a difference? We predict that, when group members discovered that they shared common values, the original attitude would be strengthened and the amount of attitude change would be correspondingly affected. When similarly prejudiced people join together to discuss a communication contrary to what they believe and feel, we expect them to strengthen each other's attitudes and to reject the attitudes supported by the communication. Furthermore, in the above experimental communication, only one side of the issue was presented. Suppose that both sides had been presented simultaneously or one after the other?

We cannot lay down specific rules to tell the teacher how and in what way he must arrange educational experiences to produce attitude change. What the psychological literature does provide is knowledge of the factors crucial in any methodology. What are these factors?

Before we move to this topic, let us review what we have learned about the method of inquiry used in the experiment discussed, since we will see it used again. The experimenter varies the characteristics of the communication; this is a variation of the independent **variable.** He tests for the original attitude, makes the communication, and tests the attitude again. He compares the pre- and post-experimental attitudes.

Where does an investigator get ideas for variables that may influence behavior change? Not too surprisingly, many ideas come from common beliefs; some have been derived from theoretical formulations. The Mitnick and McGinnies experiment illustrates many of the problems in making a communication persuasive. Teachers use similar procedures. The research problem is to separate out the variables in a communication and to determine their effects. In the following sections we consider those variables whose effects have been studied experimentally.

VARIABLES INFLUENCING THE PERSUASIVENESS OF A COMMUNICATION

PRESTIGE AND CREDIBILITY OF THE COMMUNICATOR

The communicator who has prestige with his audience, or whom his audience regards as trustworthy, will effect changes in attitudes and opinions in the direction that he advocates.[3] If the source of the communication is suspect in any way, if the listener feels that the communicator personally has something to gain by persuading people, his prestige and authority is diminished.

Kelman and Hovland [4] used an identical communication with three different kinds of communicators. High school seniors were asked to listen to a recording of an educational program, ostensibly to judge its educational value. The guest speaker was introduced in three different ways to three different groups of students. The first speaker was identified as a judge of a juvenile court, a highly trained and experienced authority. The second communicator was identified as a member of the studio audience chosen at random. The third communicator was presented as if selected from the audience, but an introductory interview with him revealed that he had been a delinquent as a youth and was currently on bail after being arrested on a charge of dope peddling. Each communicator gave exactly the same communication, a statement advocating extreme leniency toward juvenile delinquents. What was the effect of the source of communication on attitude change? As the data in Tables 9–1 and 9–2 indicate, a large percentage of students thought that the judge, the positive communicator, was completely fair in his presentation, whereas the former juvenile delinquent was regarded by only a small percentage of students as being fair in his presentation. Furthermore, the largest amount of attitude change occurred in the group that heard the communication from the judge. In other words, the communicator of a message has a definite effect upon the attitude change of the individuals who hear his message.

The situation is not as simple as this conclusion seems to indicate. Kelman and Hovland found three weeks later, when they again studied the attitudes of these students, that the differences in attitudes had disappeared and that the three groups of students, each of whom had heard a different communicator, had now substantially their original attitudes. However, when some of the students were reminded of the source of the communication, changes obtained the first time again occurred. Apparently, the prestige and authority of the communicator has its greatest effect on immediate opinion change; changes in attitude can be

[3] C. I. Hovland and W. Mandell, "An Experimental Comparison of Conclusion-Drawing by the Communicator and by the Audience," *Journal of Abnormal and Social Psychology*, 47 (1952), 581–588.

[4] H. C. Kelman and C. I. Hovland, "Reinstatement of the Communicator in Delayed Measurement of Opinion Change," *Journal of Abnormal and Social Psychology*, 48 (1953), 327–335.

maintained only by continually associating the communicator with his message.

A communicator has only relative prestige; a person speaking on a subject on which he is presumed to know little has comparatively little effect in producing attitude change. If we want to know something about the effects of atomic testing on genetics, we are likely to be influenced by the opinions and attitudes of scientists who are most informed on this subject. However, some individuals have so much prestige that they can influence attitudes and opinions on a wide variety of subjects, including those on which they are not experts. Also, some social roles represent

TABLE 9-1. *Audience evaluation of a talk on juvenile delinquency—the same talk delivered on tape by three different speakers (adapted from Kelman and Hovland).*

Source of communication	Judgments *
Judge	73† (N = 110)
Audience member	63 (N = 60)
Juvenile delinquent	29† (N = 102)

* Per cent of each group giving speaker a rating of "completely fair" or "fair" presentation.

† The significance of the difference between 73% and 29% is p < .001.

sufficient prestige that the ideas and opinions of individuals in these roles carry great weight. A study on prestige symbols illustrates this latter point.[5] Two groups of high school students heard a recorded communication made up of sentences logically unrelated to one another, or to any underlying theme. One group of students was told that this was a communication from a college president; the other, that it was a communication from a PTA member. In both cases the same voice and content were involved. The students were asked to indicate whether they understood the communication. They were also asked to indicate the sense of the communication if they thought they understood it, or to explain why they did not understand it if they had indicated that they did not. Students who heard the communication as given by a "college president" claimed to understand the communication; students who heard the same com-

[5] A. P. Coladarci, E. Elson, and K. Finis, "The Effect of Prestige Symbols in 'Critical Listening,' " *California Journal of Educational Research*, 5 (1954), 202–208.

munication "from a PTA member" said they did not understand it. The former group more frequently attempted to make sense out of the communication than did the latter, which characteristically recognized that the communication did not make sense. In other words, even a communication that is nonsense is treated as if it were important when the communication source carries prestige.

Teachers commonly resort to positive communication sources in their efforts to promote attitude changes. The mottoes and maxims of great men adorn many classrooms. The argument from authority is one of the commonest arguments used in attempting to prove a point. However, the use of credibility sources is not likely to produce drastic changes unless the child identifies with the communication source and unless the au-

TABLE 9–2. *The mean of the opinion scores of listeners who heard each communicator (adapted from Kelman and Hovland).*

Group	N	Mean *
Judge	97	46.7
Audience member	56	45.7
Juvenile delinquent	91	42.8

* A high score represents the position of leniency advocated in the communication. Significance of difference between scores: judge and juvenile delinquent, $p < .001$; judge and audience member, not significant; audience member and juvenile delinquent, $p < .01$.

thority figure remains imaginatively present so that his influence on the communication can be maintained. This method of persuasion even contradicts one of the school's objectives—namely, the critical evaluation of information, opinions, and principles in the light of evidence rather than on the basis of authority for the statements.

What about the teacher himself as a prestige figure who can affect attitude change? Little can be said by way of experimental evidence to suggest in what ways the teacher's influence is likely to be crucial in producing attitude change. The fact that "teacher says so" may influence younger children, but the teacher's prestige as such probably has comparatively little influence on attitude change. In any event, when students can get the facts for themselves or when they can arrive at a solution to a problem by their own efforts, it probably is advisable to avoid a process in which they are rewarded for accepting answers on the basis of what somebody else says.

INFLUENCE OF FEAR-AROUSING APPEALS

Teachers frequently use strongly worded and emotional appeals in endeavoring to change attitudes of children, particularly younger children. How effective are such presentations? If a teacher is trying to develop positive attitudes toward dental hygiene and wants his pupils to brush their teeth regularly, should he give a coldly dispassionate presentation of the facts of dental hygiene, or should he enliven the presentation with dramatic pictures of the harmful effects of improper dental care? If he is trying to develop a positive attitude toward conservation of natural resources, should he give the "cold facts" about the effects of poor conservation practices on our natural resources, should he present films of raging forest fires, depleted farms, and migrants from the dust bowls?

Experimental data indicate that when a persuasive communication is designed to create sustained preferences or attitudes, a strong emotional appeal, based on *arousal of fear,* is not so effective as a minimal emotional appeal. Janis and Feshbach [6] studied the effects of fear-arousing communications on changes in attitudes. First, they surveyed the dental-hygiene practices of a group of high school students. The group was then exposed to a fifteen-minute illustrated lecture on the causes of tooth decay; the presentation included recommendations about proper oral hygiene. Three forms of the talk were presented to three different groups of children: Form 1 contained a strong appeal pointing out the consequences of diseased gums, tooth decay, and all the other defects that result from improper dental hygiene; Form 2 presented a milder and more factual description of essentially the same information; Form 3 presented a minimal appeal, in which the consequences of tooth neglect were referred to infrequently. The experimenters found that Form 1 produced the greatest amount of worry and concern about dental-hygiene practices. But, as the data in Table 9–3 indicate, Form 3 produced the greatest amount of change in the direction of conformity to dental practices. At a later date the experimenters introduced another communication, which contradicted the original communication in at least one important feature. When the attitudes were studied after this countercommunication, the group given the minimal amount of appeal was again the group that was most resistant to the countercommunication (see Table 9–4).

Strongly worded appeals and fear-producing pictures and words

---

[6] I. L. Janis and S. Feshbach, "Effects of Fear-Arousing Communications," *Journal of Abnormal and Social Psychology,* 48 (1953), 78–92.

arouse strong tensions within the individual, which he must handle in some way. Consequently, he attends to his own anxiety and tensions rather than to the content of the message or his attitudes about it. He may stop listening altogether, or he may direct his anxiety against the communicator of the message. Radelfinger [7] hypothesized that if a fear-producing communication would give a clear directive or propose a way of taking action immediately, more individuals would follow the suggestion. His experimental design was analogous to that used in the Janis and Feshbach study. The communication, about the seriousness of tetanus, said that this disease frequently results from wounds and cuts,

TABLE 9-3. Effect of illustrated talk on conformity to dental-hygiene recommendations (from Janis and Feshbach).

Type of change	Group: Strong (N = 50)	Moderate (N = 50)	Minimal (N = 50)	Control (N = 50)
Increased conformity	28%	44%	50%	22%
Decreased conformity	20	22	14	22
No change	52	34	36	56
Total	100	100	100	100
Net change in conformity	+8%	+22%	+36%	0%

and described the terrible effects of this disease. The subjects were told that the health center gave anti-tetanus shots to anybody who wanted them, and the hours of service were listed. At one college, one of ninety student subjects went to the health center for a shot. At another college, with more flexible hours of service, five out of sixty students went for shots (one of whom would have gone anyway, since she was going overseas). In a modification of this experiment, when half of the subjects in the high fear group were told they could receive the shots immediately (they were available in a nearby room), significantly more subjects went for shots.

A reasonable conclusion about the general effects of threats and fear arousal seems justified. Threats, warnings, and vivid descriptions of evil consequences to follow have comparatively little effect in producing desired long-term attitude change. Furthermore, when fear-arousing techniques produce high anxiety, subjects must be shown positive and

[7] S. Radelfinger, Some Effects of Fear-Arousing Communications on Preventive Health Behavior, unpublished doctoral dissertation, Stanford University, 1963.

constructive and immediate ways of relieving the anxiety.[8] For some topics and for some age groups, a strong emotional appeal may be more effective than a minimal appeal. However, the weight of evidence at the present time suggests that extreme appeals are not likely to be highly effective in producing the attitude changes in which the school is interested.

TABLE 9-4. *Effect of illustrated talk on reactions to counterpropaganda: percentage now agreeing with statement "It does not matter what kind of toothbrush a person uses" (from Janis and Feshbach).*

Type of change	Group: Strong (N = 50)	Moderate (N = 50)	Minimal (N = 50)	Control (N = 50)
More agreement	30%	28%	14%	44%
Less agreement	38	42	54	24
No change	32	30	32	32
Total	100	100	100	100
Net change	−8%	−14%	−40%	+20%
Net effect (experimental minus control)	−28%	−34%	−60%	

INFLUENCE OF LOGICAL ARGUMENTS

The dental-hygiene study suggests that logical argument and careful presentation of factual evidence are more effective than emotional appeals in producing attitude change. Common sense, however, suggests presenting facts in a cold, logical manner is not likely to be highly

---

[8] The experimental data on the effects of punishment and the effects of success and failure are consistent with the above conclusion, if we assume that punishment and failure arouse anxiety. Experimental studies have determined the predisposition of children to be influenced by anxiety-evoking stimuli and have related this predisposition to behavior change in an anxiety-producing situation. The results indicate that subjects who become highly anxious in learning situations do not learn easily and efficiently. See, for example, R. R. Waite et al., "A Study of Anxiety and Learning in Children," *Journal of Abnormal and Social Psychology*, 57 (1958), 267–270. See also I. E. Farber and K. W. Spence, "Complex Learning and Conditioning as a Function of Anxiety," *Journal of Experimental Psychology*, 45 (1953), 120–125. A theoretical discussion of the relation of anxiety to motivation and a comprehensive bibliography can be found in J. A. Taylor, "Drive Theory and Manifest Anxiety," *Psychological Bulletin*, 53 (1956), 303–320. Of interest because of its obvious relevance is S. Sarason et al., *Anxiety in Elementary School Children* (New York: John Wiley and Sons, 1960).

effective in promoting attitude change. There are many ways in which facts can be presented. We can present the facts on only one side of an issue or on both sides. We can present the attitude-supporting facts first, followed by the attitude-contradicting facts; or, we can present the facts and arguments against an attitude position first, followed by the arguments for it. The effects of the kinds of presentations will vary, depending upon the initial attitude of the individuals listening to the arguments. A comprehensive study of these factors was conducted during World War II,[9] and the results of these experiments have implications for teaching.

What are the effects of presenting either one side or both sides of an issue on which people already have attitudes and opinions? A person initially opposed to the position advocated by the teacher is more likely to be influenced by a presentation giving both sides of the argument. However, if a person is initially favorable to the position being advocated, he is more likely to be influenced by a presentation of arguments on the fa-

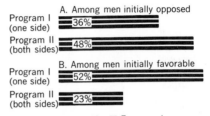

Net percent of individuals changing opinion in direction of position advocated by communicator.

FIGURE 9–5. *Effects of a one-sided vs. a two-sided presentation on beliefs (adapted from Hovland, Lumsdaine, and Sheffield).*

vorable side (see Figure 9–5). In the same experiments the effects of the educational level of the audience were studied. The two-sided argument was more effective with better-educated individuals irrespective of their initial stand. As might be expected, the one-sided presentation was mainly effective with the less well-educated group—particularly those who had already taken a stand. The more capable a person is of thinking critically, the more likely he is to evaluate the evidence for himself. A teacher in a classroom, discussing an issue on which the students already have attitudes and opinions, probably should present both sides of the issue. The students who are most capable of thinking for themselves will most likely be influenced by the arguments for the position advocated if the evidence for it is solid. Also, presenting the counter-arguments may stimulate their thinking and lend credibility to the teacher's objectivity.

Teachers discuss many issues on which there are numerous points of view. In such subjects as social studies, art, and literature, a range of

[9] C. I. Hovland, A. A. Lumsdaine, and F. D. Sheffield, *Experiments in Mass Communication: Studies in Social Psychology in World War II* (Princeton: Princeton University Press, 1949), Vol. 3.

TABLE 9–5. *Answers to question regarding students'*
opinion of their teachers' manner of presenting controver-
sial topics (from Remmers and Radler).

Total	Present all sides 60%	Prejudiced 23%	Don't know 17%
Boys	59	26	15
Girls	62	20	18
Grade 9	58	17	25
Grade 10	55	28	17
Grade 11	62	22	16
Grade 12	63	22	15
East	57	28	15
Midwest	62	20	18
South	63	20	17
Mountain-Pacific	58	22	20
Population to 2,500	63	19	18
2,500 to 25,000	56	29	15
25,000 to 250,000	63	19	18
Over 250,000	58	26	16
Low income	60	21	19
High income	61	25	14

opinions and attitudes is possible on a wide variety of subjects. On some
of these issues the weight of evidence will be on one side rather than the
other, but on other issues the teacher's presentation probably will be
influenced by his own opinions. If a teacher is discussing modern art, or
the works of Faulkner, or even such tried-and-true classics as the works of
Dickens or Scott, students' attitudes and opinions may differ considerably
from those of the teacher. Probably the best presentation and discussion
of such comparatively controversial subjects would be one in which a
variety of opinions are presented, and in which the students are allowed
to express freely their own reactions, attitudes, and opinions. If the
teacher, at the same time, strongly encourages critical thinking and intelligent evaluation based upon careful gathering of facts and logical argument, the students are more likely to accept an attitude or an opinion
when the weight of evidence favors this attitude or opinion. Haranguing

TABLE 9–6. *Answers to question regarding desirability of a teacher's expressing personal opinions and judgments on classroom material (from Remmers and Radler).*

	On art			On history and government			On present political and economic system of U. S.			On science		
	Yes	No	?	Yes	No	?	Yes	No	?	Yes	No	?
	%	%	%	%	%	%	%	%	%	%	%	%
Total	73	15	12	58	34	7	53	35	11	71	16	9
Boys	69	18	13	59	33	7	51	35	11	71	18	8
Girls	78	12	10	57	34	8	54	34	11	72	15	9
Grade 10	71	15	14	55	35	9	48	38	12	72	16	9
Grade 11	71	17	12	59	33	7	54	33	13	73	14	9
Grade 12	78	13	9	61	32	5	57	33	8	70	19	8
Rural	69	17	14	57	33	9	54	32	13	71	16	10
Urban	77	13	10	58	34	7	52	37	10	72	17	8
East	75	15	11	55	36	8	53	34	11	75	15	8
Midwest	76	15	10	57	35	8	49	38	12	69	18	9
South	68	18	14	64	28	7	57	31	10	71	16	8
West	76	13	11	57	36	6	52	35	10	72	15	10

students about what they ought to think or feel is not likely to be effective. Presenting only one side of an issue is likely to be convincing only to those who already agree with the position.

Students do not uniformly agree that teachers present all sides of an argument, although the majority of them feel that teachers are fair in their presentation of controversial subjects (see Table 9–5).[10] Students also agree that teachers should express their personal opinions and judgments about the material that they are teaching (see Table 9–6). A teacher has a reasonable certainty that if he is fair in his presentation and if he advocates a point of view while presenting all sides of an argument, most students will not resent his personal advocacy.

[10] H. H. Remmers and D. H. Radler, *The American Teenager* (Indianapolis–New York: Bobbs-Merrill Company, copyright 1957), p. 132 (Table 9–5) and p. 136 (Table 9–6). Used by special permission of the publisher.

INFLUENCE OF GROUP MEMBERSHIP

We have discussed the effects of group membership on the formation of attitudes. What happens when we attempt to change the attitudes of a group? Does the group attitude preclude attitude change? We would predict that members who have strong ties with the group, those for whom the group is a reference group, will be least influenced by an attempt to change attitudes on which the group sets standards.

Kelley and Volkart [11] studied this problem with a group of Boy Scouts. The experimenters first determined how closely each Boy Scout in twelve Boy Scout groups valued the scouting program. A week later, an adult appeared before the troops and gave a talk criticizing many Scout activities. He said tht modern boys would profit more from learning about their cities than from studying the outdoors. The experimenters then retested the attitudes of the Scouts. The results showed that Scouts who valued scouting least were most influenced by the communication from the adult, and those who valued it most were the least influenced (see Figure 9–6). In fact, the attitudes of the boys who strongly valued scouting were even stronger after the communication against scouting.

These data have implications for teaching. One of the most powerful means of influencing attitudes is by developing strong group identifications. This technique has been used consistently by teachers. Teachers urge students who are not doing well in school to "get in with" a group of students who are actively interested and successful in school. This technique is not uniformly successful because the group may not accept the proposed member; but when a student can be inducted into a group of this kind, startling changes in attitudes are frequently observed. If a student already has some attitudes he shares with members of the group, the rewards of group membership strengthen these attitudes and facilitate the learning and adoption of new attitudes.

Teachers also attempt to minimize the negative influence of groups by encouraging students to leave these groups. This technique would be useful if the student who is encouraged to leave one group can enter other groups providing satisfactions and rewards for him. Encouraging a student to leave a group whose attitudes are interfering with his success in school will only isolate the student and leave him without the satisfactions

[11] H. H. Kelley and E. H. Volkart, "The Resistance to Change of Group-Anchored Attitudes," *American Sociological Review*, 17 (1952), 453–465.

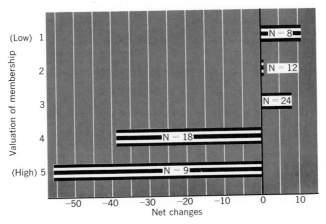

FIGURE 9-6. *Effect of listening to a communication against one's group. Percentage changing opinion of group, based on original strength of attachment to the group. When categories 1, 2, and 3 combined are compared (in terms of net change) with 4 and 5 combined, the difference in amount of change is significant: p < .02. Net change equals the per cent of change in the direction advocated by the communication, minus the per cent of change in the opposite direction. (From Kelley and Volkart.)*

he was seeking by belonging to the group in the first place.

INFLUENCE OF PERSONAL INVOLVEMENT

One factor does seem to be especially effective in changing attitudes—namely, *active participation* in the processes being used to effect attitude change. By active participation we mean that, in the process of producing attitude change, the individuals whose attitudes we are attempting to influence are involved in the appeals.

King and Janis [12] presented groups of college students with a communication about the prospects of military service. The communication argued that over 90 per cent of college students would be drafted within one year after graduation and that the length of military service required of the majority of college students would be at least three years. This communi-

[12] B. T. King and I. L. Janis, "Comparison of the Effectiveness of Improvised versus Non-Improvised Role-Playing in Producing Opinion Changes," *Human Relations,* 9 (1956), 177–186; see also C. I. Hovland, I. L. Janis, and H. H. Kelley, *Communication and Persuasion* (New Haven: Yale University Press, 1953), pp. 222–225.

cation was used because the students would be personally involved in its content and would have given thought to it. Their opinions indicate their attitudes, which are mixtures of information, thinking, and feeling about this topic. All of the subjects in the experiment were college students of draft age and were not deferrable. The students were divided into two major groups. In the first group all students read the communication aloud and into a tape recorder. The second group read the communication silently. The students in the first group were then told that their speaking ability was to be assessed. Some of these students were asked to read a prepared script based on the communication as if they were giving a talk. The remainder of the students in this group were asked to improvise a talk based on the communication.

In this experiment we have three levels of participation, or personal involvement, in the communication. All students read the communication; one group, however, read the communication into a tape recorder and then made a talk from it (improvisation group); a second group read the communication and a script based on it (oral-reading group); and the third group merely read the communication. Before the experiment the students were tested on their attitudes toward military service. The test was repeated after the experiment. Table 9–7 presents the changes in opinion taking place under these experimental operations. The students who were most involved in the communication process itself were also the students who changed the most.[13]

The degree of active participation provided in this experiment was limited. The students merely gave a talk based upon information presented to them by somebody else. However, as the student gave the talk, he was playing a **role;** he was acting as the communicator of the information. As he attempted to communicate the information and arguments realistically, he began to think and feel as the "real" communicator would think and feel. He became involved in the role; he began to take on the attitudes and feelings of the person who ordinarily lived this role.

Role playing is a device that has been used to bring about attitude changes.[14] In any role-playing technique the participants are asked to

---

[13] For additional evidence on the effects of active participation, see I. L. Janis and B. T. King, "Influence of Role-Playing on Opinion Change," *Journal of Abnormal and Social Psychology,* 49 (1954), 211–218. Also discussed in Hovland, *Communication and Persuasion,* pp. 219–221.

[14] S. M. Corey, "Role-Playing as Training in Learned Behavior," *Nation's Schools,* 53 (1954), 52. Also, H. H. Jennings, "Sociodrama as an Educative Process," in *Fostering Mental Health in Our Schools,* NEA Yearbook of the Association for Supervision and Curriculum Development (Washington, D. C.: National Education Association, 1950); J. L. Moreno, *The Theatre of Spontaneity* (New York: Beacon House, 1947).

TABLE 9-7. *Effect of role playing on opinion changes following exposure to a communication concerning the prospects of military service for college students (from King and Janis).*

Opinion Items	Improvisation Group A (N = 32)	Oral Reading Group B (N = 23)	Silent Reading Control Group (N = 20)
	Net Percentage Who Changed in the Direction Advocated by the Communication *		
1. Estimates of required length of service for draftees	41	27	5
2. Estimates of percentage of college students who will be deferred	44	26	25
3. Estimates of percentage of college students who will become officers	70	47	45
4. Personal expectations of length of military service	59	46	50
5. Personal expectation of being drafted	50	26	55
6. Combined index: per cent influenced on three or more of the five opinion items	87½	54½	65

* Significance of differences between group A and group B: p = .01; between A and C: p = .03.

portray as realistically as possible the life, the behavior, the feelings, the emotions, the attitudes, the opinions of some other person. One of the major effects of role-playing seems to be illustrated in the foregoing experiment: the individual playing the role begins to think like the other person. He begins to understand how a person living this role thinks, and his attitudes may change in the direction of those of the person whose role he is playing. Certainly the person who understands racial segregation better than anyone else is the person who has to live a life in which he has been segregated because of his race. If we have had no experience of this kind of life, our feelings about it are likely to be highly intellectualized. Through role playing we do not actually live the life, but we approach it; by approaching the experience of another person, we may take on his attitudes and feelings.

At the present time there is little experimental evidence on the effects of role playing in educational settings.[15] However, there is some indication that by utilizing role-playing techniques in our classrooms we can produce attitude changes which would not be produced by other methods.[16] Although we do not have definitive evidence on the value of role playing, the teacher ought to experiment with the procedure.[17]

IMITATIVE BEHAVIOR AND COMMUNICATION

The following experiment supplies us with an opportunity to relate interpersonal influence to the question of persuasive communication and attitude change. Although the experiment was conducted in a military setting, the general procedures used approximate educational methods.[18]

In this experiment, part of a training program for 427 air crewmen undergoing survival training, an attempt was made to influence trainees to eat a ration that was not particularly appetizing. For experimental purposes the trainees were divided into six groups. The experimental operations used in the six different groups were as follows:

1. The instructors made no effort to influence the trainees to accept the ration. They were instructed to say as little as possible about it, but were cautioned to avoid any impression of personal dislike for the ration.

2. The instructors tried to influence the trainees to accept the ration. They were instructed to set a good example for the men by eating the ration themselves and casually expressing favorable reactions to it.

3. The instructors gave information about the value of the ration for emergency purposes and about ways of preparing it. The presentation was objective and factual, and given in a "take-it-or-leave-it" manner.

4. In addition to giving facts about the value of the ration and ways of preparing it, the instructors emphasized psychological factors which might influence the men in accepting the ration.

[15] A critical analysis of experimental research on role playing can be found in J. H. Mann, "Experimental Evaluations of Role-Playing," *Psychological Bulletin*, 53 (1956), 227–234.

[16] The following studies contain descriptions of classroom experiments on the use of role-playing techniques: B. Hansen, "Sociodrama—A Methodology for Democratic Action," *Sociatry*, 1 (1948–49), 347–363; B. Hansen, "Sociodrama in the Classroom," *Sociatry*, 1 (1947), 334–350; A. Kaminsky, " 'You Are There' in the Social Studies Classroom," *High Points*, 36 (1954), 43–45; F. B. Moreno, "Sociodrama in the Sociology Classroom," *Sociatry*, 1 (1948–49), 404–413.

[17] Results in role-playing studies are not always positive. For a discussion of factors influencing role-playing activities, see W. Coleman, "Role-Playing as an Instructional Aid," *Journal of Educational Psychology*, 39 (1948), 429–435.

[18] E. P. Torrance and R. Mason, "Instructor Effort to Influence: An Experimental Evaluation of Six Approaches," *Journal of Educational Psychology*, 49 (1958), 211–218.

5. Essentially the same experimental operations were used as in Group 4, except that the procedures were done in individual discussions with the men rather than a group basis.

6. The instructors used mildly coercive techniques in the form of "grading down" the trainees if they did not "really" try the ration.

Data were gathered on how many trainees were persuaded; on the amount of the ration that was eaten; and on the trainees' reactions to the ration. With these data, the experimenters could rank each trainee on the degree to which he accepted or rejected the ration.

The greatest amount of change was produced in Group 6—the group in which mildly coercive techniques were used. Relate these effects to a principle cited earlier—namely, that attitudes are learned when rewards are produced for learning these attitudes. Positive results were also obtained in experimental Group 3, in which the information concerning the ration was presented in an objective and factual manner; and in Group 4, in which the same information and general explanations of personal factors were given. In this experiment logical arguments were effective.

In Groups 2 and 5, where personal influences of the instructors were used, negative results were obtained; the trainees were more opposed to the ration at the end of the experiment than they were when it began. The authors suggest that these trainees saw themselves as quite different from the instructor; consequently, they not only did not adopt his attitudes, but they took attitudes widely different from, and even opposing, his. This phenomenon has been called **negative identification.** In this experiment the instructors were not members of an air crew, as were the trainees; furthermore, the instructors frequently were young and in outstanding physical condition, whereas the trainees were older and in comparatively poorer physical condition. These instructors were not relevant models for these trainees.

The experiments discussed in this section amply illustrate that many variables in a communication influence its effectiveness. The Torrance and Mason experiment included several, and we saw that only some combinations were successful. The following decision rules, however, may be helpful: (1) The source of communication will influence its acceptability; but the positive effects occur at the time the communication is received and are not maintained by this variable. (2) A method of obtaining a reward for changing must be associated with the procedure. (3) Appeals to change based on strong emotions may initiate some changes, but used alone are less effective. (4) Changing an attitude requires that a person change his ways of looking at things; role playing and other procedures that involve him in this process are more likely to be effective.

THE INFLUENCE OF ATTITUDES ON COGNITION

Running through all the above experiments is the suggestion that what a person brings to the communication is an important determinant of its effect upon him. Persuasive communications do not always produce changes in the individual; even though he says he feels differently as a result of them, he may not act differently. Festinger [19] has found only three studies in which a persuasive communication has produced any behavioral change other than a verbal one. And, as we have seen, even some of these effects dissipate with time.

A person's attitudes will influence his reactions to communications. It is therefore important to know how attitudes influence these reactions.

FORMS OF INFLUENCE

The human organism does not respond equally and unselectively to all stimuli that impinge upon it. A person tends to organize and select among

TABLE 9–8. *Stimulus words representing six value categories (from Postman, Bruner, and McGinnies).*

Theoretical	*Economic*	*Aesthetic*	*Social*	*Political*	*Religious*
theory	income	beauty	loving	govern	prayer
verify	useful	artist	kindly	famous	sacred
science	wealthy	poetry	devoted	compete	worship
logical	finance	elegant	helpful	citizen	blessed
research	economic	literary	friendly	politics	religion
analysis	commerce	graceful	sociable	dominate	reverent

the stimuli. One of the major determinants of the manner in which he recognizes and selects is his previous learnings, as reflected in the concepts, attitudes, and values that he has already acquired.

A person's attitudes influence his cognitive processes in three ways: (1) The person does not respond as quickly to stimuli which are inconsistent with or contradictory to his attitudinal-value system. (2) A person recog-

[19] L. Festinger, "Behavioral Support for Opinion Change," *Public Opinion Quarterly*, 28 (1964), 404–417.

nizes and assimilates more quickly stimuli consistent with his attitudinal-value system. (3) When the stimulus situation is ambiguous, a person uses his attitudinal-value system to facilitate his interpretations of his environment.

In an experiment on attitudes and perception,[20] subjects were exposed to words that can have value meanings. In Table 9–8 are lists of words used and their categorization into some major value dimensions. Each of the subjects took a test to determine his pattern of values. These values were classified as theoretical, economic, aesthetic, social, political, and religious. For example, a person whose dominant value system is theoretical is a person whose major interests lie in the "discovery of truth." A person whose dominant value is economic is interested primarily in "usefulness and practicality." [21]

The words associated with each of the value dimensions were exposed on a tachistoscope, a device which permits the experimenter to expose the words at varying speeds. A word that is rapidly exposed is difficult to recognize. Each subject in this experiment was requested to give his idea of what the exposed word was.

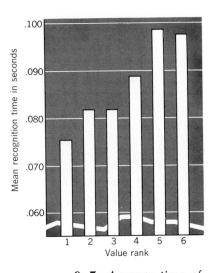

FIGURE 9–7. *Average time of recognition for the words representing the six values of the All-port-Vernon scale, arranged in rank order. A value rank of 1 is the person's dominant value. (From Postman, Bruner, and McGinnies.)*

The experimenters determined the recognition time for each of the words. The data indicated a significant relationship between the kinds of words quickly recognized and the dominant value system of the subject (Figure 9–7).

[20] L. Postman, J. S. Bruner, and E. McGinnies, "Personal Values and Selective Factors in Perception," *Journal of Abnormal and Social Psychology*, 43 (1948), 142–154.

[21] A more precise meaning is given to each of these value systems by the constellation of items checked on the test used to measure the dominant value systems. The test used was constructed by G. W. Allport and P. E. Vernon; see *A Study of Values* (Boston: Houghton Mifflin Company, 1931); the latest version is G. Allport, P. Vernon, and G. Lindzey, *A Study of Values*, rev. ed. (Boston: Houghton Mifflin, 1951).

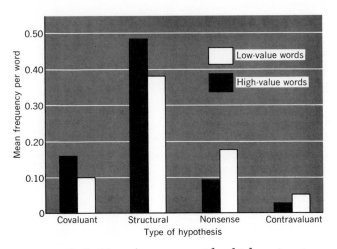

FIGURE 9–8. *Mean frequency with which various types of prerecognition hypotheses were given in response to high-value and low-value words (from Postman, Bruner, and McGinnies).*

Another purpose of the experiment was to find out whether there was any relationship between the kinds of prerecognition responses the subjects gave and their dominant value systems. For example, if the word on the tachistoscope was "sacred," and the subject said that he saw the word "sacrifice," he supplied a word which has a value connotation like the word on the tachistoscope (called "covaluant" words by the experimenters). Other words (called "contravaluant" words) had opposite value connotations to the words on the tachistoscope—for example, "scornful" when the word was "helpful," or "revenge" when the word was "blessed." Finally, two other kinds of prerecognition responses were identified. One of these was a nonsense kind of response; for example, "linone" for "income." Another kind of response, which the experimenters called "structural," consisted of words which had some of the characteristics of the exposed words—for example, "mowing" or "lowing" for "loving." The subjects who made such responses typically arrived at the correct response.

The results of the analysis are shown in Figure 9–8. As the bar graph illustrates, the subjects gave more covaluant and structural responses to exposed words that were consistent with the value system of the subject. The subjects also gave more nonsense and contravaluant responses to exposed words not consistent with their dominant values.

INCOMPATIBLE COGNITIONS AND
ATTITUDE CHANGE

In the preceding section we saw that attitudes influence how we see information presented to us. But we do not always distort or resist communications so thoroughly that we do not receive any information. If a person receives a communication that differs from the attitudes he holds, he must resolve the discrepancy between what he believes and feels and what he is told he ought to believe. The distortion process may reduce the discrepancy between the person's attitudes and the attitude advocated in the communication.

Festinger has proposed the theory of **cognitive dissonance** to describe and explain what happens in these cases.[22] He begins by making a plausible assumption: that persons may have incompatible cognitions. For example, the smoker thinks smoking is a good thing, but knows he may contract lung cancer. You buy a car that has attractive features, but it doesn't have all the horsepower you want. You have an important exam tomorrow, but there's a party you want to go to tonight. These incompatible cognitions are said to be *dissonant.*

Festinger stipulates that incompatible cognitions of this kind have motivational effects. The person is impelled to reduce the dissonance because it is uncomfortable. This he may do either by taking action or by seeking new information. If he takes action by making a choice, he will remove the dissonance by valuing more highly the choice made. However, he may seek information to remove the incompatibility between the cognitions.

Figure 9–9 portrays the theoretical relation between the magnitude of the dissonance, seeking of new information, and an expectation about the effect of the communication on the dissonance.[23] This model may be used to answer, theoretically, such questions as the following: Will a person seek information only when he is experiencing no dissonance? Does the amount of the dissonance affect information seeking? What does knowing or guessing that the information will reduce the dissonance do?

Read the figure as follows. Pick a point along the horizontal axis, the magnitude of dissonance dimension, then read up to one of the expecta-

---

[22] L. Festinger, *Theory of Cognitive Dissonance* (Evanston, Ill.: Row, Peterson & Company, 1957). See also L. Festinger and E. Aronson, "The Arousal and Reduction of Dissonance," in D. Cartwright and A. Zander, *Group Dynamics: Theory and Research,* 2nd ed. (Evanston, Ill.: Row, Peterson, & Company, 1960), pp. 214–231.

[23] Festinger, *Theory of Cognitive Dissonance,* p. 130.

tion lines, and then across to exposure dimension along the vertical axis. For example, pick a point between moderate and none, and go vertically to the line labeled "expectation new information will increase dissonance." If you now read across, you see you meet the avoidance side of the exposure dimension. The relation may be stated: if a person has moderate dissonance, and expects that the communication will increase it, he will avoid exposure to new information. Follow the same procedure except this time up to the higher line, and make a generalization.

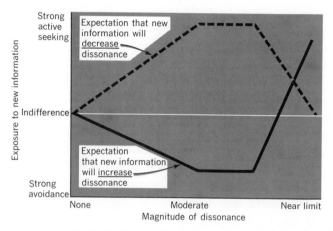

FIGURE 9–9. *Relation between magnitude of dissonance and active seeking of new information (from Festinger).*

In general, a person avoids information that is likely to increase his dissonance. However, if the dissonance is great, he is more likely to seek information as a way of reducing it. Festinger and his associates have provided solid experimental support for the general premises of the theory.[24]

It is apparent that the critical variable is how the person expects the communication to affect his thinking. Will it create, increase, or decrease dissonance? In one experiment[25] students told they were going to hear a speech against teenage drivers were relatively uninfluenced by the speaker. Other students were not told the content of the speech but were

[24] L. Festinger, *Conflict, Decision, and Dissonance* (Stanford, Calif.: Stanford University Press, 1964).
[25] J. Allyn and L. Festinger, "The Effectiveness of Unanticipated Persuasive Communications," *Journal of Abnormal and Social Psychology,* 62 (1961), 35–40.

asked to listen carefully because they would be asked questions about the speaker's personality. This group, hearing the same speech, were more influenced by it.

The teacher may too readily assume that providing information about an attitude object will be sufficient to change attitudes. The studies and theory described above clearly suggest that providing information is not sufficient, and that the teacher must consider the effects of many other variables. The prospective teacher reading this discussion may be somewhat pessimistic about the possibilities for producing attitude change. Such is not our intent, although we wish to suggest the complexity of the problem facing the teacher. For too long we have probably assumed that attitudes are easily changed, and we have been somewhat naive in our assumptions about the methods which are likely to produce attitude change. The schools have not fully explored the possibilities for producing attitude change; they have tended to rely upon what have been assumed to be the effective methods of the past, principally emotional appeals and logical arguments.

To this point we have discussed specific variables and experimental studies. The schools have attempted attitude change—sometimes in ignorance of this work, at other times by applying common-sense notions. In the next section we will look at some of these attempts. The experience gathered from them is worth analyzing to avoid their inadequacies.

SCHOOL PROGRAMS TO PROMOTE ATTITUDE CHANGE

Educational programs generally attempt to change attitudes in one or both of two ways: (1) provide information about an attitude object; (2) expose people to each other so that their attitudes toward each other will change.

INFLUENCE OF INFORMATION ON ATTITUDE CHANGE

In the learning experiences provided by schools, considerable information is given to students on subjects toward which they have attitudes. For example, questions of racial differences will be raised and answered in a sociology or an anthropology course. Information about the characteristics of racial groups is typically provided. Such information is frequently introduced into high school courses in civics and social studies. Do these courses produce changes in attitudes? The evidence for attitude change is inconclusive.

Apparently, mere exposure to the content of a course does not guarantee that students' attitudes will change on the topics being studied.[26] When classroom procedures are developed specifically to influence attitude change, such changes are more likely to occur. A classroom experiment will illustrate how carefully organized learning experiences, using some of the principles previously discussed, successfully influenced attitudes.

Bond[27] used the materials of a genetics course to attempt to influence attitude change toward national groups, races, and imperialism. The course was built to emphasize generalizations about people from the subject matter of genetics. The instructor emphasized problem solving and critical thinking rather than merely giving information to be absorbed by the students. The students were encouraged to draw their own generalizations based upon the available evidence. Other groups of students taking genetics were taught the course in a traditional manner, which emphasized providing information and generalizations for the students. Bond found that the experimental technique produced greater understanding of the generalizations and also induced positive attitude changes toward national groups, races, and imperialism.

We can speculate, in line with data cited earlier, that the process of requiring students to think critically and solve problems induces greater personal involvement in the problems being studied. The students apparently think about the material and relate it to their own ideas and conceptions. In the usual strategy, the students need not become personally involved in the material as long as they can remember it well enough to pass an examination.

Other studies[28] also suggest that when procedures are used requiring greater personal involvement, attitude changes are more likely. A common feature in many of these studies is student participation in discussion about the attitude problem. We can speculate that the discussion process

[26] A summary of some of these studies can be found in R. Williams, *The Resolution of Intergroup Tensions* (see note 1). See also J. C. Lagey, "Does Teaching Change Students' Attitudes?" *Journal of Educational Research,* 50 (1956), 307–311; C. M. Stevenson, "Effect of a Course in Minority Group Relations on the Attitudes of College Students," *Progressive Education,* 32 (1955), 19–21.

[27] A. Bond, *An Experiment in the Teaching of Genetics* (New York: Columbia University Press, 1940), Teachers College Contributions to Education, No. 797.

[28] See, for example, D. S. Laird and C. F. Cumbree, "Experiment in Modifying Ethnic Attitudes of College Students," *Journal of Educational Sociology,* 25 (1952), 401–409.

provides a student with an opportunity to express his feelings and to clarify his thinking. Again, we must warn that the factors in the discussion method which influence attitude change are not presently clear.

The common assumption at the present time is that if attitudes have not been strongly formed, information is more likely to shape the attitude. However, contrary to this common-sense notion, a person may have a strong attitude with little information. Grace [29] tested students' attitudes toward ten countries and also the amount of knowledge they had of these countries. Grace found two kinds of relationships. One group of persons was most intense in like and dislike for those nations about which they knew the most, and were neutral about those they knew the least. A second group of persons liked best the nations about which they knew the most, and liked least those about which they knew the least. Twice as many students were in the first group as in the second. The best conclusion seems to be that there is only a moderate correlation between amount of information about something and attitudes toward it.

PEOPLE AS INFORMATION SOURCES

Teachers frequently invite speakers from foreign countries or minority groups into their classes to discuss the problems of these people. Another common procedure is to invite members of national or racial groups to participate in discussions of intergroup problems. One of the assumptions underlying the use of such procedures is that contact with and exposure to members of these groups will reduce negative attitudes and will increase positive attitudes. Again, the evidence is not conclusive that such procedures are uniformly successful. In an early study, Horowitz [30] surveyed attitudes of children living in the North and the South toward Negroes. Horowitz also compared the attitudes toward the Negro of children in segregated and unsegregated schools in New York City. He found no significant differences in attitude toward the Negroes among these groups of children and concluded that familiarity with or contact with Negroes is not an important determinant of the children's attitudes. The important determiner seemed to be the children's contact with the

---

[29] H. A. Grace, "Information and Social Distance as Predictors of Hostility toward Nations," *Journal of Abnormal and Social Psychology*, 47 (1952), 540–545.

[30] E. L. Horowitz, "The Development of Attitude toward the Negro," *Archives of Psychology*, No. 194 (1936). J. Silver, University of Mississippi professor, author of *The Closed Society*, in a radio interview (KCBS, San Francisco), pointed out that students rioting at Ole Miss at the admission of James Meredith were expressing deeply held attitudes learned through their childhood and adolescence. They called themselves Freedom Fighters.

prevalent social attitude toward the Negro. Children living in New York City who had little or no exposure to Negroes formed their attitudes on the basis of what adults in their environment thought about the Negro. This conclusion is consistent with our previous discussion of the influence of adults on the attitude formation of children, where we pointed out that adults provide rewards for adopting adult attitudes.

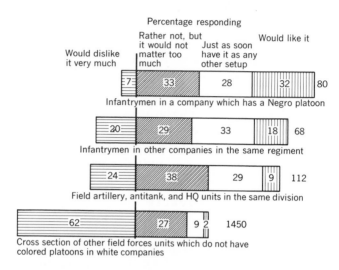

FIGURE 9–10. *Attitudes toward serving in a company containing Negro and white platoons among men who have done so and men who have not (Europe, June 1945). The numbers following the bars are the number of cases on which percentages are based. (From Stouffer.)*

As we noted above, the evidence on this point is not always in the same direction. Since World War II, service units of white and Negro soldiers have been progressively integrated. A study has been made of the attitudes of white soldiers toward the integration process.[31] Some of the data from this study are recorded in Figure 9–10. As the data suggest, soldiers in mixed companies are more favorable to integration than are soldiers who are not in mixed companies. This kind of study does not permit us to make definitive statements about cause-and-effect relationships. We cannot say that placing soldiers in mixed companies produces a favorable attitude toward Negroes; however, the relationship suggests the possibility that exposure to Negroes tends to reduce hostility toward them.

[31] S. A. Stouffer et al., *The American Soldier: Studies in Social Psychology in World War II* (Princeton: Princeton University Press, 1949), Vol. I.

Comparable results were obtained in a study of integrated and segregated housing projects.[32] The data in Table 9–9 illustrate the relationship between integrated and segregated housing and the extent to which Negroes are in contact with people in the projects. Negroes are fairly well known by whites when the opportunity for contacts between Negroes and whites is increased. Again, cause-and-effect relationships cannot be definitively established. We do not know, for example, if initial attitude disposition is a factor that determines which kinds of people will live in an integrated housing situation. If only individuals with neutral or positive attitudes toward Negroes enter such housing projects, then increased knowledge about Negroes would be expected. Furthermore, there is evidence in this study to suggest that the group norm in the integrated housing project is quite different from that in the segregated housing project. Housewives in the integrated project expect to be rewarded for contacts with Negroes, whereas housewives in the segregated housing expect to be ostracized if they are friendly toward Negroes.

Exposure to the attitude object occasionally has an effect opposite to that desired. For example, Smith[33] studied the effect of intercultural experiences on students' attitudes toward different national groups. The students in this study were 183 high school and college students who had spent some time in Europe in an experiment in international living. One of Smith's findings was that students who were exceptionally nationalistic in their attitudes tend to become more so after exposure to other national ways of living.

This study also provided an opportunity to compare two different kinds of intercultural experiences. Some of the students participated in an experiment in international living in which they lived with members of different national groups. Others lived in a camp composed mainly of American students. Greater changes took place in the second group of students than in the first.

From the above discussion, two conclusions can be drawn. If the process of gathering data about the attitude object requires a student to become actively involved in the process, familiarity is more likely to induce attitude change. Second, initial predisposition of the student

[32] M. Deutsch and M. E. Collins, *Interracial Housing. A Psychological Evaluation of a Social Experiment* (Minneapolis: University of Minnesota Press, 1951).

[33] H. P. Smith, "Do Intercultural Experiences Affect Attitudes?" *Journal of Abnormal and Social Psychology*, 51 (1955), 469–477. Mixed results were also obtained by S. W. Webster; see "The Influence of Interracial Contact on Social Acceptance in a Newly Integrated School," *Journal of Educational Psychology*, 52 (1961), 292–296. This author thinks that the "contact hypothesis" needs reconsideration. He thinks the general social milieu of the contact determines the positive or negative effects of contact.

TABLE 9-9. *Percentages of housewives indicating their most likely contacts with Negro people (from Deutsch and Collins).*

Meeting place	Integrated interracial projects		Segregated biracial projects	
	Koaltown*	Sacktown*	Bakerville*	Frankville*
As neighbors in the building	60	53	0	0
Through laundry facilities located in or near building	13	17	0	0
Outside on benches	46	64	7	21
In office, etc.	2	1	7	17
At tenant meetings	2	17	28	28
Shopping in stores, in the streets around project	12	13	81	60
Through the children's schools	1	3	14	0
Total cases†	102	86	43	42

* The project names are pseudonyms.
† Only the people who responded "yes" or "uncertain" to the question of getting to know Negro people are included. The percentage figures add up to more than 100 because many people named more than one place.

appears to be an important factor. Where student attitudes have not been formed, information and evidence are more likely to be influential in forming attitudes. Where strong attitudes have been formed, evidence that contradicts the attitude held is not likely to have an effect in producing attitude change.

COMPREHENSIVE SCHOOL PROGRAMS

A number of school systems have initiated comprehensive programs to bring about attitude changes. Most of these have been concerned with influencing attitudes toward minority groups.[34] Because of the compre-

[34] See A. Halligan, "A Community's Total War against Prejudice," *Journal of Educational Sociology*, 16 (1943), 374-378; H. E. Amerman, "Perspective for Evaluating Intergroup Relations in a Public School System," *Journal of Negro Education*, 26 (1957), 108-120; F. T. Smith, *An Experiment in Modifying Attitudes Toward the Negro* (New York: Teachers College, Columbia University, 1943); H. H. Cummings, *Improving Human Relations*, National Council for the Social Studies Bulletin, No. 25, 1949; M. Levine, "The Changing School Community," *Social Education*, 10 (1946), 348-350; S. E. Dimond, "The Detroit Citizenship Study," *Social Education*, 12 (1948), 356-358.

hensiveness of these programs, reliable experimental data are occasionally lacking. In general, reports on these programs suggest that positive results have been obtained with the procedures. Because a variety of procedures have been used, it is not possible to determine which factors were most influential in producing the observed changes.

A survey of these programs suggests that they have incorporated, in one way or another, many of the factors that we have indicated as important determinants of attitude change. In the first place, the programs were set up to influence the attitudes of parents and teachers, as well as those of students. Many of the experimenters recognized that attempts to influence students' attitudes toward minority groups would be unlikely to succeed if these attitudes were not reinforced in the home and community environment. Second, most of the programs included procedures for bringing the various groups together on a basis of equality. These groups then discussed and worked on common problems. Third, members of minority groups chosen to participate in these programs of discussion and problem solving were frequently individuals of high prestige within their own group, or in the larger community. Fourth, the school programs and administrative procedures were revised to implement democratic principles. Fifth, many of these programs began with the elementary school child because children at this age are more likely to be influenced than older children.

In these programs the experimenters usually report that the individuals involved obtain greater insight into their own feelings and attitudes—particularly teachers and parents who apparently had not realized the extent to which their attitudes were being manifested in subtle ways. An obvious but important conclusion from the programs used in these studies is that attitude change can be produced, but that attitude change must be planned for and systematically implemented. When a school engages in a comprehensive program to foster attitude change, we would expect the rewards for such changes to become increasingly greater. This factor, combined with the other factors that we have noted, probably ensures some success for such programs in producing the desired changes.

THE EVALUATIVE PROCESS AND
THE LEARNING OF VALUES

A distinction is sometimes made between attitudes and values, or between the attitudinal and the evaluative processes. This distinction is not always clear, and it is difficult to maintain. We will suggest a definition of values and the evaluative process, but the teacher should remember that the two terms are used interchangeably in this text. At the present time, there is no reason to believe that different psychological processes are involved in the acquisition of attitudes and values, or that the attitudinal and evaluative processes are psychologically distinguishable.

DEFINITION OF A VALUE

A value is a preference based upon a conception of what is desirable. Values, like attitudes, are orientation processes by which the person is prepared to respond to his environment in predetermined ways. Values, also, are states of readiness, or predispositions to act and to be motivated in specific kinds of ways. Attitudes and values are alike in that both represent preferences of the person; however, values are preferences based upon conceptions of what is desirable, whereas attitudes need not be based upon such conceptions.

Attitudes are reflected in such words as "like" and "dislike." Values are reflected in such words as "good" and "bad." A child may say, for example, that he likes swimming and thinks that stealing is wrong. In the first case he is expressing a preference, which may not reflect any conception of the rightness or wrongness of his preference. In the second case he has indicated his conception of what is desirable. However, this conception of desirability may be unrelated to personal preferences.

Values, like attitudes, have an intensity factor, and an individual may feel more or less strongly about a particular value that he holds. One child may be cognitively aware that stealing is wrong and hold this proposition as a value. Another child may have the same value but feel very strongly about the "badness" of stealing.

HOW VALUES ARE LEARNED

Values, like attitudes, are presumably learned as ways of obtaining need satisfaction. As we have stressed in previous chapters, the socialization process of a child ensures the learning of certain behaviors by the application of rewards and punishments. Out of this process the child learns what is regarded by society as desirable and undesirable behavior. From these conceptions he forms his value standards. A child, for example, cannot learn that stealing is wrong unless he is exposed to adults who, in effect, teach him this value and reinforce its learning by rewarding behavior consonant with this value.

Similarly, the identification process appears to be crucial in the development of a value system.[35] The process is presumed to be the same for attitudes and values. The result of the identification process, whether identification be with individuals or groups, is an individual who has an integrated system of attitudes and values. This system of attitudes and values is a determinant of specific behaviors, and influences the ways in which an individual can be motivated.

The experimental evidence suggests that the same influences affect both the acquisition of values and the acquisition of attitudes. For example, home influences seem to be a major determinant in the acquisition of values. In a classical study, Hartshorne, May, and Shuttleworth [36] correlated children's ideas of right and wrong with the ideas of their parents, friends, club leaders, day school teachers, and Sunday school teachers. These experimenters found the highest agreement to be between children's ideas and those of their parents. The relationship with parents is likely to be the strongest because parents exercise a primary and initial influence on the development of children's values.

However, the development of a value system is not as simple as the above description suggests. Obviously, not all children acquire values that their parents try to transmit to them. For example, some children learn antisocial behavior, perhaps of an agressive and hostile nature, in homes in which there is considerable punishment for such behavior. Recent studies have thrown light on the characteristics of the parent-child relationship which influence the learning of acceptable social values.

VALUES AND THE PARENT-
CHILD RELATIONSHIP

The child's initial relations with his parents are dependent in character. The infant, of necessity, relies upon his mother to provide him with the requisites for the sustenance of life. Obviously, the child cannot be independent in satisfying his own biological needs. Out of this dependency relationship with the mother the child typically acquires a dependency need; that is, he finds his mother a source of need satisfaction. With increasing age, the child must also develop independence needs so that he can acquire the behavior which will free him of dependency on his parents.

Complicating this relationship is the necessity for the child to acquire

[35] See R. R. Sears et al., *Patterns of Child Rearing* (Evanston, Ill.: Row, Peterson & Company, 1957), Chapter 10.
[36] H. Hartshorne, M. A. May, and F. K. Shuttleworth, *Studies in the Organization of Character* (New York: Macmillan Company, 1930).

his proper sex role. The male child must establish male identification achieved through identification with the father. Thus, a male child comes to depend upon his father as a source of rewards for typically masculine behavior. Consequently, satisfaction of the dependency need takes many different forms at different stages in the child's life. But the dependency need, because of the nature of the parent-child relationship, tends to be a prevalent and strong need in children.

Parents may reward or punish dependency behavior. Typically, the very young child is rewarded for dependency behavior; but, as he grows older, he is encouraged to think and act for himself within the limits set by the parents. In this process, repeated punishment for dependency behavior as the child grows older can lead to frustration of his dependency needs. If the dependency need is persistently punished, the identification process may itself be inhibited. As a consequence, the child, in not identifying with the parents, does not learn the attitudes and values necessary for social control, or the development of "conscience." One result of the frustration of dependency needs appears to be the development of aggressive behavior.[37]

Bandura and Walters [38] studied the relationship between antisocial behavior of adolescent boys and the parent-child relationship. In this study the investigators chose a sample of boys who had a record of antisocial behavior and carefully matched them with a sample of boys of comparable age and social status who had not manifested antisocial behavior. Through a series of personal interviews with the parents of both groups of boys and with the boys themselves, the investigators determined the relationships between the character of the parent-child interaction and the presence or absence of antisocial behavior in the boys' behavior patterns.

One of the major findings was that the parent-child relationship for aggressive boys was frequently characterized by a lack of warmth and affection. The aggressive group of boys manifested little overt emotional dependency on either their mothers or their fathers. The mothers of these boys, while encouraging the dependency relationship, discouraged it at the same time. The consequence was that the aggressive boys generally tended to inhibit their dependency relations with their parents and other adults. Furthermore, the parents of the aggressive group tended to control their children principally by physical means.

[37] R. R. Sears et al., "Some Child Rearing Antecedents of Aggression and Dependency in Young Children," *Genetic Psychology Monographs*, 47 (1953), 135–234.
[38] A. Bandura and R. Walters, *Adolescent Aggression* (New York: Ronald Press, 1959).

The establishment of male identification for these boys depended upon a rewarding relationship with their fathers. The fathers of the aggressive boys had not established affectionate relationships with their sons, had spent little time with them, showed little warmth, acceptance, or esteem for the boys, and were more punitive than the fathers of the nonaggressive boys. In other words, the parents of these children did not provide rewards for identification with the male parent.

These data suggest the complexity of the relationships between parents and children and the influence of these relationships on the development of the value system. In the homes of the aggressive boys, value standards were upheld, but the manner in which they were upheld emphasized forms of punishment that tended to cut the boys off from identification with their parents. The data from this study tend to support the hypothesis that, if the identification process is not fostered, values will not be internalized. But the identification process itself depends heavily upon the character of the child's relations with his parents and is fostered when the parents, in addition to indicating what is right and wrong, become a source of rewards for the child.

INFLUENCE OF SCHOOL ON DEVELOPMENT OF A VALUE SYSTEM

The problems that we have discussed concerning the school and the development of attitudes are the same problems that characterize the relationship of the school to the development of a value system. If a child has not learned to identify with adult figures, and has found relationships with these adult figures to be punishing and frustrating, he probably will not identify with a teacher.

We have discussed the problem of conflict and attitudes, and the principles that we cited in that discussion are applicable to conflict and values. The school, through teachers, tends to reinforce the general value standards of society. The teacher's relationship with the child is similar to that of the parents, in that both parent and teacher are sources of reward and punishment for desirable behavior. We can again hypothesize that identification with teachers and the teachers' value systems will be facilitated by the same kind of relationship that facilitates identification with parents. We would predict that using ridicule, deprivation of privileges, and, in extreme cases, physical punishment and a cold and harsh manner would suggest to a child that the teacher is rejecting him as a person. The child will learn, as with his parents, that his dependency needs cannot be satisfied by identification with the teacher. In such cases we would expect the teacher to have comparatively little influence on the development of the child's value systems.

On the other hand, where children have established identifications with parental figures, identifications with teachers probably depend on similarities between teachers and parents. If the child is treated by the teacher in the same way as he is by his parents, and if the value standards of teacher and parents are similar, we would expect the teacher to have influence in reinforcing and strengthening the learning of values.

Again, we have suggested the complexity of the problem of value standards. We have emphasized that the psychological processes for the acquisition of values are similar to those for the acquisition of attitudes. The same general principles of learning and the same variables appear to be crucial in the development of both attitudes and values. The major factor in the development of a value system appears to be the identification process. The identification process is fostered and facilitated when an adult figure is a source of rewards, and when adopting the adult's behavior is need satisfying. We have hypothesized that, as in the case of the parent-child relationship, the identification process will be fostered if the teacher's relationships with the child are characterized by warmth, acceptance, and esteem.

COMPLEX SYSTEMS OF ATTITUDES AND VALUES

Those integrations of attitudes and values which have persistently been reinforced apparently tend to produce stable and consistent personality characteristics. Some psychological research has been devoted to determining what these major systems of attitudes and values may be. One of the purposes of the test devised by Allport and Vernon, which was used in the experiment cited above (p. 363), is to determine to what extent individuals have developed dominant attitudinal-value patterns. One of the most comprehensive studies of this kind was concerned with a personality type called *the authoritarian personality*.[39] A major finding of this study was the complexity of the attitude-value system of individuals and its influence on behavior. The investigators began their research by studying fairly specific attitudes, such as attitudes toward Negroes and Jews. As their research progressed, they found that these more specific attitudes ap-

---

[39] A complete discussion of the original research on this subject can be found in T. W. Adorno, E. Frenkel-Brunswik, D. J. Levinson, and R. N. Sanford, *The Authoritarian Personality* (New York: Harper, 1950).

peared to be embedded in a general attitudinal-value orientation which resulted in a fairly specific kind of personality type, which they later called "the authoritarian personality." The authoritarian personality is a prejudiced person. His prejudice takes the form of being submissive and respectful to members of what is called the in-group—that is, the group with which he identifies—and of being aggressive, hostile, and punitive to members of the out-group. Thus, the authoritarian personality can be found in any social group, whether or not it is a minority group.

The researchers found that this basic attitude-value orientation is related to and integrated with a wide variety of other specific attitudinal-value orientations. Else Frenkel-Brunswik, in a study of prejudiced children, observed the following characteristics, which are also the characteristics attributed to the authoritarian personality: [40]

1. The ethnocentric child (that is, a child prejudiced toward out-groups and strongly attached to the in-groups) tends to have a stereotyped, rigid, and glorified concept of himself and the in-group to which he belongs. Furthermore, he tends to reject the minority and out-group, perhaps with open aggression and hostility.

2. He rejects all that is "weak" and "indifferent."

3. His rejection of "weakness" is related to an admiration of the "strong," "tough," and "powerful."

4. He emphasizes the dichotomy of sex, and the opposite sex tends to become an out-group.

5. His admiration for success, power, and prestige appears to be related to a submission to authority based on fear of punishment.

6. He tends to give approval on the basis of external moral values, frequently including such values as "cleanliness" and "politeness." He also values conformity to accepted social standards.

7. He is intolerant, inflexible, rigid, and incapable of facing ambiguous situations.

8. He has a fearful and catastrophic conception of the world and tends to be superstitious.

Note the complexity in the attitudinal-value system of the ethnocentric child. He is not simply a child who likes people in his own group and dislikes people outside of it. He has a basic attitudinal-value orientation which includes his relationships with his own group and the out-group, and a wide variety of other subjects. His attitudinal-value system tends to be inflexible and rigid, with the consequence that he falls back on his

[40] E. Frenkel-Brunswik, "A Study of Prejudice in Children," *Human Relations*, 1 (1948), 259–306.

basic values to interpret the world around him. He likes the strong and dislikes the weak. He admires success, power, prestige. At the same time, he is submissive to authority and conforms to approved social values.

The development of an attitudinal-value system of this kind of personality occurs over a long period of time. Children are not born with these characteristics. Specific kinds of attitudes are integrated into more complex attitudes and values, which set a pattern of personality development. Consistent with our discussion above on the influence of attitudes and values on the cognitive processes, we note that ethnocentric children tend to prefer sharply defined situations rather than ambiguous ones. In ambiguous situations, these children tend to redefine the environment in terms of sharply defined and rigid categories of what is right and wrong.

At the present time, the determinants of a personality development of this kind are not completely known.[41] Research evidence suggests that this kind of a personality develops out of a specific kind of parent-child interaction. These children typically come from homes in which there is considerable emphasis on conformity and submission to authority, usually accompanied by strongly coercive systems of punishment. We can speculate that children develop authoritarian personalities by identifying with adults with this kind of personality, who reward them for identification.

We have discussed the concept of the authoritarian personality to illustrate the complex ways in which attitudes and values become integrated into personality systems.[42] At the present time, psychological research has not progressed to the point where we can describe well-defined personality types and the attitudinal-value systems which particularly characterize them. The significant point here is that attitudes, values, concepts, and generalizations are not held in isolation, but are interrelated and integrated into complex systems for interpreting and responding to the environment. The more highly integrated the system, the more predictable the individual's behavior.

INSTRUCTIONAL STRATEGIES

Review the discussion of this topic at the end of the preceding chapter. We will add only a few points about persuasive communications here.

[41] There is disagreement as to whether the characteristics of the ethnocentric person constitute a personality *type* as such. For a critical review of research in this area, see R. Thristie and M. Jahoda, *Studies in the Scope and Method of "The Authoritarian Personality"* (Glencoe, Ill.: The Free Press, 1954).

[42] For further developments in this line of research see, M. Rokeach, *The Open and Closed Mind* (New York: Basic Books, 1960).

The first step in designing a strategy is an assessment of the existing attitudes of students. An information-giving, emotionally appealing strategy is likely to be effective only when the students have no discernible attitudes on the topic or with students already favorably disposed. For permanent effects with these students and to modify the attitudes of other students, strategies consistent with the following principles seem necessary. The change in attitude must provide need satisfaction; the behavior change must be stimulated and rewarded when it occurs.

If a persuasive communication is used, the only reasonable approach seems to be to get as many of the critical variables into the situation as possible. It is also necessary to have repeated experiences which reinstate the influence of these variables.

SUMMARY

1. Attempts to change attitudes consist essentially in communications designed to persuade individuals to adopt a new attitude position. The influence of these communications is enhanced by such factors as the prestige and credibility of the communicator.

2. The effect of these communications is varied when the form of the communication emphasizes logical argument or emotional appeal. These factors, in addition to the prestige of the communicator, have varying degrees of influence in producing attitude change.

3. An important determinant of the extent of attitude change is the predisposition of the person whose attitude is being influenced. Logical argument is most likely to be effective in producing attitude change if the individual does not have a sharply defined attitude, or if he is already somewhat favorably disposed toward the attitude position advocated. An emotional appeal is less likely to be effective if it is anxiety-arousing.

4. Procedures used to influence attitude change, in general, are most likely to be effective the more the individual is actively involved in the process itself. Active participation probably enhances identification with the role of the communicator of the attitude and tends to bring about attitude change.

5. Any factor that facilitates identification, either with an individual or with a group, tends to enhance attitude change. For the same reason, attitude communications contrary to attitudes based upon strong identifications are not likely to be effective.

6. Attitudes influence a person's reactions to communications—specifi-

cally, his readiness to respond to stimuli that are consistent with his attitudes. The theory of cognitive dissonance provides an explanation for a person's reactions when he resolves a discrepancy between what he believes and what he is told he should believe.

7. The school is necessarily involved in attempting to influence attitudes and values of the students. The school as a social agency reinforces the dominant attitudes and values of society. The school also acts as an agency to promote desirable changes in attitudes and values. The process of bringing about these attitude changes is complex. The teacher who organizes learning experiences designed to produce these changes again must act as a hypothesis-maker, taking into account the factors discussed in this chapter. The concepts and principles presented in this chapter provide a basis for making hypotheses about learning experiences likely to produce changes in attitudes and values.

8. Values and attitudes have many characteristics in common. Insofar as values are distinguished from attitudes, the distinction is made on the basis that values imply some conception of what is desirable.

9. The processes by which values are acquired are similar to the processes by which attitudes are acquired. The parent-child relationship is particularly influential in the formation of conscience and the value system. If the parent-child relationship, and presumably any other adult-child relationship, is characterized by mutual warmth, acceptance, and esteem, the identification process is likely to be enhanced. The result of this enhancement is that the individual assimilates and internalizes the values of the identification figure.

10. Finally, we have noted that attitudes and values tend to become integrated into complex systems which, in some cases, evolve into marked personality types.

STUDY AND DISCUSSION QUESTIONS

1. Refer to the Mitnick and McGinnies study presented at the beginning of this chapter. What hypotheses about attitude change would you offer if the experimental conditions had been arranged so that the discussion of the problem treated in the film took place before the film was shown? What predictions would you make about attitude changes in students who discussed the problem treated in the film but did not see the film?

2. Assume that in a situation of the kind described in the Mitnick and McGinnies study the students could infer from the teacher's behavior that his attitude was at variance with the attitude advocated in the communication

presented in the film. Suggest hypotheses that predict the effect on attitude change of the teacher's behavior in this context. Under what conditions might the teacher's behavior have little, if any, influence? Under what conditions might the teacher's behavior have more influence than the film communication?

3. Assume that you are teaching a class in which some of the students have a negative attitude toward members of racial groups other than their own. You find through questioning that the students view the members of these racial groups in terms of the typical stereotypes associated with such groups. You present information to demonstrate that the stereotypes are inappropriate. Formulate hypotheses about the effects of this procedure on attitude change. What variables need to be considered in making these predictions about attitude change?

4. Suggest some prestige figures that may influence the attitudes of students on these subjects:

   a. Attitudes toward drinking alcoholic beverages.

   b. Attitudes toward participation in the affairs of civic government.

   c. Attitudes toward athletics.

   In each case describe the group whose attitudes you are trying to influence and suggest your reasons for believing that these individuals will be prestige figures for these groups.

5. How do you explain the fact that the influence of a prestige figure on attitude change is relatively impermanent? Suggest ways in which you may test the hypotheses that comprise your explanation.

6. In this chapter it has been suggested that younger children may regard the teacher as a prestige figure and a source of credible statements. Assuming that this may be the case, what factors would account for this fact? What factors would explain the fact that older children may be less likely to regard the teacher as a prestige figure and credible commentator?

7. Assume that you are trying to influence students' attitudes toward maintaining a healthy regimen of eating and sleeping. Assume also that you portray the beneficial effects of such a regimen rather than the harmful effects of not following healthy practices in this respect. Suggest some hypotheses about attitude changes under these conditions. Would a minimal emotional appeal of this kind be more effective than a strong emotional appeal?

8. Many people feel that a positive appeal is more likely to produce attitude changes than a negative approach to fostering the same kinds of changes. Offer some hypotheses that would support this point of view.

9. Suppose that you wish to persuade students that the use of the atomic bomb in World War II was a commendable action. Predict the effects of using logical argument, of fear-arousing communications portraying the ef-

fects likely to have occurred if the bomb had not been used, and of the authoritative opinions of the President and military experts.

10. Assume that you have a group of students in your class who have a negative attitude toward the subject you are teaching. Suggest some procedures that you might use which might influence them to change their attitude to a more positive one. Predict the probability that any of these procedures is likely to effect a change. Explain the limitations of the procedures that you suggest and the factors that are likely to reduce the effectiveness of these procedures. What information would you need about these students before you could decide on appropriate procedures?

11. The American school typically holds as one of its objectives the promotion of behavior changes in attitudes toward the American way of life. What learning experiences do schools typically use to produce positive attitudes toward the American way of life? Which of the variables that we have discussed in this chapter seem to be operative in these activities? Suggest the limitations of these activities for effecting this attitude change.

12. Some people argue that the extracurricular program of the school fosters attitude changes which interfere with the development of positive attitudes toward "more intellectual" activities. Evaluate this argument.

13. Some people argue that the extracurricular program of the school has greater influence on producing desirable attitude changes than do many classroom activities. Assume that this statement is correct. What factors in the activity program may account for this relatively greater influence?

14. Refer to the Kelley and Volkart study discussed in this chapter. Assume that the communicator had praised the activities of scouting and strongly favored them. What effects would you predict that this kind of a communication would have on the scouts who were the least interested in scouting? Assume that the communicator presented both sides of the question on the value of scouting. What effects would you predict this kind of a communication would have had on the attitudes of the most interested and least interested scouts?

15. A teacher wishes to influence students to acquire a more positive attitude toward the United States' participation in the United Nations. He organizes the students into a mock UN Assembly. What difficulties might be involved in stimulating the students to play the roles of UN members? Assume that one of the students had a negative attitude toward the United States' participation in the UN. What is the probability that this role-playing procedure will influence attitude change in this student?

16. Review the experiment on attempts to influence air crewmen to eat a survival ration. How do you account for the fact that in this experiment the presentation of information in an objective manner influenced behavior change? Relate the results in this respect to the discussion of the influence of logical argument presented earlier in the chapter. In what ways are the procedures used in this experiment similar to the ones cited earlier? In what ways are they different?

17. Some people argue that students need to know the facts of American history if they are to develop patriotic attitudes. Evaluate this argument in the light of the principles discussed in this chapter.

18. We have suggested that "warmth" in relations between parents and children, or teachers and children, may influence the child to identify with these adults. Can a teacher be both "warm" and "strict"?

19. Describe the behavior patterns that you would expect to characterize a teacher who "rejects" a student. How could you determine whether the teacher's behavior is seen as "rejecting" by the student?

20. Is the teacher likely to influence the students' values even though the students may not identify with the teacher?

21. What are the criteria for determining that a child has internalized the values which his parents and teachers have encouraged him to learn?

22. Assume that you observe a student who apparently conforms to the principal attitudes and values of a group to which he belongs. How could you determine whether the student has internalized the attitudes and values? In general, how could you distinguish public conformity without internalizing values from genuine internalization of attitudes and values?

23. Suggest some of the specific behaviors that you might observe from which you could infer that a child had the characteristics described as associated with the authoritarian personality. Refer to the list of characteristics presented in this chapter. What kinds of need-satisfactions would a child with these characteristics be likely to be obtaining with the attitudes that he has acquired?

RECOMMENDED READINGS

L. Festinger. *A Theory of Cognitive Dissonance.* Stanford, Calif.: Stanford University Press, 1957.

J. D. Frank. *Persuasion and Healing.* New York: Schocken Books, 1963.

C. I. Hovland, I. L. Janis, and H. H. Kelley. *Communication and Persuasion.* New Haven: Yale University Press, 1953.

C. I. Hovland, A. A. Lumsdaine, and F. D. Sheffield. *Experiments in Mass Communication: Studies in Social Psychology in World War II*, Vol. 3. Princeton: Princeton University Press, 1949.

K. Lewin. *Resolving Social Conflicts.* New York: Harper & Brothers, 1948.

R. Williams. *The Resolution of Intergroup Tensions.* New York: Social Science Research Council, 1948.

CHAPTER TEN

THE LEARNING OF COMPLEX PERFORMANCES

The schools and other educational and training institutions foster the acquisition of complex behavior patterns. These patterns, sets of manipulative and movement behaviors, are not classifiable as concepts or attitudes or problem solving, but are amalgams of them all. Typing, playing a musical instrument, painting a picture, engaging in competitive games and musical or dramatic productions—these are examples of complex performances. A prospective surgeon learns a set of complex performances called "performing an operation," a lawyer learns a performance called "trying a case," a teacher learns one called "teaching a class."

Performances cannot be defined as distinctive aspects of personality. Rather, they are integrations of response patterns. A highly integrated response pattern appears to an observer as a single, unitary response. Words and phrases such as "typing," "walking," "singing," "playing the piano," and "playing football" reflect our tendency to conceptualize these response patterns as unitary responses. Usually, learning experiences are designed to achieve this integration, and we do not consider that the performance has been acquired until some minimal integration of responses has been achieved. A student has not learned to "type" or "play the piano" if he can make only the basic finger movements.

These performances usually require a high level of skill. We will refer to them here as **skill performances.** We have chosen to use this term rather than the word "skills" to emphasize an important distinction. The word "skill," as it is used in everyday speech, generally applies to any activity that is conducted with a high level of facility. We speak of skill in playing football, in playing the violin, in typing, in vocabulary, in English usage, in playing chess. From a psychological point of view, playing football or chess or using a typewriter or the English language correctly demands complex sets of responses—some of them cognitive, some attitudinal, and some manipulative. For example, "skill" in playing baseball requires that the baseball player be able to perform sets of responses with ease, quickness, and economy of motion. A baseball player must be able to hit, throw, and catch a baseball, and to do each of these under a variety of conditions. But the baseball player must also *understand* the strategy of the game. The player who can throw accurately but does not know which base to throw to or how to hold a runner on base is not a skilled baseball player. This player is not lacking manipulative facility, but he fails to understand the **concepts** and **generalizations** about the strategy of the game. The player must also have attitudes about the game. He must like to play the game and find playing the game satisfying. He must have attitudes about sportsmanship and winning. The total performance that we observe when we watch this player is a complex set of processes —cognitive, attitudinal, and manipulative. This complex integration of processes is what we usually mean when we refer to "skill in playing baseball."

During the period of his development, a child must acquire skill performances that are essential for manipulating his environment and learning his **roles** in society. Strong rewards are attached to the acquisition of these skills, and society fosters the acquisition of the needs which will motivate the learning of these skill performances (see Chapter 11, pp. 425–430). Failure to acquire skill performances of this character will interfere with a child's adaptation to society. Personality development will be correspondingly affected, since the child cannot obtain the rewards society provides for the acquisition of these performances.

In this chapter we consider the learning of skill performances. In some ways this chapter integrates many of the ideas previously discussed. The instructional issues discussed may also be generalized to the other kinds of behavior changes we have studied.

KINDS OF PERFORMANCES
AND THEIR EVALUATION

Performances are of such diverse character that some distinctions among them may be useful. Such distinctions serve to demonstrate the many components typically involved in all except the simplest performances.

STRUCTURED AND
UNSTRUCTURED PERFORMANCES

A structured performance has form and limits. Its beginning and end are specified in advance: a product is produced, a football game continues for a specified period of time, a 1-mile race is run, a king is checkmated.

An unstructured performance continually evolves and changes as the performance is enacted. Here, the performer determines for himself when the performance will end. The author of a book determines its content, its arrangement, and style; he also controls the amount of writing he will do and the time in which he will do it. Eventually, the cover goes on the typewriter; the job is done. There are mop-up operations, the editorial revisions and the proofing; but the performance is finished. The artist, the musical composer, the inventor, the scholar as theorizer, the scientist as experimenter are engaged in performances of this kind.

INVENTIVE AND CONTROLLED PERFORMANCES

An inventive performance is controlled by the performer. A controlled performance has prescribed characteristics. In some forms of dance, for instance, the dancer is free to modify and create while he is performing; in others, the dancer enacts the performance according to the directions of the choreographer. A symphony orchestra's performance is controlled by the conductor; a jam session, by its members.

PUBLIC AND PRIVATE PERFORMANCES

Every performance has some public feature, in the sense that the product is ultimately offered to the public. The actual performance, however, may be conducted alone. As I write, I am alone, and have been for many hours. Nobody watches me as I write. Similarly for the painter or composer. But if I were in a drama or a golf match or a bridge tournament, most of the performance would be public. Some of these performances, such as giving a speech or performing a play or musical composition, depend on an immediate public response. In both public and private performances, one must know his audience, but public performances demand an intimate knowledge of audience reaction, a receptivity to cues, and a responsiveness to their meaning.

CRITERIA FOR EVALUATING PERFORMANCES

All performances, except those enacted for personal pleasure and privately, are eventually evaluated by others. Some criteria for evaluation— e.g., criteria for evaluating an experiment—are sharply defined and well accepted. Other criteria—e.g., for evaluating a novel—are vague and not universally agreed on. Some criteria are functional. The object of a competitive performance is to win; and, despite the moral maxims to the contrary, the performance is frequently judged by its achievement of this goal. Many products are designed to serve a purpose, and are evaluated accordingly. When an appliance fails, the craftsmanship that produced it is suspect. The learner needs to learn the criteria that will be used to evaluate his performance. He also needs to know how to make preliminary tests when possible.

UNDERSTANDING VS. MANIPULATIVE BEHAVIOR

To learn a performance an individual must acquire the specific responses involved in the performance and the integrated sequence that forms the pattern of performance. Some of these responses are overt and observable. We can observe the person "doing something," and we assess his facility in performance from this observed behavior. For example, we judge a person's facility in driving a car or playing a piano from the responses that we can observe. If a driver grinds gears or does not brake the car properly, or if a pianist makes errors in striking the keys, we make inferences about his facility in these performances.

Although we judge a performance either by observing (seeing, hearing, or feeling) a set of actions or a product, the performer may have had to learn responses which we cannot observe. A performance called "playing the piano" usually means a set of actions involving the striking of piano keys. By the melodious sounds produced by these actions, we judge the piano-playing performance. But to learn to play the piano, the performer had to learn to read music and to study musical interpretation. He had to acquire concepts such as phrasing, rhythm, and tempo. "Playing the piano" also may require the learning of emotional responses such as control of one's anxiety about performing in public. Motivation to play must also be acquired, and certainly the motives of the performer are not easily nor directly observable.

An interesting theoretical and practical question arises when we consider all these kinds of responses to be learned by a performer. Are the covert responses—the concepts, for example—necessary to acquire the manipulative behavior? In some cases, it is not clear that they are necessary. We have seen pianists who seem to have an intuitive sense of rhythm; such a performer probably has the concept even though he may not be able to describe it in formal terms. Other covert responses are obviously necessary for performance enactment. As I typed one of these sentences on an unfamiliar typewriter, I needed to locate the margin release. On this machine this key is marked by a particularly unhelpful symbol, arrows going in two directions. Without understanding the symbol, I am handicapped in my typing.

Can the manipulative aspects of a performance be learned directly? An attempt to answer this question can be made if we have a clearer conception of the character of manipulative behavior.

Manipulative behavior is a pattern of observable responses, usually an integrated sequence of movement. A person "moves" himself, as in walking, or "moves" some environmental object, as in playing a piano, hitting a baseball, or typing a letter. Such responses can be attached to internal or external stimuli, called **cues,** so that, when the stimuli occur, the appropriate response follows. For example, a person can learn to shift the gears in a car by responding to the "feel" of the gear lever as it is moved from one position to another. In a typing class, students are taught to position their hands on the keys of the typewriter by "feel." A player attempting to hit a pitched ball responds to external stimuli, such as the position of the ball, and to internal stimuli from muscle movements.

If responses can be learned directly by association with stimuli, the manipulative aspects of a performance can be acquired directly. For example, a person can learn to shift gears without understanding the pattern of movement required. An important question is—Can such learning be facilitated by understanding the movement pattern? This kind of question needs to be investigated for each of the performances we attempt to teach. In the latter part of this chapter we will outline some general principles governing this relationship between understanding and manipulative behavior. At this point, however, we can say simply that some cognitive processes merely facilitate the learning of a manipulative sequence, and some cognitive, attitudinal, and evaluative processes are an integral part of a total performance. For example, concepts and attitudes relevant to safe driving are integral aspects of the performance of driving a car. The performance is not adequately learned if these concepts and attitudes are not acquired.

The essential characteristics of a performance are a matter of definition and description. When we decide what constitutes a performance pattern, we can determine what concepts, attitudes, and manipulative behaviors must be perfected to learn the total performance.

CHARACTERISTICS OF A SKILL PERFORMANCE

What are the characteristics of a skill performance? The fan sitting in the stadium can quickly distinguish the good players from the poor. An executive can easily determine the level of typing skill of his secretary. Parents attending the school's musical concert have little trouble in identifying the skilled musicians. What distinguishes the skilled performance and the skilled performer from the less skilled performance and performer?

ACCURACY

The skilled performer makes relatively few errors and seldom repeats those that he has made The sour note, the dropped pass, the misspelled word—all indicate a lack of skill. The errors may be apparent either in the performance itself or the product of the performance. We can observe an incorrect movement; for example, we can tell that a golfer is not moving back far enough on his back swing. We also can observe the effects of an error when a football player drops a pass, or when we find that a woodworker's chair falls apart when it is sat upon.

COORDINATION

By coordination we mean the integration of the specific responses required in the performance. The skilled performer has so integrated the responses in his performance that they appear to be one continuous movement. Hitting a golf ball requires a complex series of specific responses. The golfer must hold the club correctly; he must move through the back swing, then through the arc; the face of the club must strike the ball at the proper angle; and the golfer must follow through. While performing all of these responses, the golfer is also shifting his hips and has already positioned his feet even before he begins the swing. The beginner at golf consciously attends to as many of these specific responses as he can. The skilled golfer moves with ease through these responses as if they were one continuous response. His movement is characterized by grace and ease; there is no hesitancy, no abrupt shifting of movement, once the sequence has begun.

The unskilled performer, or the person who is just learning the skill, makes many unnecessary and occasionally conflicting responses. The diagrams in Figure 10–1 are paper-tape recordings of the foot movements of an operator as he practices the movement over a long period of time.[1] For successful operation, the operator must acquire the proper speed, form, rhythm, and pressure pattern in a complex hand and foot action. As the diagrams suggest, the operator has added some responses over this period of time (compare the right-hand sides of the curves from 9 hours to 239 hours) and has dropped others (compare the left-hand sides of the curves). Also, the sequence of movement is smoother in the latter stages of practice than in the earlier stages.

A simple laboratory experiment illustrates the characteristics of skill performance that we have outlined here.[2] In this experiment (see Figure 10–2) the subject is placed in front of a mirror and a star pattern is placed on a sheet of paper in front of him. He cannot see the star pattern except

[1] See L. G. Lindahl, "Movement Analysis as an Industrial Training Method," *Journal of Applied Psychology*, 29 (1945), 420–436.

[2] H. L. Kingsley, *The Nature and Conditions of Learning*, 2nd ed. (Englewood Cliffs, N. J.: Prentice-Hall, Inc., copyright 1946, 1957), pp. 304–305. Reproduced by permission.

in the mirror and must trace this star pattern between the lines on the pattern by looking in the mirror. Because of mirror reversal, the subject must learn to move in directions opposite to the way he appears to be moving in the mirror. A complex set of integrated responses to what he sees and of his hand movements is necessary if this subject is to perform the task at all. In this experiment an error is defined as touching either of

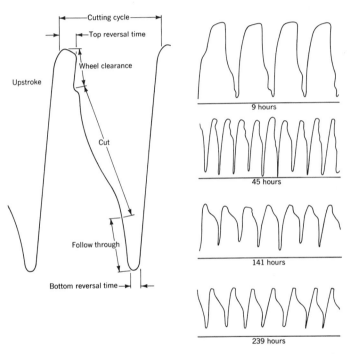

FIGURE 10–1. A view of the disk-cutting cycle. Disk cutter foot-action patterns of a trainee, showing improvement with training. The records were made after 9, 45, 141, and 239 hours of supervised operation. (From Lindahl.)

the boundary lines of the star. In Figure 10–2 are pictures of the tracings on a series of trials, two at the early stages and two at the later stages. As these diagrams illustrate, the subject makes fewer and fewer errors as he becomes more skillful. His pattern of movement, as reflected in the line that he is drawing, becomes smoother and more integrated. Figure 10–3 shows the reduction in number of errors and in time required to make the tracing over fifteen trials.

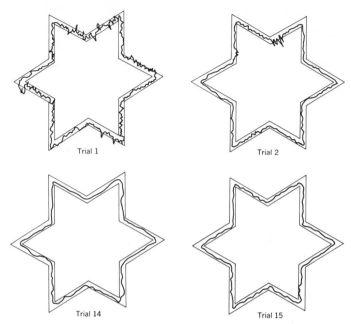

FIGURE 10–2. *The tracings of the star outline made by one subject in the mirror-drawing experiment. The drawings for the first two and the last two of fifteen trials are shown. The stars were 5 inches from tip to opposite tip, and the distance between the lines was ⅛ inch.* (*From Kingsley.*)

SPEED

Speed may or may not be a characteristic of a skilled performance. The first student who finishes a task does not always receive the highest grade for accuracy. Johnny, who fills out the answers to the multiplication tables quickly, may make a large number of errors. Where speed is a recognized component of a skill performance, the acquisition of speed, accompanied by a reduction in error, is an indicator of skilled performance. A typist who can type ten words a minute without error is not skilled, because this skill performance requires both accuracy and speed.

THE USE OF CUES

The skilled performer is distinguished from the unskilled performer in another way. As a performer moves through the behavior pattern, he is continually responding to stimuli originating both internally and externally. As the golfer swings the club, he responds to internal stimuli from his muscles and adjusts his movements accordingly. As he begins his back swing, he responds to internal stimuli which tell him whether he has reached the appropriate point to start his forward motion. As he swings, he also responds to external stimuli—the image of the ball in relationship

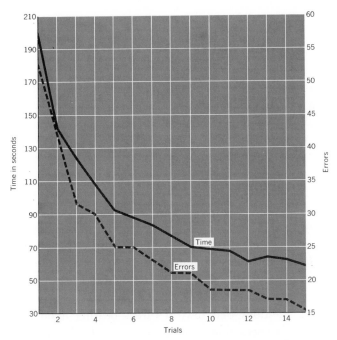

FIGURE 10-3. *Learning curves for time and errors, based on the mean scores of fifty subjects in the mirror-drawing experiment. (Adapted from Kingsley.)*

to the club, the distance from the ball to the green, and the position of the tee in relation to the green. The process of learning a skilled behavior involves learning appropriate responses to stimuli. The beginner must learn which cues to respond to and which to ignore. As the skilled performer learns the cues to respond to, he also learns to respond to fewer cues. A beginning typist may watch his hands on the keys and may look at the letters on the keys, but he is taught to touch the keys without having to look at the letters on them. A skilled typist can place his fingers in the correct position and move them without looking at his hands or the letters that he is typing.

The skilled performer also responds to subtler cues than does the beginner. The batter standing at the plate notices movements of the pitcher which "telegraph" the kind of pitch that he is going to throw. To the beginning golfer, all greens look alike; the professional is sensitive to the slope of the green and even to the texture of the grass. The skilled performer's greater sensitivity to cues enables him to anticipate potential errors and to avoid them.

THE ACQUISITION OF SKILL PERFORMANCES

Although we have described the characteristics of a skilled performance and a skilled performer, the description alone does not help us organize learning experiences. The important educational question is how learning experiences should be organized so that skill performances can be developed. The common-sense notion of skilled behavior is that it is essentially an automatic performance and that this automatic act is developed by continual practice. Does practice alone produce a skilled performance, and by "practice" do we mean merely the repetition of a response sequence? What are the effects of motivation on the acquisition of skilled behavior? What effect does fatigue have on the acquisition of a skill? Can a skill such as swimming be learned at any age, or does the stage of physical and mental development of the learner determine the optimum time for learning a skilled behavior? These are the important psychological questions that have a direct bearing upon the kinds of educational experiences that can be organized to develop skilled performances.

In this section we will study the variables that influence the acquisition of skill behaviors. Some are *task variables,* factors in the learning situation that facilitate the acquisition of a skilled behavior; others are *individual variables,* characteristics of the learner that facilitate the acquisition of skilled behavior.

INFLUENCE OF DEMONSTRATION OR GUIDANCE

Performance behaviors are observable. For this reason, the manipulative aspects of a skilled performance can be demonstrated. A teacher can illustrate by his own actions many, if not all, of the responses which characterize the skilled behavior.

Amount of Guidance

An important variable affecting the facility with which a skilled behavior is acquired is the *amount of guidance* provided in the learning experience. Experiments requiring the learning of fairly simple skilled behavior illustrate this principle.[3] In these experiments, the subjects were to learn a maze with a progressive reduction in number of trials and errors so as to achieve a criterion level of improvement; varying amounts of guidance were provided. As Figure 10–4 indicates, the amount of guidance is related to improvement in skilled performance, with some qualifications. In these experiments, guidance did facilitate the acquisition of the skill performance if an adequate amount of guidance was given at the right time—usually early in the learning series.

Once the learner has clarified the character of the response required and is able to make interpretations of the learning situation, additional guidance may only confuse him. He may be given more information than he can assimilate at the time, or he may not yet be able to integrate new responses into the pattern that he has already learned. The student reaches points in learning a complex sequence of responses where he must integrate sets of responses and assimilate the information that has already been provided. Until this process of assimilation and integration is completed, addition of new information, or the demonstration of new responses, interferes with the assimilation and integration process. If we are teaching a child to play a musical instrument, we first familiarize him with the instrument, showing him the various parts of the instrument, the way it is to be held, and the basic movements. Once he has acquired the basic movements, we teach him the refinements of these movements and the more complex aspects of the skill.

Unfortunately, no rules are available so that the teacher can know just how much information to provide at any stage of the learning of a skilled behavior. If the teacher is himself a skilled performer, he is likely to overlook the complexity of the responses involved in the skilled behavior. He may give the student too much information simply because he is thinking of the total pattern of the skilled behavior rather than of the

[3] H. L. Koch, "The Influence of Mechanical Guidance upon Maze Learning," *Psychological Monographs*, No. 5 (1923); K. E. Ludgate, "The Effect of Manual Guidance upon Maze Learning," *Psychological Monographs*, No. 1 (1923).

particular response, or segments of responses, that the learner is acquiring at this time in the learning process. However, guidance at any phase of learning is beneficial, provided the learner is ready to assimilate the additional information that the guidance or demonstration provides.

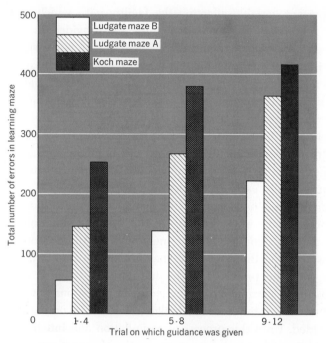

FIGURE 10–4. *When should guidance be given? In all three studies shown here, guidance given on trials 1 to 4 resulted in fewer errors than when no guidance was given, and fewer than when guidance was introduced later in the series.* (*Adapted from Koch, Ludgate.*)

Kinds of Demonstrations

We have been using the word "guidance" in this section in the sense of *demonstration.* There are many ways in which responses can be demonstrated. The teacher can explain verbally what the response ought to be; he can show the student by his own behavior what the appropriate responses can be; he can even move the student through the response, literally taking him by the hand. When teaching a child to write, we can guide or demonstrate the appropriate responses in several ways: the child can trace the letters or copy them from models; the teacher can hold the child's hand and help him to make the appropriate movements; a film demonstrating the appropriate movements can be shown to the class.

Any method of guidance is useful if it clarifies the manner in which a response is to be made. However, the learner must spend most of his time actively attempting the response himself. Therefore, the films, filmstrips, and slides frequently used to demonstrate skilled behavior—although they have the advantage of presenting a demonstration to large numbers of students at the same time—have certain limitations. In the first place, if the film attempts to teach too much, the student will receive more information than he can assimilate. Second, the film may provide so much guidance at one time that the student does not have adequate opportunity to attempt the responses on his own. Third, since the movie observer usually is limited to a verbal and imaginative rehearsal of what is to be done, the film may not require him to attempt the response actively and physically. Generally speaking, a demonstration method that requires the student to participate actively will be superior to a method that requires less active participation.

Gates and Taylor [4] tested two methods of active participation: the values of copying and tracing letters in learning to write. One group of children traced the letters *a, b, c, d,* and *e* through tissue paper. A second group, of comparable ability, age, and intelligence, copied the letters from models during the learning period. When the children were given a copying test, the group that had practiced copying the letters did twice as well as the group that had traced the original letters. When the children were called upon to copy letters that they had neither copied nor traced previously, both groups did poorly; but the copying group still was superior. The copying method proved superior partly because students in the copying group developed responses that they could apply to later tasks.

EFFECT OF REINFORCEMENT

In the Gates and Taylor experiment, the children who had the opportunity to make mistakes by copying performed better than the children who had limited opportunities for making errors in the same kinds of movements and responses. The learner must have an opportunity to attempt the response; however, when he has to attempt a large number of

[4] A. I. Gates and G. A. Taylor, "The Acquisition of Motor Control and Writing by Pre-School Children," *Teachers College Record*, 24 (1923), 459–468.

responses, he must receive information about the correctness of each response he makes. Experimental evidence clearly indicates that knowledge of correct performance or performance errors rapidly improves the learning of a performance pattern. (In other chapters, we have called this information, or knowledge of results, **feedback.**)

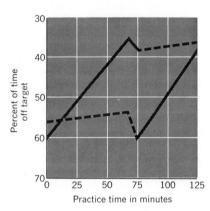

Percent of time off target

Practice time in minutes

FIGURE 10–5. *Effect of knowledge of results in learning tracking. The solid lines represent practice given with knowledge of results (a buzzer sounding whenever the tracker was off target); the dashed lines represent practice given without knowledge of results. (Adapted from Biel et al.)*

Figure 10–5 shows the results of an experiment conducted in training men to use army gun directors.[5] The instructor, who used a check sight to determine whether or not the men were accurately sighting the target, sounded an electric buzzer to indicate when the tracker was off target. The group which received immediate information about the correctness of responses improved rapidly. When the second group, which had not been receiving this information, was given the additional information, improvement was marked and immediate. Neither group showed any improvement in tracking when knowledge of the results was withheld.[6]

As the learner attempts responses, he can revise his performance only on the basis of information about its accuracy. Without this information, he may continue to make the same error over and over again. Even with the information, he may continue to make errors, but cannot correct the errors without the information. Feedback information can be obtained in two ways: (1) The learner knows immediately whether he has made an

[5] W. C. Biel et al., *The Effectiveness of a Check Sight Technique for Training 40-mm Gun Pointers* (Medford, Mass.: Tufts University, 1944), OSRD Report 4054.

[6] For additional experimental evidence, see J. L. Elwell and G. C. Grindley, "The Effect of Knowledge of Results on Learning and Performance," *British Journal of Psychology,* 29 (1938), 39–53. See also S. J. MacPherson, V. Dees, and G. C. Grindley, "The Effect of Knowledge of Results on Learning and Performance: II. Some Characteristics of Very Simple Skills," *Quarterly Journal of Experimental Psychology,* 1 (1948), 68–78.

error—a musician blowing a flat note, a ball player missing the ball, a golfer slicing into the woods. (2) Some other person or mechanical device must inform the learner about his accuracy—a child attempting a multiplication problem cannot tell whether he has made a mistake unless the teacher checks the correctness of his answer.

An operation that indicates to the learner the correctness of his response is called a **reinforcement.** When a golfer drives a ball straight down the fairway, he tries to carry out his swing in the same way the next time he drives. The batter who knocks out a home run receives reinforcement from many different consequences of hitting this home run: The home run reinforces the pattern of batting responses; in addition, the batter receives reinforcement through need satisfaction from the prestige that he receives for performing a socially valued action. If the consequences of a response have reward value, either by indicating to the learner that he is making the correct response or by obtaining **need satisfaction** for the person, the response pattern is strengthened, and it is likely to occur more frequently the next time the response pattern is attempted.

Even a punishing consequence, when it indicates a right response, may have the same effect. Jones [7] required a group of thirteen- and fourteen-year-old boys and girls to learn to operate a punchboard maze. In order to find the correct solution, the learner had to make choices, some of them correct and some incorrect. Under one experimental condition, a pattern of lights, an agreeable stimulus, was flashed on when the child made a correct choice. Under another experimental condition, a disagreeable vibration in the subject's stylus was set up when he made a correct choice. There was no difference in learning under these two conditions (see Figure 10-6). Evidently, as long as the learner is receiving information about the correctness of his response, he may tolerate and even be "rewarded" by mild punishment.

Responses that are not reinforced are usually dropped. Through the selective application of reinforcement, a performer learns to discriminate between desirable and undesirable, or correct and incorrect responses. A mother may reward the correct behavior of a small child by smiles, pats on the head, and affectionate gestures. The child learns to distinguish between the responses for which he will receive rewards and those for

[7] H. E. Jones, "Trial and Error Learning with Differential Cues," *Journal of Experimental Psychology,* 35 (1945), 31–45.

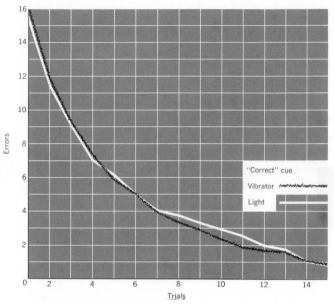

FIGURE 10–6. *Learning curves with "right" indicated by agreeable or by disagreeable stimuli. The subjects were 114 junior high school students, who learned two maze patterns in which the right choice was indicated by a pleasing light pattern in one and by a disagreeable vibration in the other. (Adapted from Jones.)*

which he will not. The unrewarded responses will tend to disappear from his behavior, and the rewarded responses will be strengthened.[8]

The teacher needs to be imaginative in devising consequences that are rewarding to students. We may assume that a given consequence is not rewarding when the learner does not see the consequence as rewarding. Teachers permit students to do library reading when they have completed an assignment in a workbook. For some of the students in the class, this consequence is rewarding; for other students, it is not, since the library reading may require additional work that they do not want to do.

[8] For an experimental demonstration of the effects of reinforcement and nonreinforcement on a learned behavior, see E. R. Hilgard, R. K. Campbell, and W. N. Sears, "Condition Discrimination: The Effect of Knowledge of Stimulus-Relationships," *American Journal of Psychology,* 51 (1938), 498–506.

In general, reinforcements must be given promptly if the consequences of making correct responses are to have a facilitating effect upon the acquisition of behavior. Prompt and frequent reinforcement while the learner is attempting responses shortens the learning time by strengthening the appropriate responses.

At present we do not know the optimum time required between attempted response and reinforcement. We do know that different schedules of reinforcement have varying effects on performance. If reinforcements are given at fixed intervals—say, every five minutes—the rate of responding is initially slow but increases as the time for reinforcement approaches. Assume that a teacher has assigned a typing exercise, and has told the students that the papers will be corrected every ten minutes. We would expect to find students working more intensely near the end of the ten-minute period than at the beginning. This effect may not be invariably found in all students, since other factors affect performance; but it will frequently be produced when reinforcements are scheduled in this manner.[9]

A suggestion is often made in methods textbooks that students be given ample opportunity to try a response before any evaluation is provided. For example, in teaching students to speak a foreign language, the teacher is counseled to let the student speak at some length before correcting his errors. Is this an efficient application of reinforcement? In the absence of clear-cut experimental evidence on this point, we can only speculate about its validity. The "response" in this example is so complex that the student requires considerable time and effort merely to attempt it. When students are attempting responses of this complexity, immediate reinforcement of specific responses probably interferes with their trying out the total response. However, they probably should not attempt this total response until they have mastered some of the specific responses. Efficiency in performance could probably be improved if the complex response is broken down into these specific responses, with adequate and immediate reinforcement for learning the specific responses. The responses requiring integration can then be attempted and reinforced as a

[9] A discussion of reinforcement and learning and the problems suggested here can be found in J. Deese, *The Psychology of Learning* (New York: McGraw-Hill Book Company, 1958), Chapters 2 and 3. Original research on these problems is presented in B. F. Skinner, *The Behavior of Organisms* (New York: Appleton-Century-Crofts, Inc., 1938); B. F. Skinner, *Verbal Behavior* (New York: Appleton-Century-Crofts, Inc., 1957); and C. B. Ferster and B. F. Skinner, *Schedules of Reinforcement* (New York: Appleton-Century-Crofts, Inc., 1957).

whole. Reinforcement would then be applied for the integration rather than for the specific responses.

Assume, however, that we are interested in encouraging the students to try to speak in the language. In this case, the response to be reinforced is the "trying" response. Rewarding precision or punishing errors in grammar or sentence structure may seem to indicate that our primary concern is formal correctness rather than the attempt to speak the language. An anecdote will illustrate this point. A young child had seen her first circus. When she came home, she rushed to her mother and said, "You should have seen them clowns!" The mother replied, "*Those* clowns." The girl repeated the original statement, and her mother again corrected her. At this point, the girl said, "I don't think you're interested in what I want to tell you." The *desired* response is the response that must be reinforced.[10]

STAGE OF DEVELOPMENT OF THE LEARNER

We have stressed the importance of the factors over which the teacher has direct control in the acquisition of skilled behavior—guidance and reinforcement. The capacity and the stage of development of the learner also are important factors. Some skilled performances are beyond the capacities of children, and the teaching of these behaviors must wait until the child is older. A one-year-old child probably cannot hold or manipulate a fork, and elaborate training is not likely to facilitate his acquisition of this behavior at this age. Sports requiring complex hand and eye coordination cannot be learned until the child has developed sufficiently to be able to acquire the coordinations. A boy cannot play baseball if he

---

[10] Most of the research on reinforcement has been done on subhuman species; however, the following studies have been conducted in classroom settings with children: D. Auble and E. V. Mech, "Quantitative Studies of Verbal Reinforcement in Classroom Situations: I. Differential Reinforcement Related to the Frequency of Error and Correct Responses," *Journal of Psychology*, 35 (1953), 307–312; D. Auble and E. V. Mech, "Partial Verbal Reinforcement Related to Distributed Practice in a Classroom Situation," *Journal of Psychology*, 36 (1953), 165–186; D. Auble and E. V. Mech, "Response Strength in a Classroom Task Related to a 'Forward' Delay in Reinforcement," *Journal of Educational Psychology*, 45 (1954), 175–181; E. Kapos, E. V. Mech, and W. H. Fox, *Schoolroom Motivation: I. Two Studies of Quantity and Pattern of Verbal Reinforcement as Related to Performance on a Routine Task* (Bloomington: Indiana University, 1957), Bulletin of the School of Education, No. 1; E. Kapos, E. V. Mech, and W. H. Fox, *Schoolroom Motivation: II. Two Studies of Quantity and Pattern of Verbal Reinforcement as Related to a Measure of Drive on a Routine Task* (Bloomington: Indiana University, 1957), Bulletin of the School of Education, No. 2.

is not strong enough to lift the bat. Printing is taught before cursive writing because the child, by learning to print, will develop muscular skill and coordination that will facilitate his learning to write cursively. Improvement of skills in children is a function of their experience, growth, and development.

The relationship between experience and maturation was demonstrated in an experiment conducted by Hilgard.[11] In this experiment two groups

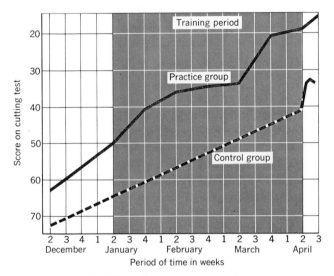

FIGURE 10–7. *Mean learning curves for two groups in cutting (ten subjects in each group). The practice group trained for twelve weeks; the control group trained for one week. (Adapted from Hilgard.)*

of fifteen children each (age 2½ years) were matched by chronological and mental age, sex, and initial ability in three skills—buttoning, cutting with scissors, and climbing. One group, the *practice group*, received intensive training in these skills for twelve weeks; a second group, the *control group*, received no training until the four days immediately following the twelve-week period. Tests were given in each of these skills at the beginning and end of the twelve-week period, and at the end of the four-day period following the twelve-week period. The data produced in this experiment are plotted in Figures 10–7 and 10–8. The curves show:

[11] J. R. Hilgard, "Learning and Maturation in Pre-School Children," *Journal of Genetic Psychology*, 41 (1932), 36–56.

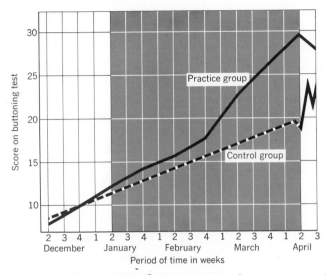

FIGURE 10-8. *Mean learning curves for two groups in buttoning (nine subjects in each group). The practice group trained for twelve weeks; the control group trained for one week. (Adapted from Hilgard.)*

1. Both groups steadily improved over the twelve-week period.

2. The control group showed marked improvement immediately after the twelve-week period and the four-day training session.

3. The practice group showed increased acceleration in learning near the end of the twelve-week period. Both groups improved, even though one group was not practicing.

This effect presumably can be attributed to maturation. As the children developed, they were ready to acquire the skill and showed increasing improvement in the skill behaviors. The practice group was consistently better than the control group, however, and this difference can be attributed to the effects of the training that this group was receiving. When the control group received intensive training, the children were at a point in development where they could profit quickly by the practice, and a rapid increase in their performance ability took place. Training, then, is evidently most beneficial when the learner has reached a sufficient level of development, both physically and mentally, to profit quickly and easily from the training.

EFFECTS OF PRACTICE

A performance process is ordinarily acquired over a relatively long period of time, and after numerous practice sessions for limited periods of time. What is the most efficient arrangement of these practice sessions? In learning to play a piano, should the student practice intensively for an hour, leave his piano for a short period of time, and then come back for another hour of intensive practice? Would his performance improve if he practiced fifteen minutes at a time and rested and then practiced for another fifteen minutes? Should he practice every day, every other day, or only once a week?

Furthermore, if a skill, such as typewriting, is made up of a variety of responses that must be integrated, should the learner practice each separate response, or should he attempt the whole response without practicing the individual movements? Should a golf player start swinging at a ball at the beginning of practice, or should he practice holding the club and then move into a backswing? In typing, is it better to learn how to strike individual letters with the appropriate finger, or should the student learn to type words immediately? These are important questions relevant to organizing learning experiences for the acquisition of skill behaviors. Enough research evidence is available on these problems to allow the statement of some general principles.

MASSED AND SPACED PRACTICE

The issue of how much time should be spent during a practice session has been described as the problem of *massed versus spaced practice.* By **massed practice** we mean intensive practice without rest between the practice trials. **Spaced practice** provides for rest periods between the trial periods.

The terms *massed* and *spaced* are relative terms. No one can practice for an indefinite period of time. The essential question is this: During a training session where successive trials in the skilled behavior can be made, how much time should be provided between each of these attempts?

In analyzing the arrangement of time in practice sessions, we first must define what we mean by a *trial* and decide on a length of time for the trial. What constitutes a trial is a function of the response that the learner is attempting to make. If by a trial we mean practicing a twenty-page piece of music which takes roughly an hour to play, then the response that is being practiced is that of playing the entire piece, and the trial time is one hour. If we define the response sequence as practicing a scale, an exercise which takes ten seconds, then the trial time is ten seconds, and the trial consists of playing the scale once. Football and baseball practice sessions are not single trials, but are arrangements of many trials of many different responses. A football player may practice punting for part of the football practice session, tackling for another part, blocking for another part. The issue of how to arrange practice time must be related to the particular set of trials with which we are concerned, the punting practice, the tackling practice, or the blocking practice.

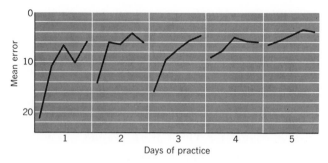

FIGURE 10–9. *Learning to depress a Morse key for a duration of .7 seconds. The approach to the "bull's-eye" was shown after each attempt; i.e. the practice was with prompt "knowledge of results." The ten daily trials were at 12-second intervals, and each data point shows the mean error for ten operators, two successive trials by each operator. The loss at the beginning of each day belongs under the head of forgetting. The error reported is in arbitrary units measured on the galvanometer scale. The figure is so drawn as to make a rise in mean improvement. (Adapted from MacPherson, Dees, and Grindley.)*

The proper arrangement of practice time is important because a player's performance drops off between practice sessions [12] (see Figure 10–9). The longer the period of time between trials or practice sessions, the greater the loss of performance skill. Athletes refer to the negative effects of "laying off" during the off-season. One of the purposes of spring

[12] S. J. MacPherson, V. Dees, and G. C. Grindley, "The Effect of Knowledge of Results on Learning and Performance: III. The Influence of the Time Interval between Trials," *Quarterly Journal of Experimental Psychology*, 1 (1949), 167–174.

training is to bring an athlete's skills back up to the performance level of the regular season. Experimental data [13] (see Figure 10–10) indicate that for a particular skilled behavior a certain length of time for rest between trials maximizes the learning. In experiments on massed versus spaced practice the time between trials is exceedingly short, probably so short

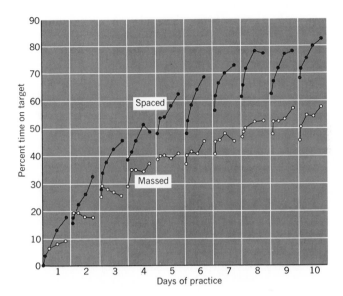

FIGURE 10–10. *The optimum intertrial rest for a particular learning task. The task was to print capital letters upside down from right to left in each line so that, if the page were inverted, the letters would appear right side up and in alphabetical order. For all groups except one, time was called at the end of each minute's work, and a rest was given before the next trial. Other groups, with rests of more than 45 seconds (up to seven days), showed no further gain. (Adapted from Kientzle.)*

that the effects produced by a rest period cannot be reliably established. Consequently, spaced practice in which the interval is relatively longer usually results in an increase in learning which is greater than that for massed practice. Too much time between trials, however, will interfere with learning.

[13] M. J. Kientzle, "Properties of Learning Curves under Varied Distributions of Practice," *Journal of Experimental Psychology*, 36 (1946), 187–211.

We might conclude that if practice sessions are spaced closely together (that is, massed), a possible decrement in performance will be reduced to a minimum. However, massing of practice may have other effects that are not desirable. The longer a person practices, the more likely he is to become fatigued or bored; as a result his performance may deteriorate. *Experimental evidence strongly favors the conclusion that spaced practice is more beneficial than massed practice for the learning of skilled performance.* The results of an experiment comparing massed and spaced practice are presented in Figure 10–11. In this experiment [14] two groups of

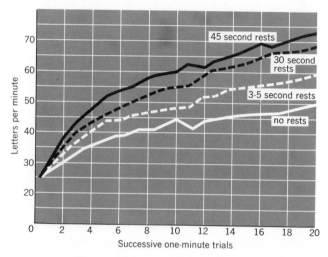

FIGURE 10–11. *Massed and spaced practice on a pursuit rotor which turned at the rate of 78 revolutions per minute. The curves are smoothed within each day, except for the first, second, and last trials of the day. (Adapted from Kimble and Shatel.)*

college students practiced a simple motor skill for fifteen trials a day for ten days; the trial time was thirty seconds. The massed group had a five- to ten-second rest between trials, but the spaced group had a sixty-five to seventy-second rest between trials. Figure 10–11 shows the curves for each day. Several features apparent in these curves are consistently found in experiments on massed and spaced practice:

[14] G. A. Kimble and R. B. Shatel, "The Relationship between Two Kinds of Inhibition and the Amount of Practice," *Journal of Experimental Psychology*, 44 (1952), 355–359.

1. The over-all superiority of the spaced group is apparent. This group after the second day of practice is consistently superior to the massed-practice group.

2. Both groups show a drop in performance on the first trial of each succeeding day.

3. Both groups improve between the first and second trials for each day's practice. This improvement is the result of warming up, during which the level of performance was generally raised to what it had been on the previous day.

4. After the warm-up, the massed group frequently declines in performance.

In a limited number of situations, however—mainly when the task to be learned is simple, and the time required to learn it is comparatively short—massed practice is usually more beneficial than spaced practice.[15] When the learning task requires considerable exploration to discover the correct responses, massed practice appears to be more beneficial than spaced practice because the learner must devote sufficient time within any given trial or set of trials to discovering the correct responses.

Realistic Practice

Realistic practice—practice under conditions similar to those where the skill will be used—is ultimately the most beneficial and efficient kind of practice. At some point the golfer must leave the putting green and the driving range and get out on the course. The batter must leave the batting cage and show his skill in a game. The musician must eventually abandon his exercises for musical compositions.

The school is limited in providing realistic practice conditions for the learning of some skills. Only a limited number of musical performances can be staged during a school year. The students learning typing for vocational purposes will probably not be using their typing in business tasks until sometime after they have acquired the basic responses of the skill. However, training devices can approximate realistic conditions. The Link trainer used in the training of pilots simulates as closely as possible the conditions under which a pilot will actually be flying; the student pilot

---

[15] See D. O. Lyon, *Memory and the Learning Process* (Baltimore: Warwick & York, 1917).

can practice many of the responses that he will be called upon to perform in identically the same way while flying. If the typing class is composed of students who are training to be secretaries, the typing exercises should provide practice exercises on business letters. Once an elementary school child has learned basic letter formations in writing, most of his practice time ought to be devoted to writing words rather than single letters or artificial combinations of letters. Modern practice in learning a musical instrument favors moving quickly to the playing of simple pieces rather than practicing exercises endlessly.

Arrangement of Practice Units

The teacher, in arranging learning sessions, should take into account the length of time required to complete the pattern of responses and adjust the number of trials and time between trials in order to maximize performance over a period of time. If a teacher notices that performance begins to drop off after a series of trials, he can hypothesize that because he is not allowing enough time between trials, the effects of fatigue and boredom have produced lower performance. If a skill is to be developed to a high level, the teacher should also provide practice sessions that are frequent enough to prevent the decrement in performance from becoming too great between sessions.

The teacher must also decide how much of a response sequence or pattern is to be practiced in any one session or during any one trial. Because performance processes are complexes of responses, it is not always possible to learn the entire pattern of responses during one learning or one practice session. If we are learning a complex skill, such as playing golf, we must acquire a number of complex patterns of responses, each of which is a skill performance in itself. Some golfers are good with woods; others have good iron shots; others are good putters. Each of these aspects of playing golf is a skill performance, and the learner will not be a skilled golfer until he has integrated each of these units into a total skill performance. He can, however, learn each of them independently, and the learning of the total skill is simplified by breaking it up into convenient practice units. Similarly, a pianist learning to play a twenty-page concerto will probably be more efficient if he breaks the concerto up into convenient units which are "wholes" that can be practiced as units.[16]

If a comparatively simple performance is broken down too finely into

[16] R. M. Gagné and H. Foster, "Transfer of Training from Practice on Components in a Motor Skill," *Journal of Experimental Psycholgy,* 39 (1949), 47–68.

units, the efficiency of learning may be reduced. If a pattern is broken up into discrete responses to be practiced separately, the individual responses may be practiced in a way in which they will never be used. In learning to type, for example, practicing with one finger at a time teaches certain basic movements. Considerable practice on these basic movements probably is a waste of time because the typist will never have to type with his first finger, and then with his second finger, and then with his third finger. Instead, he must make a series of movements that are integrations of each of the individual movements and involve coordination between hands.

Another danger in breaking up a response sequence into the smallest responses is that the learner may never see the importance of integrating these responses. A pianist who can play scales beautifully and efficiently, but never learns to play a piece of music, has limited technical competence.

INSTRUCTIONAL STRATEGIES

At the end of almost every preceding chapter, we have stressed the importance of component task and behavior analysis. Nowhere is its necessity more clear than when preparing and executing an instructional strategy to produce learning of a complex performance.

The teacher should begin by identifying the major component tasks of the performances to be learned; he must then select their order and identify the interdependency among them. For example, English teachers frequently prepare students to write essays by beginning with sentence construction. They reason, logically, that a good paragraph is a combination of well-written sentences. They should ask themselves, however, "Are there other tasks that must be mastered before a student can write a good paragraph? Does the mastery of these tasks depend on ability to write good sentences?" A third question: "Is it true that a student must be a good sentence writer before he can learn to write a good paragraph?"

At the same time, the teacher should analyze what behaviors the student must acquire in order to master the component tasks and the performance itself. At this point, the concepts and principles, the motives and attitudes required for the performance are identified; and the teacher decides whether the student needs to learn concepts in order to acquire the performance behavior. Does a student have to be able to define and recognize sentences in order to write them well? Does a physics student have to know the principle of combustion in order to use a Bunsen burner? It was thinking about this kind of problem that led to the development of the aural-oral methodology in foreign-language instruction. Why not skip initial vocabulary drill, and work directly on speaking a language?

PATTERNS OF INSTRUCTIONAL STRATEGIES

Two general strategies are conceivable for producing learning of a performance. One of these relies heavily and perhaps even exclusively on demonstration procedures. In this type, the desired performance may be modeled by an experienced performer—the violinist who demonstrates bowing technique or the pitcher who shows how to hold a curve ball. Models of good prose may be provided the novice writer. The intern watches the senior surgeon perform operations. Sets of instructions for carrying out the performance, as in "how-to-do-it" manuals and animated films with illustrative diagrams, may be given.

The other strategy does not employ a demonstration but uses **operant-conditioning** procedures to produce the desired behavior. In this strategy, the learner in a controlled environment attempts the desired responses and is rewarded as they occur. In the early phases, reinforcement is used to "shape" the desired response. Parts of the response (operants) are rewarded as they occur. The general characteristics of this process were discussed in Chapter 3. We are simply applying the ideas discussed there to the learning of complex performances.

Which of these two strategies to use? The answer depends in part on whether the teacher has enough control over the learning sequence to utilize reinforcement procedures consistently and selectively. Repeated and careful correction of themes, of steps in solving mathematics problems, of patterns of oral responding in class, of laboratory procedures are instances where the teacher has considerable freedom to reinforce desired responses. He has less control over the many instances of thinking behavior in which students engage but of which he is unaware. Only if the teacher can elicit this thinking behavior in verbal responses or in a product or set of actions can he reinforce the behavior, and then usually only the **terminal behavior.**

The efficiency of the procedure must also be considered. I could teach a child to play the piano by selectively reinforcing his poking away at it. Eventually, he would learn; but the process might be painfully slow. Appropriate demonstrations shorten this process.

Practically, the teacher will probably use some combination of these strategies. The teacher will need to test various combinations of demonstration and reinforcement by comparing one variation with another on comparable samples of learners. Also it should be remembered that demonstrations may take many different forms, and the inventive teacher will experiment with a variety.

THE PRACTICE COMPONENT OF THE INSTRUCTIONAL STRATEGY

Some teachers call any attempt to make a desired response "practice," and in the ordinary sense of the word it is. But the teacher will need to distinguish between those kinds of practice in which a learner is trying to make a response and the kinds in which he is developing his skills to a high level.

In the first phase, demonstration and reinforcement procedures are essential and probably should occupy relatively more of the instructional-strategy time. In the second phase, the learner is less dependent on instruction for mastery of the basic components of the performance. Instruction at this point is to remedy defects that have crept into the performance and to convey the subtleties and nuances.

As we have pointed out at several places in this chapter, the teacher must observe the effects of practice sessions on student behavior. So little is known at present about their appropriate length and spacing that the teacher must proceed empirically and test for himself his hypotheses about the effects of these variables.

EVALUATION DECISIONS

The principal decision in evaluating the learning of a performance is to define the **criterion performance.** Part of this phase of decision making is to identify acceptable levels of performance. Good writing, for example, is a matter of degree. One can be an excellent pianist but not a virtuoso, a good golfer but not a pro. Obviously, the levels of acceptability must be related to the potentialities of the student. We do not expect fourth graders to write like Faulkner or to speak like Churchill.

An equally obvious point is that learning should be evaluated on tasks relevant to the performance. It makes little sense to ask questions about music theory if we want to evaluate a performer's music skill. Or, if we want to evaluate a student's writing performance, it is hardly relevant to ask him to define a sentence or to describe the characteristics of a good paragraph. Knowledge of art history is not highly correlated with skill in painting. The evaluation principle is: *Measure and judge the perform-ance itself or behavior on some task known to be highly correlated with performance behavior.* Teachers will need to learn the technical skills of constructing appropriate devices for this purpose. These skills will be discussed in greater detail in Chapters 16 and 17.

SUMMARY

1. A performance is a complex integration of behavior patterns. These response systems are integrations of cognitive, attitudinal, evaluative, and manipulative behaviors. We infer the acquisition of these complex pat-terns from their overt aspects; that is, the manipulative behavior that we can observe. When the elements of the performance are known, different kinds of learning experiences can be organized to facilitate learning of these elements and their integration.

2. The term *skill performance* refers to performance behaviors that have been developed to the point where they can be carried out easily and efficiently. The term *skill* is used in everyday language to describe complex organizations of behavior, which include cognitive, attitudinal, evaluative, and performance processes.

3. Performances may be structured or unstructured, inventive or con-trolled, public or private; and are subjected to various kinds of evaluative criteria.

4. In some instances, manipulative behavior may be acquired directly; in others, an understanding of concepts is necessary before the perform-ance can be adequately learned.

5. Skill performances have the following characteristics: (a) A skill performance is characterized by accuracy; that is, few errors are made in carrying out the appropriate behaviors. (b) Skill performances require coordination of responses into a smooth pattern of performance. (c) Speed is sometimes but not always a characteristic of a skill performance. (d) The skilled performer is sensitive to more cues, and subtler ones, than is the unskilled performer.

6. The major variables that influence the acquisition of a skilled per-formance are: (a) demonstrations of the appropriate responses; (b) reinforcement of the appropriate responses; (c) the stage of development of the learner; (d) practice on the appropriate responses.

7. A teaching procedure is most efficient when the procedure requires

the learner to participate actively in the process. Demonstration facilitates learning when the appropriate responses are clearly indicated and described, and when the response being demonstrated is not too complex for the learner.

8. Reinforcement strengthens appropriate responses and is most useful in facilitating learning when applied frequently and promptly.

9. One of the most important individual variables is the learner's stage of development. Unless the learner has a background of experience and a level of maturity adequate for the performance process, it is uneconomical to attempt to teach this skill. When the learner has reached the stage of development required for the skill performance, he will learn it more rapidly than at an earlier time.

10. *Spaced practice,* which provides for rest periods between learning trials, is generally more efficient in facilitating learning than is *massed practice,* intensive practice without rest.

11. Realistic practice—practice under conditions similar to those where a skill will be used—is ultimately the most efficient kind of practice.

12. There are two general strategies for producing learning of performances: (a) through demonstration, (b) through operant-conditioning procedures—where reinforcement is used to shape the desired response. Probably, a combination of the two strategies is most practical.

STUDY AND DISCUSSION QUESTIONS

1. Describe the patterns of specific responses involved in the following performances:

   a. Driving a car under ordinary driving conditions.

   b. Writing a letter of thanks for a gift.

   c. Singing a solo in a musical production.

   d. Giving a talk on student problems before a student assembly.

2. For each of the above performances, describe the requirements of a skill performance. What kinds of errors in performance would be regarded as evidence of a lack of skill?

3. Describe the concepts, generalizations, and attitudes that must be learned as part of the pattern of performance for each of these performances.

4. What environmental interactions are facilitated by skill in each of the following performances:

a. Typing.

b. Arithmetical computing.

c. Giving a talk.

d. Playing tennis.

5. As we have seen, guidance may be most beneficial in the early phases of learning. Under what conditions is guidance likely to facilitate improvement of performance in the later stages of acquiring a skill performance?

6. Describe the kinds of demonstrations that might be provided to facilitate learning the following performances:

a. Using the card catalogue in the library.

b. Using a laboratory scale to weigh chemicals.

c. Wiring an electric bell in a simple circuit.

7. For each of the demonstrations that you have suggested for the skill performances in Question 6, predict the relative effects of each in facilitating learning. How would you explain the assumed relative superiority of some of these methods of demonstration?

8. How is feedback information obtained in the learning of each of the following performances?

a. Typing.

b. Using correct grammar.

c. Translating a foreign-language passage correctly.

d. Giving a class talk.

9. Review the learning curves from the Hilgard experiment. How do you account for the fact that the control group showed a steady improvement in performance without practice?

10. For each of the following performances, specify the specific patterns of response that need to be acquired to learn the total performance. Analyze these patterns and specify the responses to be practiced in successive trials. Estimate, where possible, the length of time to be allotted a trial for each of these responses, and suggest arrangements of practice time that may facilitate the learning of these responses.

a. Dialing a telephone number.

b. Jumping rope.

c. Playing checkers.

d. Throwing a baseball.

11. Suggest some realistic practice situations for the learning of the following performances:

a. Using English grammar correctly.

b. Spelling.

c. Working percentage problems in arithmetic.

d. Using a slide rule.

RECOMMENDED READINGS

The following chapters in R. M. Gagné, ed., *Psychological Principles in System Development* (New York: Holt, Rinehart and Winston, 1962): J. J. Wulff and P. C. Berry, "Aids to Job Performance," pp. 273–300; W. C. Biel, "Training Programs and Devices," pp. 343–386.

E. J. Gibson. "Perceptual Development," in H. Stevenson, ed., Sixty-second Yearbook of the National Society for the Study of Education, Part I, *Child Psychology*. Chicago: University of Chicago Press, 1963, pp. 144–195.

The following chapters in R. Glaser, ed., *Training Research and Education* (Pittsburgh: University of Pittsburgh Press, 1962): E. A. Fleishman, "The Description and Prediction of Perceptual-Motor Skill Learning," pp. 137–176; P. M. Fitts, "Factors in Complex Skill Training," pp. 177–198; J. Deese, "Skilled Performance and Conditions of Stress," pp. 199–222; R. M. Gagné, "Simulators," pp. 223–246; A. A. Lumsdaine, "Instructional Materials and Devices," pp. 247–294.

N. L. Munn. "Learning in Children," in L. Carmichael, ed., *Manual of Child Psychology*, 2nd ed. New York: John Wiley and Sons, 1954, pp. 387–407.

C. E. Ragsdale. "How Children Learn the Motor Types of Activities," Forty-ninth Yearbook of the National Society for the Study of Education, Part I, *Learning and Instruction*. Chicago: University of Chicago Press, 1950, pp. 69–91.

D. Wolfle. "Training," in S. S. Stevens, ed., *Handbook of Experimental Psychology*. New York: John Wiley and Sons, 1951, Chapter 34.

R. H. Seashore. "Work and Motor Performance," in S. S. Stevens, ed., *Handbook of Experimental Psychology*, Chapter 36.

CHAPTER ELEVEN

PERSONALITY AND THE SELF-CONCEPT

In the preceding chapters, we have been discussing ways in which aspects of personality are acquired, and we have conceptualized personality development as a process of behavior change.

The process of behavior change has two principal characteristics: (1) patterns of behavior become progressively *differentiated* through new discriminations; (2) the patterns become progressively integrated through a process of *generalization*. Thus, differentiation and generalization characterize the changes both in particular aspects of personality and in the development of personality as a whole.

In other words, personality structure becomes both more complex and unified: more complex in the sense that the individual responds to his environment in more diversified ways; more unified because response patterns are generalized to many particular situations.

In this chapter we will be following two lines of thought. We will first study complex aspects of personality structure—specifically, the learning of roles and behaviors necessary for social interaction within a given culture and the development of a concept of self. With this analysis, we will have completed our description of major components of personality. We will then relate the development of personality to the socialization process.

ROLES AND ROLE BEHAVIOR

A **role** *is a set of expectations about how a person in a given position in a social system should act and about how the individuals in a reciprocal position should act.* **Role behavior** or **role action** is the observable behavior related to these sets of expectations.

Let us follow John as he comes to school in the morning and meets various people. As he enters the school, he happens to meet the principal, whom he greets in a friendly manner. The principal asks him how he is doing in school, and John answers that he is doing "fine." After a brief chat, during which the principal does more talking than John, John moves down the corridor and meets a group of his fellow students in front of the lockers. As they talk, John becomes a little more boisterous, speaks somewhat more frequently, tells Bill that he's a "stoop." In this brief meeting there is much good-natured kidding and jostling, an exchange of information about last night's dates, and expressions of hope that the day won't be "too tough." John then moves into his first-period class. He takes a seat quietly and gets out his books and papers. As Mr. Henning, the teacher, begins the lesson, John follows attentively, asks questions, and participates in discussion. He carefully notes down the assignments. At the end of the class hour, John stops to ask Mr. Henning some questions that occurred to him during the lesson. They chat in a friendly way, and John listens attentively to the information and opinions offered by his teacher.

In this brief description, we see some rather obvious changes in John's behavior as he interacts with different people. We notice the respect and deference that he accords both the principal and the teacher. With them he is quiet and reserved, though with the teacher he does not hesitate to ask questions and exchange ideas. With his fellow classmates he is much less reserved, is freer in his comments, expresses his feelings about them as individuals, and puts up with some good-natured "ribbing" from them. If we observed John over a period of time, we would notice a general consistency in the ways in which he interacted specifically with the principal, his fellow classmates, and his teacher. We may observe some variations from day to day, but these variations in behavior will be within relatively well-defined limits. If John exceeds these limits—that is, if his behavior becomes inconsistent with what is expected of him as a student —his deviations may be explained in one of two ways: (1) that he has not learned what behavior is expected of students; (2) that his deviations [1] from expected behavior give him **need satisfaction** that he cannot gain by behaving consistently with expectations. Except in such cases, John's behavior is consistent with a general set of expectations about what constitutes "appropriate" student behavior.

In each interpersonal situation, John is enacting a role. To enact this role, John has had to learn what behavior is expected of him and has had to learn what behavior to expect of his principal, his fellow students, and his teacher. He does not expect to be kidded by his teacher in the same way that his fellow students can kid him, and he would probably be horrified if the principal jostled him around in the same way that his classmates do. John also knows that he cannot treat the principal or the teacher the same way that he would treat his fellow students.

When we know an individual's relation to some members of a social system, we can predict the behavior patterns he will probably follow when he interacts with the others. These relatively predictable patterns of behavior vary with the relation of one person to another within a social system. The relation of one member to another is defined by their **positions** in the system.

ROLES AND POSITIONS IN A SOCIAL SYSTEM

Positions in a social system are typically defined by the functions that may be carried out by many different individuals. The position of teacher is occupied by many persons, and though these individuals may vary in the way in which they carry out the functions of the position, we agree that the common function of the position "teacher" is to teach. In other words, positions tend to have stabilized conceptions of functions associated with them, even though the functions may change with time and although there may be disagreements about the specific characteristics of a function.

In any social system, the concept of the function of a position is shared

---

[1] "Deviation" as used here refers only to behavior patterns that are markedly different from those expected in a given social situation. It does not refer to "abnormal" personality patterns or "personality deviations" in the sense in which these terms are typically used.

by the members of the system. Positions in the system are interdependent and often reciprocal. The function of teaching cannot be carried out if the function of learning is not also carried out. In other words, the functioning of the system as a whole requires that the members occupying different positions perceive the relationship of their position to other positions in the system. The members of the system share common assumptions (although not necessarily formalized or explicitly stated) about who does what and for what purposes. If we look at societies or groups as a whole, we find this:

All primary societies, irrespective of whether they stand alone or function as units of larger integrations, have certain features of organization in common. All of them divide their membership into various categories based on differences in age and sex. All of them differentiate certain individuals or groups of individuals from the rest of society on the basis of specialized occupations. All of them include within their organization smaller, internally organized units of two sorts: (1) family groups, membership in which is established on the basis of biological relationships, real or assumed, and (2) association groups, membership in which is established on the basis of congeniality and/or common interest.[2]

An individual almost always belongs to more than one social system, and, as a consequence, he occupies many different positions in various social systems. An adolescent, for example, occupies one position as a member of his family, another as a student, and perhaps still others as a member of various school organizations. He also occupies the position of adolescent in the general structure of American society, within which he will also occupy a position as member of a particular social class. John is a student in the school social system and a child in the family social system. He may be a member of school organizations, such as the athletic teams and clubs; he may belong to the Boy Scouts; he may be a member of the church choir; he may be a newsboy. Each of these memberships represents a different social position, and each requires John to have certain role expectations and behaviors. John shifts roles as he moves from one social position to another. In his home he lives the role of a son and a brother; in school, the role of a student, a member of the football team, a member of the band, a member of the French club. In his neighborhood he may enact the roles of the boy next door and of the local newsboy. As

[2] R. Linton, *The Cultural Background of Personality* (New York: Appleton-Century-Crofts, Inc., copyright 1945), pp. 61–62. Reprinted by permission of the publisher.

John moves in and out of each of these social situations, his behavior changes in accordance with his expectations of how he and the other people should act in these situations.

Some positions are temporary; that is, individuals remain in these positions for only a portion of their lives. Other positions, such as male member of society, are occupied for an individual's entire life. Some positions, such as the position of marriage partner, may be occupied only once. Some types of positions will be occupied by all members in a society, such as those defined by age, sex, and social class. Other positions will be occupied by an individual only if he belongs to a particular social system.

ROLE EXPECTATIONS

Role expectations are complex concepts acquired by an individual occupying a position in a social system. They are essentially shared conceptions of appropriate or desirable ways of behaving. These expected ways of behaving are assumed to be consistent with maintaining position functions so that group goals can be attained. For example, a child who is a "discipline" problem is behaving inconsistently with the role expectations for a student; for, although his behavior may satisfy his own needs, it interferes with the attainment of the group goals and is therefore considered deviant. He will be urged to acquire the shared role concepts and behavior. Considerable social pressure may be brought to bear on him to understand and act in accord with these expectations. In these cases the course of action taken by the individual whose role behavior is deviant depends on the likelihood that acquiring the appropriate role behavior will lead to need satisfaction for him. For example, the need satisfaction associated with membership in a group may be such that the deviant individual will exert continued effort to acquire the expected behavior. In other cases, the individual may leave the social system and enter another in which the likelihood of obtaining need satisfaction is greater; at the same time, he can preserve his present pattern of behavior. For example, a college student may join a fraternity expecting to attain the need satisfactions associated with the social prestige of being a fraternity member. However, he may decide to leave the fraternity if he experiences difficulty in acquiring the appropriate role behavior, if he can obtain need satisfaction in other ways, or if other need satisfactions are more important to him.

Deviancy, as we have defined it here, is relative to particular social systems; a pattern of role behavior may be deviant in one social group but not in another. However, some patterns of behavior—extremely hostile behavior, extreme physical aggression, lying, stealing, cheating—are regarded as deviant in practically all social groups within our society. Nevertheless, there are some social groups in which these behaviors are "expected"; the delinquent group, for example, may value some or all of these behaviors.

An individual's adjustment to a social system is facilitated by his learning of role expectations and behaviors. In any social system, once an individual has identified his position with respect to the other members of the system, he knows how to act, provided that he has learned the role expectations for that position. If John meets someone in the corridor whom he has never met before, he knows how to act toward him as soon as he has identified him as another student.

HOW ROLES ARE LEARNED

A child must be motivated to learn a role. The acquisition of role expectations and behavior is a way of attaining goals that will satisfy the child's needs. As the five-year-old entering kindergarten learns the role behaviors of a child in school, he receives approval from his parents and his teacher; this satisfies the child's need for approval. In a similar manner, the satisfaction of other needs—for affection, for achievement, for status—may be associated with acquiring appropriate role expectations and behavior.

Learning some roles requires abandoning others. A student may give up one role and learn another one (for instance, a role in business) because he thinks that the new role will produce more need satisfaction. If he has a relatively strong need for independence, he may feel that by getting a job he will satisfy this need. Other students will continue the student role through college because it is likely to lead to need satisfaction for them.

The concepts, attitudes, and specific performances associated with role behavior are learned in the same way that any other concept, attitude, or performance is learned. John's concept of his masculine role can be learned if he sees instances or examples of masculine behavior. As he perceives examples of masculine behavior, he forms a concept of its characteristics. He learns attitudes about being a man by identifying with male individuals. As John identifies with his father, he takes on his father's attitudes about being a man. Similarly, he learns the performance requirements of the masculine role. He learns, for example, that men dress a certain way and have characteristic ways of talking, and he acquires these behaviors by imitating them.

Because a role involves many concepts, attitudes, and actions, the learning of a role is a complex and frequently time-consuming process. Some information about roles is acquired incidentally, and some of it is taught formally. However, it is usually communicated through socializing agents who have themselves acquired relevant role behavior. John's father will comment to John on appropriate masculine behavior. He may provide need satisfactions for appropriate masculine behavior and withhold satisfactions when the behavior is inappropriate. Boys are told, "Don't act like a girl" or "Crying is for girls." A girl is told, "Ladies don't act that way." Through such communications, a child learns the behaviors expected of him in a given role. Many social systems have formalized training programs for teaching rituals associated with membership. When the initiate demonstrates that he has acquired the appropriate behavior for a role in the group, he is given the privileges of full membership.

McClelland,[3] in discussing a case history, presents an analysis of how a child learned certain role expectations and behaviors from his father (see Table 11–1). In the left-hand column of the table are classifications representing broad categories of roles that Karl will have to learn; in the middle column, some of the specific problems associated with the learning of these roles; in the right-hand column, Karl's statements about these particular problems and how his father solved them. Karl, for example, has learned something about the control of children by observing the fairly strict discipline in his own home. He has learned something about work habits by observing the thoroughness of his father. From these interactions with his father, Karl learns how he can meet these same problems and also what to expect of men who occupy positions similar to those of his father. Out of these observations, Karl develops a conception of the masculine role. He will not necessarily think and act like his father; the mere presence of a potential model does not guarantee that the person will take on the behavior of that model. He will do so only if he wants to learn the role, perceives the model as a representative of it, and identifies with the model. Under these conditions, we would expect Karl to adopt some of his father's concepts, attitudes, and ways of acting.

To summarize, two general conditions facilitate role acquisition: (1) the learning of a role must be associated with need satisfaction; (2)

[3] D. C. McClelland, *Personality* (New York: Dryden Press, 1951), pp. 299–300.

TABLE 11–1. *Role adjustments made by Karl's father (from McClelland).*

Status classification	Associated problems	Role adjustments
I. *Family or kin*	*Problems facing a father*	
	1. Family support	"My father has always made a living for his family even during the depression."
	2. Nurturance of children	"My parents always took time to read us the funnies and play games with us . . . (they) love all their children."
	3. Control of children	"Our discipline at home was fairly strict."
II. *Age-sex*	*Problems facing an adult male*	
	1. Work habits	"My father is very thorough in all that he does . . ."
	2. Outlook on life	". . . but is excitable and constantly worried by everyone's troubles."
	3. Recreation	"His chief diversion is gardening."
III. *Occupation*	*Problems facing a skilled tradesman*	
	1. Job fluctuations	"My father is a skilled mechanic. During the depression he worked at everything."
	2. Job adjustment	". . . dislikes his present job to the point where he would like to quit and raise chickens."
IV. *Association*	*Problems facing a Christian*	
	1. Belief	"My father says very little though he claims Christianity as his faith."
	2. Church attendance	"Neither parent goes to church."
	3. Ethical dealings with others	"Nevertheless both parents are kind, rather generous, and have done quite a bit of community work in the past."

stimulus events must be available to the learner from which he may infer the relevant characteristics of the role. Role acquisition is a complex form of problem solving, in which the learner tries alternative ways of enacting a role.

To illustrate the principles that we have been discussing, consider the following example of a highly specialized role. One of the most important roles in Wabash School was the "queen role." [4] The complexity of that role is apparent in the following description:

The queen's throne was a slippery place, made so by the intense competition for the office with accompanying risks in the social capital for any aspirant who chose to compete for the honor and failed.

Functioning as a model for behavior among girls throughout the school, the office of queen was highly selective in the social type that achieved it. Its behavioral counterpart, the "queen role," integrated a complex set of expectations centered in the primary values of the adolescent female sex role: namely, beauty, approved dress, moral character, democratic personality, scholastic achievement, exercise of influence, and school service. . . .

As a type the queen had to be "sweet and natural in appearance," to have beauty, "prettiness," or at least "good looks." She must be physically attractive, but not "sexy"; careful in tasteful grooming and appearance; not "cheap in makeup"; well, but not expensively dressed according to the approved pattern and not "showy" nor a style setter in dress. Democratic behavior ranked high in the requirements for the queen; it was necessary for her to be "friendly to everyone and not snobbish," and equally popular with boys and girls. Clique membership was a liability, for many a girl had wrecked her hopes by exclusiveness in her associations.

The queen type had to be datable but usually did not "go steady" unless she dated a politically useful boy, who tended to be a casual or "nondater." A middle ground between too much and too little success with boys had to be maintained, or else she alienated both boys and girls. Better still, she had to lean in the direction of a "girl's girl," for queens were heavily supported by the Girls' Athletic Association. . . .

The moral character of the queen had to be above reproach. Drinking, smoking, and profanity were disapproved unless indulged with discretion. Virtue, and unquestioned virtue, was a major qualification. Girls who were "cheap" need not aspire (pp. 68–69).

The expectations for the queen role are clearly defined and universally known among students. Previous queens serve as role models both for girls who aspire to the role and for students who vote for the queen. The

    [4] C. W. Gordon, *The Social System of the High School* (Glencoe, Ill.: The Free Press, 1957), p. 67 ff.

following quotation from an eleventh-grade girl who was not successful in the queen competition illustrates the process by which the students acquired the role expectations for the queen role:

In my Freshman year I attended Waterville High School, and I don't think I thought anything about being a queen. But in my Sophomore year when I came to Wabash, one of the first things that I noticed was the girls in my class and their desire to be on the court.

The first day at school I heard a discussion of who in 1951 would be on the coronation court. Various girls were named, so I thought I was as likely a candidate as any of them. So a girl friend and I set out to be popular.

This friend and I gave pajama parties to help make the girls like us. When the day was over, we would get together and add up our progress. Such things were included: what older boys had asked us for a date, or had talked to us? If any popular boy in our class talked to us or acted interested, what things could we do or say that would attract favorable attention from him?

When we did get dates, with older boys particularly, we tried in a subtle way to have them ask us to go steady. We also tried to be friends with the girls whom we heard would be 1951 Crest Court candidates. Then we tried to join every club we could, so it would look like we had done a lot for the school (pp. 72–73).

This girl clearly had learned the significant characteristics of the queen role: the queen must be popular, she must be datable, and she must be of service to the school. The role expectations have been communicated and are widely shared, and the girls strive to acquire the appropriate behaviors for nomination for queen. That these expectations influence the selection of the queen is apparent in the following statement of one of the senior boys:

We wanted someone we could be proud of. Even though Pritty Plenty was in our crowd, I voted for Violet. So did all the rest of the fellows in our bunch. Pritty had the looks but is less the queen type. We wanted someone who was sweet, who had contributed a lot to the school (p. 69).

The need satisfactions associated with being queen were so great that girls strove for nomination and election to this position. A girl's need for approval, prestige, and status could be satisfied by acquiring the appropriate behavior and being elected to the queen role. For the girls, trying to be queen required problem-solving behavior. They brought to the solution of the problem all that they had learned from previous experience. The girls had learned something about being "feminine," and they used this learning in acquiring the behaviors of the queen role. They utilized their observations of the role models; they tried out appropriate role behaviors. Candidates for the role had been more successful in acquiring the requisite behavior. Though the "queen role" is temporary, the behavior patterns acquired by the candidates for it can be transferred to other roles; such transfer promotes continuity of personality development.

ROLE ADJUSTMENT

The development of a personality requires the learning of roles. The process of learning roles may be conceptualized as a series of developmental tasks which must be accomplished if an individual is to adjust to his society. Some roles have such great social utility that, unless they are learned, an individual cannot lead the normal life of a member of his society. A boy who does not acquire the masculine sex role has a difficult time with a wide variety of tasks in which successful performance is required by our society. He may have difficult occupational adjustments, and he may not be able to establish a satisfactory marital relationship. He is seen as a man, and he feels the social pressures reflected in the expectation that he enact the masculine role. Unless he can learn this role, he may find his adjustment to social interactions difficult and painful.

Is an individual who learns to enact a large number of roles a better-adjusted member of his society? There is no simple answer to this question. Obviously, an individual must learn certain essential roles if he is to maintain his position in a social group. Once a child has learned the essential characteristics of the student role and has learned appropriate student behaviors, he can shift easily from one classroom to another and is prepared to maintain his position in almost any kind of a school environment. He may experience some difficulties in moving from one particular environment to another, but his adjustment to these environments is facilitated if he has learned the essential characteristics of the role. Some roles, such as one's sex role, also require progressive adjustments at different ages, but learning the role at each stage prepares a person for these adjustments.

Since an individual will occupy positions in social systems at every stage in his life, he will need to acquire the appropriate role expectations and behaviors for many positions. Learning some of these roles is expected of all members of society; such learning is required for successful adaptation to society. The learning of other roles is not required for successful adaptation in society, but may contribute to successful adaptation because the behaviors acquired may be transferred to the learning of required roles. For example, we do not expect all children to learn the role of the local newsboy, but a child who learns this role may acquire behaviors—such as handling a job responsibly—that are relevant to other roles.

Role adjustment, defined as successful role enactment, depends on several factors.[5] We have already discussed two of these: the association of role learning with need satisfaction, and the availability of appropriate information on expected role behavior. A third factor is related to the general problem of **transfer** of learning: role expectations and behavior relevant to one learned role may be seen as applicable to other roles; when such **generalization** occurs, role adjustment is facilitated. On the other hand, previous learning may inhibit new learning. For example, dependency behavior is consistent with the role expectations for younger children, but is inconsistent with the expectations for older children. An individual who has obtained need satisfaction by acquiring a pattern of dependency behaviors may have difficulty in learning new roles because he transfers these behavior patterns to situations in which they are not appropriate.

Role adjustment is also difficult when the expectations are vaguely defined or when there is disagreement on the essential characteristics of the role. The role of the adolescent in our society may be such a role. This role typically contains incompatible expectations. The adolescent is expected to preserve some of the characteristics of a younger child— dependence on adults, for example. At the same time, he may be expected to demonstrate that he is capable of assuming some adult responsibilities. In such cases, the individual learning a role is likely to experience difficulty in determining the relevant role expectations and behavior.

THE SCHOOL AND ROLE ACQUISITION

As we have suggested, the learning of roles may be regarded as a problem to be solved. The successful solution of these problems contributes to the progressive and consistent development of personality. The learning of social roles is an essential aspect of the socialization of the child. Since the school is one of the agencies of socialization in our society,

---

[5] For a comprehensive discussion of variables influencing role enactment, see T. R. Sarbin, "Role Theory," in G. Lindzey, ed., *Handbook of Social Psychology* (Cambridge, Mass.: Addison-Wesley Publishing Company, 1954), Vol. I, pp. 223–258.

we may inquire in what ways the school contributes to the learning of social roles.

The school contributes to the learning of some roles because teachers and students, along with parents and other family and community members, communicate the general social expectations for role behavior. In addition, the school communicates role information not generally available from other sources. For example, a course in vocational guidance is designed to give students role information about various occupations, even though some students may acquire this information in other ways. A course in home economics or family and marriage is designed to teach students role expectancies and to give them some preliminary practice in role actions such as cooking and keeping house. The school also attempts to develop role expectancies related to the role of a citizen in a democracy. Finally, the school alone is responsible for preliminary training for some roles. Initial role training for such occupational roles as those of engineer, doctor, lawyer, and teacher is provided by the school and specifically required by society.

Occasionally, role expectations as conveyed in school (for example, through the readings provided) may be overidealized, unrealistic, and inconsistent with the conception of the role as it is shared by the larger society.[6] One study of readings used in the schools found marked **stereotyping** in the portrayal of male and female roles.[7] Men were characterized as typically aggressive, achievement-oriented, and constructive, whereas women were portrayed as typically inactive, unambitious, uncreative, but sociable and kind. The extent to which such stereotypes affect role expectations and role adjustment is not known; if assimilated, they would probably affect role adjustment adversely in some respects. In any case, we need to determine the probable consequences of a student's acquiring specific information on role adjustment and the relevancy of this information to society's conception of the role.

THE SELF-CONCEPT

In the course of a day, a week, or over a period of time, a person enacts many roles. Yet, in each of the roles, though his behavior varies from one

[6] For an interesting discussion of the discrepancies between role expectancies taught in some courses and the role as it is lived in the social system, see D. Lee, "Discrepancies in the Teaching of American Culture," in G. D. Spindler, ed., *Education and Anthropology* (Stanford: Stanford University Press, 1955), pp. 163–176.

[7] I. L. Child, E. H. Potter, and E. M. Levine, "Children's Textbooks and Personality Development: An Exploration in the Social Psychology of Education," *Psychological Monographs*, No. 279 (1946).

environmental context to another, he sees himself as essentially the same person. This conception of one's integral unity as he moves from role to role is his **self-concept**—the way he sees himself; the set of characteristics he associates with himself; the set of inferences, drawn from self-observation in many different situations, that describe his characteristic behavior patterns.

These self-descriptions may take many different forms. John might say that he is 5 feet, 10 inches tall and weighs 150 pounds. He might mention the color of his eyes and hair. He might use descriptive trait names, such as "shy or open," "friendly or withdrawn," "talkative or quiet." He might say that he is interested in fishing and football, that he likes woodworking and mathematics, that he wants to be an engineer or a doctor.

In Table 11–1, we presented a list of Karl's perceptions of his father's solutions to role-adaptation problems. We suggested that these perceptions influenced Karl's conceptions of these roles. Here is Karl's picture of himself as an adolescent. What aspects of Karl's self-concept seem to have been influenced by his concepts of the roles outlined in the table?

I was always cooperative and obedient, a good student, but influenced by others who sometimes led me into trouble. I was always sensitive and my feelings were and still are easily hurt.

I went to school, grammar school, at five, graduated at thirteen years of age. Very good marks, head of the class of eighteen. I always liked geography and history. Got the best marks in these courses. Liked math least of all although I received good marks in it. I had many friendships (got along alright with the teachers) and was regarded favorably by other boys and girls. I was always bashful around girls and was kidded a lot about it. I was very gregarious. In the younger days, third and fourth grade, I was occasionally picked on, but after a couple of fist fights I was goaded into I was left alone.

In high school my marks were excellent. I was at the head of the class, in many activities, president of the class for four years, on the football team, all-state guard, editor of the school paper. I worked well with all groups. My high school days were very happy and gratifying ones. I was very ambitious, wished to become a chemical engineer. I always did my work conscientiously and thoroughly and never wasted a minute. I always went to Sunday School, kept myself pure and led a model life. I graduated when seventeen years of age. I was confident working in groups when I knew the people, received cooperation and was usually chairman or a "wheel." I was very anxious to get ahead in the world and was very zealous toward going to college.

For amusement I played sports, went to the movie shows, etc., but not as much as the average. I was sometimes more content to sit home and read. I did a great deal of reading during my youth. I had no particular heroes. I always liked the cowboy heroes of the Westerns, Tarzan and others in the Saturday serials. I looked up to my football coach to an extent but not too greatly.[8]

In this description of himself, Karl gives us an abundance of factual data, as well as his impressions of himself. He says that he is sensitive and that his feelings are easily hurt; he also says that he was gregarious, although bashful around girls. He tells us what he wants to be—a chemical engineer. He gives us some conception of his values by telling us that he led a fairly model life.

Karl's self-concept was formed on the basis of his experiences with himself in a wide variety of situations over a long period of time. As Karl went through elementary and secondary schools, he formed impressions of what he was like. He found that he could get along with groups, that he was frequently elected chairman. He found that he had no trouble operating in a group situation. He then formed a picture of himself as an individual capable of working effectively in a group. Since he continually got good grades, he also saw himself as a successful student. Similarly, every individual has a concept of himself. His concept may not always be an accurate or objectively complete description of his personality. Other people may see him quite differently from the way he sees himself. In any case, the task of making a complete description either for the individual himself or for an observer would be an unending one. We do know that older and younger adults, men and women, have characteristically different ways of describing themselves.[9] However, the more important task is explaining why an individual chooses to describe himself as he does. This question is partially answered when we understand what factors influence development of the self-concept.

DEVELOPMENT OF THE SELF-CONCEPT

From our definition of it, it is clear that the self-concept will change with an individual's experiences. A preschool child interacts with a limited number of people, mostly with his parents, brothers, and sisters. His picture of himself is determined by his experiences in these interactions. When he enters school, he interacts with his teacher and with his classmates. New tasks are set for him, and, as he is successful or unsuccessful in the accomplishment of these tasks, he makes inferences about

[8] McClelland, *Personality* (see note 3), p. 531.
[9] See J. F. T. Bugental and S. L. Zelen, "Investigations in the 'Self-Concept': I. The W-A-Y Technique," *Journal of Personality,* 18 (1950), 483–498.

himself. Even the children in first grade learn quickly who is best at reading or art, though the teacher may attempt to disguise these facts. As the child progresses through school, he learns what his physical and mental capabilities are; he makes inferences about his ability to get along with other people, and he develops a pattern of likes and dislikes. During this process of assimilating new experiences, the child is continually revising his self-concept, trying to develop a fairly clear picture of himself. The self-concept probably changes throughout life.

Again, a self-concept is the set of inferences a person makes about himself on the basis of his experience. Some of these inferences may be tested in a relatively direct manner. A child's inference that he is stronger than other children may be tested in any task that requires strength for its performance. With repeated tests of this inference, the child may revise and refine his conception of his strength. He finds that he is stronger than most children his age but not as strong as most older children. In similar ways, he may repeatedly check other inferences about himself. Karl, for example, checked his inferences that he could work well in groups by participating in group activities.

Since a person is interacting with other people at every stage in his life, he frequently receives descriptions of himself from other people. He may be told by his teacher, for instance, that he isn't very good at mathematics or that he is bright; his parents may tell him that he is stubborn or that he is a friendly child. The child may accept these descriptions as reliable and may include these descriptions in his self-concept, saying about himself, "I'm not very good at mathematics" and "I'm stubborn." In other cases, the child may make inferences about himself from the way he is treated by other people. He notes that few of his classmates choose him as a friend, and he infers that he is not likable.

That a person will accept other people's evaluations of himself should not surprise us. A parent or teacher or classmate may be an important source of need satisfaction for a child. Accepting another person's evaluation of him may seem necessary to preserve the need satisfaction that person provides. The child may also accept the evaluations because he has learned to trust his parents or teachers or even a classmate as a source of reliable information: "My mother says I'm stubborn; she should know."

In these ways a person's self-concept may be compounded from his own observations of himself and from other people's descriptions of him. Earlier, we raised the question of why a person sees himself as he does. In general, the significant aspects of a person's self-description are the product of his inferences from self-observation and from others' descriptions of him that he has accepted. We can determine why a particular individual's self-description takes the form it does when we know what data he has used in forming his self-concept.

PRESERVATION OF THE SELF-CONCEPT

Experience that is inconsistent with one's self-concept is often anxiety-arousing. A person who sees himself as friendly but finds himself in a group that is unfriendly to him may come to believe that he is unfriendly and that the unfriendliness of the group is a response to his own disagreeableness. Why should such an interpretation of his own behavior, an interpretation that contradicts his self-image, be threatening to an individual?

Within an individual personality, the self-image is a *mediating variable* between the experiences of the individual and the dependent variable of behavior. An individual behaves and interprets environmental influences in accordance with his image of himself. If a child sees himself as friendly, he is likely to behave in ways consistent with this self-image. He may say, for example, "I will get along in this group because I like people." In so behaving, he obtains need satisfactions, such as love and approval, from other people. But if experience tends to contradict his image of himself, the whole behavior sequence that has led to need satisfaction is threatened. The child perceives that the self-concept, which has been regulating behavior, may be influencing behavior so that need satisfactions may not be obtained; this possibility is anxiety-provoking.

Defense Mechanisms

To assimilate his experiences and to integrate them into a comparatively consistent picture of himself, and to reduce the anxiety provoked by experiences that do not bear out his self-concept, the child learns **defense mechanisms** for interpreting what he knows and what he experiences about himself.[10] There is little experimental evidence on the factors that influence the learning of these mechanisms; but an abundance of clinical evidence, and even common-sense observation, supports the hypothesis that they are fairly typical means by which individuals maintain their self-concepts.

These mechanisms for interpreting experiential data in relation to an

[10] A detailed discussion of defense mechanisms may be found in P. M. Symonds, *The Dynamics of Human Adjustment* (New York: Appleton-Century-Crofts, Inc., 1946).

individual's self-concept involve complex interactions with his environment. For example, a child may have a picture of himself as friendly, warm, and agreeable. In school he attempts to make friends, but one student in the class consistently rejects his overtures of friendship. The child can interpret this rejection in several ways, but he is most likely to interpret it so that his self-image will remain relatively unchanged.

One way of handling this inconsistent information is to explain it away, or to **rationalize**. When the child rationalizes, he offers an explanation, more or less adequate, which enables him to reject the inconsistent information and maintain his original conception of himself. He says, for example, that the other child is really a very disagreeable person who never gets along with anybody anyway. If he has found that other people see him as friendly, warm, and agreeable, his explanation may be valid. If his actions do not evoke friendly behavior from others, if he is not seen by other people as a warm and agreeable child, his explanation is probably a rationalization.

Another way of handling experiential data inconsistent with one's self-concept is to attribute one's own disagreeable qualities and traits to other people, through the mechanism of **projection**. The child who is easily angered may contend that other people are easily angered, and that he is only responding to their hostility and aggressiveness. Posner [11] performed an experiment that illustrates this phenomenon. He divided his subjects, a number of eight-year-old children, into two groups and gave them two toys to play with—one of them a preferred toy and the other a relatively nonpreferred toy. In one group the experimenter asked the children to give a toy to a friend. Each child could give away either his preferred or his non-preferred toy. If a child gave away the toy that he did not like, he would presumably feel guilty—he had made a selfish choice. The child was then asked which toy the friend would have given away. If the child now says that he thinks the friend would give away the non-preferred toy, we may assume he is projecting his own feelings onto the friend. In other words, he sees the friend acting as he himself acted, and in this way relieves his guilt feelings. In the second group the children were not asked to give away toys. When the two groups were compared, much less projected selfishness was found in the second group than in the group requested to make choices.

Still another mechanism by which a person handles experiential data

[11] B. A. Posner, "Selfishness, Guilt Feelings and Social Distance," unpublished master's thesis, University of Iowa, 1940; cited in R. R. Sears, *Survey of Objective Studies of Psychoanalytic Concepts* (New York: Social Science Research Council, 1942), pp. 125–126.

inconsistent with his self-concept is **denial** or **repression**. Some data that a child may receive about himself may be so threatening to his concept of himself that he cannot accept or tolerate it. A child who sees himself as a "good boy," but who lies or cheats on a test, may completely repress the memory of inconsistent behavior. He selectively remembers what has happened to him on the basis of what fits in with his concept of himself. Repressions are largely unconscious and cannot ordinarily be recalled by the individual. Memories and feelings thus repressed can be recalled or re-experienced only in therapy, where the individual talks out his feelings and memories.

The consistency of the self-concept may also be maintained by self-selection of experiences likely to strengthen an individual's concept of himself. Individuals leave social systems in which the patterns of interpersonal relationships are markedly different from their preferred patterns.[12] There is some evidence to suggest similarities in personality types among the members of social systems.[13] The evidence does not prove that individuals select environments in which they are likely to have experiences compatible with their self-concepts, but this hypothesis is nonetheless consistent with this evidence.

Development of Self-Understanding

The self-concept is one of the orientation processes by which an individual is predisposed to interpret his environment in consistent ways. In this sense, the self-concept is an adaptive function of personality; however, the mechanisms for preserving the consistency of the self-image may interfere with successful adapting if the image that is preserved inhibits behavior change likely to lead to need satisfaction. The following example illustrates the way in which these mechanisms might preserve a self-concept that is likely to lead to need deprivation rather than need satisfaction.

A high school student who wants to be an engineer but has little mathematical ability may persist in his efforts to become an engineer despite the fact that he is persistently failing in mathematics. He sees himself as having the abilities and qualities necessary to be an engineer. He also expects to achieve need satisfaction by becoming an engineer, but

[12] See G. G. Stern, M. I. Stein, and B. S. Bloom, *Methods in Personality Assessment* (Glencoe, Ill.: The Free Press, 1956).

[13] See A. Roe, *The Psychology of Occupations* (New York: John Wiley & Sons, 1956).

he may infer from his failure in mathematics that he does not have the ability to become an engineer. To preserve his image of himself as a potential engineer, he may reject conflicting data about himself in several ways. He may deprecate the importance of mathematical knowledge in engineering. He may attribute his failure in mathematics to poor teaching or poor texts or to the fact that he was doing too much other work to concentrate on mathematics. He may remember that he was quite good at arithmetic in the fourth grade and may completely ignore the fact that he failed mathematics in high school. Thus, he preserves the consistency of his self-concept; however, this self-concept may influence him to continue working for unattainable goals.

This student is probably obtaining some need satisfaction by imagining himself as a potential engineer. He may associate with engineering students whom he admires and win their approval by participating in their activities. He may receive parental approval because he has chosen an occupational goal that his parents regard as desirable. However, he lacks self-understanding to the extent that he does not perceive the discrepancy between what he thinks he can attain and what he is likely to attain. We say that he does not have **insight,** because he does not understand the discrepancy between what he thinks he can or will do and what he is likely to be able to do.

Failures in self-understanding inevitably handicap a child, since he will interact with his environment on the basis of his concept of himself. A child who sees himself as friendly, but who is not seen as friendly by his classmates and who by every objective criterion is not friendly, is not likely to change his behavior until he acquires some insight into the fact that he is a hostile and aggressive child. The greater the discrepancy between an individual's experiences and his concept of himself, the more difficult it will be for him to adjust to his environment, particularly to the interpersonal relationships that his environment requires of him.

THE TEACHER AND THE CHILD'S SELF-CONCEPT

In formulating hypotheses about behavior change, the teacher will need to consider the influence of a child's self-concept. Let us take a child who is not doing very well in arithmetic. One of our problems is to determine the factors likely to be influencing his performance. He may have inadequate mathematical concepts; he may not be interested in arithmetic; he may not be very intelligent. However, he may be doing poorly because he sees himself as poor in arithmetic and, consequently, does not select the means necessary to do reasonably good work. Or these factors may be interrelated in complex ways. The child may have inadequate concepts and, as a consequence, has done poorly in arithmetic, and now sees himself as poor in arithmetic. In some cases, the child may be intelligent and may have done adequate work in arithmetic but, because of a few poor performances, has concluded that he is not proficient. Or a child may have formed a conception of abilities from some remark made by an adult, such as "girls aren't good at arithmetic."

We formulate hypotheses that his poor performance may result from the influence of these factors. We may then proceed to check these hypotheses by gathering information on the child's previous performance in arithmetic, his intelligence level, and his self-concept. By making an analysis of this kind, we may determine to what extent the child's self-concept is relevant to or an important determinant of his behavior.

In what ways can the teacher influence a child's self-concept? As we have noted before, the teacher is one of many adults who describes and evaluates a child's behavior to him. The teacher may be an important source of the child's information about himself—for example, about his ability to learn. Through guidance programs, designed to help children clarify their self-concepts by providing them with reliable information about themselves, and in many less formalized ways, the teacher may help children develop self-understanding.[14]

Assume that the child who is doing poorly in arithmetic is handicapped principally because of his conception of his abilities, since his general level of intelligence and previous experience indicate that he should be doing reasonably well in arithmetic. Can we influence the child's self-concept so that he sees himself potentially as good in arithmetic? We might try several procedures, such as discussing his abilities with him. Or we might arrange his arithmetic experiences so that he is successful—in the hope that he will perceive himself differently afterward. Here again, the teacher proceeds as a hypothesis maker. Each alternative procedure is tried on the hypothesis that it is likely to promote a desirable change in the child's self-concept. Our understanding of the variables which influence the development of a child's self-concept should improve the quality of our hypotheses. For example, if we know that a child has serious deficiencies in his previous training, we are not likely to hy-

---

[14] However, some children lack self-understanding to such an extent that they require professional help before any pervasive change in their self-concepts is likely to occur. Teachers do not usually have the training to provide this kind of help, and will have to refer the child to trained therapists.

pothesize that encouragement alone will result in a change in his self-concept.

Teachers are frequently urged to help children accept themselves as they are and to respect their own intrinsic worth. This recommendation would be indefensible and naive if it meant that all patterns of personality development are in some vague sense "good." The recommendation is psychologically sound if it means that teachers may help a child to achieve a degree of self-understanding adequate for his age and developmental status, or that they may help a child use his conception of himself in obtaining need satisfactions. In these ways a child is helped "to accept himself." The child may be made aware of his "intrinsic worth" by being helped to achieve his goals in socially acceptable ways; he may then assume a place in a group which will value his contribution to the attainment of the group's goals. Presumably he will see himself as a "valuable" person because he can make a contribution that is valued by the group.

PERSONALITY ADJUSTMENT

Personality development, as we have conceptualized it, is a process of progressive **adaptation,** or **adjustment.** We have described each of the major aspects of personality as "orientation" processes; that is, processes that prepare an individual to interact with his environment in specific ways. However, we sometimes refer to a person as "adjusted" or "maladjusted," and, when we do, we are typically referring to his personality adaptation as a whole. "Personality adjustment" is another label for behavior change, which, however, frequently implies some criterion of "good" adjustment. In this section, we explore the concept of adjustment and its effect on personality development.

We say that an individual is adjusted if he has learned responses that enable him to interact with his environment so that he obtains need satisfactions while behaving in ways acceptable to the members of his society. An individual in a particular social situation can adapt or adjust to it in many different ways. In any classroom there are children with widely different personalities; yet the majority of the children have learned ways of interacting in this environment so that they obtain need satisfactions and successfully enact the roles required of them.

At least two possible meanings may be associated with the term **maladjustment.** One meaning is basically a social concept: an individual is not adjusted if he cannot interact appropriately in a given environment.

The other meaning describes an individual as maladjusted if he is not obtaining need satisfactions, even though his behavior may be appropriate for his society. These two concepts of maladjustment are interrelated. A child who shouts out in class is not conforming to the standards of appropriate classroom behavior, but he may be satisfying his need for approval or prestige. Delinquent behavior may be a way of satisfying a need for aggression or prestige, but a delinquent is not an adjusted member of society. A child is motivated by certain needs and attempts to achieve goals that will satisfy them. Since the child is a social being, society attempts to develop needs that will motivate the child to seek goals and thereby acquire behavior consistent with the expectations for appropriate behavior in a given society.

Poor adjustment—or maladjustment—results from inadequate or inappropriate learning. The learning process can break down at a number of points. The child may fail to acquire appropriate needs to motivate him toward desirable goals. In American society, for example, value is placed upon achievement. A child who does not develop some need for achievement will not seek goals and will not learn striving behaviors that are regarded as appropriate in some segments of society. Or, in the process of satisfying his need for achievement, a child may acquire behaviors that are not socially approved. We punish a child who cheats on an examination; we do not encourage stealing or lying as ways of acquiring goals to satisfy achievement needs. We do not encourage dependent behavior; rather, we attempt to satisfy a child's need for approval by rewarding independent behavior.

Failures in adjustment may take place at all levels of personality. A child who is physically weak has difficulty in acquiring skills involving strength. The child who is not intellectually bright may have difficulty adjusting to the requirements of schooling. Inadequate concepts or inappropriate attitudes are potential sources of maladjustment. If a child fails to learn appropriate roles or is required to enact incompatible roles, he may become maladjusted. Finally, a discrepancy between how one sees himself and how others see him is a potential source of maladjustment. The individual may have to learn new modes of responding to himself and to his environment. He may have to learn new concepts, attitudes, or roles, or he may have to revise his self-concept in order to obtain need satisfaction in socially acceptable ways.

Persistent difficulty in obtaining need satisfaction or inability to learn socially acceptable ways of obtaining need satisfaction frequently results in the development of behavior patterns so maladaptive that the individual cannot adjust adequately in any situation. Such an individual requires special treatment to restore his ability for adapting successfully to his environment.

THE SOCIALIZATION PROCESS AND PERSONALITY

The adjusted person, according to our definition of adjustment, is the *socialized* person; that is, the person who obtains need satisfactions by acquiring the behavior patterns expected from members of his society. The **socialization** processes in a society promote this development. We may profitably conclude our discussion of the development of personality by studying the influence of the socialization process on the development of personality.

Society is not a disembodied entity, but a living complex of individuals. Within any society there are members who are already socialized; and these individuals, usually adults, communicate the values and standards of the society to the child.[15] A child learns the appropriate behavior and develops the appropriate personality for his society largely through interaction with these socializing agents—in American society, principally parents and teachers. A child's peers also may influence his socialization insofar as they reflect cultural expectations in their interactions with him. By these means, the general pattern of behavior development is fostered in directions consistent with the cultural expectations.

COMMUNICATION OF CULTURAL EXPECTATIONS

Cultural expectations are communicated to the child in two ways: (1) through a set of tasks, which he must master if he is to be a socialized or adjusted member of his society; (2) through need satisfactions provided to facilitate his learning of behavior patterns required for mastery of these developmental tasks.

The relation of particular learning experiences to socialization may be more or less direct. A course in advanced nuclear physics appears to be relatively remote from the socialization process, although a student may be taking such a course in preparation for a career of research in physics. The choice of a career and successful preparation for one are parts of the

---

[15] For an interesting comparison of cultural differences in socializing processes, see M. Mead and M. Wolfenstein, *Childhood in Contemporary Cultures* (Chicago: University of Chicago Press, 1955).

socialization process. Other learning experiences are more obviously related to socialization. In the study of American history, for instance, the school attempts to communicate to the child certain values and ideals that are directly relevant to his total development as an American citizen and as a personality who can adjust to American society. Being told that America is a land of equal opportunity, the great melting pot of civilization, the child may learn to value democracy and democratic processes. Learning about the conquering of the American frontier, the child may appreciate the high value placed on achievement striving in American society.

Cultural expectations also are communicated in subtle ways, as the following example makes clear; the setting is a second-grade classroom:

TEACHER: What would you think would be one of the first things to do for our play?

STUDENT: Get scenery and conversation. Get kids who can memorize it. Tell the name and speak with expression.
(Teacher nods head and replies affirmatively to each answer.)

TEACHER: But what is *the most important thing?*

STUDENT: The characters.

TEACHER: Name them.

STUDENT: Billy Goat, Gray Pony, Red Cow, Calf, Jolly Pig, Mrs. Pig.

TEACHER: What else?

STUDENT: Scenery.

TEACHER: Have you ever been in a play?

STUDENT: No, but I've seen one.

TEACHER: He's *using his head;* he's got *ideas.* Now what kind of scenery do we need?

STUDENT: Apple tree, pies, house, sky, fence, ground.

TEACHER: Would you have the outside and the inside of the house in one part? What do you call it when you divide a play? [16]

In this example of interaction between teacher and pupil, the children learn cultural values in addition to solving the particular problem of constructing a play. The teacher's emphasis on the "most important thing" reflects an important cultural value; namely, deciding what comes first. He is also emphasizing the importance of order and arrangement by

[16] J. Henry, "Culture, Education, and Communications Theory," in G. D. Spindler, ed., *Education and Anthropology* (Stanford: Stanford University Press, 1955), p. 193.

discussing what is needed for the play and how it is to be arranged. Both of these values are reflected in common maxims such as "first things first" and "everything in its place." Notice that the child who thinks receives special approval—"He's got *ideas.*"

The teacher may not even be aware that he is communicating these values. But as a socialized member of society himself, he has assimilated these values into his attitudinal and value system, and his behavior is influenced by these values. As a socializing agent, he is communicating the expectations of society to the children in his class.

VARIATIONS IN SOCIALIZATION PROCESSES

The socialization process in American society is not quite so uniform as the above discussion may suggest. Although there is a pattern of socialization common to all aspects of this society (for example, the dominant cultural expectation that children will prepare themselves to be self-supporting), social classes, as well as ethnic and racial groups, may vary in the particular form that this cultural expectation takes. Since a child lives within a limited number of social systems, his pattern of development tends to be relatively consistent and reflects the cultural expectations for individuals in the groups to which he belongs.[17] In a comprehensive study of child-rearing practices, Sears found substantial differences between middle-class and working-class mothers (see Table 11–2).[18] A somewhat different system of rewards and punishments is used in the two kinds of homes. The middle-class mother, for example, apparently permits more dependent behavior than does the working-class mother, whereas the working-class mother punishes dependency more frequently than does the middle-class mother. The middle-class mother is somewhat permissive of mild sexual experimentation, whereas the working-class mother is not. A greater percentage of middle-class mothers expect their

[17] Students interested in the structure of American society and variations in cultural behavior patterns may find the following profitable reading: J. A. Kahl, *The American Class Structure* (New York: Rinehart & Co., 1957); R. Bendix and S. M. Lipset, eds., *Class, Status and Power: A Reader in Social Stratification* (Glencoe, Ill.: The Free Press, 1953).

[18] R. Sears, E. E. Maccoby, and H. Levin, *Patterns of Child-Rearing* (Evanston, Ill.: Row, Peterson and Company, copyright 1957), pp. 426–427. Reprinted by permission of the publisher. For other studies in social-class differences in child-rearing practices, see A. Davis and R. J. Havighurst, "Social Class and Color Differences in Child Rearing," *American Sociological Review*, 11 (1946), 698–710; and E. E. Maccoby et al., "Methods of Child Rearing in Two Social Classes," in W. E. Martin and C. B. Stendler, eds., *Readings in Child Development* (New York: Harcourt, Brace & Co., 1954), pp. 380–396.

TABLE 11-2. *Differences in child-training practices between mothers of two social classes (from Sears).*

Scales	Middle class	Working class
Median age at completion of bowel training	18.8 months	16.4 months
Percentage rated *high* on:		
Severity of toilet training	15	26
Permissiveness for dependency	42	29
Punishment, irritation, for dependency	44	56
Sex permissiveness (summary)	53	22
Permissiveness for aggression toward neighborhood children	38	31°
Permissiveness for aggression toward parents	19	7
Severity of punishment for aggression toward parents	36	51
Amount of restriction on the use of fingers for eating ..	66	81
Pressure for conformity with table standards and restrictions	23	39
Restrictions on care of house and furniture	65	78
Pressure for neatness and orderliness	43	57
Strictness about bedtime	28	38
Strictness about noise	28	38
Keeping track of child (frequency of checking whereabouts)	26	33°
Extent of father's demands for instant obedience	53	67
Importance of child's doing well at school	35	50
Percentage who expect child to go to college	70	24
Percentage rated *high* on:		
Use of praise if child gives no trouble at table	49	63
Use of ridicule	31	47
Deprivation of privileges	34	42°
Use of physical punishment	17	33
Amount of caretaking of infant by person other than mother or father	18	11°
Mother's warmth to child	51	37
Father's warmth to child	60	56°
Percentage showing some rejection of child	24	40
Percentage of mother "delighted" over pregnancy	73	65
Percentage rated *high* on:		
Mother's esteem for father	54	37
Parents' disagreement on child-rearing policies	15	19°
Family authority exercised primarily by:		
Father	29	25°
Both equally	62	59°
Mother	9	16°

° Differences between these percentages are not statistically significant.

children to go to college. The child of the working-class mother is praised more frequently for giving no trouble at the table than is the middle-class child. The working-class mother uses ridicule, deprivation of privileges, and physical punishment more frequently than the middle-class mother.

The significance of these differences is that they foster the development of differential behavior patterns. The child of the middle-class mother has typically learned more aggression control, or at least has learned not to express his aggression in overt ways. The child of the working-class mother, though punished for aggressive activity, has a persistent model of aggression in his parents. He learns to use aggression in other interpersonal relationships, though he may learn to control his aggressive feelings within the home.

Different values and needs are acquired by the children in these two kinds of homes. The middle-class child is typically achievement-oriented.[19] From early childhood he learns that his parents expect him to extend his schooling and probably to enter one of the professions or to aspire to the executive level in business. The working-class child learns that the "here and now" is important, that security is not to be sacrificed to striving for distant goals. He does not expect to go to college and does not learn to want to go to college.

The effects of the socialization process are reflected in the systems of concepts, attitudes, values, skill performances, roles, and self-concepts that an individual acquires. The totality of these systems is what we call personality. The kinds of personalities that emerge in a society depend on the kinds of socialization processes that characterize it.

INSTRUCTIONAL STRATEGIES

It seems pretentious to talk about instructional strategies for the development of personality. The point of view taken throughout this book is that the teacher is always influencing this development. Although the study of how different educational systems produce different personalities is an intriguing problem, little is known that is specific enough to guide educational policy and practice. That is, we cannot say precisely how to organize the total environment to produce certain kinds of personalities even if we knew what we wanted.

Ideally, a teacher ought to know enough about the personality develop-

[19] See B. C. Rosen, "The Achievement Syndrome: A Psycho-Cultural Dimension of Social Stratification," *American Sociological Review,* 21 (1956), 203–211.

ment, the motivations, and response patterns of his students to adapt his instructional strategies. *A general decision rule is that the design of the strategy must account for the stable characteristics of the learner.* A technical skill needs to be learned if the teacher is to acquire and utilize this information. This is the skill of behavioral observation. The relevant principles have been given before—careful description of the behavior to be observed and systematic sampling of behavior occasions. These are necessary conditions. They do not protect the teacher from faulty inference. Faulty inferences are irradicable, but they can be minimized and corrected. The method is to predict from the inference, and observe to test the validity of the prediction. Here the teacher applies what he has learned about critical inquiry.

An unending process of studying individuals is required if we are to gain insight into the personality characteristics of our students. The teacher needs to view learners not simply as a vague abstraction called students but as individuals. We mean this in the best clinical sense, much as the physician, while thinking in the general categories of anatomy and physiology, comes to recognize and understand the significance of individual variation. The teacher has no special powers for this task, no magic intuitive sense. He can observe, hypothesize, predict, and observe again. He can organize and theorize, and he can test his theories. And so he learns.

SUMMARY

1. Personality development may be conceptualized as a process of progressive differentiation and integration of response systems.

2. *Roles* are expectations about the behavior of individuals in given positions in a social system. Role behavior is behavior consistent with these expectations.

3. An individual needs to learn many different roles in order to occupy positions in different social systems. Some roles, such as age and sex roles, are expected learnings for all members of a society. Other roles may be enacted by an individual for periods of varying length; some roles may be enacted only once in a lifetime; and some roles need to be learned only by individuals belonging to particular social systems. Since an individual occupies a position in some social system at every stage of his life, role acquisitions are an important aspect of the development of personality.

4. *Positions* in a social system are the functions necessary to group operation and through whose maintenance group goals are attained.

5. *Role expectations* are shared conceptions of appropriate or desirable ways of behaving.

6. Social systems foster role learning by providing need satisfactions for the learning and by communicating the social expectations for appropriate role behavior. Role learning may be conveniently conceptualized as one kind of complex problem solving. Successful problem solution requires that the learner attempt role behavior, making successive behavior changes until the appropriate role behavior is acquired.

7. Successful role adjustment depends on (a) the extent to which the learner is likely to obtain need satisfactions by acquiring role expectations and behavior; (b) the availability of relevant information on role expectations; (c) the extent to which the learner can transfer other learned response patterns to the learning of the role. Role adjustment is particularly difficult when role expectations are not clearly defined or when there are conflicting conceptions of the role.

8. The school shares with other agencies the responsibility for encouraging role learning relevant to an individual's adjustment to society. The school communicates cultural expectations on appropriate role behavior, though the role expectations communicated through the school should be examined for their consistency with general cultural expectations.

9. The *self-concept* is the set of characteristics that a person associates with himself. It is formed by inferences from an individual's experiences. Such inferences may be made from direct observations of one's own behavior or from other people's descriptions and evaluations of one's behavior.

10. The sequence of behavior processes leading to need satisfaction is threatened by information inconsistent with the self-concept; and this threat is anxiety-provoking. Such information may be handled in three ways: (a) by rationalizing; (b) by projecting; (c) by denial or repression. Each of these mechanisms is essentially a way of dissociating from one's self characteristics inconsistent with the self-concept.

11. An individual lacks self-understanding to the extent that there is a discrepancy between his self-concept and his experience. Lack of self-understanding handicaps an individual in his adjustment to his environment, since the individual relates to his environment on the basis of his self-concept.

12. The teacher's understanding of a child's behavior may be improved if he understands the child's self-concept. Teachers may improve children's self-understanding by providing them with reliable information about themselves. In some cases, teachers may also help a child to change

his self-concept, but specific procedures for accomplishing this change cannot be given. Each procedure used by the teacher for this purpose embodies a hypothesis about the likelihood that the procedure will produce changes in the self-concept.

13. Personality development is a process of progressive adaptation, or *adjustment*. A person is considered *maladjusted* if he is not interacting appropriately in his environment or if he is not obtaining need satisfactions.

14. The socialization process is the means used by society to foster the development of personality. The socialized person is adjusted to his society in the sense that he obtains need satisfactions by acquiring socially acceptable behavior patterns. The socialization process provides (a) a series of developmental tasks that children master and, in the process, acquire the behavior patterns needed for adjustment to their society; (b) a system of need satisfactions to encourage the learning necessary for mastery of these developmental tasks.

15. The development of behavior patterns consistent with cultural expectations is accomplished through organized learning experiences, as in the school, and in the interactions of the child with socializing agents such as parents and teachers.

16. Variations in specific socialization practices may be found in social systems, such as social classes, which are a part of the total society. These variations result in differences in personality development among members of these systems.

17. *Personality* is the complex integration of the components of personality that we have studied—the cognitive, attitudinal, and evaluative processes, patterns of skill performance, learned roles, and the self-concept. The development of specific behavior patterns in these components, as well as their integration into a personality, is fostered through the socialization process. Thus, personality development is a process of progressive socialization in which an individual develops the patterns of behavior which enable him to adapt successfully to his society.

STUDY AND DISCUSSION QUESTIONS

1. Using some social organization with which you are familiar, such as a club, describe the positions that comprise this organization. Identify the functions of each of these positions in relation to the achievement of the goals of the social system.

2. Using the same organization, describe the roles associated with each of the positions you have identified. What are the role expectations and behaviors

for each of these roles? How does an individual occupying a given position learn the role expectations for that position? In what ways do the members of the social system ensure that the appropriate role expectations are learned? Are you familiar with any instances in which an individual deviated remarkably from the expected role behaviors? What were the consequences of his failure to enact the role in the expected way?

3. Describe the positions occupied by a ten-year-old child in his family, in his school, on his local baseball team, and in some club to which he might belong. What role expectations and behaviors are associated with each of these positions? What kinds of experiences are provided so that he may learn the appropriate role expectations and behaviors? What role expectations and behaviors learned in one social system may transfer to the learning of roles in the other social systems to which he belongs?

4. Describe some differences in role expectations for a student in elementary school, in high school, and in a college or university. Identify role expectations common to the student role in these three different social systems.

5. Describe the principal concepts, attitudes, and role actions associated with each of the following roles:

   a. Son or daughter.

   b. College student.

   c. Member of a club or social group.

6. What need satisfactions might a person obtain by learning the following roles?

   a. The student role in college.

   b. One's own sex role.

   c. An occupational role.

7. Identify several roles that you think a person must learn for successful adjustment in our society. Explain why you think that the learning of these roles is essential. By way of contrast, identify several roles that do *not* appear essential for successful adjustment in our society. Again, give your reasons for hypothesizing that the learning of these roles is not required for successful adjustment. How could you test your hypotheses in this respect?

8. What kinds of role expectations and behavior associated with the role of a high school student may interfere with successful learning of the role of a college student? What aspects of the high school student role may be generalized to facilitate learning the role of a college student?

9. What learning experiences provided in the elementary and secondary schools contribute to learning the following roles?

   a. One's sex role.

   b. An occupational role.

   c. One's role as a citizen.

10. Assume that an individual receives contradictory evaluations of himself from other people. What factors are likely to influence his acceptance of one of these evaluations?

11. In what sense is the self-concept a hypothesis about one's self? In what ways may an individual test these hypotheses about himself?

12. In each of the situations described below, explain how an individual might use one of the defense mechanisms, such as rationalization, to preserve the consistency of his self-concept. Also explain ways in which an individual may react to these situations without resorting to defense mechanisms.

   a. An average student is refused admission to a college which he wishes to enter.

   b. A muscular high school junior fails to make the varsity football team.

   c. An attractive girl is not invited to the class dance.

13. A student in your class tells you he would have done better on his last test if he had studied harder. How can you determine whether his explanation is or is not a rationalization? What kinds of information would you need in order to test the hypothesis that his explanation is, in fact, a rationalization?

14. Describe some ways in which an individual's self-concept may influence his behavior in each of the following situations:

   a. Choosing a career.

   b. Selecting a marriage partner.

   c. Selecting social organizations to join.

   d. Deciding whether or not to study a foreign language.

15. What kinds of behavior patterns are necessary for successful adjustment in each of the following situations:

   a. A child entering kindergarten.

   b. A high school graduate attending a residential college.

   c. A beginning teacher meeting his first class.

   d. A high school junior attending his first dance.

16. To what extent may the persons described in the above question be initially maladjusted in these situations? What are likely to be the consequences of failing to acquire the behavior patterns necessary to adapt to the situations described?

17. What kinds of cultural expectations may be learned in each of the following situations?

   a. In an American history class.

   b. In an algebra class.

   c. At a school dance.

   d. At a varsity football game.

18. Describe the social values emphasized in your own home. Describe incidents when emphasis was placed on the learning of these values. In what ways has the learning of these values enabled you to adapt successfully to other social situations?

RECOMMENDED READINGS

H. H. Anderson. "Social Development," in L. Carmichael, ed., *Manual of Child Psychology*, 2nd ed. New York: John Wiley and Sons, 1954, Chapter 19.

E. Hilgard. "Human Motives and the Concept of the Self." *American Psychologist*, 4 (1949), 374–382.

A. R. Luria. *The Nature of Human Conflicts*. New York: Grove Press, 1960.

D. C. McClelland. *Personality*. New York: The Dryden Press, 1951.

G. Murphy. *Human Potentialities*. New York: Basic Books, 1958.

T. M. Newcomb. *Social Psychology*. New York: The Dryden Press, 1950, Chapters 8–13.

P. S. Sears and V. S. Sherman, *In Pursuit of Self-Esteem: Case Studies of Eight Elementary School Children*. Belmont, Calif.: Wadsworth Publishing Co., 1964.

M. Stein, A. J. Vidich, and D. M. White, eds. *Identity and Anxiety*. Glencoe, Ill.: The Free Press, 1960.

The following chapters in H. Stevenson, ed., Sixty-second Yearbook of the National Society for the Study of Education, Part I, *Child Psychology* (Chicago: University of Chicago Press, 1963): J. A. Clausen, "Sociological Correlates of Behavior," pp. 62–107; L. Kohlberg, "Moral Development and Identification," pp. 277–332; W. W. Hartup, "Dependence and Independence," pp. 333–365; A. Bandura and R. Walters, "Aggression," pp. 264–315; V. J. Crandall, "Achievement," pp. 416–459.

C. Tryon and W. E. Henry. "How Children Learn Personal and Social Adjustment," in Forty-ninth Yearbook of the National Society for the Study of Education, Part I, *Learning and Instruction*. Chicago: University of Chicago Press, 1950, pp. 156–182.

R. W. White, ed. *The Study of Lives*. New York: Atherton Press, 1963.

CHAPTER TWELVE

PATTERNS OF DEVELOPMENT

Children are not born with concepts; they acquire them. Attitudes, values, and patterns of skill performance are also learned. At any stage of his life, the child is a unity—a personality. However, his personality changes as he acquires new concepts, attitudes, skills, and problem-solving facility. We say that he is developing, or "maturing." Implicit in our concept of "mature" behavior are culturally shared expectancies of what a child ought to be like at a given age. We do not expect a twelve-year-old child to whine and cry when he wants something. We would be surprised to hear a ten-year-old learnedly discussing foreign policy. Such behavior does not accord with our general expectations for children at these ages.

The concept of "development" suggests that we may classify the behavior changes we observe in children at various ages. And an important portion of psychological and educational research has been devoted to developmental behavior. These studies are essentially descriptive; that is, they provide data on the relation between increases in age and changes in behavior. With such data, we may formulate a picture of the amount and kind of behavior change that may be expected over a period of time. In addition, we can determine the variable factors in change; for example, if we know the pattern of behavior of the *average* ten-year-old, we have a standard for assessing and evaluating the behavior of an individual ten-year-old.

Behavior changes at given ages depend on physical growth and on changes that result from learning. In this chapter we will explore the concept of development. We will be concerned only with general patterns of development, and not with details on the development of many specific functions.[1]

Maturation in the strict sense is a biological process over which we have little control. The process of maturing cannot be stopped, but only interfered with through accidents and massive infections, or retarded through improper nutrition. The human organism grows in height and weight. The brain matures; the nervous system is myelinized. Changes of these kinds, which depend exclusively on genetic factors, and the prenatal and postnatal chemical environment of the organism, may be called *physical maturation*. Other changes—for instance, the growth of intelligence—depend exclusively or heavily on the experience of the organism.[2] "Mental maturity" develops mainly from learning opportunities. Social and emotional "maturity" is largely the product of social experience. Such changes may properly be thought of as *psychological maturation*.

It is extraordinarily difficult, however, to distinguish sharply between these two aspects of maturation. Perhaps some behavior previously thought to be exclusively the product of learning will prove to have a significant biogenetic component. But at the present time, we prefer to assume that behavior development is largely the product of learning. This assumption is most likely to be valid for behaviors (such as social habits and those that are modified by training or schooling) that differ from one social group to another.

The practical significance of this distinction is that we attend more to

---

[1] A comprehensive survey of developmental studies of many different personality functions may be found in the following: L. Carmichael, ed., *Manual of Child Psychology*, 2nd ed. (New York: John Wiley and Sons, 1954); P. H. Mussen, ed., *Handbook of Research Methods in Child Development* (New York: John Wiley & Sons, 1960). The *Annual Review of Psychology* periodically reviews research on development; see, for instance, E. E. Maccoby, "Developmental Psychology," in P. Farnsworth et al., eds., *Annual Review of Psychology* (Palo Alto, Calif.: Annual Reviews, Inc., 1964), Vol. 15, pp. 203–250.

[2] J. McV. Hunt, *Intelligence and Experience* (New York: Ronald Press, 1961).

the influence of learning on behavior development. Behavior is not modifiable if its development is controlled solely by hereditary factors (except by evolution, usually a slow process). The pattern of development will emerge inevitably, or only those individuals with the appropriate heredity will profit from the learning experiences that stimulate its emergence. One constantly hears, "Give him time, he'll mature," when the referent is social behavior. The misjudgment here usually leads to a decision to do nothing or to provide supportive conditions while the change is awaited.

In this chapter, we will be concerned with general patterns of development, progressive age changes, and the factors that may be related to them. These changes are typically the product of physical and psychological maturation.

THE PROCESS OF DEVELOPMENT

DIFFERENTIATION OF RESPONSES

The process of development requires differentiation of responses. At birth, the infant has a limited number of responses. He appears to be a mass of undifferentiated and undirected movement. As the weeks and months pass, his movements become refined, and he acquires response patterns. The swinging of his arms and hands develops into a response of grasping. His kicking movements eventually change into pushing movements, and still later into the specific movements required for crawling and walking. In this pattern of change, finer responses are developed from the earlier gross movements.

This refinement of response also characterizes changes in other functions. The child's initial response to men may be to call them "Daddy," but he learns to differentiate his father from other men, and still later he learns how to call people by their names. He learns a complex set of familial relations, which enables him to categorize people as mother, father, brother, sister, grandmother, and grandfather.[2] As the child's concepts become more differentiated, so do his attitudes, interests, and values. A child initially has a diffuse affectional tie with his parents and his family. He learns to react in a variety of emotional ways to other people. He may learn to love or hate his teacher, his schoolmates, and other adults whom he meets. *The mature person, or the relatively mature*

[2] For a general treatment of these ideas, see C. M. Solley and G. Murphy, *Development of the Perceptual World* (New York: Basic Books, Inc., 1960).

person, is capable of fine discriminations and refined and controlled responses to his environment.

INTEGRATION OF RESPONSES

The process of development also requires integration of responses. To walk, a child must not only learn a number of specific responses, but he must also integrate them into response patterns. Grasping requires coordinating hand and eye movements. Learning to read requires developing eye movements, associating words and sounds, acquiring concepts and vocabulary, and developing attitudes of interest and effort. Each of these responses has to be learned. But they must also be integrated into sets of responses—moving eyes and recognizing words, recognizing words and identifying meanings, combining sets of words into ideas. Differences in ability to read are related to differences both in level of acquisition of particular response sets and in integration of these response sets. For example, a child who makes many eye movements may have difficulty in reading efficiently—even though he has facility in such response patterns as sight recognition and phonetic analysis of words. Another child may read inefficiently because he has difficulty in relating these response patterns to one another in a continuous process of reading—even though he performs any one set of responses quite well. Both of these children may be somewhat retarded in their development, but for different reasons.

Behavior patterns become progressively more complex as the individual integrates new responses with previously learned responses. Therefore, the behavior patterns of the "mature" person—that is, the individual at an advanced stage of development—may be quite different in their totality from that of the beginner or relatively "immature" person. A "mature reader," for example, has greater and more diversified interests in reading, is able to get more and deeper meanings out of what he reads, and can read selectively to achieve many different purposes.[3] He is distinguished from the less mature reader in the specific responses he can make, as well as in the total pattern of his reading behavior.

Any stage or sequence of behavior development may be described in terms of the response discriminations and integrations required to achieve a given level of development. For example, a child learning to read begins by identifying the letters of the alphabet by sight and sound. But as he

[3] W. S. Gray and B. Rogers, *Maturity in Reading* (Chicago: University of Chicago Press, 1956).

acquires new responses, we may describe "stages" in his development in terms of the kinds of discriminations and integrations of responses he is making. The child who can recognize words by sight is further in the development of his ability to read than a child who can recognize only the letters of the alphabet. However, we have yet to account for his progression from one stage to another; we have merely described it.

FACTORS INFLUENCING DEVELOPMENT

INFLUENCE OF HEREDITY

How does heredity influence behavior? We may begin this discussion by indicating in what way heredity does not influence behavior. Behavior, or the psychological characteristics of the person, is not directly inherited. For example, behavior that we describe as relatively more or less intelligent is not inherited. We observe a child's responses on an "intelligence test," his ability to perform school tasks, his vocabulary development, and his ability to solve complex problems. We may compare his performance on these tasks with the performance of other children, and from these comparative data make inferences about his relative brightness. The "intelligent behavior" we have observed is not inherited as such, but some of the factors that influence the extent to which "intelligent behaviors" are acquired may be influenced by hereditary factors.

Popular thinking fails to distinguish between inherited factors and behavior development that may be influenced by hereditary factors. For example, we observe that a child who is more intelligent has parents who are more intelligent. Research studies have also demonstrated a substantial correlation between parent-child intelligence-test scores.[4] From the available data we cannot conclude that heredity determines the development of intelligent behavior. Such an interpretation is consistent with the data, but other hypotheses are also consistent with the same data. Children of intelligent parents probably have superior environmental stimulation toward the development of intelligent behavior.[5] The data also support the hypothesis that the interaction between heredity and environmental opportunity influences the development of intelligent behavior.

[4] H. S. Conrad and H. E. Jones, "A Second Study of Familial Resemblance in Intelligence," in *Original Studies and Experiments*, Thirty-ninth Yearbook of the National Society for the Study of Education, Part II (Chicago: University of Chicago Press, 1940), pp. 97–141.

[5] E. A. Milner, "A Study of the Relationship between Reading Readiness in Grade One School Children and Patterns of Parent-Child Interaction," *Child Development*, 22 (1951), 95–112.

Efforts to distinguish and isolate hereditary and environmental influences on behavior development have not been notably successful. "How" either heredity or environment can influence behavior development is probably a more profitable inquiry.

An individual's heredity consists of the specific genes that he receives from his parents at conception. Any behavioral characteristic that is hereditary must be linked to specific genes or gene combinations. However, the problem of determining the genetic base of some characteristics is complicated by the fact that genes combine in an infinite variety of ways, and the genetic influence on behavior may be more or less direct. Anastasi has pointed out four ways in which hereditary factors may influence behavior.[6]

1. A genetic deficiency may preclude the possibility of normal development. For example, certain metabolic disorders are genetic and impair development to such an extent that environmental stimulations cannot compensate for the deficiency.

2. A genetic defect may interfere with development by inhibiting the individual's ability to interact efficiently with his environment. Hereditary deafness, for example, interferes with normal social interaction, and the individual's development is correspondingly affected. However, in these cases, appropriate training may compensate for the handicaps imposed by genetic deficiency. The genetic deficiency does not preclude "normal" development if appropriate training experiences can be developed.

3. Genetic deficiencies may make an individual susceptible to certain physical diseases. If the individual actually contracts the disease, development may be inhibited because he cannot attend school regularly or because he develops patterns of social interaction that interfere with his ability to profit from educational experiences. However, the individual may also compensate for the effects of illness, such as restricted social activity, by developing interests and abilities which enhance other aspects of his development. The genetic deficiency in these instances has a relatively less direct influence on behavior development, since retardation in development depends on the contraction of the disease to which the individual is susceptible and his reaction to the effects of the disease.

4. Genetic factors determine many physical characteristics of the individual. Some physical characteristics influence the extent to which environmental opportunities will be available to the individual. Sex, skin pigmentation, and body build, all of which have a hereditary base, are related in particular cultures to the environmental opportunities available to an individual. The boy whose body build is comparatively small may not be able to participate in athletics. Certain need satisfactions and opportunities for development will not be available to him. He is not

[6] A. Anastasi, "Heredity, Environment, and the Question 'How?'" *Psychological Review*, 65 (1958), 197–208.

doomed to defective development, but his pattern of development will differ in some respects from that of a boy with a larger and more muscular body build.

These examples indicate that the influence of heredity on development is relatively indirect, and that behavioral characteristics are not directly inherited. Moreover, many aspects of behavior development are modifiable even when they are influenced by hereditary factors. Heredity sets the initial limits to the organic conditions under which behavior development occurs, although the mere presence of requisite organic conditions does not guarantee behavior development.

INFLUENCE OF ENVIRONMENT

Discussing motivation and learning in the preceding chapters, we assumed that variations in environment influence behavior change. Each experiment demonstrates that changes in the environment (experimental manipulations) produce a behavior change (when significant changes occur); and therefore that the behavior is controlled by environmental influences. In this section we will discuss the more general ways in which environmental influences affect the pattern of development.

By **environment** we mean all the stimuli that impinge on an individual from conception to death. Environment includes the physical setting in which the individual lives. However, we will consider such a setting an environment—in the psychological sense—only if it is a *stimulus* influencing the responses an individual is likely to make. A child growing up in a slum, whose parents are divorced, and whose companions are mostly delinquents, is influenced only to the extent that these characteristics of the setting are stimuli which evoke certain kinds of behavior. That such differences in physical and social settings are likely to be correlated with differences in psychological environment has been amply demonstrated.[7]

We may distinguish between two general classes of environmental

[7] See J. Clausen and J. R. Williams, "Sociological Correlates of Child Behavior," in H. W. Stevenson, ed., *Child Psychology*, Sixty-second Yearbook of the National Society for the Study of Education, Part I (Chicago: University of Chicago Press, 1963), pp. 62–107; A. Davis and R. Havighurst, "Social Class and Color Differences in Child-Rearing," *American Sociological Review*, 11 (1946), 698–710; E. E. Maccoby and P. K. Gibbs, "Methods of Child-Rearing in Two Social Classes," in W. E. Martin and C. B. Stendler, eds., *Readings in Child Development* (New York: Harcourt, Brace & Co., 1954), 380–396; J. R. Williams and R. B. Scott, "Growth and Development of Negro Infants: IV. Motor Development and Its Relation to Child-Rearing Practices in Two Groups of Negro Infants," *Child Development*, 24 (1953), 103–121; R. Sears, E. Maccoby, and H. Levin, *Patterns of Child-Rearing* (Evanston, Ill.: Row, Peterson & Co., 1957).

influences. The first of these classes may be called *organic* environmental influences; that is, the environment may be directly or indirectly responsible for organic changes in the individual. Inadequate prenatal environment and birth injuries are examples of organic environmental factors that may influence development. Dietary deficiencies of pregnant women, for example, appear to be related to the intellectual development of their children.[8] Severe incapacitation from disease without accompanying injury to the higher neural centers is another example of an organic environmental influence on development. In this case, however, the influence is less direct. Incapacitation, either permanent or temporary, may inhibit the individual's interaction with the environmental influences likely to stimulate his development, but it does not necessarily doom him to complete or permanent retardation. Other kinds of organic environmental influences may influence behavior development. A physically weak boy may take advantage of environmental opportunities to build up his body strength and muscular development. His associates will react differently to him now that he is stronger, and his own self-concept and subsequent behavior will probably change correspondingly.

The second class of major environmental influence is called *behavioral;* that is, environmental influences serving as direct stimuli to behavior change. The variables discussed in the preceding chapters are behavioral environmental influences, designed to bring about some degree of behavior change. For example, a class discussion of the rise of dictatorships is designed to encourage increased understanding of certain historical events. The environmental influence is the class discussion, and its immediate effect is supposed to be the behavior change of increased understanding.

While environmental influences are direct stimuli, the scope and permanence of their influence vary considerably. The socioeconomic setting in which a child grows up has, typically, a pervasive influence on his development. An illustration of the effect of a restricted environment on development is provided in Table 12–1. Two groups of children were studied.[9] The mountain children lived in isolated valleys in the Blue Ridge Mountains; the village children lived at the foot of the mountains in a less isolated area. The mountain children also attended less adequate schools. Both of these groups were from "deprived" environments. The

---

[8] R. F. Harrell, E. Woodyard, and A. I. Gates, *The Effect of Mothers' Diets on the Intelligence of the Offspring* (New York: Bureau of Publications, Teachers College, Columbia University, 1955).

[9] V. Sherman and C. B. Key, "The Intelligence of Isolated Mountain Children," *Child Development*, 3 (1932), 279–290.

effect of these environments is reflected in the test scores of the children. Both groups scored, on the average, below 100, which is the average score usually obtained from an unselected group of children; however, the scores of the mountain children run lower than those of the village children. Successive decreases in score are also apparent through the older ages, but once again the decreases are smaller for the village children. The data illustrate only one aspect of retarded development, but intellectual retardation would have pervasive effects on other aspects of development. The gradual regression also suggests the pervasive influence of the total environment. Other studies of similar environments provide comparable data.[10]

TABLE 12-1. *Mean IQ of mountain and village children in relation to age (from Sherman and Key).*

Age	Pintner-Cunningham Test		National Intelligence Test		Goodenough Draw-a-Man Test		Pintner-Patterson Performance Tests	
	Mt.	*Vill.*	*Mt.*	*Vill.*	*Mt.*	*Vill.*	*Mt.*	*Vill.*
6– 8	84	94			80	93	89	
8–10	70	91		117	66	82	76	93
10–12	53	76	66	101	71	69	70	87
12–14			67	91	69	73	83	
14–16			52	87	49	70	73	

Bilingualism in childhood is an environmental factor that may have a more or less pervasive influence on development depending on the accompanying circumstances. In some cases, bilingualism adversely affects personality development; [11] in others, it serves as a symbol of status, which in turn enhances emotional adjustment and personality development.[12]

The various environmental influences we have described suggest the variety of ways in which such factors are related to behavior development. Again, caution is recommended to the teacher making inferences

[10] See, for example, H. M. Skeels and E. M. Fillmore, "Mental Development of Children from Underprivileged Homes," *Journal of Genetic Psychology, 50* (1937), 427–439.

[11] N. T. Darcy, "A Review of the Literature on the Effects of Bilingualism upon the Measurement of Intelligence," *Journal of Genetic Psychology, 82* (1953), 21–57.

[12] A. Anastasi and F. A. Cordova, "Some Effects of Bilingualism upon the Intelligence Test Performance of Puerto Rican Children in New York City," *Journal of Educational Psychology, 44* (1953), 1–19.

about the "causes" of a particular pattern of development he observes. Such inferences are hypotheses which must be tested. Extensive knowledge of a child's genetic and environmental background, as well as of present influences on his development, are required before we can assess the relative influence of any of the factors.

INTERDEPENDENCE OF HEREDITY
AND ENVIRONMENT

A commonly held theory is that heredity and environment are mutually interdependent.[13] That is, the contribution of either set of factors to behavior development is determined by the contribution of the other set. An environmental factor, such as an intellectually stimulating home environment, will have different influences on individuals with different genetic backgrounds, since genetic background will influence the extent to which an individual is likely to profit from this environment. Similarly, two individuals of identical genetic background, such as identical twins, will develop differently if environmental influences on them are different.[14] Behavior development depends on the combination of hereditary and environmental influences.

Because the relationships among factors influencing development are extremely complex, we would expect to find many variations in the developmental patterns of children; however, we also find relative consistencies in these patterns. In the following section we will outline several principles accounting for the variation in developmental patterns; at a later point in the chapter, we will discuss the factors contributing to the relative consistencies we observe.

VARIATIONS IN DEVELOPMENT
PATTERNS

DIFFERENCE IN RATE OF DEVELOPMENT
AMONG INDIVIDUALS

Children differ from one another in their rates of development. The rate of development may be estimated by plotting behavior change against

---

[13] For a critical analysis of theories about the relationship of heredity and environment, see A. Anastasi, *Differential Psychology,* 3rd ed. (New York: Macmillan Company, 1958), Chapter 3.
[14] H. H. Newman et al., *Twins: A Study of Heredity and Environment* (Chicago: University of Chicago Press, 1937).

time. For example, suppose that we measure a child's height at successive ages. We may then estimate the changes in height for successive years by plotting the child's height at each age level. We obtain a picture of the child's rate of growth from this curve. If we obtain data on the growth of a large number of children and compute the average height of these children at each age level, we obtain a picture of "average" development at various ages. However, such "average" curves mask the range of variation

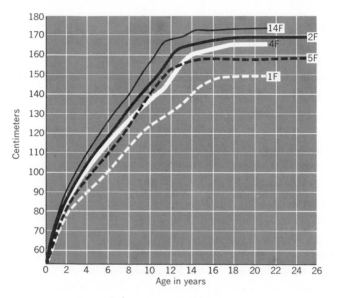

FIGURE 12–1. *Curves of stature by age for five girls in the Berkeley Growth Study, including the tallest female in the group (14F), the shortest, and three girls of intermediate height (from Bayley).*

in height at any age and the differences in rate of development for individual children.

In Figures 12–1 and 12–2 are plotted individual curves of development for two different kinds of behavior change.[15] Note the steady progression in development apparent in both sets of curves. Observe also the variation in attained level at any one age level. Compare also the amount of change per year for each of these curves. In Figure 12–1, we note that early

[15] N. Bayley, "Individual Patterns of Development," *Child Development,* 27 (1956), 45–74.

superiority or inferiority is not necessarily maintained except for the most obviously superior or inferior children. Child 4F, for example, is eventually taller than child 5F, even though at age 12 their relative positions were reversed.

For all of these children the developmental pattern is relatively simi-

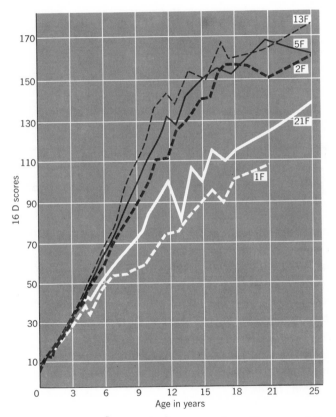

FIGURE 12-2. *Individual curves of intelligence of five girls (from Bayley).*

lar when plotted over a long period of time, though rates of development vary considerably. Development is also more or less rapid at different periods in each child's life.

The variations in the rate of development depend upon both physiological changes and the kinds of experiences that children are having. Changes in physical structure will affect development, and these changes in turn may influence other aspects of development. The boy who is slow in developing physically may feel inferior because he is smaller and weaker than other boys of his age. The fact that he is not so strong or tall as other boys of his age may prevent him from participating in sports and receiving need satisfactions that come from participating in these highly valued activities of boys. His feelings of inferiority may spread to other

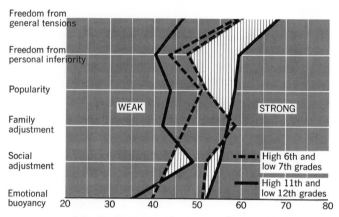

FIGURE 12–3. *Contrasts between the ten highest and and the ten lowest of 78 boys on total score on strength tests at 17.5 years. Popularity and emotional buoyancy as rated by staff observers during "free-play" activity; general tensions, personal inferiority, and adjustments as shown on a personal-social inventory filled out by the boys. The ten strongest boys are shown to have been high on freedom from general tensions in grades 6–7 and higher yet in grades 11–12, but the ten weakest were more inferior in this respect in grades 11–12 than earlier. (From Jones.)*

activities. He reacts to his experiential opportunities in a limited way, and his development is correspondingly affected.

In one extensive investigation of the relationship between motor performance behavior and general development, Jones compared the ten strongest and the ten weakest boys in a class on a variety of social and emotional factors at two different periods in their schooling.[16] The data are diagramed in Figure 12–3. In elementary school the two groups are comparatively similar, particularly on such traits as amount of tension and

[16] H. E. Jones, *Motor Performance and Growth* (Berkeley: University of California Press, 1949).

popularity. However, by the senior year of high school the two groups are farther apart, the weaker group scoring lower and the stronger group scoring higher on these traits. In this period of the boys' schooling, the culture places great value on physical prowess and physical attributes. The child's physical appearance affects his social relations with other children and determines the extent to which he can participate in the highly valued athletic activities of the school. We are not surprised to find the weaker boys feeling more inferior and being less popular in their senior year than they were in grade school.

The teacher, who sees a child for a relatively short period of his life, must be careful in drawing conclusions about the child's rate of development. Generally, a child who is *markedly* advanced or retarded in development will remain that way over the period of growth. However, a child who is advanced in development at one time in his life may not be at another, because other individuals have caught up with and surpassed him. Neither will a child who is behind others in development necessarily remain there; he too may catch up by very rapid growth in a relatively short period of time.

DIFFERENCES IN RATE OF DEVELOPMENT IN EACH CHILD

The psychological functions of each child vary in their rate of development. When we say that the child develops as a whole, we do not mean that every aspect of the child's personality is developing at the same rate or that, if we measure different functions of personality, we will find each of these functions at the same general developmental level. Some children will be comparatively advanced in all aspects of development, and others will be comparatively retarded. But the typical pattern, when the rates of development of the behavior patterns of an individual child are compared with each other, is a differential pattern of rate of development. In Figure 12–4, several different kinds of behavior change in one child are plotted.[17] Here, again, we see the same pattern as we observe when two children are compared. The various functions plotted in this diagram follow an over-all pattern of increasing development, but the rate at which any one function develops varies with time, and the pattern of variation is different for each function.

[17] W. C. Olson and B. O. Hughes, "Concepts of Growth: Their Significance for Teachers," *Childhood Education,* 21 (1944), 54.

DIFFERENCES IN CULTURAL EXPECTANCIES AT VARIOUS AGE LEVELS

Parents and teachers continually observe the changes in children. The results of the extensive studies of child growth and development have been diffused throughout our society through the media of mass communication. As a consequence of this widespread attention to child development, there has emerged an *expected* pattern of child development. For descriptive purposes, we divide the course of development into periods, such as infancy, early childhood, late childhood, prepuberty, adolescence, and adulthood. Each of these periods is frequently considered as an age span, and is understood to describe common levels of development in children who have reached these age levels.

Perhaps the most prevalent example of conceptualizing development as a series of stages with given characteristics is reflected in the popular picture of the adolescent and the expectations associated with it. The adolescent is commonly expected to be moody, irresponsible, rebellious, a daydreamer, perhaps somewhat awkward, moon-struck, difficult to live with, and generally a remarkably different person from what he was five or ten years earlier in his life. This general cultural expectancy frequently predisposes us to see the adolescent in terms of this stereotype rather than in terms of his own unique patterns of behavior. More important, we fail to see how social influences are producing his characteristics. We frequently do not understand changes in these stimuli may lead to changes in his behavior, desirable or not.

One of the major consequences of widely shared cultural expectancies for age groups is that children in these age groups are accorded differential treatment. We do not expect to treat the eight-year-old and the sixteen-year-old in identically the same way. However, not all eight-year-olds are alike. Some eight-year-olds are more like nine- or ten-year-olds than they are like eight-year-olds. Other eight-year-olds are not so well developed as the typical eight-year-old child. While children within any age span typically are more like other children within that age span than they are like children in other age groups, the range of variability within any age group is great.

This age-grouping conception of development ignores the interdependence of all phases of development and the complexity of the interrelationships among factors affecting behavior development. Until the child approaches the point of maximum development within the limits imposed by his native endowment and environmental opportunities, his pattern of development is essentially continuous. For example, a child's rate of development in height and weight gradually decreases, but the child is getting taller and heavier until he reaches his maximum development in

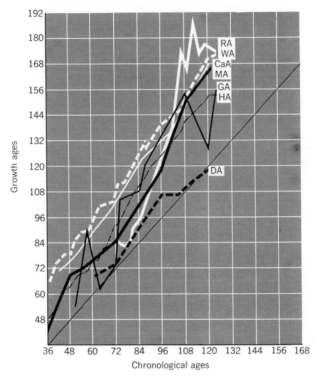

FIGURE 12–4. *Contrasted growth in reading age (RA), weight age (WA), carpal age (CaA), mental age (MA), grip age (GA), height age (HA), dental age (DA) (from Olson and Hughes).*

these functions. At some periods in his development, he will appear to the casual observer not to be growing at all, but his growth is being maintained although it is less apparent. Such variations in rates of development may influence us to overlook the continuities in development. There are no sharp breaks in the pattern of development; an eight-year-old does not drop suddenly the behavior patterns of an eight-year-old and immediately take on the behavior patterns of a nine-year-old.

In Figure 12–5 the mental ages of 167 girls at age eight, twelve, and sixteen are plotted.[18] The mental ages of some sixteen-year-old girls are below those of some eight-year-old girls. Some of the twelve-year-old girls have higher mental ages than over half of the sixteen-year-old girls. However, a sixteen-year-old girl is different in many ways from an eight-year-old girl, even though the eight-year-old girl may be brighter than the sixteen-year-old. One of the explanations for these differences is that

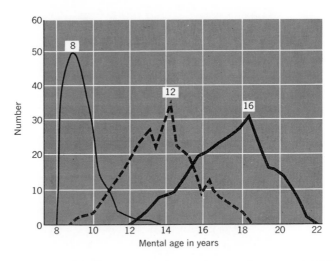

FIGURE 12–5. *Distributions of mental ages of 167 girls at ages 8, 12, and 16 (after Dearborn and Rothney).*

differential treatment is accorded to the two age groups. For example, in a fifth-grade class, we will typically find some fifth graders who are as bright as eighth graders, but these fifth graders are not treated in the same way as eighth graders. We do not expect as much of the fifth grader as we do of the eighth grader. Parents typically supervise more of the younger child's activities. The younger child's present stage of development necessarily limits his opportunities for learning. He is not strong enough to participate extensively in body-contact sports, as an older child is both permitted and frequently encouraged to do. Many of the environmental stimuli which evoke development in the older child are not provided for the younger child. In other words, the psychologically different environments of children of different ages result in substantial differences in

[18] W. F. Dearborn and J. W. M. Rothney, *Predicting the Child's Development* (Cambridge, Mass.: Sci-Art Publishers, 1941), p. 325.

development, even though a younger child may be more advanced developmentally in some respects.

RANGE OF DIFFERENCES
IN INDIVIDUAL DEVELOPMENT

The discussion of development in the preceding two sections has emphasized the variation in patterns of development. The reader may have gained the impression that this variation is so great that developmental patterns cannot be ordered in any systematic way. We may think that a

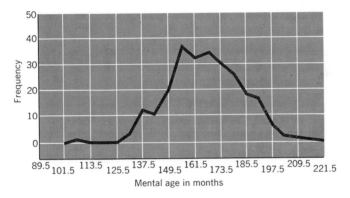

FIGURE **12–6.** *Distribution of mental ages of 256 girl subjects at age 12 in Harvard Growth Study (adapted from Dearborn and Rothney).*

teacher should expect infinitely varied patterns of development in his class. But data on differences in patterns of development may be organized in such a way that the range of variation in any behavior pattern for a group of children is predictable.

DISTRIBUTIONS OF INDIVIDUAL DIFFERENCES

We have noted that the complex interaction of hereditary and environmental influences results in considerable variation in behavior development. We expect to find various levels of development for any behavior pattern in a group of children. We may order these differences in the following way. First, select a particular behavior pattern that we may wish to study, such as intellectual development. Second, choose a random sample of a group within which we wish to study variation, such as school-age children or sixteen-year-old girls. Third, obtain a measure of development status for each child in the sample—by giving an intelligence test, for example. At this point we will have scores for each child in the group, and we may count how many children have obtained each score. These data may be conveniently plotted as in Figure 12–6.[19]

Note the clustering of frequencies around the average; the majority of children obtain scores at or near the average. We find decreasingly fewer students with progressively higher and lower scores. This ordering of the data gives us a picture of how variation in developmental status for one behavior pattern is distributed, and it enables us to make predictions about the variation in this kind of behavior to be expected in a random sample of children.

This kind of distribution of differences is obtained for many behavior patterns, both over a wide age range and within specific age levels.[20] Such a distribution does not give us information on individual developmental rates, for which we would need plots of individual changes over time. Neither may we infer from these data the relative influence of particular factors affecting the development of a child. What we do have is a picture of how variation is distributed for a group. But other data are required before we can make judgments about individual rates of development and the factors influencing them.

INDIVIDUAL DIFFERENCES IN SCHOOL ACHIEVEMENT

Within any class, the achievement in school subjects may range anywhere from two to six or more grades above and below the grade at which the child is actually placed. Hildreth,[21] in summarizing a series of studies on the range of achievement in classes, notes that scores for one group of seven-year-olds ranged from the first- to the sixth-grade level; for a group of ten-year-olds they ranged from the first- to the ninth-grade level. Cook has pointed out:

[19] Dearborn and Rothney, p. 175.

[20] Not all behavior patterns are distributed in this way. Another kind of distribution is illustrated in F. H. Allport, "The J-Curve Hypothesis of Conforming Behavior," *Journal of Social Psychology*, 5 (1934), 141–183.

[21] G. Hildreth, "Individual Differences," in W. S. Monroe, ed., *Encyclopedia of Educational Research*, rev. ed. (New York: Macmillan Company, 1950). See also F. Tyler, "Individual and Sex Differences," in C. W. Harris, ed., *Encyclopedia of Educational Research*, 3rd ed. (New York: Macmillan Company, 1960), pp. 680–688. See also W. W. Cook, "Individual Trait Differences in Public Schools with Implications for School Organization and Curriculum Development," *Teachers College Journal*, 19 (1947), 56–59, 67–70.

When a random group of six-year-olds enters the first grade, two percent of them will be below the average of four-year-olds in general mental development and two percent will be above the average of eight-year-olds. Disregarding the extreme two percent at either end, there is a four-year range in general intelligence. By the time this group has reached the age of twelve (sixth-grade level) the range will have increased to almost eight years.[22]

REDUCING THE RANGE OF INDIVIDUAL DIFFERENCES

Most teachers are aware of the range of differences in their classes, and they have tried to provide learning experiences appropriate to the various levels of developmental status. One common assumption is that "good teaching" will reduce the *range* of individual differences—or, in other words, given appropriate learning experiences, all students can achieve the same level of development in school achievement. Although differences among students result in part from the influence of factors over which the teacher has no or little control, nonetheless, "good teaching" *may* reduce the range of individual differences in some behavior patterns. The evidence on this latter point is mixed. Some investigators have found increased variability after a specific learning experience; others have not.[23] This research does suggest that the assumed relationship between learning experience and reduction in range of individual differences is too broadly conceived to permit precise investigation.

Note that we have not yet defined "good teaching"—having used only a vague and general conception, as it is frequently stated. Consider for a moment what might be meant by "good teaching." We are probably referring to many variables, each of which in turn may be composed of still other variables. "Good teaching" probably presupposes that students are motivated to learn; we have already seen how complex is the variable called "motivation." In fact, every variable we have discussed in the

[22] W. W. Cook, "Individual Differences and Curriculum Practice," *Journal of Educational Psychology*, 39 (1948), 141. For these reasons, some schools are trying ungraded primary classes. The effects of this innovation have not been fully assessed as yet; evaluating this change is complicated because other organizational changes, such as team teaching, are made concurrently. See J. Goodlad and R. Anderson, *The Nongraded Elementary School* (New York: Harcourt, Brace, 1959), and R. Anderson, "Organizational Character of Education: Staff Utilization and Deployment," *Review of Educational Research*, 34 (1964), 455–469.

[23] For one summary and analysis of this research, see L. E. Tyler, *The Psychology of Human Differences*, 2nd ed. (New York: Appleton-Century-Crofts, Inc., 1956), 466–472. F. Tyler (see note 21), evaluating studies on this problem, concludes that variability increases under training with complex tasks, decreases with simple tasks.

preceding chapters is related in some way to "good teaching." To explore this problem adequately, we will have to investigate the influence of variation in each and all of these variables on individual differences. From this kind of research we could determine precisely which variables in a learning experience are likely to reduce the range of individual differences in a specific behavior pattern.

At the present time the safest generalization we can make is this: The range of individual differences is not likely to be reduced by the learning experiences typically provided for children in a system of mass education. The range of individual differences is a fact with which every teacher must contend. There is no way to eradicate the differences among children. These differences originate because children have different capacities, have had different learning experiences, and are developing at different rates. However, some differences—differences arising from living in inferior or degrading home environments such as slums, or from being exposed to an inferior education, or from being treated as inferior persons—among children are remediable. But even when these conditions are changed, some differences among children will remain because their capacities are different and their environments will not be identical.

When a teacher meets a class, he must expect a range of differences. Such a range will typically be found at every age and grade level. We label children "third graders" and "fourth graders," but we cannot think of the children in the third-grade class as identical units. The educational significance of this fact is that a uniform curricular experience cannot be provided for every child at a given age level. Learning experiences are more likely to be effective in promoting development when they are geared to individual levels of development.

PREDICTING DEVELOPMENTAL STATUS

Data on developmental patterns are gathered in two ways: by a *longitudinal* study, in which a group of children is tested or measured on a given behavior pattern over a period of time; or by a *cross-sectional* study, in which children at different age levels are measured on the behavior pattern. Using data from both kinds of studies, we may compute the average of these measurements at each age level, and plot a continuous curve of averages. Figure 12–7 is an example of curves derived in this way. Such curves give us a picture of the typical pattern of development for specific kinds of behavior.[24] These curves reflect *relative consistencies*

[24] Dearborn and Rothney (see note 18), p. 312.

in development for many children. The relative consistencies suggest that the factors influencing development affect large numbers of children in substantially the same ways. Environmental opportunities may be relatively constant within a culture or subculture, so that children in it tend to profit from the opportunities in substantially the same manner. As the data on the mountain children illustrate (see Table 12–2), when the

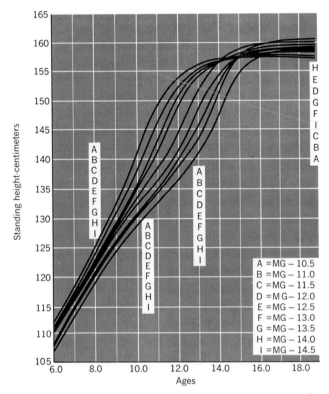

FIGURE 12–7. *Growth trends in average standing height of nine groups of girls having different ages at maximum growth* (MG). (*From Dearborn and Rothney.*)

environmental opportunities are different from those in other parts of the culture, the pattern of development may be also different.

Another factor contributing to consistency in development among children is physical growth toward maturity, which provides the biological basis for behavior development. Again, when physical maturation is inhibited by some environmental influence, such as disease, or by hereditary deficiency, the pattern of development may be affected. The observed consistencies in development are the basis for the concept of "normal" development. The usual meaning associated with this concept is this: A child's development is "normal" when it approximates the average pattern of development for children of his age and with his environmental opportunities.

The term "normal" has unfortunate connotations. Its use by some people is meant to include the idea that marked deviations from the average are "abnormal" and therefore undesirable. However, although an exceptionally bright child is markedly deviant from the average of his age group—he obtains high scores on intelligence tests, and he may perform in a superior fashion both academically and socially—he is rarely "abnormal" in all the ways connoted by this term.[25] Some people also use the concept to mean that the pattern of average development is the "expected" pattern of development for all children. The use of the term "normal" to connote "expected" is inappropriate if we mean by "expected" that children should be like the "average." But a defensible meaning may be given to the term "expected" because we may use curves of average development to make predictions about children's development. If, for instance, a distribution of differences in developmental status is similar to that in Figure 12–6, we would predict that a majority of the children tested have attained a developmental status approximating the average. Less than half the children will be markedly different from the average of the group. In other words, "expectations" may be predictions about the developmental status of a group of children.

It is important to distinguish between the data provided in developmental curves and the inferences we make from them. A developmental curve describes developmental status. *We cannot infer from this curve what children ought to be like, although we may predict what a group of children will probably be like in developmental status if they are similar to the children on whom the measurements were made.*

EARLY AND LATE MATURATION

The concept of "normal" development has limited usefulness, but it has been the basis for the development of the concepts of *early* and *late* maturation. A boy or girl who matures early reaches maximum development before the average age for attaining it. A boy who matures late is

---

[25] L. M. Terman et al., *Mental and Physical Traits of a Thousand Gifted Children* (Stanford, Calif.: Stanford University Press, 1925). The latest volume on this study is L. Terman and M. Oden, *The Gifted Group at Mid-Life* (Stanford, Calif.: Stanford University Press, 1959).

one who attains his maximum growth beyond the average age for reaching it. Figure 12–7 illustrates an application of these concepts to one aspect of physical growth. The girls who reached their maximum height at an earlier age are early-maturing girls; as the curves indicate, these girls were consistently taller than the late-maturing girls until all girls had reached their maximum growth. This fact illustrates another important principle. Since the curves indicate that the early-maturing girls eventually fell below the average height for these groups, it is clear that early superiority or inferiority is not necessarily maintained over a long age span. We cannot predict on the basis of relatively early maturity in any one behavior pattern that the child will necessarily be superior in that pattern at a later date.

The concepts of early and late maturing cannot be applied to all developmental patterns, but mainly to those that are closely tied to physical maturation. Because early and late maturing are defined in terms of the average age of maximum growth, a pattern of development must reflect a point or period of maximum growth before the concepts may be used appropriately. Maximum growth cannot be defined for some behavior patterns because the pattern of development continues throughout the life span. For example, recent evidence suggests that intellectual development may continue through adult life, even though the rate of development is not as rapid as in the early years of life.[26] The concepts of early or late maturation have little meaning in relation to this kind of development.

Some people have argued that there are consistencies in over-all development—that, for example, a person who is developing rapidly in one respect is likely to be developing rapidly in all others; in other words, that developmental rates among behavior patterns are positively correlated. Research evidence does not support this hypothesis. For example, rates of change in physical and intellectual functions are not highly correlated.[27] The relation between physical and mental development is probably indirect. A child who is experiencing rapid physical development is more likely to expand his environmental contacts, which in turn may facilitate his intellectual and social development.

[26] N. Bayley, "On the Growth of Intelligence," *The American Psychologist*, 10 (1955), 805–818.
[27] E. M. Abernethy, "Relationships between Mental and Physical Growth," *Monographs of the Society for Research in Child Development*, No. 7, (1936). The most recent comprehensive review of the literature on this problem may be found in D. H. Eichorn, "The Biological Correlates of Child Behavior," in H. W. Stevenson, ed., *Child Psychology*, Sixty-second Yearbook (see note 7), pp. 32–52.

RELIABILITY OF PREDICTIONS OF
DEVELOPMENTAL STATUS

The teacher should be concerned with a child's probable pattern of development, as well as with his present status. Many decisions about appropriate learning experiences require predictions of future developmental status. At the end of the elementary school period a decision is made about the kind of high school curriculum in which a child is most likely to succeed. A comparable kind of decision may be made by the elementary school teacher about the child who has demonstrated musical talent. Should this child be encouraged to develop his talent on the assumption that he may be able to succeed in a musical career? Implicit in both of these decisions is a prediction that on the basis of the child's present development he will or will not reach a level of development requisite for success in some activity.

How reliably can future status be predicted? Our discussion of the factors influencing variability in development suggests that such predictions are not likely to be perfectly reliable. Obviously, we cannot know all the factors which may influence development at some future date; we can only assess the probability that a person at a present level of development will be at a comparable level at some future time. We can ask this sort of question: What is the probability that a child who now demonstrates intellectual superiority will be intellectually superior in five years?

The general question whether future status can be reliably predicted cannot be answered until we ask a host of more specific questions—questions like the one posed about intellectual superiority. Still, some general principles have emerged from the extensive investigations of this question:

1. A long-term prediction is likely to be less reliable than a short-term prediction.[28] For example, we are more likely to be accurate in predicting a fifth-grade child's sixth-grade school achievement than in predicting his high school or college achievement.
2. The greater the superiority or inferiority in development, the more likely it is that this superiority or inferiority will be maintained. The child

---

[28] R. L. Thorndike, "The Effect of Interval between Test and Retest on the Constancy of the IQ," *Journal of Educational Psychology*, 24 (1933), 543–549; " 'Constancy' of the IQ," *Psychological Bulletin*, 37 (1940), 167–186; "The Prediction of Intelligence at College Entrance from Earlier Tests," *Journal of Educational Psychology*, 38 (1947), 129–148.

who is highly superior to his age-mates in intellectual development is likely to maintain his superiority.

Important qualifications of both these principles must be made. A long-term prediction is more likely to be reliable if it is made at a later phase in the development of a behavior pattern. For example, predictions of a child's mature intellectual status tend to be more reliable the older the child is at the time the prediction is made. There are important technical reasons for this greater reliability of prediction at later ages. For example, intelligence tests administered to younger children probably do not measure the same aspects of intellectual development that are measured by tests used with older children. Performance on early tests is not highly correlated with performance on tests administered later.[29] Still, the greater reliability of these predictions in later phases of development may also result from the cumulative effects of development. An older child may be reaching the point of maximum growth in the development of a behavior pattern, and the stabilization of development contributes to the improvement of prediction. In other aspects of development, previous learning influences the extent to which a child is likely to profit from new experience. Finally, development may have stabilized because environmental opportunities for additional development are not available. In all of these cases, our prediction of future status is more likely to be reliable because development has stabilized.

A qualification must also be made to the second principle. Recall the description of changes in height for early- and late-maturing girls (see Figure 12-7). Relative superiority in this kind of development was not uniformly associated with later superiority. The more direct the influence of native endowment on behavior development, the less reliable are our predictions of relative future status. In other words, early superiority is not highly correlated with final status in this development pattern. Again, if the prediction of future status is made near the time of maximum growth, it is more likely to be accurate.

Our predictions of future developmental status are probability statements made on the basis of present knowledge. Such statements are more or less reliable depending on the information available for making them. Many factors—the kinds of test instruments we use to assess develop-

[29] N. Bayley, "Consistency and Variability in the Growth of Intelligence from Birth to Eighteen Years," *Journal of Genetic Psychology*, 75 (1949), 165–196. See also K. P. Bradway and C. W. Thompson, "Intelligence at Adulthood: A Twenty-Five Year Follow-up," *Journal of Educational Psychology*, 53 (1962), 1–14.

mental status, the stability of the environmental conditions in which the child is developing, and the time interval between present and predicted status—are related to the accuracy of our predictions.

The following example will illustrate the difficulties in making predictions of future developmental status.

Intensive study of life-history data and intelligence-test performance frequently reveals events in a child's life that have probably affected his general level of intellectual functioning.[30] Figure 12–8 shows the IQ performance and life events for three children. There is no proof that the

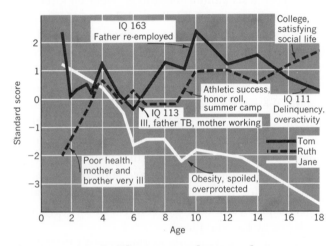

FIGURE 12–8. *Three cases showing changes in general ability from two to eighteen years (from Honzik, MacFarlane, and Allen).*

life events listed in the figure caused the changes in IQ score. There is reason to believe, however, that events of this kind will affect intelligence test performance and general intellectual functioning. Compare the performance of Ruth and Jane. Ruth's initial performance is relatively low, but she gradually progresses: after a series of rewarding experiences, the curve continues on up through college. Jane, on the other hand, starts high and shows a progressive decline. Tom shows considerable variability, with his intelligence-test scores ranging from very high points to

[30] M. P. Honzik, J. W. MacFarlane, and L. Allen, "The Stability of Mental Test Performance between Two and Eighteen Years," *Journal of Experimental Education,* 17 (1948), 309–324.

much lower points. The teacher who had Tom in class at age 10 may have thought that he was an exceptionally intelligent boy. If the teacher had been asked at that time to make a prediction about Tom's future status, he perhaps would have suggested that Tom ought to go on to college and enter one of the professions. If a teacher were studying Tom's intelligence test performance at age 16, he would predict that Tom's academic future was not particularly bright.

In this discussion we have emphasized two important principles: (1) The development of a child's psychological functions may vary considerably over a period of time. (2) Predictions of future status may be more or less reliable, depending upon the time when the child is being studied and the stage of development of the particular functions being studied. The teacher's primary task is to test the child's present stage of development, since learning experiences are planned for this stage of development. The relationship of present to future status is crucial when important decisions for the child's life must be based on predictions about his future. When such predictions must be made, they can probably be improved if we take into account the whole pattern of the child's previous development, the comparative development of the specific functions we are assessing, and the span of future time bridged by our prediction. If the child's pattern of development in any function has been irregular, if he is at a stage in which the function has not reached its maximum level of development, and if we are making a long-term prediction, then our predictions are likely to be less reliable. On the other hand, if the functions we are assessing are relatively stabilized, if there has been a relatively consistent pattern of development, and if our prediction is for a relatively short period of time, then the prediction is more likely to be reliable.

THEORIES OF DEVELOPMENT

We have been emphasizing both the variability and the consistency in behavior development. Now we will discuss some theories that attempt to account for the consistencies in behavior development and relate development to effective socialization. One theory links two familiar ideas: (1) that similarities in behavior development result in part from common processes of maturing; (2) that similarities also result from the influence of common environmental opportunities. As we have seen, these two categories of influence on development are mutually interdependent.

DEVELOPMENT AS MASTERY OF DEVELOPMENTAL TASKS

The theory of *developmental tasks* proposes that these two factors are interrelated in such a way that a pattern of expectations for development emerges. This pattern of expectation is reflected in the kinds of behavior patterns a child is expected to acquire and in the developmental goals he is expected to attain. In turn, socializing agents, such as parents and teachers, reward the child for attainments and punish him in some way for failures to achieve developmental expectations.

Concept of a Developmental Task

We can conceive of the entire span of development, from infancy into adulthood, as a series of tasks which the individual must perform successfully. Some of the tasks are closely related to bio-physical development: a child must learn to walk and to feed himself. Other tasks have been set by the society in which the child is growing up. In our society, for example, a child is expected to prepare himself for gainful employment. As a child masters the sequence of tasks set for him, he becomes an adjusted member of his society; that is, he acquires behavior that is rewarded and valued in his culture.

Havighurst, who introduced the concept of the developmental task into psychological and educational thinking, defines *a developmental task* as follows:

. . . a task which arises at or about a certain period in the life of the individual, successful achievement of which leads to his happiness and to success with later tasks, while failure leads to unhappiness in the individual, disapproval by the society, and difficulty with later tasks.[31]

Note that the definition of a developmental task relates behavior development to social expectations for development. But social expectations are not associated with every aspect of behavior development. Hobbies, for example, may have little if any direct social significance since there are no uniform and consistent social expectations that children develop hob-

---

[31] R. J. Havighurst, *Developmental Tasks and Education* (New York: Longmans, Green & Co., 1952), p. 2.

bies. In other words, developmental tasks represent accomplishments expected of all children unless there are special incapacitating conditions, such as the effects of disease, that make these accomplishments impossible. The definition also requires a systematic time sequence in the arrangement of these tasks. They do not occur at random; instead, one accomplishment sets the stage for the next.

What are these developmental tasks? Empirical investigation is needed to identify the general social expectations for development, as well as to find the extent to which accomplishment of any one task affects the accomplishment of other tasks and general social adjustment. Lists of such tasks, at present, are based on inferences from sociological and psychological investigations. As might be expected, such lists vary with the preferences of different authors for classifying social expectations. These descriptions, however, have some common characteristics, which suggest the general nature of developmental tasks.

Characteristics of Developmental Tasks

Table 12–3 gives a list—adapted from Havighurst—of developmental tasks in American society. The following factors should be noted:

1. *Some of the tasks are common to all cultures and occur at about the same period of time in every culture.* The tasks are closely tied to the biophysical structure and development of the child. In all cultures children learn to walk—and they learn to walk at about the same age.

2. *The character of some of the tasks is closely tied to specific cultures.* The age for choosing an occupation varies from culture to culture, as does the age for marriage. The kinds of occupations available in a society, the mores of courtship, the social customs associated with marriage, vary from one culture to another. While children in different cultures may be mastering the same general tasks, the specific behavior patterns differ and the ages at which the tasks are to be accomplished are different. For culturally-bound tasks, variations may take place even within a given culture over a period of time. The age of marriage is gradually changing in American society, so that the average age of marriage is now a younger one than it was twenty or thirty years ago.

3. *Some of the tasks need to be learned only once at a given period in life.* The child learns to walk, and, once he has mastered this task, he is never required to learn it again unless he is handicapped in some manner. A child learns to take solid foods and to feed himself; and, again, except in

TABLE 12–3. *List of developmental tasks (from Havighurst).*

Age Span	Developmental Tasks
Infancy and Early Childhood	Learning to walk
	Learning to take solid foods
	Learning to talk
	Learning to control elimination of body wastes
	Learning sex differences and sexual modesty
	Achieving physiological stability
	Forming simple concepts of social and physical reality
	Learning to relate oneself emotionally to parents, siblings, and other people
	Learning to distinguish right and wrong, developing a conscience
Middle Childhood	Learning physical skills necessary for ordinary games
	Building wholesome attitudes toward oneself as an organism
	Learning to get along with age-mates
	Learning an appropriate masculine or feminine social role
	Developing fundamental skills in reading, writing, and calculating
	Developing concepts necessary for everyday living
	Developing conscience, morality, and a scale of values
	Achieving personal independence
	Developing attitudes toward social groups and institutions
Adolescence	Achieving new and more mature relations with age-mates of both sexes
	Achieving a masculine or feminine social role
	Accepting one's physique and using the body effectively
	Achieving emotional independence of parents and other adults
	Achieving assurance of economic independence
	Selecting and preparing for an occupation
	Preparing for marriage and family life
	Developing intellectual skills and concepts necessary for civic competence
	Desiring and achieving socially responsible behavior
	Acquiring a set of values and an ethical system as a guide to behavior

TABLE 12-3. *List of developmental tasks (from Havighurst).—Continued*

Age Span	Developmental Tasks
Early Adulthood	Selecting a mate Learning to live with a marriage partner Starting a family Rearing children Managing a home Getting started in an occupation Taking on civic responsibility Finding a congenial social group
Middle Age	Achieving adult civic and social responsibility Establishing and maintaining an economic standard of living Assisting teen-age children to become responsible and happy adults Developing adult leisure-time activities Relating oneself to one's spouse as a person Accepting and adjusting to the physiological changes of middle age Adjusting to aging parents
Later Maturity	Adjusting to decreasing physical strength and health Adjusting to retirement and reduced income Adjusting to death of spouse Establishing an explicit affiliation with one's age group Meeting social and civic obligations Establishing satisfactory physical living arrangements

unusual circumstances, the essential features of development need not be relearned.

4. *Some tasks are recurrent, and new aspects of the tasks must be learned at different ages.* The child's learning of his sex role is a continuous kind of task. The child begins to learn his sex role quite early in life and establishes his major expectations about how a boy or a girl is to behave. His conceptions of his sex role will vary with increasing experience, and he will modify his behavior accordingly. The adolescent, for example, discovers a whole new dimension of his sex role with the advent of puberty.

5. *Some of the tasks occur at different ages or in different forms within*

a given society. A child from a lower socioeconomic group will probably make decisions about occupations and marriage earlier than the middle- or upper-class child who postpones marriage and career for more years of education. A child from the lower socioeconomic class also learns different attitudes and values for some tasks. A middle- or upper-class child is taught to inhibit aggression or to express it in more subtle ways—restrictions not characteristically placed on the child in a lower social-class environment. Sexual mores also vary with social classes.[32]

Developmental Tasks and Personality Development

The basic assumption in the theory of developmental tasks is that failure to meet developmental tasks successfully results in poor adjustment because failure in one task increases the probability of failure in others. This assumption appears to be reasonable. As the child develops, his needs are met through social interaction. His needs for approval, affection, prestige, and status can be satisfied if he acquires behaviors that are socially valued. Society ties the satisfaction of needs to the achievement of developmental tasks, and it also fosters the development of needs which motivate the accomplishment of these tasks. Failure to master a task prevents need satisfaction, and inadequate behavior development interferes with adaptive goal-seeking behavior. Inappropriate behavior development also evokes social punishment and exclusion.

Research evidence suggests that this assumption is tenable. Schoeppe and Havighurst [33] studied intensively the achievement of thirty adolescents on five developmental tasks: (1) learning an appropriate sex role; (2) achieving emotional independence of parents and other adults; (3) developing conscience, morality, and a set of values; (4) getting along with age mates; (5) developing intellectual skills. From their data the investigators concluded that the early period of adolescence is the crucial one, in which changes in level of accomplishment take place, and that the level of achievement on these specific tasks is largely determined by age 13. (This and the other conclusions might be modified with an investigation of a larger number of students.) They also found that satisfactory relations with fellow students seem to be closely linked to accomplish-

[32] See A. C. Kinsey, W. B. Pomeroy, and C. E. Martin, *Sexual Behavior in the Human Male* (Philadelphia: W. B. Saunders Co., 1948).
[33] A. Schoeppe and R. Havighurst, "A Validation of Developmental and Adjustment Hypotheses of Adolescence," *Journal of Educational Psychology,* 43 (1952), 339–353. See also R. F. Peck and R. J. Havighurst, *The Psychology of Character Development* (New York: John Wiley & Sons, 1960).

ment of the other tasks, that achievement of the appropriate sex role is important, and that failure to accomplish one task adequately may be compensated by more successful accomplishment of another task.

The data also indicate that adolescents do not move through these developmental tasks in lock-step fashion. A variety of factors will determine whether a child will accomplish a particular task. A highly socialized adolescent is successful on most, if not all, of these tasks, whereas a child making a generally poor adjustment has failed at one or more of the tasks.

The differences in rate of accomplishment on the tasks result in part from the particular environmental influences that children meet. The influence of the culture is transmitted through significant individuals in the culture, such as parents and teachers. A study of the factors affecting success in the accomplishment of developmental tasks has revealed "that children whose parents exercise severe control in their formative years were hindered on accomplishment of the tasks. . . . Such severe parental control stifles the growth of emotional, personal security and results in the child's sensing himself as worthless as an individual; when he feels ego-impelled this inner feeling brings with it guilt feelings which he must repress." [34]

The social conditions under which children learn developmental tasks affect both the level of accomplishment and the manner in which they learn the tasks. A convenient way of conceptualizing the developmental tasks is to visualize them on a continuum of dependence-independence. As the child accomplishes each of the developmental tasks, he acquires greater personal autonomy and also greater social freedom. Each of the tasks requires some assumption of personal responsibility and initiative by the child. The successful accomplishment of a task is hampered if parents and teachers in his environment rigidly restrict freedom so that his learning opportunities are limited. Developmental tasks are essentially problems that the child must face; and, as we noted when studying problem solving, a problem cannot be solved unless the problem solver has freedom to explore his environment and to investigate alternatives for the solution of the problem. Freedom to explore and test alternative solutions to the problems posed by developmental tasks is a necessary condition for successful accomplishment of these tasks.

[34] A. Schoeppe, E. A. Haggard, and R. J. Havighurst, "Some Factors Affecting Sixteen-Year-Olds' Success in Five Developmental Tasks," *Journal of Abnormal and Social Psychology*, 48 (1953), 49.

The School and Developmental Tasks

The theory of developmental tasks, according to Havighurst, has important implications for the organization of learning experiences:

First, it helps in discovering and stating the purposes of education in the schools. Education may be conceived as the effort of the society, through the school, to help the individual achieve certain of his developmental tasks.

The second use of the concept is in the timing of educational efforts. When the body is ripe, and society requires, and the self is ready to achieve a certain task, the teachable moment has come. Efforts at teaching, which would have been largely wasted if they had come earlier, give gratifying results when they come at the *teachable moment*, when the task should be learned.[35]

This point of view does not demand that the entire curriculum be organized around developmental tasks. However, the school assumes responsibility for the achievement of many of these tasks, while sharing the responsibility for some tasks with other social agencies. The essential point of this conception is that relating the learning experiences provided by the school to the accomplishment of developmental tasks would presumably insure consistency in the development of the child. Furthermore, the arrangement of learning experiences into "teachable moments" (though this concept must be defined behaviorally or operationally) is likely to increase the chance of a child profiting from the learning experiences provided by the school.

This theory suggests a way of relating the factors influencing development to the pattern of learning experiences which are provided to promote development. The theory calls our attention to the fact that social demands as well as maturational factors influence the course of development. Further, it relates development to the adjustment of the child as a member of society. In these respects, it is useful for clarifying our conception of the relation of development to the organization of learning experiences.

The theory does not solve all the problems associated with analyzing and predicting development that we have outlined in this chapter. All the concepts bearing on variability of development are also applicable to the

[35] Havighurst (see note 31), p. 5.

accomplishment of developmental tasks. Individuals will vary in the rate at which they accomplish the tasks, but a general consistency in the total pattern of development will be apparent—largely because the opportunities for learning many of the tasks are age-graded. The probable relationship between accomplishment of developmental tasks and success in the many specific tasks the child must accomplish in school suggests the relevance of this theory. Radical or frequent failure in the major phases of development probably has a pervasive effect, spreading over the entire life of the child and affecting his performance in many particular learning activities.

CONCEPT OF A CRITICAL PERIOD
FOR LEARNING

Recent experimental work has suggested that there may be a *critical period* for some behavior acquisitions,[36] a period when the organism must learn or the learning will never be achieved. The behavior acquired during critical periods is that necessary for the organism's survival and existence as a member of a species. The concept has little application to educational practice at present, though it may have some meaning for understanding the development of personality, particularly during the early periods of socialization.

Concepts such as critical periods and developmental tasks and a popular educational concept, readiness,[37] are all used to account for a commonly observed phenomenon; that is, that some organisms appear to have difficulty achieving new behavior acquisitions, even though their general capacities for learning are adequate. Critical-period notions account for lacks in primary socialization. Developmental-task ideas account for the relation between successive socialization achievements. Readiness, the most general concept, describes what a learner needs as he enters a new learning experience.

Critical-period phenomena, if they exist, have the most drastic consequences for behavioral development. If the learner does not acquire a

[36] J. P. Scott, "Critical Periods in Behavioral Development," *Science*, 138 (1962), 949–958; E. H. Hess, "Imprinting," *Science*, 130 (1959), 133–141; E. H. Hess, "Imprinting in Birds," *Science*, 146 (1964), 1128–1139.

[37] For a critical review of this concept and its educational applications, see F. T. Tyler, "Issues Related to Readiness to Learn," in Sixty-third Yearbook of the National Society for the Study of Education, Part I (Chicago: University of Chicago Press, 1964), Chapter IX, pp. 210–239.

behavior change linked to such periods when they occur, he is handicapped and development suffers. These consequences would appear in difficulties in learning during the child's formal educational experience. In theory, such deficiencies would not be remediable.

Concepts such as those of developmental tasks and readiness assume that amelioration is possible by a proper arrangement or rescheduling of learning opportunities. However, specific steps for remedying deficiencies usually must be invented by the teacher.

Final judgment cannot be rendered on the notion of critical periods. The major implication of developmental-task concepts has been indicated by Havighurst. The notion of developmental readiness, while enjoying considerable popularity among educators, has little specific value for the teacher except in alerting him to diagnose the child's present behavioral capacities as a prelude to planning a learning experience. It also encourages him to arrange learning opportunities sequentially, so that the learner is prepared by one experience for the next. Remediation may be necessary before new learning experiences can take place. In brief, learning begins where the learner is.

PIAGET'S DEVELOPMENTAL THEORY

Jean Piaget has proposed one of the most comprehensive of developmental theories.[38] His theory is enjoying considerable popularity at present; and, if valid, it has many implications for both educational theory and practice.[39] His methodology, however, has been criticized by many psychologists in this country. He does not perform experiments in the ways described in the first chapter of this book—with control groups, random assignment of subjects to treatments, and similar ways of creating an experiment. In addition, for many of his results, he has not used, or at least has not regularly reported, tests of statistical significance.

Piaget begins by making systematic observations of some behavioral phenomenon; he then relates his observations to a theoretical framework that he has developed. He calls his method "the clinical interview," and in it he explores a child's thinking about some natural phenomena with which Piaget has confronted him. His summaries of these observations and his theorizing about them constitute his reporting.

---

[38] For a critical analysis and comprehensive description of this theory, see J. Flavell, *The Developmental Psychology of Jean Piaget* (New York: D. Van Nostrand Company, 1963).

[39] J. Piaget, "The Genetic Approach to the Psychology of Thought," *Journal of Educational Psychology*, 52 (1961), 275–281.

Piaget's Theory and Learning

Piaget's theory—a complete description of cognitive development over the significant early years of life, with implications for a total theory of personality and intelligence—is not a learning theory in the same sense that the concept is used in this book. It is a developmental theory designed to account for the major changes observed in the life span. Such a theory must inevitably be related to theories of learning. However, it has not been to date, nor is it at all obvious how such interrelations can be made—at least at any level below the most abstract one. Therefore, because this book has taken a learning rather than a developmental approach to instructional problems, we have not studied Piaget to this point. Here, we will simply note the major features of his theory and indicate how they might influence our thinking about educational problems.

Structure and Function in Piaget's Theory

Piaget's theory is basically a qualitative description of the development of intelligence. He is primarily concerned with describing the changes in the structure of intellectual activity; intellectual functions do not change, content does, by accretion. The major intellectual functions are adaptation and organization, the former having two components: assimilation and accommodation.

Adaptation is a process whereby the person changes as he interacts with his environment in such a way that beneficial future interactions are promoted. Through accommodation, the person fits himself to those aspects of the environment with which he is interacting. A child, for example, seeing a heated bimetallic bar bend upward must necessarily adapt to this observation; he must assimilate the observation to what he already knows about objects and their properties. He must accommodate his conceptions to the new observation.

Adaptation proceeds through organizations called schema. It is not simply a process of change, but of change within stability, where stability is provided by cognitive structures. As we have seen, these structures change, either by reorganizing within themselves in assimilating or by accommodating. The purpose of Piaget's investigations is to describe the kinds of changes that occur in these structures.

The processes of adaptation are the invariant functions in this developmental process. The contents of intelligence, as noted earlier, vary widely from age to age. Structures change more slowly, but their changes are the major landmarks in Piaget's theory.[40]

Stages of Development in Piaget's Theory

The first period, from birth to approximately age two, is the *sensory-motor period of development*. As we saw early in this chapter, development proceeds by finer discriminations; Piaget adopts a similar point of view. The new-born child is a set of reflexes. During this first period of development, the child organizes his sensory world. He acquires more differentiated responses to particular stimuli—he reacts to objects as single things, not as classes of things. Symbolic thought is not apparent.

During the major stage following this period, the child begins the process of symbolization, eventuating in the stage of *concrete operations*, in which the child begins to group objects. At this time the child is capable of performing logical operations on these classes—combining them, reducing them; and he also learns the logical properties of measurement, such as its invariant characteristics under certain transformations. Weights of objects do not change when their shapes are rearranged; lengths remain invariant under movements. This stage is completed roughly by age eleven. The relation of these changes to the school experience of the child is obvious when the whole span of this period is considered. Not so obvious is the occurrence of changes under direct educational experiences; that is, does it make a difference in how the child learns about addition of groups—whether he is taught counting as enumeration of sets or of single objects? Will the changes be hastened?

The last stage, that of *formal operations*, is reached in the adolescent period. Here the child learns to think in the structure of hypothetical-deductive thinking. He learns to consider the possible, to see what he has observed as one instance of it. He learns to experiment and to theorize. At this point, he has reached intellectual maturity; he has acquired the structures appropriate to mature thought.

This concept of stages has caused the most difficulty in understanding and evaluating Piaget's theory. The earlier notion was that he thought the stages occurred at fixed points in development. Evidence simply did not

[40] M. Wallach, "Research on Children's Thinking," in H. Stevenson, ed., *Child Psychology*, Sixty-second Yearbook for the National Society for the Study of Education, Part I (Chicago: University of Chicago Press, 1963), pp. 236–276.

support this notion.[41] However, Piaget's idea seems to be that the ages he provides are approximations of when changes are likely to occur.

The essential notion here is that the stages do occur in the order described, and that the emergence of the stages is in the order described and necessarily so. This is, of course, the most important theoretical concept, and the one on which the theory hinges.

This notion of stages also exemplifies the genetic character of the theory. If the theory were not genetic in this sense—predetermined evolution of stages—it would be developmental only in the very general sense of successive changes. The changes could then be reinterpreted as the products of learning. Experimenting would ferret out the variables controlling these changes, which then could be explained as the products of learning.

Implications of Piaget's Theory

The genetic character of Piaget's theory is the point on which its acceptability turns for many psychologists. The ferment around Piaget's ideas at present is largely on this point. Its significance is fairly obvious.

Any genetic theory assumes a built-in determinism. If intellectual development proceeds as Piaget describes it, certain kinds of intellectual experiences are precluded; for instance, can you teach an elementary school child to experiment while he is in the stage of concrete operations? The notion of genetic determinism in intellectual development opens up a host of theoretical questions of this kind and raises practical issues about what the learner brings to the learning experience. As we have seen throughout this chapter, developmental theories force us to consider where the learner is at the time of learning, how modifiable he may be at that moment. Piaget's kind of theory forces us to look still further. Is the learner's present state simply the sum or product of his previous learnings, or does it reflect the stage he has reached in a predetermined growth sequence?

The learning psychologist claims that behavior changes are largely the result of learning experiences; they are acquisitions, extinctions, modifications under the control of environmental variables. The developmental psychologist leans to the argument for a predetermined growth sequence.

[41] See data, for example, presented in A. Bandura and F. J. McDonald, "Influence of Social Reinforcement and the Behavior of Models in Shaping Children's Moral Judgments," *Journal of Abnormal and Social Psychology*, 67 (1963), 274–281.

These two ways of looking at behavior change are not irreconcilable, but they have yet to be integrated into one systematic theory. Piaget has stimulated theorizing and experimenting about these issues. We will inevitably have to rethink these problems. More important, the whole realm of intellectual development has been brought into this controversy. It remains to be seen what the specific implications of his theory will be for educational practice. We have seen some preliminary attempts at applying Piaget's ideas in Suchman's and Taba's work (Chapters 7 and 6).

SUMMARY

In this chapter we have studied how behavior patterns change with time. We have explored such questions as: Is there a consistent pattern of personality development? To what extent are there similarities in the personality development of individuals in the same culture? To what extent are there differences in development among individuals? What are the sources of both consistency and variability in personality development?

1. Development may be described as a continual process of acquiring new responses and integrating them with previously acquired responses. The possibilities for future development are determined in part by the individual's present state of development; that is, the effects of development are cumulative. An individual's present state of development is the "equipment" with which he meets new opportunities for development. Present developmental status determines the likelihood of continued development—as well as the ways in which this development is likely to progress.

2. The pattern of personality development is influenced by hereditary and environmental factors. Behavior patterns as such are not directly inherited, but hereditary factors may have a more or less direct influence on behavior development. Some environmental factors have a relatively indirect influence on development; others are direct stimuli to behavior development.

3. Hereditary and environmental factors influence both the consistency and the variability of personality development. Hereditary and environmental influences form a pattern from which we can determine the probability of relatively consistent development. Varying combinations

of hereditary and environmental influences account for the variations in behavior development among individuals.

4. Variations within general patterns of consistency characterize individual development. The behavior patterns of an individual vary in rate of development. When individuals are compared in terms of their developmental status within a specific behavior pattern, a wide range of variation in developmental status is typically found. This range of individual differences reveals the effect of the compound influence of hereditary and environmental factors.

5. Teachers must frequently make, or help children to make, decisions based on predictions of future developmental status. Variations in the rates of individual development make such predictions difficult.

6. Growth curves derived from measuring the developmental status of large groups of children provide us with a picture of average developmental change within a given group of children. However, individual development may vary considerably, although not necessarily, from this "typical" pattern of development.

7. Long-term predictions of developmental status tend to be less reliable than short-term predictions. Such long-term predictions are more likely to be reliable if the development of the behavior pattern being studied is relatively superior or inferior. In general, predictions of developmental status require adequate information on the genetic and environmental history of the child as well as on factors likely to influence present development. Caution is urged in making predictions about the developmental status of behavior patterns more directly influenced by maturational factors, for advanced or retarded status in these patterns is not highly correlated with final developmental status.

8. The theory of developmental tasks has been introduced to account for the relative consistencies in development among members of the same culture or subculture. Developmental tasks require the acquisition of behavior patterns and the attainment of goals which satisfy cultural expectations for development within a society. A major hypothesis in this theory is that successful accomplishment of developmental tasks increases the likelihood of progressive development and a correspondingly successful adjustment to and assimilation into society. This conception of development as a succession of problems to be solved may be used to coordinate the efforts of the school and other social agencies in promoting the development af the child.

9. Another major conception of development states that behavior de-

velopment is strongly influenced by changes occuring at critical periods. At these periods, certain kinds of learning must occur or the organism will never acquire these behaviors in his subsequent development. Although this theory has little application to education presently, because research is not sufficiently advanced, it would have considerable significance for education if found to be relatively valid.

10. Theories of this kind and the concepts of development tasks and learning readiness alert the teacher to an important idea: The effects of learning are relatively permanent. Each new learning experience must contribute to future development. Remediation of past deficiencies may be necessary before progress can be made.

11. Piaget's theory of cognitive development is one of the most comprehensive developmental theories, one potentially having important implications for educational practice. Although Piaget has presented data to support his idea, many psychologists have criticized his experimental method. To date, his ideas have not been integrated into the major theories of learning; nor has his theory been completely accepted.

Piaget's theory describes the evolution of intellectual behavior through a series of stages from the sensory-motor stage to the acquisition of formal operations (by which Piaget means *the use of the hypothetical-deductive mode of thinking*). These stages represent cognitive structures the person acquires through the processes of adaptation and organization. The major implication of this theory for educational practice is not yet clear. Presumably, as in other developmental theories, educational practice would be geared to the stage of the child's cognitive development. A few educational applications are being tried in which the child is led through the preliminary stages to the more advanced one of complex thinking.

STUDY AND DISCUSSION QUESTIONS

1. Listed below are three broad categories of behavior patterns. Describe the kinds of expectations that adults hold for an eight-year-old, a fourteen-year-old, and an eighteen-year-old for each of these behavior patterns.

   a. Table manners.

   b. Personal grooming.

   c. Friendship relations.

2. At each age level in the above behavior patterns, what kinds of experience related to the age of a child might facilitate the learning of the expected behaviors?

3. Again, using the same behavior patterns as in Question 1, describe the response differentiations required as the child develops more complex patterns of behavior. What response integrations are required as the behavior patterns become more complex?

4. In what ways may a "mature" ten-year-old and a "mature" sixteen-year-old be alike? In what ways may these two children be different? What criteria are you using to evaluate maturity?

5. You may have heard some adults refer to a characteristic, such as becoming "easily angered," in the following way: "He gets that from his father's side of the family." Can you offer a different explanation for the development of this particular characteristic?

6. Describe some learning experiences that may be available to boys that are not available to girls. Describe some kinds of learning experiences for girls that may not be available to boys. In what ways will these different kinds of experiences influence development?

7. A teacher, in discussing a child with his mother, suggested that the child might be mentally retarded. The mother stated that she was not surprised, since an older brother and sister had been slow in school. These children were first-generation Mexican-American. How would you account for this child's apparently low level of achievement and intelligence test performance?

8. Refer to the Kahl study presented in Chapter 4. Discuss the influence of hereditary and environmental factors on the college aspirations of the boys studied in this investigation.

9. Classify each of the following as an organic or behavioral environmental influence. Suggest some of the ways each of these environmental factors may influence behavior development.

   a. A poor diet.

   b. A nagging mother.

   c. A home in a "deprived" neighborhood.

   d. An older brother.

10. Review the data presented on the intelligence test performance of the mountain children. How might heredity have influenced the development of intelligence among these children? How might the interaction of heredity and environment account for the performance of these children on intelligence tests?

11. You observe a boy in your class who is somewhat smaller than the other boys in the class and who is also comparatively shy and quiet. Do you see any relationship between these two observations? Suggest some hypotheses that would relate physical size to personality traits such as shyness or quietness. What other factors may account for the development of these traits?

12. Describe what seem to be the characteristics of adolescents as many adults expect to find them. Suggest factors in the experiences of children which may account for the development of these characteristics.

13. A parent complains that his son is irresponsible in taking care of his personal property, such as his clothes and athletic equipment. The parent attributes this irresponsibility to the fact that the boy is now an adolescent. Trace the kinds of experiences that this child may have had over a period of years that would account for his failing to learn responsible behavior.

14. Assume that you are counseling a high school sophomore who wants to become an engineer. What predictions about future development status will you have to make in order to counsel this pupil? What information do you need in order to make these predictions?

15. Assume that you are studying an eighth-grade student with a view to counseling him about his high school program. Which of the following predictions can you make most reliably?

    a. A prediction of his grades in senior English.

    b. A prediction of his probable performance in junior-year mathematics.

    c. A prediction about his height and weight when he is a junior.

    d. A prediction about his sociability when he is a junior.

    What information would you need in order to make any of these predictions.

16. Refer to Figure 12–8. In what ways might the life events listed in this figure account for the changes in intelligence test performance for each of the three children whose scores are reported in this figure?

17. Refer to Table 12–3. Note that Havighurst has listed "achieving a masculine or feminine social role" as a developmental task for middle childhood and adolescence. In what ways might the period of infancy and early childhood influence the learning of an appropriate sex role? Does the omission of this developmental task from later periods in life imply that the appropriate sex role is to have been learned by the end of the adolescent period?

18. Describe some ways in which a child in the period of middle childhood learns to "achieve personal independence." What kinds of experiences may contribute to successful accomplishment of this developmental task?

19. Select any one of the periods from infancy to adolescence and describe the kinds of learning experiences that the home, school, and other social institutions provide to facilitate the accomplishment of the developmental tasks listed for that period.

20. Suggest some ways in which failing to select and prepare for an occupation in adolescence may interfere with the total development of a child.

21. Describe the ways in which various aspects of the curriculum and extra-curriculum may contribute to the accomplishment of the developmental

tasks of adolescence. In what ways do the experiences provided in the elementary school contribute to the accomplishment of the developmental tasks of middle childhood?

RECOMMENDED READINGS

A. Anastasi. *Differential Psychology*, 3rd ed. New York: The Macmillan Co., 1958, Chapters 3 and 4.

A. Baldwin. *Behavior and Development in Childhood*. New York: The Dryden Press, 1955.

L. Carmichael, ed. *Manual of Child Psychology*, 2nd ed. New York: John Wiley and Sons, 1954.

S. Pressey and R. Kuhlen. *Psychological Development through the Life Span*. New York: Harper & Brothers, 1957.

J. H. Flavell. *The Developmental Psychology of Jean Piaget*. New York: D. Van Nostrand Company, 1963.

J. L. Fuller and W. R. Thompson. *Behavior Genetics*. New York: John Wiley and Sons, 1960.

R. Havighurst. *Developmental Tasks and Education*, 2nd ed. New York: Longmans, Green & Co., 1952.

J. Piaget. *The Language and Thought of the Child*. New York: Harcourt, Brace & Co., 1926.

——————. *Judgment and Reasoning in the Child*. New York: Harcourt, Brace & Co., 1948.

——————. *The Moral Judgment of the Child*. New York: Harcourt, Brace & Co., 1932.

H Stevenson, ed. *Child Psychology*. Sixty-second Yearbook of the National Society for the Study of Education, Part I. Chicago: University of Chicago Press, 1963.

H. Werner. *Comparative Psychology of Mental Development*, rev. ed. New York: International Universities Press, 1948.

PART THREE

THE SOCIAL
CONDITIONS OF
LEARNING

CHAPTER THIRTEEN

TEACHER - STUDENT INTERACTIONS

In the preceding chapters we studied ways in which many different variables influence behavior change. Some of these variables were characteristics of the environments in which learning takes place. Others were characteristics of the individual learner. Still others, which we will discuss in this chapter, are characteristics of the relations between people—for instance, teacher and student.

At several places we discussed variables over which the teacher has relatively direct control; among these were amount of guidance, arrangement of practice sessions, and provision of opportunities for need satisfaction in learning experiences. We assumed that the teacher plays an important role in organizing learning experiences. And, of course, the teacher's role is never confined to the impersonal; once he has arranged the environment, he is a major force in it. His own behavior is a stimulus influencing pupil behavior.

These ideas may be illustrated in a hypothetical case. Mr. Johnson announces that he will deduct one point for every error in punctuation in the themes to be turned in by his senior English class. This announcement presumably follows some hypothesizing on Mr. Johnson's part about the probable effect of these penalties in reducing punctuation errors. The students in Mr. Johnson's class probably see this announcement as consistent with what they have come to expect from him: he is not likely to ignore errors; he expects careful work; he usually penalizes mistakes. He may also be friendly or unfriendly, kind or harsh, quick to praise good work or sparing in his praise. These patterns of expected behavior are the students' impressions of Mr. Johnson's personality. From your own experience as students, recall the descriptions that have been applied to teachers you have known: "rough," "demanding," "a nice guy," "tough but fair," "too easy on students," "a tough marker." Each of these terse phrases conveys an impression of a person. When we say someone is a "tough marker," we expect that only a few "A" grades will be given to students in his class; we expect to meet a "no-nonsense" kind of person—a person who expects maximum effort and performance from students.

We expect the students' impressions of the teacher's personality to influence their interactions with him. Mr. Johnson's announcement takes on additional meaning when seen in the light of what students think of him as a person. Assume for the moment that they know from previous experience that he is not likely to enforce his penalties. How would you expect his announcement to influence the punctuation of student themes? Conversely, suppose that the announcement is one of a long list of penalties that Mr. Johnson has been imposing and enforcing. Making any prediction is difficult without more information about the class, but we can imagine a number of possible reactions. This latest addition to the penalty list might be the "last straw" for the students; they might revolt, either openly or covertly. On the other hand, errors in punctuation might decline, but a marked decrease in creativity might appear in the themes; the students might be less willing to "let themselves go." And yet none of these unfortunate reactions might occur if the penalty is seen as a reasonable demand, which Mr. Johnson tempers with understanding and encouragement. We cannot decide which of these alternatives is likely to occur until we know more about the students' conceptions of Mr. Johnson as a person. However, these alternative results appear to be reasonable possibilities when the meaning of the announcement is studied in the total context of teacher-pupil relations.

A MODEL OF INTERPERSONAL INTERACTION

In this section we describe a simple **model** of two-person interactions.[1] That one person acts as a stimulus event for another person is a simple idea to understand. Imagine the following incidents. You are walking down the street, you meet a friend, you say "Hello." There may have been a hundred other people on that street, none of whom you addressed. The sight of your friend evokes a response. In turn, he says "Hello"; you are a stimulus evoking his behavior.

However, it is apparent that your behavioral patterns vary from person to person, and from group to group. With some people you are more cautious, more reserved; with others, you work freely and easily. Let us imagine for a moment a matrix such as that drawn in Figure 13–1. Along the horizontal axis, we represent at each point some response that you are able to make in the presence of another person. There are a very large number of these responses. Along the vertical axis are the responses that another person can emit in your presence. Which of all these responses will be linked in an interaction pattern? These links will not be created randomly, that much we can be sure of.

Apply a principle we have used throughout this book. If the responding is rewarding by providing need satisfaction, interaction patterns will evolve; if a set of pairings is aversive or costly, they will not appear or, if they do, will be abandoned. You and your friends chat because the verbal interchanges are pleasant. You avoid topics, questions, and ways of saying things that are aversive. We avoid the grouch, are careful around the touchy person, watch ourselves around the cynic and the person given to quick sarcasm.

These examples describe general patterns of rewarding and costly interactions. Americans have been socialized to be friendly and open. Not all people nor all interactions even in our society are of this character, but the same principle applies. A "rough" character is receiving some rewards, perhaps in the form of achieving social control, for his behavior. Some social groups have established interaction patterns which on the surface appear to be aversive. However, the group members have learned the

[1] This model is described in greater detail and applied to many different kinds of interactions in J. W. Thibaut and H. H. Kelley, *The Social Psychology of Groups* (New York: John Wiley and Sons, Inc., 1959).

meaning of the responses; and, to maintain a position in the group, they interact in ways that seem strange to the nonmember. In such groups, gentility may be costly.

Apply these ideas to teachers and students. A student will talk with a teacher when such talk is rewarding; when the costs of the interaction go up, it will be avoided. The same idea applies to the teacher. The teacher is most likely to interact with those students whose responding is rewarding to him. This may be easily observed in many classes. Watch whom the teacher calls on when questioning. You will find some teachers persist-

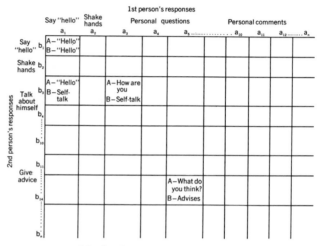

FIGURE 13–1. *A matrix of interaction patterns.*

ently calling on the same students—the students who most frequently give the right answer. McNeill found some empirical support for this observation.[2] He used an auto-instructional program to teach boys and girls some reading skills. In this treatment—in which each child had identical opportunities to respond and identical lessons, including words of praise—the boys were not inferior to the girls in reading acquisitions. But in the subsequent and comparable learning task directly under a teacher's control, they were. When the teachers were asked to nominate students who were not ready or motivated for reading, they nominated significantly more boys. The drop from the first to the second test was positively correlated with the number of negative comments about the children received from the teacher.

[2] J. D. McNeill, "Programed Instruction versus Usual Classroom Procedures in Teaching Boys to Read," *American Educational Research Journal*, 1 (1964), 113–119.

Although a superficial observer may be quick to say that they were "playing favorites," these teachers did not malevolently intend to deprive the boys of reading opportunities; they were probably even unaware of their different modes of responding. They simply found interactions with girls more rewarding, those with boys more costly. It hardly comes as news that adult females are not overly fond of some boys' characteristics, such as their aggressiveness or impulsiveness; but we may not have suspected how easily this attitude may lead to teacher behavior that impedes learning.

COMPARISONS AMONG INTERACTION OPPORTUNITIES

Although there are constraints on our freedom to select interaction opportunities, a person may drop out of an interaction or initiate a new one. What determines the stability of an interaction? Let us assume that a person has a set of evaluative concepts of the potential interactions available to him. That is, he knows which are likely to be rewarding and which are not. This conception need not be precise; it may even be erroneous, but it is what he thinks will happen. It may be the product of direct experience or a generalization from this experience, or based on indirect evidence, such as somebody else's judgment ("Oh, you won't like him").

For every interaction in which a person is engaged, he has alternatives that may be more or less attractive. If an alternative interaction is more attractive, he is likely to seek it out. A simple form of the phenomenon may be seen in a classroom. The students are interacting with the teacher; they may also interact with each other. Generally, though not invariantly, we would expect the interactions among peers to be more attractive. Although there are rewards to be gained from interaction with the teacher, it also puts costly demands on the student—most notably in the form of task orientation, work, and effort. Is it surprising that students will talk to each other or attempt to engage in other interactions with each other, which the teacher sees as "discipline problems"?

THE SOCIAL POWER OF THE TEACHER

In the overwhelming majority of teaching situations, the teacher is not free to choose his students, and the students are not free to choose their teacher. A class is a kind of captive audience; and, though you may not have thought so, the teacher is a captive of his class. Obviously, the pattern of interaction that emerges depends on what each member brings to this situation, what each does in it. However, the teacher has a social position that differs from that of his students. His social role has psychological significance independent of his personal style.

Social power may be defined as *the ability to influence the behavior of another person*. Both the teacher and the student have some social power over each other. French and Raven have described five kinds of social power which will be useful to consider.[3]

One kind is *reward power*, in which one person controls the rewards another person seeks. The teacher may provide many different kinds of need satisfaction for students, some clearly related to their long-term goals. A second type is *coercive power*, the power to administer aversive stimuli or punishments, to make the interaction costly. Obviously, the teacher has some coercive power, but it is limited. He can fail a student; he can be harsh or sarcastic; he can demand excessive amounts of work. The third kind of power is *legitimate power*, in which the person to be influenced recognizes the legitimacy of the influence efforts. He accepts the "right" of the other person to influence him in certain respects. This "right" derives from a common set of values that both persons share and of which one of them is regarded as the custodian. A teacher, for example, prohibits fighting in his class—not on the grounds that he is personally offended by it, but because he has the right to enforce the code to prohibit it. When the values are not shared, the teacher is not usually accorded this kind of power, though he may control students in some other way. Fourth is *referent power*, that based on identification with the other person. This kind of power was considered when we discussed imitative behavior and reference groups. The fifth kind of power is *expert power*, where a person is influenced because he recognizes the superior knowledge and skill of another person. A teacher may have any or all of these sources of social power, whereas students have only reward and coercive power.

These types describe what one person attributes to another or recognizes another person as having. A teacher controls such rewards as praise, but a student who does not need this kind of reward from a teacher does not see the teacher as having reward power. The teacher's social position

---

[3] J. R. French and B. Raven, "The Bases of Social Power," in D. Cartwright and A. Zander, eds., *Group Dynamics: Research and Theory*, 2nd ed. (Evanston, Ill.: Row, Peterson & Co., 1960), pp. 607–623. There is fragmentary evidence that the bases of a teacher's social power are perceived differently when students respond positively or negatively to the teacher's control measures. See W. J. Gnagey, "Effects on Classmates of a Deviant Student's Power and Response to a Teacher-Exerted Control Technique," *Journal of Educational Psychology*, 51 (1960), 1–8.

gives him legal power to influence; the students' recognition of his "right to influence" is what gives him legitimate power. There are many students who simply do not attribute this power to the teacher. I have heard students announce to teachers, "You can't change my ideas," where the implication was clearly "You have no right to try."

Many people want the teacher's social influence to derive from legitimate, referent, and expert power. This would be ideal. But the problem is not that simple. A student may not accept the teacher's having social power in these ways. For example, the student who has rejected such values as the worth of intellectual enterprise, critical thinking, and objective inquiry is not likely to accept the teacher as a legitimate controller of his behavior in these respects. He may not revolt openly or publicly disclaim the teacher's social power, but he will not permit the teacher to influence him.

The teacher must also act consistently with these bases for influence. He must portray in his behavior an image consistent with them. One can hardly have expert power if he has no expertise. A beginning teacher is advised to distinguish between being friendly and helpful and being "buddy-buddy" with students. The friendliness recommended is professionalized friendship, not the highly personal kind common among peers. Professional behavior, ritualistic as it may be at its worst, has the advantage of creating an image consistent with legitimate power.

PATTERNS OF TEACHER-STUDENT INTERACTION

This discussion makes clear that any interaction situation requires reciprocity. Two people so involved are trying to maximize their rewards and to minimize their costs, both of which are multiple and diverse. A classroom is meant to be a task-oriented interaction. It is a work situation; the class ideally is a work group. It is not a group of friendly fellows mutually joined for merriment. Nor is the classroom an oppressive place with the teacher as taskmaster and the students as slaves. It is a social device for facilitating learning, and the teacher's responsibility is to create that device in fact as well as in theory.

MAINTENANCE OF GOAL ORIENTATION

A teacher's interactions with pupils may be conceptualized as ways of ensuring goal orientation on the part of pupils, whatever the particular goal may be. One teacher may be friendly and encouraging, because he believes that treating students in this way will facilitate their interest in and stimulate their activity toward goal attainment. Another teacher may remain relatively aloof from his students and have many rules designed to maintain "classroom order," again on the assumption that such procedures will facilitate goal attainment. Some teachers often praise students' efforts; others rarely praise them. Some use ridicule and sarcasm. Still other teachers feel that making classroom relations pleasant and interesting will guarantee goal orientation.

The kinds of teacher behaviors with which we are concerned in this section are those by which the teacher treats students as persons in order to facilitate their goal orientation. Again, we ask this general question: What are the effects of teacher behavior of this kind on change in pupil behavior?

THE TEACHER'S NEED SATISFACTION IN INTERPERSONAL RELATIONS

Organizing the educative act is presumably need satisfying for the teacher. In some cases, a particular act of a teacher may be a way of satisfying his own needs, but it may inhibit goal attainment by a pupil. For example, in punishing a disrespectful student, a teacher may be satisfying his own needs rather than fostering desirable pupil change. We would predict that if the student is aware of the intent behind his teacher's behavior, his own behavior is not likely to improve.

THE TEACHER'S CONTROL OF NEED SATISFACTIONS

As we have seen, behavior change begins in a motivated state of the individual: the individual must want or need something. Energized by this need, he will seek goals to satisfy it. One of the ways in which the teacher controls learning is by controlling the need satisfactions available to pupils. Some of these need satisfactions will be intimately tied to the learning experience itself; others will be provided by the teacher in his interaction with the pupils, and these may indirectly facilitate behavior change. A learning experience that does not provide need satisfaction for the pupils is not likely to produce desired behavior changes.

One of the problems facing the teacher is that the means children have already learned for satisfying their needs are frequently incompatible with the goals of a learning situation. A child who continually requires the teacher's approval may be so preoccupied with securing approval that he does the class work inadequately. Here is how one teacher attempted to solve a problem like this. The teacher describes her first try at resolving the difficulty:

Pat, a pampered first grader who lives with his grandparents, had a unique response to my suggestion that each time he required my attention without justifiable cause I would remember the times that I had to call his name before the class. (As, "Pat, get back to your seat—that is the fifth time that I have had to call your name this afternoon.") Pat loved every minute of this "game" and responded with "Mrs. S., watch me, that is number twenty-three." [4]

When the teacher first tried the technique of numbering the times Pat required her attention, the technique failed to reduce Pat's attention-seeking behavior. On analysis, an observer discovered that the teacher "lectured" Pat each time, in addition to indicating the number of times that Pat had tried to attract attention. The observer suggested that the teacher avoid "lecturing" and merely number the times Pat attempted to attract her attention. This technique proved successful, for Pat gradually abandoned his customary attention-getting devices.

This case illustrates the importance of recognizing the motives for a pupil's classroom behavior. These motives may be utilized to get the pupil involved in the learning experience and to seek satisfaction from it. While Pat was giving up his attention-getting behavior, he still needed the teacher's approval; at this point the teacher could help Pat learn that he would obtain approval by doing successful work rather than by causing disturbances in class.

UTILIZING STUDENTS' NEEDS FOR PRODUCTIVE ACTIVITY

One of the teacher's more difficult problems is motivating students in a particular learning experience. Children in a classroom are always motivated in some way, but the problem is to help them seek the goals implicit in the learning situation and to obtain satisfaction from the attainment of these goals. The class "cut-up" is motivated and is obtaining need satisfac-

[4] R. Dreikurs, *Psychology in the Classroom* (New York: Harper & Brothers, 1957), p. 115.

tion from the laughter and approval he gets from his classmates. The problem is utilizing his need for approval or attention in constructive ways, so that he can profit from the learning experience and obtain satisfactions from it. Al was a boy who continually argued with the teacher. When a paper was returned to him, he would argue with the teacher about the grade that he had received; he had learned to obtain satisfaction from getting into this kind of an argument with people. The teacher solved this problem of motivation in the following way:

Recently I forgot to tell the boys and girls to look for the eclipse of the moon. I felt that here I had an opportunity to direct Al into a constructive channel. I called his home and told him to watch the eclipse and to report to the class the next day. I thought this would also give him a chance to contribute to the class on the useful side, thus giving him status within his group. He does not feel a part of his group; he complains that the children will not play with him.

The next day Al was quite excited about giving his report to the class. He brought his source of information, a little bit about the solar system which he had in his collection of books. His report and his presentation were excellent. We decided to put Al's report in the newspaper which we publish monthly, and put his name under it (Dreikurs, p. 124).

The teacher in this case was attempting to teach Al new ways of satisfying his needs. He was capitalizing on the boy's need for approval and status with his classmates by involving him in a learning experience that could satisfy these needs. If Al learned that he could satisfy his needs for status and approval by participating intelligently and cooperatively in the class activities, he would probably abandon his destructive ways of satisfying his needs.

THE USE OF REWARD AND PUNISHMENT

From the viewpoint of the teacher, reward and punishment are **incentives** to induce and strengthen behavior change. An "A" grade may be an incentive of this kind. The teacher assumes that if a child wants a high grade, he will work to achieve the goals of the learning experience. Subtracting points for errors may be a punishment; it may also be an incentive for inducing behavior change—in this case, the avoidance of errors. However, what the teacher assumes to be rewards and punishments may not be so regarded by the students. Some children may not work for high marks because the attaining of a mark has little if any goal value for them. A supposed punishment may actually provide a child with need satisfaction, as in the case of the child who attracts the teacher's attention only when he talks out in class. The teacher, thinking to punish him, may reward him by paying attention to him.[5]

In general, if the rewards provided by the teacher are seen as potential sources of need satisfaction, they are likely to induce and strengthen behavior change; however, before we can predict that certain students will work for particular rewards, we must consider another factor. A particular reward may be attractive to a child, but he may have little hope of attaining it. His past experience in working for such rewards and his estimates of his own ability to attain the reward influence his expectancy of attainment.[6] As a case in point, a child may have little expectancy for attaining high grades even though they represent highly desirable goals for him. Similarly, the child's understanding of a given punishment may determine whether or not he avoids the behavior for which it may be administered.

In general, the effects of punishment are more variable than the effects of reward. Sears,[7] in a study on child rearing, investigated the effectiveness of a wide variety of punishments, such as isolation of the child, spanking, withdrawing of love, deprivation of privileges. The investigators concluded:

. . . punitiveness, in contrast with rewardingness, was a quite ineffectual quality for a mother to inject into her child training . . . our evaluation of punishment is that *it is ineffectual over the long term as a technique for eliminating the kind of behavior towards which it is directed.*

The evidence for this conclusion is overwhelming. The unhappy effects of punishment have run like a dismal thread through our findings. Mothers who punished toilet accidents severely ended up with bed-wetting children. Mothers who punished dependency to get rid of it had more dependent children than mothers who did not punish. Mothers who punished aggressive behavior severely had more aggressive children than mothers who punished lightly. They also had more dependent children. Harsh physical punishment was associated with high childhood aggressiveness and with the development of feeding problems (p. 484).

[5] A comprehensive analysis of the effects of punishment may be found in R. Solomon, "Punishment," *American Psychologist,* 19 (1964), 239–253.

[6] L. Worell, "The Effect of Goal Value upon Expectancy," *Journal of Abnormal and Social Psychology,* 53 (1956), 48–53.

[7] R. Sears, E. Maccoby, and H. Levin, *Patterns of Child-Rearing* (Evanston, Ill.: Row, Peterson and Co., 1957).

In some cases, punishment does not eliminate the behavior it is designed to eliminate, as when a child punished for dependency behavior becomes more dependent: the punishment does not remove the child's need for dependency, and he continues to seek need satisfaction by being dependent. In other cases, punishment of undesired behavior may eliminate *that* behavior, but a related and equally undesirable behavior emerges, as with the child who bed-wets after he has been punished for toilet accidents. In still other cases, the punished behavior is eliminated in one context, but manifested in another—as with the child who avoids being aggressive at home but who is highly aggressive in school.

Punishment may sometimes cause a child to avoid an undesired behavior, but it does not necessarily stimulate him to acquire a desired behavior pattern. A child may learn to control his aggressiveness without learning to become friendly; or he may learn to keep quiet in class without learning to ask appropriate questions.

Effects of the act of punishing are frequently undesirable. The threatening aspects of punishment may produce emotional tension in the child, and he may learn to hate the punisher because he fears the punishment. He may also acquire many undesirable behaviors to avoid being punished: he may lie or cheat to avoid it.

Teachers are frequently concerned with controlling classroom behavior that interferes with appropriate goal orientation. Teachers do not want pupils shouting out in the classroom, leaving their seats unnecessarily, talking to their companions, or practicing arithmetic when they should be doing reading assignments; and they frequently use punitive measures to eliminate these undesirable behaviors. A child may be put in the back of the classroom, he may be ridiculed, or he may be deprived of some privilege accorded the rest of the class. We expect that in a certain number of cases the child will stop doing these undesirable things to avoid punishment; but in other cases the child may not learn to take an interest in his class work, and, knowing no other ways, he may continue to seek need satisfaction by talking with his companions or shouting out in the classroom.

Other factors also must be considered in using reward and punishment techniques. Thompson and Hunnicutt studied the effects of praise and blame on the work achievement of **introverts** and **extroverts**.[8] In this experiment, fifth-grade pupils from five classes were presented with a

---

[8] G. G. Thompson and C. W. Hunnicutt, "The Effects of Repeated Praise or Blame on the Work Achievement of 'Introverts' and 'Extroverts,'" *Journal of Educational Psychology*, 35 (1944), 257–266.

simple learning task. The experimenters gave a personality test to the children that classified them as "introverts" and "extroverts." Then the experimenters divided the children into five groups. Two groups were made up of extroverts, one of which was praised and the other blamed; two groups were made up of introverts, one of which was praised and the other blamed; and the fifth group received neither praise nor blame. It is important to know that in this study "praise" consisted in the teachers placing a mark of "G," meaning "Good," and that the "blame" consisted in the teacher placing a "P," meaning "Poor," on the pupil's test paper. The experimenters came to these conclusions:

1. The work output of both introverts and extroverts, praised or blamed, is significantly higher than that of children in the control group; that is, the group that has not received rewards or punishments at all.
2. If repeated often enough, praise increases the work output of introverts until it is higher than that of extroverts who are praised or introverts who are blamed.
3. If repeated often enough, blame increases the work output of extroverts until it is higher than that of extroverts who are praised or introverts who are blamed.

These results are plotted in Figure 13–2. As the graph illustrates, the group showing the largest gains was the extrovert-blamed group, and the group showing the least improvement was the introvert-blamed group.

The conclusions from this study do not comprise rules for applying praise and blame to the behavior of students. The character of the "praise" and "blame" used in this experiment is limited and highly specific. All we know about the personality characteristics of these children is that they are introverts and extroverts as described by test scores on a personality test. Generally, however, praise is found to be more effective in almost all research done on this point. The exceptions have been underachieving children, very bright adolescents, and Negro children working under Negro examiners.[9] These few and somewhat surprising exceptions suggest that the child's previous history of praise and blame determines how he is likely to respond in the classroom. The teacher is well advised to inform himself on this point.

The experimental evidence from animal research, research on child-

[9] The literature on the use of praise and blame is reviewed in W. A. Kennedy and Herman C. Willicutt, "Praise and Blame as Incentives," *Psychological Bulletin*, 62 (1964), 323–332.

rearing practices, and classroom investigations consistently suggests the superiority of rewarding over punishing in producing effective change in behavior.[10] Punishment has a limited usefulness as a control technique, but it may have real disadvantages in terms of the total learning of a child. From this evidence we would certainly be safe in concluding that a teacher whose interactions with pupils are largely characterized by punitive relationships is likely to be ineffective in promoting a wide range of desirable behavior changes.

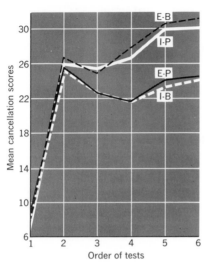

FIGURE 13-2. *Effects of praise (P) and blame (B) on introverts (I) and extroverts (E) (from Thompson and Hunnicutt).*

Kounin and Gump studied the reactions of children under punitive and nonpunitive teachers.[11] They selected from ratings the three most punitive and three least punitive first-grade teachers in three different schools. They interviewed each of the children in these teachers' classes, asking them "What is the worst thing you can do in school?" They categorized the children's comments, classifying statements about the content and quality of misconduct and the explanations for it, the role of the individual in the misconduct, how much aggression the actions selected seemed to contain, and how much concern with school objectives was revealed. They then compared the two groups of children by these categories.

They found that children under punitive teachers describe as the worst thing more acts of sheer aggression and more extreme forms of aggression than children under the nonpunitive teacher. "Children with nonpunitive teachers talk more about learning, achievement losses, and violations of

[10] An experimental study supporting this point and usually cited as evidence is W. K. Estes, "An Experimental Study of Punishment," *Psychological Monographs*, No. 263 (1944); see also U. E. Whiteis, "Punishment's Influence on Fear and Avoidance," *Harvard Educational Review*, 26 (1956), 360–373. The Solomon article (see footnote 5) is the latest summary of the research on this problem.

[11] J. S. Kounin and P. V. Gump, "The Comparative Influence of Punitive and Nonpunitive Teachers upon Children's Concepts of School Misconduct," *Journal of Educational Psychology*, 52 (1961), 44–49.

school-unique values and rules" (p. 48). Children under punitive teachers were concrete in their descriptions ("hit George in the mouth") rather than abstract ("be mean to people"). Although these children under punitive teachers express more abhorrence of the misdeeds they describe, the deeds they describe require forethought—suggesting that their aggressive thoughts and, perhaps, acts are deliberate. To hit George in the mouth usually requires a little thought and planning. These children are thinking more about their aggressive impulses, apparently, than they are about school.

This is a dismal picture. These first-grade teachers may have been punitive, but one can only be so punitive to a small child. Their punitiveness was mainly in their attitudes. But note the effects on the children. Even what these teachers probably thought they wanted, commitment to school objectives, was not achieved. Of what value was the punishment?

THE TEACHER'S BEHAVIOR AS A STIMULUS EVENT

We pointed out earlier that the teacher's behavior is a stimulus likely to evoke certain kinds of responses from students. In the preceding sections, we discussed one way in which this stimulus behavior may be seen from the viewpoint of the student—namely, as a source of control over need satisfactions. These stimulus events may also be considered as ways in which the teacher *forces* or *leads* a child toward goal attainments.

Anderson and his students investigated teacher-child relations to ascertain the effects of "forcing" (dominating) and "leading." In so doing, they discriminated various degrees of what is sometimes called "teacher control." [12] In this investigation, domination was classified in three categories: domination with evidence of conflict, domination with no evidence of conflict, and domination in working together. In general, a "dominating" teacher sets the goals of a learning experience and uses some measure of direction to ensure that students work for these goals. A teacher's behavior is classified as *domination with conflict* if the goals of the teacher and the pupil appear to be incompatible, and if the teacher is punitive in enforcing the pupils' goal orientation. *Domination without conflict* is also teacher control of the goals, but the students accept the teacher's direc-

---

[12] A summary with bibliography of these studies can be found in H. H. Anderson, "Domination and Socially Integrated Behavior," in R. G. Barker, J. S. Kounin, and H. F. Wright, eds., *Child Behavior and Development* (New York: McGraw-Hill Book Company, 1943), pp. 459–483.

tion and show no signs of resisting his influence. A teacher's behavior is classified as *domination in working together* if the teacher sets the goals and expected patterns of behavior but works cooperatively and nonpunitively with students to attain these goals. These categories represent points on an assumed continuum of "forcing."

Anderson classified "leading" behavior in two categories: *working together with conflict* and *working together without conflict*. A teacher's behavior was classified in the first of these two categories if he allowed students to be more self-directive but did not succeed in producing goal orientation. A teacher's behavior was classified in the second category if he encouraged self-direction that secured goal orientation.

What is the effect of these kinds of teacher behavior on the behavior of pupils? The major finding in this series of studies was that a particular kind of teacher behavior tended to evoke a similar kind of pupil behavior. Dominating behavior in a teacher tended to produce dominating behavior in his students. A teacher working with the pupils found that they worked with him. Such important characteristics of child behavior as spontaneity and participation in classroom activities decreased under the dominating behavior of a teacher.

In one of the studies in the Anderson series, the children were observed over a two-year period; for one year they had a teacher whose behavior was principally dominating; in the second year they had a teacher whose behavior was essentially that of working with them. The children's behavior was characteristically dominating and resisting under the dominating teacher, and cooperative and more spontaneous under the teacher who worked with them. These studies provide an analysis of some ways in which specific kinds of teacher behavior are likely to influence pupil behavior. We may not draw detailed rules of action from them, but the data suggest some ways in which teacher behavior and pupil behavior are related.

PUPILS' PERCEPTION OF THE TEACHER'S BEHAVIOR

Common sense suggests that the pupil's response to teacher behavior is likely to be influenced by many factors. A particular instance of teacher behavior may not be seen as harsh or punitive, or, if it is, the student may still regard it as justifiable. In these cases a dominating or resisting pupil response may not occur.

One factor that may influence students' perceptions of the teacher's behavior is their awareness of the status differences between teacher and pupil. To some extent, the teacher is regarded as having higher status. He is an authority on many matters for the students. Pepitone and Wallace found that individuals viewed the positive and negative actions of a higher-status person as more justified if they were relevant to his status.[13] A teacher's actions may then be regarded as justifiable even though the students find them disagreeable. Students expect teachers to evaluate their work and to maintain "classroom order." The teacher's behavior is viewed as justified when he acts in ways consistent with these expectations.

As other studies indicate, students may not view all restrictions imposed by a teacher as justified simply because the teacher is a person of higher status. They may find such restrictions arbitrary and hence unjustified. Pastore conducted an experiment to study the relationship between hostility and the arbitrariness of a frustration.[14] He described a series of situations to his subjects and asked them to describe how they would feel in these situations. Each situation involved a frustration of some kind; for example, a date is broken or a bus does not stop. One set of these situations supplied reasons for the frustrations—for example, a date's being broken because the girl was ill. The same situations were described to a second group in such a way as to indicate that the action was arbitrary. A significantly higher number of hostile responses were made by the subjects who received the arbitrary situations. In other words, if a disagreeable and frustrating situation is regarded as justifiable, people are less likely to respond to it in a hostile manner.

Rosenfeld and Zander explored these phenomena by extensively questioning a sample of four hundred male junior high school students.[15] They found that students distinguished between disapproval of poor performance and disapproval when the student had done as well as he could. The latter produced negative reactions in students. Reward, except when indiscriminate, was related to the amount of influence the teacher had on students. Consistent with our earlier discussions on sources of social power, students accept teacher influence when the sources of his power are reward, legitimate, referent, or expert power. Students tend to ignore or oppose influence mediated by coercive power.

[13] A. Pepitone and W. Wallace, "Experimental Studies on the Dynamics of Hostility," discussed in A. Pepitone, "Attributions of Causality, Social Attitudes, and Cognitive Matching Processes," in R. Tagiuri and L. Petrullo, eds., *Person Perception and Interpersonal Behavior* (Stanford, Calif.: Stanford University Press, 1958), pp. 258–276.

[14] N. Pastore, "The Role of Arbitrariness in the Frustration-Aggression Hypothesis," *Journal of Abnormal and Social Psychology*, 47 (1952), 728–731.

[15] H. Rosenfeld and A. Zander, "The Influence of Teachers on Aspirations of Students," *Journal of Educational Psychology*, 52 (1961), 1–11.

The above discussion suggests that an important determinant of one person's response to the behavior of another is his perception of the intent behind the behavior.[16] A reasonable hypothesis is that students will respond positively to a pattern of teacher behavior insofar as they trust the teacher's intention. If they believe that he is working for their best interests and is not arbitrary in his decisions, they are more likely to respond positively to him.

Dominating and punitive behavior is more likely to be interpreted as ill-intended or arbitrary. The teacher who hands out excessive punishments for mild digressions from acceptable classroom behavior, or who makes unreasonable assignments, may be seen as hostile by his students. In such cases their responses are likely to be hostile and resisting.

CLASSROOM CLIMATE

The casual observer going from classroom to classroom will notice gross differences between the psychological "climates" of different classrooms. The term *climate* refers to the general pattern of social interaction observable in the relations of a group of individuals. These general patterns appear to be relatively consistent in a stable group, such as a class, and considerable variation in climate exists between the classes of different teachers.[17] In one classroom the students are working industriously and effectively; the teacher is a source of information and guidance; the teacher's and the pupils' goals do not appear to be incompatible. In another classroom a continual state of conflict exists between the teacher and the pupils; the teacher must use harsh and punitive methods to maintain minimum order; the pupils do not seem to be involved in the learning experience.

These differences in classroom climate may be described on several dimensions. One such dimension is the method of behavior control typically used in the classroom. A "democratic" classroom, for instance, may be described as one in which there is a large degree of permissiveness in the teacher-pupil relationship: pupils are allowed selection of the work projects, and they participate in decisions about the learning activities; they are not closely supervised, but are allowed to work independently. In contrast, an "autocratic" classroom may be described as one dominated by

---

[16] A. Pepitone and J. Sherberg, "Cognitive Factors in Interpersonal Attraction," *Journal of Personality*, 25 (1957), 257–266.

[17] J. Withall, "Assessment of the Social-Emotional Climates Experienced by a Group of Seventh-Graders as They Moved from Class to Class," *Educational and Psychological Measurement*, 12 (1952), 440–451.

the teacher: the teacher decides on and attempts to impose the goals of learning activities; the pupils do not participate in either the selection of learning activities or the goals of these activities. These two descriptions of methods of behavior control represent end-points on a continuum of "self-directed"–"other-directed." There are many variations between the extreme of the "democratic" class and the extreme of the "autocratic" class. Also, while the definitions of the extremes are comparatively clear-cut, it is much more difficult to define the points between them. Some climates may be characterized by both "democratic" and "autocratic" procedures.

INFLUENCE OF CLASSROOM CLIMATE ON PUPIL BEHAVIOR

Do these differences in classroom climate produce differences in pupil behavior? Lewin, Lippitt, and White conducted a series of experiments in which they tested the effects of three kinds of adult leadership on group behavior.[18] Table 13–1 describes the characteristics of each of these kinds of leadership. The experimenters kept a complete record of the behavior of the boys under each kind of leadership. The following results were obtained:

1. Hostile and aggressive behavior occurred more frequently under autocratic leadership than under democratic leadership.
2. Aggressive behavior tended to generalize to other situations. There was a sharp rise in aggression when the autocratic leader left the room. The boys also became more aggressive when they moved to a freer atmosphere.
3. Two "wars," more or less playful, broke out between clubs meeting in the same room at the same time. These wars broke out either when there was no adult present or when a "hostile stranger" came into the room.
4. There were at least two striking instances of aggressive attacks on impersonal objects.
5. Under autocratic leadership "scapegoating" of some of the boys in the group occurred, a phenomenon that decreased under democratic leadership.
6. The boys were almost unanimous in disliking the autocratic leader and practically unanimous in liking the democratic and even the laissez-faire leader.

[18] K. Lewin, R. Lippitt, and R. K. White, "Patterns of Aggressive Behavior in Experimentally Created 'Social Climates,'" *Journal of Social Psychology*, 10 (1939), 271–299. A more extensive report on this and related studies may be found in R. K. White, *Autocracy and Democracy* (New York: Harper & Brothers, 1960).

TABLE 13-1. *Characteristics of authoritarian, democratic, and laissez-faire styles of leadership (from Lewin, Lippitt, and White).*

Authoritarian	Democratic	Laissez-faire
1. All determination of policy by the leader.	1. All policies a matter of group discussion and decision, encouraged and assisted by the leader.	1. Complete freedom for group or individual decision, without any leader participation.
2. Techniques and activity steps dictated by the authority, one at a time, so that future steps were always uncertain to a large degree.	2. The activity perspective gained during first discussion period. General steps to group goal sketched, and where technical advice was needed the leader suggested two or three procedures from which choice could be made.	2. Various materials supplied by the leader, who made it clear that he would supply information when asked. He took no other part in work discussions.
3. The leader usually dictated the particular work task and work companions of each member.	3. The members were free to work with whomever they chose, and the division of tasks was left up to the group.	3. Complete nonparticipation by leader.
4. The dominator was "personal" in his praise and criticism of the work of each member, but remained aloof from active group participation except when demonstrating. He was friendly or impersonal rather than openly hostile.	4. The leader was "objective" or "fact-minded" in his praise and criticism, and he tried to be a regular member of the group in spirit without doing too much of the work.	4. Very infrequent comments on member activities unless questioned, and no attempt to participate or interfere with the course of events.

The results of this experiment were clear-cut. Under autocratic leadership the children were frustrated, and they resolved their frustration by aggressive acts of one kind or another. They were also more apathetic and less personally involved in the work of their club. Control in the group and task orientation disappeared when the autocratic leader was not present. The effects in the democratic group were just the opposite: the children were responsive and spontaneous; they did not need the supervision of the leader to continue working, and they showed less evidence of aggression and hostility.

The above study is frequently cited as evidence that democratic leadership produces more task orientation and more socially adaptable behavior than does autocratic leadership. However, the results of this study should not be overgeneralized. The terms democracy and autocracy have more than one meaning. The results of this study apply only to the definitions used. Further, the learning tasks used in the experiment represent one kind of activity. Behavior in other kinds of activities may not be similarly influenced. For example, learners may prefer more direction when the learning task is ambiguous or when they are in the early stages of learning. Is direction given at this time likely to be resented? (Would such direction be what we mean by authoritarianism?) We do not know whether these same effects would be obtained for a wider range of activities, but they are consistent with the experimental data cited previously: an aggressive, hostile, punitive leader stimulates aggressive, punitive, and hostile behavior in children. If the children cannot express their hostility to the teacher, they may direct it toward impersonal objects or their companions. From the discussion of the Lewin experiment, we may be tempted to conclude that a given set of procedures automatically produces the pupil behavior described in that experiment.[19] But we would also expect the pupils' expectations about or perceptions of the classroom climate to influence their behavior.

Experimental work suggests that both the students' perceptions of the typical pattern of control and the teacher's consistent maintenance of these patterns substantially influence pupil behavior.[20] In one experiment,

---

[19] That these results have been difficult to obtain consistently is amply illustrated in the following article: R. Anderson, "Learning in Discussions: A Résumé of the Authoritarian-Democratic Studies," *Harvard Educational Review*, 29 (1959), 201–213.

[20] M. Horwitz, M. Goldman, and F. J. Lee, *A Further Study of the Effects of Power Reduction on Arousal of Hostility*, Office of Naval Research Technical Report, 1956, discussed in M. Horwitz, "The Veridicality of Liking and Disliking," in R. Tagiuri and L. Petrullo, eds., *Person Perception and Interpersonal Behavior* (Stanford, Calif.: Stanford University Press, 1957), pp. 191–208. See also M. Horwitz, "Hostility and Its Management in Classroom Groups," in W. W. Charters and N. L. Gage, eds., *Readings in the Social Psychology of Education* (Boston: Allyn and Bacon, 1963), pp. 196–211.

two kinds of classroom climates were established: first, a "teacher-centered" one, in which the vote of the teacher on a problem of mutual interest counted twice as much as the votes of the students; second, a "student-centered" one, in which the teacher's vote on a common problem was given only one fourth the weight of the student vote.

As part of the experimental procedure, both groups were required to vote on continuing the work in which they were involved. The teachers in both groups overrode the students' decision. This behavior was consistent with the expectations of the students in the "teacher-centered" classroom, where the teacher's vote counted twice as much; but it contradicted the expectations established in the "student-centered" classroom. When the students were asked to rate their teacher, expressions of hostility and dislike were significantly greater in the "student-centered" classroom.[21]

How are the results of this experiment reconciled with those of the Lewin experiment? Some of the differences in results may be related to the different kinds of teacher control used, even though we may think that "teacher control" and "autocratic" are similar. The reader should note the ways in which the variables describing "'climate" are defined in each of these experiments. In the "teacher-centered" classroom in the above experiment the rules of operation seemed generally understood, whereas in the autocratic group of the Lewin experiment the "climate" was established primarily by the way the leader treated the group. In the "teacher-centered" group the rules were apparently "accepted." The boys in the autocratic group did not "accept" the leader's directives; that is, they did not recognize his right to exercise social power in these ways. Another difference between the experiments is that the different effects obtained refer only to one behavior pattern; namely, expression of hostility.[22]

Despite these methodological differences, we may hypothesize that some patterns of classroom climate, such as the extreme form of "autocratic" control, usually have the same effects. But in many other cases, student behavior is more likely to be influenced by the expectations for control, assuming that such expectations are "accepted." In general, we would predict that the more extreme forms of autocratic control are less likely to be "accepted." We need not assume that the democratic pattern

[21] Similar results were obtained in the experimental work reported in F. J. Lee, M. Horwitz, and M. Goldman, *Power over Decision Making and the Response to Frustration* (Washington, D. C.: Office of Naval Research, 1954).

[22] Rate and retention of learning were investigated in the following experiment, but the different experimental treatments did not produce significant differences between the groups. See M. Horwitz and M. Goldman, "Veridicality of Attitudes toward Authority and Effects on Rates of Learning and Psychological Oversatiation," described in M. Horwitz, "The Veridicality of Liking and Disliking" (see note 20).

of control will necessarily be accepted. Although it is more likely to be accepted, its effectiveness depends upon the extent to which students "accept" it. In all cases the students' behavior will probably be influenced by the degree to which the teacher's behavior is consistent with established and accepted expectations.

From our review of the experimental evidence on the teacher-pupil relationship, we cannot conclude that the teacher should act in one prescribed way in order to produce desirable pupil behavior in all situations. One limitation of most of the experiments we have discussed is that they have investigated only a limited number of variables. Or they have studied variables so complex that we do not know which particular procedures produced the experimental effects.[23] In the Lewin, Lippitt, and White study, for example, democratic leadership involved many specific operations, such as the manner in which the leader treated the boys, as well as the operations that were permitted in the group, such as participation in policy decisions. The obtained effects may have been due to one or both of these aspects of democratic leadership. But, although specific operations cannot be recommended, a reasonable rule is: Reward rather than punish, lead rather than force, stimulate rather than coerce. Another decision rule: Act consistently with students' expectations of desirable teacher behavior; change the expectations when they are undesirable, acting consistently with the desired expectation.

COMPARATIVE INFLUENCE OF TEACHER AND CLASS BEHAVIOR

How does the teacher's interaction with a student affect other students' feelings about this student? An easy assumption is that if the teacher is punitive to a student, the other students will sympathize with him. If he is praised highly, they will think he is "teacher's pet." These effects do occur. In some classes, in fact, the teacher's rejection or disapproval is a mark of success, a status symbol. However, these reactions do not occur invariantly.

Teachers obviously try to influence student action and thought, using logical arguments or some other form of appeal. A teacher is also likely to reward those students who are persuaded. In such a situation, will other students be influenced by the teacher rewarding those who are persuaded, or will they ridicule and reject these students? If most of the students seem to be persuaded, will the rest go along?

[23] See Anderson's critique of studies on these variables (note 19).

Flanders and Havumaki [24] designed an experiment to test two hypotheses related to this problem: (1) If a teacher appeals to the individuals in his class, addressing his arguments to each person rather than to the group as a whole and rewarding the student's response, more students will be persuaded. (2) Students will be influenced more readily if they perceive that other students are also being persuaded. These investigators placed 330 tenth-grade students in two kinds of experimental situations: in one, the teacher appealed directly to individuals, addressing them by name and praising their contribution; in the other, he spoke to the group as a whole. The students were continuously informed of the group's decisions on a discussion topic by a mechanical device indicating each member's choice and displaying the results to the group.

Students came to the laboratory rooms in groups of ten, and were told that they had been selected to participate in a Quiz Kid type of show. They had to decide whether to appear on radio or TV. They also had to select five of their number as participants and five as helpers to act as consultants during the program. After an orientation period in which this information was given to them, a teacher-trainer led a discussion on the choices to be made.

All groups were initially told that they, in a preliminary vote, had preferred to appear on TV. The teacher-trainer, in leading the discussion, pointed out the values of performing on radio. During the discussion a display panel showed how the group was voting, each student periodically recording his preference. Actually, the experimenters manipulated the results to show in some groups that students were shifting to the teacher's side (performing on radio). In other groups, the board showed that the group was not changing its preference. In this way, four kinds of experimental groups were created: (1) a group receiving individual treatment and apparently shifting to the teacher's side; (2) a group also receiving individual treatment but not shifting; (3) a group addressed as a whole and shifting; and (4) a group receiving the same treatment and not shifting.

At the end of the discussion the students filled out a questionnaire, expressing their preference for radio or TV, nominating the participants, and expressing a desire to work or to discontinue working with the teacher-trainer. The students also rated how well the teacher had explained the radio vs. TV issue, his fairness, their awareness of his prefer-

---

[24] N. A. Flanders and S. Havumaki, "Group Compliance to Dominative Teacher Influence," *Human Relations*, 13 (1960), 67–82.

ences, and whether he seemed more interested in individuals or the group.

Two major results were obtained supporting the validity of the hypotheses being tested. First, more students shift to the teacher's side (perform on radio) when the teacher treats them as individuals and when they perceive the group being persuaded (in this experiment, the gradual change displayed on the board). Second, this shift is minimal when individual treatment is used but the group does not shift. Third, students' preferences are more like those of their group (for example, more students treated individually wanted to transfer out when in groups opposed to the teacher).

Two other results are interesting: (1) When the students in individual treatments were asked who should select the program participants, significantly more of those who interacted with the teacher said the teacher should. (2) When these same students were asked whom they nominated, more students who interacted with the teacher were nominated.

A few cautionary words. These students met for the first time as a group in the experiment. Very few had known each other previously. Long-term associations might have altered the observed effects. The teacher also was unfamiliar, so that the students had not adapted to his style or learned his idiosyncrasies. Also, the task was a cooperative one, and the students did not know at the beginning that only some of them would be selected. If they had been obviously competing, the praise might have had a different effect.

The effects of teacher behavior, then, are dependent on a set of conditions, chief of which are the communality of ideas and values among the teacher and students, the established pattern of teacher-pupil relations, and the students' perceptions of the teacher's typical behavior.

INFLUENCE OF THE CLASS ON TEACHER BEHAVIOR

Students have long suspected that their actions have some influence on teachers' behavior. That they do, and that their influence may be beneficial to the teacher, is illustrated in a study by Gage, Runkel, and Chatterjee.[25]

[25] N. L. Gage, P. J. Runkel, and B. B. Chatterjee, "Changing Teacher Behavior through Feedback from Pupils: An Application of Equilibrium Theory," in W. W. Charters and N. L. Gage, eds., *Readings in Social Psychology of Education* (note 20), pp. 173–181.

These investigators studied teachers' reactions when they were told what their pupils thought of their behavior. The investigators constructed a twelve-item list of teacher behaviors (such as "Tells pupils about some interesting things to read" and "Acts disappointed when a pupil gets something wrong") and asked students to say whether an item was like or unlike their teacher. They checked the same kinds of responses for the "best teacher they can imagine."

The students made these ratings twice, approximately five months apart. A total of 176 teachers and 3,600 pupils in their classes participated in the study. In between the two sets of ratings, half of the teachers received information on their students' first set of ratings of them. This information showed them how many of their students said each of the behaviors was like or unlike them, and how they compared to the students' picture of the ideal teacher. The investigators then analyzed the second set of ratings to see whether the teachers receiving the information were rated differently. Although there were only four significant differences between ratings of the teachers who had received the information and those who had not, ten of the twelve differences showed the first group moving in the direction of the pupils' conception of the ideal teacher. **Feedback,** it was reasonable to conclude, had changed the teachers' behavior in the direction their students valued. The changes were not large, but the feedback was very limited—information from one set of ratings.

INFLUENCE OF PERCEPTION ON INTERPERSONAL INTERACTIONS

Our interactions with another person are influenced by the way we perceive him, the kind of person we think he is. We have a language—mainly adjectives—for describing other people. If I see a person coming down the street, I may say to myself, "Here comes poor, pathetic George," or "practical George," or "clever George" or "intelligent George" or "humorous George." My response to George will depend to a large extent upon my adjectival labels for him.

In making judgments about the personality characteristics of other individuals, we frequently overlook the fact that our descriptions are really inferences from our observations of their behavior. These inferences are useful and meaningful if we have sampled their behavior adequately and if our descriptive labels are clear. For example, describing a child as a "bad actor" tells us very little about the child until we know what is meant or implied by the category "bad actor." More impressive but equally vague categories such as "maladjusted" or "socially competent" tells us little about the kind of behavior that we might expect of an individual so described.

SYSTEMS OF TRAIT ASSOCIATIONS

If you described a child as "intelligent," you would not also call him "stupid" unless you obtained information that required a revision of your judgment. While the meaning of these terms is not always perfectly clear, we do recognize that they cannot be applied to the same person at the same time. Similarly, a child who calls a teacher "cold" is not likely to describe him as also being "warm." What traits would you expect to be associated with "intelligent"? What descriptive terms occur to you immediately? You may say that a person described as "intelligent" could have almost any trait name applied to him, depending on his other characteristics. Agreed; but what traits do you *expect* to find associated with a person described as "intelligent"? Research evidence [26] suggests that we tend to associate trait descriptions in related patterns. For example, if a number of people are asked about a set of traits they associate with "intelligent," the majority will say they expect a person so described to be "imaginative," "clever," "active," "conscientious," "deliberate," "independent," "reliable."

Some trait names apparently have greater influence in forming our impressions of a person than do others. Asch [27] gave groups of students lists of trait descriptions; the lists were alike in all respects except one. The list received by one group included the trait "warm," whereas the list received by the other contained the trait "cold." The students were then asked to write a description of the person whom the traits seemed to suggest. Asch found remarkable differences between impressions of the "warm" and "cold" persons. Kelley [28] used the trait lists to describe instructors whom students were to meet briefly. Again, when the impressions of the students were collected, the marked difference in group impressions depended upon whether the instructor had been described as

[26] J. S. Bruner, D. Shapiro, and R. Tagiuri, "The Meaning of Traits in Isolation and in Combination," in R. Tagiuri and L. Petrullo, eds., *Person Perception and Interpersonal Behavior* (see note 20), pp. 277–288.
[27] S. E. Asch, "Forming Impressions of Personality," *Journal of Abnormal and Social Psychology,* 41 (1946), 258–290.
[28] H. H. Kelley, "The Warm-Cold Variable in First Impressions of Persons," *Journal of Personality,* 18 (1950), 431–439.

"warm" or "cold." Other research [29] indicates that some trait names are less likely to produce differences of this kind and that the location of the trait name on the list also influences impressions.

This research evidence suggests that we tend to form relatively consistent patterns of personality descriptions, so that we see certain traits as "going together." In other words, we acquire expectations about patterns of personality, as perhaps best exemplified in our tendency to describe individuals as "types." The significance of this tendency is that it may operate independently of our observations of an individual, and in many cases may inhibit our observations. For example, a teacher who sees a child as "intelligent" may assume that he is "imaginative" or "reliable" without observing behavior from which he could appropriately infer either of these traits.

Just as certain traits give rise to associated traits, certain social roles or positions are associated with specific traits. For example, what traits do you expect in a football coach? Do you expect him to be "dynamic" and "energetic" or "shy" and "withdrawn"? Sarbin [30] played a variety of recorded statements to students and asked them to identify the role of the person making the statement. One statement, "All right, boys, get in there and fight!" was recorded in a shout by an actor described to the students as a middle-aged man. Ninety per cent of the students identified the actor as a coach. The students were responding to role behavior, but perceptions of role behavior may be and frequently are organized into conceptions of traits associated with the role.

Some trait associations may be learned as ways of interpreting behavior significant in some situations but not others. In studies of teacher characteristics valued by pupils, for instance, traits such as "kindliness," "patience," and "fairness" are chosen as traits characterizing teachers who were most helpful to students. In other words, the pupils respond to characteristics most desirable to them as students.[31]

---

[29] S. E. Asch, *Social Psychology* (Englewood Cliffs, N. J.: Prentice-Hall, Inc., 1952), pp. 205–221. See also M. Haire and W. F. Grunes, "Perceptual Defenses: Processes Protecting an Organized Perception of Another Personality," *Human Relations,* 3 (1950), 403–412.

[30] T. R. Sarbin and J. D. Williams, "Contributions to Role-Taking Theory: V. Role Perception on the Basis of Limited Auditory Stimuli," cited in T. R. Sarbin, "Role Theory," in G. Lindzey, ed., *Handbook of Social Psychology* (Cambridge, Mass.: Addison-Wesley Publishing Co., 1954), Vol. I, p. 230.

[31] P. Witty, "An Analysis of the Personality Traits of the Effective Teacher," *Journal of Educational Research,* 40 (1947), 662–671. Evidence supporting this point, based on correlations between teacher and pupil behavior, may be found in D. G. Ryans, "Some Relationships between Pupil Behavior and Certain Teacher Characteristics," *Journal of Educational Psychology,* 52 (1961), 82–90; D. G. Ryans, "Inventory

A study of teachers' evaluations of pupil behavior suggests the same tendency: to note characteristics of pupil behavior directly related to the attainment of the teachers' goals. Schrupp and Gjerde [32] prepared a list of traits and asked a group of teachers and a group of clinicians (mental hygienists) to rate these traits on a scale from "of no consequence" to "an extremely grave problem." In Table 13–2 is a list of traits rated by teachers and clinicians as most serious. In a list of fifty traits, there were only sixteen on which the rank difference (that is, the difference between the rank given by the clinicians and the teachers) was 15 or greater. These differences between teachers and clinicians cannot be compared directly, since the two groups were given different instructions for making their

TABLE 13–2. *Traits on which greatest disagreement appears when rated by 1,951 teachers and clinicians (from Schrupp and Gjerde).*

Traits rated more serious by teachers	Rank difference	Traits rated more serious by clinicians	Rank difference
Impertinence, defiance	26.5	Shyness	31
Impudence, rudeness	26	Suspiciousness	27.5
Obscene notes, pictures, etc.	24	Dreaminess	25.5
Disobedience	24	Fearfulness	22
Disorderliness	24	Sensitiveness	20.5
Heterosexual activity	23	Overcritical of others	19
Masturbation	20	Imaginative lying	16
Untruthfulness	16	Nervousness	16

ratings: the teachers were asked to rate the problems *presently* serious, and the clinicians were to rate those likely to indicate *future* difficulties in adjustment.

These differences are merely suggestive of the relative importance that teachers attach to various kinds of pupil behavior. The traits rated as more serious by teachers are overt demonstrations of behavior which usually interfere with classroom order; those rated more serious by clinicians are symptoms of personality conflict and maladjustment. The two groups evaluated the seriousness of behavior in relation to two different

---

Estimated Teacher Characteristics as Covariants of Observer Assessed Pupil Behavior," *Journal of Educational Psychology,* 52 (1961), 91–97.

[32] M. H. Schrupp and C. M. Gjerde, "Teacher Growth in Attitudes toward Behavior Problems of Children," *Journal of Educational Psychology,* 44 (1953), 203–214.

contexts (induced at least in part by the differences in directions).[33] Fragmentary as this evidence may be, it is nevertheless consistent with the hypothesis that trait associations may be learned as ways of interpreting the significance of behavior in particular social relations.

An individual's self-perception, taken with his attitudes and values, appears to influence his perceptions of the characteristics of other people. Stagner[34] determined the attitudes of students toward labor, and then asked the students to check traits characterizing factory workers and executives. The students also checked the traits that they thought characterized themselves and rated the pleasantness and unpleasantness of all the traits in the list from which they worked. Pro-labor students, for example, ascribed more traits to themselves that they had ascribed to factory workers and generally rated these traits more favorably. These data are consistent with the hypothesis that we are more sensitive to characteristics which we associate with ourselves.[35]

ACCURACY OF TEACHERS' PERCEPTIONS OF PUPILS

If an individual is influenced more by his conception of trait consistencies than he is by his observations of behavior, his conception of the other person is not likely to be accurate; that is, the traits he ascribes to this person have limited usefulness in predicting and explaining his behavior. If we assume that an "intelligent" student is also a "responsible" person, we are likely to err in our estimates of the responsibility traits of students. And such inaccuracies in our perception of pupils' personalities will probably affect their development adversely because of the way we will treat them. Inaccurate perceptions will also interfere with planning of appropriate learning experiences. We might be handicapped in our understanding of goals likely to motivate a particular student; we might also err in evaluating the factors likely to stimulate pupil change, or in our estimates of the factors inhibiting change.

[33] Studies of friendship and partner choices also indicate the relevance of the *conditions* under which a choice is made. For data on this point, see H. H. Jennings, "Sociometric Differentiation of the Psychegroup and the Sociogroup," *Sociometry*, 10 (1947), 71–79. H. H. Jennings, *Leadership and Isolation*, rev. ed. (New York: Longmans, Green & Co., 1950).

[34] R. Stagner, "Psychological Aspects of Industrial Conflict: I. Perception," *Personnel Psychology*, 1 (1948), 131–144.

[35] H. Fensterheim and M. E. Tresselt, "The Influence of Value Systems on the Perception of People," *Journal of Abnormal and Social Psychology*, 48 (1953), 93–98.

Ojemann and Wilkinson [36] studied the effects on pupil growth of providing teachers with more information about pupils. The investigators set up two groups of students, an experimental and a control group. The teachers of the experimental group received detailed summaries and analyses of personality, as well as environmental data on the students in their classes. In personal interviews the teachers were given suggestions for improving their understanding of the children's behavior and for planning appropriate learning experiences. The investigators made periodic visits to these teachers' classes to discuss the pupils' progress. At the end of the year the investigators found significant differences in grade-point average, attitudes toward school, and personal adjustment—all in favor of the experimental group.

We may not conclude from this study that providing teachers with more data about pupil behavior *will necessarily* improve their understanding of pupil behavior or *will necessarily* lead to marked changes in pupil progress. Many different procedures were used in this study, and care should be taken not to attribute the measured changes to any one of these procedures. In addition to detailed information, the teachers were given interpretations of the data and suggestions about ways of interpreting and controlling pupil behavior. The teachers who participated in the experimental program commented that they felt they had greater understanding of pupil behavior. The experimental procedures used and the teachers' comments suggest that a reorganization of their perceptions was achieved. These changes may have made the teachers more amenable to suggestions which, if implemented, were likely to be effective in promoting behavior change.

The relationship between the teacher's understanding of pupil behavior and its changes is not a simple one; this is clearly indicated by the data from a study by Hoyt,[37] who also studied the effects of teachers' knowledge of pupils on achievement of pupils and on their attitudes toward class work. Hoyt established three levels of teachers' understanding of pupils. One group of teachers was urged to refrain from obtaining specific knowledge about individual pupils; a second group was asked to limit their study of their pupils, but was provided with copies of achievement and IQ scores for individual students in their classes, as well as distribu-

[36] R. H. Ojemann and F. R. Wilkinson, "The Effect on Pupil Growth of an Increase in Teachers' Understanding of Pupil Behavior," *Journal of Experimental Education,* 8 (1939), 143–147.

[37] K. B. Hoyt, "A Study of the Effects of Teacher Knowledge of Characteristics on Pupil Achievement and Attitudes toward Class Work," *Journal of Educational Psychology,* 46 (1955), 302–310.

tions of the scores for the classes; the third group was given considerable information about individual pupils, and also participated in discussions about them. Subject content and the general approach in teaching methods were uniform for the three groups.

When pupil achievement and pupil attitudes were studied, however, no relationship between the teachers' knowledge of the pupils and pupil achievement was found. In other words, teachers who presumably knew more about their pupils did not produce greater pupil achievement (as measured by standardized achievement tests). However, the greater the teachers' knowledge of the pupils, the more favorable were the pupils' attitudes toward teachers.

The negative evidence presented by the Hoyt study—that there is little relation between the information about pupils acquired by teachers and the achievement of their pupils—may serve to remind us that many variables influence behavior change. The teacher's perception of his pupils has been assumed to be one of these variables, but the evidence presented here suggests that the influence may be an indirect one.

Both the Hoyt and the Ojemann studies treated the teacher's perception of his pupils as the independent variable and assumed that other factors influencing behavior change were relatively constant. This latter assumption probably is questionable. In the Ojemann study, for example, the teachers in the experimental group presumably individualized their instruction to a greater extent than did teachers in the control group; this effect illustrates the way in which a change in teachers' perceptions is likely to influence pupil change.

Both experiments produced attitude changes. This fact suggests the likelihood that changes in a teacher's understanding of pupils may influence some kinds of pupil change directly and other kinds indirectly. Attitudes toward school and toward the teacher changed in the favorable direction, presumably predisposing the students to be more interested in their work. Given other requisite conditions for behavior change, we would predict that pupil achievement would improve as it did in the Ojemann study, in which the pupils were studied over a longer period of time.

Devising ways of promoting behavior change is a problem for the teacher. The solutions he tries are likely to be influenced by his perception of the situation. The teacher's perception of the pupil's characteristics is one aspect of his total conception of the problem to be solved.[38] A reorien-

---

[38] See O. K. Moore, "Problem-Solving and the Perception of Persons," in R. Tagiuri and L. Petrullo, eds., *Person Perception and Interpersonal Behavior* (see note 20), pp. 131–150.

tation in his picture of the student may thus stimulate new approaches to the problem. Reorganizing, expanding, modifying, or generally changing one's perception of a student is likely to be effective in promoting pupil change if these perceptual changes lead to more effective choices of ways to promote pupil growth.

THE ORGANIZATION OF CLASSROOM GROUPS

Students are frequently placed in classes according to similarity of age, interest in a subject, preparation for study of a subject, or level of ability. A group formed on the basis of such general characteristics is usually composed of children who are different in many other characteristics. Consider a few of the differences that might characterize any one of these collections of individuals. Students in a class organized by age may differ in home backgrounds, previous academic achievement, interest in the subjects studied, and attitudes toward school and the teacher. Students in classes organized by interest in a subject may differ in terms of general level of ability, specific talents, and need satisfactions they hope to obtain by studying the subject. One student may be interested in algebra because he wants to be an engineer; another student, because algebra is required for college admission; and still another, simply because he likes mathematics. Typically, the students in any class are different in more ways than they are alike.

These differences among pupils are significant if the difference affects the achievement of learning goals. The students who are interested in algebra for different reasons may still work effectively for the attainment of the goals involved in the learning of algebra. Other differences among them may be indirectly related or unrelated to the attainment of these particular goals. Still other differences, such as differences in ability or previous preparation, may be highly relevant to the attainment of the learning goals.

THE INSTRUCTIONAL GROUP

We will call the group organized to work for a common goal in a learning experience the **instructional group.** The organization of such a group assumes (1) that the attainment of the common goal represents the desired behavior changes attainable by the students in the group; (2) that the pupils in the group to some extent share those characteristics relevant to the attainment of the goal; and (3) that students in the group are motivated to work for the common goal.

Such groups will vary in size and composition. For some goals and learning experiences, the instructional group may be the entire class. If a foreign visitor is invited to talk to the class on the customs of his country, the goal of the learning experience is probably acquiring certain basic facts and generalizations about his country. Assume, by way of contrast, that several students in the class are particularly interested in the customs of that country. They might be organized into a group to pursue the common goal of gaining greater understanding of the culture and life of that country. They may share such common learning experiences as a personal discussion with the speaker after his talk. In these two examples, note that the particular goals of the learning experiences and the character of the learning experiences themselves are different. The students are grouped together because they have similar goals and the abilities for attaining them.[39]

GROUP AND INDIVIDUAL GOALS
IN INSTRUCTIONAL GROUPS

Groups are typically organized to attain goals sought by the members of the group and more easily attained through common efforts. A distinction may be made between *group goals*—goals each group member is working for by combining their efforts—and *common goals*—goals shared by many individuals but attained principally by independent individual efforts. For example, a class of students may be working on a common set of problems where the goal of each student is to work the problems correctly. The goal in this case is shared, but it is not a group goal, since a cooperative effort is not required or utilized to attain the goal.

Other goals may be *individual goals* in the sense that they are the goals of a particular student and are not shared by the other members of a class. Learning experiences may be organized to facilitate the achievement of these individual goals. The English teacher may organize a "free" reading period in which students pursue their own reading interests; the science

---

[39] For a discussion of ways to group students, see H. A. Thelen, "Classroom Grouping of Students," *The School Review*, 67 (1959), 60–78. Bush and Allen argue for greater flexibility in grouping, variation in time spent in a learning experience, and other changes that diversify the size and composition of the instructional group. See R. Bush and D. Allen, *A New Design for High School Education* (New York: McGraw-Hill Book Co., 1964).

teacher may encourage students to develop their own projects or experiments.

The organization of a class group implies the hypothesis that such an organization is more likely to lead to the behavior change involved in goal attainment than is some other organization. We may not assume that grouping procedures are necessarily more effective for all purposes than other arrangements; furthermore, the effectiveness of such groups depends on factors related to group organization and operation. These factors will be discussed in the following sections.

FACTORS AFFECTING GROUP EFFECTIVENESS

A group is effective in attaining group goals only if the members are committed to achieving the group goal. What factors influence their willingness to commit themselves to a group goal? One important factor is the extent to which the members participate in deciding what the group will work for and how they will attain it. The evidence for this conclusion is derived from experiments performed elsewhere than in the school.[40] The conclusions from these experiments, however, are clear-cut. When individuals have an opportunity to participate in the decision-making process, rather than being "lectured at" or told what to do, desired behavior changes are much more frequent. However, the specific procedures that will produce involvement in goal setting have not been worked out. In fact, studies applying these ideas have yielded mixed results (see Anderson, note 19). The principle is sound, but effective technologies remain to be found. Experimenting is the teacher's recourse in this instance.

Need Satisfaction and Group Effectiveness

What is the influence of varying degrees of commitment to group goals on individual behavior? An individual in a group is more or less committed to attaining the group goal. Individuals join groups for a variety of reasons; the need satisfactions provided by achieving group goals may be only part of the need satisfaction that a person obtains by being in a group. For example, the members of a class research committee may achieve need satisfactions by carrying out their tasks successfully, but

[40] L. Coch and J. French, "Overcoming Resistance to Change," *Human Relations,* 1 (1948), 512–532; J. Levine and J. Butler, "Lecture versus Group Discussion in Changing Behavior," *Journal of Applied Psychology,* 36 (1952), 29–33.

they may also achieve need satisfaction from social interaction in the group. They may like to be with each other; they may like working together; and they obtain a certain amount of need satisfaction from these relationships.

An individual's goals are not necessarily compatible with the group goals. One may be so preoccupied with preserving, maintaining, or improving his own status that he cannot work effectively for the group goal. Consequently, he may interfere with the effectiveness of the group—especially when his needs cannot be satisfied by attaining the group goal. A group of investigators, studying the conflict between attempts to satisfy individual needs and attainment of the group goal, rated discussion groups on the extent to which the members apparently attempted satisfying their individual needs even though their needs were incompatible with attaining the group goal.[41] When the observers rated the effectiveness of the groups, they found that the ones in which there was little common goal orientation spent a longer period of time working on their agenda and completed fewer items on it. The members of these groups were also more dissatisfied with the meetings and the way in which they were conducted.

Allowing group members to define their goals and procedures presumably permits an individual to relate his individual goals to those of other members. Commonality of purpose may be clarified, and shared expectations developed. The development of common standards in turn increases the likelihood that pressures toward group attainment will be exerted on the individuals in the group.[42]

Group effectiveness also depends on the character of the leadership in the group. We have seen that at least a minimal leadership is necessary.[43] However, leadership which interferes with the full participation of the group members tends to reduce individual need satisfaction, although the group may still be effective in achieving its goal.[44] One of the major functions of leadership in the group is to preserve an open communication

[41] N. T. Fouriezos, M. L. Hutt, and H. Guetzkow, "Measurement of Self-Oriented Needs in Discussion Groups," *Journal of Abnormal and Social Psychology*, 45 (1950), 682–690.

[42] S. Schachter, N. Ellertson, D. McBride, and D. Gregory, "An Experimental Study of Cohesiveness and Productivity," *Human Relations*, 4 (1951), 229–238.

[43] N. Maier and A. R. Solem, "The Contribution of a Discussion Leader to the Quality of Group Thinking: The Effective Use of Minority Opinions," *Human Relations*, 5 (1952), 277–288.

[44] A. Bavelas, "Communication Patterns in Task-Oriented Groups," *Journal of the Acoustical Society of America*, 22 (1950), 725–730; also in D. Cartwright and A. Zander, eds., *Group Dynamics: Research and Theory*, 2nd ed. (Evanston, Ill.: Row, Peterson & Co., 1960), pp. 669–682.

system so that members of the group can effectively exchange information and ideas.

There is probably a limit below which need satisfaction may not drop without the group's also becoming ineffective. A research committee may appoint a chairman whose job is to lead the discussions in which the group analyzes its research findings. If the leader controls the amount and kind of communication between the members to get a report prepared, he may be effective in getting the report prepared, but he may also have a committee that is less satisfied with the job it is doing. If the group members become too dissatisfied, they may relieve their frustration by activities that interfere with accomplishment of the group task. For a group to be successful, a balance probably needs to be maintained between achieving the group task and providing individual satisfactions for the members of the group. Compatibility between the goals satisfying individual needs and the group goal is likely to facilitate both group effectiveness and individual need satisfaction.

Cooperation, Competition, and Group Effectiveness

The foregoing discussion stresses the importance of compatability between group and individual goals. It is possible to organize a group in such a way that the group goal may be attained by either individual or cooperative effort—as, for instance, when a teacher organizes a research committee to prepare reports for the social studies class, yet each student is to turn in an individual report for a grade. The students work together to prepare their reports. But if they are required to submit individual reports, which will be graded, they may be motivated to work for purely individual goals. The group goal in this case is largely a fiction; the students have the common goal of getting a good grade. If they can really help each other, they do have a group goal; if they cannot, the point of doing group work is not clear.

An experiment conducted by Deutsch [45] illustrates the kinds of effects that may occur in such situations. Deutsch formed groups of students working in a problem-solving situation, using two kinds of groups. In one set of groups, the students had to work cooperatively in order to attain the group goal; in the other group, the students could work together, but each attained the group goal independently of the others. The students

[45] M. Deutsch, "The Effects of Cooperation and Competition on Group Process," in D. Cartwright and A. Zander, eds., *Group Dynamics* (see note 44), pp. 414–448.

worked on two kinds of problems—puzzle problems and human-relations problems. In the cooperative groups, the groups were rated as a whole on their performance on the problems, each person in the group receiving the group rating as his rating. In the competitive groups, while the individuals worked together by discussing the problem, each could present his own solution and was rated on this solution independently of the solution achieved by the others.

What were the effects of cooperation and competition? The following are some of the characteristics of cooperative groups as opposed to competitive groups: greater coordination of efforts, greater diversity in the amount of contributions, more subdividing of activity and responsibility, more achievement pressure, more attentiveness to fellow members, more common understanding of communication, more common evaluation of communication, more orientation and orderliness, more productivity per unit of time, better discussions, more friendliness during discussions, and more favorable evaluation of the group and its work. In short, the members of the cooperative group worked harder and accomplished more than the members of the competitive groups. Some of the success in problem solving in the cooperative groups occurs, of course, because there are individuals in the cooperative group who can solve the problems and communicate the solutions to other members.

Note that many of the behavior patterns characterizing the cooperative groups are necessary for effective problem solving (e.g., achievement pressure, problem orientation, and greater understanding and evaluation of communications). Others are behavior required for students to work effectively with other people, such as more attentiveness to fellow members, greater coordination of efforts, and more widespread division of activity and responsibility. Generalizing the results of this experiment to the classroom, we would say that a cooperative organization of group activities is more likely to promote widespread behavior changes than would a competitive organization. The successful accomplishment of a group task increases the cohesiveness and attractiveness of the group and tends to develop greater task orientation and interest in the class work.

THE TEACHER'S USE OF
GROUPING PROCEDURES

In using grouping procedures, the teacher must attempt to answer two questions: (1) Are grouping procedures likely to promote the desired behavior changes more effectively than some other arrangements? (2) Is this particular grouping arrangement with its relevant procedures likely to be effective in facilitating the attainment of specific group goals?

We may not assume that children naturally prefer to work in groups or that they necessarily learn better when working in groups.[46] Grouping procedures are not a panacea for the problems of classroom "discipline." Grouping of pupils is one of many general procedures a teacher may use to foster behavior change.

SUMMARY

Much school learning is controlled in some way by a teacher. The teacher's behavior and the way he interacts with pupils substantially influences what students want to learn and how they approach learning opportunities. Teacher and student interactions may be conceptualized broadly in the following model.

1. Any behavior of one person may be matched with any behavior of the second person—that is, may occur as a response to it.

2. However, if we observe persons interacting, we are aware that only some of these behaviors do in fact occur and seem to occur with regularity.

3. These matchings may be assumed to be those which each person finds most rewarding and least costly. When the costs of the interaction are greater than rewards, the relationship will be broken if possible.

4. Interactions among teachers and students may be viewed as one kind of interaction, which we expect to be explainable in terms of these ideas. One deduction is that teachers are more likely to interact with those students who in some way reward them. Similarly, students will interact with teachers in ways they find rewarding. Both are likely to avoid interactions they find costly.

5. In general, a person is likely to change the pattern of his interactions with other people in the direction of finding more satisfying relations. Some pupil behavior, frequently seen by the teacher as a "discipline problem," is an instance of this phenomenon.

6. The teacher is assumed to be free to exercise some control over students, a function accorded him by virtue of the social role he is expected to play. This control is *social power,* which is the ability to influence the behavior of another person. Social power may be one of five

[46] H. B. Gerard, "Some Factors Affecting an Individual's Estimate of His Probable Success in a Group Situation," *Journal of Abnormal and Social Psychology,* 52 (1956), 235–239.

kinds: (1) *reward power,* or the ability to control the rewards another person seeks; (2) *coercive power,* or the ability to administer punishments; (3) *legitimate power,* where the person who is influenced accepts the right of the other person to influence him; (4) *referent power,* when one person, who is influenced, identifies with another, who influences; and (5) *expert power,* when a person exerts influence because of his superior knowledge and skill. A teacher may have all of these sources of social power to some degree. Theoretically, the teacher's social power ought to be primarily based on legitimate, referent, and expert kinds of social influence.

7. Teachers' interactions with pupils are presumably meant to promote pupils' attainment of the goals of learning experiences. In interacting with his pupils, the teacher attempts to maintain goal orientation and to eliminate behavior patterns that interfere with goal orientation. The teacher stimulates goal orientation by providing need satisfactions that will be attained by goal achievement. One of the major tasks in organizing learning experiences is to relate the kinds of need satisfactions for which students have learned to strive with the particular goals of a learning experience.

8. Teachers use rewards and punishments as ways of maintaining goal orientation in learning experiences. The effectiveness of rewards and punishments depends on their relation to the kinds of goals that satisfy students' needs. Rewards that provide need satisfactions for students are likely to facilitate goal orientation. The effects of punishment are less predictable. Students may acquire many undesirable behaviors to avoid punishment. Punishment may be effective in teaching students to avoid undesirable behavior, but may be ineffective in stimulating them to acquire desired behavior. Punishment frequently fosters the kind of behavior that it is designed to eliminate.

9. The pupil's perception of the justifiability and the intent of the teacher's behavior influences his response to that behavior. Actions of the teacher which are seen by pupils as justifiable and well intended inspire less hostility from pupils, even though the teacher's behavior may be disagreeable to them. Some forms of teacher behavior are more likely to be viewed either as unjustified or as inspired by personal hostility to the student. Dominating behavior is probably seen in this way, and it is likely to evoke dominating and resisting behavior from the student.

10. Teacher control of pupil behavior is related to the kinds of expectations pupils have about the patterns of control. Pupils are less likely to be hostile and aggressive in their response to patterns of teacher control

when the teacher acts consistently with established expectations. But some patterns of control are more likely to evoke undesirable responses from students. Autocratic patterns of control are likely to evoke many undesirable kinds of pupil behavior, such as aggressiveness, unwillingness to assume responsibility without teacher direction, and lack of sustained interest in the learning experience.

11. Generally, the consensus of the students on matters of opinion, or on ideas and actions expressing attitudes and values, determines how much the teacher will affect individuals.

12. The class also influences the teacher's behavior by rewarding him for some actions and not others, although this rewarding may not be easily detected and the teacher himself may not be aware of it.

13. How people perceive each other, what they think other persons are like, determines how they will act toward them.

14. Traits are descriptive classifications of perceived characteristics of another person. These categories may be more or less precisely defined in terms of observable behavior and are based on inferences from these observations.

15. Individuals tend to develop systems of trait associations, in which they see certain traits as necessarily or typically associated with other traits. In this way, individuals may be attributed traits they do not possess.

16. Perceptions of another individual's characteristics are frequently influenced by the relevance of these characteristics to environmental factors. This is seen in the way some teachers tend to perceive traits that interfere with classroom order as more serious than other characteristics. In other words, a teacher may be predisposed to attend to certain kinds of pupil behavior and to ignore other kinds. In this way the teacher's perceptions of a pupil's characteristics are limited to the kinds of behaviors that the teacher sees as desirable or undesirable in the classroom setting.

17. As teachers acquire more adequate information and greater understanding about their pupils, desired changes in pupil behavior are more likely to occur. The relationship between the teacher's perceptions of a pupil's behavior and the influence of these perceptions on pupil change is probably indirect. Changes in the teacher's perception of the pupil may stimulate the teacher to think of more alternatives for influencing pupil change, and in this way contribute indirectly to pupil change.

18. Students may work either individually or cooperatively in groups to attain the goals of a learning experience. A group is effective to the

extent that group action leads to the attainment of the group goal. The effectiveness of groups depends upon the willingness of members in the group to work for the attainment of the group goal. Group members are likely to work cooperatively for the attainment of the group goal when their individual need satisfactions and the satisfactions associated with goal achievement are compatible.

19. Individual group members may interfere with the attainment of the group goal by striving for personal need satisfactions rather than striving for the attainment of the group goal. The procedures for attaining the group goal may be organized in such a way that individual need satisfaction may be obtained only by attaining the group goal. Cooperative groups of this kind foster a wide range of behavior change in group members.

STUDY AND DISCUSSION QUESTIONS

1. Observe some simple interaction between two people. List and describe the behavior of each in sequence. In what ways is the behavior of each acting as a stimulus to the other? In any one interaction sequence, could either of the persons have behaved differently? If you think they might have, hypothesize about why the behavior you observed occurred.

2. Using this same observation, identify the ways in which each person rewards or makes costly the behavior of the other.

3. How is a student's classroom behavior costly to a teacher? List some specific behaviors (other than the most obvious violations of good manners and decorum) that you think are costly. (Hint: Is a student's not being able to answer a question likely to be costly to the teacher?)

4. How is a teacher's behavior likely to be costly to a student? List some specific kinds of teacher behavior you think may be costly—again find some kinds other than the more obvious ones, such as being sarcastic.

5. List teacher and student behaviors that each is likely to find rewarding.

6. Some people think that the more things a teacher is competent at, the more his students will respect him. Evaluate this hypothesis. Do you think that a history teacher's expertise on automobiles will inspire students to accept his expertise on ideas related to history?

7. Suggest some ways in which each of the following aspects of teacher behavior may influence teacher-pupil relations.

    a. The teacher's physical appearance and grooming.

    b. The quality of the teacher's voice.

    c. A teacher's posture habits.

8. For each of the above behavior patterns, suggest some variations in behavior that may be observed among teachers. What inferences may students be predisposed to make about the teacher's personality on the basis of the different behavior patterns apparent in the teacher's behavior?

9. List the principal kinds of need satisfactions that may be provided in the typical classroom by the teacher. What kinds of teacher-pupil relations may develop if the teacher provides these need satisfactions?

10. In what ways may the teacher be limited in providing satisfactions for student needs? Predict some effects that difficulty in providing these need satisfactions may have on teacher-pupil relations.

11. What kinds of need satisfactions may be provided by a teacher who is:

    a. Friendly but firm.

    b. Friendly but not firm.

    c. Strict and demanding.

    Describe the behavior that you associate with each of the above traits, and predict the kinds of teacher-pupil relations that may result.

12. Recall your first day in some class. What impressions did you form of the teacher? What inferences did you make about his personality characteristics? What expectations did you have about teacher-pupil relations? Were your predictions in this respect confirmed?

13. What traits do you associate with each of the following traits?

    a. Smart.

    b. Practical.

    c. Clever.

    d. Shy.

    e. Hard-working.

    What experiences have you had that lead you to expect that these traits are associated? Can you recall instances of people who may have the given traits but not the associated traits?

14. If you were told that an instructor whom you were to have in the near future has a "warm personality," what other characteristics would you expect him to have? Explain why you think that these characteristics may be associated with the characteristics of "warmth."

15. For each of the statements listed below, describe the kinds of persons you think are likely to have made such a statement:

    a. It is essential that a study of science be included in a modern curriculum.

    b. Children do not mean to be malicious; this kind of behavior usually results when they are frustrated.

    c. Studying history is a waste of time; it has no practical value.

16. Refer to the Schrupp and Gjerde study presented in this chapter. If the teachers had been asked to describe the traits they considered most serious for the future development of the child, do you think they would have given a different rank order? Would there have been greater agreement between teachers and clinicians? Explain the reasons for your predictions.

17. Describe some of the ways in which a teacher may respond to a student whom he sees as:

    a. Friendly.

    b. Unfriendly.

    c. Intelligent.

    d. Not very bright.

18. Compare the Ojemann and Hoyt studies. What differences in procedures may have accounted for the differences in results obtained in these two investigations?

19. What kinds of need satisfactions may a teacher be obtaining who is:

    a. Friendly with students.

    b. Firm with students.

    c. Strict with students.

    d. Unfriendly with students.

    Define and describe the behavior that you associate with each of these terms and make your predictions in terms of the descriptions that you provide.

20. What kinds of motives may initiate the following instances of student behavior?

    a. A student regularly asks for extra work.

    b. A student offers answers to questions only when called on.

    c. A student regularly ignores assignments.

    d. A student appears to avoid any close relationship with the teacher.

21. In what ways may isolating a child in the back of a classroom provide the child with need satisfaction? Are there any circumstances in which the use of this procedure may effectively eliminate undesirable classroom behavior?

22. Suggest some ways in which students might explain to themselves the following behaviors in teachers:

    a. Assigning extra homework.

    b. Requesting a student to leave class.

    c. Asking a student to have his parents visit the teacher.

    d. Organizing a class picnic.

23. For what kinds of learning experiences may students "expect" relatively more direction from teachers?

24. List a number of "teacher controls" that students are likely to find disagreeable. Suggest the probable effects of these teacher-control procedures on pupil behavior. What kinds of pupil behavior change would a teacher be attempting to achieve by using these procedures? What alternative forms of teacher-pupil relations may be available to achieve the same purposes?

25. Some people argue that students need to be placed in competitive situations in order to learn how to compete successfully. Evaluate this argument. Is the use of group procedures in the organization of learning experiences likely to inhibit the development of "competitive" behavior?

26. Some people argue that emphasis on the use of group procedures in the school tends to produce "conformity." They claim that this emphasis does not develop individuals who can think for themselves. Evaluate this argument in the light of the principles of group operation discussed in this chapter. Under what conditions might this criticism be justifiable?

27. In organizing project work, some teachers of social studies will assign the brighter students to a research committee and the other students to construction activities, such as painting a mural. Are such arrangements likely to lead to group effectiveness in problem solving? What kinds of behavior changes might not be facilitated by these arrangements?

28. Assume that you mixed the students randomly on both committees. What effect would you predict that these arrangements would have on group effectiveness and satisfaction?

RECOMMENDED READINGS

K. D. Benne and G. Levit. "The Nature of Groups and Helping Groups Improve Their Operation," *Review of Educational Research*, 23 (1953), 289–308.

R. N. Bush. *The Teacher-Pupil Relationship*. Englewood Cliffs, N. J.: Prentice-Hall, Inc., 1954.

D. Cartwright and A. Zander. *Group Dynamics: Research and Theory*. Evanston, Ill.: Row, Peterson & Co., 1953.

B. Collins and H. Guetzkow. *A Social Psychology of Group Processes for Decision-Making*. New York: John Wiley and Sons, 1964.

M. Horwitz. "The Conceptual Status of Group Dynamics," *Review of Educational Research*, 23 (1953), 309–328.

R. Strang. *Group Work in Education*. New York: Harper & Brothers, 1958.

R. Tagiuri and L. Petrullo, eds. *Person Perception and Interpersonal Behavior*. Stanford, Calif.: Stanford University Press, 1958.

J. Thibaut and H. Kelley. *The Social Psychology of Groups*. New York: John Wiley and Sons, 1959.

CHAPTER FOURTEEN

THE SCHOOL AS A SOCIAL SYSTEM

Social systems may be distinguished from each other by differences in the arrangement of **positions** and their various **roles**. The family may be viewed as a three-position system, the positions being those of mother, father, and child. The system increases in complexity with additional children, who will have positions with respect to each other. Contrast this social system with that of a small town, which is characterized by a more complex organization of social positions. The number and kinds of positions in these two systems and their relationship to each other influence the kinds of interactions likely to occur among the members. These differences in patterns of interaction create differences in role expectations and behavior. The character of a social system influences the behavior of its members by stimulating learning behavior patterns requisite to membership.

The school is a social system because it is an organization of social positions.

Three principal kinds of positions characterize this system—administrator, teacher, and student. These positions are part of the formal organization of the school as a social system. The school also embraces the complex of social positions in the formal and informal organization of student activities. A child located in the social position of "student" also occupies positions in such organizations as the athletic team or the band, and may have other positions in the informal groupings of friends and associates.

An understanding of this system is necessary to recognize the variables that influence behavior change. Formally organized learning experiences embrace only some of the variables influencing learning. A child's attitude toward "school achievement," for example, may be influenced more by the the attitudes of his friends than by his teacher's conception of desirable achievement. Many aspects of a child's personality development may be influenced by the specific experiences associated with the positions he occupies in the social system of the school.

SOCIAL POSITION AND
SOCIAL STATUS

A status system based on prestige is typically associated with the arrangements of positions in a social system. The status associated with a position may derive from the character of the formal organization. The higher status of some positions is based on the greater responsibilities and privileges associated with their occupancy. The positions of principal and teacher involve responsibilities not required of students, and they have some privileges associated with them that are not accorded to students. The presidency of a school club is another example of this kind of status associated with a position.

In other cases the status associated with a position reflects the dominant values of the members of a system. In a school the members of the varsity football team may have high status associated with their position as team members. This status is based on some generally shared values about the importance of the activities of the football team.

The status of a position may vary depending on the particular social system of which it is a part. The presidency of a club may have high status within the social system of the club, but relatively low status in the system of clubs in the school. A position may be given high status by some members of a system but not by others. However, we are concerned here only with the most stable status relations of positions in the school's social system.

The school's social system may be described in terms of its *formal* and *informal* organizations. The positions in the formal organization may be represented along several status dimensions. One dimension of status includes all of the individuals within the school, and the major positions on this status dimension are principal, teacher, student. The formal organization of classes also defines students' status positions with respect to each other. Seniors generally have higher status than do the juniors, and juniors have higher status than sophomores and freshmen. In most schools, activities and clubs—with varying degrees of prestige—define another status dimension.

Within the formal organization in the school, many informal groupings develop through associations of students for which the school system as such does not systematically provide. In Wabash School, for example, we saw that there were a number of cliques, and that the group with the highest status was the "athletic crowd."

INDIVIDUAL SOCIAL STATUS IN THE SCHOOL

In general, the social status of an individual student in the school depends on the prestige of the positions he occupies within both the formal and the informal organizations of the school. A student who is a senior is assured of a relatively high prestige position within one aspect of the formal organization of the school. But if he is not a member of one of the informal organizations with high status, his general social status will probably be lower than that of another senior who belongs to a high-prestige organization.

Variations arise from school to school in the importance of positions in both the formal and the informal social systems. The student's position in the formal organization may be more influential in determining his general social status if his school places little emphasis on participation in clubs and activities, so that most of his personal associations exist outside the school. The informal organization may be more influential in determining a student's general social status if most of his personal associations are with other students in school activities. In most schools, the student's status in the social system is a complex combination of his status in both the formal and informal organizations.

INFLUENCE OF FORMAL ORGANIZATIONS
OF STUDENTS ON STATUS

At the student level, three kinds of formal school organizations may be identified: (1) grade-sex groups, (2) class groups, (3) classroom groups.

A *grade-sex group* would be, for example, all the eighth-grade boys, or all the eighth-grade girls. It is an association based upon sex and common grade in school. The members of the freshman class would constitute a *class group*. A *classroom group* would be the students in Mr. Day's class. These groups are the principal organizational units in a school, and the principal roles within these organizational units are teacher and student roles.

The formal organizations are typically controlled by the administration and the teachers in the school, and they tend to be "achievement oriented." The major goal of these systems is likely to be "success in school." "Success in school" frequently, though not always, means success in achieving grades. "Success in school," as measured by grades attained, may embrace more than academic achievement. The following statement from the grading policy of Wabash School indicates the factors implicit in some systems of grading:

E and *S* indicate that the pupil is above the class in school average and that superior work is done. *F* indicates that the pupil is failing and will not pass the course unless improvement is made. An *I* is unsatisfactory. Absence or tardiness without a good reason is inexcusable. *Grades are not determined by knowledge of subject matter alone.* Other extremely important factors are regularity, punctuality of attendance, attitude, effort, and contribution to class discussion.[1] (Italics added.)

The probable result of a policy of this kind is that students learn what achievement and appropriate classroom social behavior mean in that school. Status within these systems depends on the extent to which a student's behavior accords with these patterns of expectation. We would hypothesize that a student's social status will be influenced by the status of his position in these formal structures if such achievement is generally valued in a particular school. The status value of achieving success in the formal system of the school is determined by three factors.

First, the value placed on such achievement is influenced by the extent to which need satisfactions are provided through other organizations in the school. In "street-car universities," where students have few associations, we expect social status to be determined mainly by achievement within the formal department structures. In elementary schools and high schools, where there are usually large numbers of clubs and activities, as

[1] C. W. Gordon, *The Social System of the High School* (Glencoe, Ill.: The Free Press, 1957), p. 34.

well as many informal student groups, social status is more likely to be influenced by the student's prestige within the informal system.

Second, occupancy of some social positions is clearly related to achievement in these structures; in other cases, status in the formal structures may have a negative correlation with general social status. The queen role was a high-prestige position in Wabash School. The girl who hoped to obtain the position of queen had to have prestige in both the formal and informal organizations of the school. Among the boys at Wabash School, the students with the most prestige were accorded the title "big wheel." The "big-wheel" status, however, depended heavily on participation in school activities. A student could not become a "big wheel" unless he belonged to a wide variety of important activities. He had to belong to the "athletic crowd," one of the informal organizations. It was impossible for a nonathlete to attain full "big-wheel" status.

Third, these formal organizations influence social status by controlling opportunities for participation in other organizations. Table 14–1 indicates the criteria for eligibility in the school organizations in an elementary school.[2] As is apparent, almost all of the organizations set a grade standard for membership, and some of them also set a sex standard for membership. Belonging to the Color Guard is possible only for a sixth-grade boy, whereas only third-graders are excluded from the Art Club, which both boys and girls are allowed to join.

INFLUENCE OF FORMAL ORGANIZATION OF ACTIVITIES ON STUDENT STATUS

In addition to class associations, schools usually provide clubs or organized activities—varsity athletic teams, foreign-language clubs, musical groups. These organizations typically have varying degrees of status in the social system of the school. In Table 14–2 is a list of clubs and activities at Wabash School, ranked according to their prestige in the eyes of the students.[3] These clubs and activities have both formal and informal standards of membership. Participating in them depends in part on the exclusiveness of their criteria for membership.

In a comparative study of the social systems of schools, the investigators found that one school, which they called "Old School," had the fewest students participating in clubs. The investigators attributed this low level

[2] H. Taba, *School Culture: Studies in Participation and Leadership* (Washington, D. C.: American Council on Education, 1955), p. 70.

[3] Gordon (see note 1), p. 61.

activities (from Taba).

Activity	No. of members possible	3	4	5	6	Sponsor Appt.	Prin. Appt.	Elected	Indiv. Choice	Talent	Scholarship	Dependability	Leadership	Grade	Sex	Initiative	Pupil Need
Safety Squad	85				✓	✓						✓	✓	✓			
Color Guard	7				✓	✓						✓		✓	b✓	✓	✓
Art Club	18		✓		✓	✓	✓			✓	✓	✓			g✓	✓	
Office assistant	5		✓									✓		✓			
Glee Club	64		✓	✓	✓							✓			g✓		
Gym captains	56				✓							✓	✓				✓
Stage crew	1	✓								✓		✓					
Upper Student Council	24		✓	✓	✓			✓				✓			b✓		✓
Orchestra	29		✓	✓	✓	✓				✓		✓					✓
Waitresses	6				✓	✓						✓					✓
Library	3	✓			✓	✓						✓					
Piano	75	✓		✓	✓	✓			✓	✓		✓		✓			
Ushers	6			✓	✓			✓				✓		✓	b✓		
Cafeteria helper	2			✓	✓	✓						✓		✓	b✓		
School Patrol	9		✓	✓				✓				✓		✓	b✓		
Milk girls	6		✓	✓	✓		✓							✓	g✓		✓
Cot girls	2			✓	✓		✓		✓	✓				✓	g✓		
Violin	35	✓								✓							
Lower Student Council	24	✓		✓	✓	✓		✓								✓	
Primary Chorus	58	✓				✓					✓						
Instrumental ensemble	5	✓				✓				✓	✓						
Total	520	7	7	10	15	11	3	4	2	7	3	15	2	9	8	3	6

TABLE 14–2. *Prestige ranks of activities in a high school (from Gordon).**

Organization	Girls' rank	Boys' rank	Combined rank
Student Assembly (Student Governing Body)	1	2	1
Varsity Basketball	3	1	2
Varsity Football	5	3	3
National Honor Society	4	8	4
Cheerleaders	2	9	5
Crest Coronation (Yearbook Queen's Court)	6	7	6
Varsity Baseball	11	4	7
Crest Staff (Yearbook Staff)	9	5	8
Varsity Track	14	6	9
Senior Play Cast	7	13	10
Junior Prom Committee	8	12	11
Scoop Staff (School Newspaper)	17	11	12
Mixed Chorus	10	14	13
Varsity Wrestling	20	10	14
Girls' Athletic Association	12	19	15
Senior Dramatics Club	16	15	16
School Band	15	18	17
"B" Basketball	18	16	18
School Orchestra	13	23	19
Quill & Scroll (Honorary Publications)	19	21	20
Junior Ring Committee	22	17	21
"B" Football	21	22	22
Varsity Tennis	28	20	23
"T-13" (Honorary Girls' Athletic)	23	26	24
Pep Club	27	24	25
Junior Dramatics	25	28	26
Junior Rotarians	24	33	27
Junior Town Meeting	26	32	28
Bowling Club	30	27	29
Rifle Club	29	30	30
Projection Staff	31	29	31
Varsity Golf	37	25	32
Intramural Basketball	40	31	33
Drum Majorettes	34	35	34
Stage Crew	33	37	35
Gym Assistants	32	42	36
Office Assistants	35	41	37
Chess Club	49	48	38
Art Club	39	39	39
Intramural Volleyball	41	36	40
Diversified Occupations (Vocational Club)	43	38	41

TABLE 14–2. *Prestige ranks of activities in a high school (from Gordon).*—Continued

Organization	Girls' rank	Boys' rank	Combined rank
Student World Federalist	36	45	42
Intramural Tennis	44	40	43
Library Club	42	44	44
Junior Red Cross	38	46	45
Roller Skating Club	45	43	46
Outdoor Club	50	34	47
Pencil Pushers (Creative Writing)	47	47	48
Riding Club (Horseback Riding)	46	49	49
Knitting Club	48	50	50

* A rank of 1 indicates the most prestigeful group. Note that boys and girls rank these groups differently; the combined rank is meaningful only when both rank a group similarly.

of participation to the exclusive standards of the clubs at "Old School." They stated:

Perhaps the chief factor in this pattern was the tradition of exclusiveness in all school clubs sponsored by a few "old clubs." The barriers to admission were, therefore, many and high. In a school with a heterogeneous population, grade requirements usually work especially against the lower economic group and racial or ethnic minorities. Because these conditions usually magnify the cleavages already inherent in such schools, a considerable proportion of students become inactive, indifferent, and even hostile to group activities. In Old School . . . the club program was such as to interest only a minority of students. School clubs had either social exclusiveness or academic pretensions as their main focus.[4]

Many of the clubs had been established at Old School by the mothers of the present generation of children. The children of these mothers were encouraged to join the same clubs to which their mothers had belonged. These parents, by encouraging their children to join, to support, and to maintain these clubs, gave the clubs importance beyond the school itself. A chess club is important to its members, and some of their parents may be interested in its activities. But the clubs in "Old School" were impor-

[4] Taba (see note 2), p. 96.

tant to the parents as well as the children. The parents helped maintain the exclusive character of the clubs and rewarded their children for belonging. In this way, the club system had similar status differences to those of the school's community.

The extent of participation in clubs and activities is one measure of differences between the social systems of schools. Participation in school activities appears to depend upon general community expectation for such participation; these differences in expectation reflect local cultural values.[5]

The hypothesis relating membership in these organizations to social status is that a student's social status will be positively correlated with the status of the activities in which he participates. This relation assumes that social positions may be maintained both in the formal administrative organizations of students and in the activity organizations. Some students may experience difficulties in achieving or maintaining status in both systems, but the above hypothesis assumes that the membership demands of the two systems are not in serious conflict with each other.

One characteristic by which the social systems of schools may be distinguished is the relative amounts of prestige that may be achieved in them. The extent to which a student achieves relatively high social status is in turn influenced by the value placed on membership in the formal structures.

INFLUENCE OF INFORMAL ORGANIZATIONS ON STUDENT SOCIAL STATUS

Informal associations or "cliques" of students may be found in every school. These groups are formed and maintained, at least in part, by the choices of students. Some of these associations are prestigeful groups. Membership in such prestige groups provides such need satisfactions as approval from classmates, special privileges, and control over the behavior of other people. The following statement from one of the "big wheels" at Wabash School reflects the privileged status accorded to a "big wheel":

Everyone enjoys privileges but no one intends to take advantage of them, although I feel that sometimes I do. I am a necessary member of the choir, and I am afraid that I take advantage most of the time. I am constantly absent or late to class.

[5] See Taba, p. 93.

Today was a typical example. At 1:07 I stole into class and took my seat. I thought that Andrews (the teacher) wouldn't say anything, but he stopped and asked me for an excuse. I gave my usual simple answer of, "Why, am I late?" He says, "Are you late? Seven minutes!" To this I just said, "Oh, do you want me to get an excuse?" He gives up and we go on singing without my giving any sort of reason for being late.

If I am just a minute or less after the bell, I just nod to him as I go in and he lets me go. What are the kids' reactions? They all think it's a big joke. Some girls come out with, "big wheel," so I may hear it. This annoys me to be called "big wheel"! [6]

EFFECTS OF SOCIAL POSITION AND STATUS ON PUPIL BEHAVIOR

As we have seen, a student's general social position and status depend on his position and status in both the formal and informal organizations of the school system. A student does not move from the formal organization to the informal organization; he is a member of both at the same time. He has a social position within each and a corresponding amount of status or prestige. For example, if a child is achieving high grades in school, if he belongs to the most important clubs in school, and if he belongs to the cliques that have high prestige, his general social status in the school is likely to be high. In other words, he meets all the criteria, both formal and informal, for high social status. Failure to meet some or all of these requirements would place him in a different social status.

The "outsider" in any school may be so for a variety of reasons. He may not be reaching an adequate achievement level in school. He may be a member of low-status organizations, or he may not be a member of any group of students. Another child may be achieving well within the formal system, but he may have relatively low social status because he does not take part in any of the important activities, or because he has not been accepted as a member of an important clique. *Why* he is not a member is another problem.

Another important consideration is related to the way in which we visualize social status as influencing behavior change. Social status, as we have described it, is an index reflecting the prestige of the positions occupied by an individual. To what extent does occupancy of relatively high- or low-status positions influence behavior?

[6] Gordon (see note 1), p. 93.

SOCIAL STATUS AND NEED SATISFACTION

An individual's social status is a measure of the associations he is likely to have. A student with relatively low social status in the school may be an individual who is not a member of important prestige groups. From this fact we might infer that the need satisfactions available to these group members may not be available to this student. We might also infer that the student may be obtaining these need satisfactions in other ways; or he may not be motivated by the needs that membership in these groups satisfies; or, in fact, his needs may not be satisfied. Each of these inferences is a hypothesis that may be tested by gathering appropriate data about the student.

A social system provides means for attaining desirable ends or objects by cooperation among the members. For example, the control that a clique exercises over the dating behavior of its members may be accompanied by provisions for guaranteeing that its members will be able to date. The prestige of the clique may attract the opposite sex to its members. Membership in these and other groups provides a way of obtaining a wide variety of need satisfactions. For this reason, a student's social positions in the school affect the kinds of need satisfactions available to him.

In some cases, a group in the school may provide a certain need satisfaction that compensates for failure to achieve another need satisfaction in another group. A clique that emphasizes popularity and participation in student activities while devaluing academic achievement may provide prestige and approval for members who could not gain these satisfactions by academic achievements. As we have seen, striving for need satisfaction is the motivational force behind behavior change. Since the kinds of need satisfaction available to a student depend on his position in the school's social system, his social position influences the kinds of goals he may seek to achieve need satisfaction.

SOCIAL STATUS AND GROUP MEMBERSHIP

Knowing a student's positions in a social system enables us to predict the kinds of behavior patterns he is likely to learn. Both the formally organized clubs and the informal associations of students are likely to be *reference groups* for their members. These groups set standards of appropriate behavior for their members.

An individual's awareness of his group identifications increases the probability of his conforming to the group attitudes and behavior patterns.

In school the pupil is with other people almost constantly. Presumably, what he does is influenced by what he thinks others expect; also by their rewarding or punishing what he does. We may hypothesize that a student's behavior will be different, to some extent, when he is with other members of groups to which he belongs and whose favorable attitude toward him he values. We would expect him to adhere to the group code rather than jeopardize his membership and consequently his status. The following study provides experimental evidence that being with fellow group members does influence how a person acts. In a subsequent study we will see how conforming to the group's standards affects a person's social status.

Charters and Newcomb[7] performed an experiment to determine the effects on behavior of informing students that they were working with individuals who belonged to the same groups they did and who, therefore, presumably knew those groups' code. They formed several groups of students on the basis of religious background. In some groups—the control groups—the students were not aware that all of the members of the group were of the same religious faith. In the experimental groups, the leader of the group made clear to the members that they were all of the same faith. The problem that the groups were to work on was the construction of a questionnaire on religious beliefs. In the experimental groups, the leader conducted a discussion on the basic and commonly shared religious beliefs of the particular religious group to which the members belonged.

Before the discussion periods, the experimenters had the students answer an attitude questionnaire on a variety of topics related to religious principles. After the discussions, the students were requested to take the same attitude questionnaire. Table 14–3 lists the average scores of the experimental and control groups on items related to their respective religious positions. A Catholic item, for example, was "Birth-control information should be provided to all married individuals who desire it." Catholic students would be expected to take a definite position on this item since their religious faith generally takes a negative position on birth control. A Jewish item was, "Under no conditions is there any justification

[7] W. W. Charters, Jr., and T. M. Newcomb, "Some Attitudinal Effects of Experimentally Increased Salience of a Membership Group," in E. E. Maccoby, T. M. Newcomb, and E. L. Hartley, eds., *Readings in Social Psychology*, 3rd ed. (New York: Henry Holt & Co., 1958), pp. 276–281.

TABLE 14–3. *Mean scores of Catholic students, classified by type of item (from Charters and Newcomb).*

Type of item	Theoretical* orthodoxy	Experimental group	Control groups	University norms
Catholic	1.00	2.09†	2.36	2.73†
General religious	1.00	2.04†	2.41	2.77†
Church	1.00	1.50†	1.80	2.15†
Protestant	1.00	2.56	2.67	2.60
Jewish	1.00	2.36	2.38	2.23
Feminist	1.00	1.76	1.78	1.65
Political	1.00	1.95	2.07	2.17

* The scores in this column are a baseline—the score that would be obtained if all members of a faith answered "their" items the way their faith prescribes. The closer the actual scores are to 1.00, the more orthodox the answers were.

† Difference between mean scores of control subjects and experimental subjects or university norms is at or beyond the .01 level of significance.

for quotas limiting admission to schools and colleges on a racial or religious basis." The general Jewish position on racial or religious prejudice should influence a Jewish student's response to this item. When the scores in the table are examined, it is apparent those of the experimental groups are much closer to "orthodoxy" on items that tested attitudes likely to be influenced by religious beliefs. In general, fewer Catholics in the experimental groups gave deviant responses than did Catholics in the control group (see Table 14–4). This experiment illustrates the effect that awareness of group membership may have on behavior. We may not conclude from this experiment that such changes are permanent, since they may be an expression of public conformity. They need not be, however, to influence one's social status.

TABLE 14–4. *Percentage of subjects with high deviation scores in each religious group (from Charters and Newcomb).*

Religious group	% Deviant* control	N	% Deviant* experimental	N
Catholic	24	58	8	46
Jewish	3	92	6	58
Protestant	9	45	16	33

* The number of subjects whose answers were markedly different from the "orthodox" answer.

Dittes and Kelly[8] explored the relationship between social acceptance and conformity, and their work sheds some light on the relationship of social status to behavior change. These investigators systematically manipulated experimental conditions so that group members were accorded two levels of acceptance by their respective groups. In each group, some members were given less than complete acceptance but were allowed to see the possibility of obtaining such acceptance. Other group members were accorded little acceptance and given no hope of gaining it. The experimental tasks required group discussions and decisions, and the group members were given opportunities and some encouragement to deviate from the common judgments of their groups about topics being discussed and what was decided. Two patterns of conformity appeared in this situation: (1) a high degree of genuine adherence to group judgments among group members who had hopes of attaining complete acceptance; (2) high public conformity to group judgments, but private rejection among group members who had little hope of complete acceptance.

On the basis of these experimental data, we would predict that the extent to which a student genuinely accepts the attitudes, values, and behavior patterns of a group will be related to his status in the group and his hopes for improving his status.

In summary, the behavior patterns of students are acquired in part from associations they have in school. Some of these associations accrue as a result of sex, age, and grade in school. Some of them result from membership in activities, and others from friendship relations and common interests.

A student's position in these social systems influences his status in the school; both his social position and its status influence the kinds of experiences that he is likely to have. Thus, the social system of the school shapes and diversifies the kinds of experiences available to a student. The character of these patterns of experience serves as a stimulus to behavior change.

EFFECTS OF THE SCHOOL'S
SOCIAL SYSTEM ON LEARNING

A social system is a system of rewards and punishments, a system for controlling learning opportunities. In the school, as in all societies, power-

---

[8] J. E. Dittes and H. H. Kelley, "Effects of Different Conditions of Acceptance upon Conformity to Group Norms," *Journal of Abnormal and Social Psychology*, 53 (1956), 100–107.

ful social stimuli control behavior. Learning of the formal kind occurs in this setting. What are the effects of the social system on both this learning and all other kinds that might be expected to occur in this environment?

As we have seen repeatedly, the success or failure of a learner determines whether he continues to learn. He comes to see himself as a success, and is ready to strive and to try again, to correct errors, to utilize learning opportunities. If he fails, he is likely to withdraw. The social system of the school presents a learning problem for the child. He must learn how to win the rewards it provides. If he does not, he has failed.

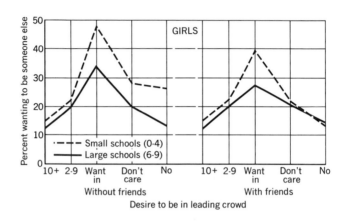

FIGURE 14-1. *Relation between desire to be in leading crowd and wanting to be someone else among those with and without friends, for large and small groups separately. Similar results were obtained with boys. (From Coleman.)*

Coleman [9] has studied intensively the social systems of ten high schools and provides data on the effect of the social system. As in the Gordon study, he was able to identify the "ins" and the "outs." He asked students whether they would like to be somebody else. A "yes" answer may be regarded as symptomatic of a negative self-evaluation. Figure 14-1 shows the relation between "wanting to be somebody else" and being an insider and outsider. It is clear that students who do not belong to the elite or the

[9] J. S. Coleman, *The Adolescent Society* (New York: Free Press, 1961).

leading crowd are more likely to want to be somebody else, and presumably have more negative self-evaluations. Coleman summarizes the problem as follows:

These results point to a dilemma in secondary education. The students most involved in the school and most identified with it—those for whom school means most—are the ones upon whom exclusion from the leading crowd has its greatest impact. Those least involved in school, the ones who can take it or leave it, are least likely to be hurt by its social system. Thus, attempts to pull more and more of a teen-ager's interests toward school and the activities within it make him more vulnerable to the whims of its social system, less able to find internal peace through some alternative means (p. 228).

How does the social system affect learning opportunities?

Coleman (pp. 236–240) again provides us with some data. Tables 14–5 and 14–6 show that, in schools where athletics are highly rewarded, the athletes spend *less time* with the mass media. A similar effect occurs in schools where scholarship is rewarded. The data are consistent if we make one assumption. If a student is receiving extensive rewards through the school's social system, he is not frustrated. Hence, he does not need to turn to the mass media as an outlet. This is Coleman's hypothesis: "Heavy mass-media use occurs when one is in a system where his achievements go unrewarded" (p. 240). The data are consistent with this hypothesis.

These data are also consistent with the idea that the lack of rewards available to a student in the school culture induces him to seek other rewards. Most of the adolescent's life is tied up in the school and is oriented to its activities. There are few other places he can seek rewards than in the mass media and fantasy behaviors.

Another way of interpreting these facts is to see that a child's and adolescent's life is bound up in the school, and that his psychological energy is invested in coping with the problems of living in that society. He cannot run the risk of psychological isolation except at the price of personal pain. He cannot simply get up and walk out of this society, again except by incurring painful consequences. On the other hand, coping with finding a place in it offers many rewards. Coleman argues that his data convincingly show that the social system of the high school controls the allocation of energies. In his words, "School forces a scholar to choose between being *selfish* by studying hard, and being *unselfish* by working for the glory of the school in its interscholastic games" (p. 240).

Although the times have produced a change in some high schools, there

TABLE 14–5. *Influence of the value system rewarding athletics on mass-media attention (from Coleman).*

| | Per Cent Who Are High Users of Mass Media | | |
	Boys named as best athletes	Others	Difference (others minus best athletes)
Athletics of high importance			
Green Junction	13.6%	24.0%	
St. John's	18.2	26.8	
Percentage average	15.9	25.4	9.5
Athletics of medium importance			
Marketville	35.3	35.1	
Elmtown	30.0	26.3	
Newlawn	15.6	30.7	
Millburg	34.4	34.1	
Executive Heights	2.4	23.4	
Percentage average	23.5	29.9	6.4
Athletics of low importance			
Maple Grove	23.5	25.3	
Midcity	26.1	20.4	
Percentage average	24.8	22.9	−1.9
Number of cases			
Green Junction	(22)	(233)	
St. John's	(44)	(597)	
Marketville	(17)	(151)	
Elmtown	(20)	(209)	
Newlawn	(32)	(335)	
Millburg	(32)	(472)	
Executive Heights	(41)	(640)	
Maple Grove	(17)	(154)	
Midcity	(46)	(760)	

are still many schools whose social systems resemble those described by Gordon and Coleman. Greater interest in curriculum by administrators and teachers, plus the public press for achievement and the difficulties of getting into "good" colleges, has changed the atmosphere of some schools and will change that of more. But there will always be a social system of some kind in a school shaping the nature of the learning opportunities.

TABLE 14–6. *Influence of the value system rewarding scholarship on mass-media attention of boys (from Coleman).*

| | Per Cent Who Are Frequent Users of the Mass Media | | |
	Boys named as best scholars	Others	Difference (others minus best scholars)
Scholarship very important			
Midcity	13.5	21.2	
Marketville	20.0	36.0	
St. John's	16.1	26.7	
Percentage average	16.5	28.0	11.5
Scholarship of average importance			
Millburg	25.8	35.1	
Maple Grove	16.7	25.9	
Elmtown	37.5	26.1	
Percentage average	26.7	29.0	2.3
Scholarship of low importance			
Green Junction	13.6	24.3	
Newlawn	34.8	30.5	
Executive Heights	15.2	23.2	
Percentage average	21.2	26.0	4.8
Number of cases			
Midcity	(52)	(754)	
Marketville	(10)	(164)	
St. John's	(31)	(550)	
Millburg	(31)	(504)	
Maple Grove	(12)	(166)	
Elmtown	(16)	(218)	
Green Junction	(22)	(243)	
Newlawn	(23)	(367)	
Executive Heights	(46)	(656)	

THE TEACHER'S ROLE IN THE SCHOOL'S SOCIAL SYSTEM

The school is a social institution, and the teacher's role implements its functions. The school as an institution defines the directions of desirable behavior changes to be expected of students; these changes represent the goals to be attained through the functioning of the school. The teacher's task is to promote these behavior changes.

VARIATIONS IN TEACHER ROLE EXPECTATIONS

The role of the teacher is seen by students, administrators, and parents as essentially that of organizing learning experiences to facilitate desired behavior changes. A student also has an institutionalized role, that of being a learner. Ideally, the teacher would enact his role—promoting learning; the student would enact his, being receptive to the teacher's prompts. Reciprocally, the teacher would be responsive to the student's learning—rewarding him for learning, giving him more opportunities to learn.

Why does the theory of the school fall short of being realized? Because neither the teacher's role nor the student's is shaped exclusively by the theory of what a school and their relation ought to be. In the preceding section we saw how the student's role was influenced by many personal associations—some of them part of the formal structure of the school; others, in informal but socially potent relations. Similarly, the teacher's role is shaped by associations other than those defined by the formal structure of the school.

Because the role of the teacher is institutionalized, many different social groups and individuals have the same general expectations of what a teacher may and should do; and in many different schools the teachers have much the same role and perform the same general functions. But variations in the role should also be expected, because the role is being enacted in a particular social system, the local school. The following statement suggests the factors influencing these variations:

In Wabash the teacher role was conditioned by the fact that he faced in the classroom a system of student organization which was differentiated by *grade rank, grade achievement, sex, social class, and prestige cliques* which were value differentiated by their participation in both the formally organized and the informal student culture. . . .

The teacher's perspective of the classroom was one in which behavior was defined according to an ideally conceived classroom situation in which performances approximated the ability and knowledge of the students. . . . Teachers accepted the personal limitations of pupils as part of the educational situation. Students understood the teacher's perception of the situation and the rules of its operation. However, the students calculated their relation to two sets of status positions, those of students of variously rated performance and those of the informal groups; namely, an adolescent in relation to same sex and opposite sex, "dater-nondater," "athlete-nonathlete," "brain," "big wheel" or "non-wheels" and "fruits" (derogated group), clique member, and isolate. Each of the above labels defines roles which incorporate expectations counter to those of the teacher. Teacher-defined roles which were not accepted resulted in strain in the role of the teacher.[10]

In Wabash School, as in other schools, the formal and informal organizations have differing expectations for the teacher role. The extent to which a teacher will enact a teacher role successfully within the social system of the school appears related to his ability to reconcile conflicting role expectations. **Role conflicts** are incompatible expectations about the desirable behavior characterizing a role. For example, students may think that teachers ought not to expect them to be "intellectuals"—meaning that studying hard, or being interested in literature or politics, should not be expected, demanded, or maybe even encouraged by the teachers. The teachers and parents may, however, expect students to be interested in these things and to work hard at learning about them. Here are two different expectations about what a teacher ought to encourage. If he acts consistently with one, he may please the students; with the other, he may please the parents and other teachers. Another example is the elementary school child who expects the teacher to reward his depending on the teacher for help, when the teacher thinks that he ought to be encouraging the child to be more independent.

As the teacher tries to resolve this conflict, his behavior tends to be influenced by the social-status system within the school. This tendency is sometimes reflected even in his evaluation of students, an aspect of the institutionalized role of the teacher. The teacher may give higher grades to a student whose achievement does not merit them, but who has considerable prestige within the school.[11] The following excerpt from a teacher's report suggests how such decisions might be made:

Art was the top student in his class, a member of the football team, and in the school play. Near the end of the school year he fell in love and his performance in class dropped considerably. When we came to the end of the marking period, on the basis of Art's performance on tests he should have been graded C or less in practically all of his subjects. Another teacher and I discussed Art and felt that his drop in performance was understandable. We did not want his record to carry a lot of

[10] Gordon (see note 1), pp. 45–46.
[11] A. B. Hollingshead, *Elmtown's Youth* (New York: John Wiley & Sons, 1949).

low grades, because this might influence his admission to college and his ranking for scholastic honors in the school. As a consequence we graded him much higher than he deserved and not really on the basis of his present performance.

In this case the teachers consciously and systematically evaluated a pupil on the basis of their general perception of his status in the school. Teachers do not invariably accept the status system of the school and grade pupils accordingly. But if the teacher insists on the achievement values of the formal system when the informal system is not achievement-oriented, he runs the risk of incurring the disapproval or hostility of students.

THE TEACHER'S ROLE IN RELATION TO THE PRINCIPAL

Conceptions of the teacher's role in a particular school may be influenced by the principal's expectations of how this role should be enacted. For example, the teacher is expected to maintain control and have authority within his own classroom; in a given school, however, the principal may define the extent to which problems of disorder or control may be handled exclusively by the teacher. A policy statement may represent a role expectation or define the role of the teacher in this particular area. More data from the Wabash School study will illustrate this point.

The number of classroom evictions over a three-year period was for successive years respectively 160, 81, and 50. Reduction in the number of evictions was related to the dissemination of a rumor among teachers that the principal kept a *mythical little "black book"* in which he records the number of students which teachers send to the office. "When he gets ready to rate your teaching he looks in the little black book and decides your salary increase for next year." It appeared that the greater the support the principal gave the teacher's authority, the more likely the formal *institutional role* of the teacher was utilized to coordinate the classroom. The less willing the principal was to support the teacher's institutional authority, the more likely was the teacher to absorb conflict in his classroom, and the more likely he was to resort to *personalized* leadership and face a situation of endemic conflict.[12]

In conceptualizing his role, the teacher will need to interrelate the expectations of the informal social system among students and the expec-

---

[12] Gordon (see note 1), pp. 44–45.

tations of the administration of his own school. The following example, again from Wabash School, illustrates how these varying role expectations influence a teacher's behavior:

Mr. Spears' class is often a topic of discussion. There is constant fun-making by the most organized group in school: Rudy, Milton, Myers, Hack, Vance, Moon, and Ash as they are all in one class. The only person who could complete this group to make it the rest home for Spears would be Arnold. Spears realized at the beginning of the second semester when Myers, Hack and I joined the rest that it would be constant conflict. We all enjoy hearing him blow up unless it happens to be directed at one of us individually. The tendency is to bother Spears as a group; secondly, to get him to bawl someone else out.

Many a time I have given myself a pat on the back for getting my trouble-making buddy, Vance, in "dutch." But today he evened up all those times by getting Spears mad enough to throw me out of class. What happened?

Vance tore the name paper off the inside cover of my book and was proceeding to stick it into Ash's shirt when I discovered my loss and in a loud voice so all the other fellows could get the full benefit of the trouble I was to cause Vance, I started saying, "What the heck are you doing, Vance, just what are you doing to my book?" Mr. Spears having been disturbed once too often this day, instead of finding out what Vance was doing, just beat on the desk and screamed as loud as he could for me to get out. All he could say was: "Moon, get out, get out, just get out."

I realized the harder the storm the sooner it's over, so I just sat there ignoring the outburst for I had no intention of leaving. I could say nothing and didn't try to. I looked him in the eye and he'd holler, "Get out." So I would just disgustedly look away, feeling he would cool off and go on, realizing that I wouldn't be giving him any more trouble for the day. Finally, he went on reading. I remained silently in class, and the class also stayed quiet for about five minutes (pp. 43–44).

If the teacher had evicted Moon, as he apparently wanted to do, he would have had to face the principal's expectation that teachers should handle such problems themselves. In evicting Moon, he would have run the additional risk of creating disapproval and resentment in the informal student system. Eviction is serious even to the members of a fun-loving group; the consequences are serious for maintaining their positions within the school. The teacher in this conflict situation was apparently immobilized: his personal frustration is apparent in his outburst; the fact that he did not adequately resolve his conflict is shown by his failure to insist that Moon leave the class.

Concepts of the roles of teacher and administrator may vary from school to school, within the general limits set for these expectations by the institutionalized concept of the roles. Some evidence is available to suggest that if the role expectations of the administrator are relatively clearly defined and known by the teachers, there is greater satisfaction among teachers.[13] That this clarification is not the only requisite for reducing conflict among role expectations should be apparent from our discussion above. In general, when role expectations are clearly defined and widely shared within a social system, personal conflict (conflict in the individual about expected behaviors) is likely to be reduced. But an understanding of the institutional roles of students, teachers, and principals, although helpful, cannot always account for the various and conflicting role expectations that may exist in a given community.

RESOLVING ROLE CONFLICT

Consider again the question of the teacher's authority in the classroom. Parents have certain expectations about the teacher's role in this respect. They expect the teacher to maintain at least enough control to ensure desirable behavior changes in the pupils. The principal and the teachers themselves also share this expectation. But when a problem situation arises, differences between the expectations are all too frequently apparent. The principal, as we noted above, may expect the teacher to keep the problem in the classroom. Assume that the teacher does, and in solving the problem of disorderly conduct uses physical punishment on the child. The parents' expectation may be that the teacher will exercise as much control as is necessary without using physical punishment, and as a consequence a disagreeable situation arises.

The teacher's behavior, therefore, is influenced by the role expectations of the principal and the students, and of parents and other members of the community. A teacher will have difficulty in adjusting to his role when there are conflicting expectations about the character of it in his school or its community. Some of these conflicts concern the teacher's relationship to students. Some concern such fundamental issues as whether the teacher

[13] See C. E. Bidwell, "The Administrative Role and Satisfaction in Teaching," *Journal of Educational Sociology*, 29 (1955), 41–47. Evidence that similarities in personality characteristics between leaders and group members increase group effectiveness may be found in W. Haythorn et al., "The Effects of Varying Combinations of Authoritarian and Equalitarian Leaders and Followers," *Journal of Abnormal and Social Psychology*, 53 (1956), 210–219.

may require students to read books that some community members think they should not read. Others concern appropriate topics for class discussion. Occasionally the teacher's rights to engage in community activities on which there are disputed issues is challenged. Even within his profession, he will encounter conflicting views of what a teacher ought to be. Difficulty in adjusting to these various conceptions will probably be accompanied by heightened anxiety; if the teacher cannot adequately resolve the conflicting expectations, his anxiety may become so acute that he may be forced to leave the teaching profession.

Role conflict is sufficiently pervasive in the teaching profession to constitute a serious problem. Probably only certain kinds of personalities can tolerate this role conflict over a long period of time. We do not know whether teachers' personalities are radically different from those of other people, although some evidence suggests that there is a characteristic pattern of needs among teachers who have remained in the profession for a comparatively long period of time.[14] These personality characteristics may be related to tolerance of role conflict.

At present, the research available on the role conflict of teachers is limited.[15] Getzels and Guba found a variety of significantly different personal reactions to role conflicts in teaching.[16] They noted that many expectations for the teacher role are inconsistent with the expectations attached to other roles the teacher typically occupies. For example, because teaching is a respected profession, the teacher may be expected to maintain a social status within the community which the salary provided him will not allow. The teacher who needs additional income to maintain a social position in the community may need to reconcile what is expected of him as a teacher and the expectation reflected in the salary paid him. We are not surprised to find that male teachers felt significantly more role conflict than female teachers. Also teachers with one dependent, as compared to teachers with no dependent, also felt significantly more role conflict, as did teachers who had part-time jobs instead of full-time positions.

[14] P. W. Jackson and E. G. Guba, "The Need Structure of In-Service Teachers: An Occupational Analysis," *School Review*, 65 (1957), 176–192; E. W. Guba, P. A. Jackson, and C. E. Bidwell, "Occupational Choice and the Teaching Career," *Educational Research Bulletin*, The Ohio State University, 38 (1959), 1–12, 27–28.

[15] For a review of research on the role of the teacher, see W. B. Brookover, "Research on Teacher and Administrative Roles," *Journal of Educational Sociology*, 29 (1955), 2–13.

[16] J. W. Getzels and E. G. Guba, "The Structure of Roles and Role Conflict in the Teaching Situation," *Journal of Educational Sociology*, 29 (1955), 30–40.

Both in Chapter 13, where we discussed teacher-pupil interactions, and in this chapter, we have emphasized the complexity of the teacher-pupil relationship. This relationship is not a single, isolated, person-to-person kind of relationship. The social system of the school has a complex structure of penalties and rewards and, as a social system, makes varying demands on its members. The teacher should be sensitive to these demands, and be able to work out an adjustment in which he fulfills to a considerable degree the expectations of both the formal and informal organizations. Considerable flexibility, awareness of the social system, and sensitivity to the expectations and demands of this complex system are probably required to effect such an adjustment. The teacher who is at least aware of the complexities of the social relationships within a school is more likely to make adjustments than the teacher who sees the role of the teacher in its institutionalized aspects as fixed and immutable in all social contexts.

SUMMARY

In this chapter we have discussed the social system of the school as a complex of stimulus variables which influence behavior change. A social system is an arrangement of social positions. Status relations are typically correlated with this matrix of social positions; status relations reflect the prestige and social acceptability associated with the various positions.

1. The social system of the school may be described by the position arrangement involved in the formal organizations of the school. These formal organizations are of two kinds: (a) the formal organization of pupils in administrative units, such as class groups, classroom groups, and age-sex groups; (b) the formal organization of clubs and activities provided for students.

2. The social system of the school may also be described on the basis of the informal organization of associations of students.

3. A student occupies positions in each of these aspects of the social system of the school. A student's general status in the school depends in part on his status in each of these organizations. A student's position in the social system and the prestige associated with that position influence behavior in several ways.

4. Social status influences the kinds of need satisfactions available to an individual. Since the individual's status depends on his positions in the

formal and informal organizations of the school, his status is an index of his associations. Many need satisfactions are mediated through the associations available in a school. Striving for need satisfaction is the motivational force in behavior change; hence, social status is likely to influence behavior change by influencing the kinds of need satisfactions available to motivate behavior.

5. Social status and positions are measures of the kinds of group influences on behavior change. An individual's social status is an index of his group membership. This group membership influences his behavior to the extent that the group is a reference group for the individual. Social status may be related to conformity to group standards to the extent that an individual hopes to improve his status by meeting group standards.

6. The teacher role is another major role in the social system of the school. The teacher's role is an institutional role in the sense that its characteristics are defined in relation to the attainment of the goals of the social institution. In this respect the teacher's role is conceptualized in terms of expectations associated with the organization of learning experiences. Such expectations are influenced, however, by the expectations characteristic of local schools.

7. These variations in role expectations arise from expectations of students and the administration with respect to the teacher's role.

8. These expectations may be at variance with the expectations associated with the institutionalized conception of the role.

9. Other variations in expectations in the role concept of a teacher arise from the conceptions of appropriate teacher role behavior held by parents and other community members.

10. These variations in role expectations may be incompatible and result in role conflict.

11. Role conflicts may be reduced in part when teachers and administrators share similar expectations for their respective roles. Role clarification may tend to reduce some aspects of role conflict. However, since role expectations are frequently influenced by local values, role conflict in particular social contexts is not unlikely.

12. A conception of the complexity of the social system of the school may make the teacher aware of the many influences on student behavior change. Expectations for both the teacher and student roles are shared in many different schools, but the role expectations also tend to be influenced by the social system of a particular school. Sensitivity to such variations may prepare the teacher to make the adjustments required for successful role enactment in a particular school.

STUDY AND DISCUSSION QUESTIONS

1. Select some organization with which you are familiar, preferably one of which you are a member. Describe the arrangement of social positions within this organization. What functions are associated with each position? What is the relative status of the various positions in this organization?

2. For the same organization, describe the criteria for membership in this organization. What are the criteria for the various positions in this organization? Who may not be a member of this social system?

3. Describe the system of formal student organizations in the school in which you are now either a student or a teacher. Describe the criteria for membership in these organizations.

4. Describe the informal organizations in the school in which you are now a student or a teacher as you see them. Check your descriptions with those of a fellow student or teacher. What are the criteria for membership in these informal organizations?

5. Select some student whom you know well and describe his or her social status in the school. To what organizations does this student belong? Of what organizations is this student not likely to become a member? How has his position in these various organizations of the school influenced his prestige with fellow students?

6. What organizations of the school use the sex of the student as a criterion for membership? What organizations in your school set grade level or department association as a criterion for membership?

7. Identify a student who appears to have relatively low prestige or social status in the school. To what organizations, if any, does he belong? How do you account for his relatively low social status in the school?

8. What personality characteristics are used as criteria for membership in the various school organizations with which you are familiar? How do the members of these organizations determine whether a prospective member has the requisite personality characteristics? What observable behaviors define or describe the personality characteristics that are used as criteria for membership?

9. Identify the club or activity which has the highest prestige in your school. What appear to be the dominant value standards of this organization? In what ways are the value standards of this organization consistent or inconsistent with achievement in school? How do the members of this organization appear to perceive the role of the teacher in your school?

10. Identify the informal organization in your school which seems to have the highest social status. What value patterns appear to be shared by the members of this organization? In what ways are these value patterns consistent or inconsistent with achievement in school?

11. Again, using the formal and informal organization with the highest prestige in your school, describe the ways in which these organizations provide need satisfactions for their members. What need satisfactions do these organizations provide that are not likely to be obtained by membership in any other organization in the school? In what ways do they provide need satisfactions that are not likely to be obtained in the typical classroom activities?

12. Refer to the Charters and Newcomb experiment described in this chapter. Assume that the investigators had used students of different political persuasions instead of members of religious groups. The experimental procedures would be substantially the same, except that the items in the questionnaire would refer to matters on which political parties have taken a position. Would you expect the results to be comparable to those obtained when students of different religious faiths were used?

13. Assume that you were trying to influence a student who is a member of a group whose attitudes are "anti-school" in character to change his attitudes toward school. What factors will affect your success in influencing this student? What is the relationship between his position in this group and the extent to which your persuasion is likely to be effective?

14. Describe the principal role expectations associated with the role of the teacher in your school.

15. Compare the general role expectations for the role of a high school teacher and a university professor. In what ways are the role expectations similar? In what ways are they different? In what ways are the role expectations for the teacher role related to the expectations for the student role?

16. Describe the different kinds of role expectations that parents, teachers, and the principal and students may have in relation to the following:

    a. Grading students.

    b. Managing "discipline" problems.

    c. The teacher's position on religious matters.

    d. The teacher's position on local political activities.

17. Are there some personality characteristics that may make it difficult for a teacher to resolve role conflicts associated with teaching? If you think so, suggest what these characteristics might be, and describe the ways in which they would be related to a failure to resolve role conflicts adequately.

RECOMMENDED READINGS

R. G. Barker and P. V. Gump. *Big School, Small School: High School Size and Student Behavior*. Stanford, Calif.: Stanford University Press, 1964.

J. Coleman. *The Adolescent Society*. New York: The Free Press of Glencoe, 1961.

C. W. Gordon. *The Social System of the High School.* Glencoe, Ill.: The Free Press, 1957.

R. Havighurst and B. Neugarten. *Society and Education.* Boston: Allyn and Bacon, 1957, Chapters 8 and 17.

T. M. Newcomb. *Social Psychology.* New York: The Dryden Press, 1950, Chapters 13, 14, and 15.

H. Taba. *School Culture.* Washington, D. C.: American Council on Education, 1955.

PART FOUR

METHODS OF EVALUATION

(

CHAPTER FIFTEEN

THE EVALUATION OF LEARNING

The teacher is always evaluating behavior change. Every question asked in class, by teacher or student, every piece of homework, every essay, every discussion gives the teacher an opportunity to evaluate behavior—motives, work orientation, interest. Furthermore, a teacher can create any occasion for evaluating what he wants to evaluate.

Some of this evaluation is unplanned and unsystematic. A teacher asks random questions to assess whether the class understands him, a kind of audience-reaction estimate. Or he makes a preliminary evaluation of a student's work in order to assess progress. However, he also needs more systematic, planned, and carefully controlled measurements of behavior change—first, because random and preliminary measurements often are not good **samples** of pupil behavior; and second, because many of the things to be learned are complex, and additional experience over time is required for their acquisition. Only a final evaluation provides a valid estimate of change, although preliminary evaluations are used to check progress. Furthermore, a practitioner who cannot measure reliably and validly the behavior he tries to produce and control is helpless. He does not know when he has succeeded or failed. He cannot estimate progress. He cannot revise instructional strategies to fit the present acquisitions of learners.

Finally, systematic evaluation of a pupil's achievements is important because it becomes a matter of public record. These records are used to make important decisions such as admission to special courses and programs. Such decisions should be based on the best data that can be obtained. To do less courts error and injustice.

In this part of the book, we turn our attention to the problems of measuring behavior change. In this chapter we study in some detail the principles of measurement. We then cover the principles of constructing testing procedures and of using available standardized tests. The material presented in these chapters is no more than an introduction to basic principles and procedures. The teacher who wishes to become thoroughly competent in developing and using evaluation procedures will want to pursue a more detailed study of these topics.

WHAT IS AN EVALUATION PROCEDURE?

Consider the following example. A first-grade teacher attempts to teach children the spelling of a list of words. Ordinarily, a child cannot spell when he enters the first grade. After presenting learning experiences designed to teach him how to spell, the teacher will determine his present level of spelling performance. The teacher may ask, "How many words on this list can the child now spell correctly?" When the teacher has determined how many words the child can spell, he has a *measure of behavior change.* A child who could originally spell few if any words may now be able to spell fifty, seventy-five, or even a hundred words.

Once the teacher has determined the amount of behavior change, he must evaluate the extent of change by referring to some standard. Since any improvement in spelling ability is desirable, the question is this: Has the child changed as much as can be expected of him? Has he come up to some expected standard of performance? We probably want a child to be able to spell all of the words correctly. Therefore, we *evaluate* the child's performance as "good" or "poor" by the degree to which he has approached this standard and by our estimate of his capacity to do so.

Again, if the teacher has organized a set of learning experiences designed to teach children cooperative behavior, he can determine the degree to which they have improved by observing them during and after the learning experience. There will be varying degrees of improvement; therefore, we must evaluate the improvement of any one child by comparing his performance with our expectations for him. These expectations contain both a conception of an ideal or relatively good performance and an estimate of the pupil's basic ability to learn.

MAJOR PHASES OF EVALUATION

The task of evaluating behavior change has several aspects: (1) a judgment of what, in general, constitutes a desirable behavior change; (2) a means of *measuring* [1] whether the behavior change has occurred and, if so, to what degree; (3) a judgment of the "acceptability" of a particular behavior change.

When a student has finished a course in American history, we find that he has learned a number of facts and generalizations about American history; this change, we say, is desirable. But if he has responded to the learning situation by doing as little as he possibly can in order to "get by," we call this change undesirable. We base these decisions on our conceptions of what behavior changes are uniformly desirable. Beyond this judgment, we know that this student's performance is good or bad only in comparison with some standard of performance. To determine how "acceptable" his performance is, we make a judgment based on our criteria of "acceptable" degrees or amounts of change.

CRITERIA FOR EVALUATION

Often, criteria for evaluation are highly subjective. For example, a teacher who rates an English composition as "highly creative" is probably evaluating the writing in terms of his own conception of "creativity." His

[1] Measurement, used in its broadest sense here, includes categorizing, rank ordering, and scaling procedures. Some authors prefer to limit the concept to scaling procedures. The technicalities of these distinctions are beyond the scope of this book. An introduction to the characteristics of the above three procedures can be found in J. M. Bradfield and H. S. Moredock, *Measurement and Evaluation in Education* (New York: The Macmillan Company, 1957). For a technical discussion of this problem, see S. S. Stevens, "Mathematics, Measurement, and Psychophysics," in S. S. Stevens, ed., *Handbook of Experimental Psychology* (New York: John Wiley and Sons, 1951), Chapter I.

conceptions may or may not be shared by others. Objective criteria for behavior like "creativity" are difficult to determine, and standards tend to be influenced by uncriticized personal preferences. Subjective criteria are not necessarily invalid or inappropriate. We would, however, expect considerable variability in ratings of students' creativity when different teachers evaluate students' writing.

In other cases value standards may be more or less generally accepted. We would expect, for example, some general agreement among evaluations of children's cooperative behavior. This agreement is possible because people in our society have some common conceptions of what constitutes "acceptable" interpersonal relations.

In still other cases we use a prediction to evaluate performance. If a student's achievement in the fifth grade is very low, we may predict that he will do poorly in the sixth grade. We might then evaluate his fifth-grade performance by calling it "unacceptable" as a basis for promotion to the sixth grade. Our criterion, then, is that students who have not performed successfully should not be promoted. When we decide that the student will not be permitted to advance to the next level, we have made a *judgment* about the "acceptability" of the student's performance. The determination of the relationship between performance in one learning experience and that in another is a *measurement* problem. If judgments of acceptability are to be made in this way, the data necessary for making predictions must be gathered.

The typical performance of students is frequently used as the basis for making an evaluation. For example, if we give a reading test to a group of fifth graders, we can arrive at an average score on the test for fifth-grade children. We can also determine the range of performance or behavior change. We can determine the highest and lowest scores achieved by fifth graders. With this information, we can compare the performance of a student to the typical performances of fifth graders. We can say that he is performing as the average fifth grader performs, or above or below this average.

Such a description of the student's performance is the result of our *measurement procedures*. We have made an *evaluation* when we decide that the performance, as represented by the test scores, is or is not satisfactory. In this evaluation we have assumed that the criterion used represents a standard for what fifth graders should be able to achieve. One must be careful about such an assumption. *The typical performance of a group of students does not necessarily set a standard for performance,* although teachers and administrators frequently assume so. In principle, we cannot determine what "ought" to be from what "is." We cannot say that, because students typically read at a certain level, a particular student *ought* to read at this level. When we go beyond the descriptive data, we are adding some criterion of "acceptability."

The process of developing appropriate evaluative criteria is complex, and is a process in which the teacher is engaged continually. The following principles describe the characteristics that evaluative criteria ought to possess if they are to be useful:

1. The criteria of "acceptability" must be explicit and clearly defined if appropriate evaluative judgments are to be made.

2. Since an evaluation determines the *degree* of "acceptability," the definition of the criteria must also define the levels or degrees of "acceptability." (See Table 15–1).

3. The value standards embodied in the evaluative criteria should be relatively stable and should be applied consistently. Recall that evaluative criteria rest in part on a judgment of what constitutes a desirable behavior change. Students will have difficulty in clearly conceptualizing desirable goals if the evaluation of their changes in the directions of these goals is inconsistent or arbitrary.

4. Evaluative criteria should be consistent with the facts of child development. We have warned that typical performance does not set a standard for performance. But such typical performances do provide us with information on the range of pupil performance in relation to such variables as age, sex, grade in school, and intelligence level. With such data we can estimate what a child might or might not be expected to achieve. For example, we will estimate that a child of below-average intelligence will probably perform below the average of his class in many respects. We will not expect him to perform as well as the brightest child in the class.

Table 15–1 provides an example of a set of evaluative criteria that are consistent with the above principles. The development of this outline of evaluative criteria began with a conception of desired behavior change, a conception embracing two objectives: (1) to develop students' ability to remember and understand the factual content of a story and (2) to develop students' ability to recognize and use the new words presented in the story. The column labeled "Performance" describes the range of possible levels of achievement of these objectives. The column labeled "Level" represents the evaluation to be made of each of these levels of achievement. In this way degrees of achievement are related to degrees of "acceptability." Note also that the criteria are clearly defined.

The above discussion on evaluative crieria stresses that the operations

TABLE 15–1. *An example of definitions of evaluative criteria (from Bradfield and Moredock).*

Level	Performance
I. Unsatisfactory	Cannot pronounce correctly the new words when seen written. Cannot answer questions about the most obvious facts contained in the story.
II. Fair	Can pronounce the new words correctly when seen written. Can answer questions about the most obvious facts contained in the story when the questions are phrased the same way as the statements in the story.
III. Good	Same as level II, and in addition: Can underline the new words from among other words when the new words are spoken. Also has a rough idea of the meaning of the new words. Can answer more subtle questions about the content of the story when the questions are phrased differently from the sentences in the story. Also can recall the sequence of the story.
IV. Excellent	Same as levels II and III, and in addition: Can correctly use new words in sentences of his own construction drawn from his own experience, and can identify when the new words are improperly used. Can relate the content of the story to his own experience and can give plausible explanations of the events in the story.

of evaluating and of measuring can be thought of as logically distinct. In general, we assume that learning is acceptable when the desired behavior change has taken place; but since change is a matter of degree, we can make judgments on the relative "acceptability" of a performance only by referring to a standard more precise than that of "desirable."

A note of caution is appropriate here; it should be recalled in reading the remainder of this chapter. We have been using tests and testing situations as examples of the evaluation process; however, the teacher is continually evaluating his students' behavior changes. When a teacher asks a question in class, he makes an evaluative decision on the student's performance on the basis of the answer he receives. If the student does not know the answer to a question, the teacher has measured some aspect of the student's knowledge. But beyond this, the teacher will probably make an evaluation based on his assumption about whether the student ought to know the answer to this question. Formalized testing procedures are merely systematic ways of gathering data about changes in pupil behavior; evaluation procedures are not limited to these formalized testing methods.

EDUCATIONAL OBJECTIVES AND EVALUATION PROCEDURES

Evaluation procedures should be consistent with the stated objectives of the learning experience; that is, the method of measurement selected must assess the attainment of a stated behavioral objective. Furthermore, the methods of measurement should cover the *range* of stated objectives.

An important problem, however, is the distinctions among the order of objectives. We earlier made a distinction between immediate and ultimate objectives: an *immediate objective* is the goal of a particular learning experience or a set of them; the *ultimate objective* is where the student will be at some later point—usually near the end of his formal schooling, or at the end of a sequence of courses, or later in life. This ultimate objective is frequently complex and is more easily stated in abstract terms. Practically, it gives meaning to immediate purposes and hopefully will suggest the necessity of ordering them.

This distinction between immediate and ultimate objectives has practical signficance for the development of evaluation procedures. Since the objectives of the learning experience in a classroom are immediate, the evaluation procedures are of necessity designed to measure the attainment of the immediate objectives. We can measure what a student knows about American history, but we cannot measure what kind of a citizen he will be as an adult. We can determine the present reading level and interests of a fifth-grade child, but we cannot measure what his reading level and interests will be ten years from now.

In developing evaluation procedures, we can nonetheless determine the relationship between the attainment of an immediate objective and some more comprehensive objective. We could, for example, study how students participate in student government, the extent to which they vote or do not vote in student elections. Then we could study the voting records of these children when they become adults and establish empirically the relationship between voting in student elections and voting in municipal or national elections. With such data we could predict whether the attainment of an immediate objective will probably lead to the attainment of some more comprehensive one.

By evaluating the degree of attainment of immediate objectives, we determine the value of a particular learning experience. By determining the relationship between the degree of attainment of immediate and ultimate objectives, we can also evaluate the contribution of the learning experience to the attainment of the ultimate objectives. Suppose that we give a test in American history and find that the majority of students have profited from the learning experience, as represented by their performance on the history test. The learning experience has apparently produced the results that it was designed to produce. But another evaluation of the relationship between learning American history and some more general objective, such as behavior at the polls, may suggest that the course in American history is making little contribution to the attainment of this objective. If the course is making little or no contribution to the attainment of the more comprehensive objectives, then the learning experiences provided in the course may need revising.

TESTS AND EVALUATION PROCEDURES

An evaluation procedure begins in measurement. The function of a measurement process is to determine whether behavior change has occurred, and, if it has, to what extent. The measurement process itself begins with observations of behavior. We cannot determine whether a behavior change has occurred unless we observe behavior. We may determine the reading level of a student by observing, for instance, what kinds of material he can read. We may make an inference about a student's reading interests by observing the number and kinds of books he reads.

TESTS AS SAMPLES OF BEHAVIOR

If we wish to measure the reading interests of students, we may gather data on the number and kinds of books they read, but we can rarely observe all of the behavior in which we are interested. If we give a test in American history, we cannot ask every conceivable question that could be asked about American history. If we are observing children's cooperative behavior, we are ordinarily limited to observing this behavior at particular times and under particular circumstances. In other words, in making a measurement of behavior we obtain a sample of behavior.

A *test* is a sample of behavior, no matter what the form of the testing procedure may be. If the teacher tests the third-grade class on a list of a hundred spelling words, he is obtaining a sample of the children's spelling performance. From a child's performance on these hundred words, we may make an inference about what his performance would be like if we had given him all of the words that he has ever studied. If the teacher is measuring the cooperative behavior of his pupils, he may observe the number and kind of acts of cooperation among the children in a particular situation, such as when they are working in a committee or organizing a game. From this *sample* of a child's cooperative behavior, the teacher may make an inference about what the child's cooperative behavior is generally like.

NECESSARY CHARACTERISTICS OF A BEHAVIOR SAMPLE

The sample of behavior must be *representative* of the total **population** of behaviors that is being measured. By the *population of behaviors,* we mean all of the behavior that could be observed if we had the time, means, and energy to observe this behavior. The population of potential behaviors in a course in American history includes the acquisition of all of the concepts, generalizations, solutions to problems, facts, attitudes, and values that the learning experience is designed to achieve. The sample of behavior that is observed in a test or test situation is only a portion of this population.

The sample of behavior observed is representative only if it is comprehensive enough and if it has the characteristics of the population of behaviors. While we cannot cover the entire range of behaviors, we must sample enough so that our conclusions about the child's behavior are reliable. We could not draw reliable conclusions about a child's knowledge of American history by his ability to answer the one question "In what year did Columbus discover America?"

The behaviors that we sample must also be representative of the population of behaviors in the sense that they must be of the same kind as the behaviors in the population. If we wish to test a child's attitudes about American history, we must use procedures to determine what his attitudes are; we cannot come to conclusions about his attitudes by testing his ability to answer factual questions. If we wish to test a child's ability to solve problems, we must place him in a test situation that requires problem-solving behavior; we cannot accurately estimate his ability to solve problems by testing his ability to produce facts. If we wish to draw conclusions about children's cooperative behavior, we must place them in situations in which cooperative behavior is likely to occur; we cannot infer from his reading habits the extent of a child's cooperative behavior. If we wish to test a child's understanding, we must have samples of the child's understanding behavior; if we wish to test a child's ability to solve problems, we must have instances of problem-solving behavior; if we wish to test a child's knowledge of facts, we must have instances of facts that the child remembers.

The basic assumption in any evaluation procedure is that the children being evaluated have had the opportunity to learn the desirable behavior changes the evaluation procedure is designed to measure. We patently violate this assumption if we construct a test that is unrelated to the kind of behavior that was to be acquired in the learning experience. When teachers construct classroom examinations, they ordinarily sample subject content that could have been acquired in the learning experience. A fifth-grade spelling test typically covers the words that were to have been learned by the fifth graders. But a test on subject content may not sample the behavior change specified as desirable. If a teacher giving a test on American history requires only knowledge of facts, he can make inferences only about the children's knowledge of the facts of American history. He cannot make reliable inferences about their understanding of concepts and generalizations or their development of certain attitudes.

Another common error is testing for the attainment of objectives for which learning experiences have not been provided. If one of the important objectives of a learning experience is to develop concepts and understanding, but the whole emphasis in the learning experiences has been on the acquisition of facts, a testing procedure designed to test understanding is inappropriate. Many courses in social studies emphasize the development of social attitudes. A test on the content of social studies, as defined by the acquisition of facts, generalizations, and concepts, does not adequately sample the attitudinal changes in behavior.

Adequate evaluation procedures presuppose a consistency between objectives, learning experiences, and evaluation procedures. We are logically inconsistent if we attempt to evaluate a behavior change for which we have not provided adequate learning experiences. It is also inappropriate to make inferences about the attainment of all of the objectives of a learning experience from evaluation procedures which measure only some of these changes. We would not attempt to determine a person's height by measuring his weight, unless there were some known and highly predictable relationship between height and weight. Neither would we attempt to make inferences about the height of ten-year-old boys by measuring the height of the first 5 ten-year-old boys whom we met.

The principles of measurement suggested in these two examples are applicable to psychological and educational measurement. A *measurement is a sample of behavior that must be representative of a class or category; that is, a population of behaviors.* We ensure a representative sample by obtaining an adequate number of specific observations which are similar in kind to the behavior about which we are making judgments.

CHARACTERISTICS OF MEASUREMENT PROCEDURES

Every measurement procedure must have certain characteristics if we are to make accurate inferences about the behavior changes we are attempting to measure. The measurement procedures used in assessing behavior change also have certain characteristics which affect the kinds of inferences we may make from data gathered by using these procedures.

THE RELATIVE CHARACTER OF MEASUREMENT

If we are measuring height, we can make a statement about how tall a person is. We can also make statements about the height of the person in comparison with other people. We can say that he is taller or shorter than the average height of his group, or the height of some other individual.

Many behavior changes that we measure, however, cannot be broken up into units of amount. For example, we cannot break up changes in spelling behavior into units of spelling ability. If we are measuring how much American history has been learned, we cannot break up the behavior changes into units of knowledge of American history. We can, however, make inferences about the *relative* amount of behavior change that takes place. We can identify, in any class, the child who can spell the most words and the one who can spell the least. We can also identify the student who knows the most about American history and the student who knows the least.

Our measurement devices are essentially procedures for *categorizing people in terms of inferred amounts of behavior change,* rather than in terms of units of behavior change. This characteristic of educational measuring devices limits us to making statements of relative position or relative change. We can determine where a child stands in comparison with other children, and we can make simple categorical judgments about the presence or absence of change. But we have no devices for measuring the "absolute" amount of any behavior that we are measuring.

Teachers frequently make evaluative judgments based on a presumed measure of the absolute amount of a student's knowledge. A teacher may say, "This student knows nothing about spelling." A more precise statement would be, "This child knows less than children of his age and experience typically know." We may also make categorical judgments such as "The child does not know the answer to this question." But we cannot infer from the failure to answer one question a complete absence of knowledge of the facts in a given subject. If a child does not know the answer to one question, we should not infer that he does not know the answer to other questions on the same topic. We may know that a child has not learned to spell all the words in a spelling list, but this measurement is only a relative measure of how much the child has changed.

RELIABILITY OF A MEASUREMENT PROCEDURE

Another important characteristic of every measurement procedure is that it must be **reliable.** When we say that a measurement must be reliable, we mean that it must be consistent; that is, repeated or comparable measures of a behavior change should place a child in relatively the same position on a scale of performance.[2] For example, if a teacher gives a child a spelling test, a second testing on the same or comparable words should place the child substantially in the same relative position, unless the child has been studying spelling between the testing sessions. An analogy from physical measurement will make this point clear. If we had a ruler that gave us differing measurements of height, assuming that we are taking the measurements one after the other or with comparable rulers, the measurement procedure would not be reliable.

---

[2] There are several different ways in which reliability can be measured. A discussion of these methods may be found in L. J. Cronbach, *Essentials of Psychological Testing,* 2nd ed. (New York: Harper & Brothers, 1960); and A. Anastasi, *Psychological Testing,* 2nd ed. (New York: The Macmillan Company, 1961).

Several factors influence the reliability of a measurement procedure. The measurement procedure must provide us with *enough instances* of the behavior that we are attempting to measure. Small samples of behavior are likely to yield relatively fewer reliable measurements. If we wish to draw conclusions about a child's ability to spell, we must give him enough words so that we can get a stable estimate of his spelling ability. We cannot reliably measure spelling ability by giving a child one word, nor can we measure a child's knowledge of social studies by asking him one question.

When we devise a measurement instrument, we also establish *optimal conditions* for measuring. We assume that a child is working at his maximum level of ability and that he is in good physical and emotional health. If a child is ill or emotionally disturbed, his performance in a test situation will be affected.[3] Ordinarily, we want to know how a child can perform when he is functioning at his best, not how he is likely to perform when he is temporarily handicapped. Test scores may fluctuate when the optimal conditions for testing are not met. The most reliable score is likely to be the one obtained under optimum test conditions. When we say a measuring device must be accurate or reliable, we mean that it must be *reliable at the time of measurement and under the assumed conditions for measurement.*

VALIDITY OF A MEASUREMENT PROCEDURE

The most important characteristic of a measurement device is that it must have relative **validity.** When we measure behavior change, we want to be able to make inferences about a particular kind of behavior change. The measurement procedure is supposed to tell us something about this change. Insofar as the measurement procedure gives information on the behavior change we are studying, it is a relatively valid basis for making inferences about this behavior.

A test has relative validity only for specific purposes; that is, for measuring specific kinds of behavior change. The validity of a test is determined by the kinds of inferences that we want to make from our measurement. If we want to determine whether a child has learned the facts of American history, we must give him a test that is a valid measure of knowledge of facts. This test is relatively valid only for determining the

[3] M. L. Hutt, "A Clinical Study of 'Consecutive' and 'Adaptive' Testing with the Revised Stanford-Binet," *Journal of Consulting Psychology,* 11 (1947), 93–103.

extent of the child's knowledge of particular facts, and may have little or no validity for measuring his understanding of concepts and generalizations or for measuring his ability to solve problems.

The relative validity of a testing procedure must be determined for each kind of inference that we wish to make from the data the test provides. In this respect a word of warning is appropriate. Many published tests have descriptive titles, which label the **variables** they purport to measure: "intelligence," "mental maturity," "social competence." A test user may assume that the test is measuring what he means by "intelligence," or "mental maturity," or "social competence," and may proceed to make inferences about these behavior patterns from students' test scores. But such a test is relatively valid only for the kind of intelligent behavior it measures. A given test may not measure, for example, the kind of intelligent behavior called "practical judgment," and inferences about students' "practical judgment" based on data from this test are not likely to be valid. Further discussions of this problem can be clarified by describing the general procedures that may be used to determine the relative validity of a test.

Content Validity

Tests have two major uses in the evaluative phase of an educative act: (1) to determine the present status of performance; (2) to predict future performance on the basis of present performance. A test may be relatively valid for both or only one of these two purposes. The tests that teachers usually construct are relevant to the first of these purposes. If a teacher constructs a test that measures the behavior specified as desirable in a statement of educational objectives, and if the appropriate learning experiences have been provided, then the test is relatively valid for assessing the extent to which pupils have acquired the desirable behaviors. We say that such tests have "logical" or "face" validity. That is, "on the face of it," the test appears to be measuring what it is designed to measure, or the tasks in the test are logically related to the kinds of behavior change specified as desirable. We have warned that we cannot too readily assume that the test actually does measure what it purports to measure. Teachers may assume that they are measuring a wide variety of behavior changes when, in effect, their tests are measuring only a limited number of such changes.

Another kind of content validity is sampling validity. A test has sampling validity when the items or tasks in it comprise a representative sample of the behavior to be tested. Three steps are required to achieve content validity: (1) the behavior to be measured is carefully defined; (2) the content area or the characteristics to be measured are subdivided into categories representing all major aspects; (3) a judgment is made that all categories and behaviors are adequately represented.

Predictive Validity

A test has predictive validity in the degree to which we can use it to predict, from the test situation, performance in some other situation.[4] Here is one example of the way in which such a relationship could be established. A typing teacher dictates a business letter to his class and has the class transcribe the letter. When the teacher has graded the typed letters, he can make statements about the students' typing performance. He knows how many errors in transcription and typing the students have made. Assume that the letter he gave the students to type is similar to letters that they would have to type in business. Even so, the test has only logical or face validity, because "on the face of it" the typing of this kind of business letter appears to be the kind of task that the student will eventually have to perform. This teacher could keep careful records of his students' performances on these exercises, and then obtain some rating of their performance on the job at a later date. If he then related perform-ances on the test to those on the job, he could determine the *predictive validity* of his tests. If his typing tests had predictive validity, he would be able to say that a student who performed at a certain level on his typing test would be likely to perform successfully or unsuccessfully on the job. His tests would have both kinds of validity, logical and predictive. If a test has neither logical nor predictive validity, we have no idea what it is measuring; it seems to be measuring some kind of behavior, but what kind we do not know.[5]

To establish predictive validity, it is necessary to have a **criterion performance** of what we are attempting to predict; that is, a standard to which we can relate present performance. For the typing class, the

---

[4] There are several kinds of empirical validity. A comprehensive discussion may be found in A. Anastasi, *Psychological Testing* (see note 2).

[5] A knowledge of statistical procedures is required to develop the kinds of predictive relationships being discussed here. Generally, such predictive relationships are estab-lished by computing correlation coefficients, the significance of which can be used to determine the predictive validity of a measurement procedure.

criterion performance was a specific performance on a job. If we relate performance in high school to performance in college in order to predict the latter, the criterion is college performance. A test of scholastic aptitude can be used to predict performance in a number of subject areas in both high school and college; in this case, performance in each of the areas is a separate criterion. Such a test has varying degrees of validity, since each of the predictions is based on a separate and distinct criterion performance.[6]

In saying that tests have relative validity for specific purposes, we mean this: predictions are probability statements about the relationship between performance on a specific test and a specific criterion performance. Consequently, it is important to determine the criterion performances that can be predicted from a test performance, and to know the relative validity of such predictions. At present, we do not have sufficient empirical data for judging many of the predictions implicit in the decisions of teachers. The predictive validity of almost all teacher-made tests is unknown; yet student performance on these tests affects many decisions made by teachers. A teacher who decides that a child should not be promoted to the sixth grade has decided, in one way or another, that performance in the fifth grade can be used to predict performance in the sixth grade. While we would assume that such a relationship exists, we may not know the relative validity of this prediction. Although tests which have logical validity may be used as the basis for inferences about the effects of a learning experience on behavior change, they should not be used to make predictions about future performance unless their predictive validity has been determined.

This same condition applies to making inferences about the relationship between attainment of immediate and ultimate objectives. Despite the difficulties in making valid predictions, the teacher's task frequently requires him to make judgments about future performance. And some kinds of validity judgments can be made; a teacher can make some general predictions from the level of a student's intelligence alone. The lower the intelligence of the student, the less likely it is that he will succeed in the next learning situation. But it is important to realize that the teacher can make errors in inference when there are no reliable data on the relationship between performance in one learning situation and that in

---

[6] The manuals of the following tests provide data from prediction studies: G. K. Bennett, H. G. Seashore, and A. G. Wesman, *Manual for Differential Aptitude Tests*, 3rd ed. (New York: Psychological Corporation, 1959); E. F. Lindquist and A. N. Hieronymus, *Iowa Tests of Basic Skills* (New York: Houghton Mifflin, 1956).

another. Such predictions should be made with caution and on the basis of as much relevant information as the teacher can gather.

OBSERVATION OF PUPIL BEHAVIOR AS A MEASUREMENT PROCEDURE

The previous examples of test situations and measurement devices suggest neither the wide range of available measurement methods nor the broad area of behavior that can be measured. Here, we will indicate some of the major types of measurement methods that can be used in evaluation procedures. We will also point out some of the problems of measurement involved in using these methods.

A technique commonly used by teachers is that of observation of pupil behavior. As we observe the behavior of our students, we note important and distinguishing characteristics. We may say, "This child is aggressive and a bully," "This child is shy and quiet," or "This child does his homework." Statements of this kind are usually based upon *observations* of what pupils do in and out of the classroom. Since these judgments are frequently evaluative, the principles for evaluating behavior change (discussed earlier in this chapter) also apply to them. But these evaluations presuppose an adequate measurement of the behavior being evaluated. In the following sections we will discuss the method of observation as a technique for obtaining measurements of behavior change.

PROBLEMS IN USING THE OBSERVATIONAL METHOD

How adequate is the method of observation as a measurement procedure? Its relative value depends upon the extent to which it can give us reliable and valid information about pupil behavior. Three problems may arise when we attempt to obtain reliable and valid samples of pupil behavior by using the method of observation. When the precautions noted below are taken, however, such samples may be obtained.

The first problem in this method of measurement is obtaining a *representative sample* of behavior. Unless we use systematic procedures designed to obtain an adequate sample of observations, our measurement of pupil behavior may lack validity. Since the teacher cannot continually watch one pupil, but must interact with a comparatively large number of pupils, he usually obtains a limited and unsystematic set of observations. The sample of observations may also be biased, because the teacher notes only unusual or deviant behavior. The teacher may be more likely to note and remember Johnny's speaking out of turn because this behavior disturbed "order." Samples of behavior based on such unsystematic observations are likely to be unrepresentative of a child's *typical* behavior.

Another potential problem in using the observational method arises when the observations are not recorded until some time after they have been made. This *lapse in time* allows the influence of **selective forgetting** to affect the observations recorded. The teacher may remember and record only unusual and striking instances of behavior. The teacher filling out a rating scale on a pupil has the problem of remembering what this particular pupil is like. His ratings, which represent the summarizations of his observations, are probably biased both by the inadequacy and unsystematic order in which the observations have been gathered, and by the effects of selective forgetting.

A third potential problem in observation is that frequently the behavior to be observed is *not adequately defined*. For example, if we are to rate pupils on aggressive behavior, we must have a clear-cut definition of what we mean by aggressiveness. Two difficulties arise in attempting to define the kind of behavior to be observed. The first arises from the character of the language we use to describe behavior. We are frequently observing behaviors for which we have everyday descriptive terms. We want to observe behaviors that we call "aggressive," "selfish," "cooperative," or "friendly." Each of these terms, while it suggests a category of behavior, subsumes a wide variety of particular responses. Such words may have different connotations for each teacher who uses them. What behavior would you associate with each of the above adjectives? Before we can observe behaviors of this kind, we must specify the kinds of responses that will be called "aggressive," "friendly," or "selfish," and agree, at least for the purposes of observation, on the meanings to be associated with these terms.

The second difficulty associated with definition is *distinguishing between overt behavior and the inferred motive* for the behavior. If one child pushes another child, we may call this behavior "aggressive." On the other hand, we may decide not to call it "aggressive" because the child's *intent* was not to harm the other pupil. In defining the behavior that we are observing, we must decide whether we shall confine ourselves to describing overt responses or whether we shall also make inferences about the motive behind the behavior. For example, a teacher may describe a pupil as a "daydreamer." This inference may be based on the observation that the child is staring out the window frequently; however, a child may be "paying attention" while he is looking out the window. We can observe that "he is looking out the window"; we can only *infer* that "he is not paying attention."

IMPROVING THE TEACHER'S OBSERVATION OF PUPIL BEHAVIOR

We can devise observational procedures that minimize the possible errors in observation. If we carefully define the behavior to be observed, if our definitions comprise descriptions rather than inferences, if we set up a systematic observational schedule, and if we sample enough behavior over a long enough period of time, the disadvantages of the observational method tend to disappear. Many experimental investigations have used systematic observation of the kind described here.[7] When such methods are used, we find a relatively high degree of reliability in the observational method. As a matter of practical consequence, however, many of these precautions cannot be implemented in the classroom. A teacher in a classroom does not have time to make completely systematic observation of his pupils; he must also perform many other functions.

This discussion of the problems in observation should make the teacher aware of the possible errors that may occur when judgments are made on the basis of observed behavior. A comparatively casual observation in the classroom or on the playground is not a proper basis for making comprehensive judgments about students' behavior. The more extensive the evaluation of the pupils' behavior that is to be made, the more comprehensive and systematic must be the observations. And the teacher should recognize that he does have some opportunities for making systematic observations of pupil behavior. Teachers may use periods when they are not working directly with students to make systematic observations and records of these observations. Such observations can be made when students are working in committees or studying at their desks, or during an assignment to "yard duty."

The teacher also can check his inferences from observed behavior by making predictions from these inferences. These predictions in turn can be checked by new observations. For example, if a teacher has observed that a child becomes angry when he is frustrated, he might infer that this

---

[7] See R. E. Arrington, "Time-Sampling Studies of Child Behavior," *Psychological Monographs*, No. 2 (1939); F. B. Newman, "The Adolescent in Social Groups," *Applied Psychology Monographs*, No. 9 (1946); P. S. Sears, "Doll Play Aggression in Normal Young Children," *Psychological Monographs*, No. 6 (1951); R. R. Sears, M. H. Pintler, and P. S. Sears, "Effect of Father Separation on Preschool Children's Doll Play Aggression," *Child Development*, 17 (1946), 219–243.

is the child's typical response to frustration. This inference can be checked by observing the child's reaction to other frustrating situations. How does he respond when he cannot work a problem? What does he do if the teacher does not recognize his attempts to get attention? The teacher who checks inferences is likely to become increasingly sensitive to the distinction between what is observed and what is inferred.

Many of the above recommendations will not improve the use of observational methods if the teacher does not clarify his conceptions of the behavior categories that he uses to describe behavior. A teacher can think through what he means by such terms as "aggressive," "friendly," and "shy." Such clarification should be in the direction of defining these categories in terms of observable behavior. Increased clarification of descriptive categories is likely to improve the validity of inferences based on observations.

A TEST SITUATION

With observational methods, we can describe behavior as it occurs in typical situations in a classroom. However, it is sometimes necessary to arrange situations that will evoke the behavior change we wish to measure.

A test situation is a "contrived" experience to which the student is systematically exposed. As distinguished from a natural situation, it usually occurs at a specified time and in a specified place; the persons being tested are usually aware of the fact that they are being tested, and the test situation is, as far as possible, the same for each of the individuals involved in it. A test situation is not a measurement procedure itself, but rather a way of arranging situations so that measurements can be made. For example, if we want to study the cooperative behavior of children, we can organize a task and situation that should evoke cooperative behavior. Then by observation, we can measure the amount of cooperative behavior that occurs in this test situation.

ADVANTAGES OF A TEST SITUATION

One advantage of test situations is that they permit us to gather data about behavior in a more systematic manner than do natural situations. We also gather comparable kinds of data on each pupil from which we can make comparisons of relative achievement. Having students answer questions on a paper-and-pencil test, for example, enables us to gather data about all of the pupils in the class. Contrast this situation with one in which the teacher asks questions in class. As soon as the teacher obtains a correct answer to the question, he ordinarily moves on to the next question. He has no way of knowing whether any of the students who did not attempt answers could have answered the questions; he knows only which pupils answered correctly and which ones did not. He does not know how many other pupils could have answered the questions asked, or whether the pupils who did answer them could answer other questions. In other words, by using a comprehensive test, the teacher gathers a larger and a more representative sample of pupil behavior.

The measurement procedures used in test situations must have the characteristics required of any measurement procedure. Test situations usually provide more reliable and valid data since they afford more control over the behavior being studied.

CHOOSING APPROPRIATE TEST SITUATIONS AND MEASUREMENT PROCEDURES

The measurement procedure we use requires the student to use the kind of behavior we want to measure. If we have organized a learning experience designed to produce certain skill performances, we will want to use a measurement procedure relevant to these performance behaviors. For example, if we are teaching a course in driver education and one of the objectives is to develop skillful drivers, a paper-and-pencil test will measure *some* behaviors related to this objective. A driver must know the rules and laws of driving; a paper-and-pencil test will measure his knowledge of these rules. But his knowledge of the rules does not give us information about his skill in manipulating an automobile. If we wish to test how skillfully he drives an automobile, we must place him in an automobile and ask him to drive it under standardized conditions. The choice of a measurement procedure should be governed by the character of the learning experience itself and its objectives.

Procedures have been developed for measuring a wide variety of personality functions. We have tests of intelligence and aptitude, achievement and skill, attitudes and values, as well as tests of more complex aspects of personality, such as measurements of the need systems of an individual and his adaptive mechanisms. (These kinds of tests are discussed in Chapter 17.) Some of these tests can be used by teachers with some training. Other tests require extensive training before they can be used. Should the teacher want a more complete description of a pupil than the available test procedures can provide, he must refer the pupil to the school psychologist or psychometrist, who has been trained to make more comprehensive and thorough measurements and evaluations.

SUMMARY

Learning experiences are designed to foster desired behavior changes. Evaluation procedures are used to determine the effectiveness of the learning experience in fostering these changes. A logical continuity exists between the character of the desired changes, the learning experiences organized to foster these changes, and the procedures used to evaluate the extent of behavior change resulting from participation in the learning experiences. This chapter has presented some basic principles of measurement and evaluation. The following points were made:

1. A logical distinction can be made between *measurement* and *evaluation*. A measurement procedure is an arrangement for determining the amount of behavior change. We evaluate behavior change when we compare the measured change to some criterion of acceptable performance.

2. These criteria may be subjective and personal, or may be matters of agreement. Generally, teachers partially define their expectations in terms of pupil capacity. Empirical data on the relationship of one performance to another can also be used as a partial basis for establishing achievement criteria.

3. The first step in developing evaluation procedures is to define carefully the *objectives* of a learning experience. Many published statements of objectives are too abstract in character; they permit us neither to organize learning experiences that promote achievement of an objective nor to evaluate behavior change. The teacher will need to work out specific statements of objectives; that is, statements that describe desired changes in terms of observable behavior.

4. Broad statements of educational objectives are useful for defining the school's general responsibilities in the education of the child. We also assume a relationship between the attainment of the immediate objectives of a particular learning experience and the attainment of the ultimate objectives described in these broader statements. At the present time, however, little empirical evidence is available to indicate the existence of such a relationship.

5. Measurement procedures can provide us with a sample of behavior.

From this sample we can make inferences about the amount of change occurring in the population of behaviors from which the sample was taken. To make reliable inferences, we must obtain representative samples of behavior. These samples of behavior must contain an adequate number of instances of the measured behavior. The measured behavior must also have all the characteristics of the population of behaviors about which we are making inferences.

6. Any measurement procedure must have two characteristics: (1) it must be *reliable;* (2) it must be adequately *valid.* A measurement procedure is reliable in the degree to which it is consistent and stable. A measurement procedure is valid in the degree to which it provides us with a sample of the behavior that we wish to measure.

7. Measurement procedures will be reliable to the degree that we obtain a representative sample of behavior. Reliability also depends on the degree to which optimal testing conditions are maintained.

8. Measurement procedures are relatively valid for specific purposes. There are two major kinds of validity—logical and predictive. A measurement procedure has logical validity in the degree to which the sample of behavior is representative of the kind of behavior that we wish to measure. A measurement procedure has predictive validity in the degree to which we can use it to predict some future performance; it is valid if the predicted behavior—the criterion performance—actually occurs.

9. We have also analyzed the observational method as a measurement procedure. We have noted that there are three potential problems associated with using observations as a method for gathering data about change in pupil behavior. First, since teacher observations are frequently informal and unsystematic, such observations may not give us a representative sample of pupil behavior. Second, the pupil behavior to be observed may be defined so vaguely that agreement on behavior change cannot be attained. A third problem in using the observational method arises when the recording of the observations occurs some time after the observations have been made. As a consequence, the report of the behavior may be affected by selective forgetting. We have also noted that, in defining the behavior to be observed, we must distinguish between observed behavior and inferred behavior. The observational method is likely to be useful if the behavior to be observed is carefully defined, and if systematic procedures are used to gather a representative sample of this behavior.

10. A test situation is an arrangement of a standardized task and of standardized conditions for performing it. Test situations differ from "natural situations," in which we observe behavior as it occurs. One of the

advantages of using test situations is that we can use them to evoke the behavior we want to measure. We can also make judgments of relative achievement in test situations since each person taking the test performs the same task under relatively similar conditions.

11. Finally, we have noted that the measurement procedure requires the student to use the kind of behavior we wish to evaluate. Irrespective of the particular form of measurement procedure used, the measurement device must provide a representative sample of the behavior to be measured and must be minimally reliable and valid.

The basic principles of measurement and evaluation will be applied in the next two chapters, in which we will discuss the principles of test construction and the use of standardized tests. The principles provided here are a starting point from which the teacher can begin to analyze his own evaluation procedures. The development of appropriate evaluation procedures is a necessary part of the teacher's task. The teacher cannot judge the value of learning experiences without using procedures which adequately measure the effects of these learning experiences on pupil behavior.

STUDY AND DISCUSSION QUESTIONS

1. Select a unit in some subject that you are teaching or may teach. Define the specific behavior changes that the learning experiences associated with this unit are intended to promote. Describe in detail the criteria that you would use for determining the extent to which the behavior changes that occurred were "satisfactory."

2. What hypotheses about child behavior have you used in establishing these criteria? In what ways can you determine whether the "acceptable" level of behavior change can be attained by the children in your class?

3. A school board member asked a sample of first grade children to identify the letters of the alphabet. He found that 12 per cent made at least one error in identification and that 10 per cent made at least two errors. He concluded that the schools were not doing a satisfactory job of teaching children the identification of the letters of the alphabet. What evaluative criteria are implicit in this person's criticism of these children's performance? What factors may be related to a first grade child's performance in identifying the letters of the alphabet? How would you account for the fact that 10 per cent of the students made at least two errors in identification?

4. The same person asked a group of children to pronounce several words that he had selected and used a tape recorder to collect their responses. When

he found several children who were unable to pronounce some of the words, he concluded that the teacher had not taught the children the use of phonetics. Evaluate his procedures and conclusion in terms of:

a. The sample of behavior obtained from each child.

b. The sample of the children studied.

c. The criteria used to evaluate performance.

d. The testing procedure.

5. You give a reading test to your sixth grade class and find that several students score considerably below grade level. What inferences would you make on the basis of these data? What information would you need to check your inferences? May you conclude that the learning experience was inappropriate for improving the performance of these children?

6. Some people argue that using the average test scores reported for large samples of students does not provide an accurate measure of what students can achieve. These people argue that the average score tends to become the expected performance for students. Evaluate this argument and suggest some qualifications of this argument that need to be made.

7. Below are listed three general objectives. Describe each of these objectives in specific terms. Relate the attainment of these objectives to particular kinds of learning experiences at different levels of education. In what ways do the experiences in elementary school and high school contribute to the attainment of these objectives? What levels of behavior change may be expected at various points in the education of a child?

a. The educated person writes the mother tongue effectively.

b. The educated person can work and play with others.

c. The educated citizen seeks to understand social structures and social processes.

8. Select the subject that you are or may be teaching and describe the ways in which the learning experiences you organize may or may not contribute to the attainment of each of the specific objectives you have listed. What kinds and amount of behavior change are to be expected as the result of the learning experiences organized in your class?

9. Given the objective: The educated citizen respects the law. In what ways do the home and school contribute to the attainment of this objective? What kinds of behavior change would you expect to observe if a child learns to respect the law? Be specific about the behavior expected and the context in which you expect to observe this behavior.

10. Assume that you have developed a testing procedure for determining the extent to which children have learned cooperative behavior. Essentially, your testing procedure consists in observing the frequency with which children share materials when working on a common project. What independent criteria could you use to determine the validity of your testing procedure? Does your testing procedure have logical validity?

11. A teacher has constructed a test on the content of Algebra I. He finds, however, that he cannot predict how students will perform in Algebra II from the scores that they obtain on his test. How would you describe the validity of his test? For what purposes may the teacher utilize this test?

12. Assume that you wanted to measure the cooperative behavior of the students in your class. Describe the procedures that you would need to use in order to obtain a relatively reliable sample of pupil behavior. Be specific in your definition of cooperative behavior and in formulating the observational methods you will use to obtain samples of pupil behavior.

13. Some people argue that test situations are "artificial." They maintain that if we want to understand pupils, we need to observe them under natural conditions. Evaluate this argument in the light of the principles of measurement discussed in this chapter.

14. Below are listed several traits on which teachers are frequently asked to rate pupils. Define each of these pupil characteristics in terms of observable behaviors. Suggest procedures by which teachers may make more reliable observations of these kinds of behavior.

a. Courtesy.

b. Application.

c. Cooperation.

RECOMMENDED READINGS

A. Anastasi. *Psychological Testing*. New York: The Macmillan Co., 1954.

B. Bloom, ed. *Taxonomy of Educational Objectives. Handbook I: Cognitive Domain; Handbook II: Affective Domain*. New York: David McKay Company, 1956, 1964.

O. K. Buros. *The Fifth Mental Measurements Yearbook*. Highland Park, N. J.: Gryphon Press, 1959. Earlier editions of this book are available, and it is periodically revised and brought up to date.

L. J. Cronbach. *Essentials of Psychological Testing*, 2nd ed. New York: Harper & Brothers, 1960, Chapters 1–6.

E. Lindquist, ed. *Educational Measurement*. Washington, D. C.: American Council on Education, 1951, Chapters 1–4.

R. Mager. *Preparing Objectives for Programed Instruction*. San Francisco, Calif: Fearon Publishers, 1962.

R. Thorndike and E. Hagen. *Measurement and Evaluation in Psychology and Education*. New York: John Wiley and Sons, 1955.

CHAPTER SIXTEEN

CLASSROOM EVALUATION PROCEDURES

In the preceding chapter we outlined some basic principles of measurement and evaluation. A teacher will also need to know some general principles of test construction if he is to develop adequate evaluative procedures. The formulation of a question, problem, or task may not serve to evoke the kind of behavior that we wish to measure and evaluate. A question asked in one form is likely to evoke one kind of behavior; asked in another form, it may evoke another kind of response. In this chapter we will discuss the relationship between the kinds of materials used in test situations and the kind of behavior we wish to measure and evaluate.

Evaluations can be made during any phase of a learning experience or prior to the initiation of a new experience. A "readiness" test, for example, measures the extent to which a student may be able to profit from a learning experience. We use this measurement to make an evaluation of his "readiness" for that new learning experience. A "diagnostic" test may be used to determine learning deficiencies either before or during a learning experience. Tests given at the end of a learning experience may be used to measure achievement and to predict probable performance in a new situation. In each of these cases the function of the measurement procedure is to provide data for the evaluation of behavior change. To make these kinds of judgments, measurement procedures must be used which evoke the kind of behavior change we wish to evaluate.

WHAT IS TO BE EVALUATED?

A statement of the objectives of a course, a unit, or a learning experience determines what is to be evaluated. But even when they are fairly specific, these statements of objectives cover a wide range of psychological functions and behaviors. In most learning experiences the student acquires a wide variety of new concepts, attitudes, values, skill performances, and problem-solving techniques.

SPECIFIC DEFINITION OF EDUCATIONAL OBJECTIVES

The first step in devising evaluation procedures is to develop a systematic outline of the desired behavior changes in a form as specific as possible. Below is a list of general objectives for a science course.[1]

1. Acquisition of Information.
2. Understanding of Important Technical Terminology and Symbols.
3. Ability to Identify Forms, Structures and Processes and to State Their Functions.
4. Familiarity with Reliable Sources of Information on Science Problems.
5. Ability to Recognize Unsolved Problems in Science.
6. Interest in Solving Science Problems for Which the Student Has No Present Solution.
7. Ability to Draw Reasonable Generalizations from Experimental Data New to the Students.
8. Ability to Plan Experiments and to Test Hypotheses.
9. Ability to Apply Scientific Generalizations to New Situations.
10. Skill in Laboratory Techniques.

The statement of these objectives must be made more specific. For example, the teacher must determine what unsolved problems in science the students should be able to recognize when they have completed the

[1] H. E. Hawkes, E. F. Lindquist, and C. R. Mann, eds., *The Construction and Use of Achievement Examination* (Boston: Houghton Mifflin Co., 1936), Chapter V.

course. They are not ordinarily required to be able to recognize all the unsolved problems of science, nor are they even required to be able to recognize all of the unsolved problems in the special field of science being studied. What forms, structures, processes should the student be able to identify? What important technical terminology and symbols are to be learned? When the teacher has answered these questions, he will have an outline of the content of the unit or course and of the specific concepts, facts, generalizations, and attitudes that the student is expected to acquire.

Statements of objectives formulated as expected behavior changes are preferable to statements of objectives formulated as content to be acquired. One of the dangers in stating objectives as content to be acquired is that we may assume that content acquisition is correlative with other desired behavior changes. Wrinkle [2] provides an example which makes this point:

Do you see why "knowing things" isn't a good objective unless something happens as a result of the learner's knowing the things that he knows? He can tell you that he should cross the street only at the intersections. He knows that is the correct answer. But what if he leaves the classroom and cuts across the street in the middle of the block? What if he knows that twenty-five miles an hour is the speed limit in the residential area in which he lives, but he drives thirty-five miles an hour?

In such cases facts have been remembered, but the desired behavior change has not occurred. Throughout this book we have emphasized that the educative act begins with a conception of desired *behavior* changes. Although the acquisition of knowledge is a behavior change, a statement of objectives in terms of content to be acquired may cause us to forget that we are often concerned primarily with other kinds of behavior change. The ideas, facts, and problems which constitute the content are the materials used to foster these behavior changes.

DETERMINATION OF RELATIVE IMPORTANCE OF OBJECTIVES

In preparing a statement of objectives, the teacher will need to determine the relative importance of each objective. Consider the objective of "understanding important technical terminology and symbols." Besides

---

[2] W. L. Wrinkle, *Improving Marking and Reporting Practices* (New York: Rinehart and Company, 1947), p. 8. Used by permission of the author.

defining the number and kind of symbols or terms to be learned, the teacher will need to decide how these terms are to be understood and remembered. The definition of some terms must be memorized exactly because the terms are so important and are used so frequently that only precise definitions will clarify the meaning of the terms for the student. The student will need to define other terms only in his own words. Still other terms need only to be recognized, and we may not require the student to be able to define them exactly. These statements about how a term is to be understood and remembered indicate the relative emphasis placed on the specific performances to be acquired.

More comprehensive objectives will have varying degrees of importance attached to them. Some teachers will place major emphasis on recognizing unsolved problems in the science they are teaching. Other teachers will place a premium on the acquisition of factual information. At this phase in the development of an evaluation procedure the teacher is answering the question, "How important is the attainment of each objective?"

The relative importance attached to the different objectives will determine the importance attached to the learning activities, as well as to the measurement procedures used to assess behavior change. Students usually do many things in a learning experience. In a social studies class the children read books for information and understanding, listen to the teacher's descriptions of events, participate in class discussion, write essays, make book reports, and organize into committees to carry out projects. The amount of time planned for each of these activities should reflect the relative importance of the objectives of the course. If a teacher decides that what can be learned by independent research is more important than what can be learned by discussing a question in class, proportionately more time should be given for research. The teacher's evaluation of this independent research should be given correspondingly greater weight. If acquisition of information and concepts is the most important objective, then the testing procedures used to evaluate the learning experience should reflect proportionately more measurement of acquisition of information and concepts.

Below is a list of concepts to be learned by sixth-grade students during a unit on India. Some of these concepts must be understood more clearly than others if the child is to attain the objectives of the unit. A test given to determine the extent to which children understand these concepts should reflect the relative emphasis the teacher has placed on the learning of these different concepts.

Culture	Irrigation	Mosque
Sari	Monsoon	Banyan
Turban	Millet	Universal
Caste	Maize	Fundamental
Desert	Bullocks	Optimistic
Mountains	Purification	Parable
Plateau	Ritual	Sorghum
Environment	Embroidery	Tamarind
Village	Shrine	Cobra
Population	Worship	Sacred
Tolerance	Scythe	Education
Brahmin	Mango	Self-confidence
Ceremonial	Bazaar	Beliefs
Betel nut	Charpoy	Resources
Chapatis	Koran	Homes
Peasant	Arable land	Diversity of beliefs
Manure	Pyre	Worth of individual

Logically, the systematic planning of objectives should precede organizing of the learning experience. Too frequently it is left until the time when the teacher evaluates behavior change. The teacher may revise his objectives in the light of pupil interest or pupil progress, but at the outset of a learning experience he needs to have some conception of why the children are participating in this particular experience. We have discussed this point at several places in the text, and repeat it here only to emphasize the relationship between the relative importance of specific objectives and the kinds of procedures used to measure behavior change leading toward achievement of these objectives.

SELECTING TEST EXERCISES

A test situation requires the person being tested to do something. We may ask the person to answer questions, supply meanings for words, perform a musical composition, write an essay, or operate a tool. We will use the term *test items* to refer to the *stimuli* designed to evoke the behavior we wish to measure. These stimuli may come in a variety of forms, requiring responses of many different kinds and of varying degrees of complexity.

TEST TASKS AS STIMULI

The test items must evoke the behavior we wish to measure. If we are testing a student's retention of a fact, we ask him a question that requires remembering the fact. For example, the question "What year did Columbus discover America?" requires that the student recall the answer "1492." If we want to test a student's ability to add a column of figures, we present him with a column of figures to add. If we wish to test a student's ability to play a piece of music, we present him with a musical score to be played.

In the following sections, a set of examples of different item forms is given. These examples illustrate how the stimulus the item provides is likely to evoke different kinds of responses. The teacher will need additional study in the technique of item construction before he can become skillful in devising test items that will evoke the kind of behavior he wishes to measure.[3]

TEST STIMULI DESIGNED TO EVOKE RECALL RESPONSES

Below is an example of an item that tests the student's ability to recall information:

The primary colors are:
(1)_____, (2)_____, (3)_____.

To answer this question the student will have had to learn the names of the primary colors and be able to recall them.

Below is another example of a test item designed to test recall, but presented in a different form from that of the above item:[4]

Directions: One letter has been omitted from each of the words below. Write it in the blank space where it should be.
1. Priv_lege
2. Ne_essary
3. Mu_ilage
4. Cemet_ry
5. Per_eived

[3] A comprehensive collection of test items can be found in J. R. Gerberich, *Specimen Objective Test Items* (New York: Longmans, Green & Co., 1956). See also R. Ebel, "Writing the Test Item," in E. Lindquist, ed., *Educational Measurement* (Washington, D. C.: American Council on Education, 1951), Chapter 7.

[4] C. W. Odell, *How to Improve Classroom Testing* (Dubuque, Iowa: William C. Brown Co., 1953), p. 54.

The following example is an item that tests acquisition of information, but requires the student only to recognize the correct answer, even though he might not have been able to recall it without this stimulus:[5]

Which one is not a lever?
1. **Pencil sharpener**
2. **Seesaw**
3. **Derrick**
4. **Fishing rod**
5. **Scissors**

Test items of this kind can be presented to students in a wide variety of forms, for example, as completion type, matching type, and true-false and multiple-choice types. To respond to each item, the student is required to recall or recognize something he should have learned previously.

Test items of this kind do not test understanding directly. If we wish to determine whether a student can use information, we must devise a test item or exercise that requires him to use information. The following is a test item of this kind.[6]

Assume that the articles displayed on Screen I are to be worn with a suit of dark-value gray, a top coat of middle-value gray, and middle-value pigskin gloves. Choose the most becoming shirt, tie, handkerchief, and socks for each man to wear with the gray suit, coat, and gloves. Write the number corresponding to your choice in the blank at the left of each item, and list no article more than once.

ARTICLES OF CLOTHING	DESCRIPTIONS OF MEN
———— 1. Shirt	
———— 2. Tie	A. Black hair, fair skin, and blue eyes
———— 3. Handkerchief	
———— 4. Socks	
———— 5. Shirt	
———— 6. Tie	B. Medium brown hair, blue eyes, and somewhat sallow skin
———— 7. Handkerchief	
———— 8. Socks	
———— 9. Shirt	
———— 10. Tie	C. Auburn (red) hair, brown eyes, and florid complexion
———— 11. Handkerchief	
———— 12. Socks	

[5] From J. G. Read, *Read General Science Test, Form A* (Yonkers, N. Y.: World Book Company, 1950).

[6] C. B. Arny, *Evaluation in Home Economics* (New York: Appleton-Century-Crofts, Inc., 1953), p. 143.

The student has presumably learned certain facts about choice of appropriate colors in clothing for men with different colors of hair, skin, and eyes. To answer this question he must remember these facts and then apply them to the particular type of man described in the test question.

TEST STIMULI DESIGNED TO EVOKE CONCEPTUAL RESPONSES

Below is an item designed to test understanding of a concept:[7]

Directions: Some of the groups of words below are complete sentences and some of them are not. You are to read each group of words and ask yourself "Is this a sentence?" If you think the group of words is a sentence, you are to cross out the Y (Yes); if you think the group of words is not a sentence, you are to cross out the N (No).
1. To stand erect is good posture. N - Y
2. Run into the house and get your doll. N - Y

To respond to this question the student cannot call on his memory. He has not memorized long lists of sentences among which are these particular sentences. The teacher has presented him with examples of sentences and with examples of non-sentences and has stressed the characteristics of the concept "sentence." If the student has acquired this concept, he will be able to recognize both examples and non-examples of the concept. This test item requires him to do just that. He must identify the examples and the non-examples of the concept "sentence."

Figure 16–1 gives another example of a test item for determining concept development.[8] If the child has the concepts and the appropriate word symbols for these concepts, he will be able to identify correctly each object in terms of its name. In this example the words are simple and familiar to most elementary school children. If they do not know what a car is, however, they cannot identify the correct picture. From this we

---

[7] R. V. Young and W. E. Pratt, *American School Achievement Tests,* Intermediate Form B, Test V, Language, Part 4, Sentence Recognition (Bloomington, Ill.: Public School Publishing Company, 1943).

[8] G. H. Hildreth, *Metropolitan Achievement Tests,* Primary I, Test 1, Reading— Word Picture (Yonkers, N. Y.: World Book Company, 1946), p. 3.

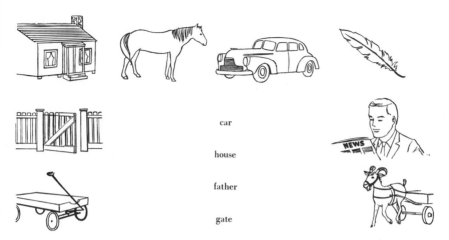

FIGURE 16–1. *An item testing concept formation. The student is required to draw a line from the words to the appropriate picture. (Adapted from Hildreth.)*

could infer that they have not yet acquired an adequate concept of "car." [9]

TEST STIMULI DESIGNED TO EVOKE GENERALIZING RESPONSES

On pages 614–615 is an example of a test item used to measure ability to draw reasonable generalizations from experimental data.[10]

TEST STIMULI DESIGNED TO EVOKE SKILL PERFORMANCES

If we want to measure a student's achievement of a performance skill—such as his ability to play a piece of music, operate a lathe, or

---

[9] The following book is recommended to the teacher who wishes to explore the problems of measuring understanding. This book discusses general principles and also provides applications of these principles to a wide variety of subject areas: N. B. Henry, ed. *The Measurement of Understanding*, Forty-fifth Yearbook of the National Society for the Study of Education, Part I (Chicago: University of Chicago Press, 1946).

[10] Hawkes (see note 1), pp. 241–242.

Directions: In the following exercise, an experiment has been described. Below the description are some statements which have been suggested as interpretations of the experiment. Assume that the facts given in the description of the experiment and in the data obtained are correct; then on the basis of these facts only consider each statement. Mark with a figure 1 every statement which is a reasonable interpretation of the data obtained; mark with a 2 every statement which is most likely true but for which the given facts are insufficient to justify the interpretation; mark with a 3 every statement which cannot be judged as either true or false because of the insufficiency of the given facts; mark with a 4 every statement which cannot be true because it is contradicted by the data obtained in the experiment.

Nine hundred seeds of a certain plant were divided into nine groups of 100 seeds each. Each group of 100 seeds was placed in a germinator. The seeds in all the germinators were under the same conditions of air and moisture, and they were all kept in the dark. Each germinator, however, was kept at a different temperature. The various temperatures and the number of seeds which germinated within 30 days are shown in the table below.

Temperature in degrees Centigrade.....	6	8	11	13	18	25	30	35	39
Number of seeds which germinated.......	0	0	0	0	16	50	84	30	0

a. More seeds of this variety will germinate at 28° C. than at any other temperature ..... (3) a.＿

b. None of the seeds germinated within 30 days at the temperatures in the experiment which were below 18° C .... (1) b.＿

c. The higher the temperature, the greater the number of seeds which germinated .... (4) c.＿

d. As far as the results of this experiment go, 30° C. is the optimum temperature for germinating these seeds .... (1) d.＿

e. Some of the seeds of this variety will germinate at 39° C. .... (2) e.＿

f. The rate at which the seeds germinated was
affected by the temperature ....(2) f.—

g. Whenever seeds of this variety are germinated at 25° C., only one out of four seeds
will germinate ....(4) g.—

h. A decrease in moisture content reduces the
number of seeds germinating more than does a
decrease in temperature ....(3) h.—

i. Beginning at 30° C, an increase of 5° C. resulted in a much greater reduction in the
number of seeds germinating than did a
decrease of 5° C. ....(1) i.—

j. More seeds would have germinated at the lower temperatures if they had been left for a
longer time in the germinators ....(2) j.—

> From the facts given, statements *b*, *d*, and *i* are reasonable interpretations. Statement *f* is most likely true, although the facts are not sufficient to justify them. Insufficient facts are given to decide whether statements *a*, *e*, *h*, and *j* are likely to be true or not, while statements *c* and *g* are contradicted by the data obtained in the experiment.
>
> The kinds of statements to be marked 2 or 3 are interpretations that go beyond the data, since they include the whole population, whereas the experiment concerned only a few individuals; or they include other kinds of populations than those in the experiment.

hammer a nail in straight—we present him with the materials required for performance and then we observe the performance. To measure achievement in such situations, we must observe the performance and rate it. Figure 16–2 contains a performance rating scale.[11] The test requires the student to fasten pieces of wood in a woodworking project. In this case only one aspect of a complex performance is being measured: how the fastenings are made. The kinds of fastenings are specified, and the characteristics of the fastenings are outlined in the column on the left. The questions in the right-hand column suggest the criteria of an acceptable performance. An observer judges the pupil's performance and rates him accordingly.

[11] D. C. Adkins et al., *Construction and Analysis of Achievement Tests* (Washington, D. C.: Government Printing Office, 1948), p. 231.

(a) NAILS:

(1) Straightness	1	2	3	4	5	6	7	8	9	10

Are nails driven straight, heads square with wood, no evidence of bending?

(2) Hammer marks	1	2	3	4	5	6	7	8	9	10

Is wood free of hammer marks around nails?

(3) Splitting	1	2	3	4	5	6	7	8	9	10

Is wood free of splits radiating from nail holes?

(4) Depth	1	•2	3	4	5	6	7	8	9	10

Are depths of nails uniform and of pleasing appearance?

(5) Spacing	1	2	3	4	5	6	7	8	9	10

Are nails spaced too close or too far apart?

(6) Utility	1	2	3	4	5	6	7	8	9	10

Will the nails hold?

(b) SCREWS:

(1) Slots	1	2	3	4	5	6	7	8	9	10

Are slots free of splitting and other evidence of driving strains?

(2) Straightness	1	2	3	4	5	6	7	8	9	10

Are screws straight, heads parallel with surface?

(3) Splitting	1	2	3	4	5	6	7	8	9	10

Is wood free of splits in the area of screws?

(4) Screwdriver marks	1	2	3	4	5	6	7	8	9	10

Is wood free of screwdriver marks near screws?

(5) Countersinking	1	2	3	4	5	6	7	8	9	10

Is countersinking neat and of satisfactory depth?

(6) Spacing	1	2	3	4	5	6	7	8	9	10

Are screws spaced too close or too far apart?

(7) Utility	1	2	3	4	5	6	7	8	9	10

Will the screws hold?

FIGURE 16–2. *Example of a performance rating scale (from Adkins et al.).*

Skill performances may be measured by rating either the products or the performances as they occur. When we rate the product as such, we assume that better products are produced by individuals with more highly developed skills. For example, in the woodworking class we could rate the finished products of the students. Since a student may need to use many different skills in completing a project, a rating of the project as a whole tells us something about the student's ability to use all of these skills. The student may be more skillful in some respects than in others; if the teacher wishes to test particular skills, he must determine the desired behavior changes and the relative importance of each of them, and then select appropriate measurement procedures for rating skill performances. If an important objective is developing students' ability to construct a well-made product, then a rating of the product is probably an appropriate measure of the extent to which students have achieved this objective.[12]

These examples illustrate how the *item form* or *test stimuli* can evoke the particular kind of behavior we want to measure. The teacher should be aware of the particular kinds of behavior evoked by the test items he uses; and he should remember continually evaluating items assures that they provide the information necessary for making judgments about pupil progress.

ITEM FORM

There are many ways of asking a question. It can be stated directly: *In what year was the Colony at Jamestown founded?* It can require identification of the correct answer: *Jamestown was founded in* (a)*1650,* (b) *1607,* (c) *1590,* (d) *1603.* Or "Jamestown" could be listed among other colonies in one column, and the founding dates of each of these colonies in another asking students to match dates with colonies. Or we could write out the statement "Jamestown was founded in 1607," and ask the students to identify it as *true* or *false.* Each of these *item forms* tests memory of a fact, although some of them test it as recall, whereas others test it by requiring the student to recognize the correct date.

Any of the alternative item forms may be used so long as it evokes the behavior that we want to measure. But other considerations also influence the selection of item forms. If we wish to test a wide range of factual knowledge, some parts of which we want the student to recall and other parts of which we want him only to recognize as being correct, we should select items that require him to fill in a blank or to check the correct response. A student can answer a large number of these questions in a comparatively short period of time.

USES OF SHORT-FORM QUESTIONS

Some forms of items—for example, *the fill-in, the true-false, and the matching items—are most useful in testing acquisition of information.* If our purpose is to determine how much information students have acquired, this kind of item allows quick and easy testing of a wide range of

[12] A comprehensive discussion of the problems of measurement involved in rating performances can be found in D. G. Ryans and N. Fredericksen, "Performance Tests of Educational Achievement," in E. Lindquist, ed., *Educational Measurement* (Washington, D. C.: American Council on Education, 1951), Chapter 12.

information. The short form of the questions makes it easy to identify errors. The disadvantage of this item form is that it places a premium on remembering isolated bits of fact.

A multiple-choice item can be designed to test remembrance of facts, knowledge of concepts and principles, or ability to draw generalizations and solve problems. We presented an item above in which the student had to draw inferences and generalizations from experimental data; that item illustrates one of the many uses of multiple-choice items. Although many teachers believe that multiple-choice items can be used only to test factual information, an imaginative test constructor can use multiple-choice items for testing a wide variety of behaviors.

USES OF ESSAY QUESTIONS

Some questions require the student to respond at length; questions of this type are usually called *essay questions.* The *essay question* can be used to test some behaviors that cannot be or are not easily tested by other item forms. Following is a list of behaviors that can be tested by an essay question.[13]

Comparing two things—on a single designated basis.
Compare essay examinations and objective tests from the standpoint of their effect upon the study procedures used by the learner.

Comparing two things—in general.
Compare standardized and nonstandardized tests.

Deciding—for or against.
Which do you prefer—oral or written examinations? Why?

Describing cause or effects.
How do you account for the great popularity of objective tests during the last thirty-five years?

Summarizing.
Summarize in not more than one page the advantages and limitations of essay examinations.

Analyzing (The word itself is seldom involved in the question).
Why are many so-called "progressive educators" suspicious of standardized tests?

Explaining relationships.
Why is it that nearly all essay examinations, regardless of the school subject, tend to be measures of the learner's mastery of English?

Illustrating principles in science, construction in language, etc.
Give two original examples of specific determiners in objective tests.

Applying rules or principles to new situations.
In the light of China's experience with state examinations what would you expect to be the effect of the Regents' Examinations in New York?

[13] W. S. Monroe and R. E. Carter, *The Use of Different Types of Thought Questions in Secondary Schools and Their Relative Difficulty for Students,* (Urbana, Ill.: 1923); Bureau of Educational Research Bulletin, No. 14.

Criticizing—adequacy, correctness, or relevancy of a printed statement, or a classmate's answer to a question on the lesson.
Criticize or defend the statement "The essay examination overrates the importance of knowing how to say a thing and underrates the importance of having something to say."

Outlining.
Outline the principal steps in the construction of an informal teacher-made test.

Reorganizing of facts (a good type of review question to give training in organization).

Name ten practical suggestions from Chapters 4, 5, and 6 that are particularly applicable to the subject you teach or plan to teach.

Formulating new questions or problems.
What are some problems relating to the use of essay examinations that require further study?

Devising new methods of procedure.
Suggest a plan for proving the truth or falsity of the contention that exemption from examinations is a good policy in high school.

If we want to test a student's ability to organize information, to criticize and evaluate points of view and data, or to hypothesize about possible solutions to problems, we can most easily evoke these functions by presenting the student with questions to which he must respond extensively. We may also want to evaluate the student's ability to write clearly and correctly and his style of writing. Then the essay question is probably the most appropriate form of question to use.

Some items often called "essay questions" do not evoke the behaviors most appropriately measured by this form. Because a student has to write out the answer to the question "In what year was the Declaration of Independence signed?" the question does not become an essay question; yet some teachers refer to five or ten such questions, which require remembering facts or generalizations, as an "essay examination" simply because the student must write out the answers. The teacher could have obtained a more representative sample of behavior by using a short-form question, the answers to which allow a more reliable estimate of the student's knowledge of facts.

Some essay questions are too vague or too comprehensive to indicate to the student the kind of response desired. Since a properly constructed essay question tests at least one complex function, if not several, the question form should clearly indicate the kind of response that is desired. The essay question "Discuss tariff regulations and American foreign relations" does not clearly indicate what kind of response the student is expected to make. The meaning of "discuss" is not clear. The student does not know whether he should list specific instances of tariff regulations and their assumed effect on foreign relations, criticize and evaluate the effects of the tariff regulations, or suggest alternative regulations which could achieve the same effect. The student can respond at length, and frequently does, by attempting to cover as much ground as he thinks the question might require. Again, we emphasize that the teacher should be clear on the behavior changes he desires before designing procedures to measure behavior change.[14] The problems that arise in scoring and grading essay examinations are discussed later in this chapter.

SCOPE OF EVALUATIVE PROCEDURES

The discussion of item forms and the range and function of measurement methods suggests the range of possible methods for evaluating behavior change. The teacher continually makes decisions about what and when to evaluate; although he may sometimes do this informally, he must often choose formal evaluative procedures and decide when to use them.

TEST FREQUENCY

One question that teachers often ask is, "How frequently shall I give tests?" The answer to this question varies with the kind of behavior being evaluated. Some behavior changes cannot be evaluated until the student has had time to integrate what he has learned. For example, to evaluate a student's ability to analyze a complex problem, we will have to wait until he has acquired the concepts, generalizations, and facts necessary for solving the problem. A student who learns the symbols for chemical elements will use them throughout a chemistry course, even though he may have studied them originally in a unit on chemical symbols. To test this student's knowledge of chemical equations, we must wait until he has learned all of the symbols required and until he has had sufficient experience in solving chemical equations.

We will want to measure some behavior changes at the time of the learning experience, and others at a later period in order to evaluate long-term change. To do this, a teacher may use a number of short tests or a series of long tests to measure immediate mastery, and a comprehensive final examination to measure long-term gains. The comprehensive exami-

[14] For a discussion of the many ways in which different item forms can be used, see Gerberich (note 3), Part III.

nation can also be designed to measure the student's ability to integrate material he has learned over a long period of time. In other words, the timing of the examination serves different functions, as do the kinds of test situations that are provided.

USE OF SHORT QUIZZES

Some teachers give short quizzes daily. Such quizzes may have two purposes: (1) to check on immediate mastery of what is being learned; (2) to motivate students to keep up with their work. We should recall that the shorter the test, the less likely its reliability.[15] The total of a series of short tests—say, of two or three items, given daily—may yield a reliable measurement; but the individual tests are not usually reliable because they do not adequately sample what the student has learned. As a consequence, the teacher must be careful in drawing inferences about behavior change from the results of short tests. And, as we have noted elsewhere, the use of tests for motivational purposes may result in rewarding inappropriate behavior.

COMPREHENSIVE EVALUATION

Let us summarize here the basic concepts a teacher must use in setting up a testing program. In the first place, the teacher must have a clear conception of the behavior changes that are expected as the result of the learning experience, and he must design measurement devices to test changes in all of these behaviors. Second, the scope of the evaluation procedures must be as broad as the statement of desirable behavior changes. Third, the importance attached to attaining different behavior changes must be given corresponding emphasis in each of the evaluation procedures that the teacher uses. Fourth, the timing of evaluation procedures is determined by the kinds of judgments the teacher wishes to make.

An example will illustrate how these principles might be applied in a particular class. In a woodworking course, we expect the students to learn certain skill performances. They also must acquire certain facts and concepts. Before we organize the learning experiences, we decide on the

---

[15] For a discussion of this principle, see L. J. Cronbach, *Essentials of Psychological Testing* (New York: Harper & Brothers, 1949), pp. 60–61.

relative importance of facts and how they are to be remembered. We decide on the relative importance of learning concepts and generalizations and learning various skill performances. After doing this, we organize a system of measurement procedures to assess changes in these various behaviors.

One of our specific objectives may be to have the student learn how to construct a table. The most appropriate evaluation procedure would be a performance test requiring the student to build a table.

At earlier points in the course, we may test the student on specific skills, such as his skill in hammering nails correctly, his skill in making fastenings of one kind or another, or his skill in sanding and varnishing. We may give short-form questions to test his grasp of information and his understanding of concepts and generalizations. Some of these measurement procedures will be used for diagnosing difficulties the student may be having, so that we can reorganize the learning experience for him. Other measurement procedures will be used to make a final evaluation of the student's performance in this course. The measurement procedures used are chosen on the basis of the evaluation the teacher wishes to make and the purposes for which the evaluations will be used.

We have chosen the example of the woodworking class because in such a class we may use a variety of measurement procedures. In many other classes, an equally comprehensive set of measurement procedures is required to determine the extent to which pupils have attained the objectives of the learning experience. No single procedure can be used to measure all of the behavior changes that are deemed desirable in any class.

We are limited in measuring some of these behavior changes by the lack of adequate measuring devices. When he lacks an adequate measuring device, the teacher should make only tentative judgments about behavior change, recognizing the very limited value of measurements of dubious reliability and validity.

Evaluating, like the organizing of learning experiences, is a process— not a single, static event. There are no simple, infallible rules for constructing and using appropriate measurement devices. In constructing and using evaluation procedures, the teacher is a hypothesis maker. He hypothesizes about the appropriate time for a test, about appropriate item forms, and about the relation of test-item responses to the kinds of behavior he wishes to measure. We have outlined some general principles from which the teacher should derive the innumerable specific hypotheses about the measurement procedures he will use in his classroom. Each of these hypotheses must be evaluated and revised if found to be relatively unsatisfactory.

SCORING AND GRADING

Ordinarily, a student's performance in a test situation is summarized by a score. This score may be the number of problems worked correctly, the number of correct answers, or the number of errors made. These are called *raw scores*. A raw score, such as the number of words spelled correctly in a test, tells us only what per cent of the student's responses were made in the appropriate manner. To gain a better understanding of the student's performance, we must translate raw scores into scores that indicate the student's relative position on a scale of performance. For example, we may arrange the scores by rank from highest to lowest, or we may group them in categories, such as "upper quarter," "middle half," and "lower quarter." Still another possible arrangement would be to group the scores by tenths—"top tenth" and on down to "lowest tenth." Each of these arrangements describes the student's status as it compares with that of other students in the class.[16]

GRADES AS EVALUATIVE SYMBOLS

When we have scored a test performance, we have quantified the learner's status or change, but we have not yet evaluated this change. Some criterion of acceptability must be established. That "70" shall be a passing grade is an example of such a criterion of acceptability. Another way of determining acceptability is to rank the students on their perform- ance and assign letter grades, such as "A" or "B," to different levels of performance. An "A" grade ordinarily means an acceptable and superior performance; a "B" grade, an acceptable and good performance; a "C" grade, an acceptable and average performance; and an "F" grade, an unacceptable performance. In using symbols of this kind, we are making evaluations on the basis of our measurements. Even when we use simpler systems of evaluating, such as labeling the student's performance "satis- factory" or "unsatisfactory," or "plus" or "minus," the symbol represents an evaluation of the performance based upon a measurement of it.

[16] The teacher will need to be familiar with several kinds of scores which indicate relative position. A fuller treatment of these scores is given in Chapter 17. For a discussion of scores indicating relative position, see R. Thorndike and E. Hagen, *Measurement and Evaluation in Psychology and Education* (New York: John Wiley and Sons, 1955), Chapter 7.

THE MEANING OF A GRADE

The major requirement for a system of symbols is that the meaning of the symbols be clear to those who will use them. The grading systems used in schools are interpreted by pupils, teachers, administrators, and by such individuals outside the school system as employers or admission officers at more advanced schools.

It is a common assumption that grades represent the degree to which the student has attained the objectives of particular learning experiences. A letter grade of "A," or a mark of "100," usually represents a high degree of such attainment. However, some teachers maintain that a grade should also represent the amount of effort a student has expended in attempting to attain the objectives. But the grade would then symbolize the teacher's judgment of the pupil's achievement and effort, and ordinarily a person using the grade to make other judgments, or the pupil himself, will not know how much of each went into the grade. If the teacher wants to convey to the student an evaluation of the progress that he is making, the grade should represent the degree of progress achieved. If the teacher wants to inform the student of his position with respect to other students who have had comparable learning experiences, the grade should represent achievement relative to that of other students. Similarly, the grades used by counselors for programing and by college admission officers for selecting students should represent the relative achievement of the student.

In any event, the final grade should reflect the relative importance attached to the attainment of specific objectives. Suppose we have a class in which we have measured the students' performance by discussion, short quizzes, an essay, and a final comprehensive examination. We have four measurement procedures. From each of these procedures, we draw some type of score or grade; and we must combine the various grades into a total summary grade. The weight we give each of the grades should reflect the relative importance of attaining the specific objectives. If we have decided that the most important objective of a course is gaining ability to criticize and evaluate a piece of literature, and if we have measured the attainment of this objective principally by using an essay test, then the grade on the essay should be given the greatest weight in determining the final grade.[17]

[17] For a discussion of weighing different evaluation procedures in determining the final grade, see Thorndike and Hagen (note 16), pp. 474–482.

It is important to remember that the assignment of grades is relatively arbitrary. The symbol systems and the meanings we give to them are matters of decision. What symbols we use and to what percentage of the class we assign various symbols cannot be determined by statistical means: we may determine the average of the class and the position of each student with respect to this average, but at what levels we establish the cutting scores for "A" grades, "B" grades, or "F" grades is basically a matter for the teacher to decide. "Marking on the curve" is an administrative policy and not something inherent in the nature of test scores. The decision to give a certain percentage of students "A's," "B's," and "F's" is made on the basis of the school's educational philosophy, the evaluative criteria used, and the functions the grades will serve. Whatever decision is made about the distribution of grades, the meaning of the grades in a particular class or school must be clear. All teachers do not have to give grades in identically the same way, but the grounds on which grades are assigned must be clear to students, teachers, and anybody else who will have occasion to use these grades in making decisions about the students.

IMPROVING GRADING SYSTEMS

One major difficulty in using a system of symbols is that a symbol summarizes a complex evaluation procedure. A grade of "A" or "F" is a summary of the evaluation of all of the changes that have been measured. As a consequence, the symbol system inadequately represents the extent of change in any student. Therefore, attempts have been made to develop more comprehensive ways of reporting pupil change. Essentially, these systems require the teacher to rate the pupil on a wide variety of factors (see Figure 16–3).[18] Unfortunately, there are both technical and practical difficulties associated with these systems. In the first place, the larger the number of factors on which a teacher must rate pupils, the more difficult it is to derive adequately reliable ratings. Consider, for example, the list of behavioral traits in Figure 16–3. A teacher with a class of thirty pupils needs reliable and valid information on all of these behaviors for each student. However, he cannot systematically observe each child over a long period of time to evaluate behavior change in each of these respects; so he frequently relies on periodic observations and memory, with a resulting drop in the reliability and validity of his ratings.

[18] Wrinkle (see note 2), pp. 108–109.

EVALUATION OF STUDENT ACHIEVEMENT

COLLEGE HIGH SCHOOL of COLORADO STATE COLLEGE OF EDUCATION at GREELEY

1 2 3 4 5 6
_____   Secondary School Year Date of This Report
Student

_____   6 8   12   36   2 1/2   5   10   15
Course of Activity   Weeks Enrolled   Regular Periods Each Week

GENERAL OBJECTIVES: The evaluation of the student's achievement of the twelve general objectives which follow is made in terms of what normally might be expected of students of similar age and school placement. O--outstanding. S--satisfactory. N--needs to make improvement. U--unsatisfactory. X--insufficient evidence or does not apply. SPECIFIC BEHAVIORS ESPECIALLY RESPONSIBLE FOR O, N, OR U EVALUATIONS ARE CHECKED. SPECIFIC COMMENTS PARTICULARLY WITH REFERENCE TO O, N, AND U EVALUATIONS ARE WRITTEN ON THE OPPOSITE SIDE OF THIS SHEET.

_____ 1. HE DIRECTS HIS INDIVIDUAL ACTIVITIES EFFECTIVELY ( ) begins work promptly ( ) makes good use of time ( ) requires minimum of supervision ( ) does more than the least that will be accepted ( ) meets responsibilities promptly
_____ 2. HE FOLLOWS PLANS AND DIRECTIONS ( ) listens to and reads directions carefully ( ) follows and completes plans and directions which have been set up
_____ 3. HE GETS ALONG WELL WITH OTHERS ( ) is considerate of rights and wishes of others ( ) is courteous and tolerant ( ) controls his temper ( ) conforms to reasonable social standards
_____ 4. HE TAKES AN ACTIVE PART IN GROUP LIVING ( ) participates in group planning ( ) volunteers his services ( ) does his share in group activities
_____ 5. HE SPEAKS CORRECTLY AND EFFECTIVELY ( ) speaks clearly ( ) adjusts his voice to the size of the group ( ) uses adequate vocabulary to express himself interestingly ( ) speaks with ease and confidence ( ) uses correct grammatical forms
_____ 6. HE TAKES GOOD CARE OF PERSONAL AND SCHOOL MATERIALS AND EQUIPMENT ( ) shows respect for property ( ) does not waste or damage materials or equipment ( ) returns things when due ( ) reports breakage and loss
_____ 7. HE OBSERVES ATTENDANCE REGULATIONS ( ) is regular and prompt in attendance except for approved cause ( ) arranges in advance for absence when possible ( ) takes initiative in making up work missed ( ) makes proper use of school health service
_____ 8. HE READS WITH EASE AND UNDERSTANDING ( ) selects important ideas ( ) understands and evaluates what he reads ( ) reads with reasonable speed
_____ 9. HE EXPRESSES HIMSELF CORRECTLY AND EFFECTIVELY IN WRITING ( ) expresses ideas clearly ( ) uses correct grammatical forms ( ) punctuates correctly ( ) spells correctly ( ) writes legibly
_____10. HE UTILIZES AVAILABLE SOURCES OF LEARNING MATERIALS ( ) selects and uses appropriate sources of information ( ) uses library and library tools effectively ( ) effectively engages in interview and observation
_____11. HE USES THE PROBLEM SOLVING METHOD ( ) recognizes problems ( ) states problems clearly ( ) collects and records appropriate information ( ) arrives at sound conclusions
_____12. HE USES THE BASIC SKILLS IN MATHEMATICS ( ) uses accurately the simple fundamental combinations ( ) computes with reasonable speed ( ) uses fractions and per cents correctly ( ) selects correct processes

SPECIFIC OBJECTIVES: The specific objectives of each course and activity have been discussed with the student and used in classroom instruction and evaluation activities.
HIS ACHIEVEMENT OF THE SPECIFIC OBJECTIVES OF THIS COURSE OR ACTIVITY HAS BEEN:

better than   consistent with   poorer than
what reasonably might have been expected of him in terms of his background and ability.

Such that full credit is not recommended on administrative records.

Such that he cannot be recommended for admission to college courses or training programs to which this course is prerequisite

Such as to justify encouraging him

to enroll in _____

not to enroll in _____

Supervising Teacher _____
This section is for record purposes and is to be detached before the report is issued to the student or his parents.

ACTUAL
ACHIEVEMENT:

OUTSTANDING   ABOVE AVERAGE   AVERAGE   BELOW AVERAGE   VERY POOR*

EXPECTED
ACHIEVEMENT:

*Adjusted credit recommendation (in full year courses only): 1/3 1/2 2/3 regular credit should be allowed.

FIGURE 16–3. *An example of a comprehensive report form (from Wrinkle).*

In addition, many teachers find these ratings difficult and tedious to make and, as a consequence, tend to become careless in making the ratings. Finally, such ratings are frequently characterized by the *halo effect,* in which the teacher has a general impression of a student and consistently rates him on all of the traits in accordance with this general impression.

When these more comprehensive reporting systems are used, parents, teachers, and students appear to find them more satisfactory; however, over a period of time, the practical difficulties of maintaining such a system seem to be too great.[19] Administrators and teachers are continuing to try to find a practical way to convey more information about the evaluation of pupil change. At present, a system satisfactory from every point of view has yet to be developed.

OBJECTIVITY IN SCORING
TEST PERFORMANCES

In the preceding chapter, we stated that any measurement device must be highly *reliable;* that is, everyone who understands and uses the measurement procedure should obtain approximately the same score for a student's performance. A measurement of pupil performance is unreliable if the scoring procedures tend to place the student in a different relative position each time the performance is scored independently.

The major advantage of the short-form question is that the *form* of the question makes scorer agreement easy to obtain. With only the master answer sheet available, the scorer can obtain the same score for a student that any other scorer would.

Essay examinations, however, are difficult to score reliably. For example, Falls [20] gave the same composition to one hundred English teachers, asking them to grade the composition on a percentage scale and to indicate the grade level at which they expected that quality of work to be done. The results of the grading are listed in Table 16–1. Notice the range of grades assigned to the *same* composition. Obviously, these scores do not place the student in the same relative position each time the paper is scored independently. In another study, Tiegs gave a set of papers to one teacher and then, two months later, gave the same teacher the same papers for re-marking.[21] Table 16–2 shows the two sets of grades. Compare these data with those in the Falls study. Several other studies support the statement that two teachers grading the same set of essay examinations do not highly agree on the grade that they give, and that the

---

[19] For a discussion of one school's attempts to develop a comprehensive reporting system and the difficulties encountered, see Wrinkle (note 2).

[20] J. D. Falls, "Research in Secondary Education," *Kentucky School Journal,* 6 (1928), 42–46.

[21] E. W. Tiegs, *Educational Diagnosis,* (Monterey, Calif.: California Test Bureau, 1952). Educational Bulletin No. 18.

TABLE 16-1. *The estimated grade value and percentage marks assigned to an English composition by one hundred teachers (from Falls).*

Grade value	Percentage mark								
	60–64	65–69	70–74	75–79	80–84	85–89	90–94	95–99	Total
XV								2	2
XIV									0
XIII							1	2	3
XII					1		2	3	6
XI			2			6	5	2	15
X		1		3	8	4	7	1	24
IX	1	1		1	8	4	4	3	22
VIII		2		2	2	3	4	3	16
VII				2	2	2	1		7
VI	1				1	1		1	4
V	1								1
Total	3		6	8	22	20	24	17	100

same teacher grading the same set of examinations over a period of time does not assign the same grades to the students.[22]

This disadvantage of essay examinations can be remedied by using a number of procedures. If the teacher defines in advance what the essay question is to measure, and then grades on this *and this only*, reliability probably will be improved. Or the teacher may, in advance of the actual scoring, assign relative weights to every aspect of performance to be graded. For example, an English teacher may decide that greater weight is to be given to the theme of a composition than to correct grammar. The number of points or the letter grade to be assigned for each aspect of the composition could be allotted in advance and applied to each composition as it is graded. Figure 16–4 gives an example of directions to the scorer of an essay question.[23] Notice that the scorer is told what to grade and what credit to allow for each item he grades.

[22] See, for example, L. M. Childers, "Report of the Research Committee on Examinations," *Proceedings of the Sixtieth Annual Meeting*, National Association of Dental Examiners, 60 (1942), 77–106; C. E. Hulten, "The Personal Element in Teachers' Marks," *Journal of Educational Research*, 12 (1925), 49–55.

[23] F. P. Frutchey and R. W. Tyler, "Examinations in the Natural Sciences," in Hawkes (note 1), pp. 218–219.

Procedures such as these usually improve the reliability of grading essay questions or any type of performance in which the behavior to be measured is complex.[24] Where several teachers are to grade essay examinations on the same subject matter, the teachers should agree in advance on the criteria for grading. This principle also applies to the assignment of

TABLE 16–2. *Re-marking of ten examinations by same teacher after two-month interval (from Tiegs).*

Pupil No.	First Marking	Second Marking
1	85	70
2	50	75
3	90	95
4	90	85
5	90	70
6	99	90
7	70	60
8	75	80
9	60	80
10	90	75

grades. In this way the grades or marks have a consistent meaning, even though they may be given by different people to different students.

LIMITATIONS OF CLASSROOM EVALUATION PROCEDURES

One of the major limitations in classroom evaluation procedures is that there are many behaviors, particularly those of a complex nature, for which the teacher does not have adequate measuring instruments. In social studies courses we attempt to influence students' attitudes, but rarely do we have reliable and valid measuring devices for determining the extent to which pupils' attitudes have changed. We are also concerned with students' interests and values; but, again, we do not have adequate measuring devices with which to measure them. Many teachers are annoyed, and rightly so, by the fact that their tests are limited to measuring knowledge of facts, concepts, generalizations, problem-solving ability, and performance processes. To measure many important behavior

[24] For suggestions for improving essay examinations, see J. M. Stalnaker, "The Essay Type of Examination," in E. Lindquist, *Educational Measurement* (note 12), Chapter 13.

Purpose of the test

This part of the test is to obtain evidence of the student's acquisition of information. If you are able to identify the meaning of his statements, do not consider his spelling, handwriting, grammatical construction, or method of presentation in your evaluation. Judge only the accuracy and adequacy of the information he stated.

Values to be assigned to answers

Question 1a--How is the volume of a kilogram of air affected by changes in the pressure applied to it?

Allow 4 points credit for answers which indicate direction and nature of relation and constancy of temperature; for example, "Volume varies inversely as pressure if temperature remains constant."

Allow 3 points for answers which indicate direction and nature of relation but do not mention constancy of temperature; for example,

$$\frac{V_1}{V_2} = \frac{P_2}{P_1}$$

or an equivalent expression.

Allow 1 point for omissions, or "I don't know" statements. This assumes that the teacher considers it better for a student to recognize that he does not know than to be mistaken in the facts he thinks he knows.

Allow no credit for mistaken conceptions, such as "Pressure has no effect on volume," "Increasing pressure increases volume."

Question 1b--Upon what other gases do changes in pressure produce similar effects?

Allow 2 points credit for answers which indicate that all or nearly all gases are affected in similar fashion.

Allow 1 point credit for omission, or "I don't know" answers.

Allow no credit for mistaken conceptions, such as, "No other gases," "Gases which are lighter than air," "Gases where molecules are composed of only one atom."

FIGURE 16–4. *Sample of directions for scoring essay questions (from Frutchey and Tyler).*

changes, the teacher must rely heavily upon his observations of pupil behavior. If the teacher is sensitive to the difficulties involved in making such observations, he can utilize data that he gathers in this way to make cautious inferences about pupil change.

The teacher can construct some instruments for measuring even complex changes for which tests may not be available. Figure 16–5 shows an example of an interest-inventory test given to a group of bright students in an experimental program. The teacher wanted to know what the interests of these students were, both at the beginning and at the end of the experimental program; and he constructed this test to measure interests. Through an interest inventory of this kind or through personal questioning, the teacher might collect data from which he could make inferences about the student's behavior. The advantage of the written interest inventory is that the teacher can gather the data in a systematic way for a large number of pupils.

Every principle that we have stated about sampling behavior and about reliability and validity of measurement is applicable to the formal and informal procedures that the teacher may use to gather data on interests, attitudes, values, and even on the self-concept of the child. Until tests are constructed to measure comprehensive behavior changes, the teacher will have to rely on procedures of unknown reliability and validity in gathering information from which to make inferences about pupil change. However, if the teacher is aware of the difficulty in making inferences with such procedures, and if he tests his inferences systematically, he is less likely to make serious errors in evaluating pupil change.

MEASUREMENT OF THE SOCIAL STRUCTURE OF A CLASS

Teachers frequently want to know the pattern of social relations in their classes. Data on these relations have important implications for the organization of learning experiences. For instance, if we know who is the least-liked student in the class, we can devise situations in which he will have an opportunity to interact more frequently with his fellow students and to become more accepted by them. The social structure of the class may also directly affect some kinds of learning experiences. For example, planning group work requires information about what students are likely to work well with each other—unless the teacher has a therapeutic strategy in mind to change pupil's attitudes to each other; but information on the social structure is also needed here.

A number of simple techniques, called **sociometric devices**, are avail-

PUPIL INTEREST INVENTORY

1. What school subjects do you like the best? Number these school subjects from 1 to 10 to show the order in which you would choose them:

   (__) Reading   (__) Social Studies   (__) Language   (__) Music   (__) Art

   (__) Handwriting   (__) Arithmetic   (__) Science   (__) Spelling   (__) P.E.

2. Are there any school subjects not taught at your school that you wish were part of the school program? _____

3. Do you have a definite time to study at home?_____

4. How many books do you read in a week at home?_____

5. What are the names of some of the books you especially enjoyed reading in the last few years?

   _____

6. How often do you use the public library? Underline the answer that is right for you.

   Never   Once in a while   Every two weeks   Every week

7. How often do you read the newspaper?   Never   Once in a while   Regularly

8. Underline the parts of the paper that you read often:

   Local News   World News   Sports   Comics   Advertisements   Society Page

   Weather   Tides   Theatre, Radio, Television   Editorials

9. Do you like to read magazines?_____

   What magazines do you read often?_____

10. Do you often read comic books?_____ What comic books do you read?_____

    _____

11. Do you listen to the radio every day?_____ What kind of programs do you like best?

    _____

12. Do you have a television set in your home?_____ About how many hours do you spend watching television on a school day?_____ On a week end?_____ Please list your Five Favorite Television Programs:_____

13. How often do you go to the movies? Underline the best answer for you.

    Never   Two or three times a year   Two or three times a month

14. Underline the names of the places where you have been. Check the ones you would like to visit again.

    Natural History Museum   Airport   Ferry   Beach   Circus

    Ball Game   Art gallery   A park on the peninsula   Lighthouse

    Junior Museum   A dam   A broadcasting station   Opera

    Observatory   Planetarium   Symphony concert   Zoo   Aquarium

    A manufacturing plant   _____   _____

15. Have you ever visited any foreign countries? _____

    Name them. _____

16. Check any clubs or organizations to which you belong and add any which are not listed below:

    Boy or Girl Scouts   Cub Scouts   Brownies   Church Choir

    School Orchestra   Campfire Girls   Blue Birds   Gray Y

    Jr. Traffic Patrol   Student Council   School Chorus   Jr. Hi Y

    _____   _____   _____   _____

Comments: (If you have any)

FIGURE 16–5

able for making gross measurements of the social structure of a class.[25] One of the simplest of such techniques is to ask each student to list the person he likes best and the person he likes least in the class. When the teacher obtains this information, he can rank all of the students by the number of times they were chosen as most liked and least liked. He can also determine who chooses whom. An example of this technique is given in Figure 16–6, which tabulates the preferences of sixth-grade students who were asked to list their first, second, and third choices of a person to sit by. Constructing a *sociogram* is another convenient way of plotting the same data; the sociogram in Figure 16–7 uses circles to represent the children, and arrows drawn between the circles to indicate choices (solid lines for boys, broken lines for girls).

Many variations on this kind of question can be asked to measure different kinds of social interaction. Ask the students with whom they would like to work on a social studies committee, or with whom they would like to play on the same team in a game, or with whom they would like to walk home from school. Each of these questions yields different kinds of information about the pattern of social relations in a class. There may not be a high relationship between the children most frequently picked as work companions and those most frequently picked as play companions. The children will make their choices on how useful or helpful the chosen person will be in a particular activity. For example, children may most frequently pick the best athlete if they are choosing team members for a game, but they may frequently choose the brightest students in class to work on a committee with them. Moreover, the teacher can determine who is the best-liked student and who is the least-liked student for a variety of purposes or activities. He can ordinarily find out which student is rarely chosen for anything and which student is most frequently chosen. With this kind of information the teacher is better able to understand pupil behavior, and he will also be able to use this information in planning learning experiences.[26]

Another variation on this technique is to disguise the purpose of the question. Instead of asking a child whom he likes, ask him to assign people to different roles. This is the "guess-who" technique.[27] Essentially,

[25] Moreno first developed these techniques, and he has suggested possible uses for them. See J. L. Moreno, *Who Shall Survive?* (Washington, D. C.: Nervous and Mental Diseases Publishing Company, 1934).

[26] For suggestions on such uses, see H. Jennings et al., *Sociometry in Group Relations* (Washington, D. C.: American Council on Education, 1948).

[27] For examples of the use of this technique in studies of child behavior, see H. Hartshorne and M. A. May, *Studies in Service and Self-Control* (New York: The Macmillan Company, 1929).

CHOOSERS \ CHOSEN	Pam	John	David	Steve	George	Brian G.	Paul	Scott J.	Scott K.	Jeff	Ruth	Marc	Libby	Sherman	Sharon	Tony	Judy	Alan	Brian S.	Jane	Wayne	Bill	Keith	Sandy	Lane
Pam													1		2		3								
John*																									
David			3	2												1									
Steve				1													3						2		
George							1									2					3				
Brian G.	1															2					3				
Paul												1	2								3				
Scott J.				2						1											3				
Scott K.							2									3					1				
Jeff			3														2				1				
Ruth													1								3				2
Marc							1										2	3							
Libby	3						2																	1	
Sherman							2											1			3				
Sharon	3								1									2							
Tony		1																			3				
Judy	3								1																2
Alan							1										2				3				
Brian S.							2											1			3				
Jane			3							1	2														
Wayne							2										3	1							
Bill						3	2																1		
Keith		2	3																			1			
Sandy							2					1									3				
Lane									1									2					3		
CHOSEN 1.		1	1		1	2		1	3	4	2	1			1	2		1	1		3	1	1		
2.		1			2	7				1	1			1	2	2	1	2				1	2		
3.	3		3	1					1			1		1	1	1	2		9	1		1			
TOTALS	3	2	1	3	1	3	9	0	1	1	3	5	3	0	2	5	3	3	4	0	9	4	2	2	2

* John absent

FIGURE 16–6. *Chart of seating preferences in a sixth-grade class. The children were told, "List the child you would like to sit next to." They were to give three names in order of preference. These choices are listed below each name.*

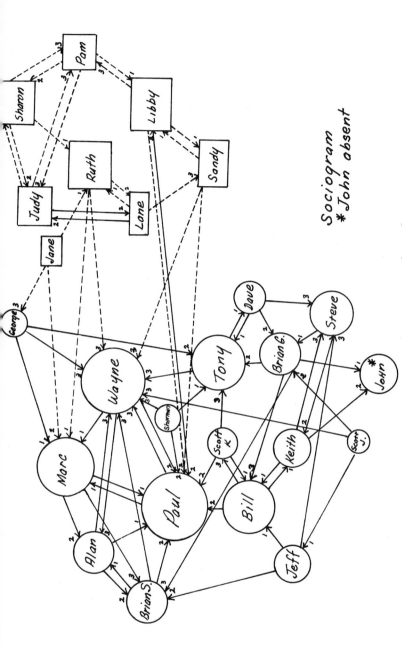

FIGURE 16–7. Sociogram based on seating preferences charted in Figure 16–6. An arrow is drawn between chooser and chosen, pointing to the person chosen. An arrowhead on each end of the line symbolizes a mutual choice. The number indicates the order of preference.

Name_____School_____Grade_____

THE CLASS PLAY

Just imagine your class was going to put on a play and you are selected to direct it. Below you will see the kinds of parts that will be needed for this play. As director of the play, you have the responsibility of selecting any boy or girl in your class for any of the parts. Since many of the parts are very small, you may, if you wish, select the same boy or girl for more than one part.

In order to make this play successful, and a lot of fun, you will need to choose boys and girls who you think would be most natural for the part. Make your choices carefully, and, if you have any questions about the meaning of a word or anything else, be sure to ask your teacher.

THESE ARE THE PARTS

Part 1 - The Hero -- someone who is good in sports and in
         school work.   _____

Part 2 - Someone who is often mean and gets into fights a great
         deal (boy or girl).   _____

Part 3 - The Heroine -- someone who gets along well with other
         boys and girls and with the teacher.   _____

Part 4 - Someone who is always getting angry about little
         things.   _____

Part 5 - Someone who could be the hero's friend - a kind,
         helpful boy or girl.   _____

Part 6 - Someone who could play the part of a bully - picks on
         boys and girls smaller or weaker than himself.   _____

Part 7 - Someone who has a good sense of humor but is always
         careful not to disturb the teacher or the class.   _____

Part 8 - Someone who could play the part of a person who
         doesn't ever say anything.   _____

Part 9 - Someone who is never mean and always friendly.   _____

Part 10 - Someone who could act like the laziest person in the
         world--never does anything.   _____

Part 11 - A boy or girl you would choose to be in charge when
         the teacher left the room.   _____

Part 12 - This person knows all the answers and usually works
         alone.   _____

Section II

A. Which part or parts would you like to play best? (Write number or numbers on line here.)_____

B. Which part or parts do you think you could play? (Write number or numbers on line here.)_____

C. Which part or parts do you think the teacher might ask you to play? (Write number or numbers on

   line here.) _____

D. Which part or parts do you think most of the other kids would ask you to play? (Write number or

   numbers on line here.)_____

FIGURE 16-8. *Assignment of parts in a play (compiled by California State Department of Education).*

it consists of asking the child to guess who is the most popular boy in class, who is the least popular, who is the brightest, and so on. In one variation the children are asked to assign parts in a play (see Figure 16–8). Again, from this kind of information the teacher can make inferences about the social structure in the class.

Sociometric devices present problems in reliability and validity; ordinarily, such devices have "face" validity only, and only for the kind of question that we ask. From the answers to one question, we should not generalize about all of the various social relations of children. Furthermore, although we assume that the children are answering honestly, some children may be afraid to state what child they dislike, and may even refuse to answer such a question. Also, changes in the social structure take place as the children become better acquainted with each other or as the teacher manipulates their social relations. At best, a single use of this technique gives us a picture of the social structure of a particular class at a particular time.[28]

SUMMARY

We have presented some techniques of test construction that the teacher may use to measure pupil change, and we have discussed the relevance of the basic principles of measurement and evaluation to the use of these techniques.

1. The evaluation procedure logically begins with a conception of the desired behavior change to be evaluated. Such a conception requires that the teacher (a) define the desired behavior carefully and precisely, describing it in terms of observable responses; (b) define the relative importance of attaining each objective, and specify what the importance is. This relative importance should be reflected in the kinds of learning experiences organized, the measurement procedures used to assess behavior change, and in the final summary evaluation of behavior change expressed in grades or marks.

2. Teachers frequently define the objectives of a course in terms of content to be acquired. While content acquisition is a behavior change, teachers are concerned with fostering other kinds of behavior changes as

---

[28] For a comprehensive discussion of these measurement problems, see L. J. Cronbach (note 15), Chapter 17.

well. Measurement procedures used to assess content acquisition may not measure other kinds of behavior change.

3. When objectives of the learning experience have been clarified, evaluation procedures need to be devised which will evoke samples of the kind of behavior described in the objectives. A test item is a stimulus designed to evoke such behaviors.

4. A primary consideration in devising test items is the kind of behavior likely to be evoked by them. The same test stimuli may be arranged in a variety of forms. Item forms are chosen so that the total set of test items will provide us with a representative sample of pupil behavior.

5. Many kinds of short-form questions, such as the completion, fill-in, true-false, and matching types, are most appropriately used in testing for recall and recognition of facts, generalizations, or principles. Multiple-choice items can be used for this and other purposes, such as testing for understanding of concepts, ability to apply generalizations, and ability to detect errors in inference. We recommend that the prospective teacher familiarize himself with specimens of these various kinds of items and the uses that have been made of them.

6. Essay questions are most appropriately used to test complex functions that cannot be tested easily or efficiently with a short-form question. Essay questions should specify clearly the character of the response desired. Some teachers assume that if it requires an extensive written answer, the question is an essay-type question. Essay questions which test retention of facts could more appropriately be recast as short-form questions, which would obtain for the teacher a more representative sample of the pupil's behavior.

7. The results of a performance in a test situation are usually quantified in the form of a score, called the "raw" score. Such scores can be given meaning by transforming them into other scores describing the student's relative position on a scale of performance. Such scores are useful to the extent that they are objective.

8. By *objectivity* of scoring, we mean that the procedures, if used by independent scorers, would place the student in the same relative position with respect to other students.

9. The scoring of essay examinations tends to be relatively unreliable unless the responses to be graded are carefully defined and appropriate weightings are specified for different levels of performance.

10. Grades or marks are symbols used to summarize the results of evaluation procedures and to convey information about those results. One of the principal disadvantages of the commonly used symbol systems is

that the letter or number grade used does not adequately convey all the available information about pupil status and change. If grades or marks are to be used effectively, the criteria employed in determining the grade must be clear to the user of the grade. Consistency in grading can be improved by defining and agreeing on the evaluative criteria to be used in judging students' performances.

11. *Sociometric* devices are measurement procedures that teachers may use to determine the pattern of social relations in their classes. In one simple form of a sociometric device, students are asked to list the fellow students with whom they would like to participate in some activity. By counting the frequency of choices, the teacher can determine which pupils were chosen the most and least frequently for this particular activity, the pattern of mutual choices, and even the hierarchy of leadership in the class. It is important to remember that such procedures describe the pattern of social relations only as it stands at the time of testing and only for the kind of activity tested by the stimulus question.

12. The teacher who wishes to become a skillful constructor of measurement devices will need additional training and experience. This chapter has suggested basic principles and techniques with which a teacher can begin to evaluate his own procedures. The process of measuring pupil status and change is a process of making inferences from data that are gathered about pupil behavior. The relative validity of the inferences depends on the relative validity and reliability of the data that the teacher gathers on pupil behavior. The teacher will need to check continually his inferences about pupil status and change.

STUDY AND DISCUSSION QUESTIONS

1. Select some unit of a subject that you are or may be teaching. Prepare a detailed list of behavior changes to be promoted by the learning experiences you will organize for this unit. Be as specific as possible in the statement of objectives. Indicate what aspects of each learning experience will facilitate the achievement of each objective. Indicate the relative importance of attaining each of these objectives. Specify the criteria for evaluating the behavior changes.

2. Describe the measurement procedures that you will use to evaluate the behavior changes specified in the statement of objectives. Construct test items, using any of the item forms discussed in this chapter. Explain the ways in which your item selection is appropriate for measuring the kinds of behavior change the item is designed to measure.

3. Now that you have constructed test items to measure the behavior changes, what procedures will be necessary to improve the test that you have devel-

oped? Be specific about the procedures you will use to determine whether the items are ambiguous and to determine the relative difficulty of the items.

4. Review your statement of objectives. Are there some behavior changes that cannot be measured, or measured only with difficulty, by using the test item forms discussed in this chapter? What procedures would you use to evaluate these kinds of behavior change? Specify the procedures that may be used to measure these behavior changes.

5. Describe the scoring procedures that you will use for evaluating behavior change. Also describe how you will use these measurements to determine grades. What may a person infer about pupil achievement in your class? What aspects of pupil achievement may be ignored by utilizing the grades that you provide?

6. Some people argue that distributing grades according to fixed percentages is an unfair and misleading procedure. Under what conditions would such a procedure be defensible? Under what circumstances might such a procedure be misleading?

7. A teacher constructs an essay examination with the following directions: "Select any five of the ten questions; each question has a value of 20 points." What difficulties in measurement and evaluation may result from the use of these directions?

8. A teacher indicates at the beginning of an essay examination that students will be penalized one point for every mistake in grammar. The essay examination covers the content of a history course. What difficulties in measurement and evaluation may result from using this procedure?

9. Some school systems use a grading system in which student achievement is reported in the following symbols: S (satisfactory), U (unsatisfactory), N (needs improvement). Some teachers argue that this kind of a grading system reduces student's motivation to work hard. Evaluate this argument. Under what conditions might this objection be valid?

10. Some parents feel that marks given on the basis of a child's ability give neither his parents nor the child a "true picture" of his achievement. How would you evaluate this argument? Under what conditions might the argument be valid? What assumptions seem to be implicit in this argument? Criticize these assumptions.

11. Some teachers feel that a grade should include some measure of the effort the student has made. What difficulties do you see in using such a procedure? Are there some conditions under which such a procedure may be defensible?

12. Refer to the sociometric diagram and data provided in this chapter. List the students who appear to be the most frequently chosen and the least frequently chosen. Can you identify any "cliques" from these data? What is

the pattern of boy-girl choices? Do the most frequently chosen boy and girl select students who are also frequently chosen?

RECOMMENDED READINGS

A. Anastasi. *Psychological Testing.* New York: The Macmillan Co., 1961, Chapters 2–7.

E. Lindquist, ed. *Educational Measurement.* Washington, D. C.: American Council on Education, 1951, Chapters 5, 14, 15, 16.

R. Thorndike and E. Hagen. *Measurement and Evaluation in Psychology and Education.* 2nd ed. New York: John Wiley and Sons, 1961, Chapters 6 and 13.

D. A. Wood. *Test Construction.* Columbus, Ohio: Charles E. Merrill Books, Inc., 1960.

CHAPTER SEVENTEEN

THE USE OF STANDARDIZED TESTS

Measurement procedures, as we have seen, provide samples of pupil behavior. Before inferences may be made from such samples, the reliability and validity of the measurement procedure must be determined. Ordinarily, the teacher has neither the technical training nor the time for determining the reliability and validity of his own tests. He is also limited in the kinds of inferences he may make from his own tests. He may not, for example, compare the performance of his students with that of other students who have had comparable learning experiences.

Standardized tests have been developed to provide such comparisons. These tests have been administered to large groups of students to provide data on comparative performances, and their reliability and validity have been determined.

The kinds of standardized tests available to teachers may be divided into two categories: (1) those that may be used

642

to measure the attainment of objectives of learning experiences; (2) those that measure pupil characteristics related to the attainment of these objectives. Achievement tests are in the former category; intelligence tests, tests of special aptitudes, and "personality" tests are in the latter category.

The administration of some group tests can be handled easily by classroom teachers. The administration of other kinds of tests, such as the Stanford-Binet Tests of Intelligence, require special training.[1] Standardized tests provide manuals with directions for test administration; these should be followed carefully if a controlled observation is to be made.

The discussion in this chapter is merely an introduction to the study of these tests. We will study the principal kinds of tests developed to measure some of the behavior patterns with which the teacher is concerned in making hypotheses about school learning. Some of these tests, such as intelligence tests, are used in practically all school systems, and the results of performance on these tests are available to teachers. The teacher needs to know what such tests measure, how to interpret the test scores, and the limitations of these measurement procedures. The administration of other kinds of tests, such as many personality tests, is reserved for individuals who have received special training in their use and interpretation. We will offer only a general discussion of the nature and uses of such tests.

One of the major advantages of the standardized test is that it provides comparative data on pupil performance; such data in turn provide additional information about the performances of students in a particular class. An understanding of the process of test standardization is required before these comparative data may be interpreted correctly.

THE PROCESS OF TEST STANDARDIZATION

In principle, a testing procedure is a controlled observation of behavior. To make this observation we obtain behavior samples that, presumably, are influenced only by the characteristic we are studying. Assume that we collect samples of "intelligent behavior" to make inferences about intellectual ability. We have an individual perform a series of tasks in such a way that his behavior is likely to be influenced only by his intellectual ability. We attempt to control all factors unrelated to intellectual ability that may influence his performance on these tasks.

---

[1] See, for example, L. M. Terman and M. A. Merrill, *Directions for Administering Forms L and M: Revision of the Stanford-Binet Tests of Intelligence* (Boston: Houghton Mifflin Co., 1937). The latest revision of this test appeared in 1960.

STANDARDIZATION OF
TEST CONDITIONS

One of the ways in which observations are controlled is to make the observation under a prescribed set of conditions. A standardized test typically provides directions about the way in which the test is to be given. Such directions usually prescribe the length of time to be allotted for the test, and the directions to be given those being examined; they also usually describe the conditions that should be controlled to ensure comparable performance. For example, maintaining time limits ensures that all individuals taking the test have equal opportunity to perform the tasks in the test. Test directions usually encourage the testee to do his best or to say what he thinks or feels. In these ways the testing conditions are made comparable for everybody, and help the individual to do as well as he can.

TEST NORMS

Standardized tests have been given to large samples of subjects, and performance *norms* have been developed from the test-performance data. These norms are scores that indicate an individual's *relative performance*—the position of his performance among those obtained by the group that has taken the test. Teachers frequently use a simple process for obtaining norms for their own tests. Assume that a teacher has administered an algebra test consisting of fifteen problems. After correcting the papers, he may construct the following frequency table:

No. of Correct Problems	No. of Students Getting This Many Problems Correct
15	1
14	2
13	0
12	4
11	4
10	5
9	6
8	4
7	4
6	3
5	2
4	0
3	0
2	1
1	0
0	0

From the table we see that approximately half the class worked nine or more problems correctly. Two students worked all but one of the problems correctly, and one had a perfect score. The student who worked only two problems correctly did quite poorly in comparison with the other students. From these data, the teacher might compute each student's rank in class. These ranks would provide a *table of norms;* that is, a set of scores that can be used to determine a student's relative performance on the test. Many different kinds of scores may be used in tables of norms. We will discuss several kinds in this chapter. A teacher needs to know how to interpret some of these scores in order to interpret students' performances on standardized tests.

The group of subjects to whom a test is given so that norms may be developed is called the *standardization sample.* The characteristics of this sample are usually given in the manual accompanying the test. To use norms, we need to compare the group taking a test to the standardization sample. If these two groups are not highly similar on the characteristics described in the manual, using the test norms may lead to erroneous inferences about the performance of our students. Assume that the standardization sample was composed of students of lower intellectual ability than the group we are testing. A comparison of the performances of the tested group with those of the standardization sample will probably show the tested group to be relatively superior. We may draw the erroneous conclusion that our group has made greater gains than expected from what is known about their aptitude. The performance of our students should be compared to that of students of similar ability.

One important caution should be emphasized concerning the use of norms: norms do not represent "ideal" performances; they are not measures of what a student "ought" to do. They represent only the actual performances of a specific group of subjects. Teachers have been criticized for a tendency to view the standardization group's performance as a *criterion* against which to *evaluate* the performance of their own students. As we will point out later, the performance of the standardization sample may be used for making evaluations, but only under certain conditions and with considerable caution.

TEST RELIABILITY AND VALIDITY

Manuals accompanying standardized tests provide information on test **reliability** and **validity**. This information is reported in the form of **correlation coefficients.** A high positive correlation, such as .90, indicates that the test probably has sufficient reliability for the purpose for which it is intended. As a rule of thumb, the kinds of tests teachers are likely to use should probably have reliability coefficients of approximately .90.[2]

You will recall (see Chapter 15) that a test may have *logical* or *predictive validity*. Tests on subject content typically have logical validity; that is, they test knowledge of the content of some subject previously studied. Standardized subject-matter tests typically have this kind of validity. We will make some qualifications concerning logical validity in the section on "Achievement Tests" later in this chapter.

The predictive validity of a test is determined by correlating test performance with a criterion performance, which is assumed or known to be an adequate measure of the behavior being studied. Information on predictive validity describes the criterion measure used and gives the correlation between test and criterion performances. High positive correlation indicates that the test is probably measuring the same kind of behavior measured in the criterion performance.

When such information is available, the predictive validity of a test is reported in the test manual. By studying the kinds of performances that may be predicted from a particular test, we obtain information on the kinds of behavior the test is measuring. An important caution is relevant here. Some test users make inferences from the test title about the kinds of behavior a test is measuring. Such inferences are likely to be valid only when the test measures knowledge of some content area. In general, what a test is measuring can best be determined from the kinds of performances that may be predicted from test performance. In the following sections we will discuss some of the principal kinds of standardized tests a teacher is likely to use.

INTELLIGENCE TESTS

One kind of standardized test used in schools is the intelligence test. Basically, these tests are designed to measure the intellectual ability of a child. How is intelligence or general intellectual ability measured?

INFERRING INTELLECTUAL ABILITY FROM TEST PERFORMANCE

Assume that we ask children to add a column of numbers. We may arrange their performances, the number of correct additions, on a scale. A

---

[2] A more extended discussion of test reliability may be found in A. Anastasi, *Psychological Testing* (New York: The Macmillan Company, 1954), Chapter 5.

child who has never studied addition will probably be at the lowest point on this scale. But we may not immediately attribute his poorer performance to lack of intelligence. We know that ability to add a column of figures requires some experience in learning the meaning of numbers and how to add them. However, if the child has had the necessary learning experience but still cannot add, we may infer that this child is not as intelligent as a child who can add these figures.

We cannot measure intellectual ability directly. We can only make inferences about it from observations of what a person has learned. Therefore, to measure intellectual ability, we present children with a series of tasks. Many of the items in intelligence tests are tasks which a child may learn to perform at some level of his schooling. Other tasks represent what a child can probably learn on the basis of his general experience. If each of the children taking the test has had the experience necessary for learning the behavior required by these tasks, differences in performances may be attributed to differences in intellectual ability. If, however, any of the children has *not* had an opportunity to learn the behavior required by the test tasks, differences in performance on intelligence tests may not reflect differences in intellectual ability.

INTELLIGENCE TESTS AS MEASURES OF RELATIVE BRIGHTNESS

Intelligence-test performance, like performance on other psychological tests, cannot be interpreted directly. Performance on these tests is measured by the number of items answered correctly. Normative data permit us to determine a child's relative performance on these tests by comparing his performance to that of children in the standardization sample. We may say that a child is more or less bright when compared to other children. We cannot determine "how much" intellectual ability he has except in this sense.

Many people are familiar with the IQ score in which intelligence-test performance is usually reported. Some people incorrectly assume that the IQ tells us "how much" intellectual ability a child has. The IQ is not a measure of some absolute amount of intelligence; neither is it, as we have seen, a direct measure of ability. A brief consideration of the general character of intelligence tests and the arrangement of the tasks in them will suggest why we may not treat the IQ score as an absolute measure.

The tasks in an intelligence test are graded to approximate what a child should be able to do at a given age level. Intelligence tests used with younger children involve fairly simple tasks with which younger children are likely to be familiar. An intelligence test given to an older child includes many items that are likely to have been learned only by a child at that age level. For example, an intelligence test for younger children may include a problem that requires a child to follow simple directions, such as "Walk to the table, then pick up the book, and bring the book to me." Intelligence tests for older children may include arithmetic problems. In either case, the tasks can probably be accomplished by children at the respective age levels. But we may not compare test performances of children of different age levels unless they have attempted the same tasks. In other words, we are simply applying the principle that inferences about relative intellectual ability assume that the persons being compared have had comparable learning opportunities.

Of course, some younger children may be able to perform some of the tasks typically performed by older children. On intelligence tests including vocabulary items, a five-year-old may identify the meaning of some words that are known by ten-year-olds, and he may answer some questions not typically answered by five-year-olds. Our inference from this performance is that he is a bright five-year-old. We may not compare directly the intelligence test performances of a five-year-old child and a fifteen-year-old child. We may state how bright a five-year-old child is by comparing him to other five-year-old children. The performance of each child is compared to that of children likely to have had comparable kinds of experiences.

VALIDITY OF INTELLIGENCE TESTS

The constructor of an intelligence test has usually developed some conception of what is meant by intelligence; he constructs test items which he thinks will evoke responses reflecting differences in intelligence as he has conceptualized it. A test constructor may conceive of intelligence as the ability to do conceptual thinking.[3] He may then decide that verbal tasks—that is, tasks whose successful performance requires the ability to formulate ideas in verbal symbols—are the most appropriate kinds of tasks to measure this ability.

Such an intelligence test may be said to have some logical validity, since the test items are selected in accordance with some conception of the meaning of intelligence. Vocabulary-test items are included in many

[3] See, for example, L. M. Terman, *The Measurement of Intelligence* (Boston: Houghton Mifflin Co., 1916).

intelligence tests, because most definitions posit verbal ability as a part of general intelligence.

Intelligence tests also have *predictive validity.* These tests have been given to large numbers of students, and performance on these tests has been correlated with other performances, such as school achievement. Performance on intelligence tests correlates fairly highly with success in school.[4] These tests measure many of the abilities required for success in school.

Many of the intelligence tests are heavily loaded with verbal tasks, tasks requiring facility and knowledge of verbal concepts and symbols. As we would expect, such tests are more highly correlated with success in those aspects of schooling that require verbal ability than they are with learning that requires less verbal ability.

Performance on intelligence tests has also been correlated with the occupations of individuals. Figure 17–1 shows the average scores on a test of intellectual ability given to people in a number of occupations.[5] These data do not mean that everyone with a score above a certain level necessarily enters a particular profession. Note the range of scores in each of the occupations and the amount of overlap in scores between occupations.

Relationships of this kind enable us to predict whether an individual is likely to succeed in a given occupation. For instance, we may be able to determine whether he will be accepted into the training program of a given occupation; or we may use a test score as an index of his general aptitude for the work required in the occupation. However, the relationship reflected in Figure 17–1 tells us nothing about the relative success of individuals in these occupations. We may not assume that the brighter people within the occupation are the more successful members. Success in any occupation depends on a variety of factors, only one of which may be intellectual ability.

Practically every teacher has met a student whose intelligence-test score is high but who is not succeeding in school. One possible explanation for this discrepancy is that the intelligence test score is inaccurate. This

[4] Q. McNemar, *The Revision of the Stanford-Binet Scale: An Analysis of the Standardization Data* (Boston: Houghton Mifflin Co., 1942), Chapter 3; A. Q. Sartain, "A Comparison of the New Revised Stanford-Binet, the Bellevue Scale, and Certain Group Tests of Intelligence," *Journal of Social Psychology,* 23 (1946), 237–239.

[5] In A. Anastasi, *Differential Psychology,* 3rd ed. (New York: The Macmillan Company, 1958), p. 516, based on the data from N. Stewart, "AGCT Scores of Army Personnel Grouped by Occupation," *Occupations,* 26 (1947), 5–41. Reprinted with permission of *Occupations.*

hypothesis may be checked. But we also know that intellectual aptitude is only one factor that contributes to success in school. Even the brightest students may have difficulty in school if they are not appropriately motivated or have poor work habits. From what we know about what the test measures, we may make a prediction about the student's probable

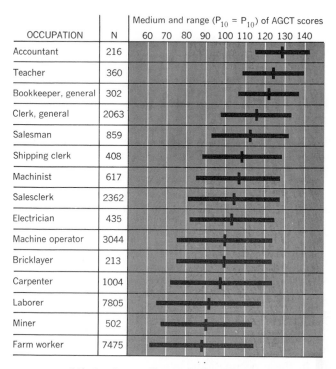

OCCUPATION	N	Medium and range ($P_{10} = P_{10}$) of AGCT scores
		60 70 80 90 100 110 120 130 140
Accountant	216	
Teacher	360	
Bookkeeper, general	302	
Clerk, general	2063	
Salesman	859	
Shipping clerk	408	
Machinist	617	
Salesclerk	2362	
Electrician	435	
Machine operator	3044	
Bricklayer	213	
Carpenter	1004	
Laborer	7805	
Miner	502	
Farm worker	7475	

FIGURE 17–1. *Army General Classification Test score in relation to civilian occupation (from Anastasi, based on data from Stewart).*

achievement, but our prediction may be in error because we failed to include data other than intellectual aptitude scores in making our prediction.

STABILITY OF INTELLIGENCE-TEST SCORES

How consistent is a child's performance on intelligence tests? What is the likelihood that a child will obtain approximately the same score at age ten or age fifteen that he received at age seven? This kind of information is frequently needed when we have to make decisions about the kinds of educational programs that children will be permitted or encouraged to enter. Such information is also relevant to the decisions a child must make about entering an occupation.

IQ scores do change over a period of time for a variety of reasons. The amount of change and the reasons for it are important considerations. Some changes reflect the effect of unreliable measurements. No intelligence test is absolutely reliable, although most of them are highly reliable. Some variations in a child's IQ score may be attributed to errors of measurement. Such variations are not usually large, and they tend to occur at random. On the average, a child's intelligence-test score may vary as much as plus or minus five points because of the unreliability of the measuring instrument itself.

Other variations in IQ will be due to changes in the child. Such variations reflect the effects of uncontrolled influences on test performance. Changes in motivation, as well as in health and emotional factors may influence his test performance.[6] When the factors influencing the test score are related to the child himself, the fluctuation in the test scores obtained may be large.

Long-term predictions of intelligence-test performance tend to be relatively unreliable. The curve plotted in Figure 17–2 shows the relationship between ages at which the tests are taken and the amount of correlation between test scores.[7] Select any age point along the bottom of the graph and erect a vertical line to one of the curves. Draw a horizontal line from the intersection point to the right side of the graph and read off the **correlation coefficient** (Pearson r) at that point. This is the correlation coefficient between scores at the age you selected and scores at age eighteen. Note that the correlations become increasingly higher as we make predictions at ages closer to age eighteen.

One of the reasons that long-term predictions are less reliable is that the tests used at an earlier age frequently require different specific abilities than do the tests at a later date. A test of intelligence appropriate for very young children cannot utilize tasks requiring verbal facility because the

[6] M. Hutt, "A Clinical Study of 'Consecutive' and 'Adaptive' Testing," *Journal of Consulting Psychology*, 11 (1947), 93–103.

[7] Compiled by H. E. Jones, "The Environment and Mental Development," in L. Carmichael, ed., *Manual of Child Development*, 2nd ed. (New York: John Wiley & Sons, 1954), p. 639, based on data in the following studies: N. Bayley, "Consistency and Variability in the Growth of Intelligence from Birth to Eighteen Years," *Journal of Genetic Psychology*, 75 (1949), 165–196; M. P. Honzik, J. W. Macfarlane, and L. Allen, "The Stability of Mental Test Performance between Two and Eighteen Years," *Journal of Experimental Education*, 18 (1949), 309–324.

child's language acquisition is limited. Because the later tests typically depend heavily on verbal materials, the earlier tests do not measure the same kinds of behavior that the later tests are measuring. We infer present learning ability, not some innate capacity, from intelligence-test perform-ance. Correlations between test performances are influenced both by the kinds of behavior tested and by the maintenance of the conditions re-quired for a controlled observation.

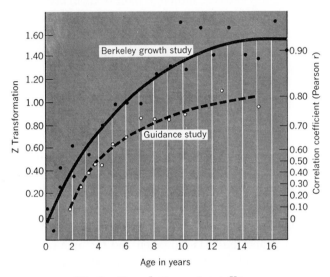

FIGURE 17–2. *Correlation of intelligence scores at eighteen years with scores at successive earlier ages. (From Jones, based on data from Bayley and from Honzik, Macfarlane, and Allen.)*

A low test score should not be immediately attributed to unreliability of the measuring instrument or to unusual dispositions in the child. Before we may conclude that a test score does not represent a child's ability, we need some corroborating evidence to suggest other factors influencing his performance. Unless we have supporting evidence, we cannot say that he did badly because he was not trying or because he was ill.

When a test score is inaccurate, the amount of error is not usually large. It is not likely that we will identify a bright child as dull or a dull child as unusually bright. Furthermore, our judgment of the intelligence of a child does not depend exclusively on intelligence-test scores; our judgments of a child's ability are also influenced by his achievement in school. If we find a child who has a high intelligence-test score and consistently achieves above the average for his class, we are reasonably certain that he is a bright child. Correspondingly, a child whose intelligence-test score is low and who does not achieve well in school is not likely to be a child of extremely high intelligence. If the teacher suspects that some factor may be influencing a child's test performance, he may refer the child to a clinical psychologist, who can analyze the child's personality.

Practically speaking, the teacher is concerned with the child's present performance level. The question of long-term stability becomes important when we attempt to make predictions about future status. In all cases, our inferences about intellectual ability are hypotheses which need to be tested by gathering all relevant data on a child's learning ability.

IQ SCORES AND PERCENTILE SCORES

Two kinds of scores are typically used to indicate a student's relative ability. One of these is the *IQ score*. Its meaning is more easily interpreted if we understand the concept of *mental age*. Suppose that on an intelligence test the average raw score for children of chronological age ten is forty-five correct answers out of a hundred items. A raw score of forty-five is equivalent to a mental age of ten. Not every ten-year-old will have a score of forty-five. Some will have answered more questions correctly; some, fewer questions correctly. But the average score of a ten-year-old is forty-five. The mental-age equivalents of raw scores are found by determining the average raw score obtained by each age group.

Now assume that the raw-score performance of an eight-year-old is forty-five. This child is performing at the level of ten-year-olds. We say that he has a mental age of ten years. In other words, once we have given the test to a large number of students, we can establish the relationships between chronological age and raw scores; from these relationships we derive a scale of mental-age scores.

We can now define what is meant by the *intelligence quotient,* or IQ. The intelligence quotient is the ratio of mental age to chronological age:

$$\text{Intelligence Quotient} = \frac{\text{Mental Age}}{\text{Chronological Age}} \times 100$$

(Multiplication by 100 merely eliminates the decimal points)

From this formula we can see that if a child's mental age equals his chronological age, he will have an IQ of 100. The more advanced the child's mental age is in relation to his chronological age, the higher his intelligence quotient will be. Correspondingly, the lower his mental age with respect to his chronological age, the lower his intelligence quotient. The intelligence quotient is a measure of relative brightness. If a child is bright for his age group, he obtains a correspondingly higher score on an intelligence test. In other words, he has profited from his experience to a greater extent than other children of his age. The IQ score is designed to show his relative superiority for a child of his age.[8]

The other form in which performance on intelligence tests is reported is the *percentile score*. Percentile scores range from 1 to 99. A percentile score tells us what percentage of students score above and below the student who obtains a given percentile score. For example, if a student's percentile score on a scholastic aptitude test is 97, we conclude that 3 per cent of students score above him. If a child has a percentile score of 15, we conclude that 85 per cent of the children score above him. The percentile score, like the IQ, establishes the relative position of a child with respect to a group of children who have taken a particular test. Percentile scores are used for reporting relative performance on many kinds of tests.

INTERPRETING INTELLIGENCE-TEST SCORES

An IQ score, as we have seen, enables us to make some predictions about what a child is capable of doing. What he actually will do, however, depends on many factors. The lower the child's IQ, the less likely he is to meet the school requirements for children his age. Below certain IQ levels, a child is not likely to profit from the typical pattern of schooling and will require special instruction or care. To determine this kind of inadequacy requires the skills of a clinician who has the training required to identify and consider all factors that may be affecting a child's intelligence-test performance.

Intelligence tests do not contain identically the same tasks. Furthermore, they may employ different scoring procedures and may be normed on quite different populations. Thus, a child may obtain different IQ's on two tests but maintain the same relative position in each case. On the other hand, a child may receive numerically the same score on two different tests; yet each score would represent a somewhat different

---

[8] Another form of IQ score is the "Deviation IQ." Such scores are not based on mental ages, but they are measures of relative brightness. Essentially they represent the extent to which an individual's score "deviates" from the mean of the standardization group. Numerically they resemble IQ scores based on mental age.

relative position. Or although he might perform in the same relative position on two tests, the tests might measure different abilities.

A comparatively easy way to decide on the meaning of an IQ score is to relate intelligence quotients to percentile scores. Table 17–1 lists IQ scores and the equivalent percentile ranks.[9] This table may be used as a rough guide for interpreting many intelligence quotients, although the teacher should refer to the test manual to learn the meaning of IQ's derived from the particular test he is using.

TABLE 17–1. *Percentage distribution of IQ's in the Terman-Merrill standardization group (from Merrill).*

IQ	Per cent of cases	Per cent of cases falling in and above each interval
150+	0.2	0.2
140–149	1.1	1.3
130–139	3.1	4.4
120–129	8.2	12.6
110–119	18.1	30.7
100–109	23.5	54.3
90– 99	23.0	77.3
80– 89	14.5	91.8
70– 79	5.6	97.4
60– 69	2.0	99.4
50– 59	0.4	99.8
Below 50	0.2	100.0

Teachers typically use intelligence-test scores to make judgments about academic ability. The following brief discussion will illustrate the complexity of factors involved in making such judgments. Suppose that we are interested in making a judgment about a student's ability to do college work. In general, we can estimate the probability of his succeeding in college from his intelligence-test performance. But, since not all colleges maintain the same standards of admission, wide ranges of intelligence-test scores may be found within colleges and from college to college. In two studies on the intellectual requirements at higher education levels, investigators found that the average Stanford-Binet IQ[10] required for

9 M. Merrill, "Significance of IQ's on the Revised Stanford-Binet Scales," *Journal of Educational Psychology,* 29 (1938), 641–651.

10 The Stanford-Binet IQ is an intelligence-quotient score derived from the Stanford-Binet Test—an individual intelligence test.

college entrance was 118; for bachelor's degree recipients, 123; for advanced-degree recipients, 126; and for persons receiving the Ph.D., 141.[11] In the colleges in which these studies were conducted, the range of IQ scores was from 95 to 180. In some colleges the average IQ of students was as low as 100, and in others as high as 133. In Wrenn's study, 10 per cent of those who eventually received the Ph.D. scored below the average of the entering freshmen in the colleges they were attending. These facts, while startling, indicate that the standards for admission to different institutions vary considerably. Although success in school may be predicted from intelligence quotients, we need to consider a variety of factors in making individual predictions. Among these factors are the particular school a student plans to enter and the particular course of study he will follow in that school.

INFLUENCE OF ENVIRONMENT

In our preliminary discussion of the character of intelligence tests, we emphasized that these tests assume that the individual has had experiences from which he can learn the behaviors the tasks require. An abundance of evidence suggests that differences in environmental opportunity yield differences in intelligence-test scores for children of comparable ages.

If we test two groups of children from different environments and find differences in their intelligence-test scores, three inferences are possible: (1) that differences in environment are responsible for the differences in test scores; (2) that differences in heredity are responsible for the differences in test scores; or (3) that some interaction of environment and heredity accounts for the obtained differences. From many of the studies demonstrating the relationship of intelligence-test-score differences to environmental differences, the second and third inferences cannot be made because the relevant hereditary factors cannot be measured.

Still, a number of studies have been conducted in which the influence of heredity has been controlled. For example, differences in intelligence-test performances between identical twins raised in different environments may be attributed to differences in environment, since in this case heredity is identical. In Table 17–2 are data from a number of studies on

---

[11] R. B. Embree, "The Status of College Students in Terms of IQ's Determined during Childhood," *American Psychologist*, 3 (1948), 259; C. G. Wrenn, "Potential Research Talent in the Sciences Based on Intelligence Quotients of Ph.D.'s," *Educational Record*, 30 (1949), 5–22.

TABLE 17–2. *Individual data on twins reared apart (from Anastasi, based on data from Woodworth, from Newman, Freeman, and Holzinger, and from Gardner and Newman).*

				Environmental Differences				Twin difference in IQ
				1. In years of schooling	2. In estimated educational advantages†	3. In estimated social advantages†	4. In estimated physical advantages†	
Pair no.	Sex	Age at separation	Age at testing					
11	F	18 mo.	35	14	37	25	22	24
2	F	18 mo.	27	10	32	14	9	12
18	M	1 yr.	27	4	28	31	11	19
4	F	5 mo.	29	4	22	15	23	17
12	F	18 mo.	29	5	19	13	36	7
1	F	18 mo.	19	1	15	27	19	12
17	M	2 yr.	14	0	15	15	15	10
8	F	3 mo.	15	1	14	32	13	15
3	M	2 mo.	23	1	12	15	12	−2
14	F	6 mo.	39	0	12	15	9	−1
5	F	14 mo.	38	1	11	26	23	4
13	M	1 mo.	19	0	11	13	9	1
10	F	1 yr.	12	1	10	15	16	5
15	M	1 yr.	26	2	9	7	8	1
7	M	1 mo.	13	0	9	27	9	−1
19	F	6 yr.	41	0	9	14	22	−9
16	F	2 yr.	11	0	8	12	14	2
6	F	3 yr.	59	0	7	10	22	8
9	M	1 mo.	19	0	7	14	10	6
20*	F	1 mo.	19	0	2	?	?	−3

* The first 19 cases are from Newman, Freeman, and Holzinger; case 20 was added by Gardner and Newman.

†Ratings are on a scale of 50 points; the higher the ratings, the greater the estimated environmental difference between the twins.

identical twins who were reared in different environments.[12] The general finding in these studies was that the better-educated twin had an IQ of 6

[12] In A. Anastasi, *Differential Psychology* (see note 5), p. 299, based on data from the following studies: R. S. Woodworth, *Heredity and Environment: A Critical Survey of Recently Published Materials on Twins and Foster Children,* Social Science Research Council Bulletin, No. 47, 1941; H. H. Newman, F. N. Freeman, and K. J. Holzinger, *Twins: A Study of Heredity and Environment* (Chicago: University of Chicago Press, 1937); I. C. Gardner and H. H. Newman, "Mental and Physical Traits of Identical Twins Reared Apart," *Journal of Heredity,* 31 (1940), 119–126.

or more points higher than that of his less-educated twin; and the greater the differences in opportunities for education, the greater the differences in IQ scores obtained. This kind of study clearly demonstrates the influence of environment on intelligence-test scores.

SOCIAL CLASS AND INTELLIGENCE-
TEST PERFORMANCE

We find similar differences in average IQ's for children from different socioeconomic backgrounds. In Table 17–3 are the average IQ's of chil-

TABLE 17–3. *Mean IQ's of children according to father's occupations (from McNemar).*

Father's Occupational Classification	Chronological Ages			
	2–5½	*6–9*	*10–14*	*15–18*
Professional	114.8	114.9	117.5	116.4
Semiprofessional and Managerial	112.4	107.3	112.2	116.7
Clerical, Skilled Trades, and Retail Business	108.0	104.9	107.4	109.6
Rural Owners	97.8	94.6	92.4	94.3
Semiskilled, Minor Clerical, and Business	104.3	104.6	103.4	106.7
Slightly Skilled	97.2	100.0	100.6	96.2
Day Labor, Urban and Rural	93.8	96.0	97.2	97.6

dren of fathers whose occupational level is indicated in the column on the left.[13] Notice that the difference in average IQ's between the highest and lowest classification levels is substantial. We should remember, however, that these are only average IQ's and that a wide range of scores may be found at any occupational level. Some children of professional men score as low as or lower than many children of laborers.[14]

[13] Q. McNemar, *Revision of the Stanford-Binet Scale* (see note 4), p. 38.
[14] For a comprehensive survey of studies of this kind, see J. Loevinger, "Intelligence as Related to Socio-Economic Factors," *Intelligence: Its Nature and Nurture,* Thirty-ninth Yearbook of the National Society for the Study of Education, Part I (Chicago: University of Chicago Press, 1940).

Although we cannot attribute these differences conclusively to differences in environment, certainly we can make a strong case, particularly at the older age levels, for the influence of environmental factors on test performance. We know that home environments are not identical. We also know that differences in the financial returns yielded by various occupations probably create differences in the kinds of opportunities provided for the child's development. In the upper-level occupations, we would expect to find a wider range of reading materials available and a greater emphasis on the advantages of schooling and achievement of school success. In general, these homes differ in the kind and amount of intellectual stimulation they provide—with consequent effects on the child's intellectual development.

Recall that comparisons of intelligence-test performance assume that the individuals compared have had equal opportunities to learn. Analysis of intelligence tests indicates that they may contain items particularly related to the experiences of middle- and upper-class children. In the studies reported by Eells et al.,[15] a number of well-known intelligence tests were administered to a large sample of children between the ages of nine and fourteen. Children's test scores were divided into groups based on the socioeconomic status of their fathers' occupation. The number of items passed or failed by children in these two groups was computed. Table 17–4 illustrates the percentage of items on which there was a reliable difference in the number of students who passed them from the two socioeconomic groups. Davis attributes this differential performance to differences in the educational opportunities available to children in these two broad categories of socioeconomic status.[16] (It should be noted that some of the items did not discriminate in this way.)

The wide variation in the amount of socio-economic difference found among items may be illustrated by citing two individual items. In the first case, 78% of the pupils in the high socio-economic group answered the item correctly, but only 28% of the pupils in the lower group did so—a difference of 46 percentage points. In the second case, the percentage answering correctly was practically identical for socio-economic groups, so that there was no statistically significant difference. The content of these two items suggests the reason for the great variation in their socio-economic differential. The first item requires the pupil to be familiar with the

[15] K. Eells, A. Davis, R. Havighurst, V. Herrick, and R. Tyler, *Intelligence and Cultural Differences* (Chicago: University of Chicago Press, 1951).

[16] A. Davis, *Social Class Influences upon Learning* (Cambridge, Mass.: Harvard University Press, 1948) p. 42.

term 'sonata'—a word which will clearly be heard more often in a home in the high socio-economic bracket than in a family from the lower socio-economic group. The second item, on the contrary, requires the pupil to apply the concept of a "cutting tool" so as to distinguish between this type and several other types of implements. Both the tools and the other implements are common to all socio-economic groups (p. 45).

TABLE 17–4. *Item discrimination between socio-economic groups (from Davis).*

| Test | Number of Pupils | | Proportion of items showing socioeconomic differential |
	High socio-economic group	Low socio-economic group	
Tests given to nine- and ten-year-old pupils:			
Henmon-Nelson	226	322	93%
Otis Alpha (nonverbal)	223	316	46%
Otis Alpha (verbal)	223	326	70%
Kuhlmann-Anderson (Grade III)	225	327	56%
Kuhlmann-Anderson (Grade VI)	225	321	85%
Tests given to thirteen- and fourteen-year-old pupils:			
Terman-McNemar	233	361	100%
Otis Beta	235	364	91%
California Mental Maturity*	235	352	69%
Thurstone Spatial	235	352	84%
Thurstone Reasoning	232	358	100%

* The figures for the California Mental Maturity test are based on only four of the six subtests. Two of the subtests were omitted because the test was too long to give in full in the time available.

The data in these studies support the hypothesis that intelligence-test performance is related to environmental factors. As the data indicate, performance on some test items is related to the socioeconomic background of a child.

Further evidence of the influence of environment may be found in studies of the relationship between home atmosphere and intelligence-test performance.[17] The atmospheres of 124 homes were rated on such

[17] A. L. Baldwin, J. Kalhorn, and F. H. Breese, "Patterns of Parent Behavior," *Psychological Monographs*, No. 3, 1945.

factors as warmth, indulgence, democracy, and activity. Children from these homes were given intelligence tests at two different ages, and the amount of change in intelligence-test scores was determined. Children from homes described as "democratic-accepting" made substantially greater gains in intelligence-test scores than did children from other kinds of homes. A "democratic-accepting" home is one in which the children are encouraged to express their preferences, and the parents consider these preferences in making decisions. Furthermore, children from such homes were consistently superior in originality, patience, curiosity, and planning—characteristics related to success in academic work and problem solving.

For a final piece of evidence on the relationship of environment to intelligence-test performance, see Table 17–5, which lists the average IQ

TABLE 17–5. *Mean Stanford-Binet IQ's of urban, suburban, and rural children (from McNemar).*

| Locality | Age Range in Years | | | | | |
| | 2–5½ | | 6–14 | | 15–18 | |
	N	Mean	N	Mean	N	Mean
Urban	354	106.3	864	105.8	204	107.9
Suburban	158	105.0	537	104.5	112	106.9
Rural	144	100.6	422	95.4	103	95.7

scores for children from urban, suburban, and rural regions.[18] The differences between suburban and urban children are not significant. However, the differences between rural children and the other two groups run, on the average, about ten or eleven IQ points.

Certainly the evidence suggests that environmental factors have an important influence on intelligence-test performance. This conclusion is of great practical significance for the classroom teacher who makes inferences about intellectual abilities from test data. If a child's family is from a cultural background other than the "American, white, urban" culture, his intelligence-test performance is likely to be below that of the typical American child. Radical changes in IQ scores may also be apparent as the child spends more time in school and has the opportunity to assimilate the experience of the typical American child. However, such a change in IQ score will not necessarily follow, because the child's intellectual ability may actually be low.

[18] O. McNemar, *Revision of the Stanford-Binet Scale* (see note 4), p. 37.

In an attempt to measure intellectual ability independently of the influence of environment, test constructors have tried to construct what are called "culture-fair tests." [19] These tests present children with tasks likely to have been met in almost any culture. Whether such tests actually are culture-fair—that is, not reflecting the influence of particular environment—is a matter of empirical test.

Some test constructors argue that we will obtain a better estimate of a child's intellectual ability if we remove from intelligence tests the items that discriminate social and cultural differences. This argument is weakened by the fact that we have little data on the predictive validity of such tests. Although intelligence tests in their present form may be used to predict school success, the same environmental factors that influence differential test performances probably influence school achievement.

If a child's intelligence-test performance is relatively poor, we may predict that he is not likely to profit from the typical learning experiences provided by schools. We cannot infer that he does not have the intelligence to profit from this environment, but only that he is at least temporarily handicapped in doing so. Unfortunately, specific procedures for remedying this handicap are not easily determined. [20]

APTITUDE TESTS

We discussed one kind of **aptitude test** when we studied intelligence tests. An intelligence test measures a *general* ability. Psychologists differ on whether intellectual ability is in fact a general trait. Some psychologists argue that intelligence is a composite of many factors.

This issue is not easily resolved. A number of tests have been constructed which purport to measure factors of intelligence. The Differential Aptitude Test Battery is a test of this kind. [21] The percentile scores of a student on the factors of this test are plotted in Figure 17–3. The names of the factors or special aptitudes that this test measures are listed at the top of each column.

Tests of this kind are constructed in such a way that performances on parts of the test tend to correlate only in a low degree. But we may not

[19] A. Davis and K. Eells, *Davis-Eells Games: A Test of General Intelligence, or Problem-Solving Ability, Manual* (Yonkers, New York: World Book Co., 1953).
[20] See K. Eells, "Some Implications for School Practice of the Chicago Studies of Cultural Bias in Intelligence Tests," *Harvard Educational Review*, 23 (1953), 284–297.
[21] G. K. Bennett, H. G. Seashore, and A. G. Wesman, *Manual for the Differential Aptitude Tests*, 3rd ed. (New York: Psychological Corporation, 1959).

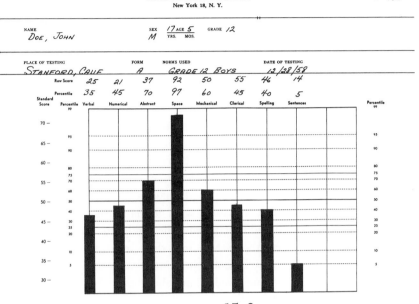

FIGURE **17–3**

conclude from this that intelligence is composed of independent factors. In other words, the "factors" measured express the way in which the test has been constructed. A general-intelligence test is constructed in such a way that it measures principally one factor—"general intelligence." In these tests, performance on any one item tends to be highly correlated with total performance on the test. In a factored test, performances on some items tend to be correlated with each other, and these performances measure performance on a particular factor, such as "verbal reasoning." But performance on the items measuring one factor is not highly correlated with performance on the items measuring another factor.

Still another way of describing these relations is to say that we cannot predict a person's performance on one factor from his performance on another factor. Note that the student whose scores are plotted in Figure 17–2 has a superior performance on the spatial-relations factor, but average or low-average performances on other factors. A student may have high, low, or average scores on one, some, or all of the factors. The factored test is designed to make discriminations among abilities on the factors measured.

A test of special aptitude is so designated because performance on this test is not predictable from tests of general ability. We determine the extent to which a test measures a distinctive performance by the degree to which it correlates with other measures of aptitude. Test manuals provide data on the correlation of the tests with other measures of ability. If the test has a high correlation with other measures of aptitude, we infer that the test is probably not measuring an independent performance factor.

Aptitude tests have been constructed to improve predictions of future performance. Aptitude tests, like other tests, may have many predictive validities. In each case, performance on the test has been correlated with some criterion performance. From these correlations we may make inferences about the abilities that the test presumably measures.

Let us take this opportunity to warn again that the test labels are frequently misleading. Some test users will select a test on the basis of the name, assuming that the test measures what its name suggests. Only by examining the test manual and by checking the predictive validities of the test can one be sure what the test in fact does measure.

One other kind of error may be made in using these tests. Aptitude tests are frequently used in making predictions about probable occupational success. A teacher may assume that the abilities a particular test purports to measure are required in a specific job. He may assume, for example, that the ability to visualize in space is required in engineering; therefore, he may be tempted to make inferences about a student's probable success in engineering from his performance on a spatial-relations test. As a matter of fact, performance on a particular test of spatial-relations ability may not be correlated with success in engineering. Again, the teacher should check the manual to determine whether the particular test of spatial relations being used does correlate with success in engineering. Some abilities, although they may be *necessary conditions* for occupational success, are not *sufficient causes* of it.

The correlation between performance on many aptitude tests and success on a job is not high, although it may be reasonably suggestive. This is not difficult to explain, since many aptitude tests are of a paper-and-pencil type and do not directly measure all the performances required by a job. As we have noted before, job success depends upon a variety of factors —not just the ability to perform a specific task.

ACHIEVEMENT TESTS

Standardized **achievement tests** are comparable to the kinds of tests teachers construct for their own use. We have achievement tests in reading, in arithmetic, and for almost every subject in the school curriculum.[22] Ordinarily, the achievement test is designed to measure the attainment of the objectives of a specific learning experience. Most of these tests have logical validity, since they sample the typical content of school subjects. They have also been given to large numbers of students; therefore, norms of performance are available for them.

AGE AND GRADE SCORES

Achievement-test scores may be reported as percentile scores, or as **age scores** or **grade scores.** An *age score* represents the performance of children of a given age; in an achievement area, it is determined in a similar way to that by which mental-age scores are determined. Assume that we give a reading test to a large group of children and we compute the average raw score for each age level. If the average raw score is 25 for age ten, a child who obtains a raw score of 25 is given an age score of ten.

A *grade score* represents the average performance of children at a given grade level. Grade scores are comparable to age scores, except that performances are averaged on the basis of grade rather than age level. The grade score is one of the most common forms in which scores on achievement tests are reported. It is particularly useful for determining a student's achievement with respect to that of students who have had comparable learning experiences. A fifth-grade teacher may give a reading test to his class. When he has scored the test, he can convert the results into grade-level scores. From these scores he can tell whether his children are reading at, above, or below grade level as it is measured by this achievement test.

A common error is frequently made in interpreting age or grade scores. We find that a child in the fifth grade is reading, according to the norms, at the seventh-grade reading level; his score is reported as grade seven in reading. This score represents the relative position of the child in reading achievement as compared to other fifth graders. He has answered more items correctly than the typical fifth grader. If this test is also used in measuring the achievement of seventh graders, he may have a score that is equal to the average score obtained by seventh graders. If the test is not usually taken by seventh graders, the symbol "seven" is being used to indicate how far above the fifth-grade level his score is.

[22] Examples of such tests are: G. Hildreth, H. Bixler, et al., *Metropolitan Achievement Tests, Manual* (Yonkers, New York: World Book Co., 1948); E. F. Lindquist, *Iowa Tests of Educational Development, Manual* (Chicago: Science Research Associates, 1948); E. W. Tiegs and W. W. Clark, *California Achievement Tests, Manual* (Monterey, Calif.: California Test Bureau, 1957).

The score does not mean that this child reads like a typical seventh grader. He may or may not, but this is something that cannot be determined from the test score alone. The test score compares his reading performance to that of children at his own grade or age level who have taken the same test. In many cases a child will be reading well above the average for his grade level, but is not reading the same as, nor is he ready to read the same as, children at a higher grade level. He may not have the reading interests of children at a higher grade level, or his general background of experiences may not be an adequate preparation for seventh-grade reading experiences.

ACHIEVEMENT-TEST NORMS

The published norms for most achievement tests have been obtained by giving the test to large samples of children. In using these norms, we assume that children taking the test are like the children in the sample from which the norms were developed. Real differences may exist between these two groups of children, either in the particular kinds of experiences that they are having in school or in their general background. We would not expect children from rural areas to perform in the same way on these achievement tests as children from urban areas. If the standardization sample has been composed of children from middle-class urban areas, then test norms represent the average performances for children from that kind of an environment.

Ideally, local norms should be developed. With such norms, a child's achievement may be compared to that of children having comparable learning experiences. However, differences between local and national performances may be significant for reorganizing learning experiences. If we find, for example, that the children in our school system are below the national average, we may raise questions about the content of the experiences that they are having. Since such differences may also be related to differences in intellectual ability between the two groups or to differences in educational objectives, a great deal of caution must be exercised at this point.

CURRICULAR VALIDITY OF ACHIEVEMENT TESTS

When an achievement test is chosen to be used in a particular class, we generally assume that it is measuring what the children have been learning in that class. This assumption may not be justified. Before a teacher uses an achievement test, he should examine it to determine to what extent the children in his class ought to be able to handle the items in the test. The standardized achievement test is a valid measure of the effects of a learning experience to the extent that it adequately samples the kind of behavior change involved in the learning experience.

A particular standardized test may not measure all the objectives of a particular learning experience. Some achievement tests contain items that require only a knowledge of factual material. Such tests measure attainment of a limited number of objectives. Recall that an evaluation program is designed to measure attainment of all of the objectives of a learning experience. Standardized tests may not be available to measure all of these objectives. A common error is to assume that a test labeled "Reading Achievement" or "Arithmetic Achievement" is measuring all of the behavior changes desired in organizing learning experiences in reading or arithmetic.

If an achievement test has curricular validity for the courses in a school, it is useful for comparing the achievement of different classes, or schools within the same system. In using achievement tests in this manner, we may not necessarily assume that the average performance of any class must be at its grade level. There will be a range of performance on any achievement test, and the average performance of the class tends to be highly correlated with the general level of intellectual ability in the class. Brighter students have the ability to profit more from experience. When the brighter pupils are grouped in the same class, the teachers are likely to provide a wider and richer range of learning experiences. These differences in pupil ability and in the learning experiences provided are reflected in higher average performance scores.

PREDICTIVE VALIDITY OF
ACHIEVEMENT TESTS

An achievement test may be used to predict future performance in the same or a related achievement area. Assume that we test students' achievement in freshman English, and that we want to use this test to predict achievement in senior English. If the test is being used for the first time, such a prediction cannot be made, since we do not know the predictive validity of the test. At some later date, however, we may obtain a measure of achievement in senior English. Test scores may then be correlated with the measures of performance in senior English. The achievement test has predictive validity to the extent that there is a substantial positive correlation between these two measures.

Test manuals for standardized achievement tests contain information on the predictive validity of these tests, when it has been determined. A relationship between achievement-test performance and some future performance may not be assumed without such information, even when achievement-test performance appears to be logically related to the future performance.

MEASURES OF
PERSONALITY CHARACTERISTICS

Teachers frequently make inferences about a wide variety of pupil characteristics. These inferences are usually based on observations of the pupil. We have repeatedly emphasized in this text that these observations must have certain characteristics if the inferences made from them are to be relatively reliable and valid. As we noted, the teacher faces many practical problems which make it difficult for him to obtain the kind of information that he needs.

Two problems in particular make it difficult for the teacher to obtain adequate information on pupils: (1) the demands on his time prevent the teacher from making systematic observations of pupil behavior; (2) observations tend to be biased because they are not based on representative samples of pupil behavior.

Another problem facing the teacher in this respect is that he observes the pupil almost exclusively in the school context. The kind of behavior the teacher observes is the kind likely to be evoked by the requirements of the learning experience. Even an elementary school teacher, who sees the pupil for a major portion of the day, observes mainly "school behavior." Pupils may and frequently do act quite differently in other contexts.

Still another obstacle to inferring from observations of students arises from the general problem of validity. Assume that a student requests a teacher's opinion on the advisability of preparing for a particular occupation. The teacher's advice will be based on his conception of the pupil's abilities, personality characteristics, and the requirements of the occupation. Even if the teacher has made reliable observations of the pupil's behavior, we may still question the relevance of these behavior samples to the kind of judgments the teacher is asked to make. If a boy says that he is interested in engineering, for example, we may obtain information on his general intellectual ability, which will help in making decisions about his general fitness for this occupation. In addition, we will need information on his special aptitudes, and we may question the strength and stability of his interest in engineering.

A wide variety of tests have been developed to provide teachers with information on pupil characteristics. Special training is required to administer many of these tests. We will discuss some of these tests briefly to suggest their value as measuring instruments. Since many school systems use them, the data they provide on student performance are often available to teachers. We will offer some warnings on using them to make inferences about pupils. This discussion will also provide us with another opportunity to stress the importance of knowing the necessary characteristics of any measurement of behavior.

INTEREST TESTS

As we suggested in the previous chapter, one simple way to determine a person's interests is by asking him what he likes and what he does not like. An **interest test** consists of a series of questions in which a person is requested to express his likes or dislikes, or his preferences for various activities. While the method of determining interests is fairly simple, the problem of reliably measuring a person's interests depends in part on the kind of interest we attempt to measure. For example, if we ask a child what TV programs he likes, we probably will get an accurate estimate of his TV interests. If, however, we ask a child what occupations he is interested in, his answer may have no practical significance. He may have only the vaguest conception of a given occupation, and his "interest" may be based upon a superficial picture of what the occupation is like. A standard interest of high school boys is engineering; yet the interest is frequently unrealistic because the student is merely reflecting his conception of a glamorous male occupation. The interest may change as the boy develops a more realistic conception of what engineers do. Standardized interest tests have been developed to measure more complex kinds of interests.

Two of the best-known interest inventories are the Kuder Preference Record and the Strong Vocational Interest Blank.[23] In each of these inventories the person taking the inventory is asked to check his preferences and his likes and dislikes. When the entire list of alternatives has

---

[23] G. F. Kuder, *Kuder Preference Record-Vocational, Manual* (Chicago: Science Research Associates, 1951); E. K. Strong, Jr., *Vocational Interest Blank for Men, Manual* (Palo Alto, Calif.: Consulting Psychologists, 1951).

been checked, the inventory is scored and a profile of relative strength of interests is obtained.

The differences between these two tests illustrate the kinds of information needed to use a test appropriately. The Kuder test, for example, reports interests in such broad categories as "scientific," "literary," and "mechanical." However, we cannot assume, for example, that the "scientific" interest measured by the test is in fact the dominant interest of individuals in a particular job until we have determined how people in that job respond on this test. The most recent test manual provides some data of this kind, although some of the occupational samples used are comparatively small.

The Strong test has been administered to successful people in a number of different occupations. The scores on the test compare the examinee's interests with those of successful people in these occupations. For example, an "A" score in an occupational category means that an individual has interests highly similar to those of successful people in that occupation. Nonetheless, the character of these interests is not defined by the test score. A score indicating similarity of interests means that a person has checked alternatives in substantially the same way that successful people in a given occupation do.

Even after we have determined a student's pattern of interests, as measured by either of these two tests, we cannot conclude that he will succeed in the occupation of people whose interests are similar to his. A student must also have other personality characteristics and the ability required for an occupation. Still, both of these tests are useful for educational and vocational counseling. They are not useful for determining a wide variety of other kinds of interests, particularly the kinds of interests with which a teacher may be concerned in organizing a learning experience.

OTHER SELF-REPORT MEASURES

The person to whom an interest inventory is administered must give information about himself. Tests which require an individual to answer questions about himself are called **self-report tests.** A large number of such tests are available for measuring many different aspects of personality.

The Allport-Vernon-Lindzey Study of Values is an example of such a test. Here are two items from this test: [24]

[24] G. W. Allport, P. E. Vernon, G. Lindzey, *Study of Values,* rev. ed. (Boston: Houghton Mifflin Co., 1951), pp. 3, 7.

Part 1. The two alternatives are rated 3 and 0 if the subject agrees with one and disagrees with the other; if he has only a slight preference for one over the other, they are rated 2 and 1 respectively.

Example:
    If you should see the following news items with headlines of equal size in your morning paper which would you read more attentively? (a) Protestant Leaders to Consult on Reconciliation; (b) Great Improvement in Market Conditions.
        (a) _____ (b) _____

Part 2. The answers are rated in order of personal preference, giving 4 to the most attractive and 1 to the least attractive alternative.

Example:
In your opinion, can a man who works in business all the week best spend Sunday in—
    a. Trying to educate himself by reading serious books?
    b. Trying to win at golf, or racing?
    c. Going to an orchestral concert?
    d. Hearing a really good sermon?

This test is designed to measure the dominant value systems of an individual. In scoring of the test, *a priori* assumptions are made about the values represented in each statement. We may infer that a person who is interested in the headline on church leaders rather than the headline on market conditions has primarily religious values. Obviously, this one item would not be conclusive evidence. The test presents a series of items in which the individual must make choices, or express preferences for one activity over another. In scoring the test, we determine what kinds of items the individual systematically prefers, and these preferences presumably reflect his dominant values.

The major advantage of these tests is that we obtain a comprehensive sample of an individual's behavior. Frequently, these tests give information about an individual that could be obtained only by an extended personal interview. The major disadvantage of such tests is that the information we obtain is based on a self-description. Previous warnings about assuming a meaning of what the test measures from the test label are appropriate here.

Because the individual's self-reporting may be unrealistic, or because the individual may consciously or unconsciously falsify descriptions of himself, personality tests have been developed using test situations in which it is difficult for the individual to know what might be a "good" response. Such tests are called *projective tests*. In a projective test an ambiguous stimulus situation is presented to the person taking the test, and he responds on the basis of his impressions. The Rorschach inkblot test and the Thematic Apperception Test are well-known examples of this kind of test. The complexities of the theory of scoring and interpreting such tests are beyond the scope of this book. The use of such tests requires special training, and they are not available to the classroom teacher unless the teacher has specialized training. The examples are presented here to suggest the wide range of tests designed to measure complex aspects of personality. These tests, as all other tests, are useful to the extent that they are reliable and valid measuring instruments and if a trained person administers and interprets them.

CUMULATIVE RECORDS

Test data gathered on pupils will be of value to teachers only if they preserve it systematically. Most schools maintain *cumulative records* on pupils. Cumulative records can be particularly useful to the teacher if certain precautions are observed in their use. The records must be kept up to date and the information in them must be correctly recorded. Many records are inadequate because they contain only a small amount of information about pupils. Into these records should go all the basic data about the child, such as his health record, his father's occupation, his test performance on intelligence and achievement tests, and his academic record. In some schools teachers are requested to write up their observations about pupils and to place these in the cumulative record.

The observations of pupils recorded by the teacher are valuable only if these have been gathered systematically and if the teacher has been careful in distinguishing what he has observed from what he infers from his observations. Many **anecdotal records,** as these observations are called, are gross, unsystematic observations of child behavior loaded with the teacher's inferences about what the pupil is like, rather than a careful description of the child's observed behavior.[25] Some teachers report only disagreeable aspects of pupil behavior in these records. Anecdotal records probably should not be used in the cumulative record unless teachers have systematic training in the observation of pupil behavior.

A major defect of many anecdotal records lies in the kinds of categories used to describe a pupil. The fifth-grade teacher who picks up a cumulative folder and reads that Johnny is a "forward and pushy child" will interpret this record in terms of his own conception of "forward and pushy." Descriptive terms used in anecdotal records should be defined

[25] See A. E. Traxler, *The Nature and Use of Anecdotal Records* (New York: Educational Records Bureau, 1939).

carefully. One way to improve these descriptions is to record the specific behavior observed. If the teacher records that Johnny is aggressive, the specific behavior that the teacher is labeling "aggressive" ought to be noted.

Another disadvantage of these anecdotal records is that they are frequently based on unsystematic observations. The teacher may record his observations when he has the time and opportunity to do so, and the record may be colored by the effects of selective memory. As a consequence, we obtain a biased picture of what the pupil's behavior is like. It is not necessary to repeat here all our previous suggestions about the limitations of and the possibilities for improving teachers' observations. The anecdotal record is simply a recording device; it is not in itself a measuring instrument. The anecdotal record is useful only insofar as it records reliable and valid observations.

The principal advantage of the cumulative record, when it is properly maintained, is that it gives a picture of the child's development over a long period of time. Some teachers object that they prefer to make their own judgments of a pupil, and they do not want to be influenced by other teachers' conceptions of what the pupil is like. This objection has validity only when the cumulative record contains scanty or inaccurate information; it makes less sense if a systematic, comprehensive program of evaluation is maintained in the school, and if the teachers are trained to make systematic evaluations. The child's present behavior is a function of his past behavior and experiences. If we want to gain greater understanding of what a child is like, we need some conception of what has happened to him and how he has reacted over a period of time. We have noted, for example, that the IQ scores of an individual child may vary over a period of time. A teacher who uses only the child's most recent IQ score has no idea of whether this performance is consistent with the child's previous performances. The same may be said about consulting the results of achievement tests and other testing devices.

The first requirement for any attempt at gaining a comprehensive understanding of pupils is the development of adequate and appropriate procedures for measuring pupil behavior. A cumulative record is useful to the extent that it contains an accurate and comprehensive report of the results of evaluation procedures.

THE SOCIAL CONSEQUENCES OF TESTING

Even the most casual reader of the press is aware that testing is not in complete public favor. Several books have attacked the idea of testing, usually picking the idiosyncrasies of tests, the errors of their users, or the worst examples of what have been labeled tests as the evidence for their view that testing is dangerous. Tests are not perfect instruments, how could they be? We have seen what the logic of measurement is, and found that it is rooted in sampling and probabilistic inferences. A test stands and falls on the evidence that it is measuring reliably and validly.

The incompetence of test users is not a valid argument against the tests themselves and certainly not against their responsible use. It may be an argument for some form of regulation, and it certainly supports the plea of psychologists for training of test users. The American Psychological Association has published a set of ethical practices for the guidance of test constructors and users.[26] But this group controls only its own members. A code of professional ethics is meant to guide and its success depends on intelligent responsiveness to its directives. You and I are not responsible for the witch doctor who uses a blood-pressure gauge to predict rainfall. We are responsible as members of a society for practices that are tolerated or ignored that harm individuals. There is no question that there are potentially and probably actually harmful testing practices. There is no question that there are poor tests. The cure for these problems is education and training and perhaps some form of regulation comparable to the control of drugs, but this kind of control will probably come very gradually. In the meantime, we hope that good tests and responsible test use will not be destroyed through unenlightened criticism.

However, even were we to achieve more intelligent test usage many people would admit to vague fears that the test somehow does not measure their "real" behavior. It doesn't really get at what they are like. There is only one logical answer to that question. The test's measured validity tells us how well the test is likely to do, and what its margin of error is likely to be. A comprehensive test program protects against the possibility of misjudging by using more than one test, by repeating tests, and by relating test information to life-history data and direct observation. A teacher who looks only at an intelligence-test score of a pupil and does not relate it to other information about the pupil needs his own intelligence-test score examined. There is no implication here that this other

---

[26] "Technical Recommendations for Psychological Tests and Diagnostic Techniques," *Psychological Bulletin*, 51 (1954) Supplement. See also *Technical Recommendations for Achievement Tests,* (Washington, D. C.: National Education Association, 1955); W. Findley, "Purposes of School Testing Programs and Their Efficient Development," in W. Findley, ed., *The Impact and Improvement of School Testing Programs,* Sixty-second Yearbook of the National Society for the Study of Education (Chicago: University of Chicago Press, 1963), pp. 1–27.

information is more reliable or more valid. It too must meet these requirements. The purpose in using additional information is to protect against the margin of error in individual measurement and against what may have been an instance of unreliable measurement.

In the last three chapters we have reviewed the principles of test construction and the use of standardized tests. Recall that the function of an evaluation program is to assess behavior change in learning experiences. One phase of this program is concerned with the assessment of the student's personality, so that decisions about appropriate learning experiences may be made. Tests are ways of obtaining more adequate and reliable information about what pupils are like. The teacher should not lose sight of the fact that one test gives only a portion of the picture of a student's personality. If we are to make adequate and reliable determinations of the personality of a child, a comprehensive evaluation program is necessary.

It is important to remember that the child's total personality affects the whole course of his learning. Knowing a child's intelligence quotient gives us only a comparatively small piece of information. On the basis of it, we cannot tell how he will act in a variety of situations, or how he *typically acts*. Many of our measures of performance measure achievement or ability, but do not give us a picture of how the student usually acts. If we are to get a picture both of abilities and typical performances, we must utilize a wide range of evaluation procedures.

SUMMARY

Most teachers do not have the training or the time to carry out all the procedures necessary for determining the reliability and validity of their own tests. Standardized tests are available for measuring the attainment of many curricular objectives. They have also been administered to samples of children with known characteristics, and they provide data on the comparative performance of these groups. The process of test standardization involves:

1. *Determining the conditions under which the test is to be administered.* These conditions must be known if the test is to be administered so that it provides a controlled observation of behavior.

2. *Determining performance norms.* Norms are relative scores which enable the test user to give meaning to the test performances. Norms of

relative performance are derived by administering the test to a group of individuals of known characteristics; this group is called the *standardization sample*. The use of test norms to interpret test performance presupposes that the examinees have the characteristics of the persons in the standardization sample.

3. *Determining the reliability and validity of the test.* Knowing the predictive validities of a test enables us to specify more precisely what the test measures.

4. An intelligence test is a measure of what a person has learned from his general experience. We infer intellectual ability from our observations of what the person has learned.

5. Intelligence tests provide a measure of relative brightness arrived at by comparing individuals who have had equal learning opportunities. IQ scores and percentile scores are used to provide estimates of relative brightness. These kinds of scores indicate a person's relative position in terms of intellectual ability within a group of people who have had comparable learning opportunities.

6. Intelligence-test performance is influenced by environmental factors. Intelligence test performance has been found to vary with differences in socioeconomic status, home atmosphere, and location in urban or rural communities.

7. Intelligence-test scores of an individual may vary considerably over a period of time. In general, long-range predictions based on intelligence-test performance tend to be less reliable than short-term predictions. This unreliability derives in part from the differences in content of tests used at various age levels and in part from changes in the individual. Gross errors in prediction are not very probable and they occur in a relatively small number of cases. Inferences about pupils' intellectual ability may be made more reliably by considering more manifestations of intellectual ability than intelligence test scores.

8. A wide variety of achievement tests is available for use. Two considerations are relevant to the use of these tests: (a) These tests may not have curricular validity for particular learning experiences. They may not sample the content included in a learning experience, or they may not sample all of the objectives of a learning experience. The usefulness of these tests is limited by the extent to which they have curricular validity. (b) The norms provided for these tests are useful if the examinees have characteristics similar to those found in the standardization sample. Differences between the examinees and the standardization sample may lead to erroneous inferences about pupil achievement.

9. Other kinds of standardized tests are available for measuring pupil characteristics—such as special aptitude tests, interest tests, and "personality" tests. Many of these tests require special training before they may be used appropriately. However, two general principles are relevant to the use and interpretation of all of these tests: (a) Most of these tests purport to measure special characteristics rather than general abilities. Independence of measurement in this respect may not be assumed. The extent to which any test measures factors measured by other tests may be determined from the correlations of the test with other tests. (b) The meanings to be associated with performance on the test are determined from the kinds of predictive validities that have been determined for the test.

10. Test information about pupil performance and pupil characteristics is most useful when it is recorded and maintained systematically. Cumulative records are one means for maintaining a file of information on pupil behavior. The cumulative record, however, is merely a device for recording information, and the usefulness of the information in the record depends on the kinds of measurement procedures that have been used to obtain this information.

11. Anecdotal records of pupil behavior are frequently included in these cumulative records. Anecdotal records are useful when systematic observations of pupil behavior have been made and the behavior itself carefully recorded. Anecdotes are misleading when they reflect biased observations and faulty inferences.

12. Three principles have been stressed throughout this chapter: (a) curricular objectives determine to some extent the usefulness of particular kinds of standardized tests, such as achievement tests; (b) the usefulness of the norms of any standardized test depends on the extent to which examinees possess the characteristics of the standardization sample; (c) the interpretation of a test score depends on the predictive validities of the test.

13. A test provides a limited sample of pupil behavior. A comprehensive evaluation of pupil characteristics and behavior change requires a comprehensive measurement program. Standardized tests may provide important information about pupils, but they should not be regarded as the only source of information about pupil behavior.

14. Standardized tests have been the objects of considerable criticism recently. Poor tests and irresponsible use cannot be defended. But the solution to these problems is improving the tests and educating their users. It is important to know what has been accomplished by using

standardized tests, such as obtaining more reliable, more valid, and more objective evidence. It is equally important to know what the tests can and cannot do.

STUDY AND DISCUSSION QUESTIONS

1. Select any intelligence, achievement or aptitude test in which you are particularly interested or which your school may use. Use the references at the end of this chapter or the test manual if it is available, and gather information on the following points:

    a. Reliability of the test.

    b. Validity of the test.

    c. The kinds of scores in which test performance is reported.

    d. Characteristics of the standardization sample.

2. What kinds of predictions about pupil behavior could you make from data on student performance on the test you have selected? What kinds of predictions could not be made from these data? Describe some student populations for which using information on this test might lead to unreliable inferences about pupil behavior.

3. You have extensive intelligence test data on a high school freshman. You note that his test scores fluctuate considerably. His most recent score would place him in the upper fourth of high school students in terms of intellectual ability. What inferences would you make about his intellectual ability? What information would you need in order to test your inferences? What inferences would you make about the fluctuations in test performance, and how would you gather data to test these inferences?

4. Below are the percentile scores received by three high school students on a scholastic aptitude test. The test items are largely verbal in character. The test has been given to a large sample of high school students. Describe these students' performances. What kinds of predictions would you make about their ability to do college work? Do you have sufficient information to make these predictions?

    a. Eighty-fifth percentile.

    b. Forty-fifth percentile.

    c. Twentieth percentile.

5. What assumptions underlie the development of age and grade norms?

6. A sixth-grade student in your class receives a reading grade score of 8.2. What inferences would you make about this pupil's ability in reading? Would you recommend that he read eighth-grade reading materials?

7. A Mexican-American child receives a low score on an intelligence test that is given to your sixth-grade class. What inferences would you make about his intellectual ability? What data do you need to check these inferences?

8. A student has received an average score on an intelligence test, but his achievement in your class is above average. What conclusions would you draw from these data? How may you test your inferences?

9. You are told that 75 per cent of the sixth-grade students in your school score above the national average on a reading test. What conclusions would you draw from these data? What additional information would you want?

RECOMMENDED READINGS

G. Adams and T. Torgerson. *Measurement and Evaluation for the Secondary School Teacher*. New York: The Dryden Press, 1956.

L. J. Cronbach. *Essentials of Psychological Testing*, 2nd ed. New York: Harper & Brothers, 1960.

W. Findley, ed. *The Impact and Improvement of School Testing Programs*. Sixty-second Yearbook of the National Society for the Study of Education, Part II. Chicago: University of Chicago Press, 1963.

J. R. Gerberich. *Specimen Objective Test Items*. New York: Longmans, Green & Co., 1956.

D. A. Goslin. *The Search for Ability: Standardized Testing in Social Perspective*. New York: Russell Sage Foundation, 1963.

E. Lindquist, ed. *Educational Measurement*. Washington, D. C.: American Council on Education, 1951, Chapters 6–13.

R. Thorndike and E. Hagen. *Measurement and Evaluation in Psychology and Education*. New York: John Wiley and Sons, 1955, Chapters 3 and 17.

T. Torgerson and G. Adams. *Measurement and Evaluation for the Elementary School Teacher*. New York: The Dryden Press, 1954.

R. Travers. *How to Make Achievement Tests*. New York: The Odyssey Press, 1950.

N. B. Henry, ed. *The Measurement of Understanding*. Forty-fifth Yearbook of the National Society for the Study of Education, Part I. Chicago: University of Chicago Press, 1946.

GLOSSARY

Achievement Test. Measurement procedure for assessing the degree to which a student has achieved the objectives of a learning experience; typically, test used to measure knowledge of content presented in courses.

Adjustment. A general concept describing a person's ability to cope with his environment; the correspondence between the demands of a task or of the environment and the responses a person has available for mastering either.

Advance Organizer. A model or a way of organizing new information to be acquired by a learner.

Aggression. An attack on a person to do harm, using either verbal or physical means.

Alternative. One of the ways of acting in solving a problem or attaining a goal.

Analysis of Goal. The process of determining the goal to be attained, of clarifying the goal to be obtained in a problem situation.

Analysis of Situation. The act of determining those factors in a problem situation relative to the solution of the problem.

Anecdotal Record. A brief description of an event observed, recorded and filed as a way of obtaining and maintaining information about a person.

Approach-Avoidance Responses. The set of responses characterizing movements to and from a goal, to and from a situation.

Aptitude Test. A measurement device used to estimate the amount of a specific ability possessed by an individual.

Arousal Phenomena. The set of behaviors associated with motivated states; behaviors characterized by mobilization of energy in goal seeking.

Arousal Strategy. A technique for producing interest, attention, curiosity.

Assimilation. A process in which an object or material perceived or remembered is integrated into previously perceived or remembered objects or materials.

Association. The link between a stimulus and a response.

Attitude. A predisposition to act in a positive or negative way toward persons, objects, ideas, and events.

Attitude Object. The persons, objects, ideas, or events toward which one has positive or negative reactions.

Attitudinal System. An intervening process—a set of responses by which a person evaluates stimulus information.

Behavioral Taxonomy. A classification of behaviors required in learning tasks.

Brainstorming. A technique of group discussion in which the participants are encouraged to give whatever ideas occur to them about a problem and in which other participants are prohibited from evaluating the ideas so presented.

Central Tasks. Tasks that must be mastered if the major goals of an instructional strategy are to be achieved (in contrast to peripheral tasks).

Cognitive Dissonance. A discrepancy or conflict between two sets of beliefs held by a person.

Cognitive Process. A complex system of organizing, interrelating, and interpreting experience.

Cognitive Strain. A term applied to concept-acquisition tasks requiring complex sorting behavior, complicated hypothesis testing, and considerable storage of information.

Cognitive System. An intervening process; a set of responses by which a person organizes and orders stimuli.

Component Task Analysis. An analytic method for determining and describing the tasks to be mastered in a learning experience.

Concept. A classification of stimuli having common characteristics.

Conflict. A state in which a person is prompted to make two kinds of incompatible responses; also, a state in which a person is attracted by two goals that cannot both be attained at the same time.

Consequences. The effects of a particular way of acting; the effects of an alternative (*see* **Alternative**).

Construct. An idea, a concept, usually offered as a way of explaining observations.

Control Group. In an experiment, a group that is as similar as possible to the experimental group—except that it receives no specific treatment or receives a treatment similar to that given the experimental group, but without the specific experimental variations.

Correlation. The degree of association between two or more variables.

Correlation Coefficient. A number expressing the degree of association between variables.

Creativity. Original behavior judged by competent peers or other people to be unusual.

Criterion Behavior. The set of observed behaviors or responses which are the resultant or product of a learning experience.

Criterion Performance (*see* **Criterion Behavior, Terminal Behavior**).

Cybernetic. A synonym for feedback, as in "cybernetic model."

Decision Rule. A principle for selecting among alternatives; a method for combining probability and value estimates to facilitate making a decision.

Deduction. A generalization derived from other generalizations by reasoning.

Deductive Strategy. An instructional strategy in which a teacher defines a concept and presents examples of it.

Defense Mechanism. A psychological process by which a person interprets his environment and experiences in such a way as to reduce their potential or actual threat to him.

Denial. A defense mechanism in which a person rejects an unfavorable interpretation of himself.

Dependent Variable. The variable whose changes are being studied; changes in this variable are predicted as the result of changes in the independent variable. (*See also* **Independent Variable.**)

Discovery Learning. The set of methodologies used to induce a learner to produce a response, an idea, a generalization with minimal help from a teacher.

Discrimination. The product of distinguishing among stimuli.

Dissonance Theory. A theory to account for what a person does when he has discrepant cognitions—that is, incompatible beliefs.

Distributed Practice (*see* **Spaced Practice**).

Drive. Stimulus evoking energy changes within a person.

Educational Objective. A statement of a desired behavior change.

Experimental Group. The group given the experimental treatment in an experiment.

Extrovert. A personality type, usually characterized by free and open participation in social interactions (in contrast to introvert).

Feedback. Information about the effects or consequences of actions taken. This information may be provided by mechanical means or by a teacher.

Feedback Schedule. A procedure for organizing the amount and timing of information given to a learner on the responses he is making while learning.

Focusing Strategy. A hypothesized process in which a *focuser* selects an instance of a concept and uses it as a basis for hypothesizing about the concept's characteristics.

Free Association. The act of producing the first response to a stimulus that occurs to an individual; also, as in psychotherapy, the act of saying what occurs to one as he talks about himself and his problems.

Generalization. The product of generalizing; that is, classifying stimuli in similar ways. Also, a statement of a relationship between two or more concepts.

Hawthorne Effect. The improvement in task performance or the behavior change accruing as the result of being an experimental subject.

Hypothesis. The statement of a relationship between variables—expressed in the form *if A, then B.*

Identification (*see* **Imitation**).

Imitation. The act of reproducing the behavior of another person.

Incentive. A proffered reinforcer; a potential goal; a reward.

Independent Variable. The variable that an experimenter manipulates in an experiment; the variable which, it is predicted, will produce changes in a second variable.

Induction. The product of inferring from observations.

Inductive Strategy. An instructional strategy in which a teacher presents examples of a concept and prompts students to formulate a definition of the concept.

Input Sequence. A term referred to a decision-making model—the information a person uses to formulate a plan.

Insight. A theoretical construct used to account for a person's ability to describe himself realistically and accurately; the ability to see one's behavior without prejudice; the ability to see oneself without impediment from one's defense mechanisms.

Instructional Strategy. An organized system for producing learning.

Interest Test. A measurement procedure for assessing an individual's preferences; most widely used in assessing preferences for occupations or occupational activities.

Interference Theory. A theory to account for forgetting; the theory postulates that forgetting is a function of intervening events occurring between the time something is learned or memorized and the time when it must be recalled.

Intervening Processes. Response systems postulated as linking observed stimuli and observed responses.

Introvert. A personality type, usually characterized by a tendency to withdraw from social interactions (in contrast to extrovert).

Learning Set. A way of organizing and sequencing learning tasks so that mastery of later tasks in the sequence is facilitated by mastery of the early tasks. Also, a hypothesized process used to account for facility in learning and offered as an alternative explanation to trial-and-error explanations of response acquisition.

Leveling. The process of accentuating similarities in perceived or remembered objects (in contrast to sharpening).

Level of Aspiration. A person's stated expectation of his success on a task, or of the goal he expects to attain.

Maladjustment. Inability to cope with one's environment; the absence of responses required for mastering a task or engaging in a relationship.

Manipulative Behavior. Observable responses characterized by movement; psychomotor actions, usually integrated in a sequence to achieve specific purposes.

Massed Practice. The sequence of practice trials arranged in close contiguity to each other.

Maturation. The biological process underlying growth; the changes in physical characteristics and associated behaviors associated with growth.

Mean Score. An average of a set of scores computed by summing the scores and dividing by their number.

Mediating Responses. A set of responses inferred to be linking observed stimuli and observed responses.

Membership Group. A group to which one officially belongs.

Model. An analogy, a representation, a simplification, a simulation.

Motivation. An energy change within a person; associated with goal-seeking behavior and directed to goal attainment.

Motivation System. An intervening process; a set of responses by which a person selects and seeks goals.

Motive. A particular instance of goal-seeking behavior.

Need. A complex system of motives; a second-order inference about stable tendencies to seek certain goals.

Need Arousal. Instances of goal-seeking behavior associated with stable tendencies called needs.

Need Satisfaction. The consequence of obtaining a goal. A person is said to have satisfied a need when he attains a goal.

Need System. The pattern of characteristic needs describing a person.

Negative Concept Example. An instance, usually introduced into concept-acquisition tasks or occurring naturally, which does not contain the characteristics of the concept to be learned.

Negative Correlation. A correlation in which the performance on one measure of a variable is in the opposite direction from that of the performance on the measure of a second variable.

Negative Identification. A theoretical construct used to account for a person's failure to respond to the instruction or to imitate the behavior of another person.

Normative Need. A statement of what a person requires to adapt successfully to the society in which he lives (in contrast to psychological need).

Null Hypothesis. A statement that observed differences or observed associations are likely to be the product of chance events; a hypothesis of "no differences."

Objective Probability. A probability estimate derived from reliable data on the previous occurrence of events; objective estimates may also be derived by using mathematical models of processes.

Operant. A response that an organism can and does make.

Operant Conditioning. The procedure of reinforcing operants as they occur to increase their strength; that is, frequency, speed, or resistance to extinction.

Operation Sequence. A term referring to a decision-making model; the phase in which the plan is enacted.

Overlearning. A procedure for increasing retention by repeating the learning task after a specified mastery level has been attained.

Pearson Product-Moment Correlation Coefficient. One type of arithmetical measure for computing the degree of association between two variables.

Peripheral Tasks. Tasks that are necessary for mastering the central tasks of an instructional strategy.

Personal Style. A characteristic way of making decisions or of acting.

Plan. A hierarchical process that controls the sequence of operations and actions a person is to perform.

Plausible Rival Hypothesis. A competing hypothesis which could explain the results of an experiment as well as the research hypothesis.

Population. A defined group or collection of people, characteristics, behaviors, or other units.

Positive Concept Example. An instance containing some or all of the characteristics of a concept.

Positive Correlation. A correlation in which performance on one measure of a variable is similar to that on a measure of a second variable.

Practice Effects. The consequences of repeating responses, usually involving an improvement in the ease with which a response may be made.

Probability. The likelihood that an event will occur—usually stated as a percentage of times in a hundred.

Probability Estimate. The numerical figure representing the percentage of times an event is likely to occur.

Problem Situation. The blocking of a goal desired by a person; the absence of alternatives for problem solution; unclear purposes and goals.

Programming. An instructional system characterized by presentation of small amounts of information, stimuli-eliciting responses, and immediate feedback on responses.

Projection. A defense mechanism in which the person attributes his own characteristics to another person without recognizing them as his own.

Psychological Need. A stable tendency to be motivated in certain ways; a tendency to seek certain kinds of goals; a want, an interest (in contrast to normative need).

Rationalization. A defense mechanism in which the person provides an explanation for his behavior; the explanation, though not usually valid, is consistent with his beliefs about himself.

Recall Behavior. The action of recalling previously learned material with minimal or no stimulus help.

Recognition Behavior. Identifying correctly a previously learned association.

Reference Group. A group with which one identifies but to which one does not necessarily belong.

Reinforcement. The process of using reinforcers; in general, any event which increases the strength of a response.

Reinforcer. An event which strengthens behavior; that is, increases the probability of its recurrence or increases its resistance to extinction.

Relearning. Procedure for measuring how much learning has been retained by evaluating the ease and speed of relearning the previously learned material.

Reliability. The accuracy of a measurement.

Replica Model. A reconstruction to scale of some physical event.

Replication. A procedure in which an experiment is repeated in all respects except that the subjects of the experiment are different from the original subjects; the purpose of replication is to validate the results of the original experiment.

Repression. Similar to denial; usually considered an unconscious process of rejecting threatening information or experience.

Response Guidance. A term referred to a model of instructional strategies; the phase of a strategy in which the learner is informed of the characteristics of the desired response.

Response Practice. A term referred to a model of instructional strategies; the phase in which the learner attempts the desired response.

Retention. The product of what has been learned; the accumulation of responses still available after the learning period.

Role. A set of expectations about how a person in a given position in a social system should act and about how the individuals in a reciprocal position should also act.

Role Adjustment. Learning the behaviors appropriate to a given role.

Role Behavior. The observable behavior associated with a role.

Role Conflict. Incompatible expectations about the behavior characterizing a role.

Role Expectation. The beliefs about the appropriate behavior associated with a role and the behavior expected of other people toward the role incumbent.

Role Playing. A procedure in which individuals enact or imitate the role behavior of another person.

Sample. The product of a sampling procedure; a selected group of persons or events or characteristics chosen to represent a larger group, called the population. Samples are similar to populations in selected significant ways.

Sampling. A procedure for selecting from a set of events, persons, or characteristics.

Scanning Strategy. A hypothesized process used by *scanners,* in which the person forms a hypothesis about a concept and then looks for instances of it.

Scattergram. A diagram for plotting the scores of subjects on two measures; a scattergram graphically portrays the correlation between the variables.

Selective Forgetting. The process of remembering aspects of what is being learned, usually determined by a person's preferences and attitudes.

Selective Perception. A person's tendency to perceive some aspects of a phenomenon and not others, as a consequence of his holding certain beliefs and attitudes.

Self-Concept. The set of a person's beliefs about and evaluations of himself as a person.

Self-Report Test. Any type of measurement procedure which requires the testee to provide information about himself (for instance, measures of personality characteristics, in which the person describes his behavior).

Self-System. An intervening process; a complex set of responses by which a person conceptualizes and evaluates himself.

Set. A predisposition, a tendency, a response system predisposing the person to view and approach a problem in a predetermined manner.

Set Induction. The actions leading to the stimulating or evoking of a set in a learner.

Set Theory. A mathematical theory in which groups and collections are the basic elements. Set theory has been used to organize mathematical concepts taught in the elementary and secondary schools as a new way of introducing mathematical ideas.

Sharpening. The process of accentuating differences in perceived objects (in contrast to leveling).

Socialization. The totality of actions taken by significant adults in shaping a child's behavior, so that he may cope with the society in which he is growing up; the process by which a child acquires the beliefs and actions necessary to be a member of the culture or society in which he is growing up.

Sociodrama. A procedure in which people play roles and reenact a social situation.

Sociometric Device. A technique for gathering data on preferences for individuals among members of a social group.

Spaced Practice. A sequence of practice trials in which intervening rest periods are provided between trials, usually of equal or greater length in time than the practice trials.

Standardization. The procedure of specifying and testing the conditions under which a measurement should be taken.

Stereotype. A concept formed from inadequate information. Usually stereotypes are limited definitions, frequently oversimplified, and derogatory in character.

Subjective Probability. A probability estimate based on inadequate, unreliable, or personalized evidence.

Symbolic Model. A representation in which abstract symbols are used to represent physical events and their relationships.

Teaching Behavior. The set of actions engaging a learner in a situation from which he acquires new or modified ways of behaving.

Teaching Strategy. A plan for producing learning, including both the decisions representing the conception of the plan and the actions representing its execution.

Terminal Behavior. A statement of the desired outcome of a learning experience; a description of the responses or behavior to be acquired or modified.

Test Sequence. The phase of decision making in which the effects of carrying out a plan are evaluated.

Transfer. Use of a previously learned response in a new situation.

Validity. The degree to which a measurement procedure represents or produces that which is allegedly being measured.

Value. A term associated with decisions; a belief about the desirability of events or persons.

Variable. A factor; a classification; a set of events, persons, or things which may vary in amount or degree.

Indexes

Author Index

Subject Index